THE BIOLOGY, HUSBANDRY AND
HEALTH CARE OF REPTILES

VOLUME I OF 3 VOLUMES
BIOLOGY OF REPTILES

Lowell Ackerman, D.V.M.

TS-297

NOTICE

The authors and editors have exerted every effort to ensure that medical information mentioned in this book is in accord with current recommendations and practice at the time of publication. However, in view of the ongoing advances in veterinary medicine, readers are urged to consult with their veterinarian regarding individual health issues.

Distributed in the UNITED STATES to the Pet Trade by T.F.H. Publications, Inc., One T.F.H. Plaza, Neptune City, NJ 07753; distributed in the UNITED STATES to the Bookstore and Library Trade by National Book Network, Inc. 4720 Boston Way, Lanham MD 20706; in CANADA to the Pet Trade by H & L Pet Supplies Inc., 27 Kingston Crescent, Kitchener, Ontario N2B 2T6; Rolf C. Hagen Inc., 3225 Sartelon St. Laurent-Montreal Quebec H4R 1E8; in CANADA to the Book Trade by Vanwell Publishing Ltd., 1 Northrup Crescent, St. Catharines, Ontario L2M 6P5; in ENGLAND by T.F.H. Publications, PO Box 15, Waterlooville PO7 6BQ; in AUSTRALIA AND THE SOUTH PACIFIC by T.F.H. (Australia), Pty. Ltd., Box 149, Brookvale 2100 N.S.W., Australia; in NEW ZEALAND by Brooklands Aquarium Ltd. 5 McGiven Drive, New Plymouth, RD1 New Zealand; in Japan by T.F.H. Publications, Japan—Jiro Tsuda, 10-12-3 Ohjidai, Sakura, Chiba 285, Japan; in SOUTH AFRICA by Lopis (Pty) Ltd., P.O. Box 39127, Booysens, 2016, Johannesburg, South Africa. Published by T.F.H. Publications, Inc.

MANUFACTURED IN THE
UNITED STATES OF AMERICA
BY T.F.H. PUBLICATIONS, INC.

THE BIOLOGY, HUSBANDRY AND HEALTH CARE OF REPTILES

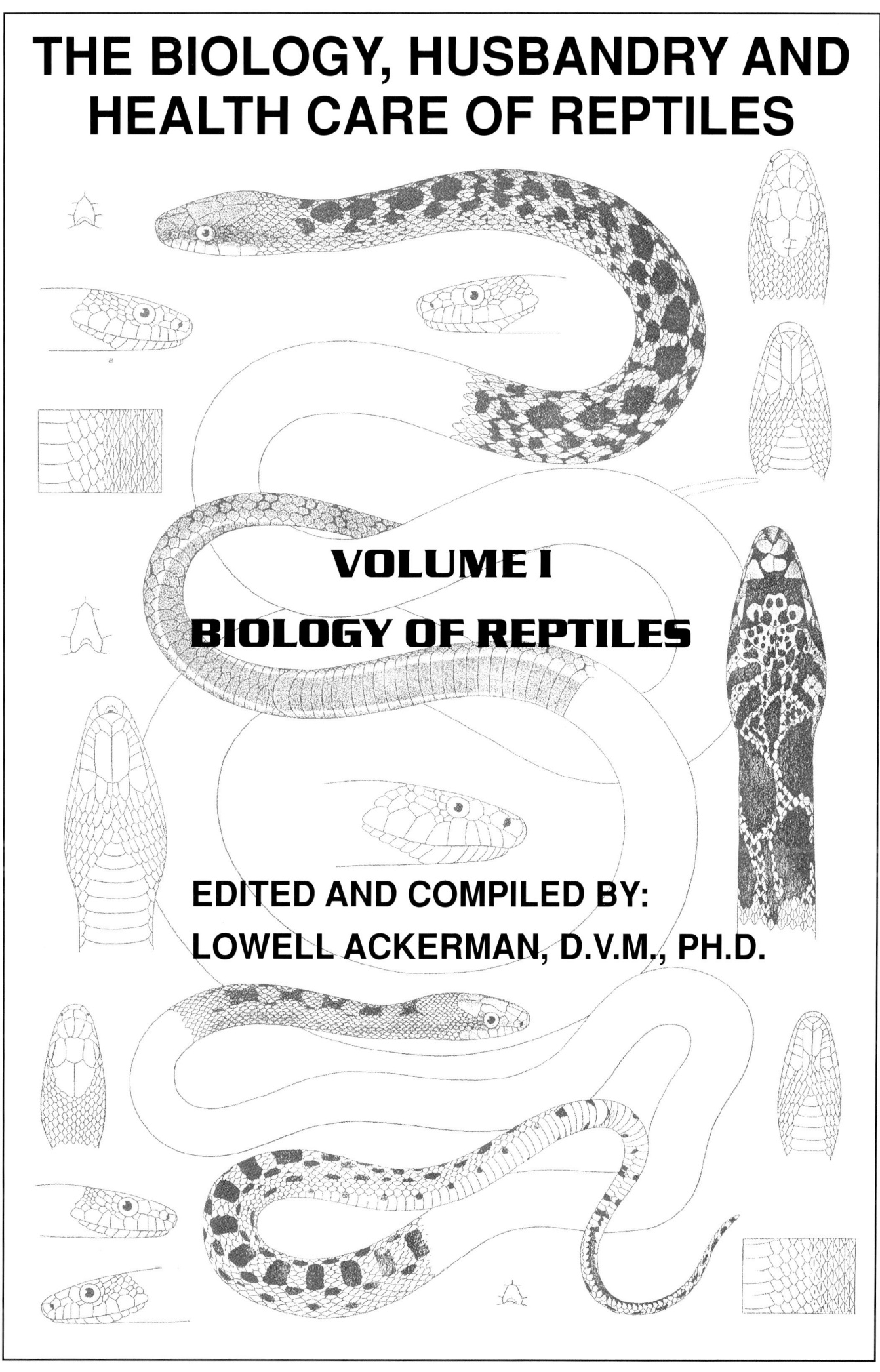

VOLUME I

BIOLOGY OF REPTILES

EDITED AND COMPILED BY:

LOWELL ACKERMAN, D.V.M., PH.D.

In addition to being available separately as individual volumes, the three books that constitute *The Biology, Husbandry and Health Care of Reptiles* are available also as a set under that title.

Volume I, *The Biology of Reptiles*

T.F.H. Publications, Inc. style number TS-297
ISBN 0-7938-0501-5

Volume II, *The Husbandry of Reptiles*

T.F.H. Publications, Inc. style number TS-298
ISBN 0-7938-0502-3

Volume III, *The Health Care of Reptiles*

T.F.H. Publications, Inc. style number TS-299
ISBN 0-7938-0503-1

The Biology, Husbandry and Health Care of Reptiles, a three-volume set comprising all three of the above-listed books:

T.F.H. Publications, Inc. style number TS-300
ISBN 0-7938-0504-X

Please Note: The following pages include the Tables of Contents of all 3 volumes.

TABLE OF CONTENTS
VOLUME I - BIOLOGY OF REPTILES

TABLE OF CONTENTS
VOLUME II - HUSBANDRY OF REPTILES

TABLE OF CONTENTS
VOLUME III - HEALTH CARE OF REPTILES

TECHNICAL EDITORS
Tara K. Harper
Lowell Ackerman DVM, PhD
Herbert R. Axelrod, Ph.D., DSC

LIST OF CONTRIBUTING AUTHORS
Lowell Ackerman DVM PhD
Pet Health Initiative, Scottsdale, Arizona

Frank Austin DVM, PhD
College of Veterinary Medicine, Mississippi
   State University

Michael J. Balsai, BA
University of Pennsylvania

Sean J. Barry, MS
Section of Evolution and Ecology, University
   of California, Davis

Brad Bolon, DVM, MS, PhD, Diplomate,
   American College of Veterinary Pathologists
Pathology Associates International Corpora-
   tion, Jefferson Arkansas

Shelley Burgin, Bsc, Msc, PhD
Faculty of Science and Technology, University
   of Western Sydney-Hawkesbury, Australia

John Coborn
P.O. Box 344, Nanango, Queensland 4615,
   Australia

James C. Cokendolpher AAS, BS, MS
Department of Biology, Midwestern State
   University, Wichita Falls, Texas

Todd Driggers, DVM
Foothills Mobile Exotic DVM, Phoenix Arizona

Chantal Dupont, DVM MS
School of Veterinary Medicine, University of
   Wisconsin-Madison

Robert E. Espinoza BS, MS
University of Nevada, Reno

Luette Forrest DVM
University Laboratory Animal Resources, University of California, Irvine

.
Mark F. Gerber
Boise State University

P. Gopalakrishnakone
Venom and Toxin Research Group, Faculty of
   Medicine, National University of Singapore

Michael S. Grace PhD
Department of Biology, University of Virginia,
   Charlottesville, Virginia

Ellis C. Greiner PhD
College of Veterinary Medicine, University of
   Florida, Gainesville, Florida

Steve Grenard RT
Staten Island University Hospital, New York

Janice S. Grumbles, DVM
Statesboro Animal Hospital, Statesboro, Georgia

Trudy Hagstrom, MA
Pathology Associates International Corporation, Jefferson Arkansas

Dr. Chris J. Harvey-Clark
University Director of Animal Care, Dalhousie
   University, Halifax Nova Scotia, Canada

Craig Hassapakis BS
Amphibian and Reptile Conservation, Provo,
   Utah

Sun Huh, MD PhD
College of Medicine, Hallym University,
   Chunchon, Korea

James L. Jarchow, DVM
Sonora Animal Hospital, Tucson Arizona

Melissa Kaplan
RepEnvirEd, Rohnert Park California

Gretchen E. Kaufman, DVM
Tufts Wildlife Clinic, Tufts University School
   of Veterinary Medicine, North Grafton Massachusetts

Michael Kiedrowski DVM
Mountain View Animal Hospital, Phoenix Arizona

David T. Kirkpatrick, PhD
Department of Biology, University of North
   Carolina-Chapel Hill

Michael Kreger, MS
Animal Welfare Information Center, Beltsville, Maryland

Khursheed Mama, DVM, Diplomate, American College of Veterinary Anesthesia

Department of Clinical Sciences Veterinary Medicine, Colorado State University, Ft. Collins, CO

Kathy Massie
Laboratory of Reproductive Ecology, Ohio University

Mark Miller
Herpetology On-line Network; President, Philadelphia Herpetological Society

Christopher J. Murphy DVM PhD
School of Veterinary Medicine, University of Wisconsin-Madison

Willard Nelson, DVM
Exotic Pet and Bird Clinic, Kirkland Washington

Kevin A. Nunan
City University of New York- College of Staten Island

Brent D. Palmer, PhD
Laboratory of Reproductive Ecology, Ohio University

M. Jane Perkins
Laboratory of Reproductive Ecology, Ohio University

Sharon Pickavance Bsc (Hons) B Vet Med, MRCVS
Royal (Dick) School of Veterinary Studies, Edinburgh, Scotland

Adrian Renshaw, B.App.Sc.
Faculty of Science and Technology, University of Western Sydney-Hawkesbury, Australia

B. J. Richardson BSc, PhD
Faculty of Science and Technology, University of Western Sydney-Hawkesbury, Australia

David C. Rostal, PhD
Department of Biology, Georgia Southern University, Statesboro, Georgia

Juergen Schumacher, Dr. med. vet
Wildlife and Zoological Medicine Service, College of Veterinary Medicine, University of Florida, Gainesville Florida

Sue Simon
Laboratory of Reproductive Ecology, Ohio University

Craig W. Stevens PhD
Department of Pharmacology and Physiology, Oklahoma State University, College of Osteopathic Medicine

Jennifer Swofford, BS
Highland Park, Illinois

M.C.A. Uribe, PhD
Lab. Biologia de la Reproduccion, Universidad Nacional Autonoma de Mexico

Craig Smith Bsc, PhD
Centre for Hormone Research, University of Melbourne, Australia

Michael B. Thompson, PhD
School of Biological Sciences, University of Sydney, Australia

C. Richard Tracy PhD
Biological Resources Research Center, University of Nevada, Reno

Stuart K. Ware, PhD
Deparment of Clinical Sciences, University of Kentucky, Lexington Kentucky

James Watson BVSc (hons) MACVSc
Animal Health Laboratory, Depatment of Primary Industries and Fisheries, Tasmania Australia

Stan Willenbring, PhD
Department of Pharmacology and Physiology, Oklahoma State University, College of Osteopathic Medicine

Bruce Young,
Department of Biology, Lafayette College, Easton , PA.

PREFACE

Reptile biology, husbandry and health care are dynamic disciplines that involve the input of various professionals, paraprofessionals and hobbyists. Until recently, these factions have been working separately, but with a similar goal - to expand the knowledge base for reptiles and their care. This book is the first to try to assimilate, in a comprehensive fashion, the diverse information collected by biologists, herpetologists, herpetoculturists and veterinarians. I believe you'll find that this makes for very interesting reading. It also provides a single source for identifying many of the fascinating aspects of reptiles and their care that aren't available in other books.

This book provides a wealth of information on many different levels. Although it is impossible to be all things to all people, there are sections in this book to address the needs of herpetoculturists, herpetologists, veterinarians, biologists, conservationists and hobbyists. The goal was to bring together experts on reptiles, but from very different backgrounds and areas of expertise. By incorporating the work of experts from different facets of reptile care, everyone benefits from the exposure. This is not an easy task, and I would especially like to thank my senior technical editor, Tara Harper, for her diligent work on this project.

Because reptile care is far from a standardized science, you will find some differences in approaches and opinions amongst the different authors. Far from being a problem, this is a wonderful forum to express different views and explore different ideas. Controversy in science is a good thing - it stops us from being complacent and keeps us searching for the real answers. Keep this in mind while reading this book and discussing the contents with others. I hope this book keeps you asking important questions and searching for the truth.

Lowell Ackerman, DVM PhD

TAXONOMY

Lowell Ackerman DVM PhD
P.O. Box 12093
Scottsdale AZ 85267-2093

John Coborn★
P.O. Box 344
Nanango, Queensland 4615, Australia

Dr. Lowell Ackerman is a practicing veterinarian, consultant, author, lecturer and radio personality. To date he has written 34 books and over 150 book chapters and articles dealing with animal health care issues..

John Coborn has written many books on various reptiles and is considered an authority in his field.

INTRODUCTION

The system of animal classification used today is an improved version of that pioneered by the Swedish biologist Carolus Linnaeus (1707-1779). In his *Systema Naturae* he set out to describe all known animal species, giving each one a two-barreled Latinized scientific name. This system of double naming is known as binomial nomenclature and is still used today. One of the first turtles to be named scientifically was the Mediterranean Tortoise, described by Linnaeus in 1758 as *Testudo graeca*. The word *Testudo* is, perhaps not surprisingly, Latin for "tortoise" and, although it is not the major species of Greece, it was nevertheless given the specific name *graeca* meaning "Greek".

The original system was primitive by today's standards, but was at least a start, and a pattern for taxonomy in the future. Even today, there are frequent arguments among scientists as the the "correct" classification of a species. Recent propositions have included breaking the large lizard family Iguanidae into eight smaller families; and including the Chamaeleonidae within the Agamidae. It seems that the iguanid proposition will become widely accepted, but more work is going to be required on the taxonomy of the Chamaeleonidae before the proposition is generally accepted. Any taxonomist, professional or amateur, can voice an opinion regarding the classification of a taxon, but whether a proposition is accepted, or rejected, depends on the decision of a board of regularly appointed scientists who operate the International Code of Zoological Nomenclature (IUZN). The board sits at regular intervals and studies the merits of various international proposals before making a decision.

Even the term "reptile" is contentious amongst herpetologists, zoologists and taxonomists but it is not the purpose of this chapter to "split hairs" when it comes to taxonomy. Here we will present widely accepted classifications of reptiles without being bogged down in the taxonomic minutia. For those looking for the definitive work on taxonomy, there are many other sources that would better suit your purposes. The term "reptile" will be used here to include the Squamata (lizards, snakes, and amphisbaenians), Rhynchocephalians, Chelonia/Testudomorpha (turtles and tortoises) and Crocodylia (alligators, crocodiles, and their relatives).

The following table gives the hierarchal classification of a well-known lizard species, the Green Iguana.

Hierarchy	Classification	Example
Kingdom	Animalia	All Animals
Phylum	Chordata	Animals with notochord
Subphylum	Vertebrata	Backboned animals
Class	Reptilia	All reptiles
Order	Squamata	Lizards, amphisbaenians, and snakes
Suborder	Lacertilia/Sauria	All lizards
Infraorder	Iguania	Iguanid lizards
Family	Iguanidae	All iguanas
Subfamily	Iguaninae	True iguanas
Genus	*Iguana*	Green Iguanas
Species	*Iguana iguana*	The Green Iguana

★Address all correspondence to John Coborn

CLASS, SUBCLASS, ORDERS, SUBORDERS AND INFRAORDER

For the purposes of our taxonomic discussions, the Class Reptilia is divided into three subclasses: Anapsida, Lepidosauria and Archosauria. Each of those are then further subdivided into orders and suborders. The subclass Anapsida consists of only one order, Chelonia, so that turtles are generally referred to by taxonomists as chelonians.

The Subclass Lepidosauria is extremely interesting and contentious and is composed of two orders, Rhynchocephalia and Squamata. Whereas Rhynchocephalia consists of the tuatara (suborder Sphenodontida, family Sphenodontidae), the Squamata consists of all lizards (suborder Sauria or Lacertilia), snakes (suborder Serpentes) and amphisbaenians (suborder Amphisbaenia). The subclass Archosauria contains the order Crocodylia (suborder Eusuchia) which, in turn, contains the Subfamilies Alligatorinae, Crocodylinae, Tomistominae, and Gavialinae.

Very large groups of reptiles, especially lizards, also make use of infraorders to group related families. An example is the Infraorder Gekkota, which include the families of Gekkonidae (Geckoes), Pygopodidae (Flap-foots) and Dibamidae (Dibamid lizards).

SUPERFAMILIES, FAMILIES AND SUBFAMILIES

In general, Family falls beneath Order in the taxonomic heirarchy. However, in some cases, families are grouped together into superfamilies with common attributes. Then, families may be subdivided into Subfamilies. A good example is the turtles of the suborder Cryptodira. They are divided into three superfamilies (Testudinoidea, Trionychoidea and Chelonioidea) which, in turn, are divided into families and subfamilies.

GENUS, SPECIES AND SUBSPECIES

Taxonomists group species into genera. A genus may contain only one or many species. A genus containing a single species is said to be monotypic. The species in a genus are all fairly similar though not quite the same.

In the binomial, the first word is the genus and is applied to groups of closely related animals. The second word is the species. Thus, *Testudo graeca* is a particular species in the genus *Testudo* ; other species in the genus include *Testudo hermanni* , *Testudo marginata* and *Testudo kleinmanni* .

In some species there may be two or more geographic variants which are slightly different (usu-

---

DIVISIONS OF CLASS REPTILIA

Subclass	Order	Suborder	Common Name
Anapsida	Chelonia	Cryptodira	Turtles
Anapsida	Chelonia	Pleurodira	Turtles
Lepidosauria	Rhynchocephalia		Tuatara
Lepidosauria	Squamata	Sauria (Lacertilia)	Lizards
Lepidosauria	Squamata	Serpentes	Snakes
Lepidosauria	Squamata	Amphisbaenia	Amphisbaenians (worm lizards)
Archosauria	Crocodylia		Crocodilians

FAMILY TIES IN THE SUBORDER CRYPTODIRA

Superfamily	Family	Subfamily
Testudinoidea	Chelydridae	Chelydrinae,
	Emydidae	Batagurinae, Emydinae
	Testudinidae	
Trionychoidea	Dermatemydidae	
	Kinosternidae	Kinosterninae, Staurotypinae
	Carettochelyidae	
	Trionychidae	Lissemyinae, Trionychinae
Chelonioidea	Cheloniidae	Carettinae, Cheloniinae
	Dermochelyidae	

ally anatomically or morphologically) but not different enough to warrant specific status. Such cases are referred to as subspecies and are given a three part name (trinomial). For example, *Testuda graeca* is often recognised as having four subspecies: *Testudo graeca graeca* (the nominate subspecies, in which the specific name is simply repeated), from Spain and northwestern Africa; *Testudo graeca ibera*, from Iberia and Turkey to western Iran; *Testudo graeca terrestris*, from northeastern Africa and Asia Minor; and *Testudo graeca zarudnyi*, from eastern Iran. Scientific names are normally printed in italics or in a style different to that of the main text. After being used for the first time in a text it is quite in order to abbreviate, thus: *T. graeca, T. g. graeca*, *T. g. zarudnyi* etc.

Note the following points regarding scentific names:

—Generic, specific and subspecific names are generally written in italics, underlined, or in a different style to the main text.

—It is quite acceptable to abbreviate in a text once the full name has been established at the beginning, and the reader is reasonably expected to know what's being discussed; for example *L. agilis* for a binomial, *L. a. agilis* for a trinomial.

—The full name should technically include the surname of the author(s) or first describer(s) and the date of description; for example *Lacerta agilis Linnaeus* 1758 (in many more popular texts, however, the author's name is often left out for practical reasons).

—If the name of the species is subsequently changed, the original author's name is still used, but placed in parentheses; for example Linnaeus first described the European Wall Lizard as *Lacerta muralis* in 1768, but the name was subsequently changed and is presently known as *Podarcis muralis* (Linnaeus, 1768).

TURTLES, TORTOISES AND TERRAPINS

The order Chelonia (sometimes referred to as Testudines, or Testudinata in older texts) today contains about 244 species in 2 suborders, 13 families, and 75 genera.

The two modern suborders developed the ability to withdraw the head into the armored shell, and thus protect it from predators (some species, however, have since partially or completely lost this ability - snappers and sea turtles for example). The means by which the head is withdrawn into the shell is the basis on which the two suborders were classified. The neck vertebrae in all species are modified to allow the neck to bend dramatically at certain points allowing the head to be withdrawn. In the Pleurodira there are three main points of neck flexure allowing the neck to be bent in a horizontal S shape and the head, on withdrawal, to be placed to one side of the shell. In the Cryptodira, there are two main points of flexure in the neck, allowing the neck to be bent in a vertical S shape and the head, on withdrawal, to be placed centrally under the shell. The families, members and locations for both suborders (Pleurodira and Cryptodira) are seen in the following table.

Suborder	Family	Members	Location
Pleurodira	Chelidae	9 genera, 37 species	Australasia and S. America
Pleurodira	Pelomedusidae	5 genera, 24 species	Africa and South America.
Cryptodira	Carettochelydae	1 genus, 1 species	Australia, New Guinea
Cryptodira	Chelydridae	2 genera, 2 species	North America to Ecuador
Cryptodira	Dermatemydidae	1 genus, 1 species	Central America
Cryptodira	Cheloniidae	4 genera, 6 species	Marine
Cryptodira	Dermochelyidae	1 genus, 1 species	Marine
Cryptodira	Emydidae	31 genera, 85 species	Cosmopolitan
Cryptodira	Kinosternidae	2 genera, 20 species	North America to Argentina
Cryptodira	Staurotypidae	2 genera, 3 species	Central America
Cryptodira	Testudinidae	10 genera, 41 species	Cosmopolitan not Australia
Cryptodira	Trionychidae	6 genera , 22 species	Cosmopolitan not Australia
Cryptodira	Platysternidae	1 genus, 1 species	Southeast Asia

SNAKES

The snakes represent the suborder Ophidia, also known as Serpentes. Within this suborder, they are arranged in 3 superfamilies, 14 families and 22 subfamilies. It is easiest to represent these groupings in chart format.

Some species have geographical races that may be somewhat different to the holotype, but are not considred different enough to warrant specific status. In our example, the Blood Python occurs in three subspecies. In captive breeding, it is important to maintain individual subspecies in a pure form. Unfortunately, many snakes with several subspecies have been bred together randomly, producing fertile subspecific hybrids which are no longer true to type. While hybrid breeding is an interesting part of herpetoculture, it is importnat that strict records are kept. Each snake should have a pedigree, just like that of a purebred dog, cat or horse. Breeding stock of original pure subspecies should also always be maintained separately from any hybrid breeding projects. Otherwise, we are likely to lose many natural species or subspecies forever.

FAMILY TIES OF THE SUBORDER OPHIDIA

Superfamily	Family	Subfamily
Typhlopoidea	Typhlopidae	
	Leptotyphlopidae	
Henophidia (Boidea)	Acrochordidae	
	Aniliidae (Ilysiidae)	
	Boidae	Boinae, Erycinae, Pythoninae
	Bolyeridae	
	Loxocemidae	
	Tropidophiidae	
	Uropeltidae	
	Xenopeltidae	
Xenophidia (Colubroidea)	Colubridae	Boiginae, Calamarinae, Colubrinae, Dasypeltinae, Dipsadinae, Homalopsinae, Lycodontinae, Natricinae, Pareinae, Sibynophinae, Xenodontinae, Xenoderminae
	Elapidae	Bungarinae, Elapinae, Notechinae
	Hydrophiidae	Hydrophiinae, Laticaudinae
	Viperidae	Crotalinae, Viperinae

SOME COMMON SNAKE FAMILIES

Common Family Designation	Family	Members
Asian wart snakes	Acrochordidae	1 genera, 3 species
Boas, Anacondas, Pythons	Boidae	23 genera, 88 species
Blind Snakes	Typhlopidae	3 genera, 200 species
Blind Worm Snakes	Anomalepidae	4 genera, 20 species
Cobras, Mambas, Coral Snakes	Elapidae	50 genera, 200 species
Colubrids (Typical snakes)	Colubridae	290 genera, 2000 species
Pipe/Cylinder Snakes	Aniliidae	3 genera, 11 species
Pit Vipers	Crotalidae	10 genera, 130 species
Sea Snakes	Hydrophiidae	16 genera, 56 species
Shield-tailed Snakes	Uropeltidae	8 genera, 44 species
Sunbeam Snake	Xenopeltidae	1 genus, 2 species
Thread/Worm Snakes	Leptotyphlopidae	2 genera, 40 species
Vipers	Viperidae	11 genera, 49 species

LIZARDS

Lizards form the suborder Sauria (sometimes referred to as Lacertilia) in the order Squamata (which includes lizards, amphisbaenians and snakes) which, in turn, is one of the four orders in the class Reptilia. The first lizards described were placed in the genus *Lacerta* (meaning lizard) and one of the first species to be catalogued was the European Sand Lizard, *Lacerta agilis*.

The Suborder Sauria (Lacertilia) is divided into five Infraorders which in turn are divided into families and subfamilies. There is a great deal of controversy regarding the taxonomic assignments of many lizards, especially the Iguanidae. For the purposes of our discussion, the taxonomy of infraorder, family and subfamily is best presented in table form. Be aware that these relationships are not fixed in stone and change on a regular basis as new scientific evidence is accumulated and presented.

FAMILY TIES IN THE SUBORDER SAURIA

Infraorder	Family	Subfamily
Iguania	Iguanidae*	Anolinae, Basiliscinae, Iguaninae, Sceloporinae, Tropidurinae
	Agamidae	
	Chamaeleonidae	
Gekkota	Gekkonidae	Diplodactylinae, Eublepharinae, Gekkoninae, Spherodactylinae
	Pygopodidae	
	Dibamidae	
Scincomorpha	Xantusiidae	Cricosaurinae, Xantusiinae
	Teiidae	Gymnophthalminae, Teiinae
	Scincidae	Acontinae, Feylininae, Lygosominae, Scincinae, Tiliquinae
	Lacertidae	
	Cordylidae	Cordylinae, Gerrhosaurinae
Diploglossa	Anguidae	Anguinae, Diploglossinae, Gerrhonotinae
	Anniellidae	
	Xenosauridae	Shinisaurinae, Xenosaurinae
Platynota (Varanoidea)	Helodermatidae	
	Lanthanotidae	
	Varanidae	

*Newly-proposed taxonomy for the Iguania would create 8 new families: Iguanidae, Hoplocercidae, Polychrotidae, Tropiduridae, Corytophanidae, Crotaphytidae, Phrynosomatidae and Opluridae. See chapter on Iguanian husbandry for more specifics.

The suborder Sauria contains 25 families (if we accept the division of the Iguanidae), about 330-350 genera, and in excess of 3000 species. Though the species are generally accepted as the lowest taxon on the hierarchal scale of classification, subspecies are frequently recognized (and many hundreds of these are recognized to a greater or lesser degree). A subspecies is usually just a geographical variation of a species, and has minor differences, but is still too close to the type species (the first described and named) to warrant its own specific status. In the case of a subspecies the binomial becomes a trinomial, thus: *Lacerta agilis agilis* (Linnaeus, 1758) was the type specimen first described and other subspecies subsequently described include *L. a. exigua* (Eichwald, 1831); *L. a. chersonensis* (Andrzejowski, 1832); *L. a. bosnica* (Schreiber, 1912) and *L. a. euxinica* (Fuhn and Vancea, 1964).

FAMILY TAXONOMY OF SOME COMMON LIZARD SPECIES

Family	Subfamily	Some Genera
Gekkonidae	Eublepharinae	*Aeluroscabotes, Coleonyx, Eublepharus*
	Sphaerodactylinae	*Gonatodes, Sphaerodactylus*
	Diplodactylinae	*Diplodactylus, Hoplodactylus, Naultimus, Oedura, Phyllurus, Rhacodactylus*
	Gekkoninae	*Afroedura, Chondrodactylus, Cyrtodactylus, Geckonia, Gekko, Hemidactylus, Homopholis, Lygodactylus, Phelsuma, Ptychozoon, Teratoscincus, Uroplatus*
Iguanidae	Iguanidae	*Brachylophus, Cyclura, Ctenosaura, Iguana, Sauromalus*
	Corytophanidae	*Basiliscus, Corytophanes, Laemanctus*
	Crotaphytidae	*Crotaphytus, Gambelia*
	Hoplocercidae	*Hoplocercus, Enyaloides*
	Opluridae	*Chalarodon, Oplurus*
	Phrynosomatidae	*Callisaurus, Holbrookia, Phrynosoma, Sceloporus, Uma, Uta*
	Polychridae	*Anolis, Enyalius, Leiosaurus, Polychrus, Urostrophus*
	Tropiduridae	*Leiocephalus, Liolaemus, Plica, Tropidurus*
Agamidae		*Acanthosaura, Amphibolurus, Agama, Calotes, Chlamydosaurus, Gonocephalus, Hydrosaurus, Moloch, Physignathus, Pogona*
Chamaeleonidae		*Bradypodioa, Brookesia, Chamaeleo, Rhampholeon*
Scincidae		*Chalcides, Corucia, Ctenotus, Dasia, Egernia, Eumeces, Hemisphaeriodon, Mabuya, Riopa, Scincella, Scincus, Tiliqua*
Cordylidae	Cordylidae	*Cordylus, Platysaurus, Pseudocordylus*
	Gerrhosauriddae	*Cordylosaurus, Gerrhosaurus, Tetradactylus, Zonosaurus*
Lacertidae		*Acanthodactylus, Adolfus, Algyroides, Bedriagaia, Cabrita, Gallotia, Lacerta, Podarcis, Psammodromus, Tropidosaura*
Teiidae		*Ameiva, Arthrosaura, Cnemidophorus, Crocodilurus, Dracaena, Euspondylus, Tupinambis*
Varanidae		*Varanus*
Lanthanotidae		*Lanthanotus*
Xantusidae		*Xanthusia, Lepidophyma*
Pygopodidae		*Aprasia, Delma, Pygopus*
Dibamidae		*Dibamus*
Helodermatidae		*Heloderma*
Anelytropsidae		*Anelytropsis*
Feylinidae		*Feylinia*
Anguidae		*Anguis, Gerrhonotus, Ophisaurus*
Anniellidae		*Anniella*
Xenosauridae		*Shinisaurus, Xenosaurus*

SOME COMMON LIZARD FAMILIES

Common Family Designation	Family	Members
Agamids	Agamidae	53 genera, 300 species
Anguids	Anguidae	8 genera, 75 species
Beaded Lizards	Helodermatidae	1 genus, 2 species
California Legless Lizards	Anniellidae	1 genus, 2 species
Chameleons	Chamaeleonidae	4 genera, 85 species
Crocodile Lizards	Xenosauridae	2 genera, 4 species
Dibamids (Burrowing lizards)	Dibamidae	1 genus, 4 species
Flap-Foots	Pygopodidae	8 genera, 31 species
Geckos	Gekkonidae	85 genera, 800 species
Iguanids	Iguanidae	55 genera, 650 species
Girdled and Plated Lizards	Cordylidae	10 genera, 50 species
Lacertids	Lacertidae	22 genera, 200 species
Mexican Burrowing Lizards	Anelytropsidae	1 genus, 1 species
Monitor Lizards	Varanidae	1 genus, 31 species
Night Lizards	Xantusiidae	4 genera, 16 species
Skinks	Scincidae	85 genera,1275 species
Skinks, Limbless	Feylinidae	1 genus, 4 species
Tegus and Whiptails	Teiidae	40 genera, 227 species
Tuatara*	Sphenodontidae	1 genus, 2 species
Worm Lizards*	Amphisbaenians	23 genera, 140 species

*Not true lizards. See section below for Tuatara and Worm Lizards

AMPHISBAENIANS

Taxonomists have had various problems with the amphisbaenians, or "worm lizards" over the years. At one time they were included among the suborder Sauria, but they are now more generally recognised as being members of a their own suborder, Amphisbaenia. Two to four families have been described by various authors and there ap-

RHYNCHOCEPHALIANS

Though superficially lizard-like in general appearance the Rhynchocephalians are sufficiently unique to demand an order of their own. The order Rhynchocephalia (Sphenodontida) once was a large reptilian group which arose during the Mesozoic period some 220 million years ago. Most species in the order became extinct about 65 mil-

Family	Members	Examples of Genera
Amphisbaenidae	16 genera, 109 species	*Amphisbaena, Ancylocranium, Chirindia, Cynisca, Dalophia, Leposternon, Monopeltis*
Trogonophidae	4 genera, 6 species	*Agamodon, Diplometopon, Pachycalamus, Trogonophis*
Bipedidae	1 genus, 3 species	*Bipes*

pear to be in excess of 140 species in 23 genera. The three most generally accepted families are the Amphisbaenidae, Trogonophidae and Bipedidae. They occur in USA (Florida, where the best known species, *Rhineura floridana* , occurs), West Indies, South America, Iberian Peninsula, North Africa, Southern Africa and the Middle East. Species length range from 10 cm (4 in) to 75 cm (30 in), but most are in the range 15-30 cm (6-12 in).

lion years ago and today there is just a single family, Sphenodontidae which, until recently, had only a single recognized species, *Sphenodon punctatus*, the Tuatara .

Commonly known as the Tuatara (from a Maori word meaning "peaked-back", referring to the spiny crest), *Sphenodon* is confined to twenty five islands off the northeast coast of the North Island of New Zealand, and in five more islands in the

Cook Strait between the North and South Islands. Tuataras once roamed all over the two main islands of New Zealand but became extinct after the arrival of humans about 1000 years ago. Recently, a second species has been reinstated, having first been described in 1877, but reduced to subpecific status in 1931. This species, *Sphenodon guntheri*, occurs only on Brother Island in the Cook Strait and estimated numbers are less than 1000 specimens.

CROCODILES, ALLIGATORS, CAIMANS AND GAVIALS

Crocodilians are an ancient group of reptiles that arose in the age of the dinosaurs during the early Mesozoic era some 225 million years ago. One of the earliest crocodilians known from the fossil record was *Protosuchus* which was found in the late Triassic rocks of Arizona. It was a relatively small reptile, perhaps no more than 120 cm (4 ft)

in length. Its hindlimbs were much larger than its forelimbs which indicates a bipedal ancestry. Though *Protosuchus* was probably not as aquatic as later crocodilians, it had many features which it passed on to them. The first close relatives of our modern crocodilians were the eusuchians which first appeared in the Cretaceous period, about 130 million years ago. From there, they evolved along three lines, characterised by the alligators, the crocodiles and the gharials.

Today we have four living subfamilies of crocodilians. The number of common names for many crocodilian species give a very good example of the importance of internationally recognised scientific names. For example *Caiman crocodilus* , which is most usually called the Spectacled Caiman in English may, in various places, also be known as Alligator, Baba, Babilla, Brillenkaiman, Cachirre, Caiman a Lunette, Caiman Blanco, Caiman do Brasil, Cascarudo, Cocodrillo, Common Caiman, Jacare de Lunetas, Jacaretinga, Krokodilkaiman, Lagarto, Lagarto Blanco, Tinga, or Yakare Blanko!

THE CROCODILIANS		
Family	**Members**	**Location**
Alligatorinae (alligators and caimans)	4 genera, 7 species	S.E. USA, C.and S. America, E. China
Crocodylinae (true crocodiles)	3 genera, 14 species	Africa, Asia, Australia, C. America, Florida, N. America.
Gavialinae (the gharial/gavial)	1 genus, 1 species	Pakistan, N. and E. India, Nepal, Bangladesh
Tomistominae (false gharial/gavial)	1 genus, 1 species	Asia

SCIENTIFIC AND COMMON NAMES FOR CHELONIANS

Scientific Name	Common Name	Scientific Name	Common Name
Apalone ferox	Florida soft-shell turtle	*Graptemys oculifera*	ringed sawback turtle
Carettochelys insculpta	Fly River turtle	*Graptemys pseudogeo-graphica*	false map turtle
Caretta caretta	loggerhead turtle, marine	*Hardella thurgi*	Brahminy River turtle
Chellonoides chilensis	Chaco tortoise	*Heiremys annandalei*	temple turtle
Chelodina sp.	snake-neck (side-necked) turtles	*Kinxys sp.*	hingeback tortoises
		Kinosternon sp.	mud turtles
Chelonia depressa	Australian Green Turtle	*Kinosternon angustipons*	narrow-bridged mud turtle
Chelonia mydas	green turtle, marine	*Kinosternon baurii*	Striped mud turtle
Chelydra serpentina	snapping turtle, common	*Kinosternon flavescens*	Yellow mud turtle
		Kinosternon hirtipes	Mexican mud turtle
Chelys fimbriata	mata mata turtle	*Kinosternon leukostomum*	White-tipped mud turtle
Chinemys reevesi	Reeves turtle	*Kinosternon scoocpioides*	Scorpion mud turtle
Chrysemys	cooter turtles	*Kinosternon sonoriense*	Sonoran mud turtle
Chrysemys picta ssp.	painted turtle	*Kinosternon subrubrum*	Common mud turtle
Claudius angustatus	narrow-bridged musk turtle	*Lepidochelys olivacea*	olive (Pacific) ridley turtle, marine
Clemmys marmorata	pond turtle	*Lissemys punctata*	soft-shell turtle
Clemmys guttata	spotted turtle	*Macrochelys temminckii*	Alligator snapping turtle
Clemmys insculpta	wood turtle	*Malaclemys terrapin*	diamondback terrapin
Clemmys muhlenbergi	Muhlenberg's turtle; bog turtle	*Malacochersus tornieri*	pancake tortoises
		Ocadia sinensis	gold thread turtle
Cuora flavomarginata	snake eating turtle	*Pelomedusa subrufa*	African helmeted turtle
Cuora sp.	Asian box turtles	*Pelusios* sp.	African side-neck turtles
Cyclemys sp.	leaf turtles	*Pelusios* sp.	East African side neck turtles
Deirochelys reticularia	Chicken turtle		
Dermatemys mawi	Central American river turtle	*Phrynops* sp.	toad-headed turtles
		Phrynops hilarii	Argentine side-neck turtle
Dermochelys coriacea	leatherback turtle, marine	*Platysternon megacephalum*	big-headed turtle
		Platemys platycephala	Bolivian side-necked turtle; twist-necked turtle
Elysea novaeguineae	New Guinea side neck turtle	*Platemys spixii*	spiny neck turtle
Emydoidea blandingi	Blanding's turtle	*Rhinoclemmys punctularia* spp.	South American wood turtle
Eretmochelys imbricata	hawksbill turtle, marine		
Geochelone carbonaria	red-footed tortoise	*Sacalia bealei*	four-eyed turtle
Geochelone chilensis	Chaco tortoise	*Siebenrockiella crassicollis*	black pond turtle
Geochelone denticulata	yellow-footed (legged) tortoise	*Staurotypus salvinii*	Pacific coast giant musk turtle
Geochelone nigra app.	Galapagos tortoises	*Staurotypus triporcatus*	Mexican giant musk turtle
Geochelone elongata	elongated tortoise		
Geochelone emys	Burmese mountain tortoise	*Sternotherus* sp.	Musk turtles
		Sternotherus carinatus	Razor-backed musk turtle
Geochelone gigantea	Aldabra tortoise	*Sternotherus depressus*	Flattened musk turtle
Gochelone impressa	impressed tortoise	*Sternotherus minor minor*	Loggerback musk turtle
Geochelone pardalis ssp.	leopard tortiose	*Sternotherus odoratus*	stinkpot turtle
Geochelone sulcata	spurred tortoise, African	*Terrapene* sp.	Box turtles
		Testudo elegans	star tortoise
Geomyda spengleri	Vietnamese wood turtle	*Testudo graeca*	Greek tortoise
Geomyda spinosa	spiny turtle	*Testudo hermanni*	Hermann's tortoise
Gopherus (Xerobates) agassizi	desert tortoise	*Testudo kleinmanni*	Egyptian tortoise
		Testudo radiata	radiated tortoise
Gopherus berlanderi	Berlander's tortoise	*Trachemys*	slider turtles
Gopherus flavomarginatus	Bolson tortoise	*Trachemys s. scripta*	yellow bellied slide turtle
Gopherus polyphemus	gopher tortoise	*Trachemys scripta elegans*	red-eared slider turtle
Graptemys geographica ssp.	map turtles	*Trionyx* spp.	soft-shelled turtles

SCIENTIFIC AND COMMON NAMES FOR SNAKES

Scientific Name	Common Name	Scientific Name	Common Name
Ahaetulloa(Dryophis) sp.	tree snakes	*Chionectis sp.*	shovel-nosed snake
Acalyptophis peronii	Peron's sea snake	*Chironius scurrulus*	green headed tree snakes
Acanthophis antarcticus	death adder	*Chondropython viridis*	green tree python;
Acrochordus granulosus	wart snake		chondropython
Acrochordus javanicus	wart snake	*Chrysopeler sp.*	flying snakes
Acrochordus sp.	elephant trunk snake	*Chrysopeler ornata*	ornate tree snake
	(or Kurung)	*Clonophis kirtlandii*	Kirtland's snake
Agkistrodon bilineatus	Mexican moccasin, cantil	*Coluber constrictor ssp.*	racer, blue
Agkistrodon blomhoffi	mamushi snake	*Coluber constrictor mormon*	racer, yellow-bellied
Agkistrodon contortrix	copperhead snake	*Coniophanes imperialis*	Black striped snake
Agkistrodon intermedius	Amur viper	*Corallus caninus*	emerald tree boa
Agkistrodon piscivorus	water mocassin	*Coronella girondica*	old world smooth crowned
Alsophis vudii picticeps	racer, West Indian		snake
Anilius s. scytale	"two headed snake"	*Crotalus adamanteus*	eastern diamondback
Arizona elegans	glossy snake		rattlesnake
Aspidelaps lubricus	cobra	*Crotalus atrocaudatus*	Canebrake rattlesnake
Aspidites melanocephalus	black-headed python	*Crotalus basiliscus*	Mexican green rattlesnake
Atractaspis sp.	Burrowing vipers	*Crotalus cerastes*	sidewinder rattlesnake
Azemiops feae	Fea's viper	*Crotalus durissus*	Cascabel rattlesnake
Bitis arietans	puff adder	*Crotalus durissus cascabel*	tropical rattlesnake; cascavel
Bitis atropos	mountain adder	*Crotalus enyo*	Baja California rattlesnake
Bitis caudalis	horned adder	*Crotalus horridus*	timber rattlesnake
Bitis cornuta	many-horned adder	*Crotalus intermedius gloydi*	small-headed rattlesnake
Bitis g. gabonica	Gaboon viper	*Crotalus lepidus ssp.*	rock rattlesnakes
Bitis gabonica rhinoceros	thorned gaboon viper	*Crotalus mitchelli pyrrhus*	speckled rattlesnake
Bitis nasicornis	rhinoceros viper	*Crotalus molossus*	Black-tailed rattlesnake
Bitis peringueyi	dwarf sand (puff) adder	*Crotalus polystictus*	lance-headed
Bitis schneideri	dwarf sand adder		(long-headed) rattlesnake
Boa constrictor sp.	Boa constrictor	*Crotalus pricei*	twin-spotted rattlesnake
Boiga dendrophile	mangrove snake	*Crotalus pusillus*	dusty rattlesnake
Boiga irregularis	Brown tree snake	*Crotalus ruber*	red diamond rattlesnake
Bothriechis [Bothrops]		*Crotalus scutulatus*	Mojave rattlesnake
schlegeli	eye lash viper	*Crotalus sp.*	rattlesnakes
Bothriechis [Bothrops] sp.	palm vipers	*Crotalus stejnegeri*	long-tailed rattlesnake
Bothrops alternatus	urutu, wutu snake	*Crotalus tigris*	tiger rattlesnake
Bothrops andianus asper	fer-de-lance	*Crotalus unicolor*	Aruba rattlesnake
boulengerina annulata	cobra	*Crotalus vegrandis*	Uracoan rattlesnake
Bungarus caeruleus sindanus	Blue krait	*Crotalus viridis cerberus*	black rattlesnake
Bungarus fasciatus	banded krait	*Crotalus viridis helleri*	southern Pacific rattlesnake
Bungarus m. multicinctus	many-banded krait	*Crotalus viridis oreganus*	northern Pacific rattlesnake
Bungarus sp.	kraits	*Crotalus willardi*	ridge-nosed rattlesnakes
Calabaria reinhardtii	burrowing Calabar python	*Crotaphopeltis hotamboeia*	cat-eyed snake; herald snake
Calloselasma rhodostoma	Malayan pit viper	*Cyclagras gigas*	Brazilian Smooth snake;
Candoia bibroni	Solomon Isand ground boa		false water cobra
Candoia carinata	Solomon Island ground boa	*Cylindrophis sp.*	pipe snakes
Candoia asper	"viper" boa	*Cylindrophis rufus*	red-tailed (Malayan)
Canoia carinata	New Guinea tree boa		pipe snake
Causus resimus	green night adder	*Dasypeltis atra*	egg-eating snake
Causus sp.	night adders	*Dasypeltis scabra*	egg-eating snake
Cemophora c. coccinea	scarlet snake	*Deinagkistodon acutus*	sharp-nosed viper
Cerastes c. cerastes	horned desert viper	*Demansia psammophis*	yellow-faced whipsnake
Cerastes c. gasperetti	hornless desert viper	*Dendrelaphis punctulatus*	Australian tree snake
Cerastes cerastes	desert viper	*Dendroaspis*	mambas
Cerastes vipera	hornless desert viper	*Dendroaspis polylepis*	black mamba
Charina bottae	Rubber boa	*Dinodon rufozonatum*	Asian big tooth snake

Scientific Name	Common Name	Scientific Name	Common Name
Diadophis punctatus	ring-neck snake	*Lampropeltis calligaster*	prairie kingsnake
Dipsas indica	snail-eating snake	*Lampropeltis getulas californiae*	California kingsnake
Dipsas sp.	snail-eating snake	*Lampropeltis getulas loridana*	Florida kingsnake
Dispholidus typus	boomslang	*Lampropeltis getulas getula*	eastern kingsnake
Drymarchon corais corais	cribo, yellow tailed	*Lampropeltis getula holbrooki*	speckled kingsnake
Drymarchon corais ssp	indigo snakes	*Lampropeltis getula splendida*	desert kingsnake
Echis carinatus ssp.	saw scaled vipers	*Lampropeltis mexicana alterna*	gray-banded kingsnake
Elaphe bairdi	Baird's rat snake	*Lampropeltis mexicana greeri*	Greer's kingsnake
Elaphe bimaculata	Chinese twin spot rat snake	*Lampropeltis triangulum elapsoides*	scarlet kingsnake
Elaphe carinata	Chinese king rat snake	*Lampropeltis triangulum*	milksnake
Elaphe climacophora	Japanese rat snake	*Lampropeltis triangulum annulata*	Mexican milksnake
Elaphe erythrura	Philippine rat snake	*Lampropeltis triangulum syspila*	red milksnake
Elaphe flavirufa	Mexican ratsnake	*Lamprophis fuliginosus*	African house snake
Elaphe flavolineata	New Guinea (copperhead) rat snake	*Laticauda* sp.	marine (or sea) snakes
Elaphe guttata guttata	red rat snake, corn snake	*Leimadophis*	Argentine green snake
Elaphe helena	Indian rat snake	*Leimadophis poecilogyrus reticulatus*	speckled snake, Argentine
Elaphe l. longissima	Aesculapian snake	*Leptodeira septentrionalis*	Cat-eyed snake
Elaphe moellendorffi	Red-headed Moerlendorff's rat snake	*Leptotyphlops*	worm snakes
Elaphe obsoleta	black rat snake	*Liasis albertisi*	white-lipped python
Elaphe obsoleta quadrivittata	yellow rat snake	*Liasis amethystinus*	amethystine python
Elaphe obsoleta spilotes	gray rat snake	*Liasis boa*	Bismark ringed python
Elaphe radiata	radiated snake; copperhead racer	*Liasis boeleni*	Boelen's python
Elaphe rufodorsata	Chinese lined rat snake	*Liasis fuscus*	brown water python
Elaphe schrenckii	Russian rat snake	*Liasis olivaceus*	water python
Elaphe subocularis	Trans Pecos rat snake	*Lichanura trivirgata*	rosy boa
Elaphe taeniua friesi	Taiwan beauty snake; Chinese rat snake	*Leioheterodon madaga-scariensis*	Malagasy hognose snake
Elaphe triaspis intermedia	green ratsnake	*Liopeltis* sp.	green snake, smooth
Elaphe vulpina	fox snake	*Lycodon aulicus*	wolf snake
Enhydris plumbea	Indonesian green water (smooth scaled) snake	*Lycophidion capense*	wolf snake
Epicrates angulifer	Cuban boa	*Lycophidion striatus*	wolf snake
Epicrates cenchria	rainbow boa	*Lystrophis* sp.	hog-nosed snake, South American
Eridiphas sp.	night snakes		
Eristocophis macmahoni	leaf-nosed viper	*Macropisthodon rudis*	false habu snake
Erpeton tentaculum	fishing snake; tentacled snake	*Malpolon m monspessulamus*	Montpellier snake
Erythrolamprus bizona	false coral snake	*Masticophis flagellum*	Coachwhip snake
Eryx sp.	sand boa	*Maticora bivirgata flaviceps*	Malayan long-glanded coral snake
Eunectes sp	anaconda		
Exiliboa	dwarf boa	*Morelia childreni*	Children's python
Farancia abacura	mud snake	*Morelia spilotes variegata*	Carpet python
Farancia e. erytrogramma	rainbow snake	*Naja* sp	cobra
Ficimia streckeri	hook-nosed snake	*Naja melanoleuca*	white-lipped forest cobra
Gyalopion sp.	hook-nosed snake	*Naja n. sputatrix*	spitting cobra
Gongylophis conicus	rough scaled sand boa	*Natix t. tessellata*	dice snake
Gonyosoma oxycephala	Asian rat snake	*Notechis scutatus*	tiger snake
Haemorrhois ravergieri	Ravergier's racer	*Oligodon formosanus*	Taiwan kukri snake
Hemachatus haemachatus	cobra	*Opheodrys* sp.	smooth green snake
Hypsiglena sp.	night snakes	*Opheodrys vernalis*	rough green snake
Imantodes cenchoa	blunt-headed tree snake		
Imantodes sp.	tree snakes		
Lachesis muta	bushmaster		
Lampropeltis sp.	kingsnakes		

Scientific Name	Common Name	Scientific Name	Common Name
Ophiophagus hannah	king cobra	*Spilotes p. pullatus*	tropical chicken (or rat) snake
Oxyuranus scutellatus	taipan snake		
Pelamis sp.	marine (or sea) snakes	*Spilotes pullatus*	tiger rat snake
Phyllorhynchus decurtatus ssp.	leaf-nosed snake	*Stilosoma extenuatum*	short-tailed snake
Pittuophis melanoleucus sp.	gopher snake (bull snake)	*Storeria dekayi*	DeKay's snake
Pituophis m. deserticola	Great Basin gopher snake	*Storeria occipitomaculata*	red-bellied snake
Pituophis m. lodingi	black pine snake	*Tantilla* sp.	black-headed snakes; flat-headed snakes
Pituophis m. melanoleucus	northern pine snake		
Pituophis m. mugitus	southern pine snake	*Thasops jacksoni*	black tree snake
Pituophis m. ruthveni	Louisiana pine snake	*Thamnophis* sp.	garter snakes
Pituophis m. vertebralis	Baja bull snake	*Thamnophis butleri*	Butler's garter snake
Pituophis melanoleucus	Bull snake	*Thamnophis couchi hammondi*	two-striped garter snake
Pituophis melanoleucus affinis	Sonoran gopher snake	*Thamnophis marcianus*	checkered gartersnake
Pituophis melanoleucus sp.	pine snakes	*Thamnophis proximus*	western ribbon snake
Porthidium [bothrops] mummifer mexicanum	jumping viper	*Thamnophis sirtalis*	common garter snake
Porthidium barbouri	Barbour's pit viper	*Thamnophis s. sackeni*	pcninsula ribbon snake
Porthidium melanurus	Blaack-tailed horned pit viper	*Thamnophis s. sauritus*	eastern ribbon snake
		Thamnophis s. similis	Blue-stiped garter snake
Porthidium [Bothrops] godmani	Godman's pit viper	*Thamnophis s. tetrataenia*	San Francisco garter snake
Psammophis sp.	sand snake	*Thelotornis kirtlandii*	Kirtland's bird snake
Pseudaspis c. cana	mole snake, African	*Trachyboa boulengeri*	rough scaled boa
Pseudohaje goldii	Gold's tree cobra	*Trachyboa* sp.	Rough-skinned boa
Pseustes poecilonotus polylepis	puffing snakes	*Trimeresurus albolabris*	white-lipped pit viper
Pseustes poecilontus polylepis	mahogany rat snake	*Trimeresurus gramineus*	Indian tree viper
Pseustes sulphureus	puffing snakes	*Trimeresurus kanburiensis*	Kanburian pit viper
Python anchietae	Angolan python	*Trimeresurus okinavensis*	himehabu
Python curtus	blood python	*Trimeresurus popeorum*	Pope's tree viper
Python molurus	Indian rock python	*Trimeresurus purpureoma-culatus*	mangrove pit vipper
Python molurus bivittatus	Burmese python	*Trimeresurus* sp.	habu snakes
Python olivaceus	olive python	*Trimeresurus stejnegeri*	Chinese tree viper
Python regius	ball python	*Trimeresurus sumatranus*	Sumatran tree viper
Python reticulatus	reticulated python	*Trimeresurus trigonocephalus*	Sri Lanken pit viper
Python sebae	African rock python	*Trimeresurus wirotii*	Wirot's pit viper
Python timorensis	Timor python	*Trimorphodon biscutatus*	lyre snake
Regina septemvittatus	queen snake	*Tropidoclonium lineatum*	lined snake
Regina sp.	crawfish (or swamp) snakes	*Tropidodipsas sartori*	snail-eating snake
Rhabdophis subminiatus	red-necked keelback snake	*Tropidophis*	wood snakes, caribbean dwarf boas
Rhadinaea flavilata	yellow-lipped (pine woods) snake	*Typhlops* sp	worm snakes, blind snakes
Rhamphiophis multima-culatus	African beaked snake	*Typhlops braminus*	Bramin blind snake
Ramphotyphlops sp.	blind snake	*Uromacer oxyrhynchus*	vine snake
Salvadora hexalepis	patch-nosed snake	*Vermicella annulata*	bandy-bandy snake
Sanzinia madagascariensis	Malagasy tree boa	*Vipera ammodytes*	long-nosed viper, sand adder
Scaphiodontophis annulatus hondurensis	neck-banded snake	*Vipera aspis*	asp
Semiatrix p. pygaea	black swamp snake	*Vipera berus*	crossed viper
Sistrurus catenatus sp.	massasauga rattlesnakes	*Vipera kaznakovii*	Kaznakov's viper
Sistrurus miliarius	pygmy rattlesnake	*Vipera palaestinae*	Palestinian viper
Sistrurus ravus	Mexican pygmy rattlesnake	*Vipera russelli*	Russel's viper
Spalerosophis diadema cliffordi	diadem snake	*Virginia striatula*	earth snake, rough
		Virginia valeriae	earth snake, smooth
		Walterinnesia aegyptia	Sinai Desert cobra
		Xenopeltis unicolor	sunbeam snake
		Zaocys dhumnades	keeled rat snake

SCIENTIFIC AND COMMON NAMES FOR LIZARDS, AMPHISBAENIANS AND RHYNCHOCEPHALIANS

Scientific Name	Common Name	Scientific Name	Common Name
Acanthodactylus pardalis	sand lizard (gecko)	*Heloderma horridum*	Mexican beaded lizard
Acanthosaura armata	mountain horned lizard	*Heloderma suspectum*	Gila monster
Agama sp.	Agama lizards	*Hemidactylus garnoti*	house gecko
Amblyrhynchus cristatus	iguana, marine	*Hemitheconyx caudicinctus*	fat-tailed gecko
Ameiva ameiva	jungle runner lizard; rainbow lizard	*Holbrookia sp.*	earless lizard
		Holbrookia maculata	lesser earless lizard
Amphibolorus barbatus	Bearded lizard	*Hoplocercus spinosus*	iguana, prickle tail
Anguis fragilis	slow "worm" lizard	*Hydrosaurus sp.*	sage brush sail finned; sail-tailed lizard
Anniella pulcra	legless lizard		
Anolis sp.	Anole lizards	*Iguana delicatissima*	iguana, lesser Antillean
Anolis carolinensis	Green anole	*Iguana iguana*	iguana, common
Anolis equestris	Knight anole	*Lacerta sp.*	lacerta lizards, misc.
Anolis opalinus	Jamaican lizard	*Laemanctus longipes*	iguana, cone-headed
Basiliscus sp.	Basilisk lizards	*Leiocephalus carinatus*	curly-tailed lizard
Basiliscus basiliscus	Common basilisk	*Lepidodactylus sp.*	common tropical gecko
Basiliscus plumifrons	Green basilisk	*Liolaemus sp.*	swifts, Latin American
Bipes biporus	worm lizards	*Liolaemus tenuis*	swift, Jewel
Blanus sp.	worm lizards	*Moloch horridus*	moloch lizard
Brachylophus fasciatus	iguana, banded	*Nactus pelagicus*	tropical gecko
Brachylophus sp.	iguana, Fiji Island	*Ophiosaurus apodus*	sheltopusik lizard
Calliopistes maculatus	dwarf tegu	*Ophiosaurus ventralis*	glass "snake" lizard
Callisaurus draconoides	zebra tailed lizard	*Oplura sp.*	Madagascan skinks
Chalcides sexlineatus	sand skink	*Petrosaurus mearnsi*	rock lizard, banded
Chameleo sp.	Old World Chameleons	*Phelsuma quadriocellata*	four-eyed day gecko
Cnemidophorus sp.	whip-tailed lizard	*Phelsuma serratocauda*	leaf-tailed gecko
Cnemidophorus tigris	Western whiptail lizard	*Phrynocephalus mystaceus*	Russian gargoyle lizard
Conolophus pallidus	iguana, ground	*Phrynosoma cornutum*	horned lizard
Conolophus subcristatus	iguana, Galapogos Island	*Physignathus sp.*	water dragon lizards
Cophosaurus sp.	earless lizards	*Podarcis sicula*	ruin lizard
Cordylus sp.	armadillo lizards	*Ptychozoon kuhli*	flying gecko
Corucia zebrata	prehensile-tail skink; Solomon Island skink	*Ptyodactylus hasselquistii*	fat-footed gecko
		Sauromalus obesus	Chuckwalla lizard
Corythophanes cristatus.	helmeted lizard	*Sauromalus varius*	San Estaban Chuckwalla
Crotaphytus collaris ssp.	leopard lizards	*Sceloporus malachitus*	Emerald swift
Crotophytus reticulatus	Reticulate collared lizard	*Sceloporus magister*	spiny lizard
Crotaphytus sp.	collared lizards	*Sceloporus poinsetti*	crevice spiny lizard
Ctenosaura palearis	iguana, Paleate spiny-tailed	*Sceloporus sp.*	fence lizards
Ctenosaura pectinata simila	spiny-tailed iguanas	*Scincus scincus*	sand "fish" (skink)
Ctenosaurus sp.	iguanas, spiny-tailed	*Sphenodon punctatus*	tuatara
Cyclura cornuta	iguana, rhinocerous	*Tarentola borgetti*	wall gecko
Cyclura nubila nubila	iguana, Cuban	*Teratoscincus S. scincus*	frog-eyed gecko
Cyclura nubila lewisi	iguana, Cayman Island blue rock	*Tiliqua sp.*	Blue tongued skinks
		Tropidurus sp.	Lava lizards
Cyclura sp.	iguana, ground	*Tupinambis nigropunctatus*	Tegu, golden
Cyrtodactylus pulchellus	Banded gecko	*Tupinambis rufescens*	Tegu, red
Dipsosaurus dorsalis	iguana, desert	*Tupinambis teguixin*	Tegu, black and white
Draecaena guianensis	Caiman lizard	*Uma sp.*	fringe-toed lizards
Eremias grammica	dwarf sand lizard	*Urocentron sp.*	spiny-tailed iguanas
Eublepharis macularious	leopard gecko	*Uromastix acanthinuris*	dab lizard
Gallotia stelini	Canary Island giant lacerta	*Uromastix aegypticus*	dab lizard
Gambelia wistizem	Leopard lizard	*Uromastix sp.*	spiny-tailed lizards
Gekko gecko	Tokay gecko	*Urosaurus graciosus*	long-tailed brush lizard
Gekko vetalus	Lined gecko	*Urosaurus graciosus*	long-tailed brush lizard
Gerrhonotus sp.	Alligator lizards	*Urosaurus sp.*	tree lizards
Gerrhosaurrus sp.	plated lizards	*Uta palmeri*	side-blotched lizards

Scientific Name	Common Name	Scientific Name	Common Name
Uta stansburiana	side-blotched lizards	*Varanus niloticus*	Nile monitor lizard
Varanus albigularis	monitor, Cape	*Varanus olivaceus*	Gray's monitor lizard
Varanus beccari	Black tree monitor lizard	*Varanus praesinus*	green tree monitor lizard
Varanus bengalensis	monitor, Bengal	*Varanus rudicollis*	rough necked monitor lizard
Varanus exanthematicus	monitor, Savannah		
Varanus flavescens	monitor, yellow	*Varanus salvadori*	monitor, Asian water
Varanus gouldii horni	monitor, argus	*Varanus salvator*	water monitor lizard
Varanus grayi	Gray's monitor lizard	*Varanus timorensis*	monitor, Timor
Varanus griseus	monitor, desert	*Varanus sp.*	monitor lizards
Varanus indicus	monitor, mangrove	*Xantusia sp.*	night lizards
Varanus komodoensis	Komodo dragon	*Zonosaurus sp.*	plated lizards

SCIENTIFIC AND COMMON NAMES FOR CROCODILIANS

Scientific name	Common Name
Alligator sinensis	Chinese alligator
Alligator mississippiensis	American alligator
Caiman sp.	Caimans
Caiman crocodylus	caiman, spectacled
Caiman latirostris	caiman, broad-snouted
Caiman yacare	Yacare (Paraguayan) Caiman
Crocodylus sp.	Crocodile
Crocodylus acutus	American crocodile
Crocodylus cataphractus	African Slender-snouted Crocodile
Crocodylus intermedius	Orinoco crocodile
Crocodylus johnstoni	Johnston's Crocodile
Crocodylus mindorensis	Philippine crocodile
Crocodylus moreletii	Morelet's crocodile
Crocodylus niloticus	Nile crocodile
Crocodylus novaeguineae	New Guinea crocodile
Crocodylus palustris	mugger crocodile
Crocodylus porosus	Estuarine crocodile
Crocodylus rhombifer	Cuban crocodile
Crocodylus siamensis	Siamese crocodile
Gavialis gangeticus	Gavial (gharial)
Melanosuchus niger	Black Caiman
Osteolaemus tetraspis	Dwarf (broad-snouted) crocodile
Paleosuchus palpebrosus	Dwarf Caiman
Paleosuchus trigonatus	Smooth-fronted (Schneider's) Caiman
Tomistoma schlegeli	False Gavial (gharial)

MUSEUM AND ANATOMICAL PREPARATION OF REPTILE SPECIMENS

Sean J. Barry, MS
Section of Evolution and Ecology
University of California
Davis, California 95616

Sean Barry completed degrees in zoology and herpetology at the University of California, Davis, and was the curator of vertebrates and preparator at the Museum of Zoology at Davis for several years. He is a researcher in endocrinology and herpetology, and is currently completing a monograph on his 20-year field study of the endangered San Francisco garter snake, Thamnophis sirtalis tetrataenia.

INTRODUCTION

This chapter is directed to individual keeper/collectors who may have occasion to preserve deceased, captive specimens and (ideally) deposit them in scientific institutions, and to those who desire to learn to prepare skeletal and other anatomical materials. Most of the objectives discussed in this chapter can be accomplished with a variety of techniques. The techniques detailed here are those in widest use for the longest time. These methods are generally satisfactory (if not perfect), and their use ensures that new specimen material is prepared by standard procedures. For example, specimen fixation in alcohol instead of the usual formalin is discouraged here. Even though alcohol fixation is safer to the preparator, few museums use this technique, and specimens so prepared may be less durable than standard museum material.

This chapter is devoted to whole-animal and gross anatomical preparation—preparative processes for histology, electron microscopy, and molecular techniques are beyond its scope.

HAZARDS, WARNINGS, AND CAUTIONS

Some of the hazards associated with the chemicals discussed in this chapter are summarized in Table 1, and are highlighted in the text. This information is based on data provided by Budavari (1989), Furr (1989), and Lewis (1993), but it does not substitute for Material Safety Data Sheets (MSDS). Before attempting to follow any procedures described in this chapter, you must familiarize yourself with the hazards of all chemicals you will be using. Take proper precautions, and do not endanger yourself or others through ignorance or carelessness.

WARNINGS

Use extreme caution in handling, using, and storing chemicals. The chemicals described in this chapter range from mildly hazardous to very dangerous. Many of the procedures described in this chapter are safe only if done with knowledge and caution, primarily because of the chemicals involved. Dangers of physical harm increase in direct proportion to ignorance and carelessness. Do not attempt any of the techniques discussed in this chapter unless you have been properly trained in the use of the chemicals involved.

Contact and exposure to chemicals can result in physical harm. Minimum handling precautions for chemicals include personal protection such as latex gloves, labcoats, closed-toe shoes, and especially face and eye protection. Volatile and certain other chemicals must be handled outdoors or in an approved fume hood. Flammables must be used outdoors, away from all ignition sources, or in a properly equipped laboratory.

None of the chemicals (including "household chemicals") described in this chapter is safe under all usage and storage conditions. Segregate incompatible chemicals and store them in a secure location away from potential access by children. (For example, you must store glycerine and acids separately; you must also store household bleach and household ammonia separately.) Store flammables in the manufacturers' containers, preferably within approved flammable material cabinets. MSDS's (Material Data Safety Sheets) typically include storage information for chemicals.

Do not wash chemicals down the sink or place in trash receptacles. Virtually all chemical waste

Table 1. Known and suspected hazards associated with the chemicals discussed in the text and Material Safety Data Sheets. This table identifies only the most important hazards, and should not be considered exhaustive. Data are derived from Budavari (1989), Lewis (1993).

Chemical	Hazard							
	inhalant	ingestion	skin	irritant	carcinogen	explosive	flammable	corrosive
acetic acid	x	x	x	x				x
acetone	x	x	x	x		x	x	x
alcian blue				x				
alizarin red				x				
ammonia (household)	x	x	x	x				x
Batson's compound components	x	x	x	x	x		x	
bleach- sodium hypochlorite	x	x	x	x				x
chloroform	x	x	x	x	x			
cyanoacrylate	x	x	x	x				
DUCO cement (wet)	x	x	x	x			x	
epoxy	x	x	x	x				
ether	x	x	x	x		x	x	
ethyl alcohol	x	x	x	x			x	
formaldehyde (formalin)	x	x	x	x	x			
glycerine								
hydrochloric acid	x	x	x	x	x			x
hydrogen peroxide, 3%		x	x	x				x
isopropyl alcohol	x	x	x	x			x	
potassium hydroxide		x	x	x				x

generated by the techniques discussed in this chapter must be disposed as hazardous waste through an approved collection facility.

Caution

A Material Safety Data Sheet (MSDS) must be obtained for every chemical to be used, including household items. These sheets are available from the manufacturers, and must be consulted before you use the material described.

LICENSING, LIVE AND CAPTIVE SPECIMENS, AND EUTHANASIA

This discussion includes information about the licensing and permits required for specimen collection, wild versus captive specimens, and euthanasia.

LICENSES, PERMITS, AND ETHICAL CONSIDERATIONS

It is sometimes necessary to collect specimens from wild populations for scientific purposes. Such activity is tightly regulated in most states, and almost every state requires that collectors have scientific collecting permits. Some states do allow reptile collecction under the authority of a sport fishing license or without a license. However, these states still typically require a collecting permit for scientific activity. Individuals not associated with academic institutions or museums are rarely allowed to collect specimens for scientific activity.

Many states also require a "salvage permit" to collect road kills. Most states prohibit the take of rare and endangered or fully protected species without special permits. Federal laws also regulate the take of federally-listed threatened and endangered species. Always check current regulations with appropriate agencies before you collect wildlife.

The scientific collector should be guided by legal and ethical constraints. He should take only as many animals as needed, and he should work to obtain maximum utility from each specimen. Rarely is it advisable or necessary for a private individual to accumulate a preserved collection. Collected specimens with locality data are too valuable to be maintained privately. In most cases a vertebrate museum is the proper place for such material. A very few private individuals have accumulated personal collections for valid reasons, but in general the practice should be discouraged.

In general, the greatest service a private individual can perform is to donate to institutions single specimens that are either deceased captives or road kills that represent hitherto poorly known populations. However, the individual should make sure in advance that the institution is willing to accept private donations. Further, most institutions prefer that specimens in their collections be fixed, tagged, and preserved by specific protocols which can vary widely among institutions. Seldom is more than one specimen required for voucher purposes; as long as the specimen is well-preserved and identifiable, and the locality data that accompany the specimen are meticulously detailed and accurate.

Collecting techniques vary with locality, habitat, season, climate, and the species sought. Standard collecting procedures are summarized by Conant and Collins (1991) and by Stebbins (1985).

LIVING AND CAPTIVE SPECIMENS

A living specimen intended for preservation in a museum collection should not be retained for more than a day or two in captivity before euthanasia. During captivity, food in the digestive system can become unrecognizable, parasites can vanish, and soft tissue proportions can change. These data are very useful in ecological studies, but not if altered by extended captivity. If a specimen is kept alive for an extended period, that fact should be noted on the tag, as should brief information about captive diet.

EUTHANASIA

Dr. Luette Forrest's chapter in the Health Care Section describes specific information about euthanasia of reptiles. The information provided here is for euthanasia of animals for museum specimens only.

Museum personnel most often use the respiratory depressant sodium pentobarbital ("Nembutal") for reptile euthanasia. Do not use pentobarbital that is cloudy or has formed a precipitate. The small dose used for euthanasia does not affect soft tissues adversely for general histological purposes.

Caution
Sodium pentobarbital is a Class II DEA controlled substance. It is available only for research or medical uses to institutions and to medical professionals.

The dosage of pentobarbital for reptile euthanasia is 100mg/kg body weight (Anderson, 1965). The preferred route for the drug is intra-cardiac. However, you can usually inject the drug effectively anywhere in the pleural or peritoneal cavity. The reptile's death is usually extremely rapid, and the specimen remains relaxed.

Other injectable euthanasia agents include the local anesthetic procaine HCl at 500 mg/kg body weight (Livezey, 1957), and the sedative tricaine (MS 222). Both drugs are available to institutions and are not currently regulated by DEA. MS 222 is rarely used as an injectable, but is used widely to sedate or euthanize fish and amphibians by adding various concentrations to the animals' water.

In the past, some euthanasia was performed with a 10% solution of formaldehyde (Table 1) by intracardiac or intraperitoneal injection. However, this is inhumane, and it is definitely less than satisfactory for museum work because it leaves the specimen contorted and stiff. Formaldehyde is not recommended for euthanasia.

Most vertebrates can be euthanized by placing the animal in a sealed container with a chloroform or ether- soaked cotton ball. Use caution because chloroform may be carcinogenic, and ether is explosive. Both substances must be handled carefully outdoors or in a fume hood (Table 1).

What of the private individual who must occasionally euthanize a captive specimen for humane reasons? The best advice is to present the specimen to a veterinarian for humane, rapid euthanasia. However, ectothermic organisms may be euthanized humanely by freezing at least overnight at or below -20°C(8°F). This temperature is normally only attainable in a chest or upright freezer—the "freezer section" of a standard household refrigerator is not cold enough, except for very small specimens. Freezing diminishes the utility of the specimen for certain techniques, and destroys its utility for most histological and immunohistochemical applications. Scott and Aquino-Shuster (1989) have shown conclusively what preparators have long understood—that freezing results in softer, darker formalin-fixed specimens, and exfoliation of the epidermis may also result.

RECORD KEEPING

Accurate and complete records are critical to the usefulness of a specimen. Always maintain a permanent record of preserved and prepared specimens.

You should follow these general steps when recording information about a specimen:

1. Assign a consecutive personal catalogue number to each specimen.
2. Record the number, specimen identification, date, and locality data in a personal catalogue that is part of a field notebook.
3. Cross-reference the catalogue data to the field book by date, locality, and species.

Hall and Kelson (1959) discuss and illustrate a good format for the catalogue-notebook.

TAGS

Tags are usually preprinted on one side with the institution name, and are quite expensive to manufacture. Thus, institutions may be reluctant to distribute tags, and adequate permanent labeling of specimens can be a real problem for private individuals. Yet, the tag is the most important part of the specimen—without tag data, almost nothing of scientific interest can be obtained from a specimen. Therefore, the private collector should try to label material carefully and as permanently as possible.

When writing data on a tag, print the data very carefully on the blank side of the tag. The other side of the tag should contain the name of the originating institution, and may also be used *by the institution* to identify the specimen.

TAG DATA

Minimum tag data include:
—precise specimen locality: county, state, and the exact distance in SI units and the direction from a permanent landmark
—date the specimen was collected
—collector's name
—collector's personal catalogue number
—the notation DOR (dead on road) if the specimen was a road-kill

If there is room on the tag, you may include further habitat detail.

LOCALITY DATA

The most common method of locality notation is from the precise to the general; for example: 1.5 airline km ESE Redwood Spring, Santa Rita Canyon, Imperial County, California. If geographic or map coordinates are known with certainty, you can also include those coordinates on the tag.

Collectors used to record distance from the post office of a town or city as a locality; for example: 5 miles east of St. Louis. However, post offices can be moved so such locality data are inherently ambiguous and their use should be avoided. Because any manmade landmark can change, you should, wherever possible, choose a natural landmark as your reference point. Also, be certain to cite the distance from a precise natural landmark rather than a general area. For example, the designation, "15 km east of temporary Interstate 495" is not very helpful.

TAG DATES

To avoid ambiguity, write out the tag date. It is preferable to write the date, followed by the month and year (for example, 23 November, 1950). However, it is acceptable to write the month first (for example, November 23, 1950).

SPECIES IDENTIFICATIONS

Some institutions discourage specimen identification on the collector's tag. These institutions prefer to leave final identification for cataloguing purposes to their own curatorial personnel. Instead of including the species identification on a specimen's tag, the identified material is stored in jars or drawers that have large labels with species names.

Remember that everything written on a tag may be scrutinized in light of new data in the distant future. If all other pertinent data are included, species identification *per se* is extraneous information which may confuse future investigators. Also, subspecific specimen identities are the most likely designations to change in fthe future. In general, individual collectors should refrain from writing either specific or subspecific identities on specimen tags unless requested by the institution.

TAG PAPERS AND INKS

TAG PAPER

The preferred paper for wet specimen tags has been Resistall Index Bristol, 100% rag (cotton fiber), 20 pound sub. However, this paper is no longer being manufactured. Many museums are now evaluating new, plastic-based materials for tags, but most continue to rely on remaining Resistall tags.

The most potentially useful tag material available in small quantities is white thesis paper. This is usually 100% rag content and is sufficiently heavy to stand some (though not excessive) abuse. Tag paper should be acid-free, and must always be white. Colored papers and attachment threads will stain the preservative and the specimen. A common size range for a tag is about 1.5-2 x 7-10 cm, although larger tags are usable.

TAG INKS

The preferred ink for tags is "Higgins Eternal" ink (Faber-Castell, Inc.). This ink does not run or smear in formalin or alcohol. You can use this ink in any of the various technical pens (point size "0" or smaller), or in an inexpensive "crowquill" pen. Always shake and agitate the ink thoroughly before use.

A sharp #2 pencil is also acceptable for wet-tag labeling. However, you should press hard and re-sharpen frequently when writing tag data, particularly if the tag will be stored in fluid.

Avoid India, ball-point, and fountain-pen inks. India inks tend to flake and fade, and thus should be avoided. Ball-point and fountain-pen inks are unacceptable for fluid-preserved specimens and not recommended for dry material. Both inks almost always run and fade in formalin, and especially in alcohol. These inks are not recommended for dry tags because most of them also run if contaminated with grease (as on a fat-stained tag). Lastly, the longevity of these two inks is unknown.

ATTACHING THE TAG TO THE SPECIMEN

Use a large needle and a length of heavy, white 100%-cotton thread (size 16 is ideal) to attach a tag to a specimen.

Follow these steps to prepare and attach a tag to a specimen:
—Drill two small (1mm or less) holes at one end of the tag.
—Loop the heavy, white, 100%-cotton tag thread through the holes, back through the resulting loop, and tie a knot about 2 cm from the edge of the tag. Make sure that at least 12 cm of the two strands of thread remain for tying the tag to the specimen.
—Using the large needle, sew the tag thread through the body of the specimen and around the vertebral column except turtles.
—Tie off the thread with a double, surgeon's knot: a simple overhand knot with an extra loop.
—Double-check the tightness of the knot.
—Cut the extra thread back to about 1 cm.

Alternatively, you can tie the thread around a limb of a lizard, salamander, frog, or turtle; or around the neck or body of a snake. When properly done, either method is satisfactory.

TAGGING DRY MATERIAL

Label dry material (such as skulls and other bones) in a similar manner as wet material. However, after tagging the dry material, use Higgins Eternal ink to number directly on the individual pieces of the dry material. You can label such material with your own catalog number, but be sure to preface your own catalog number with your initials, to differentiate that label from any future museum number.

RETAGGING AND REMOVING TAGS

Specimens should not be re-tagged. The only exception to this is when the original tag remains attached to the specimen, and the fact, reason, and date of re-tagging is noted on the new tag. If a specimen's original tag is lost, some institutions allow re-tagging, with a notation that the original was lost. In this case, however, re-tagging is usually done only if some other cross-referencing system exists (such as separate catalogue number tags).

The only conceivable reason to remove a tag from a specimen is that the tag interferes with an absolutely necessary examination or dissection. Even then, most institutions will not permit removal of the tag. If you must remove a tag, safeguard that tag carefully. Once the tag is separated from the specimen, an element of doubt will always exist as to the specimen's origin.

If possible, do not handle the tag directly, except to examine the reverse side. Such precautions may seem a bit extreme, at stake is the integrity and longevity of the material. Properly preserved and curated wet material can last at least 150 years, but not if it is mishandled. A lost tag virtually terminates the scientific utility of a specimen.

FIXATION AND PRESERVATION

This discussion describes and explains advantages and disadvantages of fixatives and preservatives. This discussion also includes procedures for fixing and preserving specimens. Molecular banking, in which tissues are stored at subzero temperatures, is described briefly at the end of this discussion. Make sure that you have recorded all required information and tagged the specimen before it is fixed and preserved. Record-keeping and specimen tagging are described in the preceding section.

FIXATION

FIXATIVE AGENTS

Formalin and ethyl alcohol have both been used as fixatives for museum specimens.

Formalin. Formalin (Table 1) is used almost universally for fixation of soft tissues for standard museum preparation. It is a "10%" solution of formaldehyde; that is, it is one part commercial (37%) formaldehyde to nine parts of distilled or deionized water.

Formalin is a true fixative, and acts by cross-linking protein with aldehyde groups. When exposed to formalin, the specimen becomes quite hard and inflexible, and tissue decomposition in properly formalin-fixed material is unlikely.

Formalin is somewhat acid, and tends to decalcify the bony skeleton. Thus, many preparators try to buffer the stock fixative, commonly with calcium carbonate. The simplest method to buffer the stock fixative is to store natural marble chips in the 10% formalin solution. However, other chemicals have been used to buffer the fixative (Edwards and Edwards, 1959).

Warning

Formalin is irritating, toxic, and potentially carcinogenic. To avoid personal injury when working with formalin, use appropriate safety gear (such as gloves, eye protection, and syringes with Luer locks) and ventilation equipment (such as fume hoods). To avoid personal injury and environmental contamination, you should dispose of the formalin as hazardous waste, even when removing it from a private residence.

Alcohols. Ethyl alcohol (70% in distilled or deionized water) has also been used as a fixative. In contrast to the cross-linking property of formalin, ethyl alcohol acts by dehydration and partial denaturation of protein (Table 1). Tax-free ethyl alcohol is not usually available to individuals, but 50% isopropyl alcohol is an acceptable substitute. Do not use "denatured" ethyl alcohol (methylated spirits).

For museum purposes, fixation in alcohol is less satisfactory than in formalin. Alcohol-fixed specimens are softer and more flexible than are those fixed with formalin, and they also tend to decompose unless fixation is extremely thorough. Further, incipient putrefaction is not halted by alcohol fixation whereas putrefaction is at least curtailed by formalin fixation. Thus, it is preferable to fix in formalin and preserve in alcohol. The process of leaching and subsequent alcohol preservation should clear nearly all free formalin from formalin-fixed specimens, so the hazards of formalin are minimized. However, individuals with only an occasional specimen to fix might consider 50% isopropyl alcohol for fixation and preservation, if the specimens are not destined for a museum.

FIXATION TECHNIQUES

Proper fixation means perfusion of soft tissues with sufficient fixative to prevent decomposition and to penetrate in adequate concentrations to all parts of the tissue. Reptiles and other animals with waterproof skin are especially difficult to fix (another reason to use the more-effective formalin instead of alcohol).

The easiest and most reliable method for fixation is as follows:

1. Make sure you are using gloves, eye protection and a syringe with a Luer Lock.
2. Slit the ventral skin with a razor or scalpel blade in several places along the body and tail.
3. Inject fixative into all parts of the specimen.
4. Immerse the tagged specimen in just enough fixative to cover it completely for 24-48 hours or until it sinks of its own accord in the fluid.
5. After the specimen sinks, discard the initial fixative.
6. Cover the specimen with at least 10 times its volume in fresh fixative.

The specimen should be immersed in fixative for at least a week, during which you should change the solution at least twice, replacing it as described in step 6 of the previous procedure. Fixation is complete when the specimen has hardened, although the effect will be less pronounced with alcohol-fixed material.

Notes

Snakes and turtles with intact shells are especially difficult to fix well, and must be injected meticulously and thoroughly. For male snakes and lizards, inject the fixative at the ventral base of the tail to evert the hemipenes, which are important taxonomic characters.

Always try to avoid bloating the specimen with fixative.

Glass, one-gallon jars are especially handy for fixing most snakes. When fixing a snake, coil the specimen upside-down in the bottom of the jar, and add just enough fixative to cover it. Change the solution twice during the week to 10 times the initial volume, as described previously.

PRESERVATION

Once a specimen is fixed, it must be preserved. You can preserve specimens in 50% isopropyl alcohol, 70% ethyl alcohol, or 5% formalin. Unless the specimen is destined for histologic study, alcohol—not formalin—is the preferred solution for specimen preservation. Alcohol-preserved material is much easier and safer to handle. If the specimen is intended for general histologic study, it should remain in buffered 10% formalin.

The first procedure in alcohol preservation of formalin-fixed material is that of leaching the free formalin from the tissues.

Follow these steps to leach the free formalin from the tissues:

1. Drain the hazardous-waste fixative from the specimen.

2. Using appropriate methods of hazardous-waste disposal, discard the old fixative.
3. Cover the specimen for at least 24 hours with as much distilled water as the container will hold.
4. Gently shake and agitate the container from time to time.
5. Drain the hazardous-waste formalin-water again, and
6. Using appropriate methods of hazardous-waste disposal, discard the old formalin-water.
7. Soak the specimen in distilled water for one more day, then discard the water and fill the container with preservative.

In general, you will not need to leach alcohol-fixed material. This is because you preserve alcohol-fixed material in the same type and concentration of alcohol that was previously employed as a fixative.

Caution

Do not leach free formalin from specimen tissues by rinsing the specimens in continuously running water. In the past, leaching of the free formalin from the tissues was accomplished by rinsing the specimen for a day or two with continuously running water. However, that method is unacceptable, because it contaminates sewage systems with formalin.

HANDLING AND STORING PRESERVED MATERIAL

Preserved material should be handled as little as possible. It must never be allowed to dry, even partially. If possible, perform dissections under distilled water—alcohol evaporation tends to desiccate and damage specimens very quickly. Investigators should always take care that the material they examine is kept moist and returned to the proper storage container.

Preserved material must be stored in leakproof containers. Use glass jars with rubber gaskets and glass lids or polyethylene disks and plastic lids instead of other jar materials and metal lids. Also, you should routinely monitor the preservative levels. When necessary, top them off or change them if they become badly discolored.

Rapid depletion of the preservative indicates a leaky container. In this case, replace both the preservative and the container, because the concentration of preservative often declines more rapidly than does the fluid level.

PRESERVING LARGER MATERIAL

Material larger than about 4 kg, such as large chelonians, squamates, and most crocodilan material is much more difficult to fix adequately. In some museums most such material is "preserved" by drying the skin/shell or preserving it in alcohol, then cleaning and drying the skull or skeleton. Such material may be fixed by extremely thorough formalin injection. It can also be embalmed by perfusing the vascular system with various fixatives. However, neither method may be practical because of the space and containers required to store such large, fixed, whole material.

PRESERVING NATURAL COLORS

Most standard fixation-preservation processes bleach the natural colors of the specimen to some degree. This is acceptable for systematics specimens because colors are normally recorded from living or freshly-killed specimens, and taxonomically significant color patterns usually survive even prolonged preservation. Some techniques have been for preserving skin-color in preserved specimens. For information about those techniques, refer to Scheim (1951), Owen and Steedman (1956), and Waller and Eschmeyer (1965).

MOLECULAR BANKING

Many museums have instituted a system of frozen tissue banking, so that DNA, allozyme, and other molecular systematics studies can be performed. Frequently, preserved tissues include serum, muscle, and liver tissues. Generally, these tissues should be frozen in screw-cap cryogenic vials or in aluminum foil in liquid nitrogen or dry ice as soon as possible after they are obtained. The muscle and liver tissues are easily obtained by simple dissection of the recently euthanized animal. Serum from blood must normally be obtained from the living animal by venipuncture or cardiopuncture, then separated from the erythrocytes by centrifugation.

In general, permanent storage of serum, muscle, and liver tissues is in -70°C to -150°C freezers or above liquid nitrogen. When freezing tissues, make sure the vials are labeled on the outside with all pertinent data. Also make sure that vials always include a personal catalogue number. Consult Dessauer et al. (1990) for specific tissue-handling instructions for various types of studies.

SKELETON PREPARATION

You can prepare virtually any reptilian specimen as a skeleton. However, you should weigh carefully the utility of a skeleton specimen against its value as a standard fixed-preserved specimen. Skulls and skeletons by themselves are never as useful in taxonomic and ecological studies as are complete specimens. It is generally best to reserve for skeletal preparation material whose identity is known but whose locality data are incomplete or unknown. Pet-trade and zoo material are good candidates for skeleton preparation.

Species identification and labeling is absolutely essential for skeletal specimens because much information about the specimen is lost during the preparation process. Again, remember that material you prepare today may be scrutinized for its scientific value in 100 years, even if you never intended it to go to a museum. Make sure you prepare and label all specimens carefully and well.

The three common methods of skeleton preparation are maceration, boiling, and cleaning with dermestid beetle larvae (or "bugging"). All three methods produce excellent specimens, but all three are also limited to certain types and sizes of material and to particular goals. In practice, most museums and preparators combine elements of two or more techniques for best results.

Connective tissue can be problematic in skeletal preparation. These tissues usually obscure the joints of specimens cleaned by controlled maceration. The same problem can occur with bugged material, but the beetle larvae usually remove most of the shrouding ligaments. Material cleaned by complete maceration or by boiling is usually clean and free of any soft tissue, but must be reassembled by hand if exhibition is the goal. Skeleton preparation for exhibition differs somewhat from museum preparation in that museum material is properly left unbleached and unassembled. Skeleton degreasing, bleaching, reassembling, and mounting procedures are described after preparative techniques.

MACERATION

Maceration can be accomplished by bacteria or by various chemicals, and it can be controlled or complete. Apart from fairly careful preparation, maceration is easy. However, you must be careful not to let the maceration progress too far, or a completely disarticulated or friable skeleton will result. For this reason, mild chemical maceration is used principally to complete the cleaning of material that has previously been cleaned by dermestid beetle larvae. However, excellent skeletons can result from maceration alone if the process is carefully monitored.

BACTERIAL MACERATION

This method is best suited to fresh specimens of 0.5-3 kg. According to Hildebrand (1968), fixed material can be used after a lengthy washing of the material in water. Smaller material is best treated chemically or bugged, and larger material is generally best prepared by boiling.

Bacterial maceration is not usually appropriate for chelonians, because chelonian scutes will swell and detach. You could use bacterial maceration for the isolated skull and girdles, and clean the shell by some other means, but there is little advantage to this approach. Chelonian skeletons and shells are best cleaned by bugging or controlled maceration with ammonia or household bleach, as discussed below.

Warning
To prevent personal infection by disease organisms wear latex gloves and eye protection, and treat all fresh material as potentially infectious.

Warning
To prevent personal injury, be careful when skinning the heads of venomous snakes. Snake venom may be dangerous long after the death of the venomous animal.

Before beginning bacterial maceration, prepare the specimen by removing the following organs and tissues:

1. Skin and viscera. Skin and eviscerate the specimen.
2. Brain. Remove the brain through the foramen magnum by one of two methods. You can inject water from a syringe through a 18-20 gauge needle into the cisterna magna. Or, you can scoop the brain out with a brain hook. To make the brain hook flatten (by pounding with a hammer) the end of short length of heavy wire, then bend the flattened end around to form a hook.
3. Eyes. For lizards and chelonians, remove the eyes carefully, then macerate them separately. Snakes and crocodilians do not have ossicles, and you can discard the eyes of those animals.
4. Spinal cord. Remove the spinal cord by teasing it out of the vertebral column with a wire. A small-gauge unwound, steel, guitar string is ideal. Form a hook at one end of the string by kinking it and cutting the string slightly forward of the kink.
5. Muscles. Dissect away all large muscle masses, and remove muscles from between the ribs.
6. Other tissue. Remove as much remaining soft tissue as possible.

Once the specimen is prepared for maceration, follow these steps:

1. Rinse the specimen in water.
2. Immerse the specimen in water in a closed glass or enameled container. Do not use a metal container. Metals may inhibit maceration and stain the bones.
3. Store the container away from human habitation (the odors of maceration are quite objectionable). The container should be stored for up to a week or more.
4. During storage, change the water in the container every second or third day.
5. During storage, check the progress of the maceration every day. When the soft tissues easily

rinse away from the bones, but the bones remain articulated, maceration is complete.

6. Rinse the specimen in water.
7. Immerse the specimen in household ammonia (nonsudsing) at least overnight to stop the bacterial action.
8. Carefully scrub macerated tissues away from the skeleton. You will need soft and hard toothbrushes, a dental or similar scraper, and a wire to probe foramina. This step completes the cleaning of the specimen.

Complete bacterial maceration is accomplished by leaving the specimen in water (change the water several times) until the bones are completely disarticulated. Disarticulation is usually very complete—even bone-fused reptilian teeth often come loose. Take care not to lose any bones when you decant the fluid. You can then complete the cleaning of the individual bones as described above in steps 6 through 8.

CHEMICAL MACERATION

The principal advantages of chemical over bacterial maceration are that odors are less objectionable, and the chemical process requires much less time than the bacterial process. Also, chemical maceration is appropriate not only for fresh specimens, but also for formalin- and alcohol-fixed material.

The three chemicals commonly used (See Table 1) for maceration include:
—household ammonia
—weak sodium hypochlorite (household chlorine bleach)
—strong alkali, such as potassium hydroxide.

Some preparators have used digestive enzymes such as trypsin and pancreatin successfully to clean skeletons (Mahoney, 1966). However, for these methods to work, you must carefully control temperature and sometimes pH for up to 1-2 days. Further, those methods also require elaborate preparation of both specimen and reagent, require somewhat exotic chemicals, and may result in a disarticulated skeleton. The advantage of enzymatic methods is that they may damage the bones less than other chemical methods, except those that employ ammonia.

You may clean chelonians by chemical maceration, but unless you saw apart the plastron and carapace, you must immerse the chelonian completely, and the scutes will swell and detach. For skeletal studies this may be of no consequence, but for exhibition, it is undesirable as it may be difficult to reattach the scutes. A sawed shell is obviously much less desirable for exhibition, and its scientific value is diminished. If you must saw the shell apart, you can macerate the specimen by using the carapace as a bowl to hold the macerating chemicals.

Household Ammonia. One of the simplest, safest, and most useful methods of controlled chemical maceration is through the use of nonsudsing, household ammonia.

Warning
To avoid a hazard from potentially lethal chlorine gas, never mix ammonia with household bleach (sodium hypochlorite). Do not store ammonia near household bleach, and do not use the same containers for ammonia as are used for bleach.

Ammonia macerates muscle and fascia efficiently, but macerates ligaments much less rapidly. Because of this, the skeleton is unlikely to disarticulate even after prolonged immersion in the ammonia. Ammonia also degreases the bones to some extent. For example, snake skulls immersed in household ammonia for several months have not disarticulated and the ammonia-based cleaning, degreasing, and bleaching of the skulls has been very thorough.

Warning
To avoid personal hazard from ammonia fumes, perform ammonia maceration only in an area with appropriate ventilation, such as outdoors or in an area equipped with a fume hood.

To macerate a specimen with ammonia, follow these steps:
1. Immerse the prepared specimen in nonsudsing clear full-strength household ammonia (Table 1) for 2-3 days.
2. Rinse the specimen in water.
3. Remove macerated tissue by gently scrubbing the specimen.
4. If necessary, return the specimen to the ammonia and repeat steps 1 through 3.

You can accelerate (sometimes too much) the maceration process if you warm the ammonia to 30°C-40°C. You can use a heat lamp, warm plate, or even a heating pad for this purpose. To macerate most of the soft tissue, it might be sufficient to place the specimen overnight in warmed ammonia in a loosely closed—but not sealed—container. However, make sure you check your specimen often to prevent the maceration from progressing too far.

Caution
Be very careful when using warmed ammonia for maceration. If the ammonia bath substantially exceeds the recommended temperature of 30°C-40°C, maceration will progress too rapidly and may destroy deep ligaments. The result can be a disarticulated specimen.

Bleach. Another common method of controlled chemical maceration uses household bleach. Follow these steps to macerate a specimen with bleach:

1. Immerse the prepared specimen in a weak ("10-50%") solution of household bleach (5.35% sodium hypochlorite—Chlorox, Purex, etc) (Table 1).
2. Monitor the maceration carefully—bleach maceration is usually complete in less than one hour.
3. Rinse the bones, particularly thoroughly.

Caution

Make sure you rinse the bones thoroughly. Bleach penetrates bones, and residual effects may render the bones friable. Even when the process is carefully controlled, bones tend to erode and later crumble.

The bleach-maceration technique, for use with alcohol-preserved material, has been perfected by Rhodin et al. (1976) at the Museum of Comparative Zoology at Harvard University. Rhodin et al. stress that skeletal material must not be left for more than 10-15 minutes in the bleach solution (full-strength). Also, Rhodin et al. use 70% ethyl alcohol to neutralize the bleach on the cleaned specimen.

Potassium Hydroxide. The third common method of complete chemical maceration uses a solution of 1-3% potassium hydroxide.

Warning

Potassium hydroxide is hazardous material and can cause personal injury and environmental contamination. Use extreme caution and wear face and eye protection in addition to latex gloves when handling potassium hydroxide. You should dispose of potassium hydroxide solutions as hazardous waste. In some localities, you might be allowed to neutralize strong basic solutions with acid, then discard the resultant material in the sanitary sewer (Furr, 1989).

Follow these steps to macerate a specimen using potassium hydroxide:

1. In a glass or glazed earthenware container, immerse the prepared specimen in 1-3% potassium hydroxide (KOH) (Table 1)
2. If rapid results are desired, warm the solution to about 40°C
3. Check the specimen hourly or daily.
4. Removed the bones as soon as they are free of soft tissue.
5. Rinse the bones.
   Make sure you remove the bones from the potassium hydroxide solution and rinse them as soon as they are clean. Bones left too long in KOH tend to become somewhat chalky.

BOILING

In general, large material is best suited to boiling.

Boiling (actually simmering) has several advantages over other methods of cleaning a skeleton. Complete maceration also results in a very clean, disarticulated product, but:

—Boiling is somewhat safer to the operator.
—Boiling is potentially much safer to most specimens than chemical maceration.
—Boiling is more pleasant for the preparator than bacterial maceration.
—Boiling is quickly and easily accomplished with a saucepan or even a coffee can and a hot plate or stovetop.
—It is simpler to prepare a specimen for boiling than for maceration (although fresh or fresh-frozen material is still by far the best). Flesh removal does not need to be as complete. However, you should remove all thick muscle masses that might obscure small, easily lost bones.
—Boiling works rapidly to produce excellent material.

Keep in mind the following considerations about boiling:

—The disadvantage to boiling a specimen is that disarticulation is relatively complete, and bones are easily lost during the cleaning of the soft tissue. Reptilian teeth fully fused in their sockets survive *"in situ"*, but younger teeth usually come free. Also, reassembly of small skulls cleaned by boiling is tedious and sometimes problematic.
—Boiling should not be used for fixed material, because such material may disintegrate during the process.
—Boiling is not recommended for preparation of snake skeletons because of the great potential for sequence mistakes in reassembly. However, boiling can be very effectively used to prepare snake and lizard skulls down to the size of a common garter snake (*Thamnophis sirtalis*).
—Boiling can be a useful technique for comparative anatomy studies. This is because the reassembly process confers a better understanding of structure and structural interaction than does simple observation of assembled components. One preparator believes so strongly in the analytic advantages of hand reassembly that he prepares extremely complex fish skulls by boiling, and reassembles this seemingly impossible material quite successfully by hand.

Follow these steps to boil a specimen:

1. Skin and eviscerate the specimen, and remove the eyes and brain.
2. Immerse the prepared specimen in water with a little added detergent or household ammonia.
3. Simmer the specimen on low to medium heat until the remaining soft tissue cooks.
4. Remove all remaining soft tissue carefully, by hand.

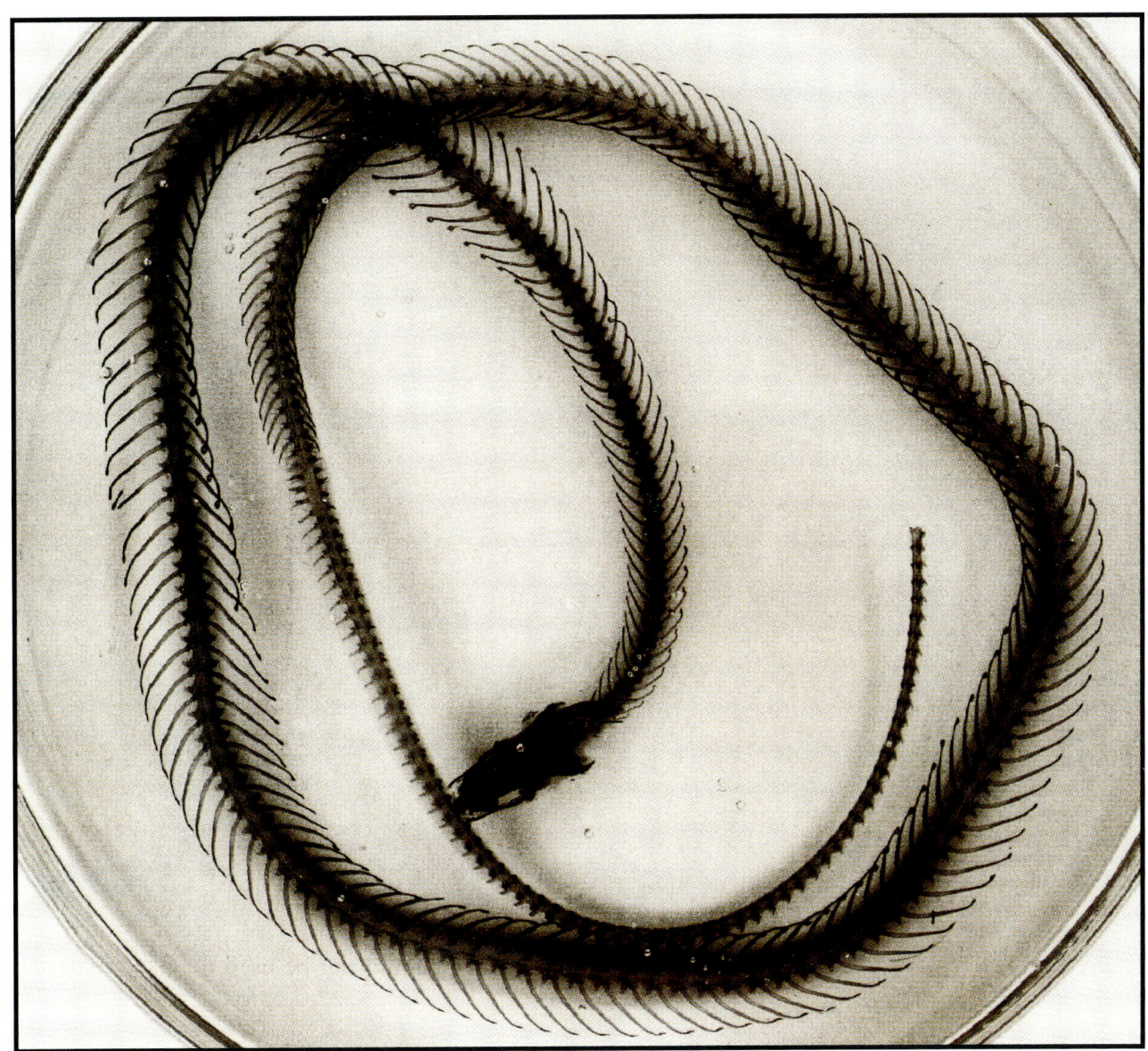

Common garter snake (*Thamnophis sirtalis*) prepared by clearing the musculature with potassium hydroxide and staining the cartilage with alcian blue and the bony skeleton with alizarin red S. Note the stained tracheal rings and spatulate cartilaginous rib termini. Photograph by Robert Munn.

5. Rinse the bones under running water.
5. Dry the bones.

Caution

Make sure you know the anatomy of your specimen. It is easy to overlook and discard small bones with the soft tissue. For example it is particularly easy to lose snake stapes, postfrontal, reserve fangs, and parts of the mandibular assembly.

A sample procedure to prepare a squamate or crocodilian skull is as follows:

1. Simmer the specimen for up to one hour in water with some added household ammonia in a stainless steel saucepan in a fume hood. (The exhaust fan over a household range usually works well enough for this application).
2. Separate the bones as they come free into right and left sections.

3. Degrease the bones.
4. Dry the bones.
5. Reassemble the bones.

Note

Chelonian skulls rarely disarticulate, and you do not usually have to reassemble those bones.

CLEANING WITH DERMESTID BEETLES

Museum staff prefer this method (called "bugging") over all others for cleaning small skeletal material. This is because cleaning small specimens with dermestid beetles takes little time and produces excellent, fully- articulated material. Large specimens and preserved material should be cleaned by other methods.

Large specimens are usually less-suited to dermestid-beetle cleaning because
—they take too much time to clean

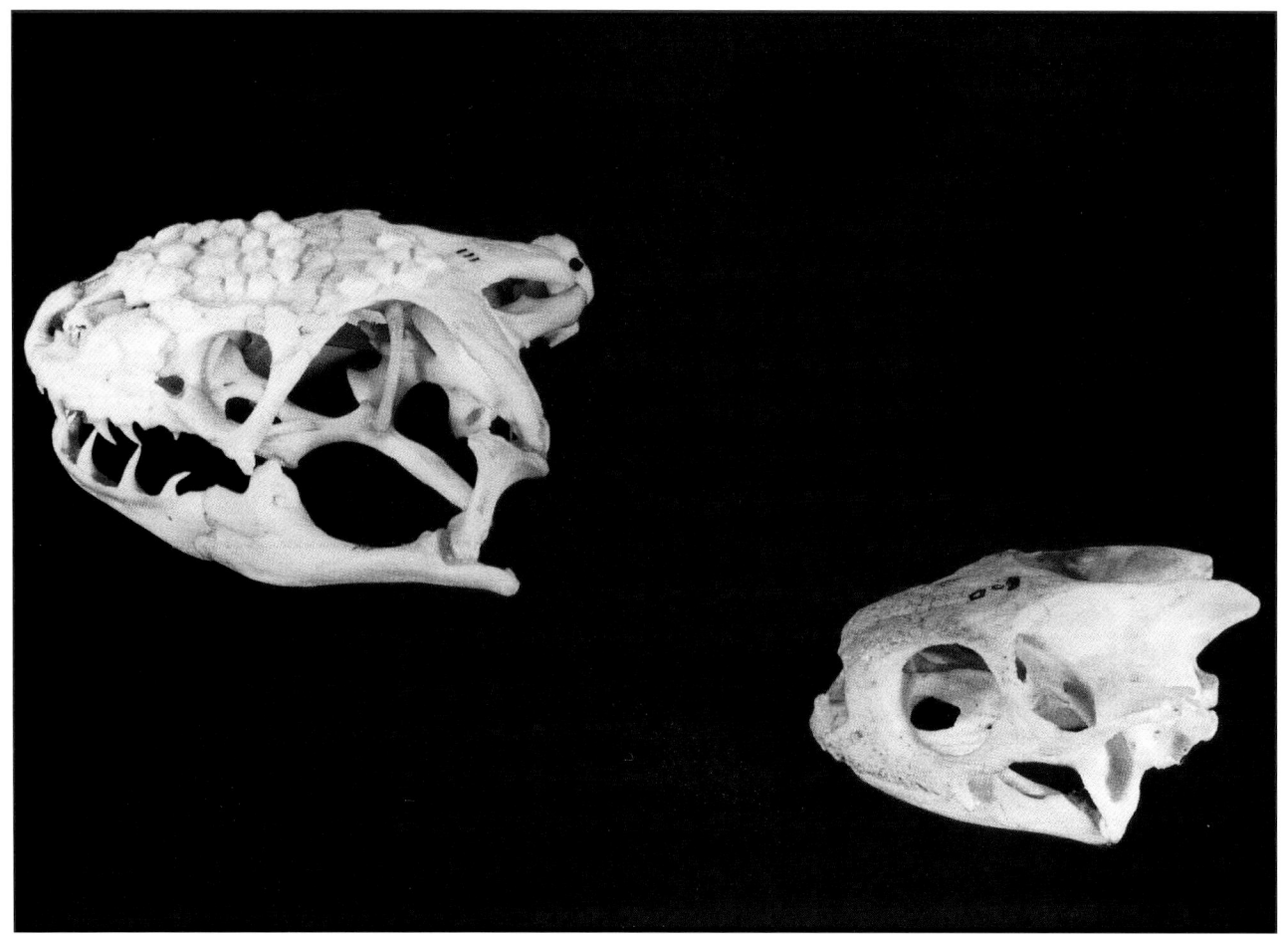

Upper left: skull of Gila monster (*Heloderma suspectum*) prepared by boiling, showing dermal ossicles and grooved mandibular teeth. Lower right: skull of desert tortoise (*Gopherus [Xerobates] agassizii*) prepared by cleaning with dermestid beetles. Photograph by Robert Munn.

—they take too much space in the colony
—they are not cleaned as well as they would have been if they had been boiled

Preserved material is usually not suitable for bugging. However, Hildebrand (1968) suggests that some such material can be rendered suitable by presoaking the specimen in broth or bullion.

The disadvantages of bugging are:
—The bugs are quite hazardous to unintended target animal material (dry museum specimens, taxidermy mounts, feather pillows, etc).
—The establishment and maintenance of a bug colony are, in general, impractical for home-based preparators and those with only occasional specimens to prepare

Dermestid Beetles. You can get dermestid adults and larvae from an extant museum colony, from partly dried carcasses found in the field, or from large cricket colonies maintained as pet food. The adult beetles are black with whitish ventral surfaces, and 5-9mm long. The larvae are fuzzy, brownish black, and about 1-14mm in length.

Larvae pass through several instars in about a month, and then remain dormant for a week. Adults lay eggs a few days after emergence, and eat far less than do larvae.

You can keep a small dermestid colony in a coffee can that is tightly and securely covered with a very small-mesh metal screen. You should house larger colonies in seamless metal-lined containers, such as old-style ice chests. Keep the colony in a warm, dark place as far as possible from any potential target material, because the beetles will infest and damage such material remarkably quickly (Hildebrand, 1968).

PREPARING A SPECIMEN FOR BUGGING.
To prepare a specimen for cleaning by dermestid beetles, follow these general steps:
1. Skin, eviscerate, and remove the eyes and brain-spinal cord from the specimen, as described in earlier procedures.
2. Remove large muscle masses, if desired.
3. *Thoroughly air-dry the material.*

4. Place entire dried skeletons in separate boxes (without lids) to avoid mixing the specimens. If you are working with several skulls, house them in different compartments of a box (cardboard egg cartons work well). An active colony will clean small skulls in a few hours, and larger material may be ready in just a day or two.
5. Remove material as quickly as possible after it is clean, as the beetle larvae will eventually disarticulate the bones.
6. Treat the material to remove live dermestid eggs and larvae. You can do this one of several ways (Hildebrand, 1968):
   a. Heat the specimen in a coffee can close to an incandescent light. This method, which forces the larvae to leave the specimen, yields the best results. Take care not to overheat and scorch the bones when using this method.
   b. Freeze the specimen. This method works well, but the larvae may remain inside bones, plug foramina, etc.
   c. Continuously (for several days) fumigate the specimen with chloroform. This method is the least reliable.
7. Finally, clean the material by immersing it in full-strength household ammonia (Table 1) for at least 24 hours. Joints will relax, and remaining bits of soft tissue are usually easily removed. This process will also degrease the bones to some extent.

Caution
Do not immerse the costal cartilages as they will warp.

DEGREASING SKELETAL MATERIAL

Even mildly greasy bones eventually become dirty and friable, and their longevity as specimens may be severely curtailed. Most reptiles do not usually present as much of a problem in this regard as do certain birds and mammals, but skeletal material obtained from long-term captives is usually quite greasy. Material cleaned by complete chemical maceration may not require further degreasing, but you should evaluate such specimens carefully and degrease if necessary. Material cleaned by bacterial maceration, controlled chemical-maceration, boiling, and bugging usually requires additional degreasing.

There are many efficient degreasing agents. However, because of toxicity or other hazards, only ordinary household ammonia (Table 1) is recommended in this chapter as a degreasing agent. Bones soaked in household ammonia changed several times over a week or two are usually adequately degreased for most purposes. Stronger ammonia concentrations than the usual

10% household variety will shorten degreasing time.

The only drawback to degreasing with ammonia is that costal cartilages will warp in ammonia. When degreasing specimens with costal cartilages, keep the cartilages dry. Position these specimens carefully, with the cartilages exposed to air.

The most efficient degreasing agents are some of the chlorinated solvents, particularly carbon tetrachloride (CCl_4), and methylene chloride (CH_2Cl_2). However, these agents are so hazardous that their routine use for anatomical preparations is not acceptable except in carefully controlled environments. Hildebrand (1968) provides a thorough discussion of solvent degreasing.

Degreasing agents that are not recommended in this chapter include the following:
—Carbon Tetrachloride. This is probably the best bone degreaser available. However, this agent is so toxic that it must be used in a fume hood, a facility normally found only in research institutions. An exhaust hood over a kitchen range most emphatically does not provide a safe work environment.
—Methylene Chloride. Though somewhat less hazardous (and less effective) than carbon tetrachloride, methylene chloride must also be used in a fume hood and disposed as hazardous waste.
—White Gasoline. White gas (camp fuel) has also been employed as a fairly efficient bone degreaser. However, because it is so flammable, its use is generally discouraged.

Degreasing a Specimen. For the long bones of animals larger than an adult box turtle, follow step 1; otherwise, skip to step 2 to begin degreasing a specimen.
1. Drill holes at each end of the long bones into the side of the shaft to facilitate ammonia penetration.
2. Immerse the bones for several days to several weeks in the ammonia. Change the ammonia at least twice a week.
3. When degreasing is complete, remove the specimen from the ammonia.
4. Rinse the specimen in clean solvent (to eliminate residual surface grease).
5. Rinse the specimen in water.
6. Set the specimen aside to dry.

BLEACHING SKELETAL MATERIAL

Skeletal material destined for a systematics collection is never bleached beyond the whitening effects of cleaning and degreasing. However, you may bleach specimens intended for exhibition or teaching.

If you want the specimen to be whiter than has been achieved by the cleaning and degreasing, follow these steps:

1. Fill an uncovered container with household-strength (3%) hydrogen peroxide solution (H_2O_2) (Table 1).
2. Immerse the bones briefly, for approximately 3-10 minutes, in the container.
3. Remove the bones before you believe they are white enough, because they will appear whiter when dry and they will continue to bleach as the peroxide decomposes to water on the surface—for this reason rinsing in water is unnecessary.

Zebra-tailed lizard (*Callisaurus draconoides*) prepared by clearing the musculature with potassium hydroxide and staining the bony skeleton with alizarin red S. Photograph by Robert Munn.

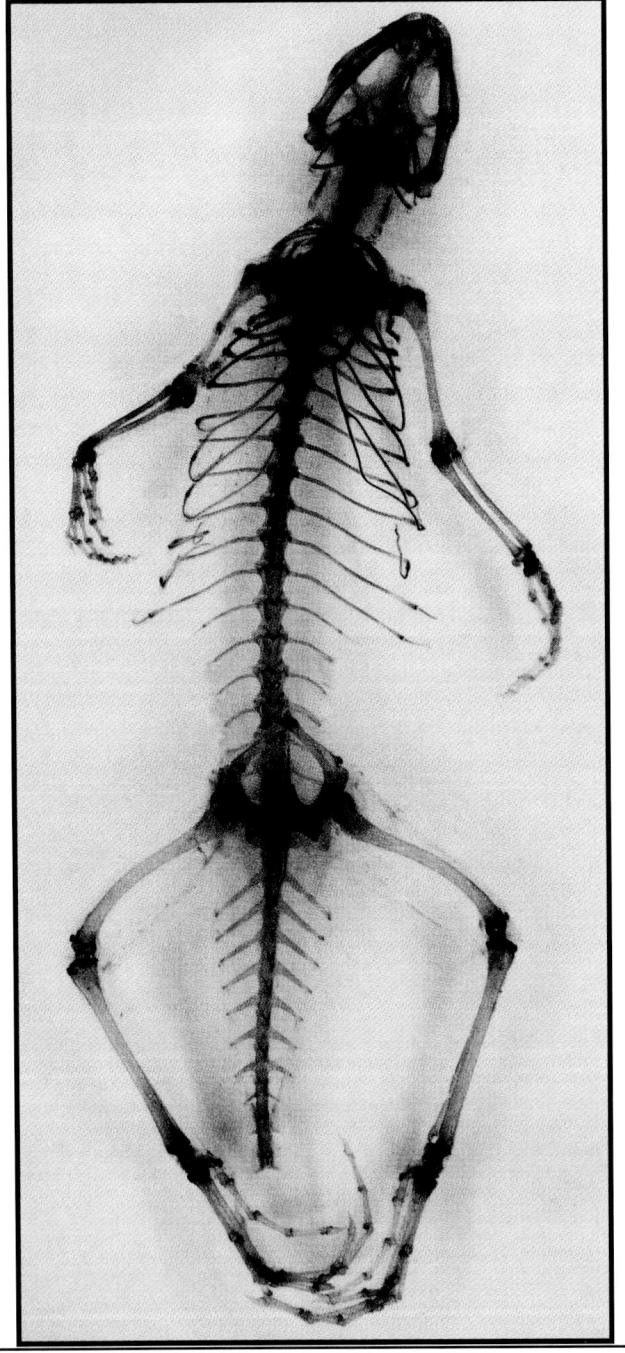

Warning
Make sure you leave the container open to prevent oxygen gas from accumulating and possibly reaching explosive pressures.

Bleaching with hydrogen peroxide is relatively safe for both the operator and the specimen. Although this bleaching process can continue for hours, take care not to overbleach. Overbleached bones tend to lose apparent dimension and will appear flat. Usually, 3-10 minutes is all that is necessary.

REASSEMBLING AND MOUNTING A SKELETON

REASSEMBLY ADHESIVES

Reassembly after skeletal preparation is a straightforward process if you know the anatomy of the specimen. In open joints, all adhesives (except epoxy) eventually fail, and regluing may be necessary from time to time. Advantages and disadvantages of adhesives used in the reassembly of skeletons are described in the next several paragraphs.

DUCO Cement. The most practical glue for reassembling small skeletons is probably DUCO cement (Table 1), which is inexpensive, strong, clear and initially colorless, and dries relatively quickly (Hildebrand, 1968). If you have to reposition a joint, you can dissolve the DUCO in acetone (Table 1). You can use DUCO glue directly from the tube, but the strongest joints are made by precoating each surface lightly, allowing the glue to dry, applying a small amount of fresh glue, and assembling the parts quickly. Be sure to wipe the tip of the tube and replace the cap immediately after each use. Dried DUCO eventually acquires a yellowish tint, and those who find this objectionable may dissolve it away with acetone and reassemble the skeleton with fresh glue. DUCO also shrinks substantially at first, and then more gradually over time, so that glued parts may eventually separate—the remedy is the same as for yellowed adhesive. Material larger than about one kilogram body weight may not be suited to assembly with DUCO.

Epoxy. Epoxy (Table 1) may be necessary for material larger than about one kilogram body weight. However, epoxy should be used only for specimens with minimal scientific value, because epoxy joints are permanent. The various "five-minute" epoxies are reasonably well-suited to skeletal assembly, although the adhesive is rather yellow.

Cyanoacrylate Adhesives. Cyanoacrylate, also called Crazy-Glue (Table 1), can be an effective adhesive, particularly for assembling skeletal components that could not be held in position

Snake skulls prepared by boiling, degreasing, and reassembly with DUCO cement. Top row (left to right): Reticulated python (*Python reticulatus*), 4.5m; Cribo (*Drymarchon corais corais*), 2.6m. Bottom row: (left to right): Spitting cobra (*Naja naja sputatrix*), 1.8m; Boomslang (*Dispholidus typus*), 1.5m; Gaboon viper (*Bitis gabonica*), 1.2m. Photograph by Robert Munn.

easily after gluing. In this situation, this glue has the advantage of setting almost instantly. However, it only works with well-fitted components; the assembly must be precise and correct. In practice, once the use of cyanoacrylates is mastered, assembly of well-fitted skeletal components progresses rapidly and cleanly.

If you are using cyanoacrylate adhesives, store them in the refrigerator, and be careful to clean up any excess from the tip of the tube. Remember that fingers contaminated with cyanoacrylate are instantly glued together, or worse, to the specimen. You can dissolve cyanoacrylate in acetone or commercial nail-polish remover. Nail-polish remover is somewhat oily and may contaminate skeletal material—it is best used only to separate fingers inadvertently glued together.

Water-Based Adhesives. Avoid water-based adhesives, such as white and wood glues, because they tend to weaken when exposed to humidity.

Contact and Rubber Cements. These adhesives dry rather dark and are thus not acceptable, and any excess is very difficult to remove.

MOUNTING A SPECIMEN

Mount skeletal material for teaching purposes in logical units or as entire mounted skeletons. The research and teaching utility of an entire, mounted skeleton may be quite limited; such whole-mounted skeletons are really best-suited to exhibition. Specimens assembled in isolated units are easier to handle, and functional morphological components are more easily perceived and understood.

Make sure you number all bones inconspicuously (except the components of an assembled skull—number the skull and mandible(s) only) with your catalogue number. Once mounted, make sure the specimen is protected from dust.

CLEARING AND STAINING SPECIMENS

Cleared and stained material has been processed in potassium hydroxide and glycerine solutions (Table 1) until the muscles are transparent, and the bony skeleton is stained with alizarin red S (Table 1), so that the skeleton is revealed *in situ* in exquisite detail. They are stored in pure glycerine, and remain quite stable if they are not handled.

This popular technique is best applied to specimens of less than 0.2 kg, because the skeletons of larger animals tend to stain unevenly, and because it is difficult to clear larger material without inadvertent maceration. Unlike dry skeleton preparative techniques, relatively precise timing and close adherence to protocol are essential to success in clearing and staining.

Cleared and stained specimens are eye-catching and attractive, but have several drawbacks. Such specimens are exceptionally delicate, and for many purposes are much less useful than are dry skeletons. The specimen is always just out of reach, and cannot be repositioned easily for examination. Also, chelonians do not make good cleared and stained specimens primarily because the shell obscures the girdles and limb bones in wet preparations. However, Hildebrand (1968) has illustrated a well-prepared juvenile softshell turtle (*Apalone*).

USING APPROPRIATELY FIXED MATERIAL

Material that has been fixed in 70-95% ethyl alcohol, either previously or during the procedure, is the best for clearing and staining, although fresh and formalin-fixed specimens can also be used. Fresh material will clear much more quickly, and formalin-fixed material will clear much more slowly than alcohol-fixed specimens. Formalin-fixed specimens should have been prepared with buffered fixative, because decalcified bone will not stain.

Alcohol-fixed material is preferred to absolutely fresh material because the clearing is easier to control. Further, my best success has been with specimens that remained for a time in 100% ethyl alcohol (Table 1), apparently because complete dehydration facilitates the clearing process greatly.

Previously-frozen specimens, fixed or not, are somewhat less satisfactory, but still usable. However, they are virtually useless for the cartilage-staining technique described in the next section.

PREPARING THE SPECIMEN

Follow these steps to prepare a specimen for clearing and staining:

1. Skin and eviscerate the specimen.
2. Depress the head and incise the connective tissue to expose the foramen magnum.
3. Introduce a hypodermic needle into the foramen magnum and flush out the brain with gentle water pressure from a syringe.
4. Remove the eyes. For lizards and chelonians, you may leave the eyes in place to reveal the sclerotic ossicles. However, refer to the paragraphs following this procedure for specific information about eyes.
5. Dissect away as much fat as possible, now and throughout the process, because fat does not clear.

After these preparations are complete, if the specimen was not previously fixed and dehydrated, you can fix and dehydrate it in 100% ethyl alcohol.

CLEARING THE SPECIMEN

Most reptiles have the dark pigment melanin distributed widely throughout the musculature, and many lizards have a darkly pigmented peritoneum that cannot be removed easily by dissection. Additionally, in specimens whose eyes have been retained, the pigmented retina will obscure the sclerotic ossicles and parts of the skull.

After skinning, evisceration, and fixation remove the melanin from the specimen. You will need a vacuum pump and chamber to complete this procedure. If you do not have a vacuum pump and chamber, you can purchase an inexpensive sink faucet vacuum adaptor and an inexpensive polycarbonate plastic vacuum chamber (Nalgene) from scientific suppliers. Use a commercial unit - do not attempt to improvise a vacuum chamber, because such a chamber could shatter and result in severe injury.

Follow these steps to remove this pigment and clear the specimen:

1. Soak the fixed specimen in 2-3% hydrogen peroxide (Table 1).
2. If eyes remain in the specimen, prepare the eyes by incising and draining these behind the ossicles so that the H_2O_2 can penetrate. Do not expect complete depigmentation of the retina. The peritoneum slowly transforms to medium brown from black within about an hour.
3. Degass the specimen under water in a vacuum chamber. This removes the bubbles generated by the hydrogen peroxide. Most bubbles will be removed after 5-10 minutes of vacuum, and remaining bubbles will eventually dissipate.
4. Once the bubbles are removed, complete the dehydration in at least two changes of 100% ethyl alcohol for at least 24 hours per change.
5. Immerse the specimen in a 1-5% (1-5 gm/

100ml) solution of potassium hydroxide (KOH) (Table 1). The precise concentration varies with the age of the specimen and type of fixation. You can clear embryonic material in very weak KOH, but you might need concentrations greater than 5% for formalin-fixed adult material. Start with 2% KOH for adult, alcohol-fixed material, and strengthen it if clearing does not progress reasonably quickly.

6. Change the solution (by aspiration or by pouring it off—do not try to transfer the specimen) if it becomes discolored.
7. Dispose of the solution by following appropriate hazardous waste handling and disposal procedures.

Caution
If maceration begins at any time during the initial clearing, aspirate or pour off the KOH (use appropriate hazardous-waste disposal procedures), rinse at least once in water, and cover the specimen with weaker KOH.

STAINING THE SKELETON
When the long bones become vaguely apparent it is time to stain the bony skeleton with alizarin red S (Table 1). Staining is best done in very weak (0.5%) KOH so that the specimen will not macerate while it is hidden in the stain solution. Use about 0.5ml of stock alizarin red S per 100ml of weak KOH, to make a medium-red solution. Use a saturated aqueous solution of alizarin red S as your stock solution, but do not store the solution for more than a few days. Make up only a small amount at a time.

The staining process takes from a few hours to over a week, depending on the size of the specimen and type of fixation.

Follow these steps to stain a specimen:
1. Immerse the specimen in the stain.
2. Reposition the specimen from time to time to allow the stain to penetrate evenly.
3. Occasionally aspirate or pour off the stain and set it aside, and cover the specimen temporarily with water to monitor the staining progress.
4. Restore the staining solution and continue until the skeleton is stained completely.

FINAL CLEARING AND PREPARATION
Once the skeleton is stained, it is time to start the final clearing and preparation for storage. In this procedure, try to clear as completely as possible without maceration, which is insidious and will destroy the specimen suddenly and quickly if it goes too far.

Caution
If maceration begins at any time during the initial

or final clearing, remove the KOH (use appropriate hazardous-waste disposal procedures), rinse at least once in water, and cover the specimen with weaker KOH.

Note
This procedure uses glycerine, which typically clears paper labels. Use pencil on 100% rag paper tags to label these specimens.

Follow these steps to clear and prepare the skeleton for storage:
1. Pour off the stain, and dispose of the solution with appropriate hazardous waste procedures.
2. Rinse the specimen with water.
3. Cover the specimen with the initial or lower KOH concentration.
4. Watch for the muscles to destain the alizarin and to complete clearing.
5. Prepare a solution of 1:1 glycerine (Table 1) and 1% KOH, which rarely causes maceration.
6. Leave the specimen in this solution until clearing is complete and the skeleton is fully revealed.
7. Using fine scissors and working under distilled water or 50% glycerine:water, finish dissecting away any fat and loose or macerated tissue.
8. Change the water or glycerine:water solution to three parts glycerine to one part 1% KOH.
9. Then, 48 hours later, change the solution to pure glycerine.
10. Lastly, change the glycerine 5-10 days later
11. Store the specimen in the pure glycerine solution in a sealed jar, away from direct sunlight.

CARTILAGE STAINING
You can stain the cartilage of reptiles and other vertebrates deep blue with alcian blue stain (Table 1) and then clear the soft tissues in a process similar to that previously detailed. Once the cartilage and soft tissues are stained and cleared, you then counterstain the bony skeleton with alizarin red S. This produces specimens with fully stained skeletons that are even more eye-catching than those already discussed.

The cartilage-staining process is quite simple for those who have mastered the alizarin red staining and clearing technique. The final product reveals the relationship between the bones and cartilages in striking detail. It also reveals certain distinctive structures, such as the spatulate cartilaginous tips of snake ribs, as no other preparation can. Amphibians prepared in this fashion are widely used for certain taxonomic studies.

The same examination drawbacks apply to cartilage-stained specimens as to other cleared specimens. One additional drawback is that prolonged immersion in the acid-alcohol cartilage stain will decalcify part of the bony skeleton and decrease its uptake of the alizarin red S stain. Also, the toluidine blue or methylene blue methods described by many authors have numerous drawbacks (Simons and van Horn, 1970). These methods have been superseded by the introduction of a simple method based on alcian blue 8GX or 8GN (Ojeda et al., 1970).

USING APPROPRIATELY FIXED MATERIAL

Use only fresh or alcohol-fixed material for this technique. Formalin-fixed material is less satisfactory. However, embryonic material fixed in formalin-based Bouin's solution has been used (Ojeda et al. 1970). Frozen material is virtually useless, because the cartilage-staining process impedes muscle clearing and destaining in such specimens. For example, a previously-frozen specimen of the Surinam toad (*Pipa pipa*) prepared in 1973 is still slowly destaining, 24 years later.

STAINING SOLUTIONS

Alizarin red S quantities in bone stain solutions can be fairly inexact and still yield consistent and reproducible results. However, alcian blue should be measured carefully for good results in cartilage staining (Simons and van Horn, 1970).

Prepare a staining (not stock) solution of alcian blue by adding 10-20mg of the stain powder to 100ml of 95-100% ethyl alcohol that has been acidified to pH 1.9-2.3 (no higher) with glacial acetic acid. Acidify the ethyl alcohol by combining 80ml of 96% ethyl alcohol with 20 ml of glacial acetic acid, then add 10-20mg of alcian blue. The pH of this organic mix should be about 2.1, but check with a pH meter. Within fairly narrow limits, you can adjust the pH to between 1.9 and 2.3. Add more glacial acetic acid to lower the pH, or add more alcohol to raise it (slightly).

If cartilage staining is inadequate, increase the concentration of alcian blue for future specimens. If you do this, be sure to maintain the pH in the effective range.

If you are not equipped to weigh milligram quantities, combine 1g of the alcian blue powder with 100ml of the acid alcohol to make a stock solution. Then add 1-2 ml of the stock to 98-99 ml fresh acid alcohol to achieve a 10-20mg% solution. Do not store the stock solution for more than a day or two. The drawback to making a stock solution is that it is wasteful, although none of the components is expensive. In any case, be sure that all of the stain is dissolved, or filter it before use.

Follow these steps to prepare the specimen for cartilage staining:
1. Skin and eviscerate the specimen.
2. Remove the eyes (if desired) and brain.
3. Immerse the fresh (not previously fixed, if at all possible) specimen in the alcian blue-acid-alcohol solution for up to two days. Do not immerse the specimen longer than two days as bone decalcification will be excessive.
4. Immerse the specimen for a few hours in 100% ethyl alcohol to dilute the acetic acid.
5. Bleach the melanin in 3% H_2O_2 (in distilled/deionized water) as described earlier.
6. Dehydrate the specimen in several changes of 100% ethyl alcohol. This step will complete fixation, dehydrate the specimen, and greatly improve final clearing.
7. After several days in 100% alcohol, remove the specimen and process it according to the clearing-alizarin staining protocol detailed previously.
8. Store the specimen in pure glycerine (as described previously), out of direct sunlight.

OTHER TECHNIQUES

Remaining anatomical techniques covered briefly here include bone-muscle and bone-ligament preparations, corrosion casting, freeze-drying, and plastic embedding. These techniques are generally more useful for teaching and exhibition than for research and museum work.

BONE-MUSCLE AND BONE-LIGAMENT PREPARATIONS

Bone-muscle and bone-ligament preparations were developed by Hildebrand (1968) as tools to teach biomechanics and the anatomy of musculature. This type of preparation reveals the mechanical relationship of the muscles to each other and to the bones in detail. Also, such a unit can be handled with care.

Success with this technique depends on
—Selection of proper material. Crocodilian, large chelonian, and large lizard girdles are best, and the head-neck musculature of medium and large reptiles may also work well.
—In-depth knowledge of the anatomy of the isolated unit.
—Experience, meticulousness and patience, which are required to isolate each muscle (undamaged) from others.

The completed bone-muscle or bone-ligament preparation is a marvel of anatomy and mechanics. It is well worth the effort.

Follow these general steps to prepare bone-muscle material:
1. Isolate a functional skeletal unit, such as a pec-

toral girdle and forelimb, with its associated musculature.

2. Fix the specimen in 10% buffered formalin, either before or after the dissection described in steps 3 and 4.
3. Peel and dissect away the fascia, fat vascular bed, and loose connective tissue.
4. Separate the muscles by blunt dissection.
5. Air-dry the specimen in a natural position, so that the muscles shrink and reveal their precise attachment points (origins and insertions).
6. Degrease the skeletal unit (in organic solvents).
7. Color the muscles with acrylic paints to restore their "natural" appearance and to make the preparation more attractive.
8. Bleach the bone by painting just the bone surfaces with 3% H_2O_2. Use a soft-bristle artist's paintbrush and do not wet the muscles.

Bone-ligament preparations are executed in a similar procedure, but the dissection is even more challenging. You must have a thorough knowledge of the anatomy of the joint to be successful in preparing bone-ligament specimens.

CORROSION-CASTING

Corrosion casting is a relatively simple technique, but it is difficult to master. It works for many types and sizes of specimens, but fresh material is usually best because fresh soft tissues yield as the casting compound fills the spaces.

You can inject any ducted system or hollow organ with one or another variety of catalyzed hardening plastic. You can tint the hardening compound several different colors. You can also independently inject different systems within the same organ or tissue. For example, the arterial and venous systems of an entire small specimen can be injected with red and blue compound to demonstrate the incredible complexity and relationship of the systems.

The most satisfactory hardening plastic is Batson's compound (Polysciences, Warrington, PA) (Table 1). See Thompsett (1956, 1959) for thorough discussions of the various techniques of corrosion casting.

Follow these steps to cast a hollow organ or ducted system:

1. Inject the catalyzed liquid plastic into the vascular system of an isolated heart, the portal and systemic veins of a isolated liver or kidney, or even into a hollow bone
2. Allow the plastic to harden.
3. Macerate away the organ or other soft tissue in strong alkali 10-30% KOH.

The remaining preparation is a perfect cast of the interior of the organ or the system.

Bone Casting. When you corrosion-cast a hollow bone, decalcify the injected bone in 1.0M hydrochloride acid, then pick away remaining matrix with forceps.

Warning

To avoid personal injury, wear eye protection when picking away matrix.

FREEZE-DRYING SPECIMENS

Freeze-drying removes ice crystals from frozen tissue under a vacuum until the tissue is dehydrated. (You might have to degrease tissues in organic solvents after freeze-drying). You can preserve many anatomical preparations, including entire small and medium-sized animals by freeze-drying. The entire musculature with small animals may be demonstrated effectively by freeze-drying. Most tissues shrink or warp very little during freeze-drying, and all tissues remain relatively inert unless rewetted.

You can also freeze-dry isolated bone-muscle units. Freeze-dried bone-muscle units shrink much less than air-dried bone-muscle preparations and some consider this undesirable because muscle shrinkage better defines their attachements. The main arguments against or disadvantages of freeze-drying systematics material are:

—Freeze-drying is a method untested by time.
—Resulting specimens cannot be dissected or manipulated.
—Many freeze-dried preparations are susceptible to attack by dermestid beetles unless stored under museum fumigation.
—Freeze-drying equipment is somewhat expensive. However, a shopmade unit can be produced locally (Meryman, 1960, 1961).

The advantages of freeze-drying are that such preparations are very useful for teaching and exhibition. The exhibition departments of many museums use this technique almost exclusively for small animals that are not amenable to standard taxidermy (such as reptiles and amphibians).

PLASTIC EMBEDDING

Plastic embedding of whole specimens, dry skeletons, corrosion casts, and of cleared and stained skeletons has long been popular, because it reinforces the eye-catching qualities of these preparations. However, embedded gross specimens may be virtually useless for scientific study. Also, such specimens are of very limited utility for teaching, because the specimen is just out of reach and unrecoverable for closer study or further dissection. Before you embed a potentially valuable scientific or teaching specimen, consider whether it might be better saved and displayed dry or in storage fluid.

For specifics about plastic embedding, refer to the information provided by major biological supply companies on components, instructions, and various accessories for the procedure. You can also refer to Lutz (1969), who discusses specimen preparation and embedding.

AFTERWORD

In this age of molecular biology and declining wild populations, the fixation, preservation, and proper labelling of museum material, as well as the production of anatomical preparations, may seem to some to be arcane and anachronistic. Yet museum collections, including anatomical and teaching material, are now more important than ever. Only now are we coming to appreciate fully the vital importance of diversity in the rapidly shrinking natural world. Hand-in-hand with that understanding is the realization that our knowledge of systematics is comparatively meager. We rely on museums as repositories of information in the form of preserved specimens and frozen tissues—a record of times, places, and species that we shall never see again. We owe to our specimen material the best possible preparation and preservation, because this material is increasingly scarce and precious. Anyone who has the opportunity to prepare museum or anatomical material should appreciate the privilege, endeavor to do the best job possible, and obtain maximum scientific and educational utility from each specimen.

ACKNOWLEDGMENTS

I thank the emeritus faculty of the Department of Zoology, University of California, Davis, for the opportunity to learn and practice curatorial and preparative techniques under their direction. In particular I acknowledge the late Tracy I. Storer, a pioneering American zoologist and museum man, for his interest, advice, and encouragement during my education in museum science.

REFERENCES

—Anderson, R. M.
Methods of Collecting and Preserving Vertebrate Animals. National Museum of Canada, Bulletin No. 69, Biol. Series. No. 18., 4th edition, 1965, 199pp.

—Budavari, S., ed.
The Merck Index, 11th edition. Merck and Co., Rahway, New Jersey, 1989, 1606pp.

—Conant, R., and J. T. Collins.
A Field Guide to Reptiles and Amphibians/ Eastern and Central North America. Houghton Mifflin Co., Boston, 3rd edition, 1991, 450pp.

—Dessauer, H. C., C. J. Cole, and M. S. Hafner.
Collection and storage of tissues. In D. Hillis and C. Moritz, Molecular Systematics. Sinauer, Sunderland, MA, 1990, pp 25-41.

—Edwards, J. J., and M. J. Edwards.
Medical Museum Technology. Oxford Univ. Pr. London, 1959, 172pp.

—Furr, A. K., ed.
Handbook of Laboratory Safety, Third edition. CRC Press, Boca Raton, FL, 1989, 704pp.

—Hall, E. R., and K. R. Kelson.
The Mammals of North America. New York, The Ronald Press Co. 1959, 2 vols, 1083pp.

—Hildebrand, M.
Anatomical Preparations. University of Calif. Pr., Berkeley, CA, 1968, 100pp.

—Lewis, R. J., Sr.
Hazardous Chemicals Desk Reference. Van Nostrand Reinhold, New York, 3rd edition, 1993, 1742pp.

—Livezey, R. L.
Procaine Hydrochloride as a killing agent for reptiles and amphibians. Herpetologica 1958, 13:280.

—Lutz, E. L.
Handbook of Plastic Embedding. Naturegraph, Healdsburg, CA., 1969, 186pp.

—Mahoney, R.
Laboratory Techniques in Zoology. Butterworth's, Washington, DC, 1966, 404pp.

—Meryman, HT.
The preparation of biological museum specimens by freeze-drying. Curator, 1960, 3:5-19.

—Meryman, HT.
The preparation of biological museum specimens by freeze-drying. II. Instrumentation. Curator, 1961, 4:153-174.

—Ojeda, J. L., Barbosa, E., and P. Gomez Bosque.
Selective skeletal staining in whole chicken embryos: a rapid alcian blue technique. Stain Technol, 1970, 45:137-138.

—Owen, G., and H. F. Steedman.
Preservation of animal tissues, with a note on staining solutions. Quart J Microsc Sci, 1956 97:319-326.

—Rhodin, S. D., Haneline. P. G., and A. G. J. Rhodin.

Skeletal preparation of herpetological specimens. Herp Rev, 1976, 7:169-170

—Scheim, M.
Color restoration and preservation of gross museum specimens. Bull Internat Assoc Med Museums, 1951, 32:117-123.

—Scott, N. J. Jr., and A. L. Aquino-Shuster.
The effects of freezing on formalin preservation of specimens of frogs and snakes. Collection Forum, 1989, 5:41-46.

—Simons, E. V., and J. R. van Horn.
A new procedure for whole-mount alcian blue staining of the cartilaginous skeleton of chicken embryos, adapted to the clearing procedure in potassium hydroxide. Acta Morphol

Neerl-Scand, 1970, 8:281-292.

—Stebbins, R. C.
A Field Guide to Western Reptiles and Amphibians. Houghton Mifflin Co., Boston, 2nd edition, 1985, 336pp.

—Thompsett, D. H.
Anatomical Techniques. Livingstone, Ltd., Edinburgh and London, 1956, 240pp.

—Thompsett, D. H:
Improvements in corrosion casting techniques. Ann R Coll Surg Engl, 1958, 24:110-123.

—Waller, R. A., and W. N. Eschmeyer.
A method for preserving color in biological specimens. Bioscience 1965, 15:361.

BASIC ANATOMY AND PHYSIOLOGY

Lowell Ackerman DVM PhD
P.O. Box 12093
Scottsdale AZ 85267-2093

Dr. Lowell Ackerman is a practicing veterinarian, consultant, author, lecturer and radio personality. To date he has written 34 books and over 150 book chapters and articles dealing with animal health care issues.

INTRODUCTION

Anatomy and physiology are dealt with throughout this book, so only a cursory introduction is provided here, in table form. Fascinating functional adaptations such as the renal-portal system are covered in the chapters on internal medicine and pharmacology while the special sensory adaptations, reproductive physiology, venom biology, sex determination and biorhythms are covered in their own chapters in the biology section.

RECOMMENDED READING

—**Beynon, PH (Ed.)**
Manual of Reptiles. British Small Animal Veterinary Association, Cheltenham, England, 1992, 228 pp.
—**Mader, DR (Ed).**
Reptile Medicine and Surgery. W.B. Saunders Co., Philadelphia, 1996, 512 pp.
—**Quesenberry, KE; Hillyer, EV (Eds.):**
Exotic Pet Medicine I. *Veterinary Clinics of North America: Small Animal Practice*, 1993; 23(6): pp 1149-1361.

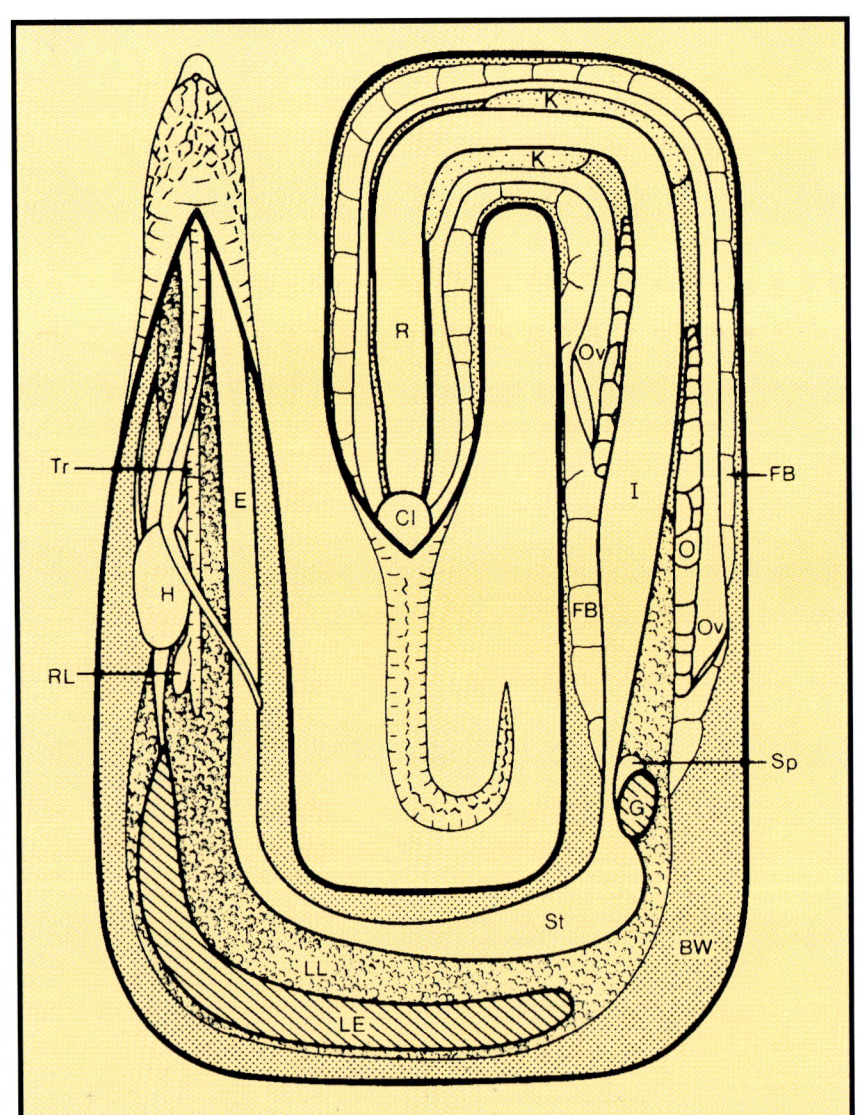

Visceral anatomy of a snake, in this case a female hognose snake. (Adapted from Cope, 1898, and Zug, 1993.) Abbreviations—BW, body wall; Cl, cloaca; E, esophagus; FB, fat bodies; G, gallbladder; H. heart; I, intestine; K, kidney; LE, liver; LL, right lung; O, ovary; Ov, oviduct; R, rectum (colon); RL, left lung; Sp, spleen; St, stomach; Tr, trachea.

Some anatomical aspects of Reptiles.

BODY SYSTEM	SNAKES	LIZARDS	CHELONIANS	CROCODILIANS
Integumentary System	Scales are larger and thicker on the ventrum (scutes) and provide support and protection. Shape and arrangement may be important in species identification. Skin is relatively aglandular except for two anal scent glands. Shedding is referred to as ecdysis and dysecdysis if abnormal. Most shed skin as one piece	Relatively thick skin that is shed in pieces. Dewlaps, spines, crests and horns are often secondary sex characteristics. Chromatophores in the skin are responsible for color change. Skin is relatively aglandular but certain species have regional pores	Thickness of scales is variable between species. The skin is shed periodically. Some families, such as the leatherback turtles (Dermochelydae) lack epidermal laminae. Nonpulmonary gas exchange via the skin is important in some species, such as *Chelydra* and *Trionyx*.	Composed of separate, tough, leather-like scales joined by elastic tissue. Each species has characteristic scales. Important route of CO_2 loss in most species. Chromatophores in the skin responsible for color variation. Integumentary sense organs present in the skin but purpose currently unclear
Musculoskeletal System	Locomotion is of two types - lateral undulation and sidewinding. Most of the process to elude predators. The tail occurs through a fracture plane. Ribs are present on most vertebrae except those in the tail.	Many species are capable of tail autonomy which is an adaptive process to elude predators. The tail loss occurs through a fracture plane. Ribs and lateral struts. Appendicular bones are similar to other vertebrates.	Shell consists of an upper carapace and lower plastron connected by bony bridges. Dermal-origin bone present in carapace, plastron, ribs and lateral struts. Appendicular bones are similar to other vertebrates.	Long, flattened tooth-lined skulls. Approximately 60–70 vertebrae. 8 pairs of true ribs and eight pairs of floating ribs.
Cardiovascular System	3-chambered heart with two atria and one ventricle; single ventricle divided into cava pulmonale, venosum and arteriosum. Two aortae fuse after leaving the heart to form abdominal aorta. Carotid arteries and jugular veins located near the trachea. Heart can vary in location since there is no diaphragm. This flexibly mobile heart may help in the digestion of large prey. Have both renal and hepatic portal circulations.	3-chambered heart, atrial septum and partially divided ventricle. Renal-portal system is very important in circulation. Medications injected into the caudal half of the body are metabolized locally in the renal-portal system and may not reach therapeutic levels in the systemic circulation.	3-chambered heart. Renal-portal system believed to be present in chelonians as in other reptiles. Recent studies have failed to show a substantial effect of a renal-portal system on antibiotic metabolism.	Only reptiles with 4-chambered hearts. Ventricular foramen of Panizza allows for mixture of oxygenated and deoxygenated blood based on pressure. Flow is typically left to right except when submerged for long periods. An adaptive mechanism to allow crocodilians to remain submerged longer. Heart rates are slow and temperature dependent.
Respiratory System	Right lung is always larger and generally stretches from the heart to the kidney; in aquatic snakes, it may extend to the cloaca. Colubrids have one functional lung. Cranial lung conducts gas exchange while caudal portion mainly functions as an air sac.	Lizards lack a diaphragm. More primitive species have lungs like hollow sacs; more advanced species have sponge-like alveoli. Nasal salt glands are present in herbivorous iguanids.	No true diaphragm separates the lungs from other organs. Lungs are large partitioned sacs. Pneumonia is particularly common in chelonians and can cause them to swim in an unbalanced fashion.	Valve-like flaps enable the throat to be sealed off from oral cavity during submergence. Important in prey capture. Well-developed lungs located in a thoracic cavity. Intercostal muscles and diaphragm involved in respiration

Some anatomical aspects of Reptiles.

BODY SYSTEM	SNAKES	LIZARDS	CHELONIANS	CROCODILIANS
Digestive System	Essentially a long tract from the mouth to the cloaca. Mucus-secreting glands are independent from venom glands. Most pet snakes have six rows of teeth, one row on each mandible and two on each maxilla. Small intestines are relatively uncoiled and empty into a colon; Boidea also have a small cecum. Pancreas, spleen and gall-bladder are located in close proximity to one another; some species have a splenopancreas.	Most species have pleurodont teeth which are shed periodically. Gila monster and Mexican beaded lizard have sublingual venom glands. Tongue used primarily to bring scents to Jacobson's organ. Most vegetarian species have extensive hindgut digestion. Cloaca divided into urodeum, coprodeum, and proctodeum.	Lack teeth. Salivary glands provide mucus but no digestive enzymes. Digestive enzymes are produced by the stomach, small intestine, pancreas, liver and gall bladder. Cloacal prolapse is not uncommon in reared chelonians.	Swallow food without chewing. Tongue has no role in moving food to the esophagus. Stomach divided into two distinct regions, the corpus and the pars pylorica. Thick muscles and gastroliths (gizzard stones) are responsible for grinding food. High acidic secretions from the stomach. In natural settings, crocodilians cease feeding when temperature are outside the range of 25-35°C.
Genitourinary System	Two kidneys located cranial to the cloaca. Ureters empty into the urodeum portion of the cloaca; there is no urinary bladder. Males have two paired hemipenes which lie in pouches in the ventral base of the tail. During copulation, the hemipenis enters the cloaca of the female. Testes are located internally between the pancreas and the kidneys. The ovaries are located in the same region in females.	In males of some species, the caudal pole of the kidney swells during breeding season and contributes to seminal fluid. Lack a loop of Henle and therefore cannot concentrate urine. Ammonia and urea are excreted in significant amounts only in aquatic and semi-aquatic species. Bladder stones may result from water deprivation or diets with excessive protein levels. Males have paired hemipenes stored inverted at the base of the tail. Only one hemipenis is used during copulation. Reproductive strategies vary and may be oviparous, ovoviviparous, viviparous or parthenogenic.	Kidneys are metanephric and lack a loop of Henle; therefore cannot concentrate urine. Urogenital ducts empty into bladder rather than urodeum. Prone to large uroliths. Terrestrial chelonians may use bladder for water storage. Single expandable penis that lies on the floor of the proctodeum Penis not used for urine excretion.	Penis is located on the floor of the cloaca and is primarily cartilaginous with little erectile tissue. In females, oviducts open on the floor of the cloaca near the clitoris.

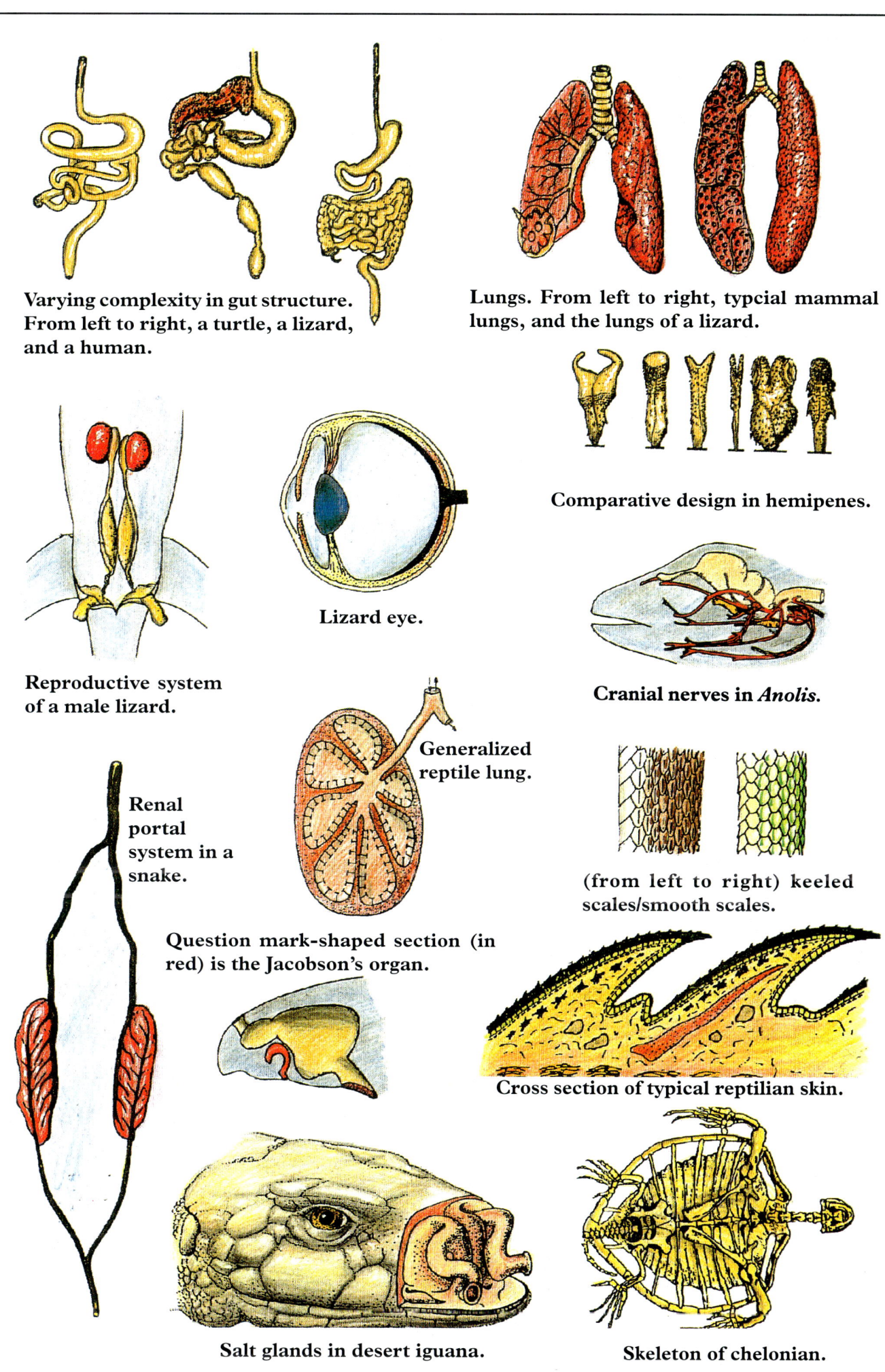

Varying complexity in gut structure. From left to right, a turtle, a lizard, and a human.

Lungs. From left to right, typcial mammal lungs, and the lungs of a lizard.

Comparative design in hemipenes.

Reproductive system of a male lizard.

Lizard eye.

Cranial nerves in *Anolis*.

Renal portal system in a snake.

Generalized reptile lung.

(from left to right) keeled scales/smooth scales.

Question mark-shaped section (in red) is the Jacobson's organ.

Cross section of typical reptilian skin.

Salt glands in desert iguana.

Skeleton of chelonian.

SEX DETERMINATION

Mark F. Gerber
P.O. Box 15143
Boise, ID 83715

Mark F. Gerber exhibited an avid curiosity for reptiles while growing up in Alexandria, Virginia and spent many hours looking throughout the Virginia woods for Herps. He moved to Boise, Idaho, in 1985 to study the native herpetofauna of that area. This interest led to educational committments within the community, at schools and at local events. He has been involved with the Idaho Herpetological Society for a number of years, and has served on it's Board of Directors. Mark also initiated the formation of a local chapter of the Idaho Herpetological Society, and served as it's President for two years. He has spent hundreds of hours in the deserts of Southwest Idaho, Southern Nevada, Southern California and Oregon, logging thousands of snakes and lizards. He is now involved in educational research for Boise State University.

INTRODUCTION

This chapter is designed as a general guideline in sexing reptiles. It would be impractical to attempt to cover all possible circumstances. In this chapter we will discuss the more common reptiles one might encounter and some of the methods used to determine their sex.

When it becomes necessary to determine the gender of a reptile, we can follow a few basic principles to make the process of finding out the sex, a fairly simple one. Sexual dimorphism in reptiles may be very obvious, but it can also be quite subtle. In attempting to determine the gender of a reptile it is often tempting to make a snap decision or jump to a conclusion, without having all the necessary information. This could lead to misidentification that can result in months of lost time in a breeding program, or it can generate a faulty set of data in a scientific experiment. It is important to be as precise as possible before reaching a conclusion.

Upon examining your animal, note the general shape of the body, particularly the head and tail. Is the head square and blocky, or is it long and slender? Is the tail long and broad based or is it quickly tapering and stout? Look at the colors and patterns. Are there bright splotches, or brightly colored appendages or scales? Make note of these observations upon examining the animal. Subtle scale colors, or anatomical shapes that may not seem important at first can often help in compar-

ing reptiles of the opposite sex in the future. In most cases, having a representative of both genders is best since sexual dimorphism is more obvious in a given reptile when compared to one of the opposite sex.

If the animal was caught in the wild, take into account and make notes if possible, any observed behavior of the reptile. Many times a combination of physical or behavioral characteristics can help to pinpoint the sex of an animal.

In many towns and almost any big city, there can usually be found, people who can confirm the sex of a reptile. Herpetological societies are an invaluable source of information particularly on local species. Often a local veterinarian can assist in gender determination or can refer you to someone who is familiar with your particular reptile. If there is an educational institute such as a university nearby, information abounds in either faculty or in the library. Most libraries carry books on reptiles that can be of some help as are many of the field guides that are available. In addition several sources are mentioned at the end of this chapter.

The reptile should always be treated with respect and gentleness when performing any sexing techniques. This ensures a safer, less stressful procedure all around. If there is any doubt as to your ability to confirm the sex of a particular reptile, it can be beneficial to consult an outside authority on the subject.

TECHNIQUES FOR SEXING SNAKES

There are a number of techniques by which gender can be determined in snakes. Do not rely too heavily on any one method since sexual dimorphism is exhibited differently in many species. With enough practice one can become proficient in all techniques of sex identification. Male snakes have a paired hemipenis, this is often covered with nubs, projections or curved spines that help hold the hemipenis in the female during prolonged copulation. One hemipenis is employed at a time and either can be used.

TAIL LENGTH

A visual identification can be used to determine the sex of a snake in many cases. Some snakes show a marked gender difference in tail structure. This is apparent in Crotalines (rattlesnakes) and other larger snakes, but in smaller snakes gender is not always readily distinguishable using this method. Often in male snakes the base of the tail is thicker and the tail in general is longer to accomodate the hemipines. In females, the tail is usually stout and appears to taper radically at the vent sometimes appearing almost constricted. In some of the racers, whip snakes and garter snakes where the tail is already long and thin, this is not an accurate technique by itself.

ANAL SPURS

Those snakes that are members of the family Boidae, have an anatomical structure unique to them. Small spurs, which are remnants of an ancient pelvic girdle project from either side of the ventral plate. In males these are usually larger. The males can sometimes be seen "scratching" these spurs on the cage floor when in the presence of a female. This technique is not 100% accurate. In many cases, two snakes of the same species and size can exhibit opposite traits than one might expect. Spurs have been known to be torn off or damaged. This could result in a male being identified as a female.

USE OF PROBES

There is some argument as to the proper use of probes or whether to use them at all. A good set of probes with six different sizes can be purchased from many herp supply houses for around $50. There has been some evidence indicating that probes can, in an occasional case, cause a prolapsed hemipines. There are also the risks of infection and damage to the organs of the reptiles. These are valid arguments that should be considered before attempting a probe. The use of a urethral catheter of appropriate size is usually preferred over metal probes. The technique is essentially performed in the same manner with a catheter.

When selecting the proper probes, there are two types of probes to consider, the straight probe and the balled probe. The former is a simple straight shaft of stainless steel that comes in a various assortment of sizes to suit the various sizes of reptiles. The latter type of probe is similar to the first type with the exception of a "ball" formed at the tip of each probe. The straight shaft is usually the preferred type. Which ever type of probe is used, there is a procedure that should be followed to ensure the snake's safety and comfort. If this procedure is followed, the probe can be done safely and successfully. The use of probes requires extreme care and much practice. Probes should always be kept clean to avoid infecting the snake. Always use a non-toxic, non-spermicidal lubricant on both probes and catheters.

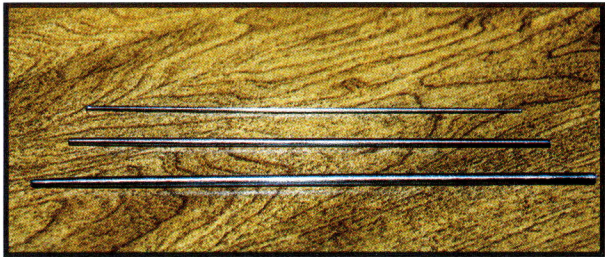

Sexing probes, available at most pet shops that stock other herpetological/herpetocultural goods. Photo by W. P. Mara.

When probing a snake, the animal should be restrained as firmly as possible without injuring it. Apply a liberal amount of the appropriate lubricant to the probe taking care to coat as much of the probe as could potentially be inserted into the snake. If the probe is too dry, there is risk of it catching on the dry skin of the sex organ and causing the tissue to tear. Insert the probe cranially under the ventral scale and then reverse caudally. When inserting the probe into the cavity containing the hemipines keep the probe to one side. There are two hemipines and it is only necessary to probe one side. If the probe is inserted too quickly there is risk to the snake by tearing the delicate tissues surrounding and comprising the sex organ. If the snake is a female the probe will only extend into the genital cavity 3-6 caudal scales. Occasionally on a female the probe goes a little deeper, but this is more the exception than the rule. On the male, if the probe can be inserted past 12 caudal scales it is a good idea to retract the probe without reaching the end of the chamber to avoid "bottoming out" and increasing risk to the snake. Under no circumstances should you put your finger or any other object over the handle end of the probe. When this is done it is difficult to tell when the end of the chamber has been reached and a tear could more readily occur.

COLOR

There does not appear to be any easily measured sexual dichromatism among snakes of the same species.

PALPATION OR MASSAGE

If done properly, palpation or massage is another effective way to determine sex. It is most effective in juvenile snakes. Utmost care must be taken not to damage the delicate skeletal structure or organs of small reptiles especially juveniles. Begin by gently pressing down on the ventral side of the tail past the end of the hemipines with the base of the thumb. Slowly roll the thumb towards the ventral opening keeping a firm and constant pressure on the region. In small males, the hemipines will usually pop out from the ventral opening. The snake will usually void its cloacal contents when handled in this manner.

BEHAVIORAL CHARACTERISTICS

Observations of snakes involved in ritualistic combat dance indicate male behavior. This includes an intertwining of the snakes bodies with the foremost third elevated above the ground. The males will attempt to knock the opposing male to the ground. Any observed male rubbing on the females can help define sex.

Two Western Fence Lizards (*Sceloporus occidentalis*). The female on the left shows much less ventral coloration than the male on the right. These lizards are often referred to as Blue Bellies. Photo by Mark F. Gerber

TECHNIQUES FOR SEXING LIZARDS

VISUAL IDENTIFICATION

Sexual dimorphism is a useful tool in sex identification, because it ususally requires little more than a visual inspection of the reptile. The morphological differences between genders may vary only minutely and result in misidentification. Always look very closely at head size and tail length. Head size can differ greatly between males and female lizards especially among the skinks (Family Scincidae). The heads of male skinks are usually much bigger and broader. Some monitor lizards may also be sexed in this manner although usually not as effectively. In many members of the family Iguanidae, the only way to differentiate between the sexes externally is two enlarged scales just caudal to the vent, or by enlarged femoral pores. The former will often stand out obviously against the smaller cyclical scales of the ventral side of the tail. Dewlaps, which are gular flaps of skin, and dorsal spines (comb) on many lizards are usually bigger or more prominent in males. Males are able to extend the dewlap in a colorful courtship display. The dewlap is also extended in a show of aggression towards other lizards.

TAIL LENGTH

Lizards, like snakes show a distinct sexual dimorphism in the length and shape of the tail. The tail is usually broader and longer in the males. This shows nicely in the monitor lizards but may not be as obvious in a small lizard such as a Western Whiptail (*Cnemidophorus tigris*). In the females the tail will usually be shorter and stouter. (See-Tail Length in Snakes)

USE OF PROBES

There is more risk involved when attempting to probe lizards because of their tendency to jerk and twirl. Lizards such as iguanas have sharp claws which can be used to make a safe probe, difficult. The probe for a lizard is performed in a similar manner as for a snake. In the female the probe will extend into the genital cavity only about a third to a half that of the male. When probing a lizard, hold the lizard firmly but gently. The cloacal opening on most lizards is not covered by a scale. This makes inserting the probe somewhat easier.

COLOR

Color plays an important part in distinguishing gender in lizards. Some members of the genus *Sceloporus* (also of the Iguanidae), have bright blue ventral sides and throat which become even more pronounced in males during the breeding season. This is the characteristic which gives rise to the common name "blue bellies". The common Side-blotched lizard (*Uta stansburiana*) is another lizard named for its sexual dichromatism. The dark grey to purple blotch just caudal to the forlimbs on these lizards becomes more prominent during the breeding season. Females in the genus *Gambelia* show much orange to red in the spring while the color contrast in the males becomes more pronounced (*Gambelia* also has the enlarged post anal scales of other iguanids).

PALPATION

This technique works well with small iguanids, skinks, and teiids which may be very hard to distinguish. If the tail of the lizard is very thin or the lizard is very young, use of this method is not advisable. On many lizards the tail will break off if handled too roughly. This will result in trauma to the lizard.

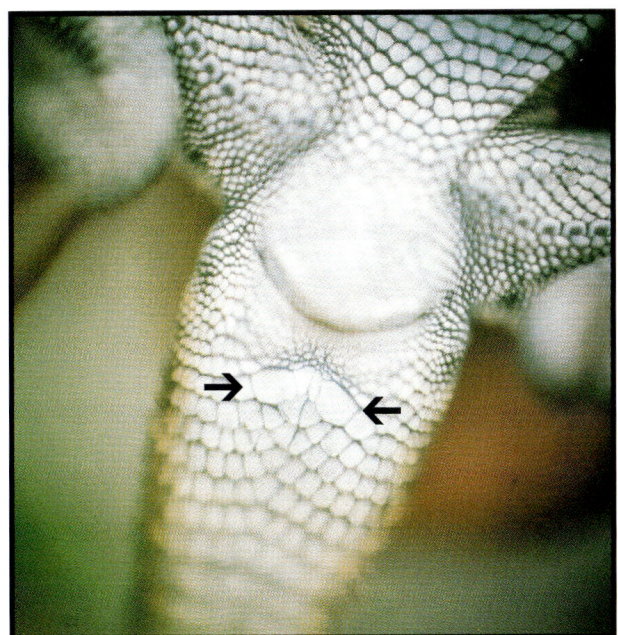

Enlarged post anal scales (arrow) on a side-blotched lizard (*Uta stansburiana*). Photo by Mark F. Gerber.

BEHAVIORAL CHARACTERISTICS

Observe the behavior of the lizard. Does it bob its head up and down and extend its dewlap if it has one? Does it become very puffed out and stand on the tips of its toes? All of these characteristics may (but not always) indicate a male.

TECHNIQUES FOR SEXING TURTLES

Many of the sexual characteristics that define sex in adult turtles, are not evident in juveniles. Perhaps of all reptiles, turtles are the most diverse in sexually dimorphic characteristics.

VISUAL IDENTIFICATION

As a general rule, tails are longer in male turtles. The base of the tail is usually broader in males but females have shorter, stubbier tails. In many aquatic species the nails on the forelimbs of the males are longer to facilitate courtship. When courting, the male can be seen waving these long nails in front of the female. The cloacal opening is usually more proximal in female turtles. In males, the cloacal opening usually extends beyond the outer margin of the carapace. Overall, female turtles are larger than male turtles but this is not always the case. Males usually have a concave plastron, especially in some aquatic species. This presumably facilitates mounting the female's carapace when mating. Males have a single penis which is occasionally erected as well as discharged, as a defense mechanism when roughly handled.

Ritual combat in male rattlesnakes.

COLOR

In some of the terrapins, including box turtles, eye color may differentiate the sexes. Do not rely too heavily on color, particularly in the eyes. There are populations which do not exhibit this trait. Male box turtles and other terrapins have red or reddish eyes and brighter colors on the forelegs. Females have brown or yellow to orange color in the eyes. and a broader shell. In some species, the overall coloration of the turtle will be brighter in males.

REFERENCES AND RECOMMENDED READING.

—**Breen, JF:**
Encyclopedia of Reptiles and Amphibians. 1974. T.F.H. Publications, Inc. Ltd.
—**Mattison, C:**
A-Z of Snake Keeping. 1990. Sterling Publishing Co. Inc. New York, NY
—**Frye, FL:**
Reptile Care: An Atlas of Diseases and Treatments. T.F.H. Publications, Inc. Ltd.

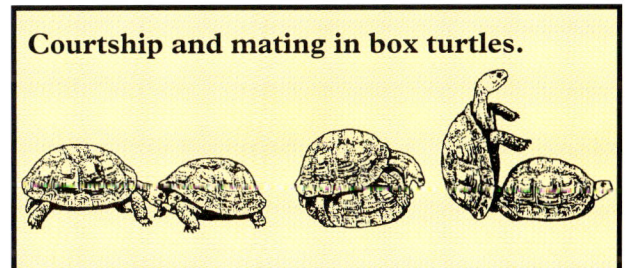

Courtship and mating in box turtles.

TEMPERATURE-DEPENDENT SEX DETERMINATION IN ALLIGATORS AND CROCODILES

by: Craig A. Smith
Department of Paediatrics and Centre for Hormone Research,
The University of Melbourne, Royal Children's Hospital, Parkville, Victoria, 3052, Australia

Dr. Craig Smith has a Bachelor Science degree (with first class Honors) in Vertebrate Physiology and a PhD in Biology. Currently he is a Post-doctoral fellow with the National Health and Medical Research Council (NH&MRC) in the Department of Pediatrics, the Univeristy of Melbourne, The Royal Children's Hospital, Parkville, Victoria, Australia.

INTRODUCTION

Females and males - the existence of separate sexes is a fundamental characteristic of all vertebrates. Anatomical and behavioural differences between males and females are often conspicuous, but how is sex determined in the first place? In humans and other mammals, the developmental decision to become either a male or a female is made at fertilization. Individuals inheriting two X chromosomes normally develop ovaries and become females, while those receiving an X and a Y chromosome develop testes and become males. This process has traditionally been termed genotypic sex determination, or GSD, because sex is decided purely by genetic factors carried on the sex chromosomes. Not all animals, however, share this rigid system of sex determination. Sex is determined by the temperature of egg incubation in a variety of oviparous reptiles, including several lizards, many turtles, and all crocodilians (crocodiles and alligators) (figure 1)(reviewed in Bull, 1980, and in Janzen and Paukstis, 1991).

Species with temperature-dependent sex determination (TSD) lack observable sex chromosomes, and sex is determined by the temperature of the nest during embryonic development. Although the mechanism by which it operates is not understood, TSD provides a novel system for studying the processes governing vertebrate sex determination in general. The following discussion gives an overview of TSD in alligators and crocodiles and how it might operate.

CHARACTERISTICS OF TEMPERATURE-DEPENDENT SEX DETERMINATION (TSD)

TSD was first reported in 1966, when Charnier noticed that hatchling sex ratios varied according to egg incubation temperature in the lizard, *Agama agama*. Today, TSD is known to occur in over 70 species of reptiles. Not all reptiles, however, exhibit TSD; many resemble mammals and birds in having GSD. Figure 2 shows the phylogenetic distribution of both forms of sex determination among the reptiles and other tetrapods (land vertebrates). Although the class Reptilia represents something of an artificial classification of quite separate groups of vertebrates, four living orders are recognised: squamates (snakes and lizards), chelonians (turtles/tortoises), crocodilians (alligators/crocodiles) and sphenodontids (the lizard-like tuataras of New Zealand). All snakes that have been examined appear to have GSD (although only a few have been tested for TSD) (Gorman, 1973; Olmo, 1986; reviewed in Viets *et al.*, 1994). Both TSD and GSD occur in turtles and lizards (Raynaud and Pieau, 1985; Standora and Spotila, 1985; Ewert *et al.*, 1994; Viets *et al.*, 1994; reviewed in Janzen and Paukstis, 1991). Among the crocodilians, TSD has been documented in all species that have been examined (Ferguson and Joanen, 1982; Webb *et al.*, 1987; reviewed in Lang and Andrews, 1994). Recent data point to the likelihood that the two species of Sphenodontids (tuataras) also have TSD (Cree *et al.*, 1995). All other land vertebrates have GSD. While TSD *per se* has not been found in amphibians, artificially elevated temperatures during embryonic development can result in sex reversal among some species (see Dournon *et al.*, 1990).

The scattered distribution of GSD and TSD across phylogenetically divergent groups suggests

Fig. 1.
Sex is determined by egg incubation temperature in *Alligator mississippiensis* and in all other crocodilians that have been examined.

that at least one of these forms of sex determination has evolved several times. It is unknown at present which system is ancestral. Since TSD occurs among ancient lineages (e.g., crocodilians and chelonians) but not among recently evolved groups (e.g., snakes, birds and mammals), it may represent the ancestral state. However, this idea remains speculative.

There are two main patterns of TSD (figure 3). In most (probably all) crocodilians, low and high egg incubation temperatures produce female hatchlings and intermediate temperatures produce males. For example, in the American alligator, *Alligator mississippiensis*, eggs incubated at 30°C yield 100% females, eggs incubated at 33°C yield 100% males, and eggs incubated at 34-35°C produce females again. Other temperatures within this viable range result in both sexes. This "female-male-female" pattern of TSD is shown in figure 3, which plots hatchling sex ratio as a function of egg temperature. Essentially all crocodilians that have been tested for TSD show this pattern, which also occurs in several species of lizards and in some terrestrial turtles (reviewed in Janzen and Paukstis, 1991). A simpler pattern of TSD is seen in many turtles, including all marine species; cool tempera-

Fig. 3.
Patterns of temperature-dependent sex determination (TSD) in the turtle, *Trachemys scripta* (A; open squares) and the crocodilian, *Alligator mississippiensis* (B; closed circles). Hatchling sex ratios (percentage male) are shown as a function of egg incubation temperature. Data from Ewert and Nelson (1991), Etchberger *et al.* (1991) and Lang and Andrews (1994)

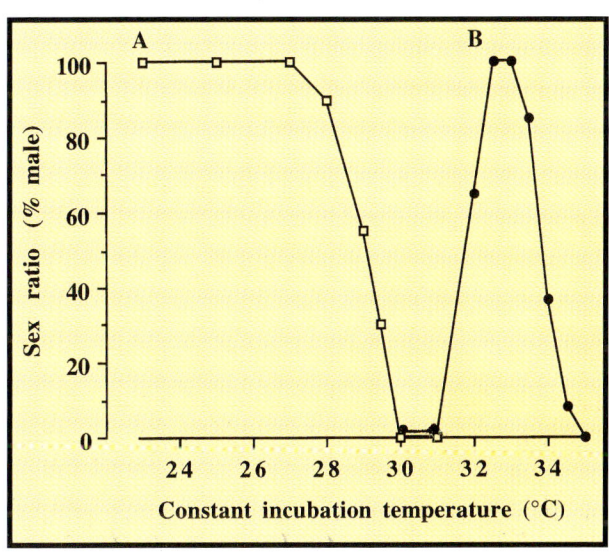

tures (around 26°C) are male-producing and warmer temperatures (around 30°C) are female-producing. Turtles such as the red-eared slider (*Trachemys scripta*) show this "male-female" pattern (figure 3) (Ewert and Nelson, 1991). Although some lizards have been reported to show a third pattern, "female-male", only part of the viable incubation temperature range has been examined, and a "female-male-female" pattern may actually exist (Viets *et al.*, 1994).

Male- and female-determining temperatures have been identified for species with TSD by incubating eggs at constant temperatures in the laboratory. However, TSD also occurs under natural conditions. In south western Louisiana, for example, alligator nests located in moist marsh habitats are relatively cool (around 30°C) and they yield female hatchlings. Nests located on levees (elevated

Fig. 4.
Alligator embryos on select days of incubation at 30°C (female-producing) and at 33°C (male-producing). On any given day, embryos developing at the male-producing temperature are larger. Hatching occurs after 62-74 days. Bar=1cm.

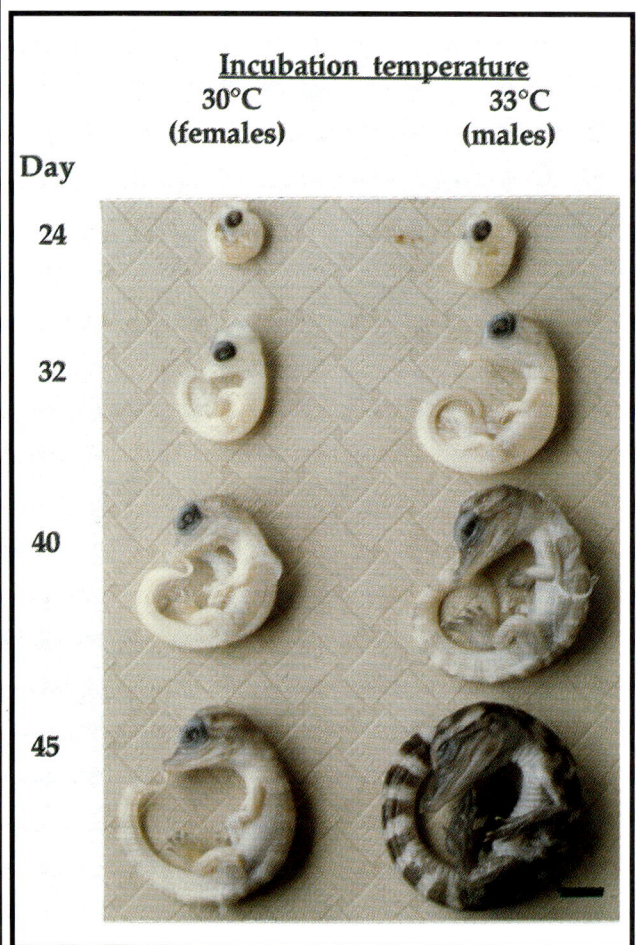

ground) are warmer (around 33°C) and they produce males (Ferguson and Joanen, 1983). For alligators and other reptiles with TSD, the temperature-determined sex of hatchlings appears to be permanent (Yntema, 1976, Ferguson and Joanen, 1983). There are no reports of subsequent sex-reversal among juvenile or adult animals.

The labile nature of sexual development in reptiles with TSD offers certain advantages for experimental analysis. The sex of embryos can be manipulated simply by changing the temperature of egg incubation. Furthermore, by shifting eggs reciprocally between male- and female-producing temperatures throughout incubation, it is possible to identify the periods during development when temperature is determining sex. These thermosensitive periods (TSPs) approximately cover the middle third of embryonic development. The sex-determining mechanism must be operating during this "developmental window". The TSPs correspond to the time that the embryonic gonads begin to differentiate into ovaries or testes. Indeed, the mechanism of TSD must act upon the gonads, either directly or indirectly, so that testis formation occurs at some incubation temperatures and ovary formation occurs at others.

CROCODILIAN EMBRYOS, INCUBATION TEMPERATURE, AND GONADAL DEVELOPMENT

Crocodilians have a lengthy period of egg incubation which varies according to temperature. *Alligator mississippiensis* eggs incubated at the female-producing temperature of 30°C hatch after approximately 74 days of incubation. Alligator eggs incubated at the warmer male-producing temperature of 33°C develop more rapidly and hatch earlier, after about 62 days. This enhanced rate of embryonic development at 33°C (male-producing) relative to 30°C (female-producing) is shown in figure 4. On any given day of incubation, alligator embryos developing at the male-producing temperature are larger than those at the cooler female-producing temperature. The developmental rate of alligator embryos incubated at 34-35°C (the high female-producing temperature) has not been reported. However, at least in one other crocodilian, *Crocodylus johnstoni*, high temperature females incubated at 34°C develop even more rapidly than males produced at 32°C (Webb *et al.*, 1987). It has been suggested that this differential growth and development of embryos at different incubation temperatures may play a role in TSD. Perhaps a specific rate of development is necessary to acti-

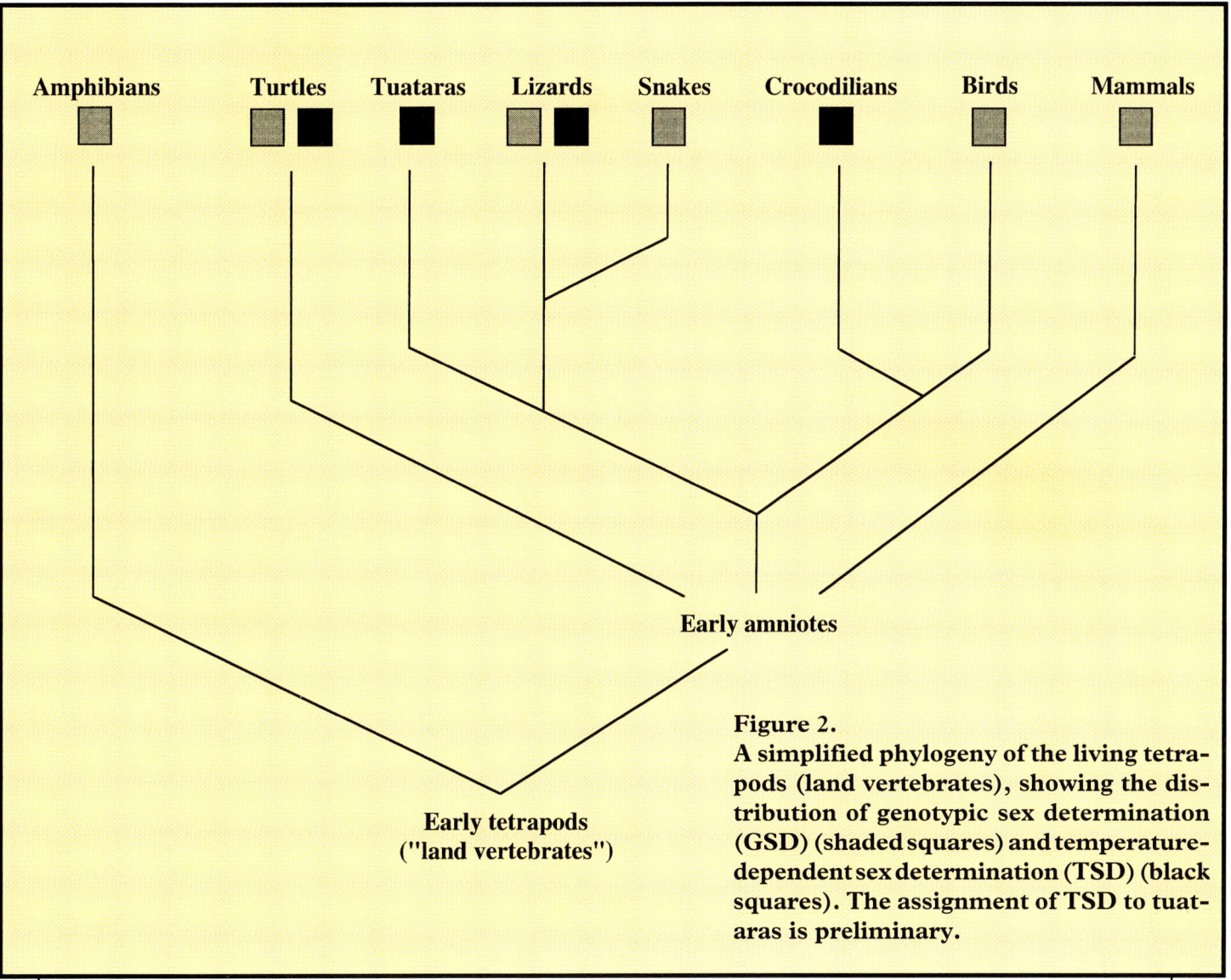

Amphibians   Turtles   Tuataras   Lizards   Snakes   Crocodilians   Birds   Mammals

Early amniotes

Early tetrapods
("land vertebrates")

Figure 2.
A simplified phylogeny of the living tetrapods (land vertebrates), showing the distribution of genotypic sex determination (GSD) (shaded squares) and temperature-dependent sex determination (TSD) (black squares). The assignment of TSD to tuataras is preliminary.

vate a testis-determining signal. This rate may only be achieved over a narrow temperature range (around 33°C in alligators). Rates of embryonic development at temperatures above or below this narrow range may result in the testis-determining signal being released too early or too late in embryogenesis, leading to ovary formation by default (Joss, 1989). However, regardless of whether it is acting upon embryonic developmental rate or through some other mechanism, the sex-determining effect of incubation temperature must ultimately be directed at the embryonic gonads. If we are to understand how TSD works in reptiles, then, it is critical to have some understanding of gonadal sex differentiation during embryonic development.

In alligator embryos, the paired gonads develop adjacent to the adrenal glands on the ventromedial surface of the mesonephric (embryonic) kidneys. Figure 5a shows one side of this urogenital system. The larger so-called metanephric kidneys lie posterior to the gonad-adrenal-mesonephric kidney complex. While the gonads derive from cells originating in the mesonephric kidneys, the metanephric kidneys play no apparent role in gonadal

development. They become the functional excretory organs in adults, as the mesonephric kidneys regress shortly after hatching. A transverse section through the urogenital system, as shown in figure 5b, reveals the close anatomical association between the gonad, adrenal gland and mesonephric kidney. In all embryos, two sets of tubes develop as part of the urogenital system, the Wolffian ducts and the Müllerian ducts (Figure 5b). These ducts are basically responsible for transferring the germ cells (sperm or fertilized eggs) from the gonads to the exterior when the animal becomes sexually active later in life. However, one set of ducts is lost according to the sex of the embryo. In females, the Müllerian ducts are retained and the Wolffian ducts regress, while in males, the reverse occurs.

At 33°C (male-producing), the gonads begin differentiating into testes between days 30 and 40 of incubation (Smith and Joss, 1993). Primordial Sertoli cells differentiate in the inner part of the gonad and seminiferous cords become defined. The germ cells (future sperm) become enclosed in these cords. The testes are well-developed in male alligators at the time of hatching (figure 6a).

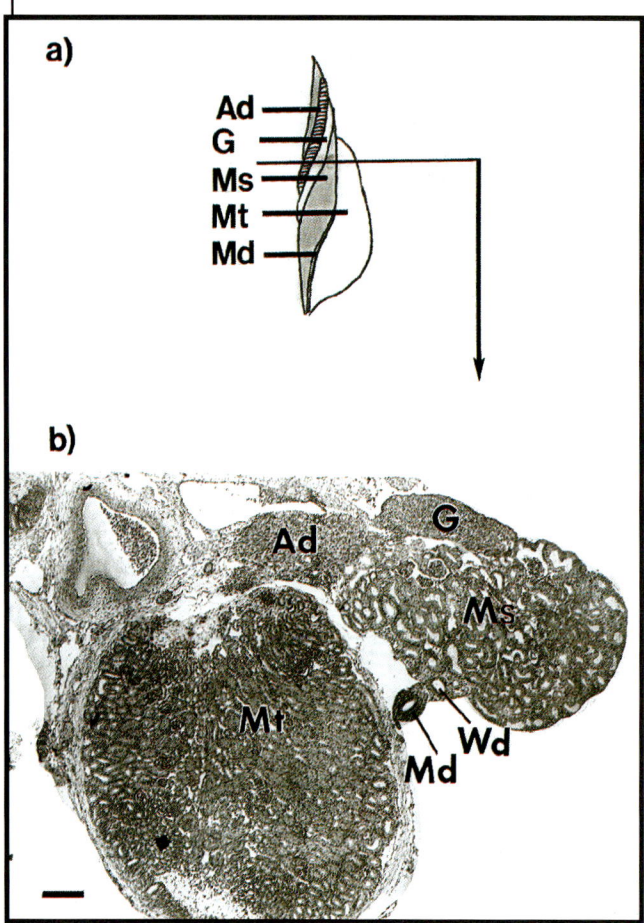

Fig. 5.
a) Semi-schematic ventral view of the urogenital system of an alligator embryo (one side only is shown, not to scale).

b) Histology of the urogenital system (one side only). This tissue was taken from a 33-day-old alligator embryo that had been incubated at 33°C (male-producing). Bar =200µm Adrenal gland (Ad); gonad (G); Müllerian duct (Md); mesonephric kidney (Ms); Metanephric kidney (Mt); Wolffian duct (Wd).

In alligator embryos incubated at 30°C (female-producing), the gonads show morphological signs of ovary differentiation a little later in development, between days 39 and 45. There is a dramatic proliferation of germ cells (future egg cells, or ova) in the outer part of the differentiating ovary. These cells then enter the earliest stage of meiosis (prophase I). The widespread proliferation of germ cells and their entry into meiotic prophase is a hallmark of female development that is not seen in male embryos. The inner part of the gonad, which is the site of seminiferous cord formation in males, becomes reduced and fragmented in fe-

males. The outer part of the ovary thickens as developing follicle cells become organised around the meiotic germ cells (oocytes) (figure 6b) (Smith and Joss, 1993). Temperature must act in some way upon these morphogenic processes underlying testis and ovary formation.

Strategies being used to investigate the mechanism of TSD have focussed specifically on the molecular and physiological aspects of gonadal development. While one or more factors controlling gonadal sex differentiation must be activated by temperature in species with TSD (either directly or indirectly), the nature of these factors is at present unknown. Deeming and Ferguson (1989) hypothesised that alligator embryos incubated at the male-producing temperature receive a threshold dose of a testis-determining factor. The level of this factor may be lower at female-producing temperatures, such that it is insufficient to trigger testis formation. Perhaps temperature has a differential effect upon gene expression, or upon the structure or function of some sex-determining protein. Current research in this area is being conducted on two broad fronts. One searches for the genes involved in TSD, while the other explores the involvement of sex hormones.

SEX-DETERMINING GENES

After many years of research, some of the genes within the mammalian sex-determining pathway have recently been identified. These genes could serve as probes to hunt for related sex-determining genes in reptiles with TSD. This approach is based upon the reasonable assumption that much of the sex-determining pathway has been conserved over evolution. Since the structure and development of the gonads is very similar in all vertebrates, especially in the amniotes (reptiles, birds, and mammals), it is likely that major components of the sex-determining pathway are shared between these groups. In mammals, the Y-linked gene, *SRY*, initiates testis formation and hence male development (Sinclair *et al.*,1990; Koopman *et al.*, 1991). *SRY* belongs to a large family of genes, called *SOX* genes, which appear to be involved in regulating various aspects of development. Another of the *SOX* genes, *SOX9*, has also recently been implicated in mammalian testis formation (reviewed in Capel, 1995). While no sex-specific *SRY* gene has been found in reptiles with TSD (or in any other vertebrate other than mammals), many related *SOX* genes have been identified in both sexes. It is possible that one or more of these genes is involved in TSD. A sex-determining *SOX* gene might be switched on or off according to temperature. For example, a SOX gene signalling ovary development might be turned on at female-producing temperatures, but not at male-producing temperatures. Alternatively, sex determination may depend upon the dose of a gene activated at all temperatures. An testis-determining *SOX* gene may be expressed at both female- and male-producing temperatures, for example, but only expressed at sufficient levels at the male-temperature. Another gene recently shown to have a key role in mammalian gonadal differentiation is *Ftz-F1*, which encodes a protein called steroidogenic factor-1 (SF-1). In mice, SF-1 is critical for the early development of the gonad in both sexes, and it also plays a role in subsequent testis differentiation in males (reviewed in Smith, 1995). It is possible that a protein similar to SF-1 participates in TSD. These molecular aspects of sex determination and gonadal development in species with TSD are only just now being examined.

SEX HORMONES AND TSD

Most studies aimed at elucidating the mechanism of TSD have focussed upon sex steroid hormones. Several lines of evidence implicate sex hormones, particularly estrogens, in TSD. If estrogens are injected into eggs incubating at the *male*-producing temperature, embryos develop as *females* (reviewed in Raynaud and Pieau, 1985, and in Wibbels *et al.*, 1994). This applies to each of the major reptilian groups displaying TSD (lizards, turtles, and crocodilians) (Pieau, 1974; Bull *et al.*, 1988; Crews *et al.*, 1989. Conversely, compounds which interfere with estrogen synthesis or estrogen action can disrupt ovarian development or cause complete testis differentiation in embryos incubated at *female*-producing temperatures (Dorizzi *et al.*, 1991; Lance and Bogart, 1991, 1992; Wibbels and Crews, 1992, 1994; reviewed in Crews *et al.*, 1994, and in Pieau *et al.*, 1994a). Collectively, this evidence suggests that some aspect of estrogen synthesis or estrogen action is naturally thermosensitive in species with TSD. Production of estrogens, or gonadal sensitivity to them, may be optimal at female-producing temperatures, triggering ovary differentiation, but sub-optimal or repressed at male-producing temperatures, allowing testis differentiation.

Radioactively-labelled estrogen injected into eggs is taken up specifically by the gonads during the period of sexual differentiation in developing saltwater crocodile (*Crocodylus porosus*) embryos. Furthermore, the steroid is taken up by the gonads at both female- and male-producing temperatures (Smith and Joss, 1994). This suggests that estrogen receptors are present in the gonads of both presumptive sexes. If estrogen can be taken up at both male- and female-producing temperatures in species with TSD, perhaps it is estrogen *synthesis* that is thermosensitive.

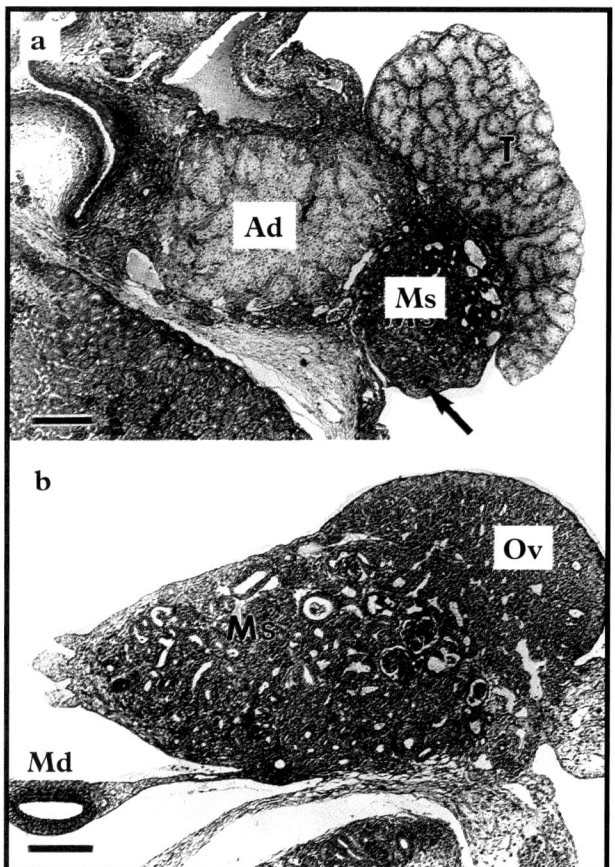

Fig. 6

Histological sections of the alligator urogential system at the time of hatching. a) Urogential system of a male hatchling. The testis (T) is well-developed and the Müllerian duct has disintegrated (arrow). Adrenal gland (Ad); Mesonephric kidney (Ms). Bar = 200μm.

(b) Urogenital system of a female hatchling. The outer part of the ovary (Ov) becomes thickened, while the inner part becomes fragmented. The Müllerian duct (Md) is well-developed. Mesonephric kidney (Ms). Bar = 200μm.

In reptiles, as in other vertebrates, estrogens and related steroid hormones are synthesised from cholesterol via a series of enzyme catalysed reactions, shown in figure 7. Two important enzymes in this pathway are 3B-HSD and aromatase. 3B-HSD is active at several points in the pathway, directly or indirectly catalysing the production of androgens (male sex hormones). Aromatase enzyme can then convert these androgens (testosterone and/or androstenedione) into estrogens (estradiol and estrone) (figure 7). A simple histochemical test can be performed on tissue sections for the presence of 3B-HSD enzyme activity. When this test carried out on sections of urogenital tissues from saltwater crocodile embryos, only the adrenal gland

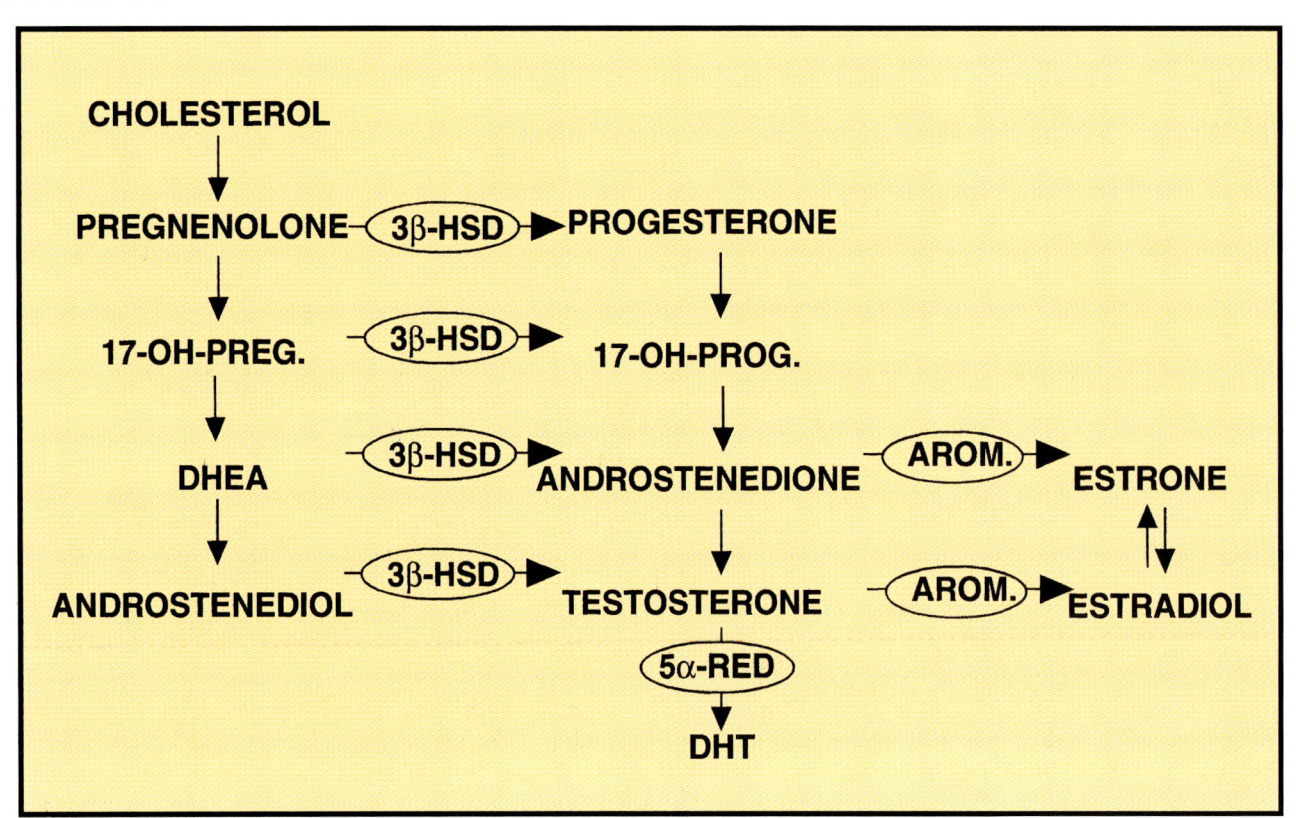

Figure 7
Major pathways of sex steroid hormone synthesis in vertebrates. 3B-HSD = 3B-hydroxysteroid dehydrogenase; Arom = aromatase; 5 -Red.= 5-reductase. Other enzymes in the pathway have been omitted for clarity.

stains positive for 3B-HSD activity throughout development. Enzyme activity is not detectable in the gonads. This occurs at both male- and female-producing temperatures (figure 8). Similar findings have been reported for two turtles with TSD, the olive ridley and the red-eared slider (Merchant-Larios *et al.*,1989; Thomas *et al.*, 1992). However, in some other species, including the alligator, both the embryonic gonads and the adrenals have detectable 3B-HSD activity (reviewed in Crews, 1994). Altogether, these studies suggest that the adrenal gland may play a role in TSD by synthesising steroid hormones. These steroids might then diffuse into the neighbouring gonad. However, do the urogenital tissues produce aromatase enzyme to convert these steroids into estrogens? Aromatase enzyme activity can be measured in tissues isolated from developing embryos. In the urogenital tissues of embryonic alligators, aromatase enzyme activity increases during development at female-producing temperatures, but not at the male-producing temperature. This is shown in figure 9. For embryos incubated at both the low (30°C) and high (34.5°C) female-producing temperatures, aromatase enzyme activity in the urogenital system increases over stages of embryonic development. In contrast, it remains very low during male development at 33°C (figure 9) (Smith *et al.*, 1995). These observations implicate increased

aromatase activity, and hence estrogen synthesis, in female development. Similar findings have been reported for turtles with TSD (Desvages and Pieau, 1992; reviewed in Pieau *et al.*, 1994b).

Aromatase enzyme assays conducted at different temperatures indicate that temperature does not directly influence enzyme activity *per se*. Rather, temperature appears to control enzyme synthesis (Smith *et al.*, 1995). Aromatase gene expression may therefore be a candidate for temperature sensitivity in species with TSD. However, it is unclear whether temperature directly or indirectly influences aromatase enzyme. For alligator embryos at least, increased aromatase activity is first detectable *after* the thermosensitive period when sex is being determined. This suggests that, while enhanced estrogen production is involved in female development, it may not represent the initial ovary-determining signal. It seems likely that other regulatory genes control aromatase synthesis, and that the action of these other genes is thermosensitive.

In view of the apparent role of estrogen synthesis in female development, one might ask whether male sex hormones such as testosterone are involved in male development. Testosterone injected into eggs incubated at the female-producing temperature has been notable in its failure to induce testis formation in species with TSD. However, the bioactive metabolite of

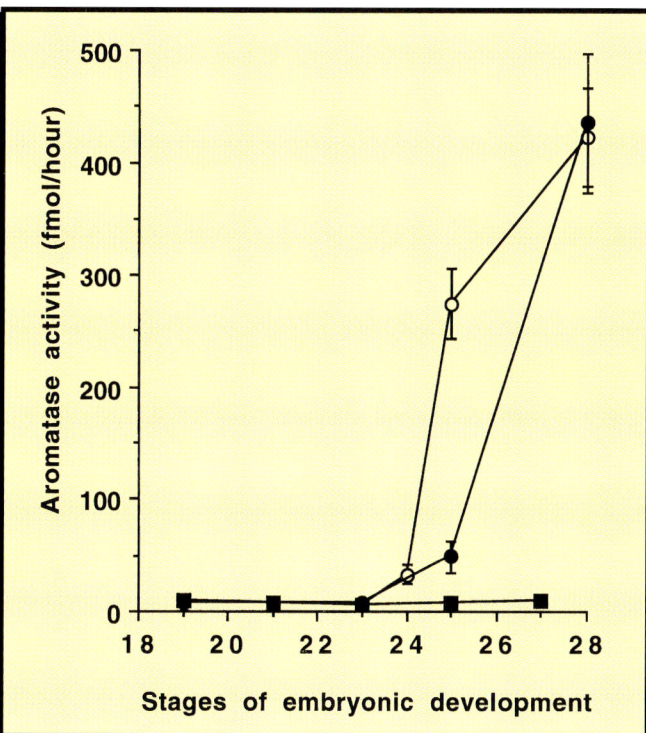

Figure 9. Aromatase enzyme activity in the urogenital system of alligator embryos during stages of development. Aromatase activity increases during female development at 30°C (◯) and at 34.5°C (●), but not during male development at 33°C (■). Stage 28 represents hatching.

testosterone, dihydrotestosterone (DHT), has attracted interest recently. In a turtle with TSD, *Trachemys scripta*, DHT can produce predominantly male hatchlings if injected into eggs incubated at temperatures that would otherwise produce both sexes (reviewed in Crews *et al.*, 1994). As shown in figure 8, DHT can be synthesised from testosterone through the action of the enzyme, 5-reductase. Recent experiments using inhibitors of 5-reductase have implicated this enzyme, and hence DHT synthesis, in testis differentiation in species with TSD (Crews and Bergeron, 1994; Crews *et al.*, 1994). Thus, different incubation temperatures might modulate female and male sex hormone synthesis as part of the mechanism underlying TSD. Further studies in this area should examine the expression of genes encoding steroid-producing enzymes during gonadal development.

TSD continues to intrigue biologists from many disciplines. While ecologists puzzle over the advantages of TSD, developmental biologists are still exploring the mechanism by which it operates. Sex steroid hormones appear to be involved, but their precise role in TSD remains to be clearly defined. Much of the interest for those studying TSD stems from its potential to shed light on the evolution of sex determination. Living rep-

Figure 8.
Tissue section showing 3B-HSD enzyme activity in the adrenal gland (A) of a female crocodile hatchling, but no detectable enzyme activity in the gonad (G). (Ms = mesonephric kidney). Bar =300μm.

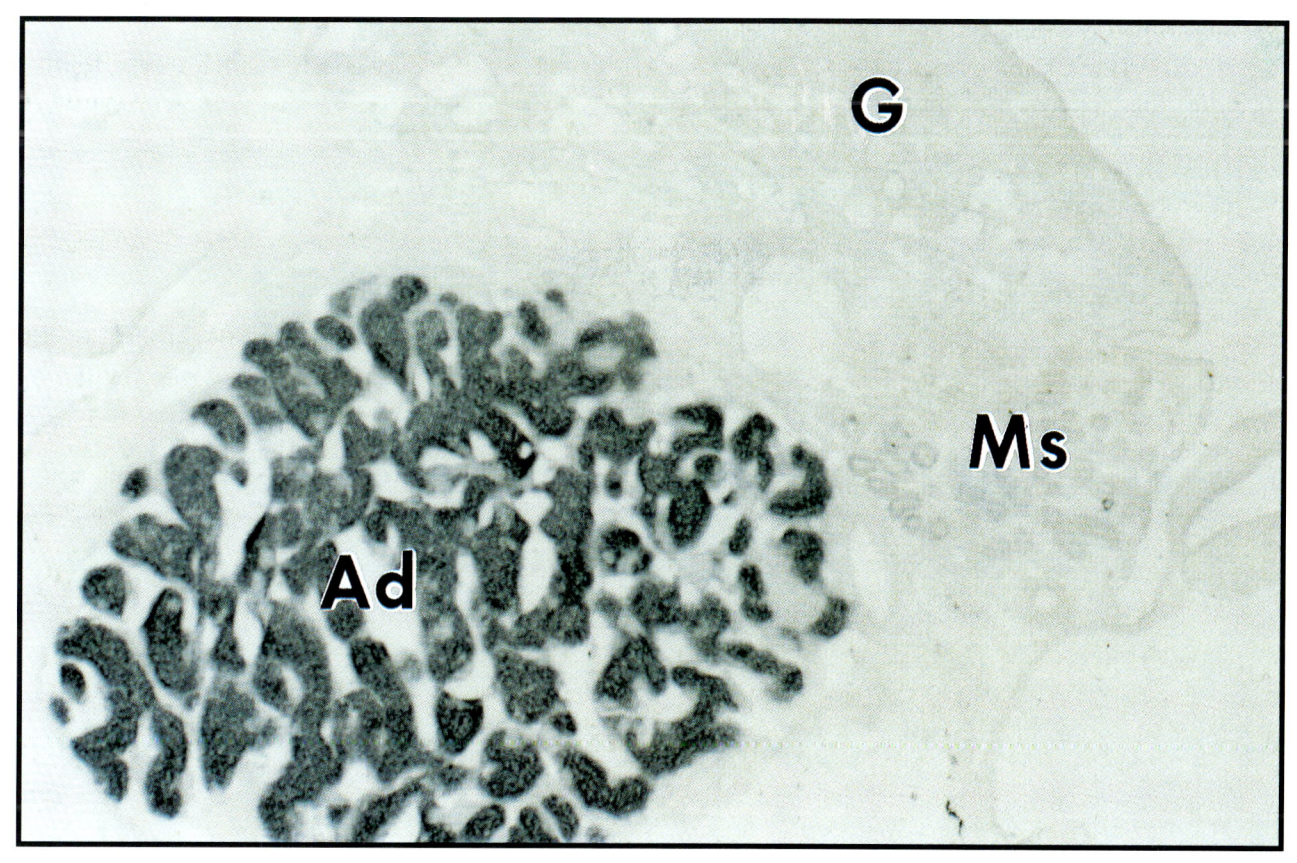

tiles, birds, and mammals are thought to be descended from a common amniote ancestor (see figure 2). By elucidating the processes underlying TSD in reptiles, we may enhance our understanding of vertebrate sex determination and how it might have evolved.

ACKNOWLEDGEMENTS

I thank Dr. Andrew Sinclair for comments on the manuscript.

REFERENCES AND RECOMMENDED READING

—**Bull, J. J. (1980).**
Sex determination in reptiles. *Quart. Rev. Biol.*, 55, 3-21.

—**Bull, J. J., Gutzke, W. H. N. and Crews, D. (1988a).**
Sex reversal by estradiol in three reptilian orders. *Gen. Comp. Endocrinol.*, 70, 425-428.

—**Capel, B (1995).**
New bedfellows in the mammalian sex-determination affair. *Trends in Genet.*, 11, 161-163.

—**Charnier, M. (1966).**
Action de la temperature sur la sex-ratio chez l'embryon d'*Agama agama* (Agamidae, Lacertilien). *Competes Rendus de la Societ+ de Biologie, Paris*, 160, 620-622.

—**Cree, A., Thompson, M. B. and Daugherty, C. H. (1995).**
Tuatara sex determination. *Nature*, 375, 543.

—**Crews, D. (1994).**
Temperature, steroids and sex determination. *J. Endocrinology*, 142, 1-8.

—**Crews, D. and Bergeron, J. M. (1994).**
Role of reductase and aromatase in sex determination in the red-eared slider (*Trachemys scripta*), a turtle with temperature-dependent sex determination. *J. Endocrinology*, 143, 279-289.

—**Crews, D., Bergeron, J. M., Bull, J. J., Flores, D., Tousignant, A., Skipper, J. K., and Wibbels, T. (1994).**
Temperature-dependent sex determination in reptiles: proximate mechanisms, ultimate outcomes and practical applications. *Developmental Genetics*, 15, 297-312.

—**Crews, D., Wibbels, T. and Gutzke, W. H. N. (1989).**
Action of sex steroid hormones on temperature induced sex determination in the snapping turtle (*Chelydra serpentina*). *Gen. Comp. Endocrinol.*, 76, 159-166.

—**Deeming, D. C. and Ferguson, M. W. J. (1989).**
The mechanism of temperature dependent sex

determination in crocodilians: a hypothesis. *Amer. Zool.*, 29, 973-985.

—**Desvages, G. and Pieau, C. (1992).**
Aromatase activity in gonads of turtle embryos as a function of the incubation temperature of eggs. *J. Steroid Biochem. Molec. Biol.*, 41, 3-8.

—**Dorizzi, M., Mignot, T.-M., Guichard, A., Desvages, G. and Pieau, C. (1991).**
Involvement of oestrogens in sexual differentiation of the gonads as a function of temperature in turtles. *Differentiation*, 47, 9-17.

—**Dournon, C., Houillon, C. and Pieau, C. (1990).**
Temperature sex-reversal in amphibians and reptiles. *Int. J. Develop. Biol.*, 34, 81-92.

—**Etchberger, C. R., Phillips, J. B., Ewert, M. A., Nelson, C. E. and Prange, H. D. (1991).**
Effects of oxygen concentration and clutch on sex determination and physiology in red-eared slider turtles (*Trachemys scripta*). *J. Exp. Zool.*, 258, 394-403.

—**Ewert, M. A., Jackson, D. R. and Nelson, C. E. (1994).**
Patterns of temperature-dependent sex determination in turtles. *J. Exp. Zool.*, 270, 3-15.

—**Ewert, M. A. and Nelson, C. E. (1991).**
Sex determination in turtles: patterns and some possible adaptive values. *Copeia*, 1991, 50-69.

—**Ferguson, M. W. J. and Joanen, T. (1982).**
Temperature of egg incubation determines sex in *Alligator mississippiensis*. *Nature*, 296, 850-853.

—**Ferguson, M. W. J. and Joanen, T. (1983).**
Temperature-dependent sex determination in *Alligator mississippiensis*. *Journal of Zoology, London*, 200, 143-177.

—**Gorman, G. (1973).**
The chromosomes of the Reptilia, a cytotaxonomic interpretation. In: *Cytotaxonomy and Vertebrate Evolution* (A. B. Chiarelli and E. Capanna, eds.), pp. 349-424. Academic Press, New York.

—**Janzen, F. J. and Paukstis, G. L. (1991a).**
Environmental sex determination in reptiles: ecology, evolution and experimental design. *Quarterly Review of Biology*, 66, 149-179.

—**Joss, J. M. P. (1989).**
Gonadal development and differentiation in *Alligator mississippiensis* at male and female producing incubation temperatures. *Journal of Zoology, London*, 218, 679-687.

—**Koopman, P., Gubbay, J., Vivian, N., Goodfellow, P. N. and Lovell-Badge, R. (1991).**
Male development of chromosomally female mice transgenic for *Sry*. *Nature*, 351, 117-121.

—**Lance, V. A. and Bogart, M. H. (1991).**
Tamoxifen sex reverses alligator embryos at

male producing temperatures, but is an antiestrogen in female hatchlings. *Experientia*, 47, 263-266.

—**Lance, V. A. and Bogart, M. (1992).**
Disruption of ovarian development in alligator embryos treated with an aromatase inhibitor. *Gen. Comp. Endocrinol.*, 86, 59-71.

—**Lang, J. W. and Andrews, H. (1994).**
Temperature-dependent sex determination in crocodilians. *The Journal of Experimental Zoology*, 270, 28-44.

—**Merchant-Larios, H., Fierro, I. V. and Urriuza, B. C. (1989).**
Gonadal morphogenesis under controlled temperature in the sea turtle *Lepidochelys olivacea*. *Herpetol. Monogr.*, 3, 43-61.

—**Olmo, E. (1986).**
A. Reptilia. In: *Animal Cytogenetics* (B. John, ed.), Vol. 4, pp. 1-100. GebrŸder Borntraeger, Berlin.

—**Pieau, C. (1974).**
Differenciation du sexe en fonction de la temperature chez les embryons d'*Emys orbicularis* L. (Chelonien). Effets des hormones sexuelles. *Ann. Embryol. Morphog.*, 7, 365-394.

—**Pieau, C., Girondot, M., Desvages, G., Dorizzi, M., Richard-Mercier, N. and Zaborski, P. (1994a).**
Environmental control of gonadal differentiation. In: *The Differences Between the Sexes* (R. V. Short and E. Balaban, eds.), pp. 433-450. Cambridge University Press, U.K.

—**Pieau, C., Girondot, M., Richard-Mercier, N., Desvages, G., Dorizzi, M. and Zaborski, P. (1994b).**
Temperature sensitivity of sexual differentiation of gonads in the European pond turtles: hormonal involvement. *J. Exp. Zool.*, 270, 86-94.

—**Raynaud, A. and Pieau, C. (1985).**
Embryonic development of the genital system. In: C. Gans and F. Billet, eds. *Biology of the Reptilia*. Vol. 15, pp. 149-300. John Wiley and sons, New York.

—**Sinclair, A. H., Berta, P., Palmer, M. S., Hawkins, J. R., Griffiths, B. L., Smith, M. J., Foster, J. W., Frischauf, A.-M., Lovell-Badge, R. and Goodfellow, P. N. (1990).**
A gene from the human sex-determining region encodes a protein with homology to a conserved DNA-binding motif. *Nature*, 346, 240-244.

—**Smith, C. A., Elf, P., Lang, J. W. and Joss, J. M. P. (1995).**
Aromatase enzyme activity during gonadal sex differentiation in alligator embryos *Differentiation* (in press).

—**Smith, C. A. and Joss, J. M. P. (1993).**
Gonadal sex differentiation in *Alligator mississippiensis*, a species with temperature-dependent sex determination. *Cell and Tissue Research*, 273, 149-162.

—**Smith, C. A. and Joss, J. M. P. (1994).**
Uptake of ^{3}H-estradiol by embryonic crocodile gonads during the period of sexual differentiation. *The Journal of Experiment Zoology*, 270, 219-224.

—**Smith, M. J. (1994)**
Turning on sex. *Current Biology*, 4, 1003-1005.

—**Standora, E. A. and Spotila, J. R. (1985).**
Temperature dependent sex determination in sea turtles. *Copeia*, 1985, 711-722.

—**Thomas, E. O., Licht, P., Wibbels, T. and Crews, D. (1992).**
Hydroxysteroid dehydrogenase activity associated with sexual differentiation in embryos of the turtle *Trachemys scripta*. *Biol. Reprod.*, 46, 140-145.

—**Viets, B. E., Ewert, M. A., Talent, L. G. and Nelson, C. E. (1994).**
Sex-determining mechanisms in squamate reptiles. *J. Exp. Zool.*, 270, 45-56.

—**Vogt, R. C., Bull, J. J., McCoy, C. J. and Houseal, T. W. (1982).**
Incubation temperature influences sex determination in kinosternid turtles. *Copeia*, 1982, 480-482.

—**Wibbels, T., Bull, J. J. and Crews, D. (1994).**
Temperature-dependent sex determination: a mechanistic approach. *J. Exp. Zool.*, 270, 71-78.

—**Wibbels, T. and Crews, D. (1992).**
Specificity of steroid hormone-induced sex determination in a turtle. *J. Endocrinol.*, 133, 121-129.

—**Wibbels, T. and Crews, D. (1994).**
Putative aromatase inhibitor induces male sex determination in a female unisexual lizard and in a turtle with temperature-dependent sex determination. *J. Endocrinol.*, 141, 295-299.

—**Webb, G. J. W., Beal, A. M., Manolis, S. C. and Dempsey, K. E. (1987a).**
The effects of incubation temperature on sex determination and embryonic development rate in *Crocodylus johnstoni* and *C. porosus*. In: *Wildlife Management: Crocodiles and Alligators* (G. J. W. Webb, S. C. Manolis and P. J. Whitehead, eds.), pp. 507-531. Surrey Beatty and sons, Sydney.

—**Yntema, C. L. (1976).**
Effects of incubation temperature on sexual differentiation in the turtle, *Chelydra serpentina*. *J. Morphol.*, 150, 453-462.

53

REPRODUCTIVE ANATOMY AND PHYSIOLOGY

(An Ecological And Evolutionary Perspective)

Brent D. Palmer, Ph.D.*; M. Jane Perkins; Sue Simon; Kathy Massie
Laboratory of Reproductive Ecology
Department of Biological Sciences
Ohio University
Athens, Ohio 45701

M.C.A. Uribe, Ph.D.
Lab. Biologia de la Reproduccion
Fac. Ciencias, Coyoacan
Universidad Nacional Autonoma de Mexico
Mexico DF, 04510, MEXICO

* Address all correspondence to Dr. Brent Palmer, Laboratory of Reproductive Ecology, Department of Biological Sciences, Ohio University, Athens, OH 45701.

INTRODUCTION

Reproduction is the critical link in the survival of all species; it ensures that subsequent generations are produced and that beneficial traits are passed on. Evolution is mediated by differential reproduction success, so that failure to produce sufficient numbers of adaptive offspring ultimately leads to extinction. The reproductive system is also extremely complex and closely tied to environmental conditions. Subtle changes can cause disastrous results. Even a slight delay in onset of sexual maturity, reduction in the number of young produced, or mistiming of reproductive events can eventually lead to a species' demise.

Unfortunately, subtle changes in reproduction often go unnoticed by wildlife biologists. Anyone who has attempted to breed reptiles knows that apparently healthy adults may not reproduce successfully. The effects that modern civilization (such as global warming and pollution) have on reptilian reproduction is largely unknown. Significant diversity in the anatomy and physiology of the reproductive system has evolved among reptilian species, further complicating matters. It is critical that the process of reproduction in all reptilian groups be thoroughly understood to ensure their survival (Fig. 1).

ANATOMY

FEMALE ANATOMY
Ovaries
The ovary has both gametogenic and endocrine functions, each of which is intimately related to

Figure 1.
Reproductive success, such as this hatching American alligator (*Alligator mississippiensis*), is the vital link for survival of all species. To ensure the future of reptiles, it is critical to understand their reproductive biology. Photo by H. Suzuki.

the regulation of reproductive events. This includes ova production, maturation and ovulation. It also includes the dynamic control of secondary sexual characteristics and behavior associated with mating, gravidity or pregnancy, and oviposition or parturition. Consequently, the ovary consists of a variety of specialized structures with distinct functions, each of which display considerable seasonal variation.

Reptile ovaries are saccular or membranous structures in which enlarged follicles are readily apparent (Fig. 2). In adult turtles and crocodilians, the ovaries are symmetrically positioned ventral to the kidneys and appear membranous. Among lizards, ova-

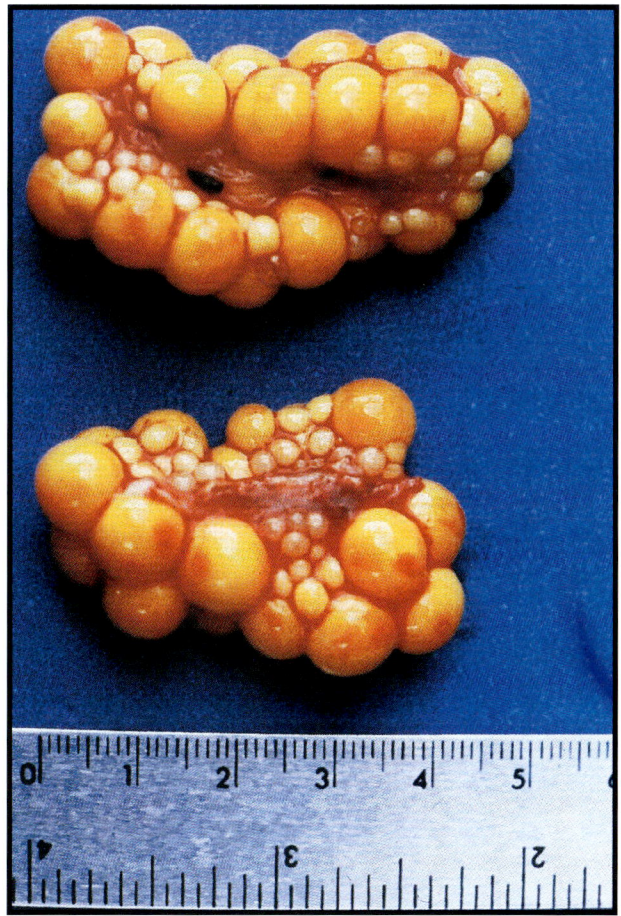

Figure 2.
Ovaries of the iguanid lizard *Ctenosaura pectinata*, illustrating various size classes of follicles. Each size class represents a progression of future clutches. Photo by MCA Uribe.

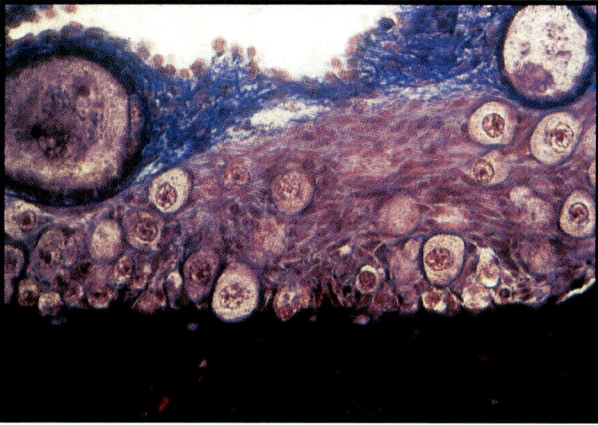

Figure 3.
Histology of the ovary of the lizard *Ctenosaura pectinata*. A germinal bed containing numerous primordial and primary follicles is evident within the ovarian stroma. Photo by MCA Uribe.

This reduces the stroma to a thin layer in which the follicles are distributed close together.

Each follicle consists of the oogonia (or oocyte) surrounded by the granulosal and thecal layers (Espey, 1978; Dodd, 1986). The granulosal cells are formed from the secondary cords during embryonic development, whereas the thecal cells are derived from stromal cells. In developing follicles, the theca is bilayered, exhibiting a theca interna and theca externa. The theca externa is fibrous with a thin matrix of collagen and fibroblasts and provides structural support for the individual follicle. The theca interna contains endocrine cells which undergo morphological, cytological, and histochemical changes throughout the reproductive cycle. The inner granulosal layer may have several layers of distinct cell types in squamates (Fig. 4).

Figure 4.
Outer layers of an ovarian follicle from the lizard *Ctenosuara pectinata*. The fibrous thecal layer rests upon the stratum granulosum, which is comprised of small, medium, and large pyramidal cells. The granulosal layer surrounds the yolk. Photo by MCA Uribe.

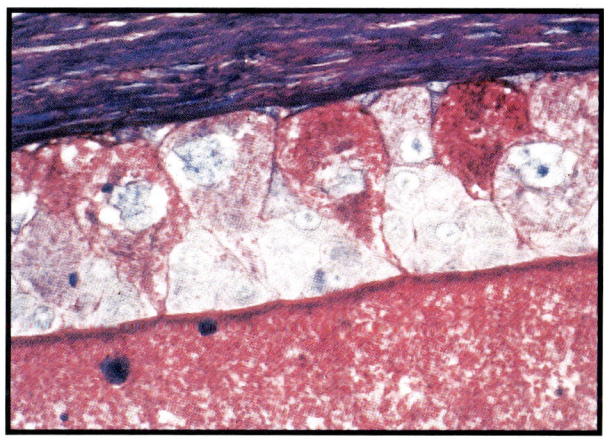

ries may be either symmetrically or asymmetrically positioned (one ovary more anterior than the other). Ovaries of snakes are elongated compared to those of other reptiles. Asymmetrically placed gonads are the rule in snakes. The right ovary is usually larger and more anterior than the left, corresponding to the length of the adjacent oviduct. The left ovary may be reduced or undeveloped. This arrangement follows from the elongated body cavity of snakes. The ovaries are supported by mesovaria attached to the dorsal body wall. Extensions of the mesovaria are continuous with mesotubaria supporting the oviducts.

The typical reptilian ovary consists of a surface layer of cuboidal epithelium (germinal epithelia) resting on a layer of dense tissue (tunica albuginea). These layers surround the ovarian cortex. The ovarian cortex houses the scattered follicles containing oogonia or oocytes among the stroma (Fig. 3). The stroma consists of loose connective tissue containing collagen fibers, scattered fibroblasts, and blood vessels. Squamate ovaries contain a central cavity or series of cavities filled with lymph and lined with squamous epithelium.

Granulosal and thecal cells function to produce steroid hormones and support the maturing oocyte.

In addition to follicles of varying maturity, the cortical stroma also contains the corpora atretica and corpora lutea. The corpora atretica consist of degenerated follicles; the corpora lutea consist of endocrine structures derived from the theca and granulosa of ovulated follicles.

During embryonic development, prolonged bisexuality or undifferentiated gonads are not uncommon in reptiles, and are typical of turtles and crocodilians. Gonadal differentiation of the ovary is marked by a thickening cortex and a regressing medulla. However, in *Alligator mississippiensis*, medullary cords may persist (Duke, 1978). Embryonic ovaries are long and oval in shape (Crews et al., 1989). After hatching, the primary sex cords of the ovary are regressed, while secondary sex cords form the cuboidal epithelium (stratum granulosa) surrounding each oogonia. In turtles and crocodilians, gender at hatching may be difficult to determine by histological inspection of the gonads. However, both oogonia and oocytes may be apparent at hatching in squamates (Fox, 1977).

In mature individuals, the ovarian cycle is divided into three phases: quiescent, vitellogenic, and gravid or pregnant. Quiescence is the period when no development of the ovaries and oviducts occurs. During the vitellogenic phase, ovarian follicles and oviducts show a rapid hypertrophy (Fig.

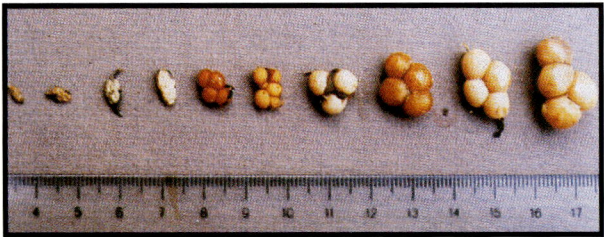

Figure 5.
Series of ovaries illustrating follicular development in the lizard, *Ctenosaura pectinata*. Photo by MCA Uribe.

5). Gravidity or pregnancy is when the eggs or embryos are held within the oviducts following ovulation. During gravidity, albumen formation and egg shelling occur before oviposition. Only lizards and snakes have evolved viviparity, or live-bearing. Pregnancy is associated with placentation during embryonic development and ends with parturition.

In most reptiles, game togenesis continues throughout life with new oogonia being formed within the germinal beds. Examination of 40 lizard species showed most species have one or two germinal beds per ovary although some had several (Jones et al., 1982). Oogonial mitoses may fluctuate seasonally, as has been shown in some turtles and lizards (Altland, 1951; Jones et al., 1978). Primordial follicles consist of oocytes in early prophase, surrounded by a single layer of granulosal cells (Dodd, 1986). In snakes and lizards, the granulosal layer thickens until small, intermediate, and large cells are present.

Ovarian recrudescence and follicular maturity are coincident with vitellogenesis, the production of vitellogenin from the liver under the influence of estrogen. Vitellogenin from the blood stream is incorporated into the maturing follicle, forming yolk (Fig. 6). Follicular development can be continuous and rapid in tropical species; it can stretch over months (or years in some turtles) in north-temperate species. In cooler climates, vitellogenesis can be interrupted by brumation or hibernation.

Within an ovary, different size classes of follicles represent future clutches/litters, with the largest

Figure 6.
Vitellogenin from the liver is deposited in growing vitellogenic follicles as yolk platelets. Note ovarian stroma at the upper right. Photo by MCA Uribe.

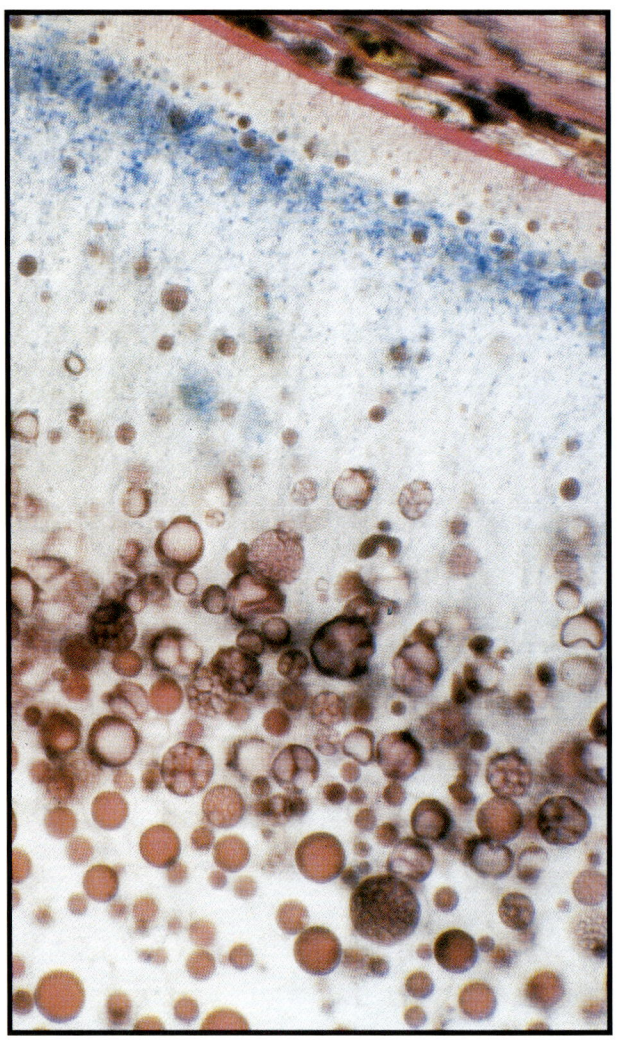

follicle class being the next to be ovulated. The size and number of ovulated follicles vary greatly among reptiles. The size of the ovulated follicle correlates to the size of the egg; the number of ovulated follicles correlates to the size of the clutch.

The thecal and granulosal layers undergo significant changes during vitellogenesis. The thecal layers of preovulatory follicles are thickened with abundant fibroblasts and collagen fibers. Theca interna and strata granulosa hypertrophy to form large, glandular cells (Uribeetal. 1995, 1996). Both thecal and granulosal cells are involved in steroidogenesis, especially of estrogen. The granulosal cells are the primary site of estrogen production during vitellogenesis (Callard and Ho, 1980; Callard and Kleis, 1987).

Ovulation is accompanied by the transformation of the follicular wall into the corpus luteum. In response to gonadotropins, Reptilian thecal and granulosal cells become luteinized. They then proliferate to transform the ovulated follicle into a corpus luteum. Although the corpora lutea of most reptiles retain a layer of thecal lutein cells surrounding the granulosal lutein cells, those of *Alligator mississippiensis* differ in having both cell types integrated—similar to that seen in mammalian corpora lutea (Guillette et al., 1995).

Corpora lutea secrete estrogen and progesterone, which may regulate oviductal function during gravidity and pregnancy. High levels of progesterone inhibit uterine contractions that might lead to early oviposition or parturition. At the appropriate time, the corpora lutea involute. This causes progesterone concentrations to drop, enabling the uterine musculature to respond to arginine vasotcin (AVT) and expel the eggs or young.

Following oviposition or parturition, the corpora lutea are gradually reabsorbed into the ovarian stroma. Corpora lutea of *Chelydra serpentina* have a life of approximately six weeks (Klicka and Mahmoud, 1973). In contrast the ovaries of, *A. mississippiensis* still exhibits luteal structures nine months after oviposition (Guillette et al., 1995).

Follicular atresia is the process by which ovarian follicles are reabsorbed prior to ovulation. Atretic follicles exhibit a proliferation of fibroblasts that disrupt the thecal and granulosal layers and macrophages that phagocytize the yolk. Atresia is a common process that may be used to eliminate defective eggs or to regulate clutch size. In *Anolis carolinensis*, corpora atretica are associated with maintaining a postbreeding season sexual-refractory period (Crews and Licht, 1974).

Oviducts

As early as 1857, Agassiz recognized that not only did the reptilian oviduct provide egg transport, but it was also responsible for the albumenous and calcareous egg coverings. Over the nearly century and a half since then, the list of oviductal functions has grown considerably. The oviduct performs these functions:

—receives the gametes
—provides active and passive transport of gametes
—is the site of maturation of the oocyte
—provides storage for sperm
—is the site of fertilization
—is the site of deposition of egg coverings; albumen, membranes, and shell
—is responsible for storage of eggs
—facilitates oviposition

The oviducts form embryologically from the paired Müllerian (mesonephric) ducts, which open into the cloaca. The paired oviducts are symmetrical with ostia adjacent to the ovaries anteriorly and joining the cloaca posteriorly. The left oviduct is reduced in some snake and lizard species, and some snake species lack a left oviduct entirely. In most snakes, even when both oviducts are functional, the majority of offspring are held within the right oviduct during gravidity or pregnancy. The oviducts are supported by mesotubaria attached to the dorsal body wall.

Longitudinally, the oviduct is divided into five morphologically and functionally distinct regions. These include (anteriorly to posteriorly):

—infundibulum
—tuba uterina (uterine tube or tube)
—isthmus
—uterus
—vagina

Many authors may subdivide these regions further into anterior and posterior portions (Fig. 7).

Figure 7.
The gravid oviduct of the tortoise, *Gopherus polyphemus*. The major oviductal regions are evident, including: the flaccid infundibulum (right), the long, convoluted tube leading into a constricted isthmus, and the uterus filled with 5 eggs (left). Photo by BD Palmer.

In crocodilians, the uterus is structurally comprised of a fibrous and calcareous portion.

The wall of the oviduct has three distinct layers:
—outermost layer: perimetrium (or tunica serosa)
—middle layer: myometrium (or tunica muscularis)
—innermost layer: endometrium (or tunica mucosa)

These three layers vary structurally in each of the five regions. The outermost layer, the perimetrium, consists of a thin layer of loose connective tissue covered by a single layer of squamous epithelium. The perimetrium is continuous with the mesotubarium. This layer is highly vascularized with blood and lymphatic vessels running parallel to the oviduct.

The middle layer, the myometrium, is composed of an inner circular and outer longitudinal layer of smooth muscle. The myometrial muscle layers generally increase in thickness along the length of the oviduct from the infundibulum to the vagina. The peristaltic contractions of these layers are responsible for the movement of eggs through the oviduct. In the vagina, the muscle layers form a sphincter to retain eggs or young until oviposition or parturition. The muscular contractions also contribute to the movement of gametes through the reproductive tract. Estrogen stimulation during vitellogenesis induces the muscle layers to hypertrophy.

The innermost layer of the oviduct, the endometrium (tunica mucosa), the most dynamic of the oviductal layers. The tunica mucosa consists of two functionally disparate layers:
—Lamina propria. The lamina propria consists of a connective tissue matrix supporting blood vessels and lymphatic spaces. The lamina propria also supports branched-tubular or compound alveolar glands lined with cuboidal epithelium.

Figure 8.
The oviduct is lined by a simple, epithelium composed of two cell types: ciliated cells, with central nuclei; and secretory cells (blue staining), with basal nuclei. Photo by BD Palmer.

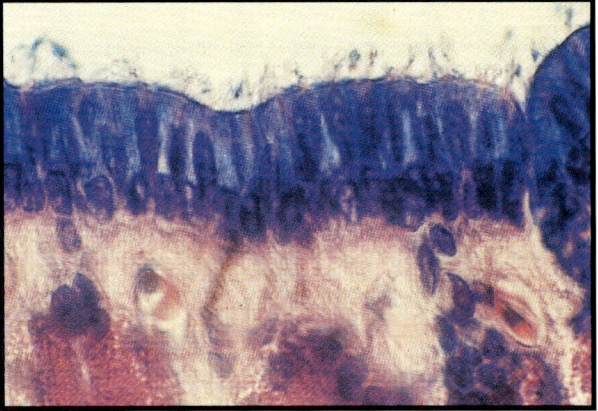

—Lamina epithelialis. The lamina epithelialis (luminal epithelium) lines the lumen of the oviduct. It consists of a single layer of epithelial cells, which may be either secretory or ciliated (Fig. 8).

Both of these layers change dramatically across the oviductal regions and with reproductive status. The relative proportion of the two types of cells changes by transmutation of one type to the other, depending on reproductive status. Ciliated cells exhibit centrally located nuclei; whereas secretory cells have basal nuclei. The secretory cells release glycosaminoglycans (GAGs) and perhaps calcium during egg shelling. Cilia are responsible for sloughing mucus from the anterior to the posterior end of the oviduct (abovarian). In some species, there is a ciliary band 1-2 mm wide, which moves in the reverse direction (pro-ovarian) in the tube. In those species, this ciliary band is credited for assisting in the movement of spermatozoa to the site of fertilization (Parker, 1928).

Infundibulum

The infundibulum is a thin, flaccid funnel, the opening or ostium of which lies nearest the ovary (Fig. 9). This anterior portion has a highly reduced muscularis consisting of scattered individual smooth muscle fibers. In contrast, the posterior

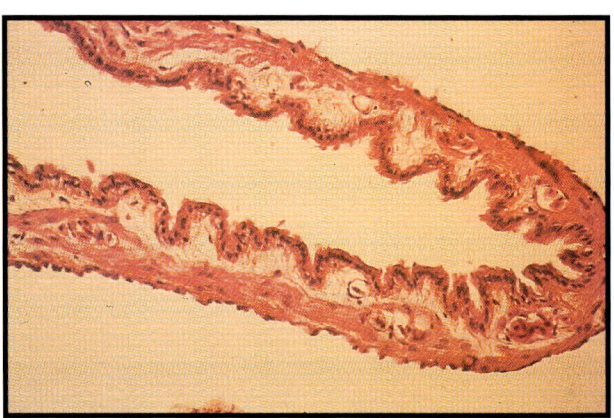

Figure 9.
The infundibulum, as seen here in *Ctenosaura pectinata*, has thin walls, limited smooth muscle, and is lined with a ciliated epithelium. Photo by MCA Uribe.

portion has a well-developed muscularis. The luminal epithelium consists primarily of ciliated cells. The few secretory cells present may secrete lubricating fluids and substances that function in the capacitation of gametes. Posteriorly, the infundibulum exhibits increasing mucosal folding and a gradual transition to the tubal region (Palmer and Guillette, 1988; Motz and Callard, 1991). In several viviparous squamates, numerous specialized sperm storage receptacles are present in the posterior infundibulum. This suggests that the posterior infundibulum is the site of fertilization (Cuellar, 1966; Halpert, et al. 1982). There appears to be little change in the infundibulum between reproductive stages or between parity modes.

Tuba Uterina or Uterine Tube

The tube is the longest portion of the oviduct in turtles, crocodilians, but it is greatly reduced in squamates. The tube is flattened, thin-walled, and highly convoluted, making it appear pleated. The diameter and thickness of the walls increase posteriorly. The myometrium increases in thickness posteriorly, although it is thin near the isthmus. The mucosal layer has low, rounded folds that form longitudinal pleats. The pleats allow the tube to expand as eggs pass.

The luminal epithelium of the tube consists of ciliated and secretory cells that secrete GAGs. Epi-

Figure 10.
The tube exhibits compound acinar glands and a simple columnar luminal epithelium. The glands, as seen in *Alligator mississippiensis*, are extensive and secrete the albumen proteins. In lizards and viviparous squamates, these glands and the albumen they secrete may be reduced. Photo by BD Palmer.

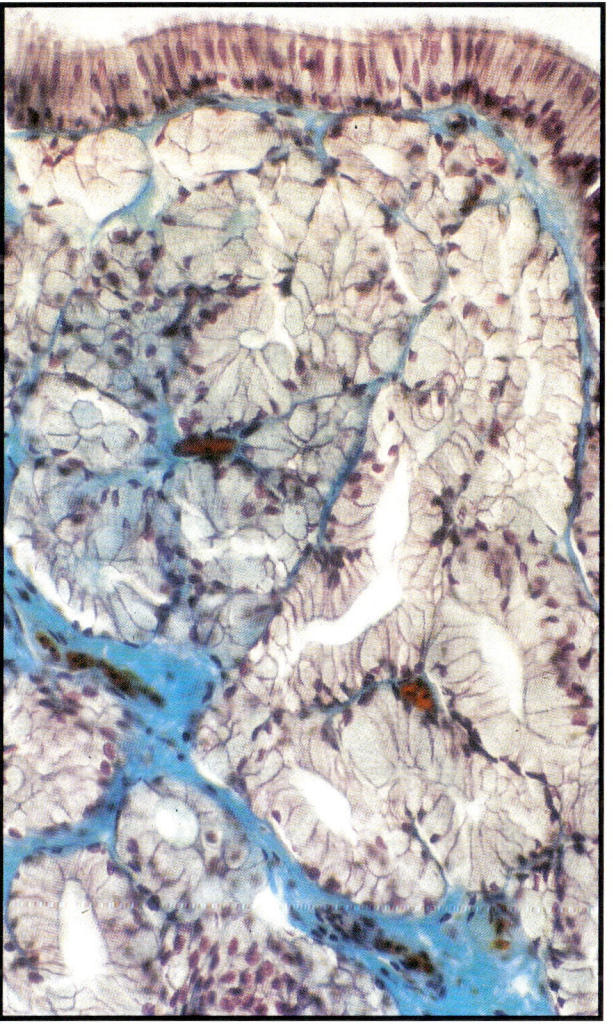

thelial cell height gradually increases from reproductive quiescence to late vitellogenesis and gravidity. The epithelial cells are more ciliated during quiescence and are more secretory at gravidity. The mucosal glands secrete the albumen layers found in their eggs. The mucosal-gland layer thickens as vitellogenesis proceeds. It reaches a peak thickness during late vitellogenesis (Fig. 10). In turtles, the posterior tube also functions in prolonged sperm storage (Fig. 11).

In squamates, the structure of the tube is more variable. The tube of snakes has limited glands, with most confined to the mesotubarial border.

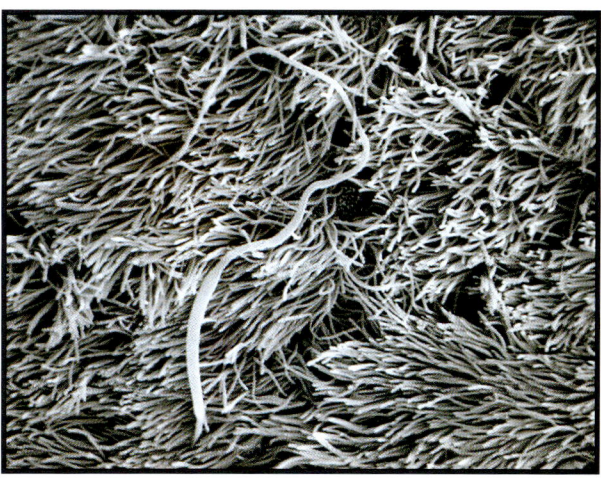

Figure 11.
Sperm are frequently stored within the oviductal glands. In *Gopherus polyphemus*, this solitary sperm is on top of the ciliated cells within the oviductal lumen. Photo by BD Palmer.

However, even fewer glands are present in some viviparous snakes. These glands, along with the epithelial cells, are thought to secrete the albumen proteins as eggs pass through the tube (Perkins and Palmer, 1995). Weekes (1927) was unable to detect any albumen secretions in viviparous species. In lizards, no mucosal glands are evident, leading to the reduced layers of albumen found in lizard eggs.

Isthmus

The isthmus is a short, thin-walled, slightly convoluted transitional junction between the tube and uterus in turtles and crocodilians. It is a narrow, nonglandular segment with a compact layer of both circular and longitudinal smooth muscle. The mucosa has small, branching folds. Sperm storage occurs within the mucosal glands of the turtle isthmus (Gist and Jones 1987, 1989; Palmer and Guillette, 1988).

Uterus

In turtles, the uterus is a thick, muscular, and nonpleated section of the oviduct. The circular and longitudinal smooth muscle layers of the myometrium are well developed (Palmer and Guillette, 1988; Motz and Callard, 1991). The uterus produces the fibrous and calcareous layers of the eggshell and retains the eggs until oviposition (Aitken and Solomon, 1976; Palmer and Guillette, 1988). The mucosa is highly folded, and it forms deep crypts lined with both secretory and ciliated cells, although secretory cells predominate. Epithelial cell height increases between early and late vitellogenesis and is maintained through gravidity. In the mucosa, the glandular layer thickens and the glands increase in diameter as vitellogenesis progresses (Fig. 12). These glands contain secretory granules that are released during gravidity to produce the proteinaceous fibers of the eggshell membrane (Palmer and Guillette, 1990).

The uterine region of squamates is similar to that found in turtles. The mucosa of oviparous species

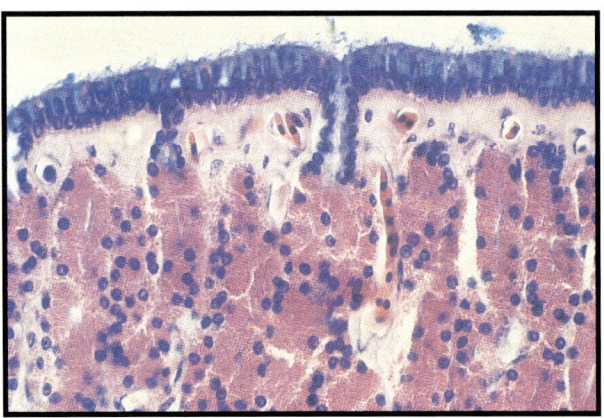

Figure 12.
The uterus of the tortoise, *Gopherus polyphemus*, exhibits simple branched tubular glands. These glands are connected by ducts to the uterine lumen and produce the proteinaceous fibers of the egg membrane during gravidity. The luminal epithelum has both ciliated and secretory cells. Photo by BD Palmer.

during vitellogenesis shows extensive development of eggshell glands (Uribeetal. 1988). These glands contain secretory granules that will form the eggshell membrane during gravidity (Palmer et al., 1993; Fig. 13). However, viviparous species exhibit poor development of the eggshell glands and an increase in abundance of blood vessels during this stage (Guillette, 1993; Perkins and Palmer, 1995). In viviparous species, embryonic implantation occurs with the formation of a placenta.

Crocodilians exhibit an advanced uterine architecture, which is structurally and functionally separated into anterior and posterior regions. The anterior uterus (fibrous portion) of crocodilians resembles the uterus of other reptiles and is the site of egg-membrane deposition (Palmer and

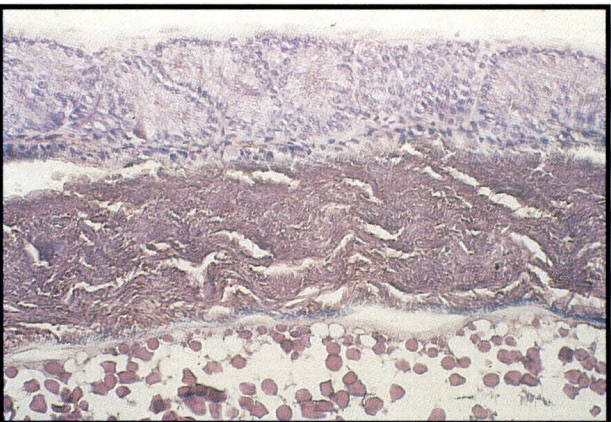

Figure 13.
During gravidity, the uterine wall (top) becomes stretched as the eggs enter into it. The secretory granules within the uterine glands produce the fibrous egg membrane surrounding the yolk, as seen here in the snake, *Diadophis punctatus*. Photo by MJ Perkins.

Guillette, 1992). However, the posterior uterine endometrial glands are specialized for the formation of the calcareous eggshell (Fig. 14). These glands release ions for development of the calcareous eggshell. The crocodilians are unique among reptiles in having egg membranes and eggshell deposited in spatially separate uterine regions. This anatomy is similar to that seen in another archosaur, the birds. Eggs are retained in the posterior uterus of crocodilians throughout calcification and up until oviposition.

Vagina

The vagina exhibits considerable variation

Figure 14.
The posterior uterus of crocodilians is substantially different than that of other reptiles. In *Alligator mississippiensis,* the endometrial glands contain none of the secretory granules observed in the fiber-producing segment. Instead, the histology and ultrastructure resembles the shell gland of the avian oviduct. This region secretes the calcareous eggshell. Photo by BD Palmer.

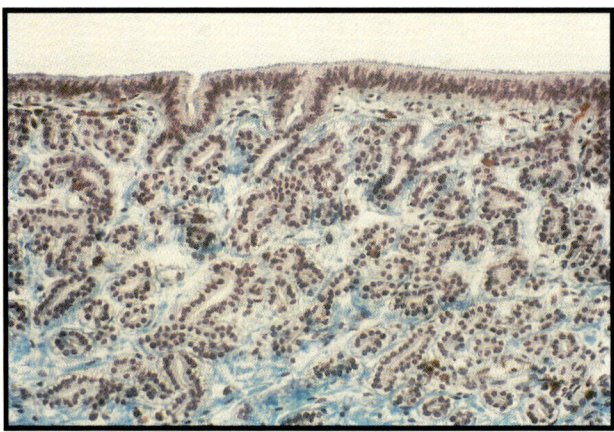

among reptiles. The vagina in turtles, lizards and crocodilians is a short, straight region of the oviduct. It has broad layers of both circular and longitudinal smooth muscle, forming a sphincter at the cloaca (Palmer and Guillette, 1988; Motz and Callard, 1991; Fig. 15). In snakes, the vagina is quite long because of the elongated body (Perkins and Palmer, 1995). The vaginal mucosa has tall, thin, longitudinal folds covered with columnar ciliated cells and very few secretory cells. The vagina serves as a conduit for eggs or offspring at oviposition or parturition respectively.

Placentas

Uterine differences between parity modes be-

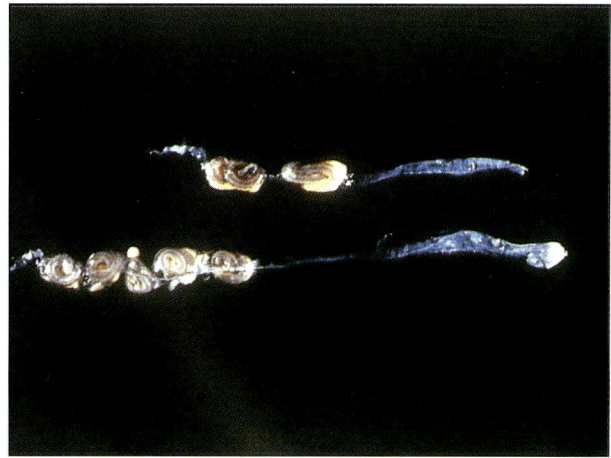

Figure 16.
Oviducts of the viviparous snake *Storeria dekayi*. Well-developed embryos are readily apparent within the thin-walled uterus. In snakes, the infundibulum and tube are reduced (left), whereas the vagina is elongated (right). Photo by MJ Perkins.

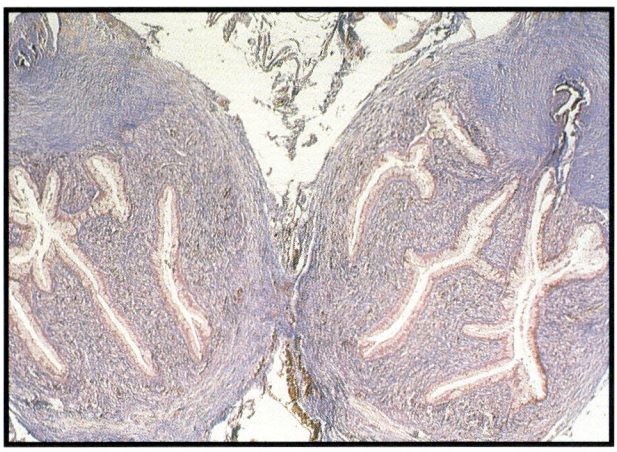

Figure 15.
The vaginal region of reptiles is often highly muscular, as seen in *Diadophis punctatus*. The extensive muscle layers serve as a sphincter to retain eggs or young during gravidity or gestation. Here, both vaginas are observed adjacent to their junction with the cloaca. Photo by MJ Perkins.

come more exaggerated during gravidity and pregnancy (Fig. 16). In viviparous species, the eggshell glands disappear entirely during gestation. The thin mucosa of viviparous squamates develops extensive capillary networks, and the epithelial cells become nearly squamous in shape. These uterine tissues surround and become associated with the tissues of the embryo to form a placenta (Fig. 17) within the uterine incubation chamber. The first published discovery of uterine gestation and placentation of reptiles was in the lizard, *Chalcides chalcides* (Studiati, 1851). Current knowledge of squamate placental structures is scattered among the lineages in which viviparity has evolved. Little is known about the degree of gaseous or nutritional maternal-fetal exchange.

Several types of placental structures have been identified (Weekes, 1935; Yaron, 1985; Stewart and Blackburn, 1988; Stewart, 1992). These include:

—choriovitelline placentas
—omphaloplacenta placentas
—omphalallantoic placentas
—chorioallantoic placentas

These categories are based on associations of extraembryonic tissues with each other and with the uterine epithelium. The extraembryonic tissues involved with placental structures are the allantois, chorion, trilaminar omphalopleure, and bilaminar omphalopleure. The uterine epithelium is involved in all categories of placentas. The following descriptions of placental structures are typical of all squamates. However, Yaron (1985) indicated that these structures may vary slightly between species, as well as vary between groups of squamates.

Figure 17.
Placenta of the lizard *Sceloporus torquatus*. A thin remnant of the egg membrane lies between the embryonic (left) and maternal (right) tissues. Photo by MCA Uribe.

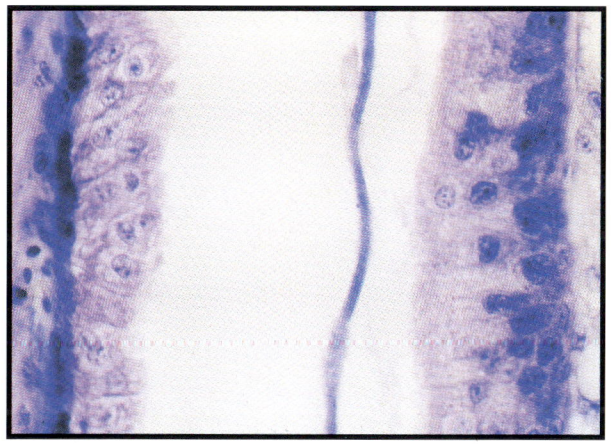

Choriovitelline placenta. The choriovitelline placenta is formed by the apposition of the trilaminar omphalopleure to the uterine epithelium. This placenta forms early in embryonic development from the ectoderm, mesoderm, and endoderm layers of the yolk sac. Later, the placenta is disrupted as the exocoelom forms (Stewart, 1992).

Omphaloplacenta. The apposition of the yolk mass (omphalopleure) with the uterine epithelium forms the second category of placentas, the omphaloplacenta. This placenta arises embryologically from the ectoderm and endoderm of the yolk sac—the intravitelline mesoderm and the yolk mass itself. However, the omphaloplacenta typically has a nonvascularized, cuboidal fetal epithelium surrounded by a thin, squamous layer of cells (Stewart and Blackburn, 1988). The uterine epithelium is vascularized and contains large columnar epithelial cells.

Omphalallantoic placenta. The third category, the omphalallantoic placenta, is formed by the apposition of the outer allantoic membrane and the bilaminar omphalopleure with the uterine epithelium. Embryologically, this placenta is derived from the same components as the omphaloplacenta, with the addition of the outer allantoic membrane. The omphaloplacenta and the omphalallantoic placenta persist throughout development in many species. In contrast, they are only transitory structures in other species.

Chorioallantoic placenta. The final category is the chorioallantoic placenta. This placental structure is present in all viviparous squamates throughout development. It arises from the somatopleure and the mesoderm and endoderm of the outer allantoic membrane. It is formed by the apposition of the chorion and amnion with the uterine epithelium. The chorioallantoic placenta is characterized by richly vascularized maternal and fetal epithelia (Hoffman, 1970). The epithelial cells are squamous in shape where they overlie the capillaries. This type of ultrastructure probably facilitates greater diffusion efficiency.

Placentas are also generally characterized according to their histology and ultrastructure. These classifications are based on the number and types of barriers between the maternal and fetal blood. The barriers can be classified as: hemichorial, which is typical of many mammals such as rodents and primates; endotheliochorial, found in dogs and cats; syndesmochorial, exhibited in most hoofed mammals; and epitheliochorial, which is found in pigs and in most viviparous squamates

The ultrastructure of the epitheliochorial placenta involves the epithelium, connective tissues, and blood vessel endothelia of both the uterus and the chorion. In addition to these barriers, a thin, shell membrane is present between the uterine epithelium and the chorionic ectoderm (Stewart and Blackburn, 1988; Blackburn, 1993).

Following ovulation, the corpus luteum produces progesterone. The progesterone primes the endometrium for the apposition of the embryo(s). The presence of the embryo in mammals triggers the formation of the placenta. Though it has not been shown in squamates, maternal recognition of the embryo probably initiates placental formation as well (Stewart, 1992).

EGG INVESTMENTS
Albumen
Egg albumen (egg white) is composed of a variety of proteins. These proteins are secreted by the oviductal tube before the eggshell is deposited. Turtle and crocodilian eggs possess an extensive coat of albumen whereas this layer is greatly reduced in squamates. The composition of albumen proteins varies among reptiles. Some of the albumen proteins—such as ovalbumin—are similar to those of avian albumen. Other proteins are unique for example, a 57 kDa protein found in alligator albumen (Palmer and Guillette., 1991).

The function of albumen remains poorly studied, but several hypotheses have been presented (Palmer and Guillette, 1991). The albumen layer is hydrated with substantial amounts of water, and may serve as a water reservoir. This may be particularly important to species nesting in arid microhabitats. However, it may serve simply as an osmotic barrier. In this capacity, the albumen may moderate fluctuations in the external environment in species with thin-shelled eggs or species that nest in microhabitats prone to hydric extremes or variations.

Albumen may also exhibit antimicrobial properties. In birds, several albumen proteins provide either mechanical barriers (such as the viscous ovomucin) or chemical defense to invading microbes. For instance, lysozyme (found in avian eggs) can directly kill invading bacteria by disrupting their cell walls. Other proteins, such as ovotransferrin and avidin (both identified in reptilian albumen), create an environment inhospitable to bacteria. These properties may be especially important in species such as alligators, which lay their eggs in a mound of muck and rotting vegetation.

Albumen may also provide a source of nutrients for the developing embryo. Besides the nutritive value of the proteins themselves, several albumens have been shown to bind minerals or nutrients. These include the biotin-binding molecule avidin, and ovotransferrin, which binds the mineral iron. Egg albumen, in conjunction with the eggshell, may help adapt reptilian eggs for survival in the great variety of nest microhabitats in which reptiles lay their eggs.

Eggshell

The shell is one of the defining features of the amniotic egg. It enabled amniotes to leave water behind and reproduce on dry land, facilitating the radiation of vertebrates into terrestrial habitats. Reptiles were the first to develop the eggshell, which retains remarkable similarity not only among reptiles, but also among birds and egg-laying mammals, the monotremes. This discussion provides an overview of the eggshell; the chapter on Egg Physiology and Biology describes eggs in detail.

The eggshell is composed of two principle parts: the fibrous egg membrane and the calcareous shell. The egg membrane is composed of proteina-

Figure 19.
The fibers that compose the egg membrane are shown as they are being extruded from the uterine glands. The uterine lining is composed of ciliated and nonciliated secretory cells. The duct openings that the fibers are extruding from lead into the branched tubular endometrial glands. Myometrial activity may be used to wrap the fibers around each egg. Photo by BD Palmer.

Figure 18.
The egg membrane is composed of proteinaceous fibers secreted by the uterine endometrial glands. These fibrous layers form a dense, protective membrane surrounding the egg. Various degrees of calcification may occur after the membrane is formed. Photo by BD Palmer

ceous fibers produced by the uterine glands following albumen deposition (Fig. 18). The fibers are extruded intact from the uterine glands and are wrapped around the egg (Fig. 19). Thick fibers are initially deposited, followed by progressively finer fibers. Eventually, a thin outer coat of particulate matter may be deposited. The eggshell membrane is present in all amniotic eggs. It forms a protective barrier to the outside environment, reducing water loss and preventing bacteria and fungi from reaching the developing embryo within.

On top of the eggshell membranes, the calcareous shell provides additional protection

from infection and the environment (Fig. 20). The degree of calcification is quite variable, ranging from the rigid-shelled eggs of crocodilians, some turtles, and geckos; to flexible-shelled eggs of many squamates. In turtles, the calcium carbonate crystals consist of aragonite. In contrast, in crocodilians and oviparous squamates, the of calcite crystals.

Calcium deposition within the oviduct begins following formation of the fibrous membrane. The time it takes for the calcium crystals to form is variable. It usually requires about 2-3 weeks, but may take up to 7-8 months (as in tuatara). Calcium crystals initially form within the upper layers of the fibrous membrane. In flexible-shelled eggs, these calcium crystals may appear as nodules, plaques, rosettes, or they may have a bubbly, frothy, or amorphous appearance. These sparse crystalline arrangements allow for gas exchange and for the eggs to swell during development. In rigid-shelled eggs, as calcification continues nodules grow outwardly, often expanding until they form tall, interlocking col-

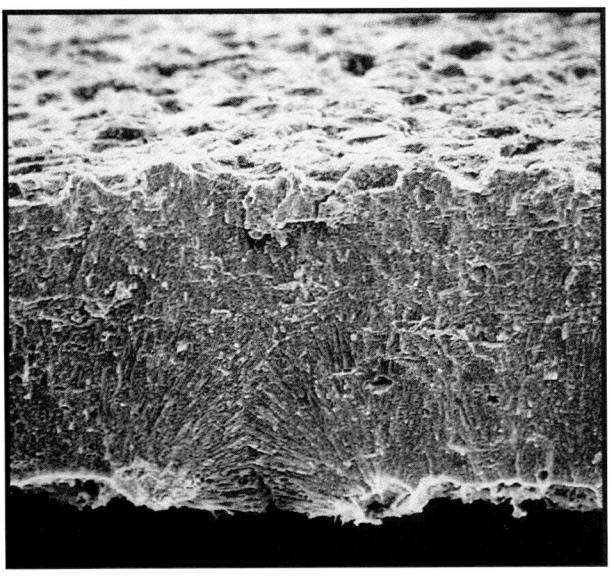

Figure 20.
This illustrates the broken edge of the highly calcified, rigid eggshell of *Gopherus polyphemus*. The egg membrane has been removed from the inside (bottom) of the eggshell. The growth pattern of calcium crystals is evident, radiating from organic nodules at the base. Photo by BD Palmer.

umns. Rigid shells, such as in desert tortoises, may possess quite extensive calcium layers. These calcium layers greatly reduce gas exchange. Small pores are left among the columns to enable diffusion of oxygen and carbon dioxide (Fig. 21).

The eggshell is more than a protective barrier to the outside world. It is also a rich source of calcium for the developing embryos. Embryonic membranes are able to extract calcium from the eggshell, thereby supplementing calcium reserves in the yolk. This is particularly important for turtles, which need substantial calcium supplies to form their shell. Whereas squamates only derive as little as 20% of their calcium requirements from the eggshell, turtles acquire up to 80% of the calcium from the shell (Packard and Packard, 1984).

MALE ANATOMY
Testis

The testes, like the ovaries, have both gametogenic and endocrine functions. These include sperm production and maturation, as well as control of secondary sexual characteristics and reproductive behaviors. Reptilian testes vary in shape from oval to elongated. They are bound to the kidneys through a fold of the peritoneum, the mesorchium (Fig. 22). In squamates and alligators, the right testis is typically found anterior to the left.

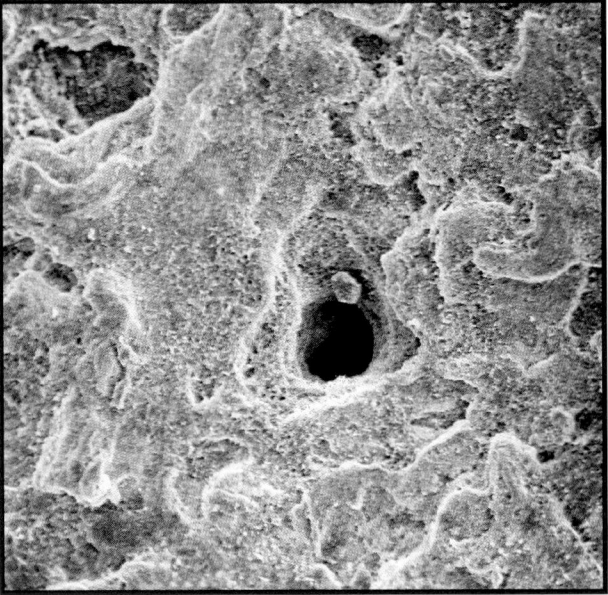

Figure 21.
Pores, such as this one in the eggshell of the gopher tortoise *Gopherus polyphemus*, allow for gas exchange as the embryo develops. Photo by BD Palmer.

The testis is encased by a fibrous capsule, the tunica albuginea, from which septa of connective tissue arise. The septa divide the testis into lobules. In some reptiles, such as *Lacerta*, the tunica albuginea contains smooth muscle fibers. Each lobule contains several convoluted seminiferous tubules and vascularized interstitial connective tissue (Fig. 23). Leydig cells, located within the interstitial tissue, are steroidogenic. A fibrous connective tissue layer, the tunica propria, surrounds each of the seminiferous tubules. Both tunica albuginea and tunica propria expand as germ cells accumulate prior to the breeding season.

During early embryonic development, both sexes exhibit male and female genital tracts. During sexual differentiation, the immature cuboidal seminiferous tubules (originating from the primary sex cords) become densely packed within the stroma (Yentma, 1981). The testes show so well-formed medulla, with regression of the cortex leaving little or no cortical remnants (Crews et al., 1989). Typically, the oviduct and mesotubaria have been resorbed in males before hatching. Histological examination at 3 months of age reveals that the characteristic female germinal epithelium is replaced by simple squamous epithelium. Although sex is often difficult to determine in turtles and alligators upon hatching, well-formed seminiferous tubules are evident at six months of age in male American alligators *(Alligator mississippiensis)*. Sertoli cells and mitotically

Many reptilian species show seasonal changes in seminiferous tubule and interstitial cell size, composition and activity. The seasonality of gonadal enlargement (associated with spermatogenesis), is correlated with environmental factors; such as light, temperature, rain, and food supply. Temperate species usually have one breeding season, followed by hibernation. However, more-tropical species tend to have multiple breeding seasons, or may even be continuous breeders.

Figure 22.
The testes of the lizard *Sceloporus torquatus* are compact organs located ventral to the kidneys (this is typical of most reptiles). The genital ducts are evident leading to the cloaca posteriorly. Photo by MCA Uribe.

active germ cells at early stages of development line the seminiferous tubules (Guillette et al., 1994).

The seminiferous tubules are lined with both developing germ cells and the somatic Sertoli cells. Sertoli cells in reptiles may be mononucleate, binucleate or even multi-nucleated, as in *Uta stansburiana*. In some lizard species, as well as snakes and turtles, the Sertoli cells are syncytial. The ultrastructure of Sertoli cells is suggestive of endocrine secretion. Sertoli cells exhibit a cyclic change in lipid droplet content, enzyme activity (3β-HSD), and ultrastructural features during the reproductive season (Mahmoud et al., 1985).

Between the seminiferous tubules and interspersed among blood vessels and lymph spaces are the steroidogenic interstitial or Leydig cells. These cells may be found alone or in small groups near blood vessels in turtles, crocodiles, lizards, and snakes. Leydig cells have large, round nuclei and vacuolated or alveolar cytoplasm. Within a species, Leydig cells may vary in size, number, and appearance during the reproductive cycle. However, among species, there may be shape variation from polyhedral, elongate, oval, to syncytial. In *C. serpentina*, Leydig cells show very little seasonal ultrastructural changes, and there is no seasonal depletion of lipid droplets (Mesner et al., 1993; Mahmoud et al., 1985). Some species also have many melanoblasts present in the interstitium, giving a characteristic black or gray appearance.

In many reptiles, the resumption of germ cell proliferation (spermatogenesis) occurs soon after the breeding season. Spermatogenesis is an involved process consisting of several stages (Fig. 24). In spermatocytogenesis, mitotic division of the germ cells results in increasing production of spermatogonia within the seminiferous tubules. Spermatogonia also divide by mitosis to produce primary spermatocytes. Sertoli cells show an increase

Figure 23.
Seminiferous tubules of the lizard *Ctenosaura pectinata*. The coiled seminiferous tubules are surrounded by interstitial connective tissue in which the steroidogenic Leydig cells are located. Spermatogenic epithelium lines the tubules, which are filled with spermatozoa. Photo by MCA Uribe.

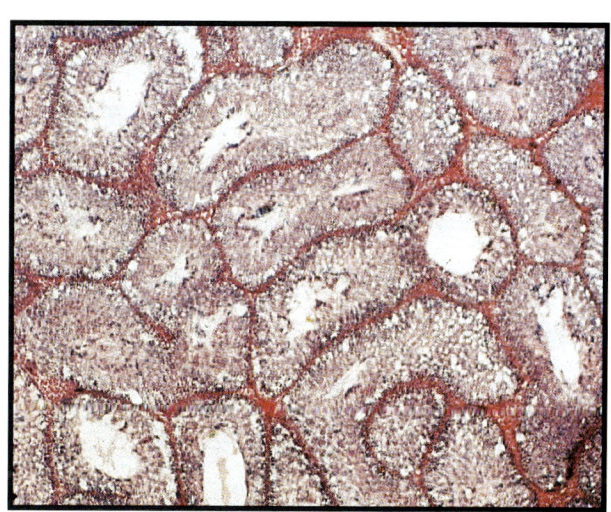

in cytoplasm and occlusion of the tubule lumen may occur.

Next, meiotic division of primary spermatocytes produces secondary spermatocytes, which then undergo the second meiotic division to form haploid spermatids. This is accompanied

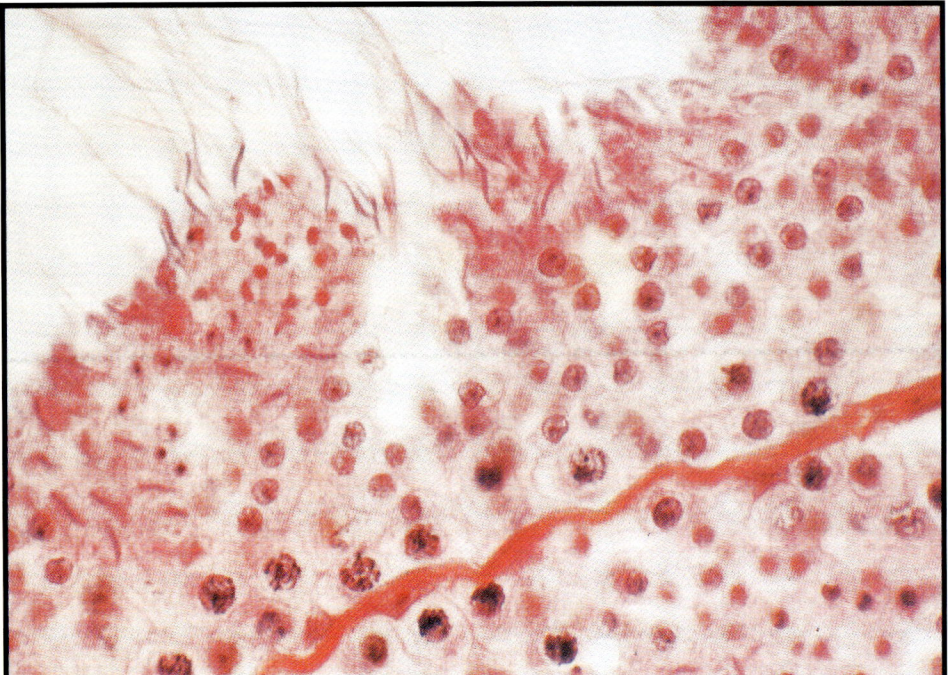

Figure 24.
The seminiferous epithelium of *Toluca lineata* illustrates spermatogonia along the basement membrane, primary and secondary spermatocytes, and spermatids attached to the surface of the Sertoli cells. The elongating flagella of the spermatids extends into the lumen of the seminiferous tubule. Photo by MCA Uribe.

by an increase in seminiferous tubule diameter.

Maturation of spermatids into spermatozoa, and their subsequent accumulation at the distal ends of Sertoli cells, occur during spermiogenesis. During this reproductive phase, seminiferous tubules exhibit maximum diameter (including several layers of germ cells). In constrast, Leydig cells show minimum size as the interstitial tissue is dispersed and compressed into tight wedges. Spermiation results in movement of mature sperm to the lumen of the seminiferous tubules and transport into the epididymis. Within temperate species, Leydig cells increase in size during germinal quiescence, and lipids associated with Leydig and Sertoli cells reach peak levels. During quiescence, the seminiferous tubules are lined with only a single layer of spermatogonia and Sertoli cells. Sperm storage may last over winter until the spring breeding season occurs.

Genital Tract

Mature spermatozoa exit the testis by convergence of seminiferous tubules into the rete testes at the dorso-medial surface of each testis. Then, ductuli efferentes exit the testis within a mesentery (mesorchium) along the entire gonadal length. The ductules are lined with a single layer of cuboidal epithelial cells (Fig. 25). The number of efferent ductules ranges from one ductule in *Lacerta* to 45 ductules in *Emys orbicularis*.

Histologically, the ductuli efferentes show two cuboidal cell types:
—ciliated cells, which aid in spermatozoa transport
—microvillous cell; which absorb fluid that is produced in the seminiferous tubules

The ductuli efferentes open into the ductuli epididymides. The ductuli epididymides may consist of two distinct regions:
—anterior portion, which is lined by high, columnar, nonciliated cells. These cells contain secretory granules during the breeding season, as in *Natrix natrix* and *Thamnophis elegans*
—posterior region, which is larger, and contains ciliated cells

The ductuli epididymides open into a single convoluted tube, the ductus epididymis, along its entire length (Fig. 25). The ductus epididymis

Figure 25.
The genital ducts of the lizard *Sceloporus torquatus*. The smaller ductuli efferentes, which are lined with cuboidal epithelia, are adjacent to the larger ductuli epididymides (bottom), which are lined with secretory columnar cells. Photo by MCA Uribe.

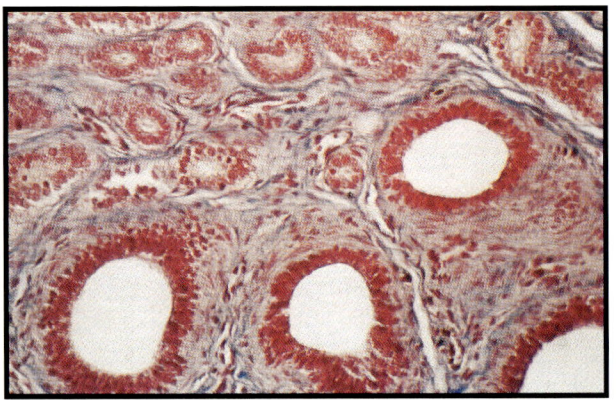

has an enlarged lumen that is filled with sperm during the breeding season. A layer of ciliated columnar epithelia forms the epididymal lining. When the epithelial lining of ductus epididymis is highly secretory, it is enlarged and contains a milky fluid. However, while nonsecretory, this duct segment is small and gray in appearance. The secretions may aid in sperm maturation and capacitation. The ductus epididymis stores sperm until ejaculation, when sperm are expelled into the ductus (vas) deferens. Circular smooth muscle fibers surround the ductus epididymis, and aid in forcing out stored sperm during ejaculation.

The ductus deferens is a highly muscular tube that transports sperm from the epididymis to the penis or hemipenes during ejaculation. The wall is extremely thick due to a large amount of smooth muscle. The smooth muscle is surrounded by connective tissue containing blood vessels and nerves. The vas deferens is lined by a nonsecretory, nonciliated epithelia. However, in *L. punctata*, the vas deferens shows two cell types in which one type (the smooth-surfaced cells) have been postulated to be involved in microapocrine secretion and phagocytosis (De and Maiti, 1985). The vas deferens shows individual variation in size reflecting differences in amounts of stored sperm.

The copulatory organs of reptiles show significant variation in morphology among groups. In turtles and crocodiles, a penis serves as the copulatory organ. The penis is a distensible, grooved, unforked organ attached to the cloacal wall. Spermatozoa enter the penis from each ductus deferens. In squamates, paired hemipenes situated in the base of the tail act as copulatory organs. The hollow, cylindrical hemipenes of snakes lie retracted within cavities on either side of the cloaca. The hemipenes of lizards, which are similar to those of snakes, are thick-walled sacs that lie inverted in cavities on either side of the median line. Variation in the hemipenis surface (spinous, reticulate, calyculate, plicate) and variation in the longitudinal groove (simple or bifurcate) serve as taxonomic characteristics. Upon cloacal contact between the male and female, one hemipenis is everted for copulation.

RENAL SEX SEGMENT

Within snakes and lizards, the preterminal and/or terminal part of the uriniferous tubule in the kidney is a sexually dimorphic structure, the renal sexual segment. In some species, the collecting ducts and ureter may also comprise the sex segment. For example, in the Indian house lizard, *Hemidactylus,* secondary and tertiary collecting ducts, as well as the short ureter, form the renal sex segment (Prasad and Reddy, 1972). Under androgen stimulation when testes are spermatogenically active, the sex segment becomes hypertrophied. During reproductive quiescence, this segment is regressed. In immature males and females, there is no development of the sex segment.

In temperate lizard species, the seasonal reproductive cycle is correlated with significant development of the renal sex segment. As the cells hypertrophy they develop abundant secretory granules. However, in continuous breeding lizards, such as the Australian skink, *Carlia rhomboidalis,* there is no seasonal variation in tubular diameter. In comparison to lizards, snakes show modest variation in sexual segment tubular diameter. In *Vipera berus*, maximum tubular diameter and cellular height occur in the spring as sperm mature; minimum size occurs in June and July. In the fall there is a gradual, slight increase in size in the sexual segment. In *Natrix natrix*, there is no obvious seasonal morphometric variation. However, the presence of secretory granules does vary and is related to cyclic testicular activity. Low secretory activity occurs during the summer, and secretion begins in the fall. Some snakes, however, such as *Thamnophis*, show more than just modest seasonal tubular size variation.

The secretory granules found in the hypertrophied renal sex segment contain high levels of phospholipids and acid phosphatase. Secretions from the sexual segment are released into the collecting duct lumen. The secretions are then transported to the cloaca and mixed with sperm. During copulation they are transported to the female cloaca. Sexual segment secretions can be found in oviductal crypts of mated females. Many possible functions for the secretions of the sexual segment have been proposed (Prasad and Reddy, 1972), including:

—serving as an activating agent or for nutrition of sperm
—transporting sperm from the male reproductive tract
—plugging the female cloaca (thereby keeping semen within the female)
—attracting females by scent

PHYSIOLOGY

ENVIRONMENTAL CONTROL OF REPRODUCTION

The reproductive cycles of reptiles are strongly correlated with climate and environmental conditions. Traditionally, photoperiod was thought to be the primary environmental factor affecting reproductive cycles. In some species of lizards, photoperiod has been shown to control gonadal recrudescence and regression. However, this phenomenon is less common in squamates that spend most of their daily and seasonal activity periods in hiding places shielded from light. Temperature is also an important driver of reproductive cycles (Lofts, 1978; Marion, 1982). High temperatures stimulate ovarian growth in many viviparous species of snakes, such as *Thamnophis* (Aleksuik and Gregory, 1974). Temperature and photoperiod may work together, since most studies reveal that high temperatures combined with long photoperiod heighten stimulation of ovarian and follicular growth (Duvall et al., 1982). In addition, rainfall and moisture levels appear to affect reproductive cycles of many tropical squamates. The appearance of vitellogenic follicles does not occur in many tropical squamates until the rainy season begins. Furthermore, many skink species do not exhibit reproductive behaviors unless relative humidity is near or above 60%. In many species of *Liolaemus*

lizards, follicular growth does not occur until temperature, as well as precipitation, peak.

Food availability also affects reptilian breeding cycles. Stored energy in the fat bodies are utilized for vitellogenin production. However, if food resources are low, the fat bodies will be used for body maintenance instead of ovarian development. This reduces reproductive success (Duvall et al., 1982). For example, most snakes in the temperate zone have the potential to breed annually (Aldridge, 1979). However, if sufficient energy reserves are not available, vitellogenesis will be inhibited, blocking reproduction.

REPRODUCTIVE ENDOCRINOLOGY

The reproductive process is a cascade of events that involves both nervous tissues and endocrine glands, such as the pineal gland, the hypothalamus, and the pituitary gland. These in turn exert their

Figure 26.
Summary of the events that follow stimulation of the pineal gland by an exogenous source, such as photoperiod.

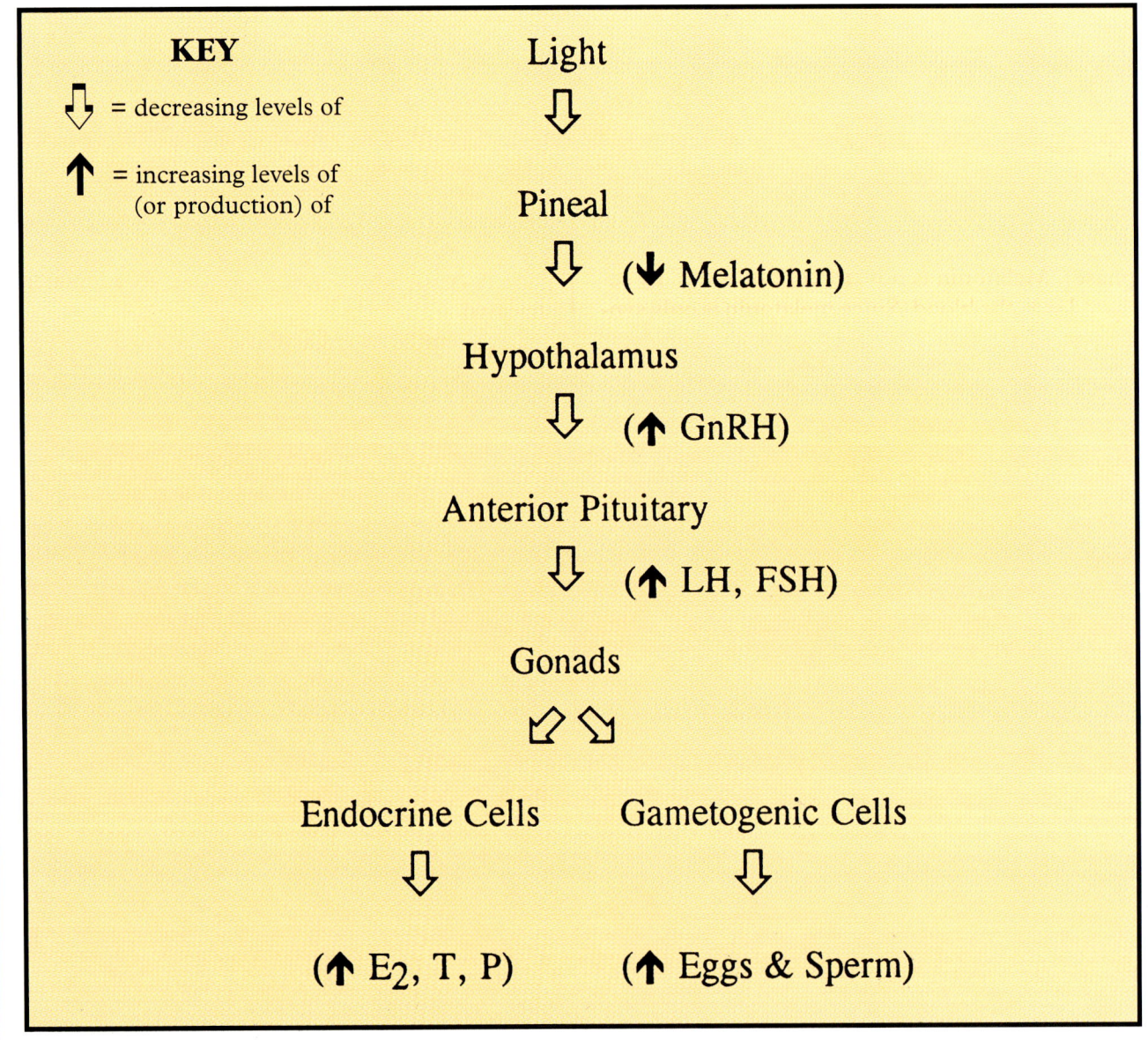

68

influence on the gonads (ovaries and testes) (Fig. 26). The endocrine glands transduce environmental stimuli into hormonal signals that regulate reproductive events. Those anatomical structures involved in the daily reception of these exogenous stimuli have been collectively termed the circadian system.

At least two sites have been shown to be of major importance in organizing the circadian system: the pineal gland and the hypothalamus. Most studies on reptilian circadian systems have concentrated on daily activities and thermoregulatory behavior, but few studies have investigated the role of the pineal and hypothalamus in "circannual" rhythms, such as reproduction.

PINEAL, HYPOTHALAMIC, AND PITUITARY GLANDS

Pineal glands are present in all reptiles except for members of the subclass Archosauria (Roth et al., 1980). The pineal gland is attached to the brain via a stalk, which carries blood vessels and afferent nerves to the brain. In lizards, the pineal contains photosensory cells, supporting cells, and neurons. The pineal of snakes lacks photoreceptive cells, but does contain pinealocytes that are considered to belong to the same cell lines as the photosensory cells (Quay, 1979; Collin and Oksche, 1981).

The pineal gland responds to changes in light both with nervous signals and with release of the hormone melatonin. Melatonin is synthesized by the photoreceptor cells during the night (dark phase). Melatonin is not stored, but is rapidly secreted into the blood. Since melatonin is only synthesized and released during the night, it serves as an indicator of day length and ultimately of season. As photoperiod increases in the spring, the duration of pineal hormone-release decreases. Fall marks an increase in the daily duration of hormone release as the photoperiod decreases. This information can be used to regulate the "internal clock" of the hypothalamus, setting up circadian rhythms and seasonal cycles.

The hypothalamus and pituitary (hypophysis) are integrated both structurally and functionally. These glands compose the hypothalamo-hypophysial axis. The hypothalamus produces small peptide hormones that regulate the release of hormones from the pituitary gland. One of these regulatory peptides is gonadotropin-releasing hormone (GnRH), which stimulates the release of gonadotropins from the pituitary.

The pituitary gland produces more types of hormones than any other endocrine gland and many of its hormones regulate the activities of other endocrine glands, including the gonads. The pituitary gland consists of two basic regions:

—the adenohypophysis, which is derived from oral ectoderm
—the neurohypophysis, which is derived from the diencephalon of the brain

The adenohypophysis is well developed in most reptiles. It consists of a pars distalis, pars tuberalis, and a pars intermedia. However, the pars tuberalis is greatly reduced and sometimes absent in many lizards. In adult snakes, the pars tuberalis is completely absent. The adenohypophysis is responsible for secretion of six pituitary hormones:
—growth hormone (GH)
—prolactin (PRL)
—adrenocorticotropic hormone (ACTH)
—thyroid-stimulating hormone (TSH)
—the two gonadotropins: luteinizing hormone (LH) and follicle-stimulating hormone (FSH)

Studies indicate that only a single gonadotropin molecule is present in squamates. In snakes, these studies also suggest that the gonadotropin is not homologous to either FSH or to LH (Licht, 1979). Gonadotropins stimulate both gametogenesis and the secretion of sex steroids by the gonads.

The neurohypophysis consists of two regions, the infundibular stalk and the pars nervosa. The neurohypophysis secretes the two nanopeptide hormones: arginine vasotocin (AVT) and mesotocin (MST). AVT plays an important role in stimulating uterine contractions which lead to oviposition and parturition in reptiles. These hormones are actually synthesized in the hypothalamus by neuroendocrine cells. The axons of neuroendocrine cells extend into the pars nervosa, where AVT and MST are ultimately released.

The pineal, hypothalamus, and pituitary gland work together to transduce environmental stimuli (such as temperature and photoperiod) into hormonal signals to regulate reproduction. Studies in mammals indicate that melatonin inhibits the release of GnRH from the hypothalamus, thereby reducing gonadotropin levels. However, low levels of melatonin allow the release of GnRH from the hypothalamus. This in turn stimulates the pituitary gland to release the gonadotropins, LH and FSH. Prolonged release of melatonin during long winter nights impedes gonadal development. This is because it inhibits the release of pituitary gonadotropin. In spring and summer, lengthening days inhibit melatonin production. This ultimately leads to increased gonadotropin levels and gonadal development.

SEX STEROIDS

The sex steroids include estrogens, androgens, and progesterone. Sex steroids are synthesized from cholesterol following a common pathway (Miller, 1988). Steroids are produced by the thecal and granulosal cells of the ovarian follicles and by the Leydig and Sertoli cells of the testes. Final steps in the hormone synthesis pathway may occur at the target cell. For instance, this may occur with the conversion (aromatization) of androgens to estrogens. Synthesis is regulated, under the influence of environmental and physiologic factors, by gonadotropins from the anterior pituitary (Callard and Kleis, 1987).

Estrogens. Estrogens have many roles in the reproductive cycle. Two forms of estrogen are common in vertebrates: estradiol-17b (E_2) and estrone (E_1), the former being more potent. Estrogen induces and regulates the synthesis of hepatic vitellogenin (which is involved in vitellogenic development of the follicles) and in the seasonal development of the oviducts (Fawcett, 1975; La Pointe, 1969; Callard et al., 1980; Callard and Ho, 1980; Licht, 1982). Positive feedback of estrogen on the pituitary produces an LH spike, inducing ovulation.

Progesterone. Progesterone (P) actions are intimately associated with those of estrogen levels. The ratio of progesterone to estrogen is largely responsible for many of their effects. Often the action of P is limited to tissues that have been primed by estrogen. Also, the presence of P may modulate the actions of estrogens (Kraus and Katzenellenbogen, 1993). Following ovulation, the remnants of the ovulated follicles develop into corpora lutea. By secreting progesterone, corpora lutea control and maintain oviductal development during gravidity or pregnancy. Gestation length is controlled in part by P released from the corpora lutea. This released P inhibits contractions of the uterine musculature involved in oviposition and parturition (Arslan et al., 1978; Xavier and Gavaud, 1986; Callard et al., 1992). Termination of gestation is correlated with luteolysis (regression of the corpus luteum) that results in a drop in plasma progesterone levels (Jones and Guillette, 1982).

Androgens. Several forms of androgens exist, the most common being testosterone (T) and dihydrotestosterone (DHT). Androgen levels are often elevated in both male and female reptiles. In females, androgens are essential precursors in the synthetic pathway for estrogens (Miller, 1988). However, androgens may also act directly on some tissues in females. Androgens play important roles in stimulating reproduction in males, and in numerous courtship and territorial behaviors. A summary of many of the known actions of steroid hormones is presented in Table 1.

Steroid Hormone Action. Steroid hormones travel through the bloodstream bound to steroid-binding proteins (SBPs). SBPs protect the steroids from degradation (Callard and Kleis, 1987; Salhanick and Callard, 1980). At the target cell, sex steroids pass into the cell and complex with specific receptors (Ho and Callard, 1984). The activated receptors associate with DNA by binding to the response element and initiating gene expression (Callard et al., 1980; Leavitt et al., 1983; Evans, 1988). In steroid hormone action, the receptors are as important as the hormones themselves. Many steroids can up- or down-regulate their own or other steroid receptors, as well as SBPs (Leavitt et al. 1983, 1988; Riley and Callard, 1988; Selcer and Leavitt, 1991; Selcer and Palmer, 1995).

GROWTH FACTORS

A group of peptides called growth factors are further associated with modulating the actions of steroid hormones. Insulin-like growth factors I and II (IGF-I and IGF-II) and epidermal growth factor (EGF) have been found to mediate hormonal action on gene expression and transcriptional activation (Ignar-Trowbridge et al., 1993). Growth factors are synthesized in various tissues of the body. Growth factors are either transported through the circulatory system, or they act in an autocrine (on the same cell) or paracrine (on nearby cells) fashion (Van Wyk and Lund, 1989). Further, gene expression for growth factors and their receptors has also been detected in reproductive tracts (Ghahary and Murphy, 1989; Yeh et al., 1993; Kennedy et al., 1994).

Estrogen may actually control the synthesis of these growth factors, which then mediate the effects of estrogen (estromedins) in the hypertrophy of reproductive tract tissues (McLachlan et al., 1991; Nelson et al. 1991, 1992). Growth factors, especially EGF and IGF-I and their specific receptors have been localized in the reproductive tracts of many vertebrates, including reptiles (Palmer and Guillette, 1991; Cox and Guillette, 1993).

REPRODUCTIVE PATTERNS AND CYCLES

Reptiles have adapted to many biomes, ranging from deserts to the sea, and from the tropics to above the Arctic circle. Within these biomes, they have further adapted to terrestrial, arboreal, fossorial, freshwater, and marine habitats. Reproductive characteristics vary among species in order to maximize reproductive output. These reproductive characteristics include:
—size, shape, and number of eggs
—rate of embryo development
—frequency of reproduction
—parity mode (oviparous or viuiparous)

In the vast majority of animals, reproduction is seasonally timed for the optimum survival of the offspring (Karsch et al., 1984; Wingfield and

TABLE 1

OVERVIEW OF ACTIONS OF MAJOR REPRODUCTIVE HORMONES.

Hormone	Action
Melatonin	Mediates circadian rhythm
GnRH	Stimulates release of FSH and LH by the pituitary gland
FSH	Initiates follicle growth
LH	Induces steroidogenesis, ovulation, formation of corpus luteum, secretion of progesterone from corpus luteum
Androgens	Stimulation of male reproduction, spermiogenesis, secondary sexual characteristics, mating and territorial behaviors
Estrogens	Stimulates vitellogenesis, proliferation of endometrium, induces LH surge
Progesterone	Maintenance of oviductal mucosa, inhibits release of gonadotropins from adenohypophysis, maintains pregnancy, inhibits oviposition and parturition
Arginine Vasotocin	Induces contraction of uterine smooth muscle during oviposition and parturition
Prostaglandins	Cause luteolysis, regulate uterine contractions during oviposition and parturition

Kenagy, 1986). In oviparous organisms, critical incubation factors control egg and embryo maturation and ultimately offspring survival. Reptile reproductive cycles are therefore synchronized to optimize extrinsic factors such as temperature, precipitation, and photoperiod—all of which vary seasonally. Due to variations in geographic range, cycles vary along a continuum from very short cycles in northern species to nearly continuous reproduction in some tropical species (Fitch 1970, 1982; Moll, 1979; Duvall et al., 1982). Species with wide geographic ranges are subject to local environmental conditions. Consequently, these species exhibit within-species variation in patterns of reproduction which may be nongenetic.

FEMALE REPRODUCTIVE PATTERNS AND CYCLES

Egg production is central to female reproduc-tion. Both oviparous and viviparous reptiles produce telolecithal eggs. Telolecithal eggs have an abundant supply of nutrients for the developing embryo in the form of yolk. Vitellogenesis is the process in which yolk is synthesized and deposited within ovarian follicles.

Vitellogenin is synthesized in the liver and released into the circulatory system. There, the vitellogenin is taken up by the oocytes and converted into two stored forms: lipovitellin and phosvitin (Ho, 1987). Vitellogenin production within the liver is under estrogen control in all egg-laying vertebrates. However, other hormones, such as T and P, may influence the effect of estrogen on vitellogenesis. Further, prolactin, P and gonadotropins influence the rate at which vitellogenin is incorporated into growing follicles (Ho, 1987). During vitellogenesis, serum lipid concentrations are increased as they are mobilized from fat bodies; and calcium concentrations are increased as they are mobilized from bone reserves.

The pattern of ovulation, as well as the number of ova produced, vary among reptiles. Most reptiles are polyembryonous, and ova for entire clutches or litters are ovulated simultaneously. The number of released ova can be as few as one or as many as 200, with turtles showing the widest range across species. Both ovaries can produce ova from the mature follicles (autochronic). In some reptiles, alternate ovaries produce the greater number of ova in consecutive years. A single ovum is produced in most anoline lizards with subsequent ovulations occurring alternately from the paired ovaries (allochronic).

The females of most turtle species have annual reproductive cycles. However, some sea turtles of the family Cheloniidae have two- to four-year cycles. Species with northern distributions generally produce one clutch per annum. In contrast, species from southern latitudes may produce multiple clutches (generally from two to six) each nesting season (Callard and Lance, 1977; Moll, 1979). For species on annual cycles, the general pattern of the cycle begins in late summer or fall as rising E_2 levels initiate vitellogenesis and ovarian recrudescence occurs. Winter hibernation or brumation interrupts vitellogenesis. The follicles may reach their maximum size before this interruption or after vitellogenesis resumes upon spring emergence.

As E_2 levels peak, androgen levels are also elevated in many turtle species. Vernal mating occurs in most species, although fall matings are not uncommon, and some species may be opportunistic breeders. In spring, E_2 levels peak and the ovaries and oviducts reach maximum hypertrophy. This leads up to the ovulation of mature follicles (Lewis et al., 1979; Licht, 1982; McPherson et al., 1982; Motz and Callard, 1991). This is followed by gravidity, a period when eggs move through the oviduct. As eggs move through the oviduct, they are fertilized and then coated with albumen proteins, egg membrane, and calcareous shell (Palmer and Guillette 1990, 1991; Motz and Callard, 1991).

During gravidity, the corpora lutea produce elevated P levels. Nesting and oviposition occur in early to late summer in northern species. However, nesting and oviposition may occur as early as January in tropical species. AVT and prostaglandins are involved in stimulating oviductal contractions that lead to oviposition (Guillette et al., 1991). A period of reproductive quiescence following the nesting season may last until late summer or early fall. During quiescence, steroids are at their lowest levels, ovaries are small with immature follicles, and oviductal tissues are regressed.

Temperate-zone squamates tend to have seasonal reproductive cycles. However, some temperate squamates may occasionally double-clutch or skip a season of reproduction. Though the seasonal patterns of temperate species are quite diverse, they follow a pattern similar to turtles: rising E_2 levels in fall or early spring stimulate vitellogenesis, ovarian recrudescence, and oviductal hypertrophy. This is followed in late spring or early summer by ovulation, fertilization, and finally gravidity or pregnancy (Fitch 1970, 1982; Fox, 1977).

It has been shown that oviparous squamates generally show spring mating and rapid follicular growth, enabling mid-summer oviposition. However, exceptions exist, such as *Diadophis* species, which also mate in the fall and some species that display initial ovarian recrudescence before hibernation in late fall (Duvall et al., 1982). Many viviparous squamates exhibit fall reproductive activity, in which vitellogenesis, courtship, and mating occur in autumn. This is followed by gestation during hibernation and parturition in the spring (Guillette and Casas-Andrew, 1980; Halpert et al., 1982; Guillette, 1983). However, some viviparous species are spring-breeders similar to most oviparous species (Hoffman, 1970; Vitt and Blackburn, 1983; Stewart, 1985). A few viviparous lizard species, such as *Liolaemus*, exhibit asynchronous reproductive activity. Reproduction patterns among tropical squamates range from strongly seasonal to continuous reproduction. Many tropical viviparous species exhibit a continuous cyclic reproductive pattern, such as the aquatic snake, *Homalopsis buccata* (Berry and Lim, 1967). In contrast, oviparous squamates have cycles strongly tied to wet/dry seasons.

Generally, female crocodilians at the higher latitudes are monestrous seasonal breeders, with the initiation of reproductive activity being largely temperature dependent (Duvall et al., 1982; Joanen and McNease, 1989; Lance, 1989; Guillette et al., 1995, 1997). In *Alligator mississippiensis*, vitellogenesis, ovarian recrudescence, and oviductal hypertrophy begin in the fall and peak in the spring. High testosterone and testosterone levels are also coincident with high estrogen levels. Copulation occurs in the spring. Ovulation usually occurs in May-June, followed by oviposition a few weeks later. Progesterone levels are elevated during gravidity. Estradiol levels become nondetectable after ovulation, and testosterone levels drop dramatically as well (Callard and Kleis, 1987; Lance 1987, 1989; Guillette et al., 1995, 1997). A quiescent period follows nesting. During this period, the gonads are atrophied until recrudescence (Joanen and McNease, 1989; Guillette et al., 1995, 1997). Females may skip breeding seasons due to low energy reserve levels.

Tropical crocodilians exhibit a stronger association between copulation/nesting and wet/dry seasons. However, within a species, geographical variations exist. *Caiman crocodilus* shows a variety of seasonal mating and nesting activity, such as: breeding and nesting during the rainy season; breeding and nesting at the end of the dry season; breeding year round except for the early wet season. *Crocodylus porosus* nests in the dry season in Sri Lanka, but nests in the wet season in northern Australia.

MALE REPRODUCTIVE PATTERNS AND CYCLES

Male reptiles in temperate regions also exhibit annual reproductive cycles, which are influenced by environmental conditions. Environmental cues influence hormonal levels to modify the timing of reproductive cycles. This ensures that young are produced under favorable conditions (Marion, 1982).

In reptiles, testosterone is produced by both Leydig and Sertoli cells. However, the amount and timing of testosterone production vary between the two cell types. Leydig cells are responsible for the majority of testosterone production throughout the testicular cycle. Testosterone is thought to initiate spermatogenesis and mating behavior (Licht et al., 1985; Mahmoud et al., 1985; Bourne and Licht, 1985). But, both Leydig and Sertoli cells actively produce testosterone during spermatogenesis and testicular growth during the fall. This signifies the importance of both cell types in the maturation of germ cells (Mesner et al., 1993). The maturation of germ cells is influenced by elevated temperatures, which are needed for testicular growth and testosterone secretion in response to increased gonadotropin levels. This is due to the binding sensitivity of testicular receptors for gonadotropins with respect to temperature (Kubokawa, 1990). Temperature also may directly regulate steroid-synthesizing enzymes (Bourne, 1991).

The male reproductive cycle can be divided into three phases:
—testicular recrudescence
—copulatory period
—testicular regression

In general, turtles typically undergo testicular recrudescence and spermatogenesis in late spring. For instance, snapping turtles exhibit a biphasic cycle in plasma T levels, with the largest peak occurring in late spring or in early summer associated with spring mating and spermatogenesis. The second and smaller T peak occurs in late summer or early fall and is associated with spermiation (release of spermatozoa into the tubular lumen) and fall mating. Testicular regression occurs as testosterone levels drop in the fall and remain low until spring (Mahmoud et al., 1985; Mesner et al., 1993).

In most turtle species, mating commonly occurs during the spring. However, fall mating and continuous breeding have also been reported for temperate species. The timing of reproductive cycles may be influenced by latitude as more southerly populations have longer cycles. For example, in *Mauremys caspica rivulata*, courtship and copulation extend from the fall to the spring with peak activity in midwinter (Gasith and Sidis, 1985). Mature spermatozoa are stored during the winter hibernation in the epididymis.

Squamates show tremendous variation in reproductive cycles among species. Often spermatogenesis occurs in late summer and fall before winter hibernation. Spermiogenesis may begin in the fall or winter but commonly occurs in the spring prior to copulation. The spring breeding season is correlated with peak testosterone levels and spermatogenesis of both males and females. Some northern temperate species of snakes and lizards show biennial reproductive cycles.

In the northern temperate lizards, such as *Tiliqua scincoides* and *Podarcis s. sicula*, spring increases in androgen levels are correlated with Leydig cell hypertrophy, testicular recrudescence, courtship and mating. Regression of testes and secondary sex organs occurs in late summer and corresponds to decreases in T levels. In the fall, spermatogenesis initiates but ceases prior to spermiation before winter (Callard and Ho, 1980; Ando et al., 1992). In more southerly temperate zone species, the reproductive cycle may show continuous testicular maintenance. In *Anolis carolinensis* spermatogenesis and androgen production begin in the fall and are completed in the spring (Duvall et al., 1982). In the tropical Jamaican lizard *Anolis opalinus*, there is less seasonal variation in reproductive stages or organ size than in temperate counterparts. For example, reproductive parameters (such as testis mass and mean epithelial cell height of epididymis, vas deferens, and sex segment) all show less variation in *A. opalinus* than in *A. carolinensis* (Jenssen and Nunez, 1994).

In temperate snakes, copulation typically occurs in the spring. However, gonadal recrudescence may be initiated from late summer to early fall. Such is the case, for example in *Nerodia sipedon*, *Pituophis melanoleucus*, *Thamnophis* species, *Tropidoclonion lineatum*, and *Crotalus viridis* (Krohmer et al., 1987). In most European snakes, summer quiescence is followed by spermatogenesis in the fall with sperm maturation and copulation in the spring. In the cobra, *Naja naja*, peak testosterone levels occur concurrently with peak spermatogenic development in the spring, which is followed by copulation. A smaller testosterone peak occurs in the fall during spermatogenic recovery. However, testosterone levels decrease during winter hibernation (Callard and Ho, 1980).

Of the crocodilians, *A. mississippiensis* is perhaps the best studied. Following winter hibernation, testosterone levels begin to elevate by February and March. This stimulates the seminiferous tubules to enlarge. By early April numerous secondary spermatocytes are evident. Maximum testes mass occurs by early May, followed by spermiation and mating in late May or early June. Testosterone levels then drop and are nondetectable from June until August. This results in the cessation of spermiation and a rapid decrease in testicular mass by mid-July. Atypically warm weather may initiate spermatogenesis in the fall (Lance, 1989). In the Nile crocodile (*Crocodylus niloticus*) spermatogenesis occurs from April to December as hibernation is absent. Copulation activity in *Crocodylus niloticus* occurs in early spring (August-September). In the Asian crocodilian species *Crocodylus palustris* and *Gavialis gangeticus*, mating events occur in January and February (Magnusson et al., 1989).

Figure 27.
A red-eared turtle (*Trachemys scripta*) ovipositing eggs in a breeding facility. The shelled amniotic eggs produced by oviparous reptiles first enabled reptiles to radiate into terrestrial habitats. Today, considerable variation in reproductive anatomy and physiology is evident among extant amniotes, due to the continuing process of evolution. Photo by BD Palmer.

STRESS AND HORMONES

Both acute and chronic stress may have a serious impact on reproduction in reptiles. Many of the effects of stress are mediated by the adrenal glands. Each gland contains two distinct regions: the adrenal medulla and the adrenal cortex. The adrenal cortex is under the influence of ACTH from the adenohypophysis of the pituitary gland. Once stimulated, the cortex synthesizes several corticosteroid hormones (such as corticosterone) involved in the stress response. Further, the adrenal cortex also produces small amounts of progesterone and androgens. Normal corticosterone levels in male lizards (such as *Podarcis s. sicula* and *Sceloporus cyanogenys*) vary

during the reproductive cycle, and reach peak levels during mating (Manzo et al., 1994).

Chronic stress is often caused by environmental factors, such as unusual temperature or moisture levels, parasites, or captivity. In *A. carolinensis*, low humidity causes a decrease in body weight, a shift in diurnal rhythm of corticosterone secretion, and suppressed ovarian function. Overcrowding and parasitic loads in captive juvenile alligators leads to inhibition of the reproductive system along with a chronic increase in corticosterone secretion and immune system suppression (Lance, 1990).

Acute stressors can also and can result in rapid changes in hormone levels. The stress of captivity of turtles, lizards, and alligators results in elevated corticosterone and reduced sex steroid levels. For example, sexually active male *A. mississippiensis* show differences in plasma testosterone levels that are correlated with duration of captivity (Lance and Elsey, 1986). In Louisiana collections, blood samples taken immediately after capture have low plasma corticosterone levels and high plasma testosterone levels. Blood samples taken much later show high plasma corticosterone and low plasma testosterone levels (Lance, 1990). Male painted turtles, *Chrysemys picta,* show significant decreases in plasma gonadotropin and testosterone levels within 24 hours of capture. However, male *Tiliqua rugosa* and female *Thamnophis sirtalis* show no changes in plasma sex steroids as a result of captivity. In male snapping turtles, there is an initial rise in testosterone after capture, but a significant decline occurs after seven days. However, the month of capture influences this response. In female snapping turtles, an increase in plasma estradiol and progesterone levels triggered by capture depends upon the stage of reproductive activity. Nongravid females show significant increases in progesterone within only six hours, but estradiol levels increase only slightly after capture. Gravid females show

**Figure 28.
Viviparous reproduction, as in this horned lizard (*Phrynosoma douglassi*) caught in the act of giving birth, offers certain advantages in some environments. Viviparity has independently evolved in numerous reptilian groups, leading to a variety of theories as to the ecological and physiological forces involved. Photo by MJ Perkins.**

significant increases in both progesterone and estradiol levels by 24 hours of capture. However, these hormone levels return to initial values within 2 to 7 days (Mahmoud et al., 1989)

EVOLUTION OF REPRODUCTIVE MODES

There are two modes of reproduction generally recognized in vertebrates:
—oviparity (egg-laying)
—viviparity (live-bearing)

Oviparity is the more primitive condition from which viviparity is derived. The shelled amniotic egg was a major factor in the radiation of vertebrates into terrestrial habitats (Fig. 27). Since the transition from anamniotic to amniotic eggs, the process by which amniotes produce shelled eggs has continued to evolve. Some species have subsequently lost the eggshell so that they now retain their offspring in utero until embryonic development is complete; thus bearing live young (viviparity; Fig. 28).

The term oviparity is generally defined as the oviposition of shelled eggs which contain relatively undeveloped embryos. Some authors have proposed that oviparity be restricted to the oviposition of an unfertilized egg, although the term ovulparous is more commonly used for this. Viviparity would therefore include all fertilized eggs, regardless of whether the fertilized egg was laid or developed internally. Currently, oviparity refers to those females that lay eggs, in which completion of embryonic development occurs outside of the female but within an egg structure (Guillette 1987, 1991; Blackburn, 1992).

Today, the term viviparity is applied to eggs that are retained within the mother's body until embry-onic development is complete, and young are borne fully formed (Shine, 1985; Shine and Guillette, 1988). This may involve a complex placenta, absence of calcified egg-membranes, and/or maternal-fetal transfer of nutrients. One exception to this definition is marsupials, in which the young are born before embryonic development is complete. The terms pregnancy or pregnant are used to describe viviparous species. The terms gravidity or gravid are used for those species which are oviparous.

Ovoviviparity describes a condition in which complete embryonic development occurs within the body of the mother, with no maternal-fetal transfer of nutrients other than the initial yolk stores laid down before ovulation or fertilization (Neill, 1964; Tinkle and Gibbons, 1977; Yaron, 1985). Ovoviviparity is generally regarded as an intermediate stage between oviparity and viviparity.

EVOLUTION OF OVIPARITY

The function of the reptilian oviduct in albumen and eggshell formation provides information on the evolution of reproductive modes. Albumen is formed in the tubal region (tuba uterina) of the tube. There is homogeneity in glandular ultrastructure and secretory nature of the oviduct. This homogeneity indicates that the tube of reptiles is less specialized than the magnum of birds (Palmer and Guillette, 1988; Perkins and Palmer, 1995). The avian magnum not only exhibits specialized cell types for producing specific proteins, but also exhibits structural organization of cell types along the length of the magnum (Gilbert, 1979; Solomon, 1983). In lizards, the tube is aglandular, so that the little albumen found in their eggs is probably produced by the luminal epithelial cells. The primitive oviparous condition is reflected in the anatomy and physiology of the tuatara, turtles, and squamates. The endometrial glands ultrastructurally resemble the fiber-producing glands of the avian isthmus. These glands extrude intact fibers that are wrapped around the egg to form the eggshell membrane. The production of fibers is controlled to form layers within the membrane. The membrane is complete shortly after ovulation (Palmer et al., 1993).

Following formation of the membranous eggshell, calcium deposition begins on all eggs while they are still retained in the uterus. Calcium deposition continues throughout the rest of gravidity. Both eggshell layers are produced in a single oviductal region (uterus). Production of the eggshell layers is usually complete in 2-3 weeks. The process of eggshell calcification may take considerably longer, such as 7-8 months in the tuatara. The uterus in turtles, squamates and tuatara is therefore dualistic in function, producing both the egg membranes and calcareous shells on an entire clutch. The amount of albumen present, as well as the thickness of the calcareous shell, is highly variable among species.

The oviparous mammals, the monotremes, have a unique egg structure. The tube produces a thin layer of albumen on each egg of the clutch virtually simultaneously. There is only a single type of albumen-secreting cell within the tube (Hughes, 1977). This is similar to the tubal structure of reptiles, which also lacks the highly specialized cell types for albumen synthesis and secretion that is typical of the avian magnum (Gilbert, 1979; Solomon, 1983). In monotremes, the uterus produces all layers of the eggshell (Hughes and Shorey, 1972; Hughes and Carrick, 1978), which are somewhat different than in birds and reptiles. Although the monotreme eggshell membranes are made from proteinaceous secretions of the endometrial uterine glands, however, the membranes are formed from particles, rather than fibers, as found in both birds and reptiles (Hughes, 1977).

The monotreme eggshell membranes may be similar to the outer layer of eggshell membrane in many reptilian species, which consists of a thin layer of proteinaceous particles (Schleich and Kastle, 1988; Packard and DeMarco, 1991). The calcareous shell is greatly reduced in monotremes, as in many squamates. This may allow for the extensive swelling of the eggs due to fluid uptake within the uterus. Both layers of the eggshell are secreted sequentially within the uterus. As in reptiles, all eggs of a clutch are ovulated simultaneously. In monotremes, therefore, the regions of the oviduct are multifunctional and can coat multiple eggs at a time, and the uterus secretes both eggshell layers. These reproductive characteristics of monotremes are closest to turtles, squamates, and tuatara, based on temporal separation of eggshell secretion within the uterus.

A more advanced reproductive mode than that of other reptiles occurs in the crocodilians. Crocodilians spatially separate formation of eggshell components along the length of the oviduct. The eggshell is thick and rigid in all species, and the albumen layer well-developed. However, the anatomy of alligator oviducts is substantially different from that of other reptiles. Alligator oviducts possess two distinct uterine secretory regions: the fiber-forming region and the calcareous region (Palmer and Guillette, 1992). The fiber-forming region histochemically and ultrastructurally resembles the eggshell fiber-forming region (isthmus) in birds and resembles the uterus of other reptiles. Further, the extrusion of eggshell fibers from the endometrial glands confirms that this region of the alligator oviduct produces the proteinaceous fibers of the eggshell membrane. The posterior region of the alligator uterus secretes the calcareous eggshell. This posterior region is ultrastructurally similar to the shell gland of birds, but distinct from the uterus of other reptiles. The calcareous shell is formed on all eggs of a clutch simultaneously. Although the oviduct of alligators resembles that of birds in having separate regions for the formation of each egg coat, it still handles all eggs of a clutch simultaneously, as in other reptiles.

In birds, the process of albumen and eggshell production became even more advanced. Birds are sequential ovulators, so only one egg of a clutch is invested with albumen and eggshell at a time by the single oviduct. This is accompanied by further specialization of cells and tissues for albumen and eggshell formation. Different populations of cell types occur along the magnum for albumen secretion. These different populations correlate with the sequential layers of albumen proteins surrounding the yolk. In birds, the fibrous and calcareous layers of the eggshell are produced in separate portions of the oviduct (isthmus and shell gland, respectively (Solomon, 1983). However, even these regions exhibit some specialization along their length.

Following ovulation in birds, an individual egg is coated with albumen in the magnum before it enters the isthmus. In the isthmus, the proteinaceous fibers of the eggshell membrane are deposited. The egg then travels into the shell gland where calcium deposition occurs. The avian oviduct is essentially an assembly line, with each region of the oviduct involved in only one specialized function. The entire process from ovulation to oviposition requires about 24 hours and is complete before the next egg of a clutch is ovulated. This represents the most anatomically complex and structurally specialized oviduct of oviparous amniotes.

Comparisons of oviductal functional morphology and eggshell formation among reptilian taxa, birds, and mammals reveal a progression of reproductive anatomy and physiology from simplest to most complex (Table 2). This assumes that:

1. The simplest anatomy and physiology is ancestral, whereas more complex features are derived, and
2. Structures with more generalized functions are ancestral to those which are more specialized.

The assumptions do not represent the evolutionary relationships among these taxa, but use those characteristics of extant groups to decipher the evolution of oviparous reproductive modes among amniotes. The range of oviparity goes from generalized oviductal functional morphology (as in turtles, squamates, and tuatara) to highly specialized oviducts of birds, with their rapid and efficient assembly-line functional morphology. The archosaurs (including birds and crocodiles) exhibit advanced anatomical separation of egg shelling events. This may have important implications for the reproductive modes of dinosaurs, which are also archosaurs (Palmer and Guillette, 1992).

EVOLUTION OF VIVIPARITY

Viviparity has evolved in several groups of vertebrates, including mammals, reptiles, amphibians, and fishes. Viviparity, however, has never occurred in crocodilians, turtles, or birds. In squamate reptiles, viviparity has independently evolved numerous times occurring at taxonomic levels ranging from family to subspecies (Shine, 1985; Shine and Guillette, 1988; Blackburn 1982, 1985). Because of the high frequency of independent origins of viviparity among squamate reptiles, the occurrence of closely related species exhibiting both modes of reproduction is high. This has made squamate reptiles an ideal group for studying the selective forces responsible for this evolutionary switch between reproductive modes.

Surveys of squamate reptiles (based on either geographic or taxonomic distributions or both) have shown that viviparity has independently arisen in different lineages of lizards and snakes. Analyses have revealed a minimum of nearly 100 independent origins of viviparity among living squamate groups (Blackburn 1982, 1985; Shine, 1985). However, the evolution of viviparity is not evenly distributed among squamates. Viviparity has evolved more in those families of squamates which have radiated worldwide—specifically, into the Americas. Among snakes, viviparity has occurred the most in the caenophidian or "advanced" families of snakes, including Colubridae, Viperidae, and Elapidae. In particular, Viperidae and Colubridae account for about three-fourths of the serpentes origins of viviparity. Viperidae and Colubridae also ac-

count for nearly 60% of all the viviparous species snakes. Furthermore, Scincidae and Iguanidae account for nearly all the origins within Sauria (Blackburn, 1985; Shine, 1985).

The selective forces associated with the evolution of viviparity have interested ecologists and biologists for years. Squamates are an excellent group for studying these mechanisms due to their high incident of independent origins of viviparity. Several hypotheses have been developed based on taxonomic, geographic, and life history characteristics of this group. For purposes of clarity, the hypotheses are grouped into three categories based upon:
—environmental factors
—ecological characteristics
—physiological or morphological factors.

ENVIRONMENTAL FACTORS

There are three hypotheses which describe the possible effect of environmental factors on the evolution of viviparity:
—cold-climate hypothesis
—unpredictable-environment hypothesis
—egg-predation hypothesis

Cold-Climate Hypothesis. The cold-climate hypothesis (Mell, 1929; Weekes, 1933; Sergeev, 1940) suggests that viviparity evolved as an adaptation to cold climates. This is based on the following sequence of criteria:

1. In cold climates, thermoregulation enables females to maintain higher body temperatures, thereby increasing the temperature of the eggs retained in utero. This causes:
2. Embryonic development to be accelerated. This leads to conditions 3 and 4:
3. A decrease in total incubation time, which thereby decreases the probability of egg mortality; and
4. Early hatching or live-bearing, which enables young to feed and accumulate energy reserves during the short, warm seasons before winter hibernation.

These assumptions have been tested in a group of Australian lizards (Shine 1983, 1985, 1987, 1989) and in high altitude *Anolis* lizards (Huey, 1988). The proportion of viviparous species increases with both higher latitudes and elevations (Sergeev, 1940; Tinkle and Gibbons, 1977; Greene, 1970). However, there are many viviparous species that inhabit hot, arid regions; such as *Crotalus* in the western United States (Shine and Bull, 1979).

Unpredictable-Environment Hypothesis. Tinkle and Gibbons (1977) have provided the basis for the unpredictable-environment hypothesis. Egg-retention and viviparity may be adaptations to variable environments, where stochastic events

TABLE 2

MAJOR ADVANCES IN THE EVOLUTION OF OVIPARITY. (MODIFIED FROM PALMER AND GUILLETTE, 1992)

SPATIAL SEPARATION PER EGG Eggshell layers formed sequentially on individual eggs of a clutch in separate oviductal regions	Aves
SPATIAL SEPARATION PER CLUTCH Eggshell layers formed sequentially on an entire clutch in separate oviductal regions	Crocodylia
TEMPORAL SEPARATION PER CLUTCH Eggshell layers formed sequentially on an entire clutch within a single oviductal region	Chelonia Lepidosauria Monotremata

such as extreme temperatures, extreme moisture levels, resource availability, etc., act as selective pressures. In highly variable environments, selection might favor females that hold their eggs through some part of this period of developmental uncertainty. For example, Packard et al. (1982) have shown that substrate moisture levels are important determinants of hatching success and also may affect hatchling size. If conditions are not suitable, selection favors females that retain eggs. However, extreme aridity may prevent evolution of viviparity because thinning of the eggshell (assumed to be a necessary precondition for viviparity) is impossible in extremely arid environments (Packard, 1966).

Egg-Predation Hypothesis. Neill (1964) proposed the "egg predation" hypothesis, based on the assumption that egg predation is reduced by uterine retention of eggs. However, Shine (1985) argued that egg predation must be balanced against increased predation upon females, which is an assumed cost of viviparity. The increased size and mass of a pregnant female may make it more difficult for her to evade predators.

ECOLOGICAL CHARACTERISTICS

The second category of hypotheses for the evolution of viviparity is based upon particular ecological characteristics:
—defense ability
—agility and speed
—arboreal or aquatic lifestyle specialization
—egg-guarding

Defense Ability. This hypothesis suggests that viviparity is more likely to evolve in those species which are large and/or venomous because the pregnant females of these species have greater defenses against predators. Since these females are less vulnerable to predation, eggs in utero would have a greater chance of survival than eggs in the nest (Neill, 1964). Data presented by Fitch (1970) indicates that 27% of the non-venomous species studied were viviparous, whereas more than 50% of the venomous species studied were viviparous.

Agility and Speed. The second ecological-characteristic hypothesis is based on agility and speed. Fitch (1970) states that viviparity may be more likely to evolve in species that do not depend on speed as a means of feeding or escaping from predators. For species that do not depend on speed or agility, the burden of carrying eggs in utero should have less impact on the pregnant female as far as her survivorship and food intake is concerned. It is possible, however, that the common cessation of feeding by both gravid and pregnant individuals may reduce the importance of this hypothesis (Shine and Bull, 1979).

Arboreal or Aquatic Lifestyle Specialization. Those species specialized for either arboreal or aquatic life styles may be more likely to evolve viviparity (Neill, 1964; Fitch, 1970). Viviparity would be an adaptation that would allow these species to remain in their native element and reproduce. However, this hypothesis offers no selective advantage for the intermediate stages of prolonged egg retention. Furthermore, live-bearing would appear to hinder the arboreal species,

TABLE 3.

COSTS AND BENEFITS OF VIVIPARITY IN SQUAMATES.

Benefits

Protection of eggs from some environmental sources of mortality

Favorable thermoregulation of developing embryos

Female can add sustenance during develop ment rather than making the entire reproductive commitment prior to ovulation

Greater predictability in placement of newborn young in sites optimal for them

Costs

Parent encumbered by enlarges eggs or embryos for prolonged periods, increasing predarory risks and pregnancy maintenance costs.

Mutiple clutches less likely

Loss of entire clutch in event of maternal mor tality

Possible decrease in genetic diversity among offspring as a result of fewer annual clutches

which depend on agility for climbing (Packard et al., 1977; Shine and Bull, 1979).

Egg-Guarding. Another hypothesis involves maternal egg-guarding. It was proposed that egg-guarding oviparous species might have prolonged uterine retention in order to feed longer. However, later studies (Aldridge, 1979) showed that both oviparous and viviparous species share the characteristic cessation of feeding during reproduction, therefore providing no advantage for egg-guarding species to evolve viviparity.

PHYSIOLOGICAL AND MORPHOLOGICAL FACTORS

Physiological and morphological hypotheses focus on increased egg retention, reduced egg-shell thickness, and the development of a placenta. That the transition from oviparity to viviparity is viewed as a continuum. Because of this, it is presumed that viviparity arises because selection favors progressively longer retention of eggs in utero associated with decreases in eggshell thickness. These conditions would eventually allow for placental development (Shine, 1984; Shine and Guillette, 1988).

Calcium Requirements. Packard et al. (1977) hypothesized that embryonic calcium requirements enabled the evolution of viviparity in squamates but not in chelonians or crocodilians. Embryonic turtles and crocodilians rely heavily on calcium from the eggshell, whereas squamates rely predominantly on the calcium stored in the yolk for their development. This would allow the adaptive thinning or loss of the egg-shell in squamates but not in chelonians or crocodilians. However, turtles exhibit embryonic diapause if oviposition is de-

TABLE 4.

MAN-MADE COMPOUNDS IDENTIFIED AS ENDOCRINE DISRUPTORS.*

INDUSTRIAL CHEMICALS	Cadmium, Dioxin (2,3,7,8-TCDD), Lead, Mercury, PBBs, PCBs, Pentachlorophenol, Penta- to nonylphenols, Phthalates, Styrenes
INSECTICIDES	Beta-HCH, Carbaryl, Chlordane, Dicofol, Dieldrin, DDT & metabolites, Endosulfan, Heptachlor & H-epoxide, Lindane (gamma-HCH), Methomyl, Methoxychlor, Mirex, Oxychlordane, Parathion, Synthetic Pyrethroids, Toxaphene, Transnonachlor
HERBICIDES	2,4-D, 2,4,5-T, Alachlor, Amitrole, Atrazine, Metribuzin, Nitrofen, Trifluralin
FUNGICIDES	Benomyl, HCB(hexachlorobenzene), Mancozeb, Maneb, Metiram-complex, Tributyl tin, Vinclozolin, Zineb, Ziram
NEMATOCIDES	Aldicarb, DBCP

layed. This eliminates any selective advantage for egg retention in turtles.

Progesterone. Progesterone levels have also been proposed as a factor in the evolution of viviparity. In environments with stressful conditions or extreme seasonal changes, the environmental stress would stimulate an increase in adrenal activity and/or a delay in luteolysis. This would result in increased and/or prolonged synthesis of progesterone (Guillette and Jones, 1985; Guillette, 1993). Progesterone inhibits uterine contractions associated with oviposition or birth, and does so in one of two ways:

—Directly, by blocking the stimulatory effects of AVT and prostaglandin F2α on the uterine smooth muscle

—Indirectly, by inhibiting release of AVT

Therefore, the stress-response to some environmental condition could bring about facultative egg retention. The resultant egg retention may increase the fitness of individuals; thus leading to the genetic fixation of prolonged egg retention by selective forces. However, prolonged egg retention would be possible only if the eggshell was also reduced.

Reduction in the Eggshell. Reduction of the eggshell is a central component to the evolution of viviparity, since the eggshell acts as a diffusion barrier between the mother and embryo. Previously, it was thought that egg shelling was simply delayed if eggs were retained. It is now clear, however, that the eggshell membranes are deposited immediately and are completed soon after ovulation (Palmer et al., 1993).

Species that display prolonged egg retention or viviparity exhibit a reduction in the numbers of endometrial glands that secrete the proteinaceous fibers of the egg membranes. In viviparous species, this enables placentation to occur. The loss of endometrial glands may occur during vitellogenesis, when the oviducts are undergoing hypertrophy. Alterations in sex steroids, such as estrogen, or their receptors may be involved. Also, reduction in eggshell thickness may facilitate maternal recognition of pregnancy, as embryonic signals will be able to reach maternal tissues (Guillette, 1993).

SUMMARY OF THEORIES OF VIVIPARITY

There are many obvious costs and benefits to viviparity (Table 3). Each of the hypotheses proposed has strengths and weaknesses, and none of them applies to all viviparous species. Since there are so many different origins of viviparity, it seems likely that there could be one or more ultimate mechanisms involved in the switch in parity modes. In order to understand the evolution of viviparity, we must understand how the selective pressures that cause the intermediate conditions (i.e. egg retention and eggshell reduction) could be adaptive.

CONCLUSIONS AND FUTURE DIRECTIONS

The study of reptilian reproduction has taken on new importance with the discovery that environmental contaminants can directly affect the reproductive system (Colborn et al., 1993). These contaminants (termed environmental endocrine disrupters) include many common and notorious pollutants (Table 4). These compounds alter reproductive endocrinology by mimicking steroid hormones. The best known are estrogen mimics, or agonists. Agonists bind to the estrogen receptor and alter hormone regulation of the reproductive tissues. Other compounds—antagonists, such as antiandrogens and antiestrogens—can inhibit steroid action by blocking steroid receptors. Some antagonists may even directly alter hormone levels by influencing steroidogenic enzymes.

Environmental endocrine disrupters can have serious effects on reproduction in exposed adults. However, the basic reproductive anatomy and physiology of adults is already in place. The most deleterious effects are seen in embryos and young, which are using endocrine signals to direct anatomical development and establish physiological set points. Embryos are therefore more sensitive to the effects of endocrine-disrupting compounds, and the effects of those compounds are often permanent. Even a single, low-dose exposure may lead to permanent damage that will only become evident years later in the form of reduced or impaired fertility in otherwise healthy adults.

In reptiles, the effects of environmental endocrine-disrupters are numerous. In adults, they can alter basic reproductive cycles, such as vitellogenesis (Palmer and Palmer, 1995). However, embryonic effects include reduced clutch sizes, hatching rates, and hatchling survival (Bishop et al., 1991). More insidious effects include direct alterations of the reproductive system, such as altered hormone levels, impaired gonad development, and reduced penis length (Guillette et al., 1994). These subtle alterations in reproduction may pose a serious threat to the survival of reptilian populations.

These environmental threats are compounded by the diversity of reproductive functional morphology and endocrine patterns found in reptiles (due to the significant evolutionary diversity of the group). Even closely related species may exhibit substantial differences in anatomy and physiology. Evolutionary diversity is one reason why reptiles are such a good model system for many studies—for example, those on the evolution of viviparity.

However, this variation further complicates efforts to unravel the impact of endocrine-disrupting chemicals on wild populations. In order to understand and protect existing species from decline, we need to further understand not only the similarities among groups, but also their differences.

REFERENCES AND RECOMMENDED READING

—**Agassiz, L:**
Contributions to the Natural History of the United States of America. The Embryology of the Turtle. Little, Brown Co, Boston, 1857, Vol. I & II. 640pp.

—**Aitken, RNC; Solomon SE:**
Observations on the ultrastructure of the oviduct of the Costa Rican Green turtle (*Chelonia mydas* L.). *J Exp Mar Biol Ecol*, 1976; 21:75-90.

—**Aldridge, RD:**
Female reproductive cycles of snakes *Arizona elegans* and *Crotalus viridis. Herpetologica*, 1979; 35:256-261.

—**Aleksuik, M; Gregory PT:**
Regulation of seasonal mating behavior in *Thamnophis sirtalis* parietalis. *Copeia*, 1974; 681-689.

—**Altland, PD:**
Observations on the structure of the reproductive organs of the box turtle. *J Morphol*, 1951; 89:599-621.

—**Ando, S; Ciarcia G; Panno ML; Imbrogno E; Tarantino G; Buffone M; Beraldi E; Angelini F; Botte V:**
Sex steroids levels in the plasma and testis during the reproductive cycle of lizard *Podarcis s. sicula* Raf. *Gen Comp Endocrinol*, 1992; 85:1-7.

—**Arslan, M; Zaidi P; Lobo J; Zaidi AA; Qoizi MH:**
Steroid levels in preovulatory and gravid lizards *(Uromastix hardwicki). Gen Comp Endocrinol*, 1978; 34:300-303.

—**Berry, PY; Lim GS:**
The breeding pattern of the puff-faced water snake, *Homalopsis buccata* Boulenger. *Copeia*, 1967; 307-313.

—**Bishop, CA: Brooks RJ; Carey JH; Ng P; Norstrom RJ; Lean DRS:**
The case for a cause-effect linkage between environmental contamination and development in eggs of the common snapping turtle *(Chelydra s. serpentina)* from Ontario, Canada. *J Tox Environ Health*, 1991; 33:521-547.

—**Blackburn, DG:**
Evolutionary origins of viviparity in the Reptilia I. Sauria. *Amphibia-Reptilia*, 1982; 3:185-205.

—**Blackburn, DG:**
Evolutionary origins of viviparity in the Reptilia II. Serpentes, Amphisbaenia, and Ichthyosauria. *Amphibia-Reptilia*, 1985; 6:259-291.

—**Blackburn, DG:**
Convergent evolution of viviparity, matrotrophy, and specializations for fetal nutrition in reptiles and other vertebrates. *Amer Zool*, 1992; 32:313-321.

—**Blackburn, DG:**
Standardized criteria for the recognition of reproductive modes in squamate reptiles. *Herpetologica*, 1993; 49(1)118-132.

—**Bourne, A:**
Androgens. In, Vertebrate Endocrinology: Fundamentals and Biomedical Implications vol. 4 part B. PKT Pang; MP Schreibman (Eds); MP Schreibman; R Jones (Assoc. Eds). Academic Press, San Diego, 1991, pp. 115-144.

—**Bourne, AR; Licht P:**
Steroid biosynthesis in turtle testes. *Comp Biochem Physiol*, 1985; 81B(3):793-796.

—**Callard, IP; Ho SM:**
Seasonal reproductive cycles in reptiles. *Prog Reprod Biol*, 1980; 5:5-38.

—**Callard, IP; Kleis SM:**
Reproduction in reptiles. In, Fundamentals of Comparative Vertebrate Endocrinology. I Chester-Jones; PM Ingleton; JG Phillips (Eds). Plenum Press, New York, 1987, pp. 187-205.

—**Callard, IP; Lance V:**
The control of reptilian follicular cycles. In, Reproduction and Evolution. JH Calaby, CH Tyndale-Biscoe; (Eds). Australian Academy of Science, Canberra City. 1977. pp. 199-209.

—**Callard, IP; Fileti LA; Perez LE; Klosternan L; Tsang P; McCracken JA:**
Role of corpus luteum and progesterone in the evolution of vertebrate viviparity. *Amer Zool*, 1992; 32:264-275.

—**Callard, IP; Ho SM; Gapp DA; Taylor S; Danko D; Wulczyn G:**
Estrogens and estrogenic actions in fish, amphibians and reptiles. In, Estrogens in the Environment. McLachlan (Ed). Elsevier North Holland, New York, 1980, pp. 213-237.

—**Colborn, T; vom Saal FS; Soto AM:**
Developmental effects of endocrine-disrupting chemicals in wildlife and humans. *Environmental Health Perspectives*, 1993; 101(5):378-384.

—**Collin JP; Oksche J:**
Structure and functional relationships in the

nonmammalian pineal gland. In, The Pineal Gland: Anatomy and Biochemistry RJ Reiter (Ed). CRC Press, Boca Raton, Florida, 1981, pp. 27-68.

—Cox, C; Guillette Jr LJ:
Localization of insulin-like growth factor-I-like immunoreactivity in the reproductive tract of the vitellogenic female American alligator, *Alligator mississippiensis. Anat Rec*, 1993; 236:635-640.

—Crews, D; P. Licht P:
Inhibition by corpora atretica of ovarian sensitivity to environmental and hormonal stimulation in the lizard, *Anolis carolinensis. Endocrinology*, 1974; 95(1):102-109.

—Crews, D; Wibbels T; Gutzke WHN:
Action of sex steroid hormones on temperature-induced sex determination in the snapping turtle *(Chelydra serpentina) Gen Comp Endocrinol*, 1989; 76:159-166.

—Cuellar, O:
Oviductal sperm storage structures in lizards. *J Morphol*, 1966; 119:7-20.

—De, TK; Maiti BR:
Scanning electron microscopic study of the male genital tract during its highest and lowest activities in the seasonal reproductive cycle of the soft-shelled turtle. *J Morphol*, 1985; 185:277-283.

—Dodd, JM:
The Ovary. In, Vertebrate Endocrinology: Fundamentals and Biomedical Implications. PKT Pang; MP Schreibman (Eds). Academic Press, Orlando, 1986, pp. 351-397.

—Duke, KL:
Nonfollicular ovarian components. In, The Vertebrate Ovary: Comparative Biology and Evolution. RE Jones (Ed). Plenum Press, New York, 1978, pp. 563-582.

—Duvall, DL; Guillette LJ Jr; Jones RE:
Environmental control of reptilian reproductive cycles. In, Biology of the Reptilia, Vol. 13, Physiology D, Physiology Ecology. C Gans; FH Pough (Eds). Academic Press, London, 1982, pp. 201-231.

—Espey, LL:
Ovulation. In, The Vertebrate Ovary: Comparative Biology and Evolution. RE Jones (Ed). Plenum Press, New York, 1978, pp. 503-532.

—Evans, RM:
The steroid and thyroid hormone receptor superfamily. *Science*, 1988; 240:889-895.

—Fawcett, JD:
Effects of Season, Ovariectomy and Hormone Replacement Therapy on the Oviduct of *Anolis carolinensis* (Reptilia: Iguanidae).

Dissertation, University of Colorado, Denver, 1975, pp. 91.

—Fitch, HS:
Reproductive cycles of lizards and snakes. University of Kansas Museum of Natural History, Miscellaneous Publications, 1970; 52:1-247.

—Fitch, HS:
Reproductive cycles in tropical reptiles. Occasional Papers of the Museum of Natural History, Univ. of Kansas, 1982; 96:1-53.

—Fox, H:
The urogenital system of reptiles. In, Biology of Reptilia, vol. 6, C Gans; TS Parson (Eds). Academic Press, London, 1977, pp. 1-157.

—Gasith, A; Sidis I:
Sexual activity in terrapin, *Mauremys caspica rivulata*, in Israel, in relation to testicular cycle and climatic factors. *J Herpetol*, 1985; 19(2):254-260.

—Ghahary, A; Murphy LJ:
Uterine insulin-like growth factor-I receptors: regulation by estrogen and variation throughout the estrous cycle. *Endocrinology*, 1989; 125(2):597-604.

—Gilbert, AB:
Female genital organs. In, Form and Function in Birds, Vol. 1, AS King and J McLelland (Ed). Academic Press, London, 1979, pp. 237-360

—Gist, DH; Jones JM:
Storage of sperm in the reptilian oviduct. Scan Microsc, 1987; 1(4):1839-1849.

—Gist, DH; Jones JM:
Sperm storage within the oviduct of turtles. J Morphol, 1989; 199:379-384.

—Greene, HW:
Mode of reproduction in lizards and snakes of the Gomex Farias region, Tamaulipas, Mexico. *Copeia* 1970; 565-568.

—Guillette, LJ Jr:
Notes concerning reproduction of the montane skink *Eumeces copei. J Herpetol*, 1983; 17:144-148.

—Guillette, LJ Jr :
The evolution of viviparity in fishes, amphibians, and reptiles: an endocrine approach. In, Hormones and Reproduction in Fishes, Amphibians, and Reptiles. DO Norris; RE Jones (Eds.) Plenum Publishing Corporation, 1987, 523-562.

—Guillette, LJ Jr:
The evolution of viviparity in amniote vertebrates: new insights, new questions. *J Zool Lond*, 1991; 223:521-526.

—Guillette, LJ Jr:
The evolution of viviparity in lizards. Bioscience, 1993; 43(11):742-751.

—Guillette, LJ Jr; Casas-Andrew G:
Fall reproductive activity in the high altitude Mexican lizard *Sceloporus grammicus microlepidotus*. *J Herpetol*, 1980; 14:143-147.

—Guillette, LJ Jr; Jones RE:
Ovarian oviductal and placental morphology of the reproductively bimodal lizard species, *Sceloporus aeneus*. *J Morphol*, 1985; 84:85-98

—Guillette, LJ Jr; Bjorndal KA; Bolton AB; Gross TS; Palmer BD; Witherington BE; Matter JM:
Plasma estradiol-17β, progesterone, prostaglandin F, and Prostaglandin E$_2$ concentrations during natural oviposition in the loggerhead turtle *(Caretta caretta)*. *Gen Comp Endocrinol*, 1991; 82:121-130.

—Guillete LJ Jr; Gross TS; Masson GR; Matter JM; Percival HF; Woodward AR:
Developmental abnormalities of the gonad and abnormal sex hormone concentrations in juvenile alligators from contaminated and control lakes in Florida. *Environ Health Perspect*, 1994; 108(2): 680-688.

—Guillette, LJ Jr; Woodward AR; You-Xiang, Q; Cox MC; Matter JM; Gross TS:
Formation and regression of the corpus luteum of the American alligator *(Alligator mississippiensis)*. *J Morphol*, 1995; 224:97-110.

—Guillette, LJ Jr; Woodward, AR; Crain, DA; Masson, GR; Palmer, BD, BD; Cox, MC; You-Ziang, Q;
The reproductive cycle of the female American alligator *(Alligator mississippiensis)*. *Gen Comp Endocrinol*, 1997; in press.

—Halpert, AP; Garstka WR; Crews D:
Sperm transport and storage and its relation to the annual sexual cycle of the female red-sided garter snake, *Thamnophis sirtalis parietalis*. *J Morphol*, 1982; 174:149-159.

—Ho, SM:
Endocrinology of Vitellogenesis. In, Hormones and Reproduction in Fishes, Amphibians and Reptiles. DO Norris; RE Jones (Eds). Plenum Publishing Corp. New York, 1987, pp. 1-29.

—Ho, SM; Callard IP:
High affinity binding of [^{3}H]R5020 and [^{3}H]progesterone by putative progesterone receptors in cytosol and nuclear extract of turtle oviduct. *Endocrinology*, 1984; 114:70-79.

—Hoffman, LH:
Placentation in the garter snake *Thamnophis sirtalis*. *J Morphol*, 1970; 131:57-88.

—Huey, RB:
Egg retention in some high altitude *Anolis* lizards. *Copeia*, 1988:373-375.

—Hughes, RL:
Egg membranes and ovarian function during pregnancy in monotremes and marsupials, In, Reproduction and Evolution. Australian Academy of Science, Canberra City, 1977, pp. 281-291.

—Hughes, RL; Carrick FN:
Reproduction in female monotremes. In, Monotreme Biology, ML Augee (Ed). Royal Zoological Society of New South Wales, Taronga Zoo, Mosman, NSW, 1978, pp. 233-253.

—Hughes, RL; Shorey CD:
Ultrastructural studies on the secretory activity of the oviduct epithelium of the platypus. *J Reprod Fertil*, 1972; 31:491-492.

—Ignar-Trowbridge, DM; Teng CT; Ross KA; Parker MG; Korach KS; McLachlan JA:
Peptide growth factors elicit estrogen receptor-dependent transcriptional activation of estrogen-responsive element. *Mol Endocrinol*, 1993; 7(8):992-998.

—Jenssen, TA; Nunez SC:
Male and female reproductive cycles of the Jamaican lizard, *Anolis opalinus*. *Copeia*, 1994; (3):767-780.

—Joanen, T; McNease LL:
Ecology and physiology of nesting and early development of the American Alligator. *Amer Zool*, 1989; 29:987-998.

—Jones, RE; Guillette LJ Jr:
Hormonal control of oviposition and parturition in lizards. *Herpetologica*, 1982; 38:80-93

—Jones, RE; Fitzgerald KT; Duvall D:
Quantitative analysis of the ovarian cycle of the lizard *Lepidodactylus lugubris*. *Gen Comp Endocrinol*, 1978; 35:70-76.

—Jones, RE; Swain T; Guillette LJ Jr; Fitzgerald KT:
The comparative anatomy of lizard ovaries, with emphasis on the number of germinal beds. *J Herpetol*, 1982; 16(3):240-252.

—Karsch, RM; Bittman EL; Foster DL; Goodman RL; Legan SL; Robinson JE:
Neuroendocrine basis of seasonal reproduction. In, Recent Progress in Hormone Research, Vol. 40. RO Greep (Ed). Academic Press, Orlando, 1984, pp. 185-225.

—Kennedy, TG; Brown KD; Vaughan TJ:
Expression of the genes for the epidermal growth factor receptor and its ligands in porcine oviduct and endometrium. *Biol Reprod*, 1994; 50:751-756.

—Klicka, J; Mahmoud IY:
Conversion of cholesterol to progesterone by turtle corpus luteum. *Steroids*, 1973; 21:483-495.

—Kraus, WL; Katzenellenbogen BS:
Regulation of progesterone receptor gene expression and growth in the rat uterus: modulations of estrogen actions by progesterone and sex steroid hormone antagonists. *Endocrinology*, 1993; 132(6):2371-2379.

—Krohmer, RW; Grassman M; Crews D:
Annual reproductive cycle in the male red-sided garter snake, *Thamnophis sirtalis parietalis*: Field and laboratory studies. *Gen Comp Endocrinol*, 1987; 68(1):64-75.

—Kubokawa, K:
Evolution and adaptation of gonadotropin receptors. In, Progress in Comparative Endocrinology. A Epple; CG Scanes; MH Stetson (Eds). Wiley-Liss, Inc, 1990, pp. 157-162.

—La Pointe JL:
Effect of ovarian steroids and neurohypophysial hormones on the oviduct of the viviparous lizard, *Klauberina riversiana*. *J Endocrinol*, 1969; 43:197-205.

—Lance, VA:
Hormonal control of reproduction in crocodilians. In, Wildlife Management: Crocodiles and Alligators, GJW Webb; SC Manolis; PJ Whitehead (Eds). Surrey Beatty & Sons, Chiping Norton, NSW, Australia, 1987, pp. 409-425.

—Lance, VA:
Reproductive cycle of the American alligator. *Amer Zool*, 1989; 29:999-1018.

—Lance, VA:
Stress in reptiles. In, Progress in Comparative Endocrinology Vol. 5. Karger; Basal (Eds). Wiley-Liss, Inc, 1990, pp. 461-466.

—Lance, VA; Elsey RM:
Stress-induced suppression of testosterone secretion in male alligators. *J Exp Zool*, 1986; 239:241-246.

—Leavitt, WW; Cobb AD; Takeda A:
Progesterone-modulation of estrogen action: rapid down regulation of nuclear acceptor sites for the estrogen receptor. In, Cell and Molecular Biology of the Uterus. WW Leavitt (Ed). (Advances in Experimental Medicine and Biology - Vol. 230). Plenum Press, New York, 1988, pp. 49-75.

—Leavitt, WW; MacDonald RG; Okulicz WC:
Hormonal regulation of estrogen and progesterone receptor systems. In, Biochemical Actions of Hormones . Vol. X. G Litwack (Ed).

Academic Press, Inc., New York, 1983, pp. 323-356.

—Lewis, J; Mahmoud IY; Klicka J:
Seasonal fluctuations in the plasma concentrations of progesterone and oestradiol-17β in the female snapping turtle *(Chelydra serpentina)*. *J Endocrinol*, 1979; 80:127-131.

—Licht, P; Khorrami-Yaghoobi P; Porter DA:
Effects of gonadectomy and steroid treatment on plasma gonadotropins and the response of superfused pituitaries to gonadotropin-releasing hormone in the turtle *Sternotherus odoratus*. *Gen Comp Endocrinol*, 1985; 60:441-449.

—Licht, P:
Reproductive endocrinology of reptiles and amphibians: gonadotropins. *Ann Rev Physiol*, 1979; 41:337-351.

—Licht, P:
Endocrine patterns in the reproductive cycle of turtles. *Herpetologica*, 1982; 38(1):51-61.

—Lofts, B:
Reptilian reproductive cycles and environmental regulators. In, Environmental Endocrinology. T Assenmacher; DS Farmer (Eds). Springer- Verlag, New York, 1978, pp. 37-43.

—Magnusson, WE; Vliet KA; Pooley AC; Whitaker R:
Reproduction. In, Crocodiles and Alligators, Ross, CA; Garnett S; Pyrzakowski T (Eds). Facts on File, New York, 1989, pp. 118-135.

—Mahmoud, IY; Cyrus RV; Woller MJ; Bieber A:
Development of the ovarian follicles in relation to changes in plasma parameters and $^5\Delta\ 3\beta$ HSD in snapping turtle, *Chelydra serpentina*. *Comp Biochem Physiol*, 1985; 82A(1):131-136.

—Mahmoud, IY; Guillette LJ Jr; McAsey ME; Cady C:
Stress-induced changes in serum testosterone, estradiol-17β and progesterone in the turtle, *Chelydra serpentina*. *Comp Biochem Physiol*, 1989; 93A(2):423-427.

—Manzo, C; Zerani M; Gobbetti A; Difiore MM; Angelini F:
Is corticosterone involved in the reproductive processes of the male lizard, *Podarcis sicula sicula*? *Horm Behav*, 1994; 28:117-129.

—Marion, KR:
Reproductive cues for gonadal development in temperate reptiles: temperature

and photoperiod effects on testicular cycle of the lizard *Sceloporus undulatus*. *Herpetologica,* 1982; 38(1):26-39.

—**McLachlan, JA; Nelson KD; Takahashi T; Bossert NL; Newbold RR; Korach KS:**
Estrogens and growth factors in the development, growth, and function of the female reproductive tract. In, Growth Factors in Reproduction. Springer-Verlag, New York, 1991, pp. 197-203.

—**McPherson, RJ; Boots LR; MacGregor R III; Marion KR:**
Plasma steroids associated with seasonal reproductive changes in a multiclutched freshwater turtle, *Sternotherus odoratus. Gen Comp Endocrinol,* 1982; 48:440-451.

—**Mell, R:**
Beitrag Zur Fauna Sinica IV. Grundzuge einer. Okaologie der chinesischen Reptilien und einer herpetologischen Tiergeographe Chinas Berlin, 1929..

—**Mesner, PW; Mahmoud IY; Cyrus RV:**
Seasonal testosterone levels in Leydig and Sertoli cells of the snapping turtle *(Chelydra serpentina)* in natural populations. *J Exp Zool,* 1993; 266:266-276.

—**Miller, WL:**
Molecular biology of steroid hormone synthesis. *Endocrine Reviews,* 1988; 9(3):295-318.

—**Moll, EO:**
Reproductive cycles and adaptations. In, Turtles: Perspectives and Research. M Harless; H Morlock (Eds). Robert E Krieger Pub Co, Malabar, 1979, pp. 305-331.

—**Motz, VA; Callard IP:**
Seasonal variations in oviductal morphology of the painted turtle, *Chrysemys picta. J Morphol,* 1991; 207:59-71.

—**Neill, WT:**
Viviparity in snakes: some ecological and zoogeographical considerations. *Amer Nat,* 1964; 98(898):35-55.

—**Nelson, KG; Takahashi T; Bossert NL; Walmer DK; McLachlan JA:**
Epidermal growth factor replaces estrogen in the stimulation of female genital-tract growth and differentiation. *Proc Nat Acad Sci USA,* 1991; 88:21-25.

—**Nelson, KG; Takahashi T; Lee DC; Luetteke NC; Bossert NL; Ross K; Eitzman BE; McLachlan JA:**
Transforming growth factor-α is a potential mediator of estrogen action in the mouse uterus. *Endocrinology,* 1992; 131(4):1657-1664.

—**Packard, GC:**
The influence of ambient temperature and aridity on modes of reproduction and excretion of amniote vertebrates. *Amer Nat,* 1966; 100(916):667-682.

—**Packard, GC; Tracy CR; Roth JR:**
The physiological ecology of reptilian eggs and embryos, and the evolution of viviparity within the class Reptilia. *Biol Rev,* 1977; 52:71-105.

—**Packard, MJ; DeMarco VG:**
Eggshell structure and formation in eggs of oviparous reptiles. In, Egg Incubation: Its Effects on Embryonic Development in Birds and Reptiles. DC Deeming; MWJ Ferguson (Eds). Cambridge Univ. Press, Cambridge, 1991, pp. 53-69.

—**Packard, MJ; Packard GC:**
Comparative aspects of calcium metabolism in embryonic reptiles and birds. In, Respiration and Metabolism of Embryonic Vertebrates, RS Seymour (Ed). Dr W Junk Publishers, London, 1984, pp. 155-179.

—**Packard, MJ; Packard GC; Boardman TJ:**
Structure of eggshells and water relations of reptilian eggs. *Herpetologica,* 1982; 38(1):136-155.

—**Palmer, BD:**
Pesticides as Endocrine Disruptors in Wildlife and Humans. *Vector Control Bulletin,* 1995; 4 (2): 21-33.

—**Palmer, BD; Guillette LJ Jr:**
Histology and functional morphology of the female reproductive tract of the tortoise *Gopherus polyphemus. Amer J Anat,* 1988; 183:200-211.

—**Palmer, BD; Guillette LJ Jr:**
Morphological changes in the oviductal endometrium during the reproductive cycle of the tortoise, *Gopherus polyphemus. J Morphol,* 1990; 204:323-333.

—**Palmer, BD; Guillette LJ Jr:**
Oviductal proteins and their influence on embryonic development in birds and reptiles. In, Egg Incubation: its effects on embryonic development in birds and reptiles. DC Deeming; MWJ Ferguson (Eds). Cambridge Univ. Press, Cambridge, 1991, pp. 29-46.

—**Palmer, BD; Guillette LJ Jr:**
Alligators provide evidence for the evolution of the archosaurian mode of oviparity. *Biol Reprod,* 1992; 46:39-47.

—**Palmer, BD; Palmer SK:**
Vitellogenin induction by xenobiotic estrogens in the red-eared slider and African clawed frog. *Environ Health Perspect,* 1995; 103(Suppl. 4):19-25.

—**Palmer, BD; DeMarco VG; Guillette LJ Jr:**
Oviductal morphology and eggshell forma-

tion in the lizard, *Sceloporus woodi. J Morphol,* 1993; 217:205-217.

—Parker, GH:
The direction of the ciliary currents in the oviducts of vertebrates. *Amer J Physiol,* 1928; 87:93-96.

—Perkins, MJ; Palmer BD:
Histology and functional morphology of the oviduct of an oviparous snake, *Diadophis punctatus. J Morphol,* 1995; 227:67-79.

—Prasad, MRN; Reddy PRK:
Physiology of the sexual segment of the kidney in reptiles. *Gen Comp Endocrinol Suppl,* 1972; 3:649-662.

—Quay, WB:
The parietal eye-pineal complex. In, Biology of Reptilia, Vol. 9, C Gans; RG Northcutt; P Ulinski (Eds). Academic Press, London, 1979, pp. 245-406.

—Riley, D; Callard IP:
Characterization of turtle liver nuclear estrogen receptors, seasonal changes, and pituitary dependence of cytosolic and nuclear forms. *J Exp Zool,* 1988; 245:277-285.

—Roth, JJ; Gern WA; Roth EC; Ralph CL; Jacobson E:
Nonpineal melatonin in the alligator *(Alligator mississippiensis).* Science, 1980; 210:548-550.

—Salhanick, ACR; Callard IP:
A sex-steroid-binding protein in the plasma of the freshwater turtle, *Chrysemys picta. Gen Comp Endocrinol,* 1980; 43:163-166.

—Schleich, HH; Kastle W:
Reptile Egg Shells. Gustav Fischer Verlag, New York, 1988, 123pp.

—Selcer, KW; Leavitt WW:
Progesterone downregulates progesterone receptor, but not estrogen receptor, in the estrogen-primed oviduct of a turtle *(Trachemys scripta). Gen Comp Endocrinol,* 1991; 83:316-323.

—Selcer, KW; Palmer BD:
Estrogen downregulation of albumin and a 170-kDa serum protein in the turtle, *Trachemys scripta. Gen Comp Endocrinol,* 1995; 97:340-352.

—Sergeev, AM:
Researches in the viviparity of reptiles. *Moscow. Soc. Nat.* 1940; pp. 1-34.

—Shine, R:
Reptilian viviparity in cold climates: testing the assumptions of an evolutionary hypothesis. *Oecologia (Berlin),* 1983; 57:397-405.

—Shine, R:
Physiological and ecological questions on the evolution of reptilian viviparity. In, Respira-tion and Metabolism of Embryonic Vertebrates. RS Seymour (Ed). Dr. W. Junk Publishers, 1984, 147-154.

—Shine, R:
The evolution of viviparity in reptiles: an ecological analysis. In, Biology of Reptilia. C Gans; F Billett (Eds.) J. Wiley & Sons Ltd, New York, 1985, 15:604-694.

—Shine, R:
The evolution of viviparity: ecological correlates of reproductive mode within a Genus of Australian snakes (*Pseudechis*: Elapidae). *Copeia,* 1987(3):551-563.

—Shine, R:
Constraints, allometry and adaptations: food habits and reproductive biology of Australian brownsnakes (*Pseudonaja:* Elapidae). *Herpetologica,* 1989; 45(2):195-207.

—Shine, R; Bull JJ:
The evolution of live-bearing in lizards and snakes. *Amer Nat,* 1979; 113(6):905-923.

—Shine, R; Guillette LJ Jr:
The evolution of viviparity in reptiles: A physiological model and its ecological consequences. *J Theoret Biol,* 1988; 132:43-50.

—Solomon, SE:
Oviduct. In, The Physiology and Biochemistry of the Domestic Fowl, Vol. 4, BM Freeman (Ed) Academic Press, London, 1983, pp. 379-419.

—Stewart, JR:
Placentation in the lizard *Gerrhonotus caeruleus* with a comparison to the extraembryonic membranes of an oviparous *Gerrhonotus multicarinatus* (Saura, Anguidae). *J Morphol,* 1985; 185:101-114.

—Stewart, JR:
Placental structure and nutritional provision to embryos in predominantly lecithotrophic viviparous reptiles. *Amer Zool,* 1992; 32:303-312.

—Stewart, JR; Blackburn DG:
Reptilian placentation: structural diversity and terminology. *Copeia* 1988(4):839-852.

—Studiati, C:
Intorno alle connessioni dell'unovo coll'ovidutto nel *Seps tridactylus. Mem Reale Accad Sci Torino* II, 1851, 15;101-113.

—Tinkle, DW; Gibbons JW:
The distribution and evolution of viviparity in reptiles. *Miscellaneous Publications Museum of Zoology, University of Michigan,* 1977; 154:1-55.

—Uribe, MCA; Velasco, SR; Guillette, LJ Jr; Estrada, EF:
Oviductal histology of the lizard *Ctenosaura pectinata. Copeia,* 1988: 1035-1042.

—**Uribe, MCA; Mendex Omana, ME; Gonzalez Quintero, JE; Guillette, Jr:**
Seasonal variation in ovarian histology of the viviparous lizard *Sceloporus torquatus torquatus. J Morphol,* 1995; 226:103-119.

—**Uribe, MCA; Portales, GL; Guillette, LJ JR:**
Ovarian folliculogenesis in the oviparous Mexican lizard *Ctenosaura pectinata. J Morphol,* 1996, 226: 103-119.

—**Van Wyk, JJ; Lund PK:**
Autocrine and paracrine effects of the somatomedins/insulin-like growth factors. In, Molecular and Cellular Biology of Insulin-like Growth Factors and Their Receptors. D LeRoith; MK Raizada (Eds). Plenum Press, New York, 1989, pp. 5-24.

—**Vitt, LJ; Blackburn DG:**
Reproduction in the lizard *Mabuya heathi* (Scincidae): a commentary on viviparity in New World *Mabuya. Can J Zool,* 1983; 61:2798-2806.

—**Weekes, HC:**
Placentation and other phenomena in the scincid lizard *Lygosoma (hinulia) quoyi. Proc Linnean Soc NSW,* 1927; 52:499-554.

—**Weekes, HC:**
On the distribution, habitat and reproductive habits of certain European and Australian snakes and lizards with particular regard to their adaptation of viviparity. *Proc Linn Soc NSW,* 1933; 58:270-274.

—**Weekes, HC:**
A review of placentation among reptiles, with particular regard to the function and evolution of the placenta. *Proc Zool Soc Lond.* 1935:625-645.

—**Wingfield, JC; Kenagy GJ:**
Natural regulation of reproductive cycles. In, Vertebrate Endocrinology: Fundamentals and Biomedical Implications. Vol. 4, Part B, Reproduction, KT Pang; MP Schreibman (Eds). Academic Press, San Diego, 1986, pp. 181-241.

—**Xavier, F; Gavaud J:**
Oviparity-viviparity continuum in reptiles. Physiological characteristics and relation with environment. In, Endocrine Regulation as Adaptive Mechanisms to the Environment, I Assenmacher; J Boissin (Eds.) Editions du CNRS, Paris, 1986, pp. 79-93

—**Yaron, Z:**
Reptilian placentation and gestation: structure, function and endocrine control. In, Biology of the Reptilia, Vol. 15, C Gans; F Billett (Eds.), 1985, pp. 527-603.

—**Yeh, J; Lee GY; Anderson E:**
Presence of transforming growth factor-alpha messenger ribonucleic acid (mRNA) and absence of epidermal growth factor mRNA in rat ovarian granulosa cells, and the effects of these factors on steroidogenesis in vitro. *Biol Reprod,* 1993; 48:1071-1081.

—**Yntema, CL:**
Characteristics of gonads and oviducts in hatchlings and young of *Chelydra serpentina* resulting from three incubation temperatures. *J Morphol,* 1981; 167:297-304.

EGG PHYSIOLOGY AND BIOLOGY

Michael B. Thompson Ph.D.,
Senior Lecturer, School of Biological Sciences (A08),
and Wildlife Research Institute
University of Sydney, NSW 2006, AUSTRALIA

*Dr Thompson graduated with a Ph.D. from the University of Adelaide in South Australia in 1983. The topic of his Ph.D. research was the physiology of eggs of the chelid tortoise, **Emydura macquarii**. Subsequently, he spent three years at Victoria University of Wellington, New Zealand, studying the egg physiology and nesting ecology of the tuatara, **Sphenodon punctatus**. His next position as the Archie Carr Postdoctoral Fellow at the University of Florida gave him the opportunity to study the physiology of eggs of alligators, as well as of freshwater and marine turtles. Dr Thompson has been at the University of Sydney since 1989, during which time he has studied the eggs, embryos and development of numerous species of lizards and snakes.*

INTRODUCTION

The egg is arguably the most vulnerable stage of the life cycle of an oviparous reptile. The egg lacks both mobility and, in most species, protection provided by the parents. With no parental incubation in most species (e.g. Congdon et al, 1983), all the requirements for successful incubation must be provided by the mother in the form of an appropriate nest. Once laid, reptilian embryos must be able to sustain any fluctuations in environmental conditions within the nest, or they will die. The requirements for successful incubation could limit the distribution of species of reptiles (Muth, 1980).

Clearly, the mother must construct a nest that is well concealed from predators. However, no matter where the nest is located, there are likely to be fluctuations in the nest environment that will elicit developmental and/or physiological responses from the developing embryo. These responses may affect the phenotype of the hatchling (Hotaling et al, 1985; GC Packard and Packard, 1988). Environmental parameters most likely to influence the physiology and development of embryos include:
—temperature
—availability of water
—concentrations of respiratory gases

Additionally, the presence and orientation of other eggs in the clutch may influence the conditions of incubation and hatching (Hotaling et al, 1985; Thompson, 1989).

Tuatara, *Sphenodon punctatus*. Photo by R. T. Zappalorti.

Reptile egg shells serve several functions. They:
—protect eggs from mechanical damage
—protect eggs from invasion by micro-organisms
—provide mineral nutrients in some species
—act as a barrier to gas and water exchanges

This chapter reviews the influence of temperature, water, gases and clutch mates on incubation of eggs of reptiles. The discussions examine the conditions experienced by eggs in the field, and also examine incubation in controlled laboratory conditions. These discussions then make inferences about the best artificial incubation practices.

STRUCTURE OF THE EGGS AND EMBRYOS

The size, shape, and shells of reptilian eggs vary greatly (Fig. 1). The following list shows a comparison of sizes between three reptilian species. You can see that the difference in size between the gecko and python eggs can be as great as a factor of 4000.

gecko, *Lygodactylus klugei* - 72 mg - (Vitt, 1986)
some species of *Crocodylus* and Komodo dragons- 100 g - (Ferguson, 1985)
Python molurus - 300 g - (van Mierop & Barnard, 1976)

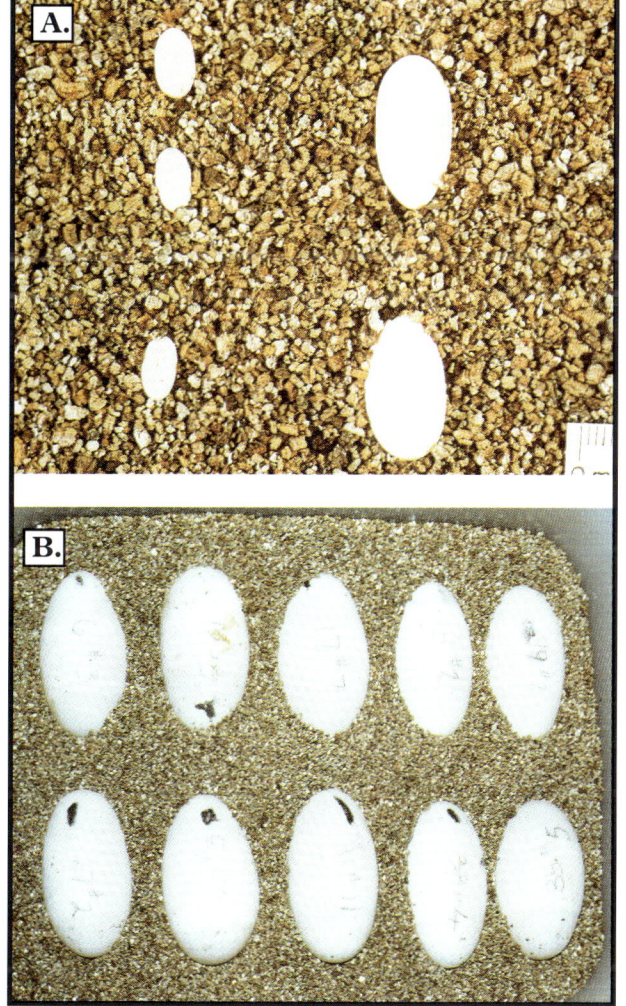

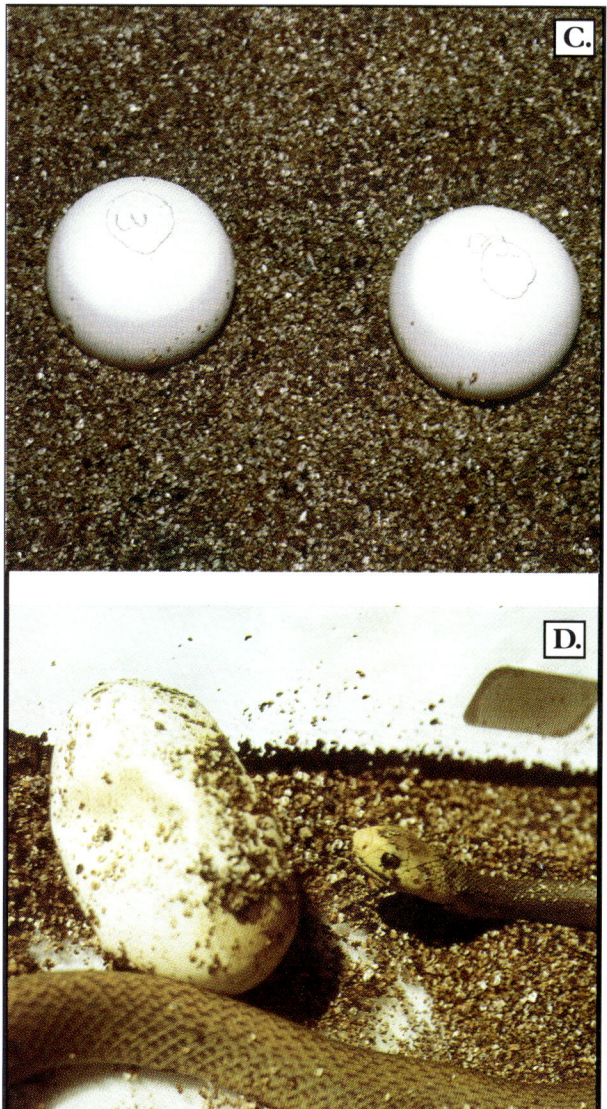

Figure 1.
Reptilian eggs vary considerably in shape and size. A. Small (100 mg) eggs of the skink *Menetia greyii* alongside the larger (1000 mg) eggs of another skink, *Ctenotus robustus*. These eggs are of similar shape. B. Developing eggs (100 g) of the American alligator, *Alligator mississippiensis*. Note the opaque banding on the surface, which is indicative of normal development. C. Spherical eggs (40 g) of the sea turtle, *Caretta caretta*. Turtle eggs also develop an opaque patch, clearly visible on the upper surface of these eggs. The pencilled circle on the eggs represents the extent of the white patch 24 hours earlier. D. Snake eggs, such as of this taipan (*Oxyuranus scutellatus*), tend to be more elongate than other reptilian eggs.

Reptilian egg shapes vary from being almost spherical to extremely elongate. They also vary in rigidity, calcium carbonate composition, and permeability. At one extreme, shells can be rigid and composed predominantly of calcium carbonate,

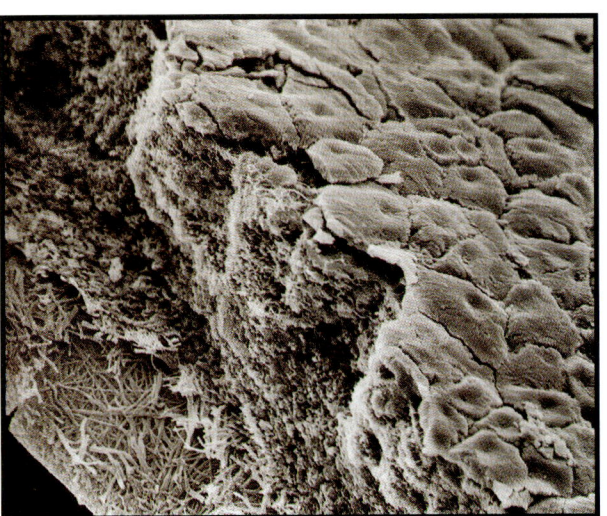

African Slender-snouted Crocodile, *Crocodylus cataphractus*, hatching. Photo by Paul Freed.

Figure 2.
Scanning electron micrograph of eggshell of tuatara, *Sphenodon punctatus*. The outside (right) of the shell is composed predominantly of calcium carbonate, which overlies fibrous membranes (left). Reptilian eggs vary in the relative developments of the calcareous and fibrous components of the shell.

with very low rates of water vapour exchange. At the other extreme, shells can be flexible (often called pliable or parchment-shelled) with little or no calcium carbonate in them (Fig. 2). Flexible-shelled eggs of turtles have more calcium carbonate than flexible-shelled eggs of squamates, but less than the hard-shelled eggs of squamates. (MJ Packard and DeMarco, 1991)

The type of shell strongly influences the rates of water loss and uptake, and flexible-shelled eggs desiccate rapidly in dry environments. (G.C. Packard et al, 1979a) The rigid-shelled eggs of many geckos are laid in relatively exposed, dry environments, such as under loose bark and crevices. Without low rates of water vapour conductance, they would desiccate rapidly. In contrast, most reptiles deposit their eggs in some kind of buried nest where humidities are high. Shells with high conductances do not suffer desiccation in such conditions, and high conductances probably enhance the water uptake by these eggs. All crocodilians and many turtle species deposit rigid-shelled eggs in buried nests. (G.C. Parkcard et al, 1979a) Rigid-shelled eggs that are

Indian Python, *Python molurus molurus*. Photo by Paul Freed.

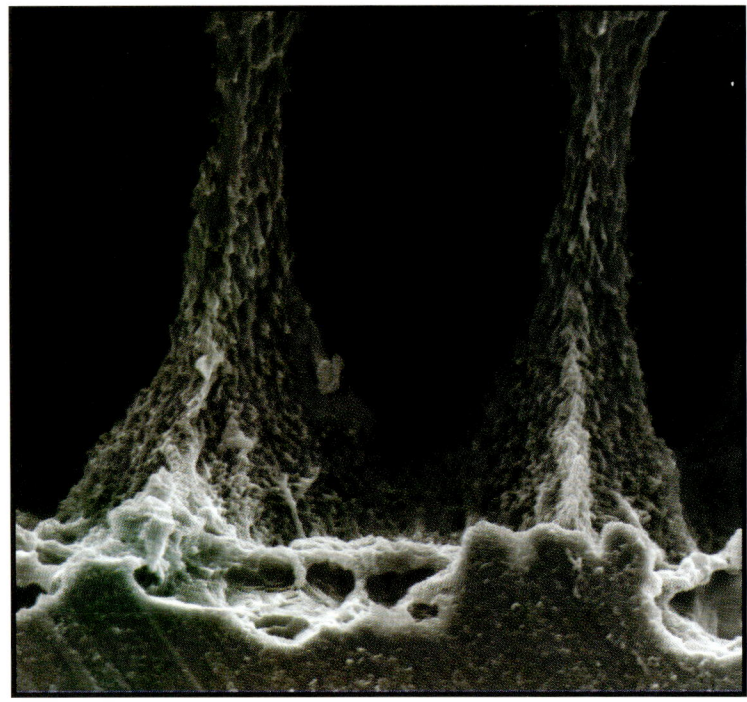

Figure 3.
A scanning electron micrograph of a resin cast of two adjacent pores through the eggshell of the chelid tortoise, *Emydura macquarri*. Pores provide an avenue of gas exchange in reptilian eggs with calcareous shells. The pores are about 20 mm at their narrowest.

ous layer of calcium carbonate over the surface; the major part of the shell is the porous, fibrous membranes. (M.J. Packard et al 1982a)

Gas exchange through the shell is necessary for proper development of the embryo. As the embryo grows, its demand for oxygen increases (Fig. 4). It is important that the shell conductance is high enough to supply that demand. If the pores become blocked—for example by liquid water on the surface of the egg—then the embryo can asphyxiate. Topical infections of fungi or bacteria may restrict gas exchange; however, that phenomenon has not been studied in detail.

When eggs are first laid, the pores in eggshells contain fluid. That fluid must be removed during development to allow adequate gas exchange. In some species, drying of the whole shell occurs more or less simultaneously. However, in crocodilians and many turtles with rigid shells, the pores dry regionally in advance of the requirements of the embryo (Thompson, 1985).

buried tend to have lower shell conductances than soft-shelled eggs. However, the conductances of rigid-shelled eggs are still high compared to avian eggs that incubate in open nests. Reptilian eggs would desiccate if incubated in open nests. (GC Packard et al, 1979a, MJ Packard et al, 1982a, Deeming and Thompson, 1991).

Despite the differences in egg size, shape, and shell structure, there are some generalisations that can be made about eggs:
—The shell and shell membranes are laid down after fertilisation, which is internal in all reptiles.
—The egg of all species contains everything that is required by the developing embryo except oxygen and, in some cases, water (Vleck, 1991; Vleck and Hoyt, 1991).
—The eggshell must be porous.

The only other material exchange with the environment is the egg's excretion of carbon dioxide. Shells must protect the developing embryo, yet be porous enough to allow the necessary exchange of gasses and liquids. In rigid-shelled eggs, there are usually discrete pores through the calcareous shell to allow exchange of gases (Fig. 3). Underlying the calcareous shell are a series of shell membranes composed predominantly of fibres which contain mucopolysaccharides (sometimes referred to as proteinaceous fibres). The mucopolysaccharides provide a mesh structure through which gases can easily pass. Flexible-shelled eggs often do not have a continu-

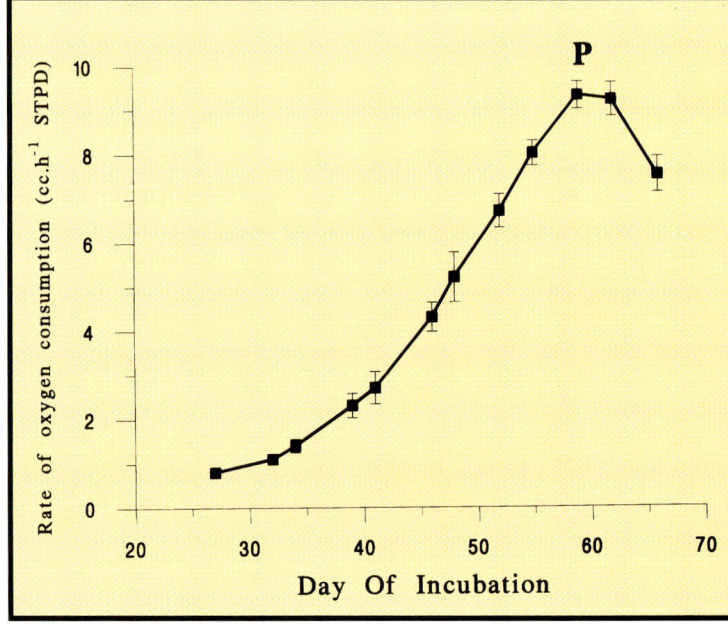

Figure 4.
Rate of oxygen consumption (measured throughout incubation) of six eggs of the American alligator, *Alligator mississippiensis*. The rate increases as the embryo grows, and reaches a peak (P) prior to hatching. The fall in the rate of oxygen consumption between P and hatching is a variable period of embryonic quiescence that allows less developed embryos to catch up to older sibs, so that hatching can occur synchronously.

92

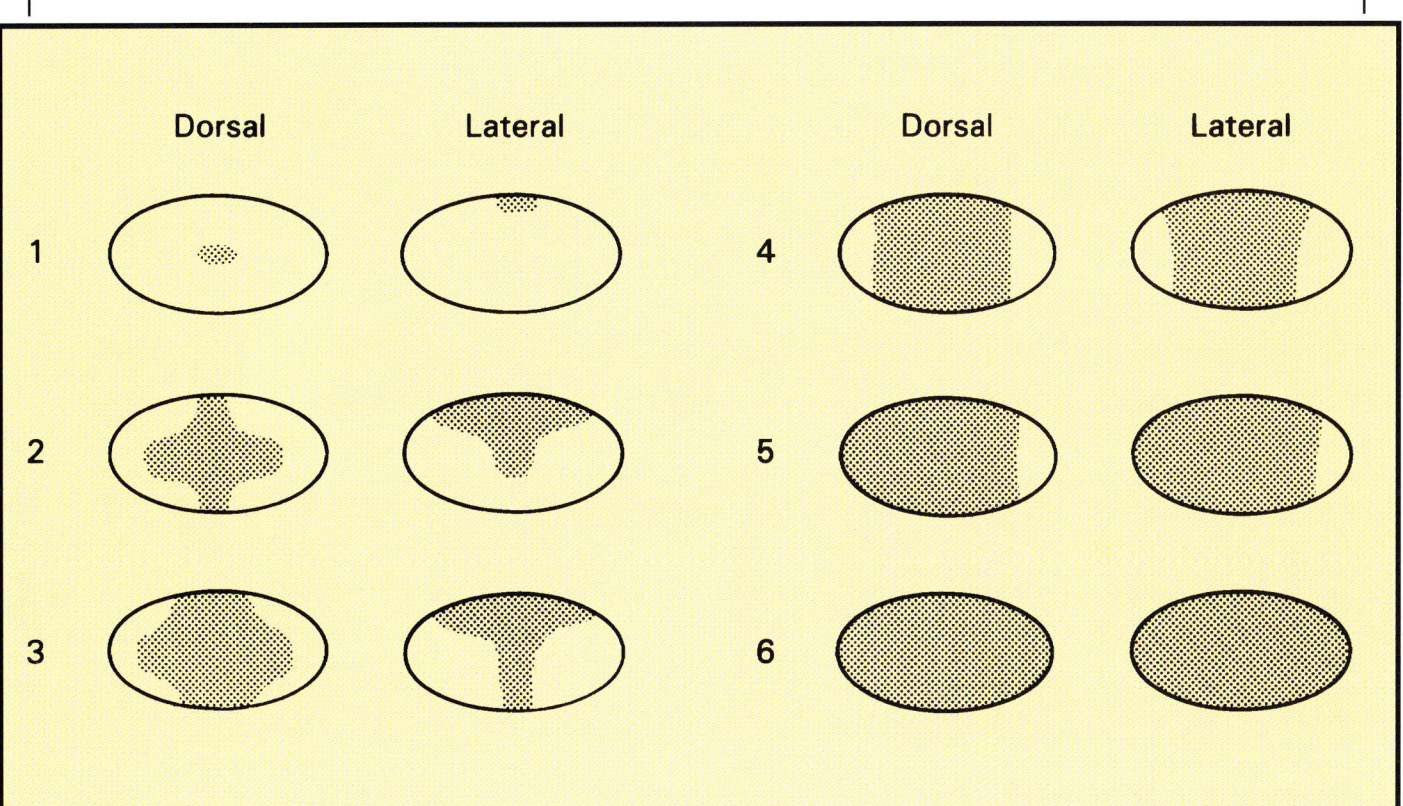

| Dorsal | Lateral | | Dorsal | Lateral |

Figure 5.
Development of opaque, white patches in eggshells of turtles and crocodiles result from regional drying of the shell. The pattern illustrated is for the chelid tortoise, *Emydura macquarri*. The small, opaque, white patch develops on the top of the egg (1) within 30 h of oviposition. Development proceeds to stage 4 in 5-10 days of a 48-day incubation at 30 C. In some eggs, white-patch development stops at stage 4; in others it proceeds to stages 5 or 6. (Redrawn from Thompson, 1985).

At oviposition, three eggs usually appear to be translucent in colour. In fertile eggs, an opaque white patch appears where the shell begins to dry on the embryonic surface of the egg, usually within 12-48 hours (Thompson, 1985). In leatherback turtles, the white patch may take up to six days to appear (Chan, 1989). That white patch expands throughout development to produce the characteristic banding pattern of crocodilian eggs and the saddle or patch pattern of turtle eggs (Figs. 1, 5). It is probably advantageous for the shell to become regionalized for water and gas exchange because gas exchange occurs best through air-filled pores, and water exchange occurs best through fluid-filled pores.

EMBRYONIC DEVELOPMENT

This section describes factors that affect embryonic development, including oviposition, incubation substrate, temperature, hydration, assistance at hatching, and so on.

EMBRYONIC STAGE AT OVIPOSITION AND EXTRA-EMBRYONIC MEMBRANES

The stage of development of embryos when eggs are oviposited varies among groups. In turtles, the embryos develop to the stage of mid to late gastrulation before oviposition. At this point, development is arrested and does not recommence until after oviposition (Risley, 1944; Ewert, 1985; Miller, 1985). The trigger for restarting the development of the embryo is not definitely known. However hypoxia may be involved in the arrest of development at gastrulation (Risley, 1944; Lynn and von Brand, 1945; Vleck and Hoyt, 1991). After oviposition, the sudden availability of oxygen outside the mother may be a factor in restarting the embryonic development.

The phenomenon of developmental arrest and its release at oviposition has been studied experimentally in turtles. Many turtles will not oviposit unless given proper conditions to do so. Consequently, it can be useful to house gravid turtles in conditions not suitable for oviposition, until a suitable date arrives at which to begin incubation. When oviposition of several females occurs on the same day, all eggs will begin developing on the same day. This greatly enhances the management of incubation. Detailed descriptions of embryonic stages in turtles are provided by Yntema (1968), Ewert (1985) and Miller (1985).

Like turtles, eggs of tuatara probably are laid at gastrulation. However, the recovery of more advanced embryos from the oviducts of a dead female (Thomas, 1890) suggests that development of a tuatara embryos are not arrested in the oviducts as it is in turtles (Moffat, 1985). However, embryos beyond late grastulation can be recovered from turtles under unusual circumstances, and the wide range of embryonic stages observed within one dead female tuatara (Thomas, 1890) casts doubt on the report. Given the extraordinarily long period between fertilisation and oviposition in tuatara (Cree et al, 1991), the possibility of preovipositional arrest should be investigated more closely.

Crocodilians appear not to have developmental arrest. They oviposit at more or less the same embryonic stage when the embryo has 9-20 pairs of somites (Ferguson, 1985). There is scant information about preovipositional development in crocodilians, but post-ovipositional embryological stages have been described (Webb et al, 1983a; Ferguson, 1985). Since not all females in a population of crocodilians ovulate simultaneously, oviposition and hatching dates will vary. Some species may produce more than one clutch in a season, also. Artificial incubation of eggs of different ages together should be carefully considered (see "Clutch mates" below).

Generalizations about developmental stage at oviposition in squamates is difficult because of the large range of reproductive modes in this group. Reproductive modes vary from oviposition at early embryonic stages to a range of modes of viviparity. No preovipositional arrest is known in squamates. This chapter discusses only oviparous squamate species.

There are different staging schemes for embryonic lizards and snakes. For lizards, the scheme of Dufaure and Hubert (1961), a full translation of which is provided by Porter (1972), is commonly used as the standard for lizard embryology. A comparison of the scheme for tuatara (Dendy, 1899) and lizards (Dufaure and Hubert, 1961) is given by Moffat (1985). Most lizard eggs are laid when the embryos are at approximately stage 30 (Fig. 6) of the scheme of Dufaure and Hubert (1961). Some may be laid as early as stage 27 (or exceptionally at stage 24, *Sceloporus woodi*) (DeMarco, 1992) but development from one stage to the next is rapid early in development, so there is little time difference between stages 27 and 30. These embryos are small, but well developed, with blood circulation and the initiation of limb buds.

Although the staging schemes are different, the earliest stage of development at oviposition is similar in snakes, lizards, and crocodilians with 9-30 somites. All squamates and crocodilians with 9-30 somites are more advanced than tuatara and turtles at gastrulation at the time of oviposition. Eggs of some lizards (e.g. *Chamaeleo lateralis*) may be laid at gastrulation, also.

Figure 6.
Photo of stage 29/30 *Eumeces laticeps*. Most oviparous lizards oviposit when embryos are at, or close to, stage 30 of the embryonic staging scheme of Dufaure and Hubert (1961). (Photo by JR Stewart)

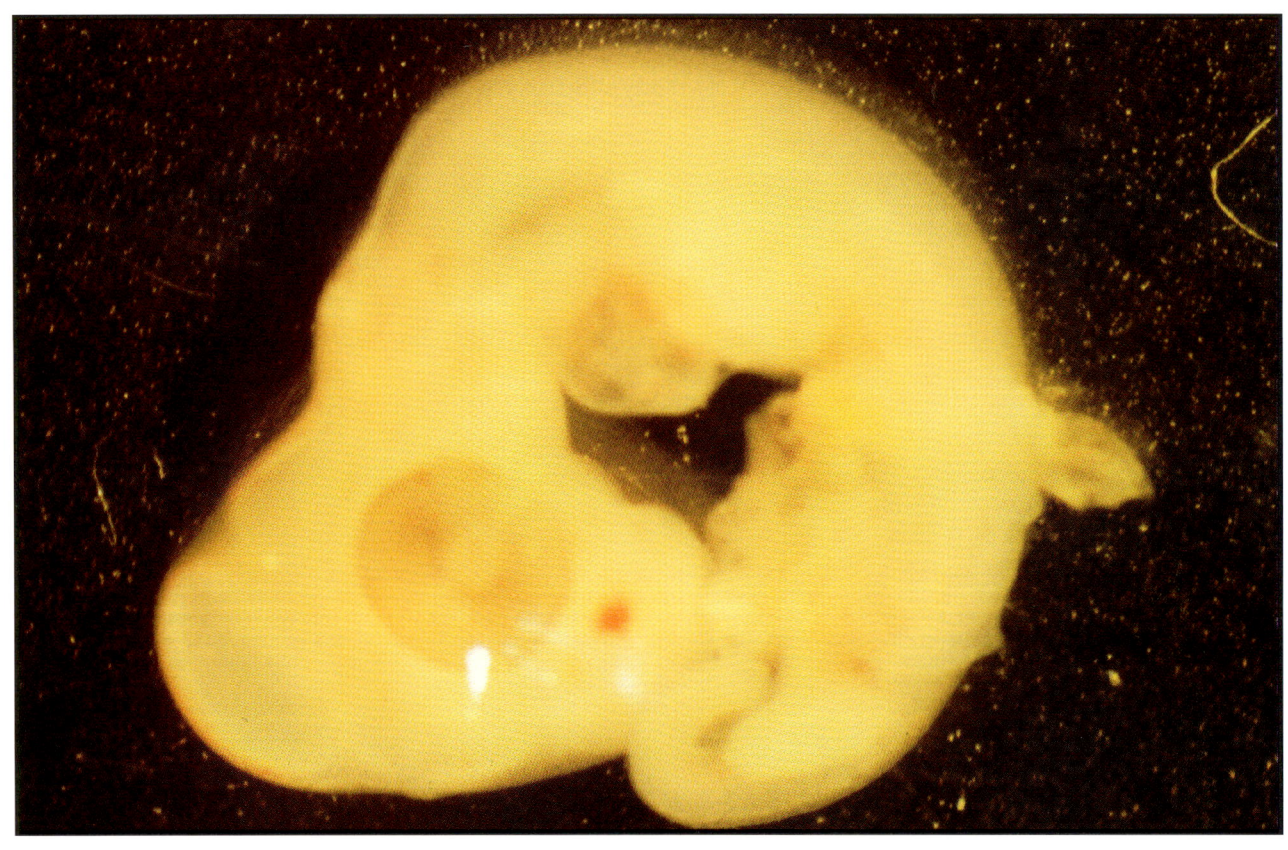

Jewelled Chameleon, *Chamaeleo lateralis*. Photo by R.D. Bartlett.

For about a third of the incubation after oviposition, growth of embryos laid at early embryonic stages is slow. This is a time of embryonic differentiation. Then, about a third of the way through development, embryonic growth rate and oxygen demand increase rapidly. Some chelonian, and crocodilian, lizard and tuatura embryos exhibit temperature-dependent sex determination. For these embryos, this stage of increased organogenesis and growth is also the stage at which the sex of the embryo is determined.

Some species of lizards and snakes (such as *Saiphos equalis, Lerista bougainvillii, Sceloporus scalaris,* and *Sceloporus aeneus;* and *Opheodrys vernalis* and *Typhlops bibroni*) retain eggs until later stages of embryonic development. For those species, incubation periods are considerably shortened, to ten days or less.

Many species of reptiles, especially among turtles and lizards, undergo some form of post-ovipositional arrest in embryonic development. This arrest can take one of three forms:

—cold torpor, as in the tuatara, *Sphenodon punctatus,* and in some snakes and lizards (Hubert, 1985),

—diapause in many turtles and chameleon lizards (Ewert, 1991)

—delayed hatching, as in the pignosed turtles, *Carettochelys insculpta,* (Webb et al, 1986) as well as other turtles and perhaps monitor lizards (Ewert, 1991).

Cold torpor is simply slowed or halted development at low temperatures, which can occur in natural nests of some species. Delayed hatching results in decreased metabolism late in development, and it is a mechanism to facilitate synchronous hatching (Fig. 4) or a suitable environment for the hatchlings.

Diapause manifests itself as a delayed initiation of development after oviposition. Complex combinations of temperatures, usually an extended (10+ days) chill, but also occasionally a warm period, are required to release diapause. Failure to release diapause will ultimately result in the death of the embryo (Ewert, 1991) . Complex diapause systems may operate in the turtle family Chelidae, especially in *Chelodina expansa* and *C. rugosa,* which probably is the only reptile to oviposit underwater. (Kennett et al, 1993)

INFLUENCE OF TEMPERATURE

Temperature probably has the most profound effects on development of reptilian embryos. Temperature affects:

—rates of growth and thus, incubation periods
—sex of offspring in many reptiles
—scalation
—body size and proportions
—incubation success (high temperatures and low temperatures may be lethal)
—post-hatching growth and behaviour (in some species)

Most artificial incubation regimes are at one constant temperature, whereas, in the field, few form of temperature fluctuation throughout incubation, even those eggs incubating in fairly stable thermal environments. Not surprisingly, some reptiles are much more sensitive to fluctuations in temperature than others; acceptable ranges of incubation temperatures vary among species. These differences reflect the differences in the environments in which natural incubation normally occurs.

Few studies have assessed the influence of fluctuating incubation temperatures compared to constant ones, but those few suggest a more complex relationship between temperature and incubation than the constant temperature studies indicate (e.g.

Pig-nosed Turtle, *Carettochelys insculpta*. Photo by K. H. Switak.

eggs incubate in constant temperatures. There may be two exceptions in which reptiles eggs are incubated in the field at fairly constant temperatures (Fig. 7): deep nests of sea turtles (Hendrickson, 1958), and brooded eggs of pythons (Pope, 1961; Hutchison et al, 1966; van Mierop and Barnard, 1976). However, in general, temperatures vary in the environment both during the day and seasonally. The eggs of most reptiles experience some

Georges et al, 1994). More research is needed on the affects of daily fluctuations in incubation temperatures.

SEX DETERMINATION

The remarkable discovery that incubation temperature can influence the sex of a reptile was made in 1966 by Charnier (1966) in the dragon lizard, *Agama agama*. There were follow-up studies con-

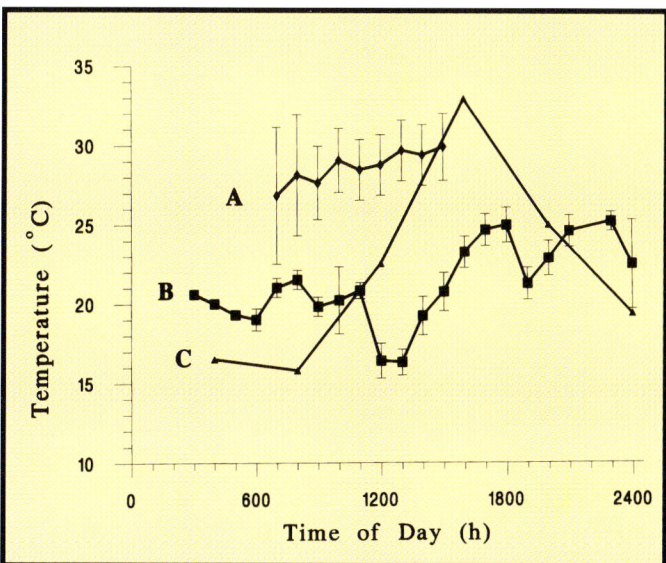

Figure 7.
In nests of reptiles, temperatures vary throughout the day, and also vary with changes in cloud cover. A. Data for five nests of the American alligator (*Alligaor mississippiensis*) on Paynes Praire, Florida, from dawn to late afternoon. B. Mean temperatures in six nests of the chelid tortoise, *Emydura macquarri*, hourly for 24 hours (from Thompson, 1988). Note the effect of clouds in the middle of the day. C. Temperature at the top of a clutch of tuatara (*Sphenodon punctatus*) eggs on Stephens Island, New Zealand, in summer (from Thompson et al., 1996).

Common Agama, *Agama agama*. Photo by Paul Freed.

ducted on turtles and lizards which were published in French. However, it was not until the mid-1970s that temperature-dependent sex determination (TSD) became known in the English literature (Yntema, 1976). Since then, the occurrence of TSD has been explored in many species of reptiles. It is likely that all crocodilians, most turtles,

tuatara, some lizards, and probably no snakes exhibit TSD. The presence of heteromorphically different sex chromosomes appears to be mutually exclusive with TSD.

TSD is not a simple phenomenon. In most species, an incubation temperature at the warm end of the successful range will result in production of hatchlings exclusively of one sex. Cool temperatures will result in production of hatchling with the other sex (Fig. 8). The intermediate temperature that re-

Figure 8.
Different patterns of temperature-dependent sex determination occur in different reptiles. In Type I, which occurs in turtles and is here represented by the sea turtle, *Caretta caretta*, females are produced at warm temperatures and males at cool temperatures. Type II, which is exhibited by some crocodilians and lizards (here represented by data for *Alligator mississippiensis*), produces males at warm temperatures and females at cool temperatures. Type III, which occurs in some turtles, some crocodilians, and some lizards, has two threshold temperatures. In Type III, females are produced at the extremes, and males at intermediate temperatures. (Figure based on Deeming and Ferguson, 1991)

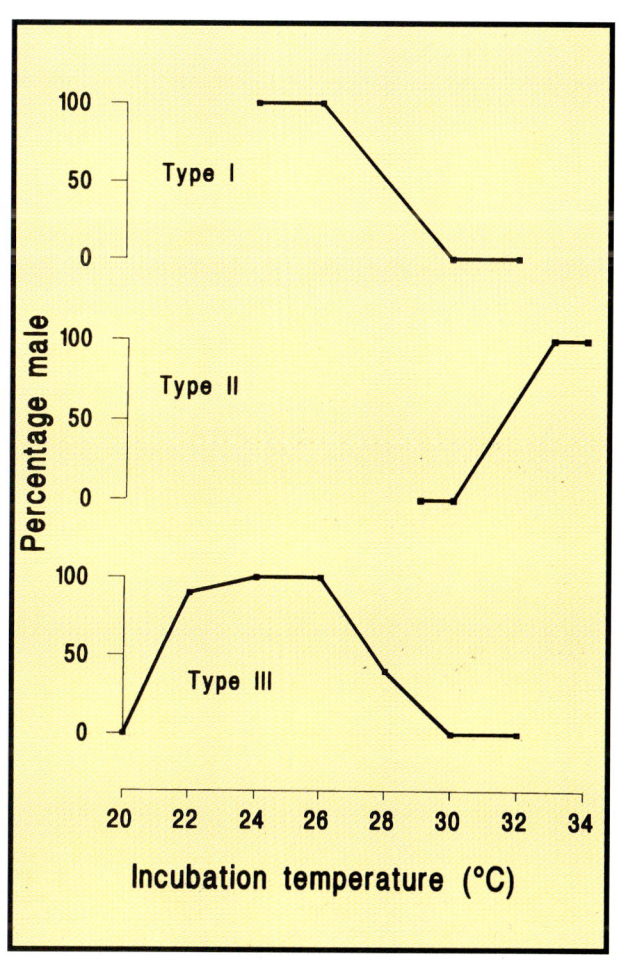

sults in males and females in equal proportions is called the threshold or pivotal temperature.

Some species have a second, lower threshold temperature (Type III). In turtles with TSD, the highest temperatures produce females, and lower temperatures produce males (Type I and III; Bull, 1980; Ewert and Nelson, 1991; Deeming and Ferguson, 1991a). In those species with a second threshold temperature, incubation below that threshold produces females again (Type III; Ewert and Nelson, 1991). In contrast to turtles, high temperatures produce males, and lower temperatures result in females in most crocodilians and lizards with TSD, (Type II; Bull, 1980). There may, however, be exceptions to this pattern in some crocodiles and lizards.

Earlier reports that water potentials during incubation influence sex (Paukstis et al, 1986) have subsequently been shown to be erroneous, and it now seems unlikely that water potentials could generally influence sex determination. However, water potential may influence egg temperature in a small way (Gutzke et al, 1987; Kam and Ackerman, 1990). Because of this, water potential could possibly influence the sex ratios of hatchlings when eggs are incubated close to the threshold temperature.

BODY PROPORTIONS

Water fluxes are influenced by water potentials and temperatures experienced by eggs during incubation. Water fluxes can influence the size and body proportions of young turtles and snakes (Miller et al, 1987; xxxx et al, 1987). Incubation temperature alone can influence the gross body proportions of hatchling tuatara by producing different body-length to tail-length ratios (Thompson, unpubl. data). Incubation temperature alone can also influence the number of vertebrae in the viviparous snake, *Nerodia fasciata* (Osgood, 1978). It is not known how common this phenomenon is or what its biological meaning is (if there is such a meaning).

SCALATION AND PIGMENTATION

Unusually cold or unusually hot periods during embryonic development may influence the final scalation of some species of snakes (e.g. Osgood, 1978) . Currently, the mechanism for development of these anomalies is not known, nor is the possible influence of temperature on post-hatching success of "abnormal" individuals.

In a similar way, incubation temperature may influence the pattern of pigmentation on hatchling alligators, turtles, and pythons. A possible mecha-

Southern Water Snake, *Nerodia fasciata*. Photo by R. D. Bartlett.

nism to explain this phenomenon has been proposed for alligators (Murray et al, 1990; Deeming and Ferguson, 1991a). The phenomenon probably stems from different rates of growth, which result in the embryos being different sizes when pigmentation and pattern develop (Murray et al, 1990). The pigmentation patterns probably remain unaltered during post hatching growth.

ARTIFICIAL INCUBATION.

When setting up artificial incubation, the most appropriate temperature for incubation is possibly also the most important, yet easiest condition to select and control. This is true especially if you use a constant-temperature incuabation regime. Constant temperature incubation works well in all groups of reptile. You can use a constant-temperature regime whenever there is no special need to provide fluctuating incubation temperatures. Before setting up the incubation regime, ask the following two questions:

1. What is the likely successful temperature range over which the eggs can be successfully incubated?
2. Does the species have TSD?

Many species have fairly narrow ranges of temperature for successful incubation at constant temperatures; those temperatures vary among species. A good guide to the range of suitable temperatures is the natural environment in which the species nests. For example, sea turtles and most crocodilians occur in tropical locations. Both types of reptiles construct nests that provide fairly even temperatures throughout incubation. The temperature range for incubation of some sea turtles is 25°C - 33°C, with the temperature centering around 30°C (Packard and Packard, 1988). The narrow range of temperatures over which tuatara can be incubated centers around 20°C (Thompson, 1990). Provision of 30 C incubation temperatures for tuatara or 20°C for sea turtles would be fatal. For some species, the temperature range is even more narrow: the lizard, *Iguana iguana*, can sustain a range of only 2°C either side of 30°C (Licht and Moberly, 1965).]

Both sea turtles and tuatara exhibit TSD. For conservation purposes, both groups are subjected to large-scale artificial incubation. Consequently, the selection of more than one appropriate incubation temperature is important to the management of these species. The need to provide different incubation temperatures to produce offspring of both sexes will result in different incubation times.

Changes in the incubation temperature can significantly change the incubation period. For example, in tuatara, low temperatures result in very much slowed or arrested development—cool torpor (Ewert, 1991). Tuatara incubated at 22 C can hatch three months earlier than tuatara incubated at 20 C (Thompson, 1990). Fortunately, many species are more rubust to temperature fluctuations than sea turtles and tuatara. Those other species can be incubated over much wider ranges of incubation temperatures. Even tuatara can sustain temperatures in natural nests as high as 32 C for short periods of time although exposure to temperatures above 25 C for extended periods would be fatal (Thompson et al, 1996).

WATER RELATIONS

Most water exchange in reptilian eggs probably occurs in the vapour phase. However, liquid water exchange can and probably does occur in favorable circumstances (Thompson, 1987; GC Packard, 1991). Unlike eggs of birds,

Figure 9.

Mass of eggs of snapping turtle (*Chelydra serpentina*) through incubation. Eggs were incubated in two positions (half buried in, and suspended above) of wet (-150 kPa), intermediate (-375 kPa), and dry (-850 kPa) subtrata. (Redrawn from GC Packard and Packard, 1984)

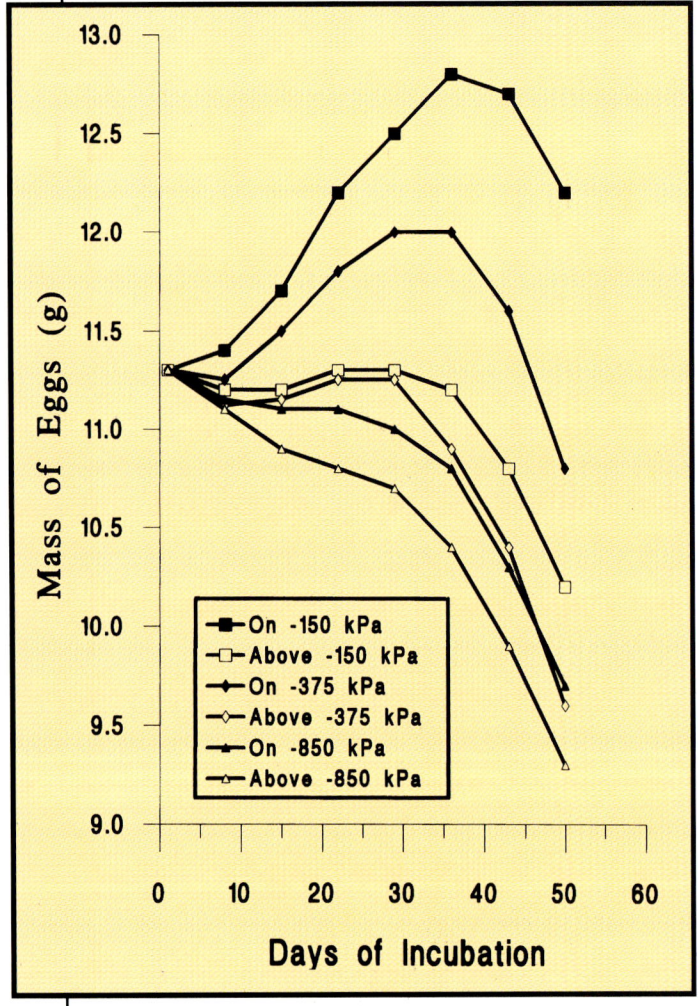

reptilian eggs can—and many probably must—take up water during development (Fig. 9; Vleck, 1991). However, too much water can drown embryos either by blocking the pores in the eggshell and asphyxiating the embryo, or possibly by upsetting some internal, homeostatic mechanism in the eggs. When a gravid female cannot

Figure 10.
Even reptilian eggs with rigid shells can absorb water if the shell cracks. Such cracking will not compromise the viability of the egg, as long as the underlying membranes remain intact. This egg is from an Australian chelid tortoise in the genus *Emydura*.

locate a nest with appropriate water-potential characteristics, the female may retain her eggs until after rainfall (Stamps, 1976; Thompson, 1983). Some female squamates may manipulate the water exchanges of their eggs after nesting by brooding the clutch.

There has been considerable research on the water relations of reptilian eggs, especially of turtles. However, to some extent, water relations of the eggs of all major reptilian fossils have been studied. The general conclusions from these studies suggest that neonates derived from rigid-shelled eggs (e.g. *Trionyx, Emydura, Alligator, Crocodylus*) are little influenced by water exchanges during incubation, as long as the eggs do not drown or desiccate (e.g. Leshem and Dmi'el, 1986). Indeed, there is no difference in hatchling size whether or not the eggs absorb or lose water. For eggs of rigid-shelled species, water absorption can occur only if the shell cracks (Fig. 10).

In contrast, eggs and neonates of most species with flexible-shelled eggs (e.g. most lizards, some turtles, some snakes) are greatly influenced by water availability during incubation (MJ Packard et al, 1980; GC Packard, 1991). Flexible-shelled eggs usually absorb water and swell during incubation. The amount of water, and speed with which it is taken up, will be influenced by two factors:

—the water potential of the substratum

—the area of surface contact the eggs has with the substratum (Fig. 9)

Flexible-shelled eggs on wetter substrates generally take up more water than those on drier substrates (Fig. 9). For many species, eggs on wetter substrates produce larger neonates that have more vigorous locomotor performance. It is possible that moister incubation media makes it easier for the embryo to harvest calcium and magnesium from the eggshell. However, incubation takes longer in wetter media, and the young emerge from such wetter media with less residual yolk (Miller et al, 1987; GC Packard, 1991). In some species (such as *Iguana iguana*) (Werner, 1988) there may be an intermediate optimal water potential for incubation. One of the exceptions to the relationship between wetter substrates and larger neonates is the *Coluber constrictor* (G.C. Packard and Packard, 1987). Like some other species with flexible-shelled eggs, *Coluber constrictor* eggs take up more water in moister environments, but the size of the neonates is not influenced by that water uptake.

Eastern Spiny Softshell, *Trionyx spinifera spinifera*. **Photo by Aaron Norman.**

In artificial situations, where hatchlings will be provided with food and shelter from the day of hatching, it is probably better to incubate eggs in moister, rather than drier, conditions. However, if conditions are likely to be difficult in the first few months of life, it may be better to deliberately produce smaller young with larger yolk reserves. You can do this by incubating the eggs in drier conditions. Internalised yolk provides energy, but little

Northern Black Racer, *Coluber constrictor constrictor*, **with eggs. Photo by R. T. Zappalorti.**

for growth of hatchling reptiles (Whitehead, 1990). Many flexible-shelled eggs will double, or even treble, their mass by the uptake of water during incubation. Because of this, incubation media that are too wet can result in the death of the embryo. In nature, death due to nest-flooding and excessive uptake of water is common.

The maximum amount of water that can be taken up varies among species, but the upper limit measured for tuatara is an approximate trebling of weight (Thompson, 1990) and may be slightly more in some lizards (Vleck, 1991; Vleck and Hoyt, 1991). It is likely to be less for many species with flexible-shelled eggs, and it is probably less for all species with rigid-shelled eggs.

Smaller eggs are more likely to have greater proportional water fluxes than large eggs (Tracy and Snell, 1985; Gutzke and Packard, 1987). You can periodically weigh eggs to get an indication of egg health. Often the first outward sign of egg death in flexible-shelled eggs is the sudden collapse of the egg. Eggs in the field may undergo net uptake and loss of water at different times of the incubation. Indeed, water potentials in field nests may fluctuate considerably. However, such resilience to fluctuations in hydric conditions means that it is easy to manipulate water uptake of eggs during artificial incubation. If eggs lose weight, or if they are taking water up only slowly, you can place them in wetter media until they recover. Conversely, you can place them in drier media to allow them to lose water if they are gaining too much.

During incubation, flexible-shelled eggs are usually in positive water balance in moist substrata for the first half to three-quarters or so of incubation. At that point, their weight may begin to fall (Fig. 9). The loss of water is probably associated with a small but significant rise in egg temperature associated with increased metabolism of the growing embryo. Thus, slow collapse of eggs in the final phases of incubation should not be of major concern in most—but not all (e.g. *Anolis*, Andrews and Sexton, 1981)—species.

There has been no study of the influence of hydration during incubation on the behaviour and physiology of young growing reptiles other than locomotion. However, in turtles, post-hatching growth may not be influenced by moisture exposure of the egg during incubation (Bobyn and Brooks, 1994). However, post-hatching survivorship of lizards is greater in the wild for eggs incubated in moist—rather than dry—substrates (Vleck, 1988).

INCUBATION SUBSTRATES

Although selecting the temperature for artificial incubation is a relatively easy decision, selecting the most appropriate hydric condition for artificial incubation is probably the most difficult decision to make. Moist environments are important for the incubation of most species of reptilian eggs.

Several media, which have been successfully used for artificial incubation, have a variety of water-potential characteristics. These media include sand, soil, vermiculite, perlite, sphagnum moss, and peat moss. To select the most appropriate medium for the eggs to be incubated, make sure you choose a medium that retains and provides as even a water potential as possible. The medium does not have to resemble natural substrates in structure; the water-potential characteristics of the medium are more important than its structure. However, knowing the percentage water content of the medium does not help much in understanding water relations between the eggs and the medium (GC Packard, 1991). The next three paragraphs describe considerations of using vermiculte versus sand.

Vermiculite is an ideal incubation medium because small changes in water content have little influence on the water potential of the medium. Remember that the water-potential of the medium can influence water exchanges with the eggs. However, vermiculite has different and generally lower hydraulic conductivity than some natural substrata (Ackerman, 1991), which means that water will not redistribute rapidly if one part of the substratum dries more than another. For that reason, you should periodically stir vermiculite to help maintain constant water potential.

It can be difficult to determine the water potential of vermiculite. The technique of thermocouple psychrometry is used for water potentials of -100 kPa or less (drier). Between 0 and -100 kPa, other techniques, such as tensiometry, are needed (Kam and Ackerman, 1990). Unfortunately, not all vermiculite has the same water-potential characteristics, so you cannot use a simple weight ratio of vermiculite-to-water to calculate water potential. Most reptilian eggs will incubate within the range of about -50 to -800 kPa. Ratios of vermiculite to water of 1:1 to 1:2 normally will provide water potentials somewhere in that range.

Small changes in the water content of sand can result in very large changes in water potential, thus changing the amount of water available to the eggs (Kam and Ackerman, 1990). Sand with 10% water may drown eggs (Thompson, 1983), because it is beyond saturation. It is possible for clay containing 20% water by weight to have less water available (lower water potential) than sand containing 5% water.

As with temperature, it is probably sensible to incubate eggs in more than one condition. You can place the eggs into the medium so that the top half of the egg is visible. This enables you to rapidly inspect the eggs and easily remove them for periodic weighing. However, if the eggs have less contact with the substrate, there will be less surface contact for water uptake. In that case, you will have to provide an incubation substrate with a higher (smaller -ve number) water potential to reach the same, final egg mass than if the eggs are completely buried (GC Packard et al., 1981a).

Atmospheric air contains 20.95% oxygen and about 0.03% carbon dioxide (Schmidt-Nielsen, 1990). However, in the soil, concentrations of oxygen often are as low as 17%. Also in soil, carbon dioxide concentrations may rise to 5% or more (Anderson and Ultsch, 1987). These differences generally result from the respiration of microorganisms, but the respiration of some large reptilian nests (e.g. sea turtles and crocodilians) may be so great that they influence their own nest gas-concentrations (Ackerman, 1977; Whitehead, 1987).

The shell conductance of an egg is a measure of

Figure 11.
American alligators, like many other species of crocodilians, construct nests of freshly collected vegetation. This nest on Paynes Prairie in Central Florida has probes to monitor temperature and tubes to sample internal gases.

RESPIRATORY GASES

Few reptilian eggs incubate in atmospheric air. Most eggs incubate where concentrations of respiratory gases in the nest may differ considerably from the composition of atmospheric gas. Specifically, most reptilian eggs develop in subterranean nests, and some incubate in mounds of rotting vegetation (e.g. some crocodilians, Fig. 11).

the ease with which gases diffuse through the shell. Shell conductance is proportional to the total area of pores through the shell and is inversely proportional to the shell thickness (Ar et al, 1974). As with bird eggs, rigid-shelled eggs of crocodilians and turtles have discrete pores that penetrate the eggshell (Fig. 3), through which gases diffuse. Flexible-shelled eggs have an open, fibrous mesh (Fig. 2), through which gases diffuse.

The conductance of the eggshell further influences the concentrations of oxygen and carbon dioxide experienced by the embryo (Deeming & Thompson, 1991). In birds, there has been selection for shell conductances that result in gas concentrations that are similar at the end of incubation to those in adult lungs (Rahn et al., 1979). Reptilian eggs may have developed shell conductances for a purpose similar to birds' eggs (Lutz and Dunbar-Cooper, 1984). Gas concentrations in the egg differ most from concentrations in the nest when the embryo is close to hatching and the embryonic metabolic rate is highest (Fig. 4). In eggs with a high shell-conductance, the embryo experiences gas concentrations not very different from those in the nest. Eggs with low conductance may experience great differences.

Shell gas-conductances have been estimated for a range of reptilian eggs. In general, shell conductances in reptile eggs are higher than in birds' eggs of equivalent size. The reptile egg conductances are higher by as much as two orders of magnitude for some flexible-shelled eggs, and higher by a factor of two in crocodilian and sea turtle eggs (Rand, 1968; Ackerman and Prange, 1972; Lutz et al, 1980; Dunson and Braham, 1981; Ackerman et al, 1985; Vleck, 1991).

Figure 12.
Gas tensions in the nests of reptiles may vary considerably from atmospheric gas tensions. Large clutches of eggs, such as those of the sea turtles represented (*Chelonia mydas*, *Caretta caretta*) may influence the nest gas environment. Smaller clutches of eggs, such as those of the chelid tortoise, *Emydura macquarii*, have much less influence. (Redrawn from Thompson, 1981).

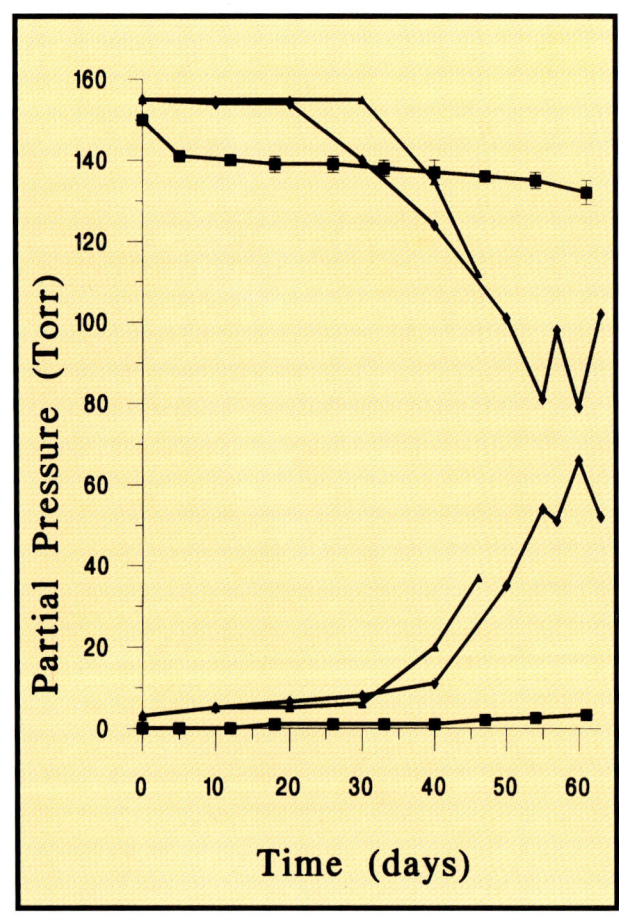

Time (days)

Most reptilian nests are not large. The gas tensions in these nests probably rarely, if ever, vary greatly from background levels (Fig. 11; Thompson, 1981). However, the background tensions in most nests are not atmospheric. Background tensions may fluctuate (Booth and Thompson, 1991).

Sea turtle nests are large and contain a large mass of respiring tissue late in development. In nests of green turtles, *Chelonia mydas*, the concentrations of oxygen in the nest may fall to 14%, and carbon dioxide concentrations may rise to 5% (Fig. 11; Ackerman, 1977; Ackerman, 1980). Gas tensions in nests of crocodilians may be similar. In an experiment that has not been repeated for other species, hatching success was shown to be greater in eggs of the sea turtles *Chelonia mydas* and *Caretta caretta* that were incubated in conditions which resembled those in natural nests (Ackerman, 1981b). If the same is true for other species, manipulation of gases during artificial incubation may raise hatching success and/or produce more vigorous hatchlings.

In most circumstances, it is not possible to vary the concentrations of respiratory gases in a controlled fashion during artificial incubation. However, during artificial incubation, eggs may be contained in sealed or partially sealed containers. As the embryos respire, the tension of oxygen will fall, and the tension of carbon dioxide will rise. As long as these changes are not too severe, they probably do not adversely affect the embryos. These changes may even have a positive influence if they reflect conditions normally experienced in nests. Notwithstanding the positive influence of natural gas concentrations of incubation in *Chelonia mydas*, it is fortunate that reptilian embryos appear to withstand incubation in atmospheric air.

In summary, the concentrations of respiratory gases are more likely to differ from atmospheric gas concentrations in covered nests than in open nests (Fig. 12). Because they incubate in covered nests, reptilian eggs in general are exposed to humid environments during incubation, and so are unlikely to desiccate. Thus, eggshell conductances can be higher in covered nests because they will not desiccate, and the higher conductances allow the eggs to tolerate the more severe gaseous conditions in the nest (GC Packard et al, 1979a; Seymour and Ackerman, 1980).

CLUTCH MATES

There are few reptiles that lay just one egg (exceptions include many geckos and *Anolis*). Most eggs are laid in clutches, some of which contain more than a hundred eggs. In general, the presence of clutch mates may influence incubation and hatching. Variations of temperature during incubation within large clutches of eggs may result in considerable developmental asynchrony, yet all the eggs in these clutches may still hatch simultaneously (Thompson, 1988). In fact, in some species (such as sea turtles), emergence from the nest may depend on the presence of many hatchlings digging together (Carr and Hirth, 1961).

The stimulus for hatching, and the means of synchronising hatching is not known. In crocodilians, the calls of the young may serve to synchronise hatching (Lee, 1968), as well as alert the mother to release the young from the nest (Magnusson, 1980). However, most other reptiles are mute. One likely means of synchronising hatching is mechanical movement. Within a clutch, most eggs are in contact with adjacent eggs. If one hatches, it will jolt the next. Thus, hatching could be stimulated within the entire clutch. However, mechanical response has not been shown experimentally.

The consequences of hatching synchronisation for artificial incubation are obvious. Within a natural nest, if developmental asynchrony occurs, but hatching occurs synchronously, some young will be more developmentally advanced than others when they hatch. This may be manifested in larger size, better coordination, and/or stronger muscles in the more advanced individuals. If longer time in the egg enhances these qualities, you should use artificial incubation protocols that increase the time spent in the egg.

Serious problems of premature hatching include yolk sacs that are not internalised or umbilical scars that have not closed. Such abnormalities may be fatal. For some crocodilians (*Crocodylus porosus* may be an exception—Magnusson, 1980), placing more-developed eggs with less-developed eggs in the same incubator may result in premature or developmentally earlier hatching in some individuals (Lee, 1968). In general, avoid placing younger and older eggs in the same incubation chamber, where hatchlings can interact with younger eggs.

Problems sometimes arise if one eggs is infertile or dies and begins to decay within the clutch. Usually, that egg collapses and the adjacent eggs take up the water that it loses. This water can pass to other adjacent eggs in contact, which is probably a mechanism to help ensure success of some eggs within a clutch incubating in desiccating environments. Most healthy eggs have some capacity to resist infection, but it is also possible for infection to pass from one egg to adjacent eggs, and for bacteria and fungi to topically invade the eggshells of adjacent eggs and reduce their gas-exchange capabilities.

Most snakes glue their eggs together. The reason for this is not clear, although it facilitates water movement among eggs. Indeed, water absorbed from the incubation substrate by one egg can be passed to another egg. Whether eggs should be separated or not at the time of oviposition before

Estuarine Crocodile, *Crocodylus porosus*, guarding her nest. Photo by Zoltan Takacs.

they stick together is much debated among snake breeders. The surface of an egg that is stuck to another egg is not available for gas exchange, nor is it available for the exchange of water with the environment. Eggs that are separated at oviposition and incubated individually can be more easily monitored; their water exchanges are more easily manipulated.

Developmental asynchrony within a clutch of snake eggs that are glued together as a mass is not very likely. When a clutch is glued together, the whole clutch experiences essentially the same thermal regime during artificial incubation. Hence, with snake eggs that are glued together, there should be no concern about eggs being stimulated to hatch early, as is possible in other groups of reptiles.

OTHER CONSIDERATIONS FOR ARTIFICIAL INCUBATION

For management of artificial incubation, the important question is, what are the most appropriate conditions in which to incubate eggs? Unfortunately, there is no simple formula for determining the most appropriate incubation conditions. The wide variety of egg types and natural incubation conditions means that you must consider a variety of incubation conditions. Also, because of the existence of TSD, you may need to provide more than one incubation protocol for each species.

The best guide in developing an incubation protocol for any particular species is to create conditions as close to those in the field as possible. Unfortunately, there are few detailed descriptions of nest environments in the field on which to base an artificial incubation protocol. There are enough, however, to provide a reasonable guide.

EMERGENCIES

For some species, there seems to be a period late in development when the embryo can "bail out" of the egg if faced with an emergency. This procedure may not be difficult for species that are adapted for developmental asynchrony (Thompson, 1989). The next two paragraphs describe examples of early hatching apparently stimulated by emergencies.

The first example involves eggs of tuatara, *Sphenodon punctatus*. On two occasions, eggs that had been infected with a fungus produced hatchlings significantly earlier than any uninfected eggs in the same incubation treatment. In both cases, the fungal hyphae had invaded the yolk sac, and the hatchlings emerged without absorbing any yolk into the abdomen. Thus, they emerged without

Nile Crocodile, *Crocodylus niloticus*, from Lake Tanganyika. Photo by Mark Smith.

Yellow-bellied Turtle, *Trachemys scripta scripta*. Photo by K. T. Nemuras.

any yolk reserves, but they emerged live. Other reptiles may also abandon yolk and hatch early when faced with emergency (Burger et al, 1987; Deeming, 1989). Turtles and crocodilians may not be able to exclude yolk at hatching (Ewert, 1991).

The second case involves eggs of the American alligator, *Alligator mississippiensis*. In this example, eggs were incubating at 30 C and had passed the peak of metabolic development (Fig. 4; Thompson, 1989) when the incubator failed and the temperature fell to about 20 C. The incubator failure and complete hatching occurred sometime within a 15-hour period, at least five days ahead of the expected time of emergence. Similar response to temperature shock occurs in the turtle *Kinosternon scorpioides* (Ewert, 1991).

HANDLING

Many reptilian eggs are very sensitive to movement, with even slight movement at critical stages of development being potentially lethal. Turtle eggs (Limpus et al, 1979; Parmenter, 1980), and to some extent those of crocodilians, can be very sensitive, although turning of some turtle eggs does not affect their development (Ewert, 1979; 1985) and may even speed incubation in *Chrysemys scripta* (Deeming, 1991). Eggs of some lizards are not susceptible to damage by turning; however, other lizard species may be damaged by such movement (Deeming, 1991). Although there are no published studies on the sensitivity of eggs of snakes and tuatara, experience with these groups leads to the tentative conclusion that they are not all that sensitive to movement during development. Indeed, many snakes and some lizards brood their eggs, so accidental movements are likely. Nevertheless, with artificial incubation, you should consider placing an identifying mark on the uppermost part of any reptilian egg when the egg is first moved into the incubation substrate. You should then maintain that orientation throughout incubation.

Sensitivity to movement results from the tendency for the yolk to rotate within an egg until it is at the top. For crocodilians and turtles, the embryo adheres to the inner shell membrane of the egg. Because of this, rotation of the egg results in rotation of the yolk within the shell. This causes tearing of the adherence of the embryo to the shell membrane.

Eggs are most sensitive to movement early in incubation (Ewert, 1979) when the embryo is adhered to the shell membrane, but is still small and delicate. Once the embryo has grown to large size (after 20 days in crocodilians and chelonians), turning of the egg seems to have little adverse affect on the embryo (Deeming, 1991). Eggs of crocodilians and chelonians have a low-viscosity albumen layer that enables the yolk to rotate within the egg (Webb et al, 1987). Eggs of squamates have no such layer. With squamates, the yolk may not be able to turn within the egg, so the likelihood of mechanical damage to early embryo is reduced.

The calcareous shell of rigid-shelled eggs may crack during oviposition or water absorption (Fig. 10). If the underlying membranes remain intact, such cracking is of no consequence to the developing embryo (Ewert, 1985; Ferguson, 1985). Accidental piercing of flexible-shelled eggs of some chelonians and squamates also may not be serious. In these cases, the hole in the eggshell often seals over, and the egg then continues as normal. The influence of such a loss of fluid on hatchling size or vigour has not been determined.

Johnston's Crocodile, *Crocodylus johnstoni*. Photo by K. H. Switak.

CANDLING

Reptilian eggs, like avian eggs, can be candled. In fact, because they usually have thinner shells than avian eggs, reptilian eggs are easier to candle. To candle an egg, place it against a bright light in a darkened room. You can then monitor the progress of the developing embryo. During this procedure, make sure you maintain the orientation of the egg.

In live eggs, you can usually see full blood vessels. If you see blotches of blood or do not see any distinct vessels, this probably indicates that the embryo has died, even though the egg remains turgid and appears normal from the outside. Late in incubation, the egg should look opaque as the fully formed neonate is not transparent.

HATCHING

Young reptiles emerge from eggs by breaching the eggshell, usually with the aid of some sort of egg breaker (Fig. 13). Chelonians and crocodilians possess a caruncle on the tip of the snout (Fig. 14), which they use to help break free of the egg. Squamates develop a true egg tooth (Edmund, 1969) to assist hatching. These egg-breakers are deciduous and are lost soon after hatching.

The process of hatching may be prolonged, 24 hours or more. The process may involve several cycles of the neonate protruding its head from the egg and then retracting it. Hatched

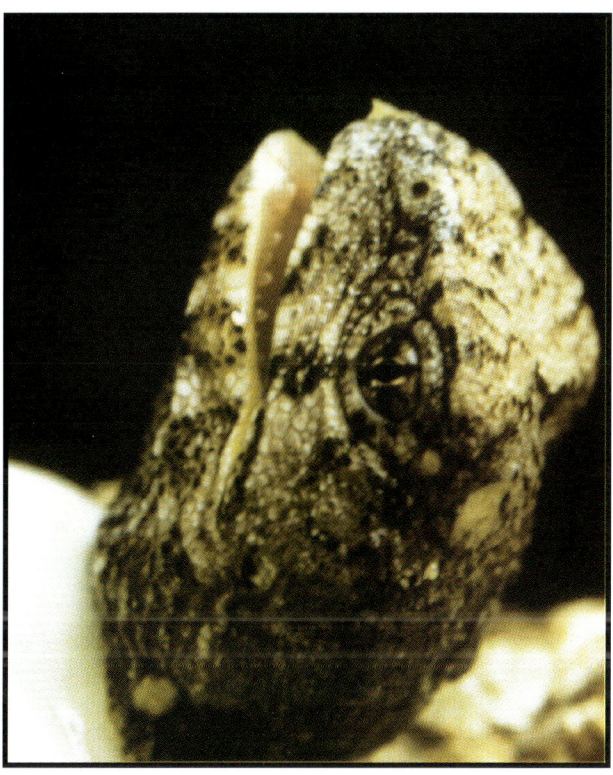

Figure 13.
Tuatara (*Sphenodon punctatus*) emerging from the egg. Note the deciduous caruncle on the nose.

snake and lizard eggshells often have many slits in them from the egg tooth (Auffenberg, 1981).

Do not assist hatchlings to emerge from the eggshell until after the head emerges. When the neonate is in the egg with its head protruding, the neonate's lungs are being cleared, and pulmonary respiration is replacing embryonic (chorioallantoic) respiration. At this time, the young swallow periodically as fluid from the lungs is being cleared. Removal of hatchlings from eggs at this stage may compromise chorio-

Tuatara, *Sphenodon punctatus*. Photo by R. D. Bartlett.

allantoic respiration before the lungs are fully cleared. It may also compromise the viability of the hatchling.

SPECIFIC GROUPS

This section briefly describes characteristics that are unusual or unique to the major groups of reptiles. The list is not exhaustive, but references to reviews are given so that you can easily research each group in more detail.

Figure 14.
Scanning electron micrograph of the caruncle of a tuatara, *Sphenodon punctatus*. Note that a caruncle, while being an "egg breaker", is not a true egg tooth.

CROCODILIANS

Crocodilians lay among the largest eggs of the modern reptiles, with some species (e.g. *Crocodylus niloticus*, *C. rhombifer* and *C. siamensis*) laying eggs larger than 100 g. All are rigid-shelled, and all are deposited in covered nests. However, while most (e.g. *Alligator mississippiensis* and *Crocodylus porosus*) nests are mounds of vegetation constructed by the mother just prior to oviposition (Fig. 12), some (e.g. *Crocodylus johnstoni*, *C. intermedius*) deposit eggs in simple "hole nests" in the ground (Ferguson, 1985; GC Packard and Packard, 1988)

Many, if not all crocodilians help release young from the nest and they form creches in the water (Magnusson, 1980), presumably for protection, for some months after hatching. Neonates can, however, emerge from eggs unassisted. Although it is probably good practice in captivity to let neonates emerge unaided, assistance from the female, at least in *Crocodylus porosus*, may be necessary (Magnusson, 1980). Crocodilians are one of the few groups of reptiles to vocalise (Ferguson 1985), and the neonates will be very vocal at the time of hatching. These vocalisations may (Lee, 1968), or may not (Magnusson, 1980), help to synchronise hatching.

TURTLES

Turtles are much more varied than crocodilians in their eggs and nesting habits. Their eggs range from rigid-shelled to flexible-shelled eggs, depending on the species (Ewert, 1985; MJ Packard and Hirsch, 1986). Even the flexible-shelled eggs contain thicker shells with a more distinct layer of cal-

cium carbonate than do flexible-shelled eggs of squamates (MJ Packard et al, 1982a; MJ Packard and Hirsch, 1986). The large size range of eggs reflects the large size range of adult turtles. With the exception of the sea turtles, eggs of turtles generally can sustain wide ranging temperature fluctuations during incubation (Fig. 7; Thompson, 1988), and can be successfully incubated over a wide range of constant temperatures. However, most species exhibit TSD, so incubation temperature will influence hatchling sex (Ewert and Nelson, 1991).

TUATARA

Considerable recent research on the eggs of tuatara, *Sphenodon* sp., shows that they share features common to both lizards and turtles. Like turtles, eggs of tuatara are oviposited at an early embryonic stage (Moffat, 1985) prior to oviposition. The hatchlings emerge with the aid of a caruncle (Figs. 13, 14), rather than a true egg tooth (Howes and Swinnerton, 1901). Like most lizards, the eggs are flexible-shelled, and they are fairly insensitive to movement during incubation. Unlike lizards and turtles, the optimal incubation temperatures for tuatara are low, centred around 20 C, and the incubation periods are long. In captivity, incubation

Red-bellied Short-necked Turtle, *Emydura subglobosa*. Photo by Jim Merli.

Above: Nest of American Alligator, *Alligator mississippiensis*. Photo by Paul Freed. Below: Estuarine Crocodile, *Crocodylus porosus*. Photo by K. H. Switak.

periods are 5-11 months (Thompson, 1990). In the field, incubation periods are commonly more than a year (Thompson et al, 1996).

LIZARDS

Lizards produce the widest variety of egg types of any of the reptilian groups, from rigid-shelled eggs

Galapagos Land Iguana, *Conolophus subcristatus.* **Photo by K. H. Switak.**

with very low shell conductances to flexible-shelled eggs with high conductances (GC Packard et al, 1977; GC Packard and Packard, 1988). For example, some geckos, and possible dibamids, produce rigid-shelled eggs with very low shell conductances.

Some species retain eggs during most of their development, so that incubation is for only a few days (Greer, 1989; DeMarco, 1992). Other species, such as the monitors, *Varanus* sp., have incubation periods of up to 10 months (Auffenberg, 1981). Some species, such as *Agama agama* (Charnier, 1966), exhibit temperature-dependent sex determination. Others, such as *Dipsosaurus dorsalis* (Muth and Bull, 1981), do not exhibit TSD.

The variety of incubation conditions also reflects the variety of lizard species. Some lizard nests are very deep within the soil; for example, *Conolophus subcristatus* (Christian and Tracy, 1982). For other species, nests are superficial. Some species require quite high incubation temperatures; for example, up to 38°C in the desert iguana, *Dipsosaurus dorsalis* (Muth, 1980). Squamates in cool environments tend to be viviparous (Shine, 1985). The hydric environments sustained by lizard eggs also varies for some periods during development. The lizard, *Conolophus subcristatus*, (Tracy and Snell, 1985) can survive incubation substrates as dry as -7,500 kPa. In contrast, *Anolis* can survive conditions wetter than -100 kPa throughout incubation (Andrews and Sexton, 1981).

SNAKES

Compared to the research available on eggs of other groups of reptiles, relatively little research has been done on snake eggs. Snake eggs are much more uniform in their characteristics than are lizard eggs. Most species produce elongate eggs (Iverson and Ewert, 1991) that are relatively larger compared to the body size of the mother than are lizard eggs. Snakes also produce the largest of reptilian eggs, which is the egg of *Python molurus* (Pope, 1961; Iverson and Ewert, 1991).

Like lizards, some snake species, such as *Opheodrys vernalis*, retain eggs until just before the eggs hatch (Blanchard, 1933; Sexton and Claypool, 1978). Other snake species have relatively long incubation periods.

Despite their similarities to eggs of lizards, there are some fundamental differences between the eggs of snakes and lizards. One distinct difference in snake eggs is their pattern of metabolic development during incubation. Like eggs of altricial birds—and unlike all other reptiles—the metabolic rate of developing snake eggs increases exponentially until they hatch (Thompson, 1989). Neonate snakes, however, are not altricial in the same way that altricial birds are, so the similarity of patterns in these groups, and the differences of neonate snakes from other neonate reptiles, have never been explained.

Another feature of snake eggs that is unusual among other reptile groups is that most snake eggs are glued together at oviposition. The significance of this condition has never been explained. Theories have been proposed to explain those conditions: it is possible that the glueing of eggs is a mechanism to keep the clutch together and to facilitate water exchange. However, those theories have not been tested.

Burmese Python, *Python molurus bivittatus.* **Photo by K. H. Switak.**

Smooth Green Snake, *Opheodrys vernalis*. Photo by R. T. Zappalorti.

CONCLUSIONS

Our knowledge and the study of the physiology of reptile eggs is still in its infancy. However, it has come a long way since the seminal review of GC Packard et al (1977) stimulated a more focused approach to the topic. Although reptilian eggs vary considerably in size and shape, incubation conditions, and incubation periods, we now know enough of the major similarities and differences to be able to make generalities that can be used to artificially incubate eggs of most species, even in the absence of detailed information about their wild nests. Many of the subtleties still await investigation.

Not all reptilian eggs can be treated the same. However, with knowledge of incubation of related species and some information about the native environment of the species, you can make educated guesses (which will most likely prove successful) about the best possible incubation regimes for artificial incubation.

There is still considerable knowledge to be discovered about the incubation of reptilian eggs. Some of the questions that could be answered are: What are the triggers that cause embryos of some turtles to enter a diapause, and what releases them? Why are there no viviparous turtles or crocodiles? Are neonate snakes altricial compared to neonate lizards? Why are eggs of most snakes glued together? The discovery of the answers to these and many other questions provides a challenge for the future and is an area of research available to a wide range of people.

REFERENCES AND RECOMMENDED READING

—Ackerman, RA:
The respiratory gas exchange of sea turtle nests (*Chelonia, Caretta*). Resp Physiol, 1977; 31: 19-38.

—Ackerman, RA:
Physiological and ecological aspects of gas exchange by sea turtle eggs. Amer Zool, 1980; 20: 575-583.

—Ackerman, RA:
Oxygen consumption by sea turtle (*Chelonia, Caretta*) eggs during development. Physiol Zool, 1981a; 54: 316-324.

—Ackerman, RA:
Growth and gas exchange of embryonic sea turtles (*Chelonia, Caretta*). Copeia, 1981b; 1981: 757-765.

—**Ackerman, RA:**
Physical factors affecting the water exchange of buried reptile eggs. In, Egg Incubation. Its Effects on Embryonic Development in Birds and Reptiles, DC Deeming; MWJ Ferguson (Eds). Cambridge University Press, Cambridge, 1991, pp. 193-211.

—**Ackerman, RA; Dmi'el, R; Ar, A:**
Energy and water vapor exchange by parchment-shelled reptile eggs. Physiol Zool, 1985; 58: 129-137.

—**Ackerman, RA; Prange, HD:**
Oxygen diffusion across a sea turtle (*Chelonia mydas*) egg shell. Comp Biochem Physiol, 1972; 43A: 905-909.

—**Alho, CJR; Padua, LFM:**
Reproductive parameters and nesting behavior of the Amazon turtle *Podocnemis expansa* (Testudinata: Pelomedusidae) in Brazil. Can J Zool, 1982; 60: 97-103.

—**Anderson, J.F; Ultsch, G.R:**
Respiratory gas concentrations in the microhabitats of some Florida invertebrates. Comp Biochem Physiol, 1987; 88A: 585-588.

—**Andrews, RM:**
Spatial variation in egg mortality of the lizard *Anolis limifrons*. Herpetologica, 1982; 38: 165-171.

—**Andrews, RM; Sexton, OJ:**
Water relations of the eggs of *Anolis auratus* and *Anolis limifrons*. Ecology, 1981; 62: 556-562.

—**Ar, A; Paganelli, CV; Reeves, RB; Green, DG; Rahn, H:**
The avian egg: water vapor conductance, shell thickness, and functional pore area. Condor, 1974; 76: 153-158.

—**Auffenberg, W.**
The behavioral ecology of the Komodo monitor. University of Florida Presses, Gainesville, 1981, 406pp.

—**Black, CP; Birchard, GF; Schuett, GW; Black, VD:**
Influence of incubation water content on oxygen uptake in embryos of the Burmese python (*Python molurus bivittatus*). In, Respiration and Metabolism of Embryonic Vertebrates, RS Seymour (Ed). Dr W. Junk Publishers, Dordrecht, 1984, pp. 137-145.

—**Blackburn, DG:**
Convergent evolution of viviparity, matrotrophy, and specializations for fetal nutrition in reptiles and other vertebrates. Amer Zool, 1992; 32: 313-321.

—**Blanc, F:**
Table de developpement de *Chamaeleo lateralis* Gray, 1831. Ann Embryol Morphol, 1974; 7: 99-115.

—**Blanck, CE; Sawyer, RH:**
Hatchery practices in relation to early embryology of the loggerhead sea turtle, *Caretta caretta* (Linni). J Exp Mar Biol Ecol, 1981; 49: 163-177.

—**Blanchard, FN:**
Eggs and young of the smooth green snake, *Liopeltis vernalis* (Harlan). Pap Mich Acad Sci Arts Lett, 1933; 17: 493-508.

—**Bobyn, ML; Brooks, RJ:**
Interclutch and interpopulation variation in the effects of incubation conditions on sex, survival and growth of hatchling turtles (*Chelydra serpentina*). J Zool Lond, 1994; 233: 233-257.

—**Booth, DT; Thompson, MB:**
A comparison of reptilian eggs with those of megapode birds. In, Egg Incubation. Its Effects on Embryonic Development in Birds and Reptiles, DC Deeming; MWJ Ferguson (Eds). Cambridge University Press, Cambridge, 1991; pp. 325-344.

—**Bull, JJ:**
Sex determination in reptiles. Quart Rev Biol, 1980; 55: 3-21.

—**Burger, J:**
Incubation temperature has long term effects on behaviour of young pine snakes (*Pituophis melanoleucus*). Behav Ecol Sociobiol 1989; 24: 201-207.

—**Burger, J; Zappalorti, RT; Gochfeld, M:**
Developmental effects of incubation temperature on hatchling pine snakes *Pituophis melanoleucus*. Comp Biochem Physiol, 1987; 87A:727-732.

—**Bustard, HR:**
The micro-environment of a natural lizard nest. Copeia, 1969; 1969: 536-539.

—**Bustard, HR:**
Temperature and water tolerances of incubating crocodile eggs. Brit J Herpetol, 1971; 4: 198-200.

—**Carr, A; Hirth, H:**
Social facilitation in green turtle siblings. Anim Behav, 1961; 9: 68-70.

—**Chabreck, RH:**
Temperature variation in nests of the American alligator. Herpetologica, 1973; 29: 48-51.

—**Chan, E:**
White spot development, incubation and hatching success of leatherback turtle (*Dermochelys coriacea*) eggs from Rantau Abang, Malaysia. Copeia, 1989; 1989: 42-47.

114

—**Charnier, M:**
Action de la température sur la sex-ratio chez l'embryon d'*Agama agama* (Agamidae, Lacertilien). Soc Biol Ouest Af, 1966; 160: 620-622.

—**Christian, KA; Tracy, CR:**
Reproductive behavior of Galapagos land iguanas, *Conolophus pallidus*, on Isla Santa Fe, Galapagos. In, Iguanas of the World, GM Burghardt; AS Rand (Eds). Noyes Publications, Park Ridge NJ, 1982, pp. 366-379.

—**Congdon, JD; Tinkle, DW; Rosen, PC:**
Egg components and utilization during development in aquatic turtles. Copeia, 1983; 1983: 264-268.

—**Cree, A; Butler, D:**
Tuatara Recovery Plan (*Sphenodon* spp.). Threatened Species recovery Plan No. 9. Department of Conservation, Wellington, New Zealand, 1993; 71pp.

—**Cree, A; Cockrem, JF; Brown, MA; Watson, PR; Guillette, LJ; Newman, DG; Chambers, GK:**
Laparoscopy, radiography, and blood analyses as techniques for identifying the reproductive condition of female tuatara. Herpetologica, 1991; 47: 238-249.

—**Cree, A; Thompson, M.B; Daugherty, C.H:**
Temperature-dependent sex determination in tuatara. Nature, 1995; 375: 543.

—**de Beer, GR:**
Caruncles and egg teeth: some aspects of the concept of homology. Proc Linn Soc Lond, 1949; 161: 218-224.

—**Deeming, DC:**
The residues in the eggs of squamate reptiles at hatching. Herpetol J, 1989; 1: 381-385.

—**Deeming, DC:**
Reasons for the dichotomy in egg turning in birds and reptiles. In, Egg Incubation. Its Effects on Embryonic Development in Birds and Reptiles, DC Deeming; MWJ Ferguson (Eds). Cambridge University Press, Cambridge, 1991; pp. 307-323.

—**Deeming, DC; Ferguson, MWJ:**
Environmental regulation of sex determination in reptiles. Phil Trans R Soc Lond, 1988; B322:19-39.

—**Deeming, DC; Ferguson, MWJ:**
Effects of incubation temperature on growth and development of embryos of *Alligator mississippiensis*. J Comp Physiol, 1989; B159:183-193.

—**Deeming, DC; Ferguson, MWJ:**
Physiological effects of incubation temperature on embryonic development in reptiles and birds. In, Egg Incubation. Its Effects on Embryonic Development in Birds and Reptiles, DC Deeming; MWJ Ferguson (Eds). Cambridge University Press, Cambridge, 1991a; pp. 147-171.

—**Deeming, DC; Ferguson, MWJ:**
Incubation and embryonic development in reptiles and birds. In, Avian Incubation, SJ Tullett (Ed). Butterworths, London, 1991b, pp. 3-37.

—**Deeming, DC; Thompson, MB:**
Gas exchange across reptilian eggshells. In, Egg Incubation. Its Effects on Embryonic Development in Birds and Reptiles, DC Deeming; MWJ Ferguson (Eds). Cambridge University Press, Cambridge, 1991; pp. 277-284.

—**DeMarco, V:**
Embryonic development times and egg retention in four species of sceloporine lizards. Funct Ecol, 1992; 6: 436-444.

—**Dendy, A:**
Outlines of the development of the tuatara, *Sphenodon (Hatteria) punctatus*. Q J Microsc Sci, 1899; 42: 1-87.

—**Douglas, RM:**
Volume determination of reptilian and avian eggs with practical applications. S Afr J Wildl Res, 1990; 20: 111-117.

—**Dowling, HG:**
Brooding behaviour in snakes. In, The Encyclopaedia of Reptiles and Amphibians, TA Halliday; K Adler (Eds). George Allen and Unwin, London, 1986; pp. 116.

—**Dufaure, JP; Hubert, J:**
Table de développement du lézard vivipare: *Lacerta (Zootoca) vivipara* Jacquin. Arch Anat Microscop Morphol Exp, 1961; 50: 309-328.

—**Dunson, WA:**
Low water vapor conductance of hard-shelled eggs of the gecko lizards *Hemidactylus* and *Lepidodactylus*. J Exp Zool, 1982; 219: 377-379.

—**Dunson, WA; Bramham, CR:**
Evaporative water loss and oxygen consumption of three small lizards from the Florida Keys, *Sphaerodactylus cinereus, S. notatus,* and *Anolis sagrei*. Physiol Zool, 1981; 54: 253-259.

—**Edmund, AG:**
Dentition. In, Biology of the Reptilia, Volume 1, C Gans; A d'A Bellairs; TS Parsons (Eds). Academic Press, 1969, pp. 117-200.

—**Erasmus, H; Branch; WR:**
Egg retention in the South African blind snake *Typhlops bibronii*. J. Herpetol, 1983; 17: 97-99.

—**Ewert, MA:**
The embryo and its egg: development and natural history. In, Turtles: Perspectives and

115

Research, M Harless; H Morlock (Eds). Wiley, New York, 1979, pp. 333-413.

—Ewert, MA:
Embryology of turtles. In, Biology of the Reptilia, Volume 14, C Gans; F Billett; PFA Maderson (Eds). Wiley, New York, 1985, pp. 76-267.

—Ewert, M:
Cold torpor, diapause, delayed hatching and aestivation in reptiles and birds. In, Egg Incubation. Its Effects on Embryonic Development in Birds and Reptiles, DC Deeming; MWJ Ferguson (Eds). Cambridge University Press, Cambridge, 1991, pp. 173-191.

—Ewert, MA; Legler, JM:
Hormonal induction of oviposition in turtles. Herpetologica, 1978; 34: 314-318.

—Ewert, MA; Nelson, CE:
Sex determination in turtles: diverse patterns and some possible adaptive values. Copeia, 1991; 1991: 50-69.

—Ferguson, MWJ:
Reproductive biology and embryology of the crocodilians. In, Biology of the Reptilia, Volume 14, C Gans; F Billett; PFA Maderson (Eds). John Wiley & Sons, New York, 1985, pp. 329-491.

—Fitch, HS:
Reproductive cycles of lizards and snakes. Univ Kansas Mus Nat Hist Misc Publ, 1970; 52: 1-247.

—Fitch, HS; Fitch AV:
Preliminary experiments on physical tolerances of the eggs of lizards and snakes. Ecology, 1967; 48: 160-165.

—Fox, W:
Effect of temperature on development of scutellation in the garter snake, Thamnophis elegans atratus. Copeia, 1948; 1948: 252-262.

Fox, W; Gordon, C; Fox, MH:
Morphological effects of low temperatures during embryonic development of the garter snake, Thamnophis elegans. Zoologica, 1961; 46: 57-71.

—Frazer, NB:
Sea turtle headstart and hatchery programs. In, Principles of Conservation Biology, GK Meffe; CR Carroll (Eds). Sinauer Associates, Massachusetts, 1994, pp. 374- 380.

—Georges, A; Limpus, C; Stoutjesdijk, R:
Hatchling sex in the marine turtle Caretta caretta is determined by proportion of development at a temperature, not daily duration of exposure. J Exp Zool, 1994; 270: 432-444.

—Gettinger, RD; Paukstis, GL; Gutzke, WHN:
Influence of hydric environment on oxygen consumption by embryonic turtles Chelydra serpentina and Trionyx spiniferus. Physiol Zool, 1984; 57: 468-473.

—Goode, J; Russell, J:
Incubation of eggs of three species of chelid tortoises, and notes on their embryological development. Aust J Zool, 1968; 16: 749-761.

—Greer, AE:
The Biology and Evolution of Australian Lizards. Surrey Beatty and Sons Pty Limited, Australia, 1989; 264pp.

—Guillette, LJ; Gongora, GL:
Notes on oviposition and nesting in the high elevation lizard, Sceloporus aeneus. Copeia, 1986; 1986: 232-233.

—Gutzke, WHN; Crews, D:
Embryonic temperature determines adult sexuality in a reptile. Nature, 1988; 332: 832-834.

—Gutzke, WHN; Packard, GC:
Influence of the hydric and thermal environments on eggs and hatchlings of bull snakes Pituophis melanoleucus. Physiol Zool, 1987; 60: 9-17.

—Gutzke, WHN; Packard, GC; Packard, MJ; Boardman, TJ:
Influence of the hydric and thermal environments on eggs and hatchlings of painted turtles (Chrysemys picta). Herpetologica, 1987; 43: 393-404.

—Gutzke, WHN; Paukstis, GL:
The influence of the hydric environment on sexual differentiation of turtles. J Exp Zool, 1983; 226: 467-469.

—Harrison, KE; Bentley, TB; Lutz, PL; Marszalek, DS:
Water and gas diffusion in the American crocodile egg. Amer Zool, 1978; 18: 637.

—Hendrickson, JR:
The green sea-turtle, Chelonia mydas (Linn.) in Malay and Sarawak. Proc Zool Soc Lond, 1958; 130: 455-535.

—Hotaling, E; Wilhoft, DC; McDowell, SB:
Egg position and weight of hatchling snapping turtles, Chelydra serpentina, in natural nests. J Herpetol, 1985; 19: 534-536.

—Howes, GB; Swinnerton, HH:
On the development of the skeleton of the tuatara, Sphenodon punctatus; with remarks on the egg, on the hatching and on the hatched young. Trans Zool Soc Lond, 1901; 16: 1-86.

—Hubert, J; Dufaure, JP:
Table de développement de la vipére aspic, Vipera aspis L. Bull Soc Zool France, 1968; 93: 135-148.

—Hubert, J:
Embryology of the squamata. In, Biology of

116

the Reptilia, Volume 15, C Gans; F Billet (Eds). John Wiley & Sons, New York, 1985, pp. 3-34.

—**Hutchison, VH; Dowling, HG; Vinegar, A:** Thermoregulation in a brooding female Indian python, *Python molurus bivittatus.* Science, 1966; 151: 694-696.

—**Iverson, JB; MA Ewert:** Physical characteristics of reptilian eggs and a comparison with avian eggs. In, Egg Incubation. Its Effects on Embryonic Development in Birds and Reptiles, DC Deeming; MWJ Ferguson (Eds). Cambridge University Press, Cambridge, 1991, pp. 87-100.

—**Janzen, FJ; Paukstis, GL:** Environmental sex determination in reptiles: ecology, evolution, and experimental design. Quart Rev Biol, 1991; 66: 149-179.

—**Joanen, T; McNease, L; Ferguson, MWJ:** The effects of egg incubation temperature on post-hatching growth of American alligators. In, Wildlife Management: Crocodiles and Alligators, GLW Webb; SC Manolis; PJ Whitehead (Eds). Surrey Beatty and Sons Pty Limited, Australia, 1987, pp. 533-537.

—**Kam, YC; Ackerman, RA:** The effects of incubation media on the water exchange of snapping turtle (*Chelydra serpentina*) eggs and hatchlings. J Comp Physiol B, 1990; 160: 317-324.

—**Kennett, R; Christian, K; Pritchard, D:** Underwater nesting by the tropical chelid turtle *Chelodina rugosa* from northern Australia. Aust J Zool, 1993; 41: 47-52.

—**Lang, J:** Incubation temperature affects thermal selection of hatchling crocodiles. Amer Zool, 1985; 25: 16.

—**Lee, DS:** Possible communication between eggs of the American alligator. Herpetologica, 1968; 24: 88.

—**Leshem, A; Dmi'el, R:** Water loss from *Trionyx triunguis* eggs incubating in natural nests. Herpetol J, 1986; 1: 115-117.

—**Licht, P; Moberly, WR:** Thermal requirements for embryonic development in the tropical lizard *Iguana iguana.* Copeia, 1965; 1965: 515-517.

—**Limpus, C.J; Baker, V; Miller, J.D:** Movement induced mortality of loggerhead eggs. Herpetologica, 1979; 35: 335-338.

—**Lutz, PL; Bentley, TB; Harrison, KE; Marszalek, DS:** Oxygen and water vapour conductance in the shell and shell membrane of the American crocodile egg. Comp Biochem Physiol, 1980; 66A: 335-338.

—**Lutz, PL; Dunbar-Cooper, A:** The nest environment of the American crocodile (*Crocodylus acutus*). Copeia, 1984; 1984: 153-161.

—**Lynn, WG; von Brand, T:** Studies on the oxygen consumption and water metabolism of turtle embryos. Biol Bull, 1945; 88: 112-125.

—**Magnusson, WE:** Hatching and creche formation by *Crocodylus porosus*. Copeia, 1980; 1980: 359-362.

—**Magnusson, WE:** Mortality of eggs of the crocodile *Crocodylus porosus* in northern Australia. J Herpetol, 1982; 16: 121-130.

—**Maritz, M.F; Douglas, R.M:** Shape quantization and the estimation of volume and surface area of reptile eggs. J Herpetol, 1994; 28: 281-291.

—**Miller, JD:** Embryology of marine turtles. In, Biology of the Reptilia, Volume 14, C Gans; F. Billett; P Maderson (Eds). John Wiley & Sons, New York, 1985, pp. 269-328.

—**Miller, K; Packard, GC; Packard, MJ:** Hydric conditions during incubation influence locomotor performance of hatchling snapping turtles. J Exp Biol, 1987; 127: 401-412.

—**Moffat, LA:** Embryonic development and aspects of reproductive biology in the tuatara, *Sphenodon punctatus*. In, Biology of the Reptilia, Volume 14, C Gans; F. Billett; P Maderson (Eds). John Wiley & Sons, New York, 1985, pp. 493-521.

—**Mrosovsky, N:** Sex ratios of sea turtles. J Exp Zool, 1994; 270: 16-27.

—**Murray, JD; Deeming, DC; Ferguson, MWJ:** Size-dependent pigmentation pattern formation in embryos of *Alligator mississippiensis*: time of initiation of pattern generation mechanism. Proc R Soc Lond B, 1990; 239: 279-293.

—**Muth, A:** Physiological ecology of desert iguana (*Dipsosaurus dorsalis*) eggs: temperature and water relations. Ecology, 1980; 61: 1335-1343.

—**Muth, A:** Water relations of desert iguana (*Dipsosaurus dorsalis*) eggs. Physiol Zool, 1981; 54: 441-451.

—**Muth, A; Bull, JJ:**
Sex determination in desert iguanas: does temperature make a difference? Copeia, 1981; 1981: 869-870

—**Muthukkaruppan, VR; Kanakambika, P; Manickavel, V; Veeraraghavan, K:**
Analysis of the development of the lizard, *Calotes versicolor*. I. A series of normal stages in the embryonic development. J Morph, 1979; 130: 479-490.

—**Osgood, DW:**
Effects of temperature on the development of meristic characters in *Natrix fasciata*. Copeia, 1978; 1978: 33-37.

—**Packard, GC:**
The physiological and ecological importance of water to embryos of oviparous reptiles. In, Egg Incubation. Its Effects on Embryonic Development in Birds and Reptiles, DC Deeming; MWJ Ferguson (Eds). Cambridge University Press, Cambridge, 1991, pp. 213-228.

—**Packard, GC; Packard, MJ:**
Coupling of physiology of embryonic turtles to the hydric environment. In, Respiration and Metabolism of Embryonic Vertebrates, RS Seymour (Ed). Dr W Junk Publishers, Dordrecht, 1984, pp. 99-119.

—**Packard, GC; Packard, MJ:**
Water relations and nitrogen excretion in embryos of the oviparous snake *Coluber constrictor*. Copeia, 1987; 1987: 395-406.

—**Packard, GC; Packard, MJ:**
The physiological ecology of reptilian eggs and embryos. In, Biology of the Reptilia, Volume 16, C Gans; RB Huey (Eds). Alan R. Liss, New York, 1988, pp. 523-605.

—**Packard, GC; Packard, MJ; Birchard, GF:**
Sexual differentiation and hatching success by painted turtles incubating in different thermal and hydric environments. Herpetologica, 1989; 45: 385-392.

—**Packard, GC; Packard, MJ; Boardman, TJ:**
Patterns and possible significance of water exchange by flexible-shelled eggs of painted turtles (*Chrysemys picta*). Physiol Zool, 1981a; 54: 165-178.

—**Packard, GC; Paukstis, GL; Boardman, TJ; Gutzke, WHN:**
Daily and seasonal variation in hydric conditions and temperature inside nests of common snapping turtles (*Chelydra serpentina*). Can J Zool, 1985; 63: 2422-2429.

—**Packard, GC; Packard, MJ; Miller, K; Boardman, TJ:**
Influence of moisture, temperature, and substrate on snapping turtle eggs and embryos. Ecology, 1987; 68: 983-993.

—**Packard, GC; Taigen; TL; Boardman, TJ; Packard, MJ; Tracy, CR:**
Changes in mass of eggs of softshell turtle (*Trionyx spiniferus*) eggs incubated on substrates differing in water potential. Herpetologica, 1979b; 35: 78-86.

—**Packard, GC; Taigen; TL; Packard MJ; Boardman, TJ:**
Water relations of pliable-shelled eggs of common snapping turtles (*Chelydra serpentina*). Can J Zool, 1980; 58: 1404-1411.

—**Packard, GC; Taigen; TL; Packard MJ; Boardman, TJ:**
Changes in mass of eggs of softshell turtle (*Trionyx spiniferus*) incubated under hydric conditions simulating those of natural nests. J Zool, Lond, 1981b; 193: 81-90.

—**Packard, GC; Taigen, TL; Packard, MJ; Shuman, RD:**
Water vapor conductance of testudinian and crocodilian eggs (Class Reptilia). Resp Physiol 1979a; 38: 1-10.

—**Packard, GC; Tracy, RC; Roth, JJ:**
The physiological ecology of reptilian eggs and embryos, and the evolution of viviparity within the class Reptilia. Biol Rev, 1977; 52: 71-105.

—**Packard, MJ:**
Ultrastructural morphology of the shell and shell membranes of eggs of common snapping turtles (*Chelydra serpentina*). J Morph, 1980; 165: 187-204.

—**Packard, MJ; DeMarco, V:**
Eggshell structure and formation in eggs of oviparous reptiles. In, Egg Incubation. Its Effects on Embryonic Development in Birds and Reptiles, DC Deeming; MWJ Ferguson (Eds). Cambridge University Press, Cambridge, 1991, pp. 53-69.

—**Packard, MJ; Hirsch, KF:**
Scanning electron microscopy of eggshells of contemporary reptiles. Scanning Electron Microsc, 1986; 4: 1581-1590.

—**Packard, MJ; Packard, GC:**
Effect of water balance on growth and calcium mobilization of embryonic painted turtles (*Chrysemys picta*). Physiol Zool, 1986; 59: 398-405.

—**Packard, MJ; Packard, GC:**
Sources of calcium and phosphorus during embryogenesis in bull snakes (*Pituophis melanoleucus*). J Exp Zool, 1988; 246: 132-138.

—**Packard, MJ; Packard, GC; Boardman, TJ:**
Water balance of the eggs of a desert lizard (*Callisaurus draconoides*). Can J Zool, 1980; 58 :2051-2058.

—Packard, MJ; Packard, GC; Boardman, TJ:
Structure of eggshells and water relations of reptilian eggs. Herpetologica, 1982a; 38: 136-155.

—Packard, MJ; Packard, GC; Gutzke, WHN:
Calcium metabolism in embryos of the oviparous snake *Coluber constrictor*. J Exp Biol, 1984; 110: 99-112.

—Packard, MJ; Packard, GC; Miller, JD; Jones, ME; Gutzke, WHN:
Calcium mobilization, water balance, and growth in embryos of the agamid lizard *Amphibolurus barbatus*. J Exp Zool, 1985; 235: 349-357.

—Packard, MJ; Phillips, JA; Packard, GC:
Sources of mineral for green iguanas (*Iguana iguana*) developing in eggs exposed to different hydric conditions. Copeia, 1992; 1992: 851-858.

—Packard, MJ; Thompson, MB; Goldie, KN; Vos, M:
Aspects of shell formation in eggs of the tuatara, *Sphenodon punctatus*.. J Morph, 1988; 197: 147-157.

—Palmer, BP; DeMarco, VG; Guillette, LJ:
Oviductal morphology and eggshell formation in the lizard, *Sceloporus woodi*. J Morph, 1993; 217: 205-217.

—Parmenter, CJ:
Incubation of the eggs of the green sea turtle, *Chelonia mydas*, in Torres Strait, Australia: the effect of movement on hatchability. Aust Wildl Res, 1980; 7: 487-491.

—Paukstis, GL; Gutzke, WHN; Packard, GC:
Effects of substrate water potential and fluctuating temperatures on sex ratios of hatchling painted turtles (*Chrysemys picta*). Can J Zool, 1984; 62: 1491-1494.

—Pieau, C:
Sur la proportion sexuelle chez les embryons de deux Chéloniens (*Testudo graeca* L. et *Emys orbicularis* L.) issus d'oeufs incubés artificiellement. C R Acad Sci Paris Ser D, 1971; 272: 3071-3074.

—Pieau, C:
Effets de la témperature sur le développement des glandes génitales chez les embryons de deux Chéloniens, *Emys orbicularis* L. et *Testudo graeca* L. C R Acad Sci Paris Ser D, 1972; 274:719-722.

—Pieau, C:
Nouvelles données expérimentales concernant les effets de la témperature sur la differenciation sexuelle chez les embryons de Chéloniens. C R Acad Sci Paris Ser D, 1973; 277: 2789-2792.

—Pieau, C:
Effets de températures d'incubation basses et élevies, sur la differentiation sexuelle chez des embryons *d'Emys orbicularis* L. (Chélonien). C R Acad Sci Paris Ser D, 1978; 286: 121-124.

—Plummer, MV:
Some aspects of nesting success in the turtle, *Trionyx muticus*. Herpetologica, 1976; 32: 353-359.

—Plummer, MV;
Snell; HL: Nest site selection and water relations of eggs in the snake, *Opheodrys aestivus*. Copeia, 1988; 1988: 58-64.

—Pope, CH:
The Giant Snakes. AA Knopf, New York, 1961, pp. 290.

—Porter, KR:
Herpetology. WB Saunders Company, Philadelphia, 1972, 524pp.

—Rahn, A; Ar, A; Paganelli, CV:
How bird eggs breathe. Sci Amer, 1979; 240: 46-55.

—Rahn, H; Paganelli, CV:
Gas fluxes in avian eggs: driving forces and the pathway for exchange. Comp Biochem Physiol, 1990; 95A: 1-15.

—Ragotzkie, RA:
Mortality of loggerhead turtle eggs from excessive rainfall. Ecology, 1959; 40:303-305.

—Rand, AS:
Desiccation rates in crocodile and iguana eggs. Herpetologica, 1968; 24: 178-180.

—Raynaud, A; Pieau, C:
Effets de diverses témperatures d'incubation sur le développement somatique et sexuel des embryons de lezard vert (*Lacerta viridis* Laur.). C R Acad Sci Paris Ser D, 1972; 275: 2259-2262.

—Ricklefs, RE; Cullen, J:
Embryonic growth of the green iguana *Iguana iguana*. Copeia, 1973; 1973: 296-305.

—Risley, PL:
Arrested development of turtle embryos. Anat Rec, 1944; 88: 454-455.

—Schmidt-Nielsen, K:
Animal Physiology. Adaptation and Environment, 4th Ed. Cambridge University Press, Cambridge, 1990; 602pp.

—Sexton, OJ; Claypool, L:
Nest sites of a northern population of an oviparous snake, *Opheodrys vernalis* (Serpentes, Colubridae). J Nat Hist, 1978; 12: 365-370.

—Sexton, OJ; Marion, KR:
Duration of incubation of *Sceloporus undulatus*

eggs at constant temperature. Physiol Zool, 1974; 47: 91-98.

—**Sexton, OJ; Veith, GM; Phillips, DM:**
Ultrastructure of the eggshell of two species of anoline lizards. J Exp Zool, 1979; 207: 227-236.

—**Seymour, RS; Ackerman, RA:**
Adaptations to underground nesting in birds and reptiles. Amer Zool, 1980; 20: 437-447.

—**Shadrix, CA; Crotzer, DR; McKinney, SL; Stewart, JR:**
Embryonic growth and calcium mobilization in oviposited eggs of the scincid lizard, *Eumeces fasciatus*. Copeia, 1994; 1994: 493-498.

—**Shine, R:**
The evolution of viviparity in reptiles: an ecological analysis. In, Biology of the Reptilia, Volume 15, C Gans; F Billett. John Wiley and Sons, New York, 1985, pp. 605-694.

—**Somma, LA; Fawcett, JD:**
Brooding behavior of the prairie skink, *Eumeces septentrionalis*, and its relationship to the hydric environment of the nest. Zool J Linn Soc, 1989; 95: 245-256.

—**Stamps, JA:**
Egg retention, rainfall and egg laying in a tropical lizard, *Anolis aeneus*. Copeia, 1976; 1976: 759-764.

—**Thomas, APW:**
Preliminary note on the development of the tuatara (*Sphenodon punctatus*). Proc R Soc Lond B, 1890; 48: 152-156.

—**Thompson, MB:**
Gas tensions in natural nests and eggs of the tortoise *Emydura macquarii*. In, Proceedings of the Melbourne Herpetological Symposium, CB Banks; AA Martin (Eds). Zoological Board of Victoria, Parkville, Australia, 1981, pp. 74-77.

—**Thompson, MB:**
The Physiology and Ecology of the Eggs of the Pleurodiran Tortoise *Emydura macquarii* (Gray), 1831. Ph.D. Thesis, University of Adelaide, South Australia, 1983.

—**Thompson, MB:**
Functional significance of the opaque white patch in eggs of *Emydura macquarii*. In, Biology of Australasian Frogs and Reptiles, G Grigg; R Shine; H Ehmann (Eds). Surrey Beatty & Sons, chipping Norton, Australia, 1985, pp. 387-395.

—**Thompson, MB:**
Water exchange in reptilian eggs. Physiol Zool, 1987; 60: 1-8.

—**Thompson, MB:**
Nest temperatures in the pleurodiran turtle, *Emydura macquarii*. Copeia, 1988; 1988: 996-1000.

—**Thompson, MB:**
Patterns of metabolism in embryonic reptiles. Resp Physiol, 1989; 76: 243-256.

—**Thompson, MB:**
Incubation of eggs of tuatara, *Sphenodon punctatus*. J Zool, Lond, 1990; 222: 303-318.

—**Thompson, MB; Newman, DG; Watson, PR:**
Use of oxytocin in obtaining eggs from tuatara *(Sphenodon punctatus)*. J Herpetol, 1990; 25: 101-104.

—**Thompson, MB; Packard, GC; Packard, MJ; Rose, B:**
Analysis of the nest environment of tuatara *Sphenodon punctatus*. J Zool, Lond, 1996; 238: 239-251.

—**Tokunaga, S:**
Temperature-dependent sex determination in *Gekko japonicus* (Gekkonidae, Reptilia). Dev Growth Differ, 1985; 27: 117-120.

—**Tracy, CR; Packard, GC; Packard, MJ:**
Water relations of chelonian eggs. Physiol Zool, 1978; 51: 378-387.

—**Tracy, CR; Snell, HL:**
Interrelations among water and energy relations of reptilian eggs, embryos, and hatchlings. Amer Zool 1985; 25: 999-1008.

—**van Devender, RW:**
Comparative demography of the lizard *Basiliscus basiliscus*. Herpetologica, 1982; 38: 189-208.

—**van Mierop, LHS; Barnard, SM:**
Observations on the reproduction of *Python molurus bivittatus* (Reptilia, Serpentes, Biodae). J Herpetol, 1976; 10: 333-340.

—**Vinegar, A:**
Evolutionary implications of temperature induced anomalies of development in snake embryos. Herpetologica, 1974; 30: 72-74.

—**Vitt, LJ:**
Reproductive tactics of sympatric gekkonid lizards with a comment on the evolutionary and ecological consequences of invariant clutch size. Copeia, 1986; 1986: 773-786.

—**Vleck, CM; Hoyt, DF:**
Metabolism and energetics of reptilian and avian embryos. In, Egg Incubation. Its Effects on Embryonic Development in Birds and Reptiles, DC Deeming; MWJ Ferguson (Eds). Cambridge University Press, Cambridge, 1991, pp. 285-306.

—**Vleck, D:**
Embryo water economy, egg size, and hatchling viability in the lizard, *Sceloporus virgatus*. Am Zool, 1988; 28: 87A.

—**Vleck, D:**
Water economy and salt regulation of reptilian and avian embryos. In, Egg Incubation. Its Effects on Embryonic Development in Birds and Reptiles, DC Deeming; MWJ Ferguson (Eds). Cambridge University Press, Cambridge, 1991, pp. 245-259.

—**Webb, GJW; Buckworth, R; Manolis, SC:**
Crocodylus johnstoni in the McKinlay River, N.T. VI. Nesting biology. Aust Wildl Res, 1983a; 10: 607-637.

—**Webb, GJW; Choquenot, D; Whitehead, PJ:**
Nests, eggs, and embryonic development of *Carettochelys insculpta* (Chelonia: Carettochelidae) from northern Australia. J Zool, Lond, 1986; B1: 521-550.

—**Webb, GJW; Manolis, SC; Whitehead, PJ; Dempsey, K:**
The possible relationship between embryo orientation, opaque banding and the dehydration of albumen in crocodile eggs. Copeia, 1987; 1987: 252-257.

—**Webb, GJW; Sack, GC; Buckworth, R; Manolis, SC:**
An examination of *Crocodylus porosus* nests in two northern Australian freshwater swamps, with an analysis of embryo mortality. Aust Wildl Res, 1983b; 10: 571-605.

—**Webb, GJW; Smith, AMA:**
Sex ratios and survivorship in the Australian freshwater crocodile *Crocodylus johnstoni*. Symp Zool Soc Lond, 1984; 52: 319-355.

—**Werner, DI:**
The effect of varying water potential on body weight, yolk and fat bodies in neonate green iguanas. Copeia, 1988; 1988: 406-411.

—**Whitehead, PJ:**
Respiration of *Crocodylus johnstoni* embryos. In, Wildlife Management: Crocodiles and Alligators, GJW Webb; SC Manolis; PJ Whitehead (Eds). Surrey Beatty Pty, Chipping Norton, Australia, 1987, pp 473-497.

—**Whitehead, PJ:**
Yolk depletion and metabolic rate of hatchling *Crocodylus johnstoni*. Copeia, 1990; 1990: 871-875.

—**Yntema, CL:**
A series of stages in the embryonic development of *Chelydra serpentina*. J Morph, 1968; 125: 219-252.

—**Yntema, CL:**
Effects of incubation temperature on sexual differentiation in the turtle *Chelydra serpentina*. J Morph, 1976; 150: 453-462.

—**Yntema, CL:**
Incubation times for eggs of the turtle *Chelydra serpentina* (Testudines: Chelydridae) at various temperatures. Herpetologica, 1978; 34: 274-277.

—**Yntema, CL:**
Temperature levels and periods of sex determination during incubation of eggs of *Chelydra serpentina*. J Morph, 1979; 159: 17-28.

—**York, DS; Burghardt, GM:**
Brooding in the Malayan pit viper, *Calloselasma rhodostoma*: temperature, relative humidity, and defensive behaviour. Herpetol J, 1988; 6: 210-214.

THE BASIS OF REPTILIAN INHERITANCE

Shelley Burgin BSc (Grif), MSc (UPNG), PhD (Macq), Senior Lecturer*
B.J. Richardson BSc (Hons), PhD (NSW), Professor of Biological Sciences
Adrian Renshaw B. App.Sc. (Hons) (UWS-H), Associate Lecturer
Faculty of Science and Technology
University of Western Sydney - Hawkesbury,
Richmond, Australia, 2753.

REPTILE GENETICS - INTRODUCTION

Understanding the processes involved in reptile breeding and evolution requires a knowledge of genetics. Attributes such as an organism's physiology and behaviour are heavily influenced by the genetic makeup of the individual. This is because the genetic code directs all cellular functions and therefore provides the underlying blue print controlling the individual's development and that of its offspring.

Despite the pivotal role that genetics plays in the understanding of the processes of life, documented reptilian examples of the basic concepts are limited. This chapter provides an introduction to these concepts utilising examples from the scientific literature.

THE BIRTH OF NEW CELLS

The functional units of heredity, genes, enable genetic material to be transmitted from one generation to the next via a family of biological molecules called nucleic acids which are contained in the chromosomes. Genes are the basis of inheritance and can be conceptually considered as small, discrete segments of DNA (deoxyribose nucleic acid) which code for a particular protein and are contained on the chromosomes. The chromosomes are therefore the vehicle by which the genes are transmitted from one generation to the next via the eggs and sperm.

In sexually reproducing reptiles two different types of cell division occur: mitosis and meiosis. Cells that divide by mitosis provide cells that are identical to the parental cells. These provide the reptile with cells for growth and the replacement of damaged cells (e.g., regeneration after tail loss in skinks). In species with only a single sex this is also the mode of cell division which produces new offspring (parthenogenesis). The second type of cell division, meiosis, produces cells with half the number as chromosomes of the parental cells. This type of division only occurs in the sex organs of sexually reproducing species to provide the gametes (eggs and sperm). The gametes then fuse during fertilisation to form a zygote. The resulting zygote grows by mitosis and differentiates to form the embryo and, in time, a hatchling. Eggs and sperm have one copy of each kind of chromosome in the set (haploid, *n*) while adults have a pair of each chromosome (diploid, 2*n*)(see Figure 1 for diagram of the two types of cell division).

INHERITANCE OF GENETIC MATERIAL

In the transmission of the chromosomes from one generation to the next, the parents provide all the genetic material for the development of a new individual. Each pair of chromosomes contains genes and each gene may exist in alternative forms called alleles. For example a reptile may carry the allele for normal skin colour on one of the chromosome pair, while on the other chromosome, it may carry an alternative allele (e.g., that codes for albinism). When there are two alternative alleles for any particular phenotypic trait, one on each of the chromosome pair, the individual is said to be heterozygous. The genotypic expression of one of the alleles may mask that of the alternative allele. Such alleles are said to be dominant over the recessive, alternative form.

There is ample evidence that this is the pattern of inheritance in reptiles, for example, throughout most of its range *Lampropetis getulua,* the Californian kingsnake, is basically yellow to white with black or brown ringed background. However three disjunct populations have more complex patterns (Zweifel, 1981). The genetics of the various components of their patterning have interested herpetologists for some time (e.g., Dunn, 1944; Klauber,

* Address all correspondence to Dr. Shelley Burgin, Faculty of Science and Technology, University of Western Sydney -Hawkesbury, Richmond, Australia 2753

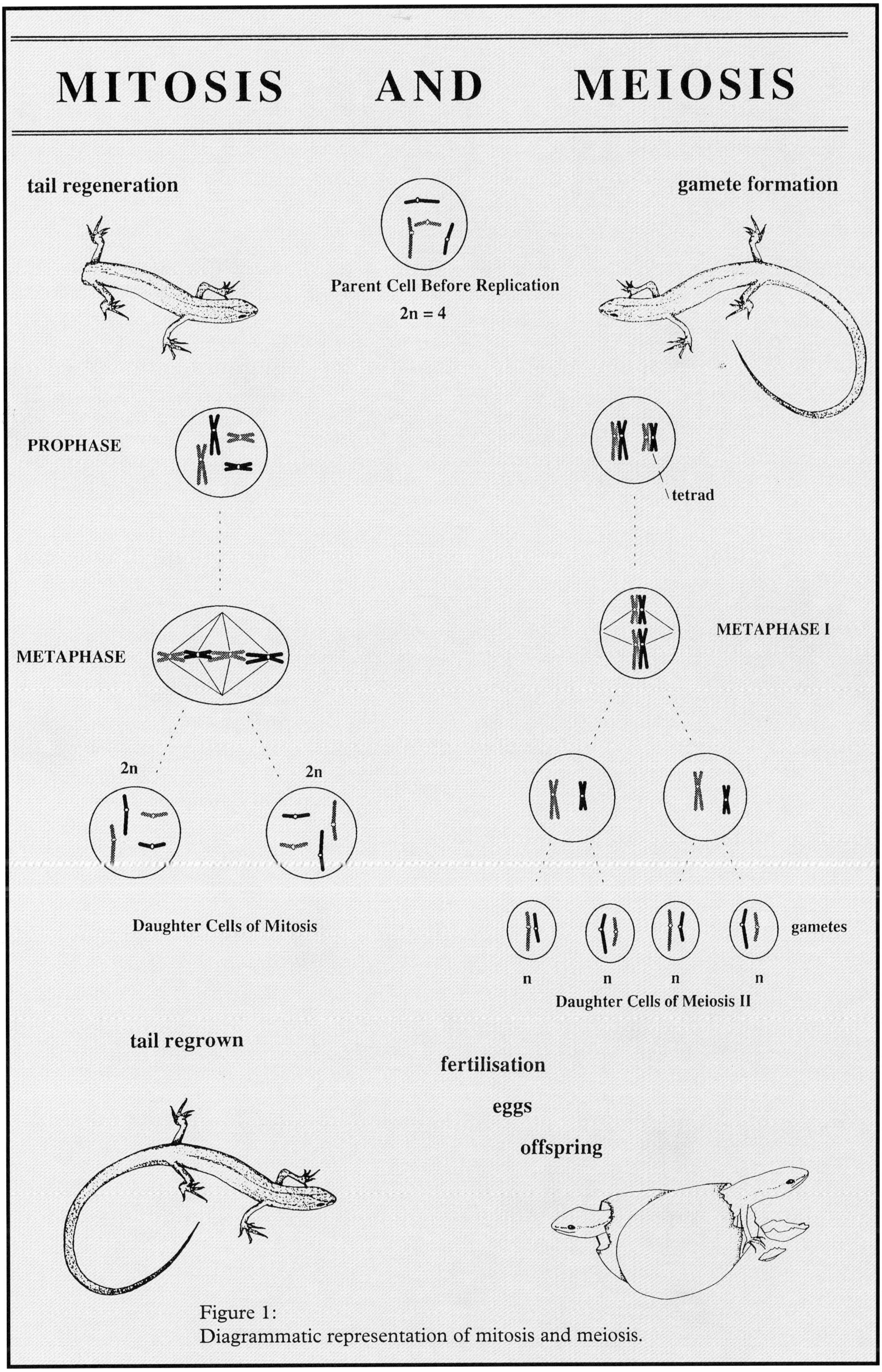

MITOSIS AND MEIOSIS

tail regeneration

gamete formation

Parent Cell Before Replication
2n = 4

PROPHASE

tetrad

METAPHASE I

METAPHASE

2n

2n

Daughter Cells of Mitosis

gametes

n   n   n   n

Daughter Cells of Meiosis II

tail regrown

fertilisation

eggs

offspring

Figure 1:
Diagrammatic representation of mitosis and meiosis.

California Kingsnake, *Lampropeltis getula californiae*. **Photo by R. G. Markel.**

1936, 1939, 1944; Mayr, 1944; Zweifel, 1981). It has been observed that although the inheritance of colour pattern in this species is complicated, involving variation at many genes, it is possible to study the inheritance of aspects of the colour patterns. When the association between the striped and banded patterns were considered in isolation, it was observed that this

Red-bellied Snake, *Storeria occipitomaculata*. **Photo by John Iverson.**

aspect of *L. getulua* colouring was controlled by two alleles (Zweifel, 1981). Each animal has two copies of this gene, one on each of two homologous chromosomes and they may be homozygous (i.e., genes of the same type on both chromosomes) or heterozygous (i.e., one of each of the alternative types). An individual may therefore carry the gene for striped pattern (*S*) on both chromosomes (genotype *SS*), the recessive gene for banded pattern (*s*) on both chromosomes (genotype *ss*) or the snake may be heterozygous (genotype *Ss*). The appearance of the offspring may be the same as one of the parents or different, depending on their genotype (see Table 1). Punnett squares are often used to demonstrate such crosses (Figure 2).

This type of genetic inheritance has also been determined for many characters in a wide range of species. For example in *Storeria occipitomaculata*, the eastern North American red-bellied snake, an investigation of inherited pattern variation of a sample of both brown and grey colour morphs provided allele frequency data equivalent to the level observed in three other natricine species. This, along with the presence of heterozygotes, was

TABLE 1:

An example of independently assorting traits: the genotype and phenotype arrangements of alleles from various hypothetical matings for banded and striped patterns in *Lampropetis getulua*, the Californian kingsnake and their offspring.

parental phenotype	parental genotype	offspring phenotype	offspring genotype
striped x striped	*SS* x *SS*	all striped	all *SS*
striped x striped	*Ss* x *SS*	all striped	1 *SS* : 1 *Ss*
striped x striped	*SS* x *Ss*	all striped	1 *SS* : 1 *Ss*
striped x striped	*Ss* x *Ss*	3 striped : 1 banded	1 *SS* : 2 *Ss* : 1 *ss*
striped x banded	*SS* x *ss*	all striped	all *Ss*
striped x banded	*Ss* x *ss*	1 striped : 1 banded	1 *Ss* : 1 *ss*
banded x banded	*ss* x *ss*	all banded	all *ss*

Figure 2:
Demonstration of a mating between two striped *Lampropetis getulua*, both heterozygous.

Parental types	heterozygote striped x heterozygote striped
Genotypes	*Ss* x *Ss*
Possible gametes	*S, s*

Maternal

	S	*s*
S	*S S*	*Ss*
s	*S s*	*ss*

Paternal

Outcome:

Phenotypes	3 striped : 1 banded
Genotypes	1 *SS* : 2 *Ss* : 1 *ss*

Common Garter Snake, *Thamnophis sirtalis*, with odd pattern. Photo by W. P. Mara.

consistent with the hypothesis that the two morphs belong to the same species (Grudzien et al, 1991). A similar pattern of inheritance of varying colour morphs have also been observed within *Thamnophis sirtalis* in western Ohio (Sattler et al, 1976) and the genetics of its melanistic forms have also been addressed (Blanchard et al, 1941).

To test the genetic stability of a particular trait, for example the banded versus striped pattern in *L. getulua* discussed above, individuals of unknown genotype may be test crossed or back crossed. This is done by crossing, for example a striped wild caught animal of unknown genotype (which could have either the genotype *SS* or *Ss*) with a homozygous recessive, banded individual (*ss*). The genotype of the wild caught animal could then be deduced from the colour patterning of the offspring. If the wild caught animal was homozygous dominant (*SS*), mated to a banded individual (*ss*), all of the offspring would be heterozygous striped (*Ss*). However if the wild caught animal was heterozygous (*Ss*) it would be expected that half of the offspring would be striped (*Ss*) and half banded (*ss*). The advantage of undertaking a test cross, therefore, is that it provides a direct reflection of the gametes produced by the individual with the dominant appearance (phenotype), because no dominant alleles are provided by the homozygote recessive to obscure the results.

CONSEQUENCES OF INBREEDING

Each offspring receives one copy of each gene from each parent, that is, it shares half of its genes with a single parent. By chance then individuals from the same clutch will share, on average, half of a half of a parent's genes. As they have the same two parents they will therefore have half of their genes in common. Individuals with one parent in common would share a quarter of their genes.

The sharing of genes between close relatives can have significant effects on the quality of offspring of crosses between relatives. This is because each individual is heterozygous, on average, for two recessive semi-lethal alleles. These very rare alleles occur for different genes in different lineages and consequently do not normally appear in the homozygous condition and so cause no ill effects. In matings between related individuals, however, the chance of producing the homozygous condition is greatly increased. In zoo studies it has been found that there is a 33% reduction in survival of offspring of inbred crosses (Ralls et al, 1988). Great care should therefore be taken in maintaining captive colonies by keeping accurate stud books and carefully selecting parents when breeding.

WHY THINGS DON'T TURN OUT AS THEY SHOULD

The previous discussion focused on an investigation of genes that were either dominant or recessive. However all traits are the result of a complex series of biochemical reactions and therefore most phenotypes are determined by a combination of two or more interacting genes. Codominance is an exception to the dominance - recessive pattern and involves the expression of both alleles in the heterozygote, usually producing an intermediate phenotype. As a result the presence of both alleles can be detected in the phenotype.

Aird et al (1989) and Wilkinson et al (1991) investigated venoms in the Mojave rattlesnake. Although not addressed directly, these works appear to provide evidence of codominance of the venom phenotype both at the inter- and intraspecific level. Two distinct venoms (A and B) are produced in *C. s. scutulatus* and these intergrade to produce a third venom with the characteristics of both venoms (Wilkinson et al, 1991). When *Crotalus atrox*, the North American western diamondback rattlesnake, hybridises with *C. s. scutulatus* the offspring have venom with the characteristics of both species, while a cross between the hybrids showed venom characteristics of *C. atrox*, *C. c. scutulatus* or both (Aird et al, 1989). From this information it can be hypothesised that the genes coding for venom are expressed codominantly in the heterozygote form.

Phenotypes of some heterozygotes may appear exactly intermediate between that of the two ho-

Western Diamondback Rattlesnake, *Crotalus atrox.* **Photo by Zoltan Takacs.**

mozygotes. Sometimes, however, they may be more similar to one of the parental phenotypes than the other. Thus the level of phenotypic expression in heterozygotes varies with degree of dominance of one allele over another.

In some instances a single gene may have multiple phenotypic effects, with no obvious physiological connection. This is referred to as a pleiotropic effect.

Stamps (1994) reported on a study by Hews and coworkers that showed that early androgen treatments affects the development of alternative male phenotypes in *Urosaurus ornatus*, tree lizards. Males can be classified into two types based on the colour of their dewlaps (an extendable fold of skin on the throat used in display), either all orange or orange with a blue patch in the centre. The two colour morphs also grow at different rates, attain different asymptotic sizes and are different with respect to social behaviour. Orange males are nomadic and relatively more passive than the 'blue' males which aggressively maintain territories against conspecific males. Distribution in dewlap colour is approximately 50 : 50 in the wild population. Males castrated as day old hatchlings nearly all developed orange dewlaps, whereas most hatchlings implanted with testosterone developed

'blue' dewlaps and the control group developed approximately 50 : 50 orange and 'blue' dewlaps. Developmentally the animals responded as expected for their acquired phenotype. If it is assumed that the genetic control of the amount of hormone is the result of alternative forms of a single gene, then this example is typical of pleiotropy in that the variation in testosterone level resulted in changes in a suite of apparently unrelated characteristics namely dewlap colour, growth and behaviour.

Although in diploid reptiles, each individual can have only one of two alleles for each gene, there may be many different alleles for the gene within the population. Based on the breeding data obtained for *L. getulua*, Zweifel (1981) hypothesised that there was a third allele within the Long Beach population at the locus for the ringed and striped phenotypes.

COORDINATED INHERITANCE OF SEVERAL GENES

To date discussion has been focused on single genes, however, frequently the inheritance of more than one gene is of interest. If each gene being

Parental phenotypes   normal orange and black pigmented skin x albino
Genotypes $OOBB$ x $oobb$
Gametes OB, ob
F_1 offspring phenotype   normal orange and black pigmented skin
Genotype $OoBb$

Cross of F_1 progeny $OoBb$ x $OoBb$
Gametes OB, Ob, oB, ob

<table>
<tr><td></td><td></td><td colspan="4">Maternal</td></tr>
<tr><td></td><td></td><td>OB</td><td>Ob</td><td>oB</td><td>ob</td></tr>
<tr><td rowspan="4">Paternal</td><td>OB</td><td>OOBB</td><td>OOBb</td><td>OoBB</td><td>OoBb</td></tr>
<tr><td>Ob</td><td>OOBb</td><td>OObb</td><td>OoBb</td><td>Oobb</td></tr>
<tr><td>oB</td><td>OoBB</td><td>OoBb</td><td>ooBB</td><td>ooBb</td></tr>
<tr><td>ob</td><td>OoBb</td><td>Oobb</td><td>ooBb</td><td>oobb</td></tr>
</table>

Genotype frequency:

1/16 $OOBB$ + 2/16 $OOBb$ +
        2/16 $OoBB$ + 4/16 $OoBb$
1/16 $ooBB$ + 2/16 $ooBb$
1/16 $OObb$ + 2/16 $Oobb$
1/16 $oobb$

Phenotype frequency

= 9/16 black and orange
= 3/16 black
= 3/16 orange
= 1/16 albino

Figure 3.
Inheritance of black and orange pigments in *Elaphe guttata*.

Corn Snake, *Elaphe guttata*. 'Reverse Okeetee' albino. Photo by Isabelle Francais.

investigated is located on a different pair of chromosomes, then they should each behave as monohybrid traits and also assort independently at meiosis. If the two genes are located in the same chromosome, they will be 'linked' and therefore may not assort independently during meiosis.

Suzuki et al (1989) provided an example of a dihybrid cross with independent assortment which resulted in varying colour morphs among *Elaphe guttata*, corn snakes. In this species the gene for dominant skin pigmentation (*OOBB*) produces a pattern of black and orange pigment. When only the alternative form of the orange gene is present which procedures a nonfunctional enzyme (*ooBB*), no orange pigment is produced and so the snake is black. Likewise when the enzyme which determines black pigment colour is defective, the snake will be orange (*OObb*). When only the defective form of both enzymes are present, the snake will be albino (*oobb*) (see Figure 3).

During meiosis sections of the DNA are exchanged between the matched pair of chromosomes (crossing over). When the genes are very close together on the chromosome they will seldom be separated by crossing over and thus move as a block and there will be more hatchlings with parental appearance than with novel combinations of both parents. At the opposite extreme the genes may be widely separated on the same chromosome, such that crossing over generally occurs between them and therefore they may approximate independent assortment. Frequently genes are at intermediate distances between these two extremes and thus the percentage of segregation would vary depending on the placement of the genes in the chromosomes. Zweifel (1981) hypothesised that in some populations of *L. getulua*, the genes for striped and banded patterns (discussed previously) were closely linked with a gene that influenced venter colour.

WHEN GENES MEET ENVIRONMENTAL INFLUENCES

The above sections have focused on differences in phenotype which result from alternative genotypes at a single locus. Examples include the ringed and banded patterns of *L. getulus* and the colour morph inheritance of *E. guttata*. Traits of this type are well suited to genetic analysis via the study of their pedigrees. This is because the genes which influence the phenotype are few in number and there is a simple correspondence between different genotypes and phenotypes. However many traits which are widely used for recognition and description of reptiles are influenced by several genes and may also be affected by environmental factors. Such characters can have varying phenotypes due to alternative alleles at various loci. In addition, local environmental conditions may influence the phenotypic expression of the genotype. Such traits will not have several discrete phenotypes but will show a single continuous range of variation.

The differences in phenotype observed with some quantitative traits are the outcome of differences in genotype, with environmental influences having minimal influence. Alternatively it may be predominantly environment which influences variability in expression of other traits, with extraneous genetic factors having little impact. More generally both environment and genetic factors interact, both contributing to the expression of the trait (Hartl, 1994). To exacerbate the problems involved, most morphological characters are adaptive such that selection may lead to only a limited number of phenotypes surviving. This can result in convergence of character states in unrelated species. Conversely it may exaggerate differences, causing additional complications (Burgin, 1989).

Despite these problems, quantitative characters such as scale counts, body proportions, scale arrangement and colour morphology, generally provide the simplest and most convenient means of identification at all taxonomic levels and so they are widely used in the classification of reptiles, at

Snapping Turtle, *Chelydra serpentina*, hatching. Photo by W. P. Mara.

least in the field (Cogger, 1992). Such traits may vary within a species and thus create problems in interpretation as to whether one or more species are involved. These problems of plasticity can frequently be overcome by examining a large number of independent traits, maximising the number of individuals investigated, ensuring that samples are drawn from the entire range of the species and submitting the data to some form of multivariate analysis or appropriate alternative. Scores of papers have been written, based on the use of quantitative traits, which provide clear taxa boundaries and thus attest to the success of the approach (Bezy, 1989; Dohm et al, 1993; Greer, 1989; Lamb et al, 1990; Taylor, 1990; Taylor et al, 1993).

ENVIRONMENTAL INTERACTION WITH GENE EXPRESSION

Virtually every aspect of the functioning and appearance of a reptile is under the control of one or more genes and the expression of such genes is frequently influenced by the environment. The extent to which there is interference with phenotypic expression is frequently difficult to isolate, identify and quantify. Despite this, numerous environmental factors have been identified which clearly influence phenotypic expression in reptiles. Characters affected include metabolic efficiency (Christian et al, 1994), caudal and ventral scale numbers (Grobman, 1992; Osgood, 1978), clutch parameters (e.g., Allsteadt et al, 1995; Howland, 1992) and it has also been widely reported that temperature of incubation can be responsible for sex determination in reptilian species (Georges, 1988).

The effects of temperature of incubation is not restricted to its influence on sex, however, for example the growth patterns of *Chelydra serpentina* (the snapping turtle) hatchlings may be influenced by temperature of incubation, in addition to factors such as maternal/paternal effects and social interaction during early growth. It has also been suggested that incubation environment may have long term consequences for the individual which are not apparent at the time of exposure (McKnight et al, 1993).

Seigel et al (1991) reported that a number of field studies have revealed that squamate reptiles show substantial phenotypic plasticity in many life history traits, especially in response to prey availability and/or rainfall. Laboratory based studies supported these field observations and demonstrated that clutch size and mass vary in response to energy intake but that relative clutch size and hatchling size were less affected, an indication that

Western Whiptail, *Cnemidophorus tigris*. Photo by R. D. Bartlett.

the latter are less influenced by the environmental parameters than the former. Studies of *Cophosaurus texanus*, the greater earless lizard, also revealed differences in clutch parameters, onset of reproduction, animal size (possibly) age at first reproduction, adult size, growth rates and differences in adult survivorship were correlated with differences in energy intake in different habitats (Howland, 1992). Variation in clutch characteristics have also been reported in many other species including *Alligator mississippiensis* (Allsteadt et al, 1995), *Crocodylus porosus*, *Crocodylus novaeguineae* (Burgin, 1981), *Cnemidophorus tigris gracilis*, *Cnemidophorus tigris septentrionalis* (Taylor et al, 1992), *Nerodia rhombifer* (Plummer, 1992) and Australian colubrid snakes (Shine, 1991).

Alvarado et al (1995) investigated the reproductive characteristics of gravid *Iguana iguana*, green iguanas, from tropical America and reported that maternal size significantly influenced the size and weight of clutches and hatchlings, although mean weight of eggs varied little with female size. Previous studies had demonstrated that *I. iguana* size varied with habitat, animals from drier areas attained smaller size than those from more moist habitats. This was attributed to differences in food availability in the different areas (Harris, 1982;

Müller, 1972). The same growth trends were observed in *Sphenodon punctatus*, the tuatara, and this also was attributed to lack of food (Newman et al, 1994). Such phenotypic plasticity therefore appears to be a widespread phenomena.

In a study of *Natrix fasciata* using five thermal regimes, Osgood (1978) observed that the number of caudal and ventral scales differed between regimes. High and low temperatures lead to an increase in the number of scales and the frequency of gross abnormalities. Likewise studies of the garter snake, *Thamnophis elegans atratus*, incubated at temperature differences of 5°C also produced differences in these scale counts, with fewer scales being counted on individuals incubated at lower temperatures (Fox, 1948; Fox et al, 1961). More recently Grobman (1992) reported on the examination of metameres (ventral plus caudal scales) in a large number of specimens of *Opheodrys vernalis* from across the range of the species. He determined that such factors as vegetation, temperature, topography, distance and past historical events such as glaciation or aridity, correlated with metamere number, implying both environmental and genetic components. For example he observed a relationship between ambient summer temperatures and total numbers of these scales, such that

131

Western Garter Snake, *Thamnophis elegans*. Photo by K. H. Switak.

for a one degree increase in mid-summer temperature the number of scales increased by approximately one and three quarters. Snakes from different habitats also characteristically had different numbers of ventral and caudal scales, for example animals from moister areas tended to have higher numbers of metameres than those found in prairie areas (Grobman, 1992).

Zweifel (1981) reported that abnormally low incubation temperatures may result in normally blotched *Python molurus* having a partly striped pattern. Thus the environmental conditions under which eggs are incubated may, in some circumstances, influence colour patterns of hatchings.

CHROMOSOMAL VARIATION

Although not universally applicable, many reptile species are represented by separate sexes and fertilisation is required for reproduction (Dessauer et al, 1986). In some taxa sex chromosomes are absent, for example the orders Crocodilia (Cohen et al, 1970) and Rhyncocephalia (Wylie et al, 1968). Conversely in other taxa, for example some snake families they are universal (Singh, 1972). In other groups, for example snakes (Mengden et al, 1980), lizards (Donnellan, 1985) and turtles (Georges, 1988), their occurrence is more infrequent.

Some reptiles with sex chromosomes have the same *XY* chromosome system as that observed in humans. Females of these taxa undergo normal, sexual reproduction and have an identical pair of sex chromosomes (*XX*) while males have two different sex chromosomes (*XY*). When chromosomes undergo meiosis they randomly segregate into different gametes. No matter what the sex determining mechanism, all sexually reproducing reptiles have this pattern of inheritance for all homologous pairs of chromosomes.

Some reptile taxa, however, are parthenogenetic and these species do not undergo normal meiotic division, instead they reproduce asexually. There are numerous recordings of parthenogenetic forms of geckos, for example the common tropical gecko, *Lepidodactylus* (e.g., Radtkey et al, 1995), tropical gecko *Nactus pelagicus* (Moritz, 1987; Donnellan et al, 1995), Taiwanese population of *Hemidactylus garnotii-vietnamenisis* (Ota et al, 1989) and *Heteronotia binoet* (Moritz, 1991; Moritz et al, 1989). Other species in which parthenogenous has been identified include *Elaphe bairdi*, Baird's rat snake (Lawson et al, 1990), several clones of the genus *Cnemidophorus*, whiptail lizards (Bickham et al, 1976; Lowe et al, 1966; McKinney et al, 1973; Parker et al, 1989; Paulissen et al, 1988,

Indo-Pacific Gecko, *Hemidactylus garnoti*. Photo by R. D. Bartlett.

1992), *Ramphotyphlops braminus*, Brahminy blind snake (Wynn et al, 1987), *Agkistrodon piscivorus leucostoma*, western cottonmouth (Tiersch et al, 1991), *Gymnophthalmus underwoodi* (Cole et al, 1993) and the iguanid complex of *Sceloporus grammicus* (Hall et al, 1973).

Many parthenogenetic species can be traced to hybridisation between two different species (Cole, 1975, 1979, 1983; Lowe et al, 1966; Vrijenhoek et al, 1989) and Radtkey et al (1995) reported that in all 'well studied' parthenogenetic vertebrates hybridisation between sexually reproducing species have been identified as the ancestors of the new species.

Goldenscale Anole, *Anolis chrysolepis*.
Photo by R. D. Bartlett.

In addition to hybridisation, changes in chromosome number may be the result of errors which occur during cell division. Polyploidy (multiplication of chromosome complement) may occur as a result of nondisjunction when the homologous chromosomes fail to separate properly and move to opposite poles. This results in one daughter cell receiving all of the homologous chromosomes and the other cell receiving none. It may also arise through the fertilisation of an egg by more than one sperm, leading to a zygote with a nucleus containing three or more sets of chromosomes. Abberant chromosomes numbers may also result from the fusion of a normal gamete with an unreduced diploid cell (Austin, 1960). The latter scenario has been suggested by several authors (e.g., Cole, 1983; Porter, 1988) for triploid ($3n$) male lizards they described. In contrast Hall et al (1973) proposed that the female *Sceloporus grammicus* he identified may have developed parthenogenetically by fusion of two ovum.

In some groups examples of polyploidy have been recorded in otherwise normal diploid ($2n$) bisexual populations, although in such circumstances the condition is generally rare. For example small numbers of chromosomally aberrant individuals of *Lepidophyma flavimaculatum* (Bezy, 1989), *Agkistrodon piscivorus leucostoma*, the west-

ern cottonmouth, (Tiersch et al, 1991), *Sceloporus occidentalis* (Cole, 1983) *Sceloporus graciosus* (Thomspon et al, 1986) *Sceloporus grammicus* (Hall, et al, 1973; Porter, 1988) and *Amphibolurus nobbi* (Witten, 1978) have been identified.

Some species such as *Platemys platycephala*, the twist-necked turtle, have varying levels of ploidy with viable diploids ($2n$), triploids ($3n$), diploid-triploid ($2n$-$3n$) mosaics and triploid-tetraploid ($3n$-$4n$) mosaics, although it has been demonstrated that males produce balanced gametes, indicating that they are sexually reproducing (Bickham et al, 1985, 1993). Such diploid-triploid mosaicism has also been recorded in the lizard genus *Lacerta* (Kupriyanova, 1989) and extreme variability also occurs at both the inter- and intra-specific level in *Sceloporus* (Porter, 1988).

An alternative form of sex determination in reptiles is temperature dependent and this is the topic of another chapter.

CHROMOSOMAL AND MOLECULAR TECHNIQUES

In the last two decades chromosomal and molecular techniques have proved useful in elucidating phylogenetic (genetic) relationships, both at the inter- and intra-specific levels. Genetic differen-

Baird's Rat Snake, *Elaphe bairdi*. Photo by R. D. Bartlett.

tiation, at the genomic level, begins at the time of reproductive isolation. The data obtained from such studies can therefore help delineate natural groups at any taxonomic level. Similarities in molecular structure may reveal common ancestry while alterations in the structure can detect divergent evolutionary pathways (Sarich, 1977a; Hillis et al, 1990).

There are various techniques available to measure the degree of differentiation among taxa. These include allozyme, immunological and various DNA sequencing techniques, all of which are broadly comparable in terms of time, effort and money per unit of information obtained (Sarich, 1977b). Within the limits of resolution for any of the biochemical techniques, that is 'the number of visible substitutions per unit time', the relative genetic distances are generally congruent. It has been demonstrated that there is a close relationship between protein structure and gene structure, so that a comparison of homologous proteins among taxa essentially provides a comparison of their genes (Gorman et al, 1971).

The limits of a particular technique may vary widely depending on the taxa being investigated and the taxonomic or phylogenetic level of interest. Basically the more distant the relationship between two taxa, the more emphasis should be placed on selecting slow evolving characters, whether morphological or biochemical. Investigating colour morphs or the number of sub-caudal scales may be useful for delineating species boundaries but at higher taxonomic levels their utility diminishes rapidly. This is because, as previously discussed, they are prone to modification in response to environmental factors. If all taxa within a group have unique characters, the data contribute nothing above the species level, and, due to environmental plasticity, it is frequently impossible to determine whether the variation is a result of convergence or retention of ancestral states. In many respects the limits of biochemical techniques are more readily identified than those of

Blackbelly Racerunner, *Cnemidophorus deppei*. Photo by R. D. Bartlett.

techniques which employ morphological characters. However it may be difficult to determine without *a priori* knowledge, the most appropriate technique for a specific problem.

Numerous studies of chromosome morphology and number addressing both evolutionary and specific level taxonomy, have been undertaken. For example investigations of Australian taxa include studies of varanids (King et al, 1975; King et al, 1982), gekkonids (King, 1977, 1979, 1982; King et al, 1977; King et al, 1982; King and Rofe, 1976), elapids (Mengden, 1985a, 1985b; Baverstock and Schwaner, 1985) and skinks (King, 1973). Although karyotype data are not useful in dating times of divergence (Baverstock and Schwaner, 1985), this technique can be a useful adjunct to molecular studies (King, 1987).

GENES AT THE POPULATION LEVEL

Since inherited enzyme polymorphism was first described by Porter and co-workers in 1962, many studies of genetic variability in natural populations have been undertaken (Graur, 1986). Since that time increasing use has been made of molecular tech-

Cottonmouths, *Agkistrodon piscivorous*. Photo by W. B. Allen, Jr.

Western Fence Swift, *Sceloporus occidentalis*. Photo by R. D. Bartlett.

niques in attempts to quantify genetic variation (Avise, 1994).

Allozyme electrophoresis has become a routine tool, widely used in this area of research. It involves the separation of soluble proteins in an electrical field on the basis of their charge, and to a lesser extent, by their shape and size (Ayala et al, 1975). Proteins which differentially migrate usually differ by a least one amino acid (Avise, 1974). Since this implies variation in at least one nucleotide base pair of the DNA sequence, the observed variation is accepted to be genetic. This variation is discrete and quantifiable, in marked contrast to the majority of conventional data, such as morphology which, as previously discussed, may be modified by several genes and influenced by environment.

Since 1968 when Throckmorton demonstrated the taxonomic value of the allozyme electrophoretic technique, many papers have included discussion of taxonomic implications. Such literature has been reviewed (e.g., Avise, 1994) and Richardson et al (1986) presented the current applications of the technique for both systematic and population genetic studies.

The utility of the technique varies considerably depending on the group being analysed. In 1982 when Avise and Aquadro reviewed the available literature, reptiles had not been widely studied using electrophoretic techniques, however, they observed that three of the five genera they examined, *Anolis*, *Bipes* and *Lacerta*, were more genetically variable than any non-amphibian genera while the two other genera they reported on, *Crrotaphytus* and *Uma* demonstrated considerable less genetic variability than other groups assayed. (Avise and Aquadro, 1982). Thus the utility of the technique varies considerably depending on the taxa being analysed. In closely related species, differentiation typically occurs at 10% of loci. At this level of differentiation the technique is useful for delineating species boundaries and elucidating relationships. Traditionally the upper limit of utility has been considered to be 60-70% divergence (Richardson et al, 1986).

In the last decade there has been a rapid expansion in the use of molecular techniques used to address genetic hypotheses. These techniques of DNA manipulation have focused around the isolation, amplification, sequence and expression of genes. They provide a suite of excellent tools to investigate genetically inherited characters.

TAXONOMIC VALUE OF GENETICALLY ASSESSED MOLECULAR VARIATION

Since population genetic studies probe the extent of variation within populations and the sys-

tematist is concerned with the delineation of biological species, and frequently phylogenetic reconstruction, there are fundamental differences in approach depending on the aim of the study. Questions concerning population genetics require investigation of frequency data (e.g., allelic frequencies). Conversely when emphasis is placed on inter-species relationships, the number of loci showing fixed allelic frequencies among species is of interest (Crozier, 1990; Richardson et al, 1986).

It is generally accepted that the basic unit of evolution in outbreeding populations is the population, since individuals within such a grouping share a common gene pool. The selection imposed on this gene pool by the fixation of mutations constitutes the basis of evolution. A population, or group of populations, constitute a species. Although many exceptions occur (generally between recently differentiated species) it is generally accepted that sexually producing, diploid individuals of one species do not inter-breed with other species to produce fertile offspring (Ferguson, 1980).

DETECTION OF GENETIC SPECIES

Since by definition a species maintains a single integrated gene pool, the demonstration that there are two different alleles, with no heterozygotes (that is two separate gene pools) at a single locality is sufficient to demonstrate that two taxa are present. When it is suspected that two species occur at the same location (i.e., in sympatry), this hypothesis can be explored using molecular techniques. This is best achieved by testing the null hypothesis, that is that random mating occurs at the locality. To address this hypothesis it is necessary to determine the expected number of heterozygotes at a single locus, achieved by calculating the deviation from expected number of heterozygotes if random breeding was occurring. The probability of not obtaining heterozygotes in a given sample of randomly mating individuals is calculated by the equation:

$$1 - 2pq$$

where p and q = relative allele frequencies and $p + q = 1$.

If the population is non-randomly mating and the frequency of two alleles p and q, occur in the population at 0.5, then the expected probability of finding a heterozygote is $2pq = 0.5$. Thus the likelihood of not finding a heterozygote among a sample of 10 individuals collected from the same population is $(0.5)^{10}$ or 0.1%. Although Richardson et al (1986) pointed out that the real allele frequency in a population may not be 0.5, they demonstrated that the proportion of heterozygotes at different allele frequencies is relatively similar between $p = 0.3$ and $p = 0.7$ and therefore an error of such magnitude does not significantly distort the data. By incorporating information from additional loci which present the same trend, increased confidence may be placed in the observation. When no heterozygotes are observed in a sample, but different allelic forms are identified, there is evidence to reject the null hypothesis and thereby accept that two species are present at the locality. However this should not be concluded on the basis of a single fixed difference, unless other evidence has been provided from morphological, ecological, behavioural, chromosomal or other molecular clues. Relying on the evidence from a single locus, may provide erroneous conclusions since it is possible that it may be a result of non-genetic variation. Some form of complex genetic control of that particular locus or chance may be responsible for the observed 'genetic' pattern.

As implied above, only a small sample is required for such a study. When it is hypothesised that two species exist, due to alternative characters, a fixed difference in a sample of ten individuals (five from each form) will provide the information to reject the null hypothesis that a single species occurs at the locality. This is because, as explained above, the chances of identifying no heterozygotes but identifying five individuals homozygous for one locus and five homozgyous at the alternative locus is 0.1%. However, since the determination of cryptic species is based on observed fixed differences between taxa, it is desirable to maximise the number of loci screened and the sample size is therefore less significant (Richardson et al, 1986).

GENETIC DETECTION OF SPECIES FROM DIFFERENT LOCALITIES

As with the detection of sympatric species, molecular techniques for studying inherited variation provide powerful tools for determining the species status of populations in different localities (allopatric species). A major advantage of the technique is that the extent of genetic divergence observed is quantifiable and each character (locus) is independent. Such techniques also measure a fixed proportion of the genome. Ayala (1976), in a discussion of the advantages of using allozyme techniques, pointed out that morphological data are frequently quantitative since the characters are not necessarily independent and problems frequently arise in the attempt to determine to what extent morphological traits represent a fixed proportion of the genome.

Unlike the related case of determining the genetic divergence required to satisfy the hypothesis of distinct species in sympatry, the extent of genetic divergence required to satisfy the hypothesis of specific status in allopatry is more difficult. Richardson et al (1986) suggested that under these conditions it is also advisable to concentrate on the null hypothesis. In this way taxa remain as a single species until sufficient genetic divergence is recognised to demonstrate otherwise. Marginal cases are therefore retained as a single unit, unless alternative data are available to support the hypotheses to split the taxon.

As with any technique it is unwise to base a decision on one form of molecular data alone. Thus if two populations show no molecular divergence with a technique, it does not necessarily mean that they belong to the same taxon but rather that the information available failed to reject the null hypothesis of a single taxon. Alternatively where it is demonstrated that the two taxa have diverged genetically, the null hypothesis may be rejected and a case made for allocation to different taxa. Always, however, the accuracy of the fixed difference estimated will be influenced by the number of loci sampled. The greater the number of loci investigated, the more reliable the result. Richardson et al (1986) also suggested that more valid decisions are possible when the data are placed in the context of genetic differentiation between conspecific populations of taxa across their geographic range and between species of congeners.

SORTING OUT THE 'FAMILY TREE'

For a technique to be utilised in phylogenetic reconstruction, it is desirable for characters to be independent and to have a genetic basis. Molecular data fulfils both these criteria and is therefore generally superior to morphological criteria for such reconstruction (Burgin, 1989).

Before investigating hypotheses concerning phylogenies, however, it is necessary to determine that the level of genetic differentiation for the group is appropriate. Hillis et al (1990) investigated popular molecular techniques and concluded that allozyme electrophoresis was most useful for comparisons of races, species and closely related genera.

Whatever approach to systematics is taken it is necessary to infer relationships on the basis of shared characters (Buth, 1984), however, where no differentiation is detected, the technique may be inappropriate and an alternative approach may be needed. Problems also occur where extensive genetic differentiation is identified and again alternative techniques need to be utilised. When two species share a small number of identical alleles, observed similarities may be due to convergence of character types.

Although genetic differences calculated from allozyme electrophoretic data occur among groups, in general (with some exceptions for example the birds which are generally invariant at the specific level) most closely related vertebrates tend to differ at approximately 10% of their loci (Avise et al, 1982) and seldom more than 15% (Baverstock et al, 1977). Richardson et al (1986) considered the upper limit of allozyme electrophoresis is 60 - 70% divergence since problems of convergence become acute above this level, although Briscoe et al (1987) considered that this limit may be extended using their data retrieval techniques. With such guidelines in mind, assessment of the utility of a technique for a specific study may be readily achieved by undertaking a preliminary study to determine the range of genetic divergence within the taxa of interest.

As with studies involving delineation of species boundaries, large numbers of individuals from a single locality are unnecessary in phylogentic investigations. Genetic distance measurements are more severely affected by the number of loci investigated than by the sample size (Nei, 1978; Gorman et al, 1979). Richardson et al (1986) suggested that as few as two or three representatives of a single population are generally sufficient. However, collection of samples over the full geographic range of the species and maximisation of the number of loci investigated is desirable.

Thus there is a fundamental difference in the approach taken to studying inter- versus intra-specific problems. Studies which involve population structure, require detailed study of a large number of individuals using some parameter which is variable among individuals (e.g., gene frequency data). Invariant characters do not contribute any information. The most appropriate approach to analysis of such information is to test the null hypothesis that the observed frequencies are not significantly different among samples. For specific loci this can be achieved by using a chi-squared test of homogeneity which measures the probability that

Twistneck Turtle, *Platemys platycephala*. Photo by R. D. Bartlett.

Above: Collared Lizard, *Crotaphytus collaris*. Photo by R. D. Bartlett.
Below: Viviparous Lizard, *Lacerta vivipara*. Photo by W. Wuster.

observed numbers deviate from expected numbers and thus gives a measure of divergence at a specific locus (Sokal et al, 1973).

When such deviation is detected at a number of loci, a measure of genetic distance or similarity may be calculated between species pairs. Various measures have been proposed (e.g., Nei, 1972; Morton et al, 1973; Rogers, 1972). Buth (1984) suggested that most are highly correlated despite varying mathematical and biological assumptions. The most widely used coefficients of variations are those of Nei (1972) and Rogers (1972).

When inter-specific relationships are of interest, the extent of genetic differentiation is of concern. All loci, whether variant or not, contribute to the interpretation. The amount of information contributed by polymorphic loci will depend on the level of polymorphism. When a taxon is monomorphic for all loci investigated, a single individual will represent the taxon. With increasing levels of polymorphism, a larger contribution to the interpretation will be made by gene frequency data. In general, however, most vertebrates demonstrate relatively low levels of polymorphism and, although variable, it is frequently approximately 15% (Richardson et al, 1986).

Historically measures of similarity, particularly Nei (1972) and Rogers (1972), which were developed to probe population substructure, were used in the analysis of systematic data. These measures rely heavily on gene frequency data which, in reality, contribute little to the study of genetic divergence. This is because most loci tend to have allele frequencies which are very similar, or alternatively fixed differently. Few demonstrate intermediate levels of polymorphism (Avise et al, 1975; Richardson et al, 1986).

Analysis of genetic divergence for classification has two possible aims. One is to categorise into groups for ease of identification (not necessarily based on genetic characteristics) and the other aims to base some genetic predictions on such relationships (Funk, 1983). There are thus basically two alternative conceptual approaches to the study of systematics. At the polarised extremes argument rages over whether systems should be based on similarities in appearance or a genetic basis, however, in reality the whole spectrum of possibilities between the two extremes are covered (Burgin, 1989; Hillis et al, 1990).

Three major schools of thought exist (Cracraft, 1983). Those advocating a phenetic approach (e.g., Sokal et al, 1973) which effectively synonomise the study of systematics with taxonomy. Such categorisation is based solely on similarities among living organisms (Fergusion, 1980) without concern for a genetic basis. At the alternative extreme the phylogenetic approach, based primarily on the work of Hennig (1966) demands that phylogenetic relationships should be the basis of classification. Between the two extremes the evolutionary systematists (e.g., Mayr, 1969, 1981; Simpson, 1961) conceive systematics as incorporating both the study of diversity and evolutionary considerations. Despite protracted argument over these various possible methods of analysis, there has not emerged a clearly definable, universally acceptable method (Hillis et al., 1990; Richardson et al, 1986). If all characters were perfectly compatible, it would seem logical to use a purely cladistic approach as the basis of classification. In reality, however, it is unlikely that such a situation will arise, therefore alternative analyses generally need to be considered and before any analyses are undertaken it would be necessary to be acquainted with the 'state of the art'.

REFERENCES AND RECOMMENDED READING

—Aird, SD; Thirkhill, LJ; Seebart, CS; Kaiser, II:
Venoms and morphology of western diamondback/Mojave rattlesnake hybrids. Journal of Herpetology, 1989; 23(2): 131-141.

—Allsteadt, J; Ibarra, L; Suazo, I:
Reproductive characteristics of the green iguana (*Iguana iguana*) population of the west coast of Mexico. The Southwestern Naturalist, 1995; 40(2): 234-237.

—Alvarado, J; Lang, JW:
Incubation temperature affects body size and energy reserves of hatchling American crocodiles (*Alligator mississippiensis*). Physiological Zoology, 1995; 68(1): 76-97.

—Austin, CR:
Anomalies of fertilisation leading to triploidy. Journal of Cell Comparative Physiology, 1960; 56(Suppl. 1): 1-15.

—Avise, JC:
Systematic value of electrophoretic data. Systematic Zoology, 1974; 23: 465-481.

—Avise, JC:
Molecular markers, natural history and evolution. Chapman and Hall, 1994.

—Avise, JC; Smith, JJ; Ayala, FJ:
Adaptive differentiation with little genic change between two California minnows. Evolution, 1975; 29: 411-426.

—Avise, JC; Aquadro, CF:
A comparative summary of genetic distances in vertebrates: patterns and correlations. Evolutionary Biology, 1982; 15: 151-188.

—**Ayala, FJ:**
Genetic differentiation during the speciation process. Evolutionary Biology, 1975; 29: 411-426.

—**Ayala, FJ:**
Molecular evolution. Sinauer Associates, Sunderland, 1976.

—**Baverstock, PR; Schwaner, TD:**
Phylogeny of Australian elapid snakes: the genetic approach. Biology of Australasian frogs and reptiles, G Grigg; Shine R; Ehmann H (Eds). Surrey Beatty and Sons Pty Ltd, Sydney, 1985, pp. 159-164.

—**Baverstock, PR; Watts, CHS; Cole, SR;**
Electrophoretic comparisons between allopatric populations of five Australian Pseudomyine rodents (Muridae), 1977; 30: 471-485

—**Bezy, RL:**
Morphological differentiation in unisexual and bisexual Xantusiid lizards of the genus *Lepidophyma* in Central America. Herpetological Monographs, 1989; 3: 61-80.

—**Bickham, JW; McKinney, CO; Mathews, MF:**
Karyotypes of the parthenogenetic whiptail lizard *Cnemidophorus laredoensis* and its presumed parental species (Sauria: Teiidae). Herpetologica, 1976; 32: 395-399.

—**Bickham, JW; Hanks, BG; Hale, DW; Martin, JE:**
Ploidy diversity and the production of balanced gametes in male twist-necked turtles (*Platemys platycephala*). Copeia, 1993; 1993(3): 723-727.

—**Bickham, JW; Tucker, PK; Legler, JM:**
Diploid-triploid mosaicism: an unusual phenomenon in side-necked turtles (*Platemys platycephala*). Science, 1985; 277: 1591-1593.

—**Blanchard, FN; Blanchard, FC:**
The inheritance of melanism in the garter snake *Thamnophis sirtalis* (Linneaus) and some evidence of effective autumn mating. Papers of Michigan Academy of Science, Arts and Letters, 1941; 26: 177-193

—**Briscoe, DAB; Gooley, AA; Bernstein, RL; McKay, GM;**
Genetic diversity in cellular slime moulds: allozyme electrophoresis and a monoclonal antibody reveal cryptic species among *Dictyostelium discoideum* strains. Genetics, 1987; 117: 213-220.

—**Burgin, S:**
Experimental examination of rearing conditions for hatchling crocodiles. Masters of Science Thesis, University of Papua New Guinea,1981, 299pp.

—**Burgin, S:**
The taxonomy and phylogenetic relationships of Australian scincid lizards (Scincidae: Lygosominae: *Lampropholis*). PhD Thesis, Macquarie University, Sydney. 1989, 234pp.

—**Buth, DG:**
The applications of electrophoretic data in systematic studies. Annals of Human Genetics, 1984; 15: 501-522.

—**Christian, KA; Conley, KE:**
Activity and resting metabolism of varanid lizards compared with 'typical' lizards. Australian Journal of Zoology, 1994; 42: 185-193.

—**Cogger, H:**
Reptiles and amphibians of Australia. Reed Books, Frenchs Forest, New South Wales, 1992.

—**Cohen, MM; Gans, C:**
The chromosomes of the order Crocodilia. Cytogenetics, 1970; 9: 81-105.

—**Cole, CJ:**
Evolution of parthenogenetic species of reptiles. Intersexuality in the animal kingdom, R Reinboth (Ed.). Springer-Verlag, New York, 1975, pp. 340-355.

—**Cole, CJ:**
Chromosome inheritance in parthenogenetic lizards and evolution of allopolyploidy in reptiles. The Journal of Heredity, 1979; 70: 95-102.

—**Cole, CJ:**
Specific status of the North American fence lizards, *Sceloporus undulatus* and *Sceloporus occidentalis*, with comments on chromosome variation. American Museum Novitates, 1983; 2768: 1-13.

—**Cole, CJ; Dessauer, HC; Markezich, AL:**
Missing link found: the second ancestor of *Gymnophthalmus underwoodi* (Squamata: Teiidae), a South American unisexual lizard of hybrid origin. American Museum Novitates, 1993; 3055: 1-13.

—**Cracraft, J:**
The significance of phylogenetic classification for systematic and evolutionary biology. Numerical taxonomy, J Felsenstein (Ed.). NATO Scientific Affairs Division, Windsheim, 1983, pp 1-17.

—**Crozier, RH:**
From population genetics to phylogeny: uses and limits of mitochondrial DNA. Australian Systematic Botany, 1990; 3: 111-124.

—**Dessauer, HC:**
Biochemical and immunological evidence of relationships in Amphibia and Reptilia. Biochemical and immunological taxonomy of animals, CA Wright (Ed.). Academic Press, New York, 1986.

—**Dessauer, HC; Zweifel, RG:**
Inheritance of transferrin, phosphoglucomu-

tase, 6-phosogluconate dehydrogenase, and prolidase in a breeding colony of kingsnakes. The Journal of Heredity, 1981; 72: 453-455.

—**Dessauer, HC; Cole, CJ:**
Clonal inheritance in parthenogenetic whiptail lizards: biochemical evidence. The Journal of Heredity, 1986; 77: 8-12.

—**Dohm, MR; Garland, T, Jr:**
Quantitative genetics of scale counts in the garter snake *Thamnophis*. Copeia, 1993; 1993(4): 987-1002.

—**Donnellan, SC :**
The evolution of the sex chromosomes in scincid lizards. Ph.D. Dissertation, Macquarie University, Sydney. 1985, 142pp..

—**Donnellan, SC; Moritz, C:**
Genetic diversity of bisexual and parthenogenetic populations of the tropical gecko *Nactus pelagicus* (Lacertilia: Gekkonidae). Herpetologica, 1995; 51(2): 140-154.

—**Dunn, LC:**
The possible genetic basis of the ringed and striped patterns. American Midland Naturalist, 1944; 31: 91-95.

—**Ferguson, A:**
Biochemical systematics and evolution. Blackie and Sons Ltd, Glasgow, 1980.

—**Fox, W:**
Effect of temperature on development of scutellation in the garter snake, *Thamnophis elegans atratus*. Copeia, 1948; 1948: 252-262.

—**Fox, W; Gordon, C; Fox, MH:**
Morphological effects of low temperature during the embryonic development of the garter snake, *Thamnophis elegans*. Zoologica, 1961; 46: 57-71.

—**Funk, VA:**
The value of natural classification., J Felsenstein (Ed.). NATO Scientific Affairs Division, Windsheim, 1983, pp. 18-21.

—**Georges, A:**
Sex determination is independent of incubation temperature in another chelid turtle, *Chelodina longicollis*. Copeia, 1988; 1988(1): 248-254.

—**Gorman, GC; Wilson, AC; Nakaniski, M:**
A biochemical approach towards the study of reptilian phylogeny: evolution of serum albumin and lactic dehydrogenase. Systematic Zoology, 1971; 20: 167-186.

—**Gorman, GC; Renzi, J, Jr:**
Genetic distance and heterozygosity estimates in electrophoretic studies: effects of sample size. Copeia, 1979; 2: 242-249.

—**Graur, D:**
The evolution of electrophoretic mobility of proteins. Journal of Theoretical Biology, 1986; 118: 443-469.

—**Greer, A:**
Overlap pattern in the preanal scale row: an important systematic character in skinks. Journal of Herpetology, 1989; 24(3): 328-330.

—**Grobman, AB:**
Metamerism in the snake *Opheodrys vernalis*, with a description of a new subspecies. Journal of Herpetology, 1992; 26(2): 175-186.

—**Grudzien, TA; Owens, PJ:**
Genic similarity in the gray and brown color morphs of the snake *Storeria occipitomaculata*. Journal of Herpetology, 1991; 25(1): 90-92.

—**Hall, WP; Selander, RK:**
Hybridization of karyotypically differentiated populations in the *Sceloporus grammicus* complex (Iguanidae). Evolutionary Biology, 1973; 27: 226-242.

—**Harris, DM:**
The phenology, growth and survival of the green iguana *Iguana iguana*, in North Colombia. Iguanas of the world: behaviour, ecology and conservation, M Burghardt; Rand S (Eds). Noyes Publishers, New Jersey, 1982, pp. 150-161.

—**Hartl, DL:**
Genetics. Jones and Bartlett Publishers, Boston, 1994.

—**Hennig, W:**
Phylogenetic systematics. University of Illinois, Urbana, 1966.

—**Hillis, DM; Moritz, C:**
Molecular systematics. Sinauer, Sunderland, 1990.

—**Howland, JM:**
Life history of *Cophosaurus texanus* (Sauria: Iguanidae): environmental correlates and interpopulatonal variation. Copeia, 1992; 1992(1): 82-93.

—**King, M:**
Karyotypic studies of some Australian Scincidae (Reptilia). Australian Journal of Zoology, 1973; 21: 21-32.

—**King, M:**
Chromosomal and morphometric variation in the Gekko *Diplodactylus vittatus* (Gray). Australian Journal of Zoology, 1977; 25: 43-57.

—**King, M:**
Karyotypic variation in *Gehrya* (Gekkonidae: Reptilia) I: The *Gehyra variegata-punctata complex*. Australian Journal of Zoology, 1979; 27: 373-393.

—**King, M:**
Karyotypic variation in *Gehyra* (Gekkonidae: Reptilia) II: A new species from the Alligator Rivers region in northern Australia. Australian Journal of Zoology, 1982; 30: 93-101.

—**King, M:**
Origin of the Gekkonidae: chromosomal and albumin evolution suggest Gondwanaland. Search, 1987; 18(5): 252-254.

—**King, M; Braithwaite, RW; Wombey, JC:**
A new species of *Diplodactylus* (Reptilia: Gekkonidae) from the Alligator Rivers region, Northern Australia. Transactions of the Royal Society of South Australia, 1982; 106: 15-18.

—**King, M; King, D:**
Chromosomal evolution in the lizard genus *Varanus* (Reptilia). Australian Journal of Biological Science, 1975; 28: 89-108.

—**King, M; Rofe, R:**
Karyotypic variation in the Australian gekko *Phyllodactylus marmoratus* (Gray) (Gekkonidae: Reptilia). Chromosoma (Berl.), 1976; 54: 75-87.

—**Klauber, LM:**
The California king snake, a case of pattern dimorphism. Herpetologica, 1936; 1936: 18-27.

—**Klauber, LM:**
A further study of pattern dimorphism in the California king snake. Bulletin Zoological Society of San Diego, 1939; 15: 1-23.

—**Klauber, LM:**
The California king snake: a further discussion. American Midland Naturalist, 1944; 31: 85-87.

—**Kupriyanova, LA:**
Cytogenetic evidence for genome interaction in hybrid lacertid lizards. Evolution and ecology of unisexual vertebrates, RM Dawley; Bogart JP (Eds). New York State Museum, Albany, 1989, pp. 613-618.

—**Lamb, T; Lovich, J:**
Morphometric validation of the striped mud turtle (*Kinosternon baurii*) in the Carolinas and Virginia, Copeia 1990, 1990 (3): 613-618.

—**Lawson, R; Lieb, CS:**
Variation and hybridisation in *Elaphe bairdi* (Serpentes: Colubridae). Journal of Herpetology, 1990; 24(3): 280-292.

—**Lowe, CH; Wright, JW:**
Evolution of parthenogenetic species of *Cnemidophorus* (whiptail lizards) in western North America. Journal Arizonia Academy of Science, 1966; 4: 81-87.

—**Mayr, E:**
Remarks on Hobart Smith's analysis of the Western King Snakes. American Midland Naturalist, 1944; 31: 88-90.

—**Mayr, E:**
Principles of systematic zoology. New York,, 1969.

—**Mayr, E:**
Biological classification: towards a synthesis of opposing methodologies. Science, 1981; 214: 510-516.

—**McKinney, CO; Kay, FR; Anderson, RA:**
A new all-female species of the genus *Cnemidophorus*. Herpetologica, 1973; 29: 361-366.

—**McKnight, CM; Gutzke, WHN:**
Effects of the embryonic environment and of hatchling housing conditions on growth of young snapping turtles (*Chelydra serpentina*). Copeia, 1993; 1993(2): 475-482.

—**Mengden, GA:**
Chromosomal evolution in Serpentes: a comparison of G and C chromosome banding patterns of some Colubrid and Boid genera. Chromosoma, 1980; 53-64.

—**Mengden, GA:**
Australian elapid phylogeny: a summary of the chromosomal and electrophoretic data. Biology of Australasian frogs and reptiles, G Grigg; Shine R; Ehmann H (Eds). Surrey Beatty and Sons Pty Ltd, Sydney, 1985a, pp. 185-192.

—**Mengden, GA:**
A chromosomal and electrophoretic analysis of the genus *Pseudonaja*. Biology of Australasian frogs and reptiles, G Grigg; Shine R; Ehmann H (Eds). Surrey Beatty and Sons Pty Ltd, Sydney, 1985b, pp. 193-208.

—**Moritz, C:**
Parthenogenesis in the tropical gekkonid lizard, *Nactus pelagicus* (Sauria: Gekkonidae). Evolution, 1987; 41: 1252-1266.

—**Moritz, C:**
The origin and evolution of parthenogenesis in *Heteronotia binoeri* (Gekkonidae): evidence of recent and localized origins of widespread clones. Genetics, 1991; 129: 211-219.

—**Moritz, C; Donnellan, SC; Adams, M; Baverstock, PR:**
The origin and evolution of parthenogenesis in *Heteronotia binoei* (Gekkonidae): extensive genotype diversity among parthenogens. Evolution, 1989; 43: 994-1003.

—**Morton, NE; Yee, S; Harris, DE; Lew, R:**
Kinship and population structure. Genetic structure of populations,. University of Hawaii Press, Honolulu, 1973, pp. 66-71.

—**Müller, H:**
Ukologische und ethologische studien an *Iguana iguana* (Reptilia: Iguanidae) in Kolumbien. Zoologische Bertrage N.F., 1972; 18: 109-131.

—**Nei, M:**
Genetic distance between populations. American Naturalist, 1972; 106: 283-292.

—**Nei, M:**
Estimation of average heterozygosity and genetic distance from a small number of individuals. Genetics, 1978; 89: 583-590.

—**Newman, DG; Watson, PR; McFadden, I:**
Egg production by tuatara on Lady Alice and Stephens Island, New Zealand. New Zealand Journal of Zoology, 1994; 21: 387-398.

—**Osgood, DW:**
Effects of temperature on the development of meristic characteristics in *Natrix fasciata*. Copeia, 1978; 1978: 33-47.

—**Ota, H; Hikida, T:**
A new triploid *Hemidactylus* (Gekkonidae: Sauria) from Taiwan, with comments on morphological and karyological variation in the *H. garnotii-vietnamensis* complex. Journal of Herpetology, 1989; 23(1): 50-60.

—**Parker, EDJ; Walker, JM; Paulissen, MA:**
Clonal diversity in *Cnemidophorus*: ecological and morphological consequences. Evolution and ecology of unisexual vertebrates, RM Dawley; Bogart JP (Eds). New York State Museum, Albany, 1989.

—**Paulissen, MA; Walker, JM; Cordes, JE:**
Ecology of syntopic clones of the parthenogenetic whiptail lizard, *Cnemidophorus 'laredoensis'*. Journal of Herpetology, 1988; 22(3): 331-342.

—**Paulissen, MA; Walker, JM; Cordes, JE:**
Can parthenogenetic *Cnemidophorus laredoensis* (Teiidae) coexist with its bisexual congeners? Journal of Herpetology, 1992; 26(2): 153-158.

—**Plummer, MV:**
Relationships among mothers, litters, and neonates in diamondback water snakes (*Nerodia rhombifer*). Copeia, 1992; 1992(4): 1096-1098.

—**Porter, CA:**
Triploidy in the lizard, *Sceloporus grammicus*. Journal of Herpetology, 1988; 22(1): 112-115.

—**Porter, IH; Schulze, J; McKusich, VA:**
Genetic linkage between the loci for glucose-6-phoshpate dehydrogenase defence and colour blindness in American negroes. Annals Human Genetics, 1962; 20: 107-122.

—**Radkey, RR; Donnellan, SC; Fisher, RN; Moritz, C;**
When species collide: the origin and spread of an asexual species of gecko. Proceedings Royal Society London, 1995; B259: 145-152.

—**Ralls, K; Ballou, JD, Templeton, A:**
Estimates of lethal equivalents and the cost of inbreeding in mammals. Conservation Biology, 1988; 2: 185-186.

—**Richardson, BJ; Baverstock, PR; Adams, M:**
Allozyme electrophoresis: a handbook for animal and population studies. Academic Press, Sydney, 1986.

—**Rogers, JS:**
Measures of genetic similarity and genetic distance. Studies in Genetic VII University of Texas Publication, 1972; 7213: 145-153.

—**Sarich, VM:**
Rates, sample sizes, and the neutrality hypothesis for electrophoresis in evolutionary studies. Nature, 1977a; 265: 24-28.

—**Sarich, VM:**
Albumin phylogenetics. Albumin structure, function and uses, VM Rosenoer; Oratz M; Rothschild MA (Eds). Pergamon Press, Oxford, 1977b.

—**Sattler, PW; Guttmam, SI:**
An electrophoretic analysis of *Thamnophis sirtalis* from western Ohio. Copeia, 1976, 1976(2): 352-356.

—**Seigel, R; Ford, NB:**
Phenotypic plasticity in the reproductive characteristics of an oviparous snake, *Elaphe guttata*: implications for life history studies. Herpetologica, 1991; 47(3): 301-307.

—**Shine, R:**
Strangers in a strange land: ecology of the Australian Colubrid snakes. Copeia, 1991; 1991(1): 120-131.

—**Simpson, GG:**
Principles of animal taxonomy. Columbia University Press, New York, 1961.

—**Singh, L:**
Evolution of karyotypes in snakes. Chromosoma; 38: 185-236.

—**Sokal, RR; Sneath, PA:**
Numerical taxonomy. W. H. Freeman and Co., San Francisco, 1973.

—**Stamps, J:**
Early hormones and the development of phenotypic variation in tree lizards. Trends in Ecology and Evolution, 1994; 9(9): 311-312.

—**Suzuki, DT; Griffiths, AJF; Miller, JH; Lewontin, RC:**
An introduction to genetic analysis. W. H. Freeman and Company, New York, 1989.

—**Taylor, HL:**
A morphological analysis of the Teiid lizards *Cnemidophorus tigris tigris* and *C. tigris gracilis* from a contact zone in northwest Arizona. Herpetologica, 1990; 46(4): 447-456.

—**Taylor, HL; Cooley, CR; Aguilar, RA; Obana, CJ:**
Factors affecting clutch size in the Teiid lizards *Cnemidophorus tigris gracilis* and *C. t. septentrionalis*. Journal of Herpetology, 1992; 26(4): 443-447.

—**Taylor, HL; Buschman, D:**
A multivariate analysis of geographic variation in the Teiid lizard *Cnemidophorus tigris septentrionalis*. Herpetologica, 1993; 49(1): 42-51.

—**Throckmorton, LH:**
Concordance and discordance of taxonomic characters in Drosophila classification. Systematic Zoology, 1968; 17(4): 355-387.

—**Tiersch, TR; Figiel, CR:**
A triploid snake. Copeia, 1991; 1991(3): 838-841.

—**Vrijenhook, RC; Dawley, RM; Cole, CJ; Bogart, JP:**
A list of known unisexual vertebrates. In Evolution and ecology of unisexual vertebrates, RM Dawley, Bogart, JP (Eds). University of New York, New York, 1989, pp. 19-23.

—**Wilkinson, JA; Glenn, JL; Straight, RC; Sites, JW, Jr:**
Distribution and genetic variation in venom A and B populations of the Mojave rattlesnake (*Crotalus scutulatus scutulatus*) in Arizona. Herpetologica, 1991; 47(1): 54-68.

—**Witten, GJ:**
A triploid male individual *Amphibolurus nobbi nobbi* (Witten) (Laceritidae: Agamidae). Australian Zoologist, 1978; 19: 305-308.

—**Wylie, AP; Veale, AMO, Sands, VE:**
The chromosomes of the Tuatara. Proceedings of the University of Otago Medical School, 1968; 46: 22-23.

—**Wynn, AH; Cole, CJ; Gardner, AL:**
Apparent triploidy in the unisexual brahminy blind snake, *Ramphotyphlops braminus*. American Museum Novitates, 1987; 2868: 1-7.

—**Zweifel, RG:**
Genetics of colour pattern in the California kingsnake. The Journal of Heredity, 1981; 72: 238-244.

West Midland Safari Park
Spring Grove
BEWDLEY
Worcestershire
DY12 1LF

South African Coral Snake, *Aspidelaps lubricus*.
Photo by Marius Burger.

Puff Adder, *Bitis arietans*.
Photo by Marius Burger.

THERMAL BIOLOGY, METABOLISM, AND HIBERNATION

Robert E. Espinoza and C. Richard Tracy
Biological Resources Research Center &
Department of Biology / FA 314
University of Nevada, Reno
Reno, Nevada 89557-0015

Robert E. Espinoza is a Ph.D. Student in the Ecology, Evolution, and Conservation Biology Program at the University of Nevada, Reno.

Dr. C. Richard Tracy is a Professor of Biology and the Director of the Biological Resources Research Center, University of Nevada, Reno.

INTRODUCTION

Aspects of reptilian* thermal biology have been studied extensively for more than 60 years, and recent progress by investigators working at the interface between environmental physiology and ecology (i.e., physiological ecologists) has substantially increased our understanding of the interactions between reptiles and their environments. An understanding of these interactions is critical because they may influence the evolution of morphology, physiology, and behavior in reptiles. Additionally, these interactions, and adaptations to them, may influence the manner in which reptiles interact with other organisms.

The most widely studied area of reptilian physiological ecology has been thermal biology, perhaps because temperature has such a profound influence on the lives of reptiles, and also perhaps because it is generally easier to study the effects of temperature than other aspects of reptilian physiology. In many respects, metabolism and hibernation are also influenced by or are closely associated with aspects of reptilian thermal biology. Therefore, these subjects have been included in this review.

---

* The term "reptile," as is currently used includes paraphyletic groups of vertebrates (see Chapter on taxonomy). Here we use this term to mean the extant Sphenodontia (tuatara), Testudomorpha (turtles and tortoises), Crocodylia (alligators, crocodiles, and their relatives), and the Squamata (lizards, snakes, and their relatives).

In this chapter, we provide an overview of the importance of body temperature. This chapter also addresses metabolism and hibernation as they relate to reptilian physiological ecology and to biology generally. Our goal is to focus on some key elements and noteworthy discoveries in these areas, rather than to attempt summarizing the vast literature in each field. The majority of the available knowledge in these areas is derived from research on lizards, particularly those from temperate and subtropical desert environments. For this reason, many of our examples are from this subset of reptiles. In some cases, what we have learned from studies on lizards is applicable to other reptiles. However, given the complexity and diversity among reptiles, generalizing beyond what is known for a handful of lizards to *all* reptiles, may lead to erroneous simplifications.

Aurora House Snake, *Lamprophis aurora*. Photo by Marius Burger.

THERMAL BIOLOGY

GENERAL REMARKS AND TERMINOLOGY

Until about 60 years ago, most biologists assumed that mammals and birds were the only organisms that could maintain high and constant body temperatures. Meanwhile, reptiles were generally assumed to have body temperatures closely resembling those of their ambient environment. An important paradigm shift occurred when Cowles and Bogert (1944) showed that reptiles were able to maintain fairly precise body temperatures by selecting specific thermal microsites within their environment. Additionally, body temperatures of reptiles are, in many cases, quite different from the ambient temperature. Some reptiles even maintain temperatures that are higher than those of so-called "warm-blooded" animals. Therefore, the use of the term "cold-blooded" in reference to reptiles is misleading and outdated.

The term **ectothermic** (Cowles, 1962) is used to characterize animals that regulate their body temperatures by utilizing thermal energy derived from external sources (e.g., solar radiation, sun-warmed objects). By contrast, birds and mammals are **endotherms**, which acquire most of their thermal energy as a byproduct of metabolism. Cowles (1962) further categorized ectothermic organisms by the two principal sources from which they acquire thermal energy:
—**heliotherms** (*helios* = sun) obtain heat from the radiant energy of the sun
—**thigmotherms** (*thigmo* = touch) exchange thermal energy by conduction with items in their environment such as warm rocks. The latter is essentially the type of thermal regimen provided in captive situations by "hot rocks," heating pads, and heat tape.

Many reptiles use a combination of both strategies for thermoregulation. The terms Cowles (1962) proposed more precisely reflect the pathways through which energy is exchanged between an animal and its environment, and they also set the stage for studies addressing thermoregulation in reptiles.

Ectothermy and endothermy are occasionally confused, or incorrectly used interchangeably with two related terms: **poikilothermic** and **homeothermic**. Poikilotherms (*poikilo* = changeable) have variable body temperatures, while homeotherms (*homoios* = similar), maintain fairly constant body temperatures (± 2 °C; Bligh and Johnson, 1973). These terms can be confusing because reptiles do change their body temperatures, and they have different body temperatures during periods of activity and inactivity. However, many reptiles maintain remarkably constant body temperatures during periods of activity. Indeed, during the daytime, some lizards maintain body temperatures that are within narrower ranges than those regulated by endotherms. Thus, the terms poikilotherm and homeotherm are inadequate in describing the patterns of body-temperature change in a few reptiles. Of course, some reptiles live in situations in which body temperatures remain constant because environmental temperatures remain relatively constant (e.g., pelagic sea turtles and sea snakes, cave-dwellers, and animals restricted to deep burrows).

Numerous terms have been used to describe the processes of temperature regulation and associated behaviors in ectotherms (Bligh and Johnson, 1973; Gans and Pough, 1982; Hutchison and Dupré, 1992). Reptiles that actively regulate their body temperatures often **choose**, **prefer**, or **select** a limited range of body temperatures from those available in the environment. Although these terms refer to the same phenomenon, different investigators insist that their term is the least anthropomorphic and, therefore the most appropriate (Hutchison and Dupré, 1992). Occasionally, the average body temperature chosen, preferred, or selected by an active reptile also may be referred to as the **eccritic** temperature. Throughout this chapter we will most frequently use the term **selection**, which we define as: the process of temperature regulation by nonrandom use of the available thermal microsites found in a heterogeneous thermal environment.

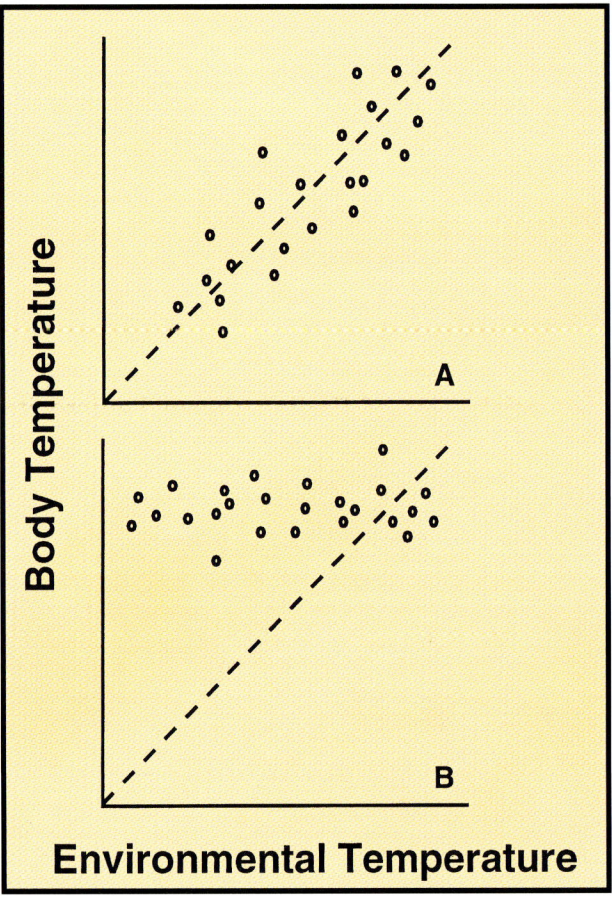

Figure 1.
Relationship for some environmental temperature variable (e.g., air or substratum temperature) and body temperature for a hypothetical reptile: A) thermoconformer; B) thermoregulator. Note body temperatures of the thermoconformer closely approximate those of the ambient environment, whereas body temperatures of the thermoregulator are independent of ambient temperature.

A large proportion of reptiles actively regulate their body temperature. However, among reptiles, the spectrum of thermal interactions with the environment ranges from little or no regulation, to precise regulation, to near endothermy. Within this continuum, reptiles with body temperatures closely resembling those of their environment are known as **thermoconformers**, while those maintaining body temperatures different from ambient temperatures, are termed **thermoregulators** (Fig. 1). Thermoconformity is largely limited to those reptiles living in aquatic or deeply-shaded environments (e.g., forest understories, leaf litter, underground burrows, caves), or those which are active at night. In these environments, few opportunities may exist for maintaining body temperatures above or below ambient temperatures. Additionally, most thermoconformers have small body sizes, which tends to limit opportunities for physiological regulation of body temperature (Claussen and Art, 1981; Bartholomew, 1982; Fraser and Grigg, 1984; also refer to the *Morphological and Physiological Aspects of Thermoregulation* section). However, thermoconformity is an appropriate strategy in environments that provide a suitable thermal regime. For example, some reptiles from tropical forests spend little time each day actively selecting particular thermal microsites within their environment (Hertz, 1974; Huey and Slatkin, 1976; Shine and Madsen, 1996). Ambient temperatures may provide these reptiles with the necessary thermal energy they require, thereby freeing them from the potential costs of finding thermal microsites throughout the day. Thermoregulators, by contrast, actively maintain their body temperatures using a suite of behavioral and/or physiological mecha-

nisms. Considering either thermoconformity or thermoregulation as a "better" strategy is not a worthy endeavor, because members of both groups are well represented in nature. However, to appreciate fully the adaptive value of either strategy, a thorough examination of the costs and benefits associated with both thermoregulation and thermoconformity must be considered (Huey, 1974; Huey and Slatkin, 1976; Pough, 1980, 1983).

Some investigators have hypothesized that reptiles have a single optimal temperature for *all* forms of performance (e.g., hearing, locomotion, digestion, prey capture, etc.; Licht, 1967c; Dawson, 1975; DeWitt and Friedman, 1979; Huey, 1982; Huey and Bennett, 1987). The **thermal optimum** is expected to be coincident with the average body temperature maintained by a reptile in nature or in the laboratory (Fig. 2). Although this hypothesis has not been tested exhaustively, recent studies have not detected a single body temperature over which performance of more than a few traits

Figure 2.
Body temperature continuum showing the terms commonly used in reptilian thermal biology. The horizontal line within the selected range is the mean (occasionally also reported as the modal) activity or selected body temperature. The thermal optimum is suggested to be coincident with the mean value, but see text regarding evidence to support this hypothesis. Note that the position of each term on the continuum may be species and individual specific. Refer to text for specific definitions.

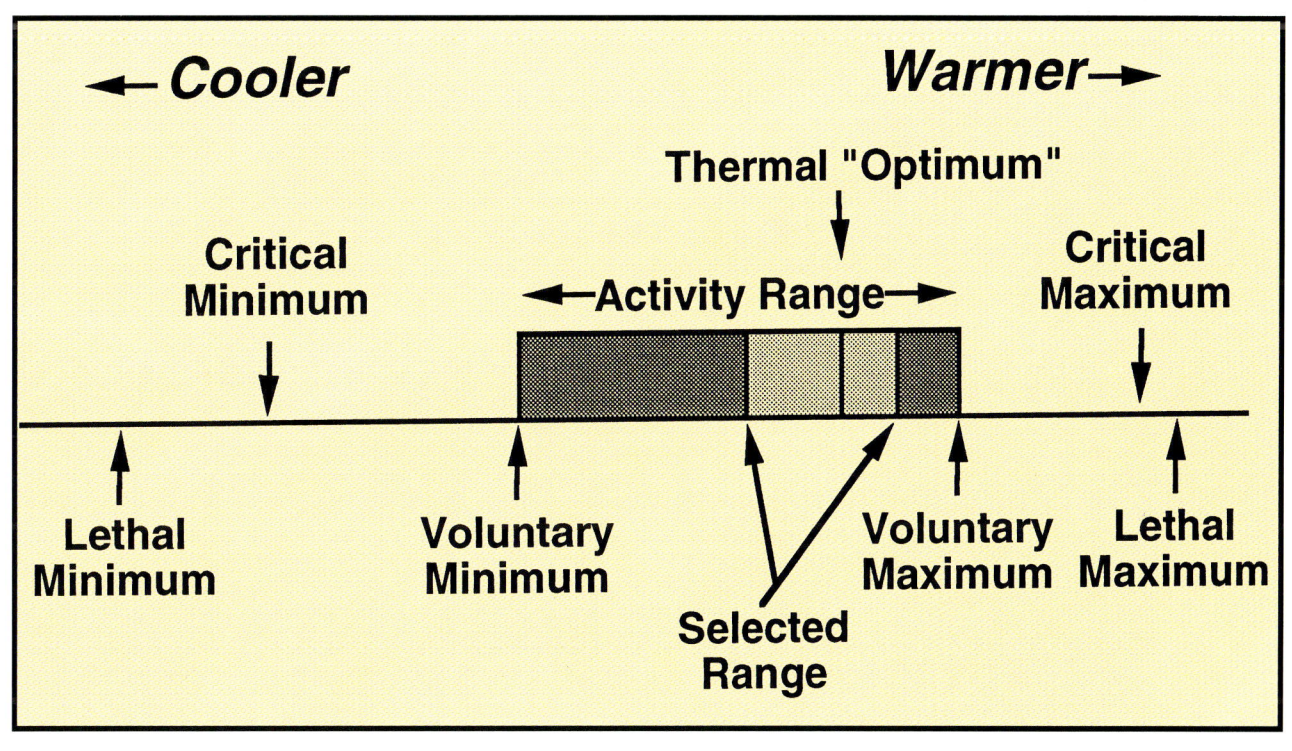

are optimized. However, performance of some single traits have been shown to be optimal within the thermal range maintained by active reptiles (Werner, 1972, 1976; Huey and Bennett, 1987; Mautz *et al.*, 1992). The existence of a single optimum temperature is not supported by evidence from one of several proposed thermoregulatory mechanisms. This hypothesis suggests that reptiles regulate their body temperature not at a single temperature, or "set point," but instead respond to the extremes of a range of temperatures (Cabanac *et al.*, 1967; Barber and Crawford, 1977, 1979; Fig. 2). In these cases, body temperatures appear to be regulated by "turning on" the appropriate cooling or warming behaviors that once body temperature has drifted out of a particular range. However, we generally know little about the abilities of reptiles to distinguish among, and respond to, small differences in body temperature. For example, reptiles may truly regulate their body temperature about a single "set point." But, if reptiles "measure" body temperature less precisely than do humans, then their patterns of thermoregulation may be misleading. For example, we might erroneously conclude from patterns of thermoregulation that 1) reptiles are selecting a range of temperatures, or 2) they are responding to upper and lower "set point" temperatures surrounding a range of body temperatures when they are actually, albeit imprecisely, thermoregulating around a single body temperature.

The range of body temperatures over which reptiles engage in their normal activities is termed the **activity temperature range** (Fig. 2). This range differs among species, and within a species for animals under different conditions (e.g., digesting, pregnant; see below). Activity ranges can start at body temperatures as low as 10 °C for the tuatara, *Sphenodon punctatus* (Stebbins, 1958), to highs approaching 46 °C for the desert iguana, *Dipsosaurus dorsalis*

Desert Iguana, *Dipsosaurus dorsalis*. Photo by Michael Cardwell.

(Norris, 1953). Furthermore, reptiles regulate their body temperatures with varying degrees of precision (e.g., Bowker, 1984), such that activity ranges may be as narrow as 4 °C, to as broad as 10 °C. Within the normal activity range, many reptiles have a more narrowly-defined range of temperatures known as the **selected** (= preferred) body temperature range (Fig. 2). Generally, the selected body temperature range is measured by recording the temperatures of animals in the field or laboratory during their activity cycle under conditions that permit unihibited thermoregulation. The selected range is typically reported as the mean (or occasionally modal) body temperature recorded for a number of individuals. The activity range and selected range are sometimes used imprecisely and interchangeably in the literature, which has led to some confusion. We suggest that the term "selected" body temperature be reserved for body temperatures that have been measured in the laboratory, and that researchers reserve the term "activity range" for (animal) body temperatures that have been measured in the field.

Bounding the normal activity range are the **voluntary minimum** and **maximum** temperatures which are also known as the thermal "set points" (Fig. 2). As body temperatures approach or reach these points, the animal will generally seek an appropriate thermal refuge such as moving into the sun or shade. Beyond these tolerances are the **critical thermal minimum** and **maximum** (Fig. 2). These are the temperatures at which an animal ceases to function normally (defined more precisely as the temperature at which the "righting reflex" is lost; Cowles and Bogert, 1944; Spellerberg, 1973). In many desert reptiles, voluntary maxima are near the critical thermal maxima (Cowles and Bogert, 1944). Similarly, reptiles living in cool environments may have voluntary minima that approach their critical thermal minimum (see e.g., Autumn *et al.*, 1994). Beyond the critical temperatures are the **lethal minimum** and **maximum** (Fig. 2). As the terms imply, sustaining body temperatures at or beyond these extremes will lead to death.

Another pair of terms groups animals by their range of tolerable body temperatures. Animals that tolerate, or are active over, a narrow range of body temperatures are called **stenothermal** (*steno* = narrow). In contrast, **eurythermal** (*eury* = wide) animals tolerate, or are active over, broader ranges of body temperatures. As with several of the terms defined above, steno- and eurythermal are relative concepts because they do not specify particular ranges of temperatures. Examples of stenothermal reptiles include: the desert iguana (*Dipsosaurus dorsalis*), and coachwhip snakes (*Masticophis flagellum*) which maintain high activity temperatures with notable precision (DeWitt, 1967; Secor, 1995, respectively). The tuatara (*Sphenodon punctatus*), box turtles (*Terrapene* spp.), and alligator lizards (*Elgaria* [= *Gerrhonotus*] spp.) are examples of eurythermal reptiles because they are often active over a relatively broad range of body temperatures (Saint-Girons *et al.*, 1980; Avery, 1982; Kingsbury, 1993, respectively).

MORPHOLOGICAL AND PHYSIOLOGICAL ASPECTS OF THERMOREGULATION

Many reptiles possess anatomical and physiological mechanisms which enable them to alter the rate at which they heat or cool. These mechanisms include altering heart rate, cardiac and vascular shunts, vasomotor dilation and constriction, and counter-current vascular exchanges (see reviews in White, 1976; Bartholomew, 1982). Reptiles can increase their heart rates during periods of heating (Bartholomew, 1982; Turner and Tracy, 1983, 1985; Turner, 1987). Pumping blood through the body increases the rate of temperature change. By the same principle, reptiles can also reduce rates of temperature change by decreasing heart rates. All reptiles, with the exception of the crocodilians, possess a three-chambered heart (see Chapter 3 this volume). The three-chambered heart is particularly well suited for altering rates of bodily heating and cooling. With a four-chambered heart, deoxygenated blood travels from the systemic circuit to the heart and is then sent to the lungs to be oxygenated. The oxygenated blood then returns to the heart and is pumped back through the systemic vessels. Generally, it is not possible for animals with four-chambered hearts to bypass either the systemic or pulmonary circuits during the circulatory cycle because the atria and ventricles are physi-

Western Coachwhip, *Masticophis flagellum testaceus*. **Photo by Paul Freed.**

Eastern Box Turtle, *Terrapene carolina*. **Photo by Aaron Norman.**

cally separated. By contrast, animals with three-chambered hearts can redirect or "shunt" blood from their single ventricle to either the pulmonary or systemic circuit. This phenomenon is generally known as **cardiac shunting**. As blood passes through the lungs and contacts the moist respiratory surfaces, it can lose heat due to evaporative cooling. By bypassing the pulmonary circuit, reptiles avoid cooling their blood, and by shunting warmed blood back to their core, they further enhance their rate of heating. Blood shunting is controlled by changing the pressure at which blood flows into the heart (Bartholomew, 1982). During heating, peripheral blood vessels are generally dilated to enhance the flow of warmed blood from the appendages, which can heat more rapidly than the core due to their smaller size and shape. When body temperatures drop due to abiotic or biotic disturbances that interfere with "normal" thermoregulatory behaviors ...and shunt blood to their core to reduce the rate of heat exchange.

Body size and shape importantly affect physiological control of thermoregulation (Spotila *et al.*, 1973; Bartholomew, 1982; Stevenson, 1985). On the basis of physical properties alone, larger animals should heat and cool more slowly than should smaller individuals. That is, larger animals have a greater **thermal inertia**, or resistance to temperature change. Thermal inertia can be an important component of thermoregulation in large reptiles. Once a large reptile has warmed itself, the physiological mechanisms discussed above can be used effectively to reduce heat loss. Moreover, these mechanisms are more effective for larger animals. For example, the giant Aldabra tortoises (*Geochelone gigantea*) can maintain particularly stable body temperatures throughout the day, despite experiencing different thermal environments (Swingland and Frazier, 1980). Some large snakes,

153

Aldabra Tortoise, *Geochelone gigantea*. Juvenile photo by R. D.

ume. By contrast, snakes and many lizards are more elongate, and have a relatively large surface-area-to-volume ratio. Therefore, more of a snake's total body area interacts with the external environment. The elongate shape of snakes also has important implications for thermoregulation. That is, snakes can exhibit remarkably different temperatures in different regions of their bodies. This phenomenon is generally known as **regional heterothermy**, and is well documented in larger reptiles which live in thermally heterogeneous environments. Because of the vasomotor abilities discussed above, a large snake can maintain some parts of its body at one temperature, while other portions of its body experience different temperatures due to their proximity to various thermal resources or sinks. Regional heterothermy is also common in smaller reptiles. For instance, smaller lizards and turtles commonly exhibit differences between head and body temperatures during periods of heating and cooling (Bartholomew, 1982). Many heliothermic lizards will first expose their heads during their initial heating in the morning, and once the head reaches a specific temperature, they will expose the rest of their body (e.g., Heath, 1965). This thermoregulatory strategy avoids exposing the entire animal when it is cool, and therefore most vulnerable to predators.

Although metabolic heat is generated by reptiles, the amount produced is thermodynamically insignificant. Even if reptiles could produce substantial amounts of thermal energy, that heat would be quickly dissipated because reptiles lack insulation, such as fur, feathers, or fat. A lack of an insulating layer is also why thigmothermy, or conductive heat exchange, can provide an effective means of changing body temperatures. There is, however,

tortoises, and crocodilians use a combination of physiological and behavioral mechanisms to maintain relatively high body temperatures through the night, despite significant declines in ambient temperatures. For instance, a large snake can lower its heart rate to physiologically reduce the rate of cooling, and coil up to further reduce its rate of heat exchange by behaviorally reducing its surface area (Heatwole and Taylor, 1987). However, the thermal tradeoff in body size is apparent once that large snake has cooled. Larger-bodied reptiles will take longer to heat up than will smaller reptiles. Smaller reptiles are said to be more coupled to their thermal environment because of their lower thermal inertia. Actually, because of their size, smaller reptiles use a greater range of thermal microsites than can larger individuals (Bowker, 1984). This may partially explain why smaller heliothermic reptiles are able to thermoregulate with noteworthy precision (i.e., exhibit narrow activity temperature ranges), despite their low thermal inertia (see e.g., DeWitt, 1967; Avery, 1982; Bowker, 1984; Pianka, 1986; Heatwole and Taylor, 1987). The minimum body mass at which physiological control is suggested to be effective in enhancing thermoregulatory capabilities is roughly 15-20 g (Claussen and Art, 1981; Fraser and Grigg, 1984). However, reptiles as small as 3-7 g may exhibit some physiological capacity to control rates of heating and cooling (Bartholomew, 1982).

Body shape varies widely among reptiles and is known to influence several aspects of their thermal biology. For example, many terrestrial turtles have domed shells, and thus their morphology roughly approximates that of a sphere. Spherically-shaped animals are generally more resistant to changes in body temperature because a small proportion of their surface area is exposed to the environment relative to their total body vol-

Leatherback Turtle, *Dermochelys coriacea*. Photo by Peter Pritchard.

at least one important exception to this generality. The leatherback turtle (*Dermochelys coriacea*) is among the world's largest living reptiles with adult body masses commonly surpassing 600 kg. *Dermochelys* also has one of the highest and broadest latitudinal ranges of all reptiles. Adults have been seen as far north as the frigid waters off Nova Scotia, yet females nest in the tropics (Mrosovsky and Pritchard, 1971). Unlike most reptiles, *Dermochelys* has a thick, oil-saturated subdermal layer which functions to insulate the animal from the cold of the northern oceans, much in the same way blubber keeps marine mammals insulated. Additionally, adult leatherbacks can generate an appreciable amount of metabolic heat which is produced primarily from their working muscles as they swim (Frair *et al.*, 1972). Leatherbacks may elevate their body temperatures by as much as 18 °C above sea water temperatures (Frair *et al.*, 1972). Rates of heat loss are low due to their large body size and insulation, and are probably further reduced by minimizing blood flow to the extremities (i.e., head, flippers, and tail), and through specialized vascular systems (see reviews in White, 1976; Bartholomew, 1982). These systems are generally known as **counter-current exchangers**. Counter-current vascular networks are relatively common among vertebrates, and are usually associated with conserving a specific physiological resource (e.g., oxygen, water, various ions, body temperature). In many cases, the blood vessels associated with these systems surround each other in dense bundles or form complex networks. In the case of reptiles such as *Dermochelys*, they function by passing vessels containing heated blood from the body core traveling in one direction, past vessels containing cooled blood from the extremities traveling in the opposite direction. In this manner, body heat can be conserved by effectively recycling the thermal energy (Greer *et al.*, 1973).

The underlying neurological control mechanisms of reptilian thermoregulation are not fully understood, and have been examined in only a few

Eastern Blue-tongued Skink, *Tiliqua scincoides*. Photo by Zoltan Takacs.

species. As with other vertebrates, the hypothalamus appears to play an important role in thermoregulation (Kluger *et al.*, 1973; Berk and Heath, 1975). In the Australian blue-tongued skink, *Tiliqua scincoides,* it appears that some neurons within the hypothalamus respond to different temperature stimuli. A subset of these neurons fire when the hypothalamic region is heated (hot neurons), while other neurons respond only when the area is cooled (cool neurons) (Cabanac *et al.*, 1967). These results are consistent with the dual-set point model of thermoregulatory responses (Barber and Crawford, 1977, 1979). That is, once the tolerable thermal maximum has been reached, heat-sensitive neurons will fire and presumably trigger the initiation of cool-temperature seeking behaviors. The inverse should follow as hypothalamic temperatures approach the tolerable thermal minimum. An alternative model for thermoregulation suggests that body temperatures are regulated about a single set value which corresponds to the animal's average body temperature selected during activity. The selected or activity body temperature was further suggested to be a fixed and inherited trait (Bogert, 1949). However, studies have generally failed to support the single body temperature hypothesis as a controlling system for thermoregulation in reptiles (Heath, 1964; Berk and Heath, 1975; Barber and Crawford, 1979; Garrick, 1979). Some researchers suggest that the mechanistic basis of temperature regulation in reptiles is best understood as a negative feedback system (see review in Huey, 1982). Under this model, the animal monitors or anticipates changes in its body temperature and compares this deflection with some internal reference or range of "set points." The animal then responds with the appropriate physiological or behavioral adjustments necessary to maintain its body temperature within the reference range (Huey, 1982).

Finally, a reptile's body color has an influence on the animal's absorptance of short-wave radiation (Norris, 1967; Pearson, 1977; Bartholomew, 1982). Changes in color can increase the absorption of radiant energy by as much as 75% (Norris, 1967; Zug, 1993). Reptiles that live in cool environments such as *Liolaemus* lizards living at high elevations in the Andes, and some aquatic turtles, may have evolved a darker body coloration to increase their absorbance of solar radiation. Other reptiles may change color as a function of their body temperature. Color change from dark to light is controlled by dispersion or aggregation of pigments such as melanin in the melanophores.

Thin Tree Lizard, *Liolaemus tenuis*. Photo by R. D. Bartlett.

Some squamate reptiles are able to alter their body coloration at different temperatures. Dark colors enhance absorbance of short-wave radiation, which increases the rate of heating (Pearson, 1977). Once the animal heats up, body coloration may lighten substantially. Lighter colors reflect more short-wave radiation and thereby reduce the radiant energy absorbed by the surface of the animal. However, color change for thermoregulatory purposes must be balanced with the need for crypsis and behaviorally communicated signals in some species.

BEHAVIORAL ASPECTS OF THERMOREGULATION

Solar radiation is the ultimate, but not necessarily the direct source of thermal energy used by living organisms. There are numerous pathways through which reptiles exchange energy with their environment (Tracy, 1982). The dynamics and direction of energy flow through each of these pathways is proportional to the differences in energetic states between the animal and its environment. For example, if a snake basking on a sun-warmed rock comes to the same temperature as the rock, no net exchange in thermal energy will result. However, the same snake would lose energy to the air if the air temperature is lower than the snake's surface temperature. To optimize these avenues of energy exchange, many reptiles **behaviorally thermoregulate** by altering their body posture and orientation with respect to thermal sources and sinks. These behavioral changes can alter the exchange of thermal energy (e.g., Norris, 1953; Heath, 1965; Heatwole, 1970; Brattstrom, 1971; Heatwole and Johnson, 1979, Autumn *et al.*, 1994).

In some environments, thermoregulatory behaviors may be subtle, while in others they may involve a complex repertoire of behaviors. These behaviors are likely to be familiar to anyone who has observed heliothermic reptiles in heterogeneous thermal environments. The behaviors (e.g., Heath, 1965; Riedesel *et al.*, 1971; Heatwole and Johnson, 1979) may include:

—posturing: flat on a rock (for rapid conductive heat exchange), or elevating the limbs (generally for convective cooling), flexing toes and raising the tail to avoid hot substrata

—orientation: to control the amount of bodily surface area exposed to the sun

—selection of the color of the substratum on which to bask (e.g., black rocks for rapid conductive heating)

—selecting a shaded crevice or burrow, or basking indirectly under or in a bush, or in full sun

—evaporative cooling by plunging into water, gaping, panting, salivating, or urinating.

Red-bellied Black Snake, *Pseudechis porphyriacus*. Photo by John Coborn.

The Australian red-bellied black snake, *Pseudechis porphyriacus*, provides an ideal, yet extreme illustration of behavioral thermoregulation in heliothermic reptiles. When cool, these snakes flatten and tilt their bodies so that they are at a right angle—fully exposing themselves to the solar radiation (Heatwole and Johnson, 1979). Postural adjustments in this snake may even include propping the entire body off the cool substratum with the aid of the tail (Heatwole and Taylor, 1987). Generally, squamate reptiles—particularly smaller ones—have greater behavioral thermoregulatory capacities than do other reptiles because of their greater vagility (Bowker, 1984). Behavioral means of thermoregulation in turtles may be limited to movements between sun and shade and/or water due to their unique morphology. However, the shell of some turtles may provide an important thermal

Desert Tortoise, *Gopherus agassizii*. Photo by K. H. Switak.

shield. Under natural thermal conditions, the carapace of desert tortoises (*Gopherus agassizii*) may be 8-10 °C above core body temperatures (McGinnis and Voigt, 1971).

In some cases behavioral thermoregulation can be energetically and ecologically costly. This may be particularly apparent for reptiles living in thermally challenging environments. Time spent thermoregulating may be time lost for foraging, acquiring mates, defending territories, and may increase exposure to predators and parasites (Huey, 1974; Porter *et al.*, 1975; Huey and Slatkin, 1976).

Emerald Swift, *Sceloporus malachiticus*. Photo by Paul Freed.

PERVASIVENESS OF THERMAL EFFECTS ON REPTILE BIOLOGY

Temperature affects nearly all physical and biochemical processes associated with reptilian physiology and behavior. Consequently, in the absence of an appropriate thermal environment, many reptiles will not thrive. Anyone who has kept reptiles in captivity is aware that providing the appropri-

ate thermal regime is often the most fundamental requirement for maintaining healthy animals (Regal, 1980). What constitutes an "appropriate thermal environment" for an individual of a given species depends upon:

—the genetically-based attributes resulting from evolutionary history

—environmental variables including season, daylength, macro-, meso-, and microclimate distribution and utilization

—attributes of the animal such as age, water balance, digestive state, reproductive status, and health

—interactions with other organisms, such as predators, prey, and parasites (Fig. 3).

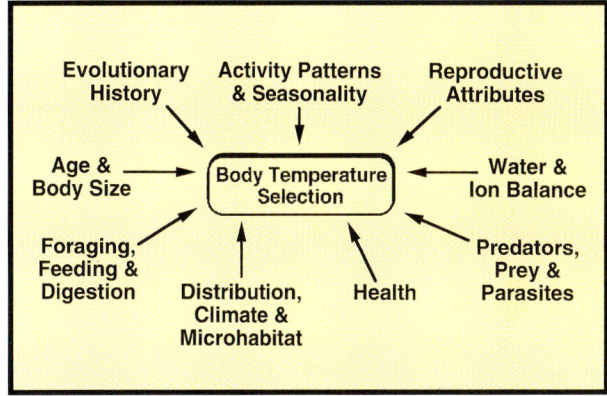

Figure 3.
Conceptual model of the abiotic and biotic variables that influence activity and selected body temperatures in reptiles. The relative importance of each variable is largely a function the individual animal.

The mechanisms by which body temperature affects these factors, and in some cases, how these factors may influence body temperature selection and maintenance, are discussed in the following sections.

EVOLUTIONARY HISTORY

The evolutionary history of a group or species provides the genetic foundation upon which all other characteristics are constructed. Thermal preferences tend to be relatively similar among species belonging to the same genus, often in spite of apparent differences in morphology, ecology, and behavior among the species within the group (Bogert, 1949; Brattstrom, 1965; Templeton, 1970; Avery, 1982; Heatwole and Taylor, 1987). For example, most spiny lizards in the genus *Sceloporus* maintain daytime activity body temperatures near 35°C (Brattstrom, 1965; references cited in Avery, 1982) despite the fact that they are distributed in a diverse array of habitats from British Columbia to Panama and from sea level to eleva-

Desert Grassland Whiptail, *Cnemidophorus uniparens*. Photo by R. D. Bartlett.

tions over 3500 m (Sites *et al.*, 1992). Apparent conservatism of activity body temperatures within a lineage has also been noted in some Chilean *Liolaemus* lizards (Fuentes and Jaksić, 1979), Australian skinks in the genus *Ctenotus* (Bennett and John-Alder, 1986), some whiptail lizards, *Cnemidophorus* (Schall, 1973, 1977), and among tortoises (family Testudinidae; Avery, 1982). Despite apparent conservatism within some reptilian clades, others may exhibit diversity within a single lineage. At the population level, differences in activity and selected body temperatures have been documented within and among populations of the northern European lizard (*Lacerta vivipara*) (Van Damme *et al.*, 1986).

DISTRIBUTION AND MICROHABITAT SELECTION

Sometimes geographic distribution, and the corresponding physical environments, can influence aspects of reptilian thermal biology. For example, some wide-ranging species (e.g., *Lacerta vivipara*) exhibit a gradient of activity temperatures across their latitudinal distribution (Avery, 1976). Caribbean anoles (*Anolis* spp.) from different latitudes have different thermoregulatory strategies (Clark and Kroll, 1974; Hertz, 1981; Huey, 1983). *Anolis carolinensis* from the southeastern United States exhibits a latitudinal gradient in critical thermal minimum with more northerly distributed populations exhibiting greater cold resistance (Wilson and Echternacht, 1987). Elevation has also been implicated in influencing activity temperatures of reptiles (Hertz and Huey, 1981; Avery, 1982). As elevation increases, environmental temperatures tend to decrease. Thus, reptiles living at particularly high elevations might be expected to possess morphological, physiological, and/or behavioral traits which are adaptive in these cooler environments. For example, Pearson (1954) stud-

ied *Liolaemus signifer* (= *multiformis*) at 4300 m in the Peruvian Andes. He found that these lizards were active when air temperatures were close to 0 °C. Despite low environmental temperatures, these lizards were able to maintain body temperatures in excess of 30 °C through careful selection of basking sites (dense clumps of bunch grasses), and by darkening their dorsal coloration (Pearson, 1954, 1977). Gorman and Hillman (1977) went as far to suggest that the geographic or elevational range limits of reptiles are generally a function of their thermal tolerances.

Climate may also influence thermoregulatory responses. Generally, diurnal reptiles living in deserts have higher activity temperatures and tend to have higher critical thermal maxima than do diurnal reptiles from mesic or wet tropical environments (see e.g., Cowles and Bogert, 1944; Pianka, 1986; Heatwole and Taylor, 1987). Reptiles that select high body temperatures either live in warm areas (e.g., in the warm tropics) or they limit their activity periods in temperate regions to the warm times of the year.

Often reptiles from similar microhabitats tend to have similar thermoregulatory strategies and select similar body temperatures. Rock dwellers and species living on unconsolidated sand (e.g., beaches and sand dunes) tend to have higher average body temperatures than do most arboreal

Green Anole, *Anolis carolinensis*. Photo by Aaron Norman.

species (see data in Avery, 1982; Pianka, 1986; Heatwole and Taylor, 1987). This relationship is at least partly due to the shading associated with an arboreal lifestyle (Hertz, 1974), but may also be due to different thermoregulatory strategies. For example, thigmothermic reptiles generally have lower body temperatures than heliothermic species (Heatwole and Taylor, 1987). It is also the case that reptiles living in environments that do not provide opportunities for thermoregulation (e.g., leaf litter, forest understories, caves) or in

Black-spotted Tree Lizard, *Liolaemus nigromaculatus*. **Photo by R. D. Bartlett.**

those that act as thermal sinks (e.g., subterranean or aquatic environments) tend to be thermoconformers. For example, thermoconformity may be the best strategy in heavily-shaded forests where patches of sunlight would have to be "chased" throughout the day in order to thermoregulate. Following patches of light may increase apparency to predators and could account for a large portion of daily activity This evergy could be used to engage in other activities (e.g., feeding, finding mates, etc.). Although life in heat sinks may interfere or preclude thermoregulation in some species, the potential advantages associated with life in a thermally stable environment should not be neglected. However, even in thermally challenging situations, some reptiles are able to sustain temperatures above that of their environment. Some aquatic species, especially turtles, crocodilians, and sea snakes, bask in the warm surface layers of water which may be somewhat warmer due to solar heating. Many aquatic reptiles may partially or completely emerge and elevate their body temperatures by basking on vegetation, logs, and other floating or exposed areas.

Finally, some investigators have suggested that the variation in the morphology and number of scales exhibited by some squamate reptiles are the result of adaptations to the physical environment. For some species, selection seems to favor larger, overlapping scales in warmer climates (Soulé, 1966; Regal, 1975), which presumably provides a small, but nevertheless important shielding effect from solar radiation. In the cooler climates of the Chilean Andes, *Liolaemus* lizards tend to have a larger number of smaller, more narrowly arranged scales (Hellmich, 1951). These differences in squamation have been interpreted as adaptations for either thermoregulation or reducing water loss (Horton, 1972; Regal, 1975).

DAILY AND SEASONAL ACTIVITY AND BEHAVIOR

Selected body temperatures and thermoregulatory behaviors may vary temporally on both a daily and an annual basis. Some diurnal reptiles select warmer body temperatures by day and appear to voluntarily select cooler body temperatures at night or during periods of inactivity (Regal, 1967). Some nocturnal species may not have the opportunity to achieve favorable body temperatures during periods of activity and may, therefore, thermoregulate by day (e.g., Bustard, 1967; Autumn et al., 1994).

During the summer months, reptiles living in temperate deserts may experience differences between daytime and nighttime temperatures exceeding 50 °C. In these regions, the activity cycles of reptiles may be highly correlated with daily cycles in temperature. On summer days in the Australian deserts, the central netted dragon, Ctenophorus nuchalis (= Amphibolurus inermis), increases its perch height as ambient temperature rises, thereby avoiding the extreme temperatures nearer the ground surface (Heatwole, 1970). Similarly, box turtles (Terrapene spp.) avoid the extreme high temperatures of summer days by shifting their normally diurnal periods of activity to dawn and dusk, or may even adopt a nocturnal lifestyle (Avery, 1982).

Desert iguanas (Dipsosaurus dorsalis), which are distributed in the temperate deserts of southwestern North America, are inactive unless environmental temperatures permit them to achieve body temperatures above 38.5 °C (DeWitt, 1967). As a consequence, individuals of this species are only active during the warmest times of the day and of the year (Norris, 1953; DeWitt, 1967). Many temperate reptiles from hot regions also exhibit changes in activity as the warm season progresses. For example, activity is typically unimodal for the desert tortoise (Gopherus agassizii) in early spring when daytime temperatures do not exceed maximum tolerance levels. However, later in the summer, when environmental temperatures often exceed the lethal maximum by midmorning, desert tortoises adopt a bimodal activity cycle surfacing only early in the morning and after sunset (Auffenberg and Iverson, 1979). Changes in thermoregulatory behaviors, selected body temperatures, and activity may be coincident with seasonal changes in the environment (Case, 1976; Huey and Pianka, 1977; Moore, 1978; Patterson and Davies, 1978; Christian et al., 1983; Van Damme et al., 1987; Christian and Bedford, 1995), daylength (Rismiller and Heldmaier, 1982), and among different age classes (Paulissen, 1988). Additionally, some reptiles may only exhibit particular behaviors, such as foraging and displays of territorial defense, once they have achieved a specific body temperature (e.g., Cowles and Bogert, 1944; Bradshaw and Main, 1968; Brattstrom, 1971; Heatwole and Taylor, 1987).

In general, diurnal reptiles in thermally heterogeneous environments (i.e., those that are not heavily shaded) tend to be heliothermic or a combination of heliothermic and thigmothermic; whereas nocturnal species tend to be limited to thigmothermy for acquiring thermal energy. This explains why some nocturnal reptiles can be found on spring and summer nights on warm asphalt roads (Brattstrom, 1965). Although nocturnal species generally select and have cooler activity temperatures than do diurnal species (see e.g., Brattstrom, 1965; Avery, 1982; Pianka, 1986; Heatwole and Taylor, 1987), some evidence suggests that not all nocturnal reptiles are thermally passive. Bustard (1967) noted that the "nocturnal" Australian gecko Gehyra variegata actively thermoregulates within its diurnal retreat by day. These geckos live under bark on trees. By tracking the position of solar illumination on the tree, these lizards are able to select warm thermal microsites during their presumed "inactivity" period. Similarly, the frog-eyed gecko (Teratoscincus przewalskii) of China is largely a thermoconformer during nocturnal activity, but raises its body temperatures throughout the day by selecting warmer temperatures within its burrow (Autumn et al., 1994). Thus partitioning some reptiles into discrete thermoregulatory categories can prove to be problematic.

Sensory perception, neurological response, and muscle reaction are the underlying physiological mechanisms of reptilian activity and behavior. Performance of many of these processes has been shown to be influenced by body temperature (Licht, 1964a,b, 1967c; Bennett and John-Alder, 1984; John-Alder and Bennett, 1987; Losos, 1988). Numerous ethological studies have corroborated the importance of temperature to behavior (e.g., Rand, 1964; Brattstrom, 1971; Bennett, 1980; Hertz et al., 1982; Mautz et al., 1992; see also Chapter 16 this volume), and temperature may even play a role in the process of learning (Krekorian et al., 1968). In cooler environments, thermoregulation can be more challenging and, thus, thermoregulatory behaviors may preempt other activities. For example, it has been suggested that southern European lacertid lizards have more complex social behaviors than more northerly distributed species because the latter must spend more of their time engaged in thermoregulatory behaviors (Avery, 1976).

In some cases, temperature can influence interactions between reptiles and other organisms including predators (e.g., Porter et al., 1975; Christian and Tracy, 1981). For example, some lizards exhibit temperature-dependent responses to **caudal autotomy**, or tail loss. Bustard (1965) found that side-blotched lizards, Uta stansburiana, may autotomize their tails more readily at higher body temperatures. However, studies on the Australian

Side-blotched Lizard, *Uta stansburiana.* **Photo by R. D. Bartlett.**

gecko, *Gehyra variegata,* showed a bimodal pattern to tail autotomy. That is, these lizards were most likely to autotomize their tails at low (4 °C) and high (19 °C), but not intermediate body temperatures (Bustard, 1968). This pattern may be interpreted as an adaptive strategy for balancing the cost of autotomy with that of would-be predation (Bustard, 1968). At low body temperatures, the geckos autotomized about 80% of their tails. At these body temperatures escape from predators would be difficult, and the writhing tail could provide a distraction. At higher body temperatures however, locomotion may be substantially improved, and only 20-25% of the tail is autotomized (Bustard, 1968). Thus, body temperature may influence the ability of these lizards to practice the "economy of caudal autotomy."

FEEDING, DIGESTION, AND DIET

Body temperature can influence the frequency of feeding, which can, in turn, influence the temperatures selected by reptiles. The efficiency of prey capture is also affected by body temperature. For example, strike accuracy and constriction in gopher snakes (*Pituophis melanoleucus*) are a function of body temperature (Greenwald, 1974).

Northern Pine Snake, *Pituophis melanoleucus melanoleucus.* **Albino specimen. Photo by W. P. Mara.**

Reptiles typically select warm microsites soon after ingesting a meal (Regal, 1966; Gatten, 1974; Lang, 1979; Sievert, 1989). This phenomenon is particularly evident in species that consume large prey items relative to their own body size. This is best illustrated in large snakes, such as boas and pythons, which can consume prey as large as 75% of their own body mass. Following ingestion, these snakes will almost immediately seek out a warm thermal environment where they can digest their meal. This behavior assures rapid and efficient digestion of the food item because most of the metabolic and enzymatic processes involved in digestion work faster at higher body temperatures. The inverse is also true, that is, reptiles experiencing even mild inanition may select cooler temperatures than satiated individuals (Gatten, 1974). Selecting lower body temperatures during periods of inanition may be a means of conserving energy.

Increasing body temperature also generally increases the rate at which digesta moves through the gut (MacKay, 1968; Throckmorton, 1973; Wilson and Lee, 1974; Diefenbach, 1975; Harwood, 1979; Naulleau, 1983; Waldschmidt *et*

Green Turtle, *Chelonia mydas.* **Photo by Zoltan Takacs.**

al., 1986; Zimmerman and Tracy, 1989; van Marken Lichtenbelt, 1992) and may also increase the efficiency with which energy and nutrients are assimilated through the gut lining (Greenwald and Kanter, 1979; Harwood, 1979).

Although most reptiles are carnivorous, some lizards and many turtle species are omnivorous. Strict herbivory is rare among reptiles but can be found in tortoises (Testudinidae), adult green turtles (*Chelonia* spp.), and within a few lineages of lizards (Pough, 1973; Zimmerman and Tracy, 1989; also see Table 1). Some evidence suggests that herbivorous reptiles are only able to process their relatively low nutrient and high fiber diets at higher body temperatures (Harlow *et al.*, 1976; Troyer, 1987; Zimmerman and Tracy, 1989; van Marken Lichtenbelt, 1992). In nature, herbivorous lizards maintain relatively high body temperatures (Table 1), suggesting a correlation with digestion of plant matter. However, the underlying requirement for maintaining high body temperatures in herbivorous reptiles is unknown. One explanation for this phenomenon implicates the thermal needs of the symbiotic microbes (bacteria, protozoa, and nematodes) exploited by herbivores to digest the fibrous components of plant tissues. Perhaps herbivorous reptiles select higher body tempera-

tures because their gut microfauna require a warm environment in which to ferment plant tissues (Schall and Dearing, 1994).

REPRODUCTION

Temperature can influence nearly every stage of the reptilian reproductive cycle including: gametogenesis, courtship and mating behavior, gestation, timing of incubation, hatchling gender and survival, and even reproductive modes (oviparous - egg producing, or viviparous - live bearing). Additionally, various stages of the reproductive cycle are known to influence patterns of thermoregulation and selected and activity body temperatures. (Refer to Chapters on reproduction and egg physiology for more in-depth information.)

The onset of the reproductive season for reptiles living in temperate regions is largely controlled by hormones which respond to abiotic cues, such as increases in daylength or environmental temperatures. For example, gametogenesis in the male green anole, *Anolis carolinensis*, is strongly correlated with daylength and temperature (Licht, 1967*a*,*b*, 1969).

Table 1.
Mean body temperatures of herbivorous lizards in nature. Although many carnivorous/insectivorous reptiles also have high body temperatures, as a group herbivorous reptiles generally maintain body temperatures above 30°C when active. Taxonomy for iguanians follows Frost and Etheridge (1989).

Taxon	Body Temperature (°C)	Source
Iguanidae		
Marine iguana (*Amblyrhynchus cristatus*)	36.0	1
Santa Fe land iguana (*Conolophus pallidus*)	36.6	4
Galápagos land iguana (*Conolophus subcristatus*)	32.0	2
Spiny-tailed iguana (*Ctenosaura hemilopha*)	37.1	14
Cuban iguana (*Cyclura nubila*)	38.6	5
Desert iguana (*Dipsosaurus dorsalis*)	40.0	10
Green iguana (*Iguana iguana*)	36.1	8
Spiny chuckwalla (*Sauromalus hispidus*)	35.8	3
Common chuckwalla (*Sauromalus obesus*)	38.3	9
Piebald chuckwalla (*Sauromalus varius*)	36.4	3
Leiolepidinae		
Egyptian spiny-tailed lizard (*Uromastyx aegyptius*)	39.9	6
Small-scaled dhabb (*Uromastyx microlepis*)	38.0	15
Tropiduridae		
Andean chuckwalla (*Phymaturus palluma*)	34.2	11
Scincidae		
Centralian blue-tongued skink (*Tiliqua multifasciata*)	34.3	10
Cordylidae		
Angolan dune lizard (*Angolosaurus skoogi*)	35.1	7
Teiidae		
Aruba Island whiptail (*Cnemidophorus arubensis*)	39.3	12
Bonaire Island whiptail (*Cnemidophorus murinus*)	38.5	13

Sources: 1. Bartholomew, 1966; 2. Carpenter, 1969; 3. Case, 1982; 4. Christian *et al.*, 1983; 5. Christian *et al.*, 1986; 6. Foley *et al.*, 1992; 7. Hamilton and Coetzee, 1969; 8. McGinnis and Brown, 1966; 9. Muchlinski *et al.*, 1990; 10. Pianka, 1986; 11. Sage, 1974; 12. Schall, 1973; 13. Schall and Dearing, 1994; 14. Soulé, 1963; 15. Zari, 1991.

Santa Fe Land Iguana, *Conolophus pallidus*. Photo by K. H. Switak.

Mate acquisition is influenced by numerous biotic variables, but temperature may also play an important role. For example, many reptiles exhibit species-specific courtship and reproductive behaviors (see review in Carpenter and Ferguson, 1977). Courtship displays typically involve both amplification of contrast and/or coloration, and physically communicated signals (e.g., "push-up" displays, head bobbing, body rubs, etc.). Performance of these stereotypic displays can be modified by body temperature (Bennett, 1980, 1982), but it is not completely understood how body temperatures of the individuals receiving the signs might influence the interpretation of the signal.

The thermal environment has substantial effects on eggs and developing reptiles. Nest incubation temperatures are known to influence hatchling viability and post-hatching performance. Warmer nest temperatures generally increase rates of development, but suboptimal incubation temperatures (i.e., too low or too high) can lead to developmental abnormalities (Beuchat, 1988; Packard and Packard, 1988) and, in extreme cases, death of the embryo (Licht and Moberly, 1965; Chris-

tian *et al.*, 1986; Packard and Packard, 1988). Temperature may also directly influence hatchling fitness. Christian and Tracy (1981) found that the ability of hatchling Santa Fe land iguanas (*Conolophus pallidus*) to avoid predators was temperature dependent. Successful dispersal from the nest sites was largely a function of a lizard's ability to achieve the high body temperatures necessary for efficient locomotory performance.

Nest temperatures not only affect rates of development, but in some cases may determine the gender of the hatchling. In some reptiles, the nest or incubating environment, not chromosomes, determine hatchling gender (see also chapters on sex determination and reproductive ecology in this volume). This phenomenon is generally known as **environmental sex determination** (ESD). In many cases temperature is the environmental variable responsible for gender determination. This type of ESD is known as **temperature-dependent sex determination**, or TSD. Nest temperatures may be affected by numerous factors including differences in season, nest depth, properties of the overlying nest material, nest moisture, com-

Incubation of python eggs. Photo by Isabelle Francais.

Leopard Gecko, *Eublepharis macularius*. Juvenile photo by R. D. Bartlett.

Northern Pacific Rattlesnake, *Crotalus viridis oreganus*. Photo by Ron Everhart.

pass orientation, substratum type (including soil texture and structure), and other microclimatic factors. Thus, at the same general locality on a given year, some nests may produce only female offspring, while other nests produce only males (Janzen, 1994). When considered at a larger scale, TSD has the potential to effect population dynamics, demography, and long-term persistence. Although TSD is known to influence the sex ratios of individual nests (Bull and Vogt, 1979; Janzen, 1994), manypopulations of reptiles with TSD equal male:female gender ratios as adults (Ewert and Nelson, 1991).

Three general patterns of TSD have been characterized in reptiles (Bull, 1980). In some turtles, low temperatures (e.g., less than approximately 25-28 °C) produce all male offspring, and high incubation temperatures (e.g., greater than about 31-33 °C) produce all females (Vogt and Bull, 1982; Ewert and Nelson, 1991). At intermediate incubation temperatures both sexes are produced. In some lizards, higher incubation temperatures produce males and lower temperatures produce females. In crocodilians, some turtles, and some eublepharid geckos (e.g., leopard geckos, *Eublepharis macularius* and African fat-tailed geckos, *Hemitheconyx caudicinctus*), males are produced at intermediate temperatures and females are produced at higher and lower incubation temperatures (Webb and Cooper-Preston, 1989; Ewert and Nelson, 1991; Viets et al., 1993; Lang and Andrews, 1994).

Variable or cyclic nest temperatures generally have an effect that is dependent on the highest temperature reached in the cycle. Gender determination typically occurs over a narrow range of nest temperatures and within a short time frame - usually during the first to second third of the incubation period (Vogt and Bull, 1982). TSD is widespread among reptiles and found in some species of all major clades of extant reptiles, except the tuatara (*Sphenodon punctatus*) (see reviews in Bull, 1980; Janzen and Paukstis, 1991; Lang and Andrews, 1994; Viets *et al.*, 1994). Despite attempts by numerous investigators, a single ecologically adaptive or evolutionarily correlated mechanism has yet to be discovered to account for the distribution of TSD in all reptiles. There is however, some recent evidence which suggests that TSD may be correlated with shifts in sexual dimorphism in some lizards and turtles (Viets *et al.*, 1994), but there are many species which do not share this pattern, and many more species yet to be examined.

Among reptiles, parental care is generally rare (Graves and Duvall, 1995), although brooding behaviors have been noted in some squamate reptiles. Two particularly large snakes, the diamond python (*Morelia* [= *Python*] *spilotes spilotes*) and the Indian python (*Python molurus bivittatus*), encircle their eggs and brood them for several months until they hatch. During the egg-brooding cycle, the female python (males do not assist in brooding) rhythmically contracts the muscles along her coils and, as a result, her working muscles raise her body temperature as much as 7 °C above the ambient temperature (Hutchison *et al.*, 1966; Vinegar *et al.*, 1970; Harlow and Grigg, 1984). This phenomenon has been termed **shivering thermogenesis**, and is one of only a few examples of "facultative endothermy" found in reptiles. The retention of

Diamond Python, *Morelia spilotes*. Photo by Aaron Norman.

Fat-tailed Gecko, *Hemitheconyx caudicinctus*. Photo by R. D. Bartlett.

the metabolic heat is undoubtedly facilitated by the large body size of these snakes and their tendency to coil around the egg mass, thereby reducing the total surface area exposed to the environment (Bennett and Dawson, 1976). During this period the brooding female may not feed or drink (Ellis and Chappell, 1987), although females of some species may leave their clutch to temporarily bask in the sun each day. Opportunistic thermoregulation may serve to conserve energy during incubation (Harlow and Grigg, 1984). Nevertheless, the energetic investment and protective behavior associated with brooding is costly, and thus the developing offspring must accrue a substantial benefit from this form of parental care for it to be adaptive. Indeed, the heat generated by the brooding mother warms the eggs and, thereby increases their rate of development (Harlow and Grigg, 1984).

Viviparity (bearing live young), has been proposed by some authorities to have evolved in squamate reptiles as an adaptive response to life in cool climates (Packard *et al.*, 1977; Shine and Bull, 1979; Shine, 1985; Guillette, 1992; see also the reproductive ecology chapter in this volume). The reasoning behind this hypothesis is simple: eggs that are deposited in nests are subject to the vagaries of the environment, whereas a pregnant female protects herself and, hence, her developing embryos, from such environmental threats. In cooler climates, the probability of eggs encountering lethally cold environments should lead to selection for shorter incubation periods (i.e., longer retention or gestation times), and under these conditions, oviparity may be evolutionarily "abandoned" altogether, and replaced by viviparity. Indeed, in many lineages of squamate reptiles, viviparous species are more frequently found in cooler environments (i.e., higher latitudes and elevations) than are oviparous species. Further sup-

Yarrow's Spiny Lizard, *Sceloporus jarrovi*. Photo by R. D. Bartlett.

port for the adaptive significance of viviparity in cooler climates is provided by groups of closely related lizards with dissimilar reproductive modes (e.g., *Liolaemus* and *Sceloporus*). Within these genera, viviparous species are typically associated with distributions at high latitude or elevation (Tinkle and Gibbons, 1977; Ramirez Pinilla, 1991, 1992).

In some cases, selection of particular body temperatures may be different for gestating females. Developing embryos of some species have different thermal requirements than do the adults. For some species, pregnant females select or maintain higher activity body temperatures (e.g., northern Pacific rattlesnake, *Crotalus viridis oreganus*; Gier *et al.*, 1989; ocellated skink, *Chalcides ocellatus*, Daut and Andrews, 1993), while other species maintain lower body temperatures (e.g., Yarrow's spiny lizard, *Sceloporus jarrovi*; Beuchat, 1986, 1988). Selection of higher body temperatures by gravid females should increase developmental rates of offspring, and therefore, shorten gestation periods. However, the thermal tolerances of developing offspring can be different from that of the adults and, in some cases, selection of high body temperatures during gestation can lead to developmental abnormalities and embryo death (Beuchat, 1988). Pregnant females of some viviparous species may also exhibit greater thermoregulatory precision than nonpregnant individuals (Stewart, 1984; Beuchat, 1986; Gier *et al.*, 1989). These embryos may be less tolerant of fluctuating temperatures, thermal extremes, and/or embryonic development is optimized over a small range of temperatures (Packard and Packard, 1988).

INFECTION AND WATER BALANCE

Body temperature may play an important role in fighting disease in ectotherms by shortening the initiation of the immune response (Tait, 1969). When humans become infected with certain pathogenic microbes, the immune system responds by increasing body temperature (i.e., creating a fever) to make the body a less hospitable environment for the pathogen. In vertebrates, fever may be induced by adjusting the internal thermostat, or the voluntary minimum and maximum temperatures. Endotherms accomplish this by increasing metabolic heat production (Kluger, 1979), whereas some reptiles do so by behaviorally selecting warmer thermal environments than they would normally prefer. In controlled laboratory experiments, desert iguanas (*Dipsosaurus dorsalis*) infected with the fever-inducing bacterium, *Aeromonas hydrophila*, behaviorally selected higher body temperatures than did uninfected lizards (Vaughn *et al.*, 1974). In subsequent studies, infected lizards were subjected to temperatures ranging from 34-42 °C. Lizards maintained at cooler temperatures died sooner than did those maintained at higher temperatures (Kluger *et al.*, 1975). Presumably, the survival rates of the lizards maintained at higher temperatures increased because of reduced bacterial growth (Kluger *et al.*, 1975; Kluger, 1979), or as a result of an enhanced immune response. However, like behavioral thermoregulation, "behavioral fever" thermoregulation may not be ubiquitous in reptiles. For instance, researchers working with the leopard tortoise (*Geochelone pardalis*) failed to demonstrate a febrile response despite subjecting the tortoises to several species of known fever-inducing microbes (Zurovsky *et al.*, 1987). Because this phenomenon has been studied in so few reptiles, it is premature to suggest any general explanations for the distribution of this behavior.

Water and ion balance may influence the regulation of body temperature in some reptiles. Following periods of dehydration, desert lizards such as the bearded dragon, *Pogona barbata* (= *Amphibolurus barbatus*) and the desert iguana, *Dipsosaurus dorsalis*, will only initiate panting at higher body temperatures (Parmenter and Heatwole, 1975; Dupré and Crawford, 1985, 1986), presumably as a water conservation mechanism. However, the precise mechanism(s) responsible for elevating the panting threshold have not been identified and may include a reduction in body fluid volume, plasma osmolality or volume, or an increase in plasma ion concentration (Dupré and Crawford, 1986). Similarly, artificially increasing ionic loads (e.g., NaCl, KCl) may increase the panting threshold and the average temperature selected by some reptiles (Dupré and Crawford, 1985; and see review in Bradshaw, 1986).

Bearded Dragon, *Pogona barbata*. Photo by R. G. Sprackland.

METABOLISM

GENERAL REMARKS AND TERMINOLOGY

Metabolism is the general term that embraces the processes associated with energy consumption and utilization by all living organisms. Metabolizable energy and other materials are acquired from the biochemical processes that convert foods into their molecular constituents. These products are used to support maintenance of normal activities, growth and repair, reproduction, and/or may be stored for later use.

Metabolism of energy can be performed through two pathways depending upon the rate of demand for oxygen and for energy production:

—**aerobic** metabolism, which is used during normal sustainable activities

—**anaerobic** metabolism, which is employed during "fight or flight" responses, such as sprinting to capture mobile prey or to avoid predation.

Unlike the aerobic pathway, anaerobic metabolism does not require an immediate source of oxygen to produce work. The distinction between, and the relative importance of, these two metabolic pathways are discussed in the forthcoming section on *Activity and Locomotion*.

ESTIMATES OF METABOLIC RATES

Metabolic rates of reptiles were first studied under controlled conditions in the laboratory. An animal's metabolic rate is often measured from the rate of consumption of materials used in metabolism. Oxygen is the most frequently measured material and metabolic rate is often expressed on a per unit body mass basis (e.g., ml $O_2/(g^\star h)$). Numerous laboratory studies have examined the metabolic rates of fasted reptiles at rest. The oxygen consumption value acquired under these conditions is termed the **standard metabolic rate** (SMR), and is assumed to be the energetic costs of "maintenance" at a specified temperature.

Recent advances using isotopically-labeled water have provided physiological ecologists with the opportunity to study reptilian energetics under natural field conditions (e.g., Bennett and Nagy, 1977; Nagy *et al.*, 1984; Christian and Conley, 1994). **Field metabolic rates** (FMRs) can provide information on changes in energy expenditure resulting from changes in season and over the reproductive cycle. Moreover, FMRs can be used to compare the activity metabolism of reptiles with different ecological attributes (e.g., herbivores vs. carnivores; terrestrial vs. aquatic, etc.).

Although metabolic rates have been measured in many reptiles, most of what we know about reptilian energetics is a product of research on squamate reptiles, and lizards in particular. Andrews and Pough (1985) developed a model for predicting the metabolic rate for squamate reptiles based on their body mass. They found that the metabolic rates (SMRs) of these reptiles were generally 10-20% that of a similarly-sized endotherm. Specifically, oxygen consumption by most squamates fell below 0.25 ml per gram of animal per hour and never exceeded 0.5 ml per gram of animal per hour. Their data show that the metabolic rates of squamate reptiles generally scale to the 0.8 power with body masses (on a log-log basis) over their normal range of activity temperatures. However, it is important to note that a single relationship based on body mass may lead to erroneous estimations of metabolism for some squamates because some evolutionary and ecological factors also explain much of the variation. For example, diurnal predators have significantly higher metabolic rates than do reclusive predators (Andrews and Pough, 1985).

In addition to differences among species in metabolic rates, there can be appreciable variation in metabolism within individuals as a function of the time of day and season of the year. The mechanisms thought to be responsible for the daily and seasonal differences in activity and metabolic rate include differences in age, gender, reproductive condition, elevational distribution, and resource availability (e.g., Bennett and Dawson, 1976; Bennett, 1982; Christian and Conley, 1994; Christian and Green, 1994; see also Chapter 10 this volume).

INFLUENCE OF BODY TEMPERATURE

In most ectotherms, temperature and metabolism are tightly coupled. Generally, metabolic rate increases exponentially with an increase in body temperature. Under aerobic conditions, a 10 °C increase in temperature will typically result in a two- to three-fold increase in the rate or function of a particular physiological process (Bennett and Dawson, 1976; Bennett, 1982). For example, digestive efficiency for a given reptile may increase two-fold over a body temperature span of 25-35°C. A few lizards and snakes have effectively decoupled this effect over a small range of body temperatures. For these reptiles, including the tuatara (*Sphenodon punctatus*) and several species of lizards and snakes, "metabolic plateaus" are observed over the range of their activity body temperatures, or during hibernation when body temperatures stabilize at lower levels (see reviews in Bennett and Dawson, 1976; Bennett, 1982).

INFLUENCE OF BODY SIZE

Body size greatly influences rates of energy exchange between reptiles and their environment. Smaller animals have higher metabolic rates per unit body mass than do larger individuals (see reviews in Bennett and Dawson, 1976; Bennett, 1982; Andrews and Pough, 1985). This relationship is generally expressed by the allometric equation

$$MR = am^b, \text{ or } \log MR = (b \log m) + \log a \text{ (Fig. 4)}$$
where: MR = standard metabolic rate;
log a = y intercept of the regression (constant);
m = body mass of the animal (g); and
b = slope of the regression (constant).

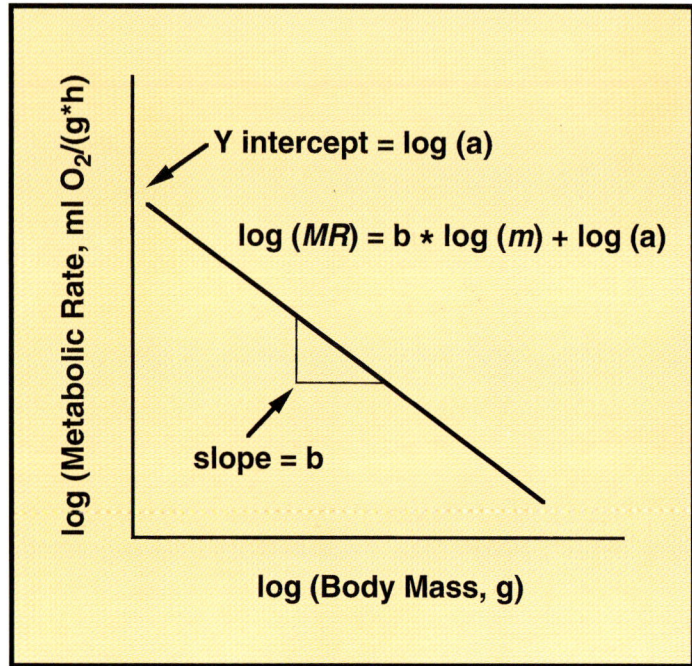

Figure 4.
General relationship for the effect of body mass on metabolic rate in reptiles

Among reptiles, metabolism increases in proportion to body mass raised to the 0.600.88 power. Because the value of the exponent is less than one, larger reptiles expend less energy per unit mass of body tissue than do smaller individuals. The variance in the exponent term b may be a function of body temperature, and/or it may be related to various ecological and/or evolutionary attributes (see Andrews and Pough, 1985).

EVOLUTIONARY HISTORY

Some reptiles have extremely low metabolic rates, while others process energy much more rapidly. Genetic constraints may account for some of the variation in energy use among reptilian lineages. The tuatara (*Sphenodon punctatus*) has a resting metabolic rate approximately two-thirds that of other reptiles, however this value does not fall

Nile Monitor, *Varanus niloticus*. Photo by K. H. Switak.

outside of the range exhibited by reptiles as a group (Bennett and Dawson, 1976). The night lizards (family Xantusiidae) have metabolic rates as low as one half that of other lizards of similar body sizes and temperatures (Mautz, 1979). By contrast, many lizards in the family Teiidae are considered "hyperactive" (e.g., *Ameiva* spp., *Cnemidophorus* spp., *Teius* spp., *Tupinambis* spp.), and indeed some of these species have high metabolic rates (Anderson and Karasov, 1981). Monitor lizards (*Varanus* spp.) also have high metabolic capacities and are generally considered to be a highly active group (Pough, 1973; Bartholomew, 1982; Andrews and Pough, 1985). However, some varanids have extended periods of inactivity over which FMRs can be substantially suppressed. Thus, as a group, monitors may be as physiologically diverse as other lizards (Christian and Conley, 1994). Generally, snakes and lizards exhibit similar metabolic rates on a mass-specific basis, though several snake lineages have not been studied. Among squamates, boas and pythons tend to have lower metabolic rates; however, these rates are statistically indistinguishable from even the high rates recorded for monitor lizards (Andrews and Pough, 1985). Fewer studies have examined the metabolic

Boa Constrictor, *Boa constrictor*. Photo by R. D. Bartlett.

rates of turtles and crocodilians, but the values for species studies in these groups fall within the range found for squamate reptiles (Bennett and Dawson, 1976; Andrews and Pough, 1985).

FORAGING, FEEDING, AND DIGESTION

Foraging behaviors vary widely among reptiles. Some reptiles, known as **sit-and-wait predators**, remain relatively motionless until prey are within striking range and then suddenly lunge out for their meal. **Active** or **widely-foraging predators** move through their environment, digging, scratching, browsing, or engaging in similar activities associated with finding prey. Not surprisingly, sit-and-wait predators have lower resting metabolic rates than do active foragers (Anderson and Karasov, 1981; Nagy *et al.*, 1984; Secor and Diamond, 1995). Generally, the cost of capturing and subduing prey for small reptiles is insignificant relative to the energy acquired from the meal, and under most circumstances, prey capture is accomplished via aerobic metabolism (Pough and Andrews, 1985; Preest, 1991).

In most cases, the energy acquired from a herbivorous diet is less than that obtained from a carnivorous diet. This is because most plant tissues contain less energy on a gram-by-gram basis than do animal tissues, and it is compounded by the fact that herbivorous reptiles digest a smaller proportion of the their diets than do carnivores. For example, digestive efficiencies for herbivorous reptiles range from 30-85%, whereas carnivorous species have efficiencies on the order of 70-95% (Throckmorton, 1973; Harwood, 1979; Ruppert, 1980; Iverson, 1982; Waldschmidt *et al.*, 1986; Zimmerman and Tracy, 1989; Davenport *et al.*, 1992; Foley *et al.*, 1992; van Marken Lichtenbelt, 1992; Barboza, 1995). However, herbivores typically expend only a small amount of time and energy acquiring their food and, thus, the "inefficiency" they experience in digestion may be offset by the low costs required for foraging (Pough, 1973; Iverson, 1982).

Recent comparative studies suggest that significant metabolic costs may be incurred when digestive structures and functions are activated to accommodate increases in food intake. Interestingly, the cost of these changes may be strikingly greater for sit-and-wait predators than for active foragers. Within 24 hours of ingestion, sit-and-wait predatory snakes, such as pythons (*Python* spp.), boas (*Boa constrictor*), and sidewinders (*Crotalus cerastes*), experience as much as a 17-fold increase in metabolic rate (Secor *et al.*, 1994; Secor and Diamond, 1995 *a,b*). Post-feeding metabolic rates of actively foraging species, such as coachwhip snakes (*Masticophis* spp.), king snakes (*Lampropeltis* spp.) and gopher

Gray-banded Kingsnake, *Lampropeltis alterna*. Photo by R. G. Markel.

snakes (*Pituophis* spp.), also significantly increase, but not as dramatically as the sit-and-wait species. These substantial differences in metabolic costs of digestion are interpreted as adaptive strategies resulting from the frequency of feeding (Secor *et al.*, 1994; Secor and Diamond, 1995*a,b*). Because sit-and-wait foragers may go for months between feeding bouts, maintaining digestive structures at their functionally operating levels is not energetically cost effective. By contrast, active foragers, which may feed daily, are expected to maintain their gut functions closer to operating levels instead of continuously turning on and off their digestive systems.

ACTIVITY AND LOCOMOTION

Activity patterns in reptiles range from sedentary species that remain virtually motionless for hours or days, to those that are nearly continuously active. Thus, for some reptiles, the energy expended in activity and locomotion can account for a substantial proportion of the total energy budget. This is particularly true for actively foraging species which spend a significant proportion of their activity period seeking prey (Bennett and Gleeson, 1979; Anderson and Karasov, 1981; Secor and Nagy, 1994). Yet for sit-and-wait reptiles, locomotion is limited to short-distance bursts used to capture prey or to avoid predation and, therefore, may not impose a significant cost relative to other behaviors (Anderson and Karasov, 1981; Secor and Nagy, 1994). Most reptiles rely on aerobic metabolism for normal locomotory activities such as foraging, migration, finding mates, dispersal, and similar behaviors. Anaerobic metabolism may be required for exertion such as sprinting, diving, or intense interactions with conspecifics and predators. Although anaerobiosis can generate energy at rates five to 10 times greater than that produced by aerobic metabolism,

the ability to sustain anaerobic metabolism rapidly degrades during such activities (Bennett and Dawson, 1976; Bennett, 1982). Moreover, recovery from anaerobic locomotion may take from hours to days depending on the intensity and duration of the activity, and body temperature (Bennett and Dawson, 1976; Wagner and Gleeson, 1996). Although the oxygen debt and lactic acid may be returned to normal levels relatively quickly, it may take longer to replace the energy consumed as a result of anaerobic metabolism because of the inefficiency with which the energy is used relative to aerobic metabolism. Indeed, anaerobic metabolism may require as much as 10 times the equivalent food energy to accomplish the same work under aerobic conditions (Zug, 1993). Interestingly, anaerobic activity is relatively independent of body temperature over much of the thermal activity range for most of the reptiles that have been examined (Bennett and Dawson, 1976). Decoupling temperature from anaerobic locomotion may permit rapid escape responses in times of need.

Numerous studies have quantified the cost of locomotion in reptiles at maximal levels, but fewer have addressed sustainable exercise. **Aerobic scope** is a measure of an animal's ability to do work without relying on anaerobiosis. Aerobic scope is measured as the difference between an animal's maximal aerobic capacity and its SMR, and is often associated with the locomotory and behavioral characteristics of the animal. A corollary of aerobic scope is locomotory endurance or stamina. Garland (1994) measured the endurance capacity of 57 lizard taxa on a treadmill and found that roughly half of the variation in endurance was attributable to body mass and temperature. Specifically, warmer and larger lizards tend to have greater endurance capacities. However, evolutionary history and various ecological attributes were also suggested to have important correlates with locomotory performance. For instance, some lineages of lizards exhibit relatively greater locomotory stamina, such as some Scincidae (skinks), Lacertidae (*Lacerta* spp.), Teiidae (whiptail lizards), Helodermatidae (Gila monster and Mexican beaded lizards), Varanidae (*Varanus* spp.), while other groups, including most of the Iguanian lineages and the Gekkota, have lower endurance capacities. Not surprisingly, the latter two groups are sit-and-wait predators, whereas the majority of the others are active foragers.

REPRODUCTION

Reproduction is a key determinant of organismal fitness, but can also be one of the most energetically costly activities. In many reptiles, mate acquisition can involve a substantial energetic investment which may be associated with costly migra-

Gila Monster, *Heloderma suspectum*. Photo by Karl H. Switak.

tions, complex behaviors and courtship displays, competition among conspecifics for mates and/or nest sites, excavating nest sites, fasting, incubation, nest guarding, gestation, and in a few exceptional cases, parental care (see Chapter 6 this volume).

Female reptiles of viviparous species might be expected to accrue the greatest metabolic costs of reproduction. Metabolic rate increases sigmoidally over the course of pregnancy in Yarrow's spiny lizard (*Sceloporus jarrovi*), and plateaus just prior to parturition (DeMarco, 1993). Litter metabolism is lowest during early pregnancy, when the litter mass consists mostly of metabolically inert yolk (DeMarco, 1993). Thus the cost of early pregnancy in this viviparous lizard is likely to closely approximate the value expected for a gravid oviparous species. However, metabolic rates substantially increase later in pregnancy, and may significantly exceed that incurred by oviparous species (DeMarco, 1993). Additionally, despite the fact that viviparous species tend to produce fewer offspring per clutch than do oviparous species, maternal investments may still be equal to or greater than that for viviparous species because the period of gestation is typically twice as long (Shine, 1985). Longer periods of pregnancy may impose additional energetic costs and may lower fitness due to an increase in total body mass which, in turn, may hamper agility, locomotory performance, and the ability to acquire prey and avoid predators.

As discussed previously, some brooding pythons produce heat via rhythmic contractions of skeletal muscles, or shivering thermogenesis. This form of incubation can be metabolically costly, because the animal's muscles may continuously twitch for more than two months. In fact, depending upon the heat differential between the mother and the environment, brooding pythons can expend anywhere from 2-22 times more energy than similarly-sized nonbrooding individuals (Vinegar *et al.*, 1970; Harlow and Grigg, 1984). Although other species

of pythons brood their eggs, shivering thermogenesis has only been recorded in the larger species (e.g., Ellis and Chappell, 1987).

HIBERNATION

GENERAL REMARKS AND TERMINOLOGY

Reptiles have been remarkably successful at invading the hot climates of the world; however, they have not experienced a similar degree of success in cooler environments. As we have discussed previously, cold temperatures, such as those associated with temperate zone winters, impose challenging or even intolerable conditions for many reptiles. **Hibernation** may be the only option available to some reptiles to avoid the unfavorable conditions of cold and limited food availability during winter. Although not all reptiles hibernate, all major reptilian clades have some hibernators. Examples are the tuatara (*Sphenodon punctatus*); most temperate and some subtropical sea turtles;

American Alligator, *Alligator mississippiensis*. Photo by R. T. Zappalorti.

alligators (*Alligator mississippiensis* and *A. sinensis*), and the Nile crocodile (*Crocodylus niloticus*); and many temperate and some subtropical squamates (Gregory, 1982).

For the purposes of this discussion, we define hibernation broadly as a state of dormancy coinciding with the cold of winter (but see Gregory, 1982 for a review of alternative definitions). Hibernation is a period of quiescence: normal activities cease, body temperature regulation may be abandoned, feeding and excretion are uncommon, and metabolism may be greatly reduced. **Brumation** was used by Mayhew (1965) to describe obligatory hibernation first seen in flat-tailed horned lizards (*Phrynosoma mcalli*). Unlike most other hibernating reptiles, *P. mcalli*, will enter and remain in a inactive state even if photoperiod and temperature are artificially increased to levels that are typical of the activity season (Mayhew, 1965). Mayhew (1965) further suggested that the term brumation be adopted to describe reptilian hibernation generally, but perhaps due to its specific definition, the term has failed to receive wide acceptance or usage (Gregory, 1982). **Estivation**, like hibernation, is a strategy to avoid harsh environments and sparse resources, but estivation generally occurs during the challenging months of summer. Like hibernation, estivation includes a reduction in activity, but unlike hibernation, estivation is generally thought to be more a strategy for conserving body water. Estivation has been commonly reported in turtles and squamate reptiles living in the hot deserts of the world.

INDUCTION AND TERMINATION OF HIBERNATION

Hibernation can be partitioned into several components or stages: fasting; entering the hibernaculum; dormancy; and metabolic depression (Gregory, 1982). The induction into each of these stages probably results from a suite of interacting exogenous and endogenous cues (Licht, 1972).

ENDOGENOUS CUES

Reptiles that hibernate in response to cues received from exogenous sources are often termed **facultative hibernators.** For most temperate reptiles, hibernation is coincident with the declining temperatures of fall and early winter. However, few studies have gone beyond simply correlating the onset of hibernation with these lower ambient temperatures. Nevertheless, the fact that some reptiles emerge on unseasonably warm days during winter suggests that temperature is an important cue. Because lower body temperatures generally inhibit appetite in reptiles (Gatten, 1974), the lower temperatures associated with seasonal cooling may also provide an exogenous cue for the initiation of fasting in hibernating reptiles (Gregory, 1982). Day length also may function as an important exogenous cue, but it is difficult to separate true day length responses from other correlated seasonal changes (Licht, 1972). Furthermore, because many reptiles hibernate in environments where they do not receive light cues, it is unlikely that photoperiod alone could serve as a controlling factor for emergence.

ENDOGENOUS CUES

Reptiles that hibernate as a result of cues received from endogenous sources are termed **obligatory hibernators**, and are probably less common than are facultative hibernators. Some investigators have suggested that the underlying hormonal mechanisms in reptiles are similar to those found in mammals (see reviews in Gilles-Baillien, 1974; Firth and Turner, 1982); however, few studies have investigated this directly. Hibernating reptiles exhibit seasonal cycles in hormone, amino acid, and neurotransmitter titers, which may play a key role in the regulation of reptilian hibernation (Firth and Turner, 1982). Several of these hormones (e.g., melatonin, serotonin, and others) are influenced by circadian and seasonal rhythms and, in reciprocal fashion, are themselves altered by daily and annual cycles. However, the mechanisms associated with these relationships are not well understood. Reproductive hormones also cycle in a similar manner, and may serve to induce reproduction upon emergence.

DURATION OF HIBERNATION

The length of the dormancy period depends upon numerous abiotic and biotic factors, including latitudinal and elevational distribution, climate, age, gender, and prehibernation condition (e.g., energy reserves) (Bennett and Dawson, 1976; Gregory, 1982). Reptiles living at high latitudes or elevations may experience longer periods of dormancy than activity (e.g., Pearson, 1954; Gregory, 1982). Different species of reptiles living in identical environments may exhibit remarkably different periods of dormancy, or hibernation strategies. Thus, the duration of dormancy is best considered a continuum spanning a few days, to longer periods interrupted by intermittent emergence, to continuous dormancy for several months (Gregory, 1982). In most reptiles, males emerge from hibernation before females. Because male reptiles can potentially mate more than once in a given reproductive season, early emergence may facilitate the establishment of breeding territories and dominance prior to female emergence, and thus enhance the probability of reproduction (Gregory, 1982).

Generally reptiles experience a substantial metabolic depression during hibernation. In most cases, metabolic rates of hibernating reptiles are lower than would be expected on the basis of the reduction in body temperature alone, and is typically accompanied by a significant reduction in cardiovascular function (Gregory, 1982; Ultsch, 1989). Some reptiles may also experience various changes in body composition during hibernation such as reductions in body fat, and water, though there is no clear pattern to these changes both among and within species and among individuals within a species (see review in Gregory, 1982). Lipid reserves are generally thought to provide the needed energy during the hibernation, but lipid metabolism may be greater before or soon after hibernation rather than during hibernation period itself, and stores generally far exceed that needed to sustain continuos hibernation (Gregory, 1982). Some hibernators may rely on these lipid reserves rather than feed during intermittent periods of activity (Derickson, 1976).

SELECTION OF THE HIBERNACULUM

Hibernacula, or overwintering sites, can function to insulate and shield the hibernator from extremes in temperature, and in some cases, predation. Selection of the hibernaculum may vary among species, populations, and individuals. Hibernacula take many forms, ranging from a pile of leaf litter, soil, or snow, to an ant or termite nest, to deep burrows or caves. Interestingly, some reptiles even hibernate under water. This strategy is well documented in fresh water turtles and alligators, some of which hibernate at the bottom of streams, ponds, or in wallows constructed especially for overwintering. Water provides a stable thermal environment for the hibernator, and because water is most dense at 4 °C, temperatures at the bottom of deeper bodies of water will typically remain above freezing. Fresh water turtles seem to be the best-adapted reptiles for submerged hibernation because they can remain under water for several months (Ultsch and Jackson, 1982*a,b*; Ultsch, 1989). However, sometimes oxygen is unavailable in these environments. To avoid anoxia, some aquatic hibernators do not bury in the mud or rocks, but simply rest on the bottom. This form of exposure may facilitate extrapulmonary respiration, such as that which can occur through the skin, which may be sufficient to meet the metabolic demands during hibernation (Bennett and Dawson, 1976; Ultsch and Jackson, 1982*a,b*; Costanzo, 1989). Nevertheless, some submerged hibernators may experience anoxic conditions which results in the accumulation of lactic acid in their tissues due to their reliance on anaerobic metabolism. For these reptiles, flushing of lactic acid may be accomplished by periodically shuttling to normoxic waters, or by breaching the surface to breathe (Ultsch, 1989).

Some reptiles overwinter in large aggregations in a common hibernaculum known as a **communal den**. This behavior is especially well documented in some temperate zone snakes (Gregory, 1984). In some cases, several different species may share a communal den. Communal denning may provide an adaptive advantage to snakes hibernating in large groups because rates of water loss can be lower than for snakes hibernating individually (Gregory, 1982). However, there is no evidence to suggest that denning clusters of snakes have a survival advantage over those that hibernate individually within the same den environment (Gregory, 1982). Nevertheless, individual snakes may re-

turn to the same den site year after year, though the factors responsible for inducing migration towards these dens have not been examined. Communal denning may also improve the probability of finding a mate upon emergence. This may be especially important for reptiles that have short activity seasons such as those living at high latitude or elevation.

FREEZE AVOIDANCE, TOLERANCE, AND SUPERCOOLING

Most temperate zone reptiles can withstand brief periods of subzero temperatures (Lowe *et al.*, 1971; Gregory, 1982; Ultsch, 1989; Costanzo *et al.*, 1993; Packard *et al.*, 1993; Packard and Packard, 1995). Survival from extremely low temperatures is achieved by one or a combination of three strategies:
—**freeze avoidance**
—**freeze tolerance**
—**supercooling**.

Freeze avoidance can be accomplished via a simplistic form of behavioral thermoregulation. For example, some hibernating snakes move periodically in an effort to find the warmest microenvironments within their hibernaculum (Sexton and Hunt, 1980). Similarly, some box turtles (*Terrapene* spp.) begin hibernation near the surface and bury deeper as the cold of winter progressively lowers the frost line. As spring approaches and ground temperatures increase, these turtles slowly "migrate" to the surface (Legler, 1960). As discussed above, some reptiles hibernate on the bottom of deeper ponds and streams, or in mud, which generally do not freeze.

Freeze tolerance may be an important adaptive strategy some reptiles use to survive the cold

Wood Frog, *Rana sylvatica*. Photo by David Green.

of winter. Two primary adaptations are thought to promote freeze tolerance in reptiles; however, these responses were developed from research on frogs (primarily the wood frog, *Rana sylvatica*), and have only been examined in a small number of reptiles. First, as the periphery of the animal begins to freeze, glucose is rapidly mobilized from glycogen stores in the liver and is carried via blood vessels to other tissues (Storey, 1990). The concentrated glucose serves as a cryoprotectant by inhibiting freeze damage to cells and tissues (Costanzo *et al.*, 1991). The second adaptation involves a redistribution of visceral and tissue water into the coelomic and subdermal spaces (Costanzo *et al.*, 1993). Reducing the concentration of water in the organs reduces the likelihood of ice-crystal formation within the tissues and may, therefore, reduce the chance of cell rupture associated with freezing (Lee *et al.*, 1990, 1992). Glucose distribution and tissue dehydration are further facilitated by a persistence of cardiac function during the onset of freezing (Costanzo *et al.*, 1993). If these mechanisms fail, the animal will die upon thawing as a result of cellular disfunction due to dehydration or mechanical rupturing of their cells resulting from ice crystal formation.

Eastern Painted Turtle, *Chrysemys picta picta*. **Aaron Norman.**

Some turtles (e.g., eastern box turtles, *Terrapene carolina* and painted turtles, *Chrysemys picta*) may tolerate freezing of extracellular fluids, while other reptiles are intolerant of freezing, but can withstand the formation of ice in a portion of their body fluids (e.g., Costanzo, 1988; Storey *et al.*, 1988; Costanzo and Lee, 1990; Costanzo *et al.*, 1993; Packard *et al.*, 1993). For example, hatchling painted turtles (*Chrysemys picta*) overwinter in their nests and commonly experience subzero temperatures which may freeze their extracellular fluids (Packard *et al.*, 1989). Similarly, American alligators (*Alligator mississippiensis*) may regularly experience and survive freezing temperatures at the northern edge of their range (Hagan *et al.*, 1983).

Supercooling occurs when an animal's body temperature falls below freezing, but the animal does not freeze because ice nuclei fail to form within the body. Hatchling painted turtles (*Chrysemys picta*) may avoid nucleation from ice and subsequent freezing, which is generally lethal at high subzero temperatures, by avoiding contact with water and by withdrawing the head and appendages into the shell during hibernation (Packard and Packard, 1995). Supercooling has been examined in only a few species of reptiles (e.g., Lowe *et al.*, 1971; Claussen *et al.*, 1990; Claussen and Zani, 1991; Packard and Packard, 1995), so little is known about the range of conditions under which this strategy is possible in nature (Packard and Packard, 1995), or the ubiquity of this phenomenon among hibernating reptiles generally.

SUMMARY

THERMAL BIOLOGY

The thermal environment plays a critical role in the lives of most reptiles. Even reptiles that do not actively thermoregulate must adhere to the countless temperature-dependent physical and biochemical processes that sustain their lives. Studies on the thermal biology of reptiles have historically focused on lizards, but many important aspects of the thermal biology of most other major groups of reptiles have been examined. Many reptiles have evolved morphological, physiological, and behavioral specializations that can be used to either enhance or reduce exchanges of thermal energy between them and their environments. The specific thermal strategies and activity body temperatures maintained or selected by an individual reptile can be strongly influenced by abiotic factors (such as distribution, climate, and microhabitat selection) as well as biotic factors (such as genetic constraints, health and reproductive status, seasonal and daily patterns of activity, and interactions with other organisms).

METABOLISM

Metabolism is the physiological process of consuming energy and is therefore useful as a tool for comparing energy utilization strategies among reptiles. Metabolism can be either aerobic or anaerobic. Aerobic metabolism is generally used for sustained activities, and is energetically more efficient; however, anaerobic metabolism can be an effective means of delivering energy during brief bursts of activity. Metabolic rate generally increases with increased body temperature, though some reptiles may have decoupled metabolism from temperature over the range of their activity body temperatures. Body size and shape also influence metabolic rates. Larger animals have lower surface-to-volume ratios and thus have lower mass-specific metabolic rates than do smaller animals. Genetic constraints may also explain some of the variation in energy use among reptiles. Indeed, some lineages are comprised of species that exhibit relatively high rates of metabolism when active, while others have remarkably low rates of energy expenditure. Metabolic rate is typically measured indirectly as the amount of oxygen consumed over a specified period of time, and can now be closely estimated on reptiles in nature as well as in the laboratory. Generally, reptilian metabolism scales to the 0.8 power with body mass; however, not all reptiles conform to this predicted value, and those that do may increase or decrease energy expenditure under certain circumstances. Numerous biotic factors, such as activity, acquiring and processing food, and reproduction, may impose important energetic demands.

HIBERNATION

Hibernation is a period of dormancy that coincides with the cold of winter and is an effective strategy for avoiding reductions in energy and other resources. Most temperately distributed reptiles hibernate, though the timing and duration of hibernation may vary widely among taxa and even among individuals at a single locality. The induction and termination of hibernation are controlled by both exogenous and endogenous cues, though the precise mechanisms are not well understood. Reptiles hibernate in a variety of sites ranging from those constructed specifically for that purpose, to more opportunistically selected sites. Some squamates and tortoises hibernate in communal dens and may return to these sites each year. Some hibernating reptiles can survive short periods at subfreezing temperatures. Survival is achieved by one or a combination of three strategies: freeze avoidance, tolerance, and supercooling.

ACKNOWLEDGMENTS

David Morafka and Gary Packard provided useful insights into the semantics and biology of reptilian hibernation and physiology. Ray Huey kindly allowed us to incorporate ideas from some of his published figures. We thank Pamela Budkovich for providing several critical references. This chapter was improved by comments and suggestions from our colleagues: Marilyn Banta, Kathy Dean-Bradley, Kimberleigh Field, Ken Nussear, Eric Simandle and Dawn Wilson. We thank the University of Nevada, Reno for providing the facilities and opportunities to pursue this project. During the preparation of this chapter, REE was supported by a Porter Fellowship from the American Physiological Society.

REFERENCES AND RECOMMENDED READING

—**Anderson, RA; Karasov, WH:**
Contrasts in energy intake and energy expenditure in sit-and-wait and widely foraging lizards. Oecologia, 1981; 49: 67-72.

—**Andrews, RM; Pough FH:**
Metabolism of squamate reptiles: allometric and ecological relationships. Physiological Zoology, 1985; 58: 214-231.

—**Auffenberg, W; Iverson, JB:**
Demography of terrestrial turtles. In, Turtles: Perspectives and Research, N Harless; H Morlock (Eds). Wiley and Sons, New York, 1979, pp. 541-569.

—**Autumn, K; Weinstein, RB; Full, RJ:**
Low cost of locomotion increases performance at low temperature in a nocturnal lizard. Physiological Zoology, 1994; 67: 238-262.

—**Avery, RA:**
Thermoregulation, metabolism, and social behaviour in Lacertidae. In, Morphology and Biology of Reptiles, A d'A Bellairs; CB Cox (Eds). Academic Press, London, 1976, pp. 245-259.

—**Avery, RA:**
Field studies of body temperature and thermoregulation. In, Biology of the Reptilia, C Gans; FH Pough, (Eds). Academic Press, New York, 1982, 12: 93-166.

—**Barber, BJ; Crawford, EC Jr:**
A stochastic dual-limit hypothesis for behavioral thermoregulation in lizards. Physiological Zoology, 1977; 50: 53-60.

—**Barber, BJ; Crawford, EC Jr:**
Dual threshold control for peripheral temperature in the lizard *Dipsosaurus dorsalis*. Physiological Zoology, 1979; 52: 250-263.

—Barboza, PS:
Digesta passage rate and functional anatomy of the digestive tract in the desert tortoise (*Xerobates agassizii*). *Journal of Comparative Physiology* B, 1995; 165: 193-202.

—Bartholomew, GA:
A field study of temperature relations in the Galapagos marine iguana. Copeia, 1966; 1966: 241-250.

—Bartholomew, GA:
Physiological control of body temperature. In, Biology of the Reptilia, C Gans; FH Pough, (Eds). Academic Press, New York, 1982, 12: 167-211.

—Bennett, AF:
Thermal dependence of lizard behavior. Animal Behaviour, 1980; 28: 752-762.

—Bennett, AF:
The energetics of reptilian activity. In, Biology of the Reptilia, C Gans; FH Pough (Eds). Academic Press, New York, 1982, 13: 155-199.

—Bennett, AF; Dawson, WR:
Metabolism. In, Biology of the Reptilia, C Gans; WR Dawson (Eds). Academic Press, New York, 1976, 5: 127-223.

—Bennett, AF; Nagy, KA:
Energy expenditure in free-ranging lizards. Ecology, 1977; 58: 697-700.

—Bennett, AF; John-Alder, HB:
The effect of body temperature on the locomotory energetics of lizards. Journal of Comparative Physiology B, 1984; 155: 21-27.

—Bennett, AF; John-Alder, HB:
Thermal relations of some Australian skinks (Sauria: Scincidae). Copeia, 1986; 1986: 57-64.

—Berk, ML; Heath, JE:
An analysis of behavioural thermoregulation in the lizard *Dipsosaurus dorsalis*. Journal of Thermal Biology, 1975; 1: 15-22.

—Beuchat, CA:
Reproductive influences on the thermoregulatory behavior of a live-bearing lizard. Copeia, 1986; 1986: 971-979.

—Beuchat, CA:
Temperature effects during gestation in a viviparous lizard. Journal of Thermal Biology, 1988; 13: 135-142.

—Bligh, J; Johnson, KG:
Glossary of terms for thermal physiology. Journal of Applied Physiology, 1973; 35: 941-961.

—Bogert, CM:
Thermoregulation in reptiles, a factor in evolution. Evolution, 1949; 3: 195-211.

—Bowker, RG:
Precision of thermoregulation of some African lizards. Physiological Zoology, 1984; 57: 401-412.

—Bradshaw, SD:
Ecophysiology of Desert Reptiles. Academic Press, NSW, Australia, 1986, 324 pp.

—Bradshaw, SD; Main, AR:
Behavioral attitudes and regulation of temperature in *Amphibolurus* lizards. Journal of Zoology, 1968; 154: 193-221.

—Brattstrom, BH:
Body temperatures of reptiles. American Midland Naturalist, 1965; 73: 376-422.

—Brattstrom, BH:
Social and thermoregulatory behavior of the bearded dragon, *Amphibolurus barbatus*. Copeia, 1971; 1971: 484-497.

—Bull, JJ:
Sex determination in reptiles. Quarterly Review of Biology, 1980; 55: 13-21.

—Bustard, HR:
Activity cycle and thermoregulation in the Australian gecko *Gehyra variegata*. Copeia, 1967; 1967: 753-758.

—Bustard, HR:
Temperature-dependent tail autonomy mechanism in gekkonid lizards. Herpetologica, 1968; 24: 127-130.

—Cabanac, M; Hammel, T; Hardy, JD:
Tiliqua scincoides: temperature sensitive units in lizard brain. Science, 1967; 158: 1050-1051.

—Carpenter, CC; Ferguson, GW:
Variation and evolution of stereotyped behaviors in reptiles. In, Biology of the Reptilia, C Gans; DW Tinkle (Eds). Academic Press, New York, 1977, 7: 335-354.

—Case, TJ:
Seasonal aspects of thermoregulatory behavior in the chuckawalla, *Sauromalus obesus* (Reptilia, Lacertilia, Iguanidae). Journal of Herpetology, 1976; 10: 85-95.

—Case, TJ:
Ecology and evolution of the insular gigantic chuckawallas, *Sauromalus hispidus* and *Sauromalus varius*. In, Iguanas of the World, GM Burghardt; AS Rand (Eds). Noyes Publications, Park Ridge, NJ, 1982, pp. 184-212.

—Christian, KA; Tracy, CR:
The effect of the thermal environment on the ability of hatchling Galapagos land iguanas to avoid predation during dispersal. Oecologia, 1981; 49: 218-223.

—Christian, KA; Tracy, CR; Porter, WP:
Seasonal shifts in body temperature and use of microhabitats by Galapagos land iguanas

(*Conolophus pallidus*). Ecology, 1983; 64: 463-468.

—**Christian, KA; Tracy, CR; Porter, WP:**
The effect of cold exposure during incubation of *Sceloporus undulatus* eggs. Copeia, 1986; 1986: 1012-1014.

—**Christian, KA; Clavijo, IE; Cordero-Lopez, N; Elias-Maldonado, EE; Franco, MA; Lugo-Ramirez, MV; Marengo, M:**
Thermoregulation and energetics of a population of Cuban iguanas (*Cyclura nubila*) on Isla Magueyes, Puerto Rico. Copeia, 1986; 1986: 65-69.

—**Christian, KA; Conley, KE:**
Activity and resting metabolism of varanid lizards compared with 'typical' lizards. Australian Journal of Zoology, 1994; 42: 185-193.

—**Christian, KA; Green, B:**
Seasonal energetics and water turnover of the frillneck lizard, *Chlamydosaurus kingii*, in the wet-dry tropics of Australia. Herpetologica, 1994; 50: 274-281.

—**Christian, KA; Bedford, GS:**
Seasonal changes in thermoregulation by the frillneck lizard, *Chlamydosaurus kingii*, in tropical Australia. Ecology, 1995; 76: 124-132.

—**Clark, DR; Kroll, JC:**
Thermal ecology of anoline lizards: temperate versus tropical strategies. Southwestern Naturalist, 1974; 19: 9-19.

—**Claussen, DL; Art, GR:**
Heating and cooling rates in *Anolis carolinensis* and comparisons with other lizards. Comparative Biochemistry and Physiology, 1981; 69A: 23-29.

—**Claussen, DL; Townsley, MD; Bausch, RG:**
Supercooling and freeze-tolerance in the European wall lizard, *Podarcis muralis*, with a revisional history of the discovery of freeze-tolerance in vertebrates. Journal of Comparative Physiology, 1990; 160B: 137-143.

—**Claussen, DL; Zani, PA:**
Allometry of cooling, supercooling, and freezing in the freeze-tolerant turtle *Chrysemys picta*. American Journal of Physiology, 1991; 261: R626-R632.

—**Costanzo, JP:**
Recovery from ice-entombment in garter snakes. Herpetological Review, 1988; 19: 76-77.

—**Costanzo, JP:**
A physiological basis for prolonged submergence in hibernating garter snakes *Thamnophis sirtalis*: evidence for an energy-sparing adaptation. Physiological Zoology, 1989; 62: 580-592.

—**Costanzo, JP; Lee, RE Jr:**
Natural freeze tolerance in the terrestrial turtle, *Terrapene carolina*. Journal of Experimental Zoology, 1990; 254: 228-232.

—**Costanzo, JP; Lee, RE Jr; Wright, MF:**
Glucose loading prevents freezing injury in rapidly-cooled wood frogs. American Journal of Physiology, 1991; 261: R1346-R1350.

—**Costanzo, JP; Lee, RE Jr; Wright, MF:**
Physiological responses to freezing in the turtle *Terrapene carolina*. Journal of Herpetology, 1993; 27: 117-120.

—**Cowles, RB:**
Semantics in biothermal studies. Science, 1962; 135: 670.

—**Cowles, RB; CM Bogert:**
A preliminary study of the thermal requirements of desert reptiles. Bulletin of the American Museum of Natural History, 1944; 83: 261-296.

—**Daut, EF; Andrews, RM:**
The effect of pregnancy on thermoregulatory behavior of the viviparous lizard *Chalcides ocellatus*. Journal of Herpetology, 1993; 27: 6-13.

—**Davenport, J; Andrews, TJ; Hudson, G:**
Assimilation of energy, protein and fatty acids by the spectacled caiman *Caiman crocodilus crocodilus* L. Herpetological Journal, 1992; 2: 72-76.

—**Dawson, WR:**
On the physiological significance of the preferred body temperatures of reptiles. In, Perspectives of Biophysical Ecology, DM Gates; RB Schmerl (Eds). Springer-Verlag, New York, 1975, pp. 443-473.

—**DeMarco, V:**
Metabolic rates of female viviparous lizards (*Sceloporus jarrovi*) throughout the reproductive cycle: do pregnant lizards adhere to standard allometry? Physiological Zoology, 1993; 66: 166-180.

—**Derickson, WK:**
Lipid storage and utilization in reptiles. American Zoologist, 1976; 16: 711-723.

—**DeWitt, CB:**
Precision of thermoregulation and its relation to environmental factors in the desert iguana, *Dipsosaurus dorsalis*. Physiological Zoology, 1967; 40: 49-66.

—**DeWitt, CB; Friedman, RM:**
Significance of skewness in ectotherm thermoregulation. American Zoologist, 1979; 19: 195-209.

—**Diefenbach, CO daC:**
Gastric function in *Caiman crocodilus* (Crocodylia: Reptilia)-I. Rate of gastric di-

gestion and gastric motility as a function of temperature. Comparative Biochemistry and Physiology, 1975; 51A: 259-265.

—**Dupré, RK; Crawford, EC Jr:**
Behavioral thermoregulation during dehydration and osmotic loading of the desert iguana. Physiological Zoology, 1985; 58: 357-363.

—**Dupré, RK; Crawford, EC:**
Elevation of the panting threshold of the desert iguana, *Dipsosaurus dorsalis*, during dehydration: potential roles of changes in plasma osmolality and body fluid volume. Journal of Comparative Physiology B, 1986; 156: 377-381.

—**Ellis, TM; Chappell, MA:**
Metabolism, temperature relations, maternal behavior, and reproductive energetics in the ball python (*Python regius*). Journal of Comparative Physiology B, 1987; 157: 393-402.

—**Ewert, MA; Nelson, CE:**
Sex determination in turtles: diverse patterns and some possible adaptive values. Copeia, 1991; 1991: 50-69.

—**Firth, BT; Turner, JS:**
Sensory, neural, and hormonal aspects of thermoregulation. In, Biology of the Reptilia, C Gans; FH Pough (Eds). Academic Press, New York, 1982, 12: 214-274.

—**Foley, WJ; Bouskila, A; Shkolnik, A; Choshniak, I:**
Microbial digestion in the herbivorous lizard *Uromastyx aegyptius* (Agamidae). Journal of Zoology, 1992; 226: 387-398.

—**Frair, W; Gackman, R; Mrosovsky, N:**
Body temperature of *Dermochelys coriacea*: warm turtle from cold water. Science, 1972; 177: 791-793.

—**Fraser, S; Grigg, GC:**
Control of thermal conductance is insignificant to thermoregulation in small reptiles. Physiological Zoology, 1984; 57: 392-400.

—**Frost, DR; Etheridge, R:**
A phylogenetic analysis and taxonomy of iguanian lizards (Reptilia: Squamata). Occasional Papers of the Museum of Natural History, University of Kansas, 1989; 81: 1-65.

—**Fuentes, ER; Jaksić, FM:**
Activity temperatures of eight *Liolaemus* (Iguanidae) in central Chile. Copeia, 1979; 1979: 546-548.

—**Gans, C; Pough, FH:**
The vocabulary of reptilian thermoregulation. In, Biology of the Reptilia, C Gans; FH Pough (Eds). Academic Press, New York, 1982, 12: 17-23.

—**Garland, T Jr:**
Phylogenetic analyses of lizard endurance capacity in relation to body size and body temperature. In, Lizard Ecology: Historical and Experimental Perspectives, LJ Vitt; ER Pianka (Eds). Princeton University Press, Princeton, New Jersey, 1994, pp. 237-259.

—**Garrick, LD:**
Lizard thermoregulation: operant responses for heat at different thermal intensities. Copeia, 1979; 1979: 258-266.

—**Gatten, RE Jr:**
Effect of nutritional status on the preferred body temperature of the turtles *Pseudemys scripta* and *Terrapene ornata*. Copeia, 1974; 1974: 912-917.

—**Gier, PJ; Wallace, RL; Ingermann, RL:**
Influence of pregnancy on behavioral thermoregulation in the northern Pacific rattlesnake. Journal of Experimental Biology, 1989; 145: 465-469.

—**Gilles-Baillien, M:**
Seasonal variation in reptiles. In, Chemical Zoology. M Florkin; BT Sheer (Eds). Academic Press, London, 1974, 13: 353-376.

—**Gorman, GC; Hillman, S:**
Physiological basis for climatic niche partitioning in two species of Puerto Rican *Anolis* (Reptilia, Lacertilia, Iguanidae). Journal of Herpetology, 1977; 11: 337-340.

—**Graves, BM; Duvall, D:**
Aggregation of squamate reptiles associated with gestation, oviposition, and parturition. Herpetological Monographs, 1995; 9: 102-119.

—**Greenwald, OE:**
Thermal dependence of striking and prey capture by gopher snakes Copeia, 1974; 1974: 141-148.

—**Greenwald, OE; Kanter, ME:**
The effects of temperature and behavioral thermoregulation on digestive efficiency and rate in corn snakes (*Elaphe guttata guttata*). Physiological Zoology, 1979; 52: 398-408.

—**Greer, AE; Lazell, JD; Wright, RM:**
Anatomical evidence for a counter-current heat exchanger in the leatherback turtle (*Dermochelys coriacea*). Nature, 1973; 244: 181.

—**Gregory, PT:**
Reptilian hibernation. In, Biology of the Reptilia, C Gans; FH Pough (Eds). Academic Press, New York, 1982, 13: 53-154.

—**Gregory, PT:**
Communal denning in snakes. In, Vertebrate Ecology and Systematics: A Tribute to Henry S. Fitch, RA Seigel; LE Hunt; JL Night; L Maralet; NL Zuschlag (Eds). Special Publications in Natural History, University of Kansas, Lawrence, 1984, pp. 57-75.

—**Guillette, LJ Jr:**
The evolution of viviparity in lizards. Bioscience, 1993; 43: 742-751.

—**Hagan, JM; Smithson, PC; Doerr, PD:**
Behavioral response of the American alligator to freezing weather. Journal of Herpetology, 1983; 17: 402-404.

—**Hamilton, WJ; Coetzee, CG:**
Thermoregulatory behaviour of the vegetarian lizard *Angolosaurus skoogi* on the vegetationless northern Namib Desert dunes. Scientific Papers of the Namib Desert Research Station, 1969; 47: 95-103.

—**Harlow, JJ; Hillman, SS; Hoffman, M:**
The effect of temperature on digestive efficiency in the herbivorous lizard *Dipsosaurus dorsalis*. Journal of Comparative Physiology, 1976; 111: 1-6.

—**Harlow, P; Grigg, G:**
Shivering thermogenesis in a brooding diamond python, *Python spilotes spilotes*. Copeia, 1984; 1984: 959-965.

—**Harwood, RH:**
The effect of temperature on the digestive efficiency of three species of lizards, *Cnemidophorus tigris*, *Gerrhonotus multicarinatus* and *Sceloporus occidentalis*. Comparative Biochemistry and Physiology, 1979; 63A: 417-433.

—**Heath, JE:**
Reptilian thermoregulation: evaluation of field studies. Science, 1964; 146: 784.

—**Heath, JE:**
Temperature regulation and diurnal activity in horned lizards. University of California Publications in Zoology, 1965; 64: 97-136.

—**Heatwole, H:**
Thermal ecology of the desert dragon *Amphibolurus inermis*. Ecological Monographs, 1970; 40: 425-457.

—**Heatwole, H; Johnson, CR:**
Thermoregulation in the red-bellied blacksnake, *Pseudechis porphyriacus* (Elapidae). Zoological Journal of the Linnean Society, 1979; 65: 83-101.

—**Heatwole, H; Taylor, J:**
Ecology of Reptiles. Surrey Beatty & Sons, Chipping Norton, NSW, 1987, 325 pp.

—**Hellmich, WC:**
On ecotypic and autotypic characters, a contribution to the knowledge of the evolution of the genus *Liolaemus* (Iguanidae). Evolution, 1951; 5: 359-369.

—**Hertz, PE:**
Thermal passivity of a tropical forest lizard, *Anolis polylepis*. Journal of Herpetology, 1974; 8: 823-827.

—**Hertz, PE; Huey, RB:**
Compensation for altitudinal changes in the thermal environment by some *Anolis* lizards on Hispaniola. Ecology, 1981; 62: 515-521.

—**Hertz, PE; Huey, RB; Nevo, E:**
Flight versus flight: body temperature influences defensive responses of lizards. Animal Behaviour, 1982; 30: 676-679.

—**Horton, DR:**
Lizard scales and adaptation. Systematic Zoology, 1972; 21: 441-443.

—**Huey, RB:**
Behavioral thermoregulation in lizards: importance of associated costs. Science, 1974; 184: 1001-1003.

—**Huey, RB:**
Temperature, physiology, and the ecology of reptiles. In, Biology of the Reptilia, C Gans; FH Pough (Eds). Academic Press, New York, 1982, 12: 25-91.

—**Huey, RB; Slatkin, M:**
Costs and benefits of thermoregulation. Quarterly Review of Biology, 1976; 51: 363-384.

—**Huey, RB; Pianka, ER:**
Seasonal variation in thermoregulatory behavior and body temperature of diurnal Kalahari lizards. Ecology, 1977; 58: 1066-1075.

—**Huey, RB; Stevenson, RD:**
Integrating thermal physiology and ecology of ectotherms: a discussion of approaches. American Zoologist, 1979; 19: 357-366.

—**Huey, RB; Bennett, AF:**
Phylogenetic studies of coadaptation: preferred temperatures versus optimal performance temperatures of lizards. Evolution, 1987; 41: 1098-1115.

—**Hutchison, VH; Dowling, HG; Vinegar, A:**
Thermoregulation in a brooding female Indian python, *Python molurus bivittatus*. Science, 1966; 151: 694-696.

—**Hutchison, VH; Dupré, RK:**
Thermoregulation. In, Environmental Physiology of the Amphibians, ME Feder; WW Burggren (Eds). University of Chicago Press, Chicago, 1992, pp. 206-249.

—**Iverson, JB:**
Adaptations to herbivory in iguanine lizards. In, Iguanas of the World, GM Burghardt; AS Rand, (Eds). Noyes Publications, Park Ridge, NJ, 1982, pp. 60-76.

—**Janzen, FJ:**
Vegetational cover predicts the sex ratio of hatchling turtles in natural nests. Ecology, 1994; 75: 1593-1599.

—Janzen, FJ; Paukstis, GL:
Environmental sex determination in reptiles: ecology, evolution, and experimental design. Quarterly Review of Biology, 1991; 66: 149-179.

—John-Alder, HB; Bennett, AF:
Thermal adaptation in lizard muscle function. Journal of Comparative Physiology B, 1987; 157: 241-252.

—Kingsbury, BA:
Thermoregulatory set points of the eurythermic lizard *Elgaria multicarinata*. Journal of Herpetology, 1993; 27: 241-247.

—Kluger, MJ:
Fever in ectotherms: evolutionary implications. American Zoologist, 1979; 19: 295-304.

—Kluger, MJ; Ringler, DH; Anver, MR:
Fever and survival. Science, 1975; 188: 166-168.

—Lang, JW:
Thermophilic responses of the American alligator and the American crocodile to feeding. Copeia, 1979; 1979: 48-59.

—Lang, JW; Andrews, HV:
Temperature-dependent sex determination in crocodilians. Journal of Experimental Zoology, 1994; 270: 28-44.

—Lee, RE Jr; Layne, JR Jr; Costanzo, JP; Davidson, EC: Systemic and organismal responses to freezing in vertebrates. Cryobiology, 1990; 27: 643-644.

—Lee, RE Jr; Costanzo, JP; Davidson, EC; Layne, JR Jr:
Dynamics of body water during freezing and thawing in a freeze-tolerant frog (*Rana sylvatica*). Journal of Thermal Biology, 1992; 17: 263-266.

—Legler, JM:
Natural history of the ornate box turtle (*Terrepene o. ornata*) Agassiz. University of Kansas Publications of the Museum of Natural History, 1960; 11: 527-669.

—Licht, P:
The temperature dependence of myosin-adenosinetriphosphatase and alkaline phosphatase in lizards. Comparative Biochemistry and Physiology, 1964a; 12: 331-340.

—Licht, P:
A comparative study of the thermal dependence of contractility in saurian skeletal muscle. Comparative Biochemistry and Physiology, 1964b; 13: 27-34.

—Licht, P:
Environmental control of annual testicular cycles in the lizard *Anolis carolinensis*. I. Interaction of light and temperature in the initiation of testicular recrudescence. Journal of Experimental Zoology, 1967a; 165: 505-561.

—Licht, P:
Environmental control of annual testicular cycles in the lizard *Anolis carolinensis*. II. Seasonal variations in effects of photoperiod and temperature on testicular recrudescence. Journal of Experimental Zoology, 1967b; 166: 243-253.

—Licht, P:
Thermal adaptation in the enzymes of lizards in relation to preferred body temperatures. In, Molecular Mechanisms of Temperature Adaptation. American Association for the Advancement of Science, Washington, DC, 1967c, pp. 131-145.

—Licht, P:
Environmental control of annual testicular cycles in the lizard *Anolis carolinensis*. I. Interaction of light and temperature in the initiation of testicular recrudescence. Journal of Experimental Zoology, 1969; 165: 505-561.

—Licht, P:
Problems in experimentation on timing mechanisms for annual physiological cycles in reptiles. In, Hibernation and Hypothermia, Perspectives and Challenges, TE South; JP Hannon; JR Willis; ET Pengelley; NR Alpert (Eds). Elsevier, Amsterdam, 1972, pp. 681-710.

—Licht, P; Moberly, WR:
Thermal requirements for embryonic development in the tropical lizard *Iguana iguana*. Copeia, 1965; 1965: 515-517.

—Losos, JB:
Thermoregulatory correlates of escape behavior by a desert lizard, *Ctenophorus isolepis*. Journal of Herpetology, 1988; 22: 353-356.

—Lowe, CH; Lardner, PJ; Halpern, EA:
Supercooling in reptiles and other vertebrates. Comparative Biochemistry and Physiology, 1971; 39A: 125-135.

—MacKay, RS:
Observations on peristaltic activity versus temperature and circadian rhythms in undisturbed *Varanus flavescens* and *Ctenosaura pectinata*. Copeia, 1968; 1968: 252-259.

—Mautz, WJ:
The metabolism of reclusive lizards, the Xantusiidae. Copeia, 1979; 1979: 577-584.

—Mautz, WJ; Daniels, CB; Bennett, AF:
Thermal dependence of locomotion and aggression in a xantusiid lizard. Herpetologica, 1992; 48: 271-279.

—McGinnis, SM; Brown, CW:
Thermal behavior of the green iguana, *Iguana*

iguana. Herpetologica, 1966; 22: 189-199.

—**McGinnis, SM; Voigt, WG:**
Thermoregulation in the desert tortoise, *Gopherus agassizii*. Comparative Biochemistry and Physiology, 1971; 40A: 119-126.

—**Moore, RG:**
Seasonal and daily activity patterns and thermoregulation in the southwestern speckled rattlesnake (*Crotalus mitchelli pyrrhus*) and the Colorado Desert sidewinder (*Crotalus cerastes laterorepens*). Copeia, 1978; 1978: 439-442.

—**Mrosovsky, N:**
Sex ratios of sea turtles. Journal of Experimental Zoology, 1994; 270: 16-27.

—**Mrosovsky, N; Pritchard, PCH:**
Body temperatures of *Dermochelys coriacea* and other sea turtles. Copeia, 1971; 1971: 624-631.

—**Muchlinski, AE; Hogan, JM; Stoutenburgh, RJ:**
Body temperature regulation in a desert lizard, *Sauromalus obesus*, under undisturbed field conditions. Comparative Biochemistry and Physiology, 1990; 95A: 579-583.

—**Nagy, KA; Huey, RB; Bennett, AF:**
Field energetics and foraging mode of Kalahari lacertid lizards. Ecology, 1984; 65: 588-596.

—**Norris, KS:**
The ecology of the desert iguana *Dipsosaurus dorsalis*. Ecology, 1953; 34: 265-287.

—**Norris, KS:**
Color adaptation in desert reptiles and its thermal relationships. In, Lizard Ecology: A Symposium, WW Milstead (Ed). University Press of Missouri, Columbia, MO, 1967, pp. 162-229.

—**Naulleau, G:**
The effect of temperature on digestion in *Vipera aspis*. Journal of Herpetology, 1983; 17: 166-170.

—**Packard, GC; Tracy, CR; Roth, JJ:**
The physiological ecology of reptilian eggs and embryos, and the evolution of viviparity within the class Reptilia. Biological Reviews, 1977; 52: 71-105.

—**Packard, GC; Packard, MJ:**
The physiological ecology of reptilian eggs and embryos. In, Biology of the Reptilia, C Gans; RB Huey (Eds). Alan R Liss, Inc., New York, 1988, 16: 523-605.

—**Packard, GC; Packard, MJ; McDaniel, PL; McDaniel, LL:**
Tolerance of hatchling painted turtles to subzero temperatures. Canadian Journal of Zoology, 1989; 67: 828-830.

—**Packard, GC; Ruble, KA; Packard, MJ:**
Hatchling snapping turtles overwintering in natural nests are inoculated by ice in frozen soil. Journal of Thermal Biology, 1993; 18: 185-188.

—**Packard, GC; Packard, MJ:**
The basis for cold tolerance in hatchling painted turtles (*Chrysemys picta*). Physiological Zoology, 1995; 68: 129-148.

—**Parmenter, CJ; Heatwole, H:**
Panting thresholds of lizards. IV. The effect of dehydration on the panting threshold of *Amphibolurus barbatus* and *Amphibolurus muricatus*. Journal of Experimental Zoology, 1975; 191: 327-332.

—**Patterson, JW; Davies, PMC:**
Preferred body temperature: seasonal and sexual differences in the lizard *Lacerta vivipara*. Journal of Thermal Biology, 1978; 3: 39-41.

—**Paulissen, MA:**
Ontogenetic comparisons of body temperature selection and thermal tolerance of *Cnemidophorus sexlineatus*. Journal of Herpetology, 1988; 22: 473-476.

—**Pearson, OP:**
Habits of the lizard, *Liolaemus multiformis multiformis* at high altitudes in southern Peru. Copeia, 1954; 1954: 111-116.

—**Pearson, OP:**
The effect of substrate and of skin color on thermoregulation of a lizard. Comparative Biochemistry and Physiology, 1977; 58A: 353-358.

—**Pianka, ER:**
Ecology and Natural History of Desert Lizards. Princeton University Press, Princeton, NJ, 1986, 208 pp.

—**Porter, WP; Mitchell, JW; Beckman, WA; Tracy, CR:**
Environmental constraints on some predator-prey interactions. In, Perspectives of Biophysical Ecology, DM Gates; RB Schmerl (Eds). Springer-Verlag, New York, 1975, pp. 347-364.

—**Pough, FH:**
Lizard energetics and diet. Ecology, 1973; 54: 837-844.

—**Pough, FH:**
The advantages of ectothermy for tetrapods. American Naturalist, 1980; 115: 92-112.

—**Pough, FH:**
Amphibians and reptiles as low energy systems. In, Behavioral Energetics, WP Aspey; S Lustick (Eds). Ohio State University Press, Ohio, 1983, pp. 141-188.

—**Pough, FH; Andrews, RM:**
Energy costs of subduing and swallowing prey for a lizard. Ecology, 1985; 66: 1525-1533.

—Preest, MR:
Energetic costs of prey ingestion in a scincid lizard, *Scincella lateralis*. Journal of Comparative Physiology B, 1991; 161: 327-332.

–Ramírez Pinilla, MP:
Estudio histologico de los tractos reproductivos y actividad ciclica anual reproductiva de machos y hembras de dos especies del género *Liolaemus* (Reptilia: Sauria: Iguanidae). Unpublished PhD dissertation, Universidad Nacional de Tucumán, Argentina, 1991, 208 pp.

—Ramírez Pinilla, MP:
Actividad reproductiva en tres especies simpatricas del género *Liolaemus* (Reptilia: Sauria: Tropiduridae). Caldesia, 1992; 17: 67-74.

—Rand, AS:
Inverse relationship between temperature and shyness in the lizard *Anolis lineatopus*. Ecology, 1964; 45: 863-864.

—Regal, PJ:
Thermophilic responses following feeding in certain reptiles. Copeia, 1966; 1966: 588-590.

—Regal, PJ:
Voluntary hypothermia in reptiles. Science, 1967; 155: 1551-1553.

—Regal, PJ:
The evolutionary origin of feathers. Quarterly Review of Biology, 1975; 50: 35-66.

—Regal, PJ:
Temperature and light requirements of captive reptiles. In, Reproductive Biology and Diseases of Captive Reptiles, JB Murphy; JT Collins (Eds). Society for the Study of Amphibians and Reptiles, Contributions to Herpetology, 1980, 1: 79-89.

—Riedesel, ML; Cloudsley-Thompson, JL; Cloudsley-Thompson, JA: Evaporative thermoregulation in turtles. Physiological Zoology, 1971; 44: 28-32.

—Rismiller, PD; Heldmaier, G:
The effect of photoperiod on temperature selection in the European green lizard, *Lacerta viridis*. Oecologia, 1982; 53: 222-226.

—Ruppert, RM:
Comparative assimilation efficiencies of two lizards. Comparative Biochemistry and Physiology, 1980; 67A: 491-496.

—Sage, RD:
The structure of lizard faunas: comparative biologies of lizards in two Argentina deserts. Unpublished PhD dissertation, University of Texas, Austin, 1974, 341 pp.

—Saint-Girons, H:
Thermoregulation in reptiles with special reference to the tuatara and its ecophysiology. Tuatara, 1980; 24: 59-80.

—Schall, JJ:
Relations among three macroteiid lizards on Aruba Island. Journal of Herpetology, 1973; 7: 289-295.

—Schall, JJ:
Thermal ecology of five sympatric species of *Cnemidophorus* (Sauria: Teiidae). Herpetologica, 1977; 33: 261-272.

—Schall, JJ;
Dearing, MD: Body temperature of the herbivorous Bonaire Island whiptail lizard (*Cnemidophorus murinus*). Journal of Herpetology, 1994; 28: 526-528.

—Secor, SM:
Ecological aspects of foraging mode for the snakes *Crotalus cerastes* and *Masticophis flagellum*. Herpetological Monographs, 1995; 9: 169-186.

—Secor, SM; Nagy, KA:
Energetic correlates of foraging mode of the snakes *Crotalus cerastes* and *Masticophis flagellum*. Ecology, 1994; 75: 1600-1614.

—Secor, SM; Stein, ED; Diamond, J:
Rapid upregulation of snake intestine in response to feeding: a new model in intestinal adaptation. Amercian Journal of Physiology, 1994; 266: G695-G705.

—Secor, SM; Diamond, J:
Evolution of the digestive response in snakes. Abstract # 340. Joint meeting of the American Society of Ichthyologists and Herpetologists and the Herpetologists League, University of Alberta, Edmonton, Canada, 1995.

—Secor, SM; Diamond, J:
Adaptive responses to feeding Burmese pythons: pay before pumping. Journal of Experimental Biology, 1995*b*; 198: 1313-1325.

—Sexton, OJ; Hunt, SR:
Temperature relationships and movements of snakes (*Elaphe obsoleta, Coluber constrictor*) in a cave hibernaculum. Herpetologica, 1980; 36: 20-26.

—Shine, R:
The evolution of viviparity in reptiles: an ecological analysis. In, Biology of the Reptilia, C Gans; F Billet (Eds). Academic Press, New York, 1985, 15: 605-694.

—Shine, R; Bull, JJ:
The evolution of live-bearing in lizards and snakes. American Naturalist, 1979; 113: 905-923.

—Shine, R; Madsen, T:
Is thermoregulation unimportant for most reptiles? An example using water pythons

(*Liasis fuscus*) in tropical Australia. Physiological Zoology, 1996; 69: 252-269.

—**Sievert, LM:**
Postprandial temperature selection in *Crotaphytus collaris*. Copeia, 1989; 1989: 983-989.

—**Sites, JW, Jr; Archie, JW; Cole, CJ; Flores Villela, O:**
A review of phylogenetic hypotheses for lizards of the genus *Sceloporus* (Phrynosomatidae): implications for ecological and evolutionary studies. Bulletin of the American Museum of Natural History, 1992; 213: 1-110.

—**Soulé, M:**
Aspects of thermoregulation in nine species of lizards from Baja California. Copeia, 1963; 1963: 107-115.

—**Soulé, M:**
Trends in the insular radiation of a lizard. American Naturalist, 1966; 100: 47-64.

—**Spellerberg, IF:**
Critical minimum temperatures of reptiles. In, Effects of Temperature on Ectothermic Organisms, W Weiser (Ed). Springer-Verlag, Berlin, 1973, pp. 239-247.

—**Spotila, JR; Lommen, PW; Bakken, GS; Gates, DM:**
A mathematical model for body temperatures of large reptiles. Implications for dinosaurian ecology. American Naturalist, 1973; 107: 391-404.

—**Stebbins, RC:**
An experimental study of the "third eye" of the tuatara. Copeia, 1958; 1958: 183-190.

—**Stevenson, RD:**
Body size and limits to the daily range of body temperature in terrestrial ectotherms. American Naturalist, 1985; 125: 102-117.

—**Stewart, JR:**
Thermal biology of the live bearing lizard *Gerrhonotus coeruleus*. Herpetologica, 1984; 40: 349-355.

—**Storey, KB:**
Life in a frozen state: adaptive strategies for natural freeze tolerance in amphibians and reptiles. American Journal of Physiology, 1990; 258: R559-R568.

—**Storey, KB; Storey, JM; Brooks, SPJ; Churchill, TA; Brooks, RJ:**
Hatchling turtles survive freezing during winter hibernation. Proceedings of the National Academy of Sciences, 1988; 85: 8350-8354.

—**Storey, KB; Storey, JM:**
Natural freeze tolerance in ectothermic vertebrates. Annual Review of Physiology, 1992; 54: 619-637.

—**Swingland, IR; Frazier, JG:**
The conflict between feeding and overheating in the Aldabran giant tortoise. In, A Handbook of Biotelemetry and Radio Tracking, CJ Amlaner; DW McDonald (Eds). Pergamon Press, Oxford and New York, 1980, pp. 611-615.

—**Tait, NN:**
The effect of temperature on the immune response in cold-blooded vertebrates. Physiological Zoology, 1969; 42: 29-35.

—**Templeton, JR:**
Reptiles. In, The Comparative Physiology of Thermoregulation, GC Whittow (Ed). Academic Press, New York and London, 1970, 1: 167-221.

—**Throckmorton, G:**
Digestive efficiency in the herbivorous lizard *Ctenosaura pectinata*. Copeia, 1973; 1973: 431-435.

—**Tinkle, DW; Gibbons, JW:**
The distribution and evolution of viviparity in reptiles. Miscellaneous Publications of the University of Michigan, 1977; 154: 1-55.

—**Tracy, CR:**
Biophysical modeling in reptilian physiology and ecology. In, Biology of the Reptilia, C Gans; FH Pough (Eds). Academic Press, New York, 1982, 12: 275-321.

—**Troyer, K:**
Small differences in daytime body temperature effect digestion of natural food in a herbivorous lizard (*Iguana iguana*). Comparative Biochemistry and Physiology, 1987; 87A: 623-626.

—**Turner, JS:**
The cardiovascular control of heat exchange: consequences of body size. American Zoologist, 1987; 27: 69-79.

—**Turner, JS; Tracy, CR:**
Blood flow to appendages and the control of heat exchange in American alligators. Physiological Zoology, 1983; 56: 195-200.

—**Turner, JS; Tracy, CR:**
Body size and the control of heat exchange in alligators. Journal of Thermal Biology, 1985; 10: 9-11.

—**Ultsch, GR:**
Ecology and physiology of hibernation and overwintering among freshwater fishes, turtles, and snakes. Biological Reviews 1989; 64: 435-516.

—**Ultsch, GR; Jackson, DC:**
Long-term submergence at 3 °C of the turtle *Chrysemys picta bellii* in normoxic and severely hypoxic water. I. Survival, gas exchange, and

acid-base balance. Journal of Experimental Zoology, 1982*a*; 96: 11-28.

—**Ultsch, GR; Jackson, DC:**
Long-term submergence at 3 °C of the turtle *Chrysemys picta bellii* in normoxic and severely hypoxic water. III. Effects of changes in ambient PO_2 and subsequent air-breathing. Journal of Experimental Zoology, 1982*b*; 97: 87-99.

—**Van Damme, R; Bauwens, D; Verheyen, RF:**
Selected body temperatures in the lizard *Lacerta vivipara*: variation within and between populations. Journal of Thermal Biology, 1986; 2: 219-222.

—**Van Damme, R; Bauwens, D; Verheyen, RF:**
Thermoregulatory responses to environmental seasonality by the lizard *Lacerta vivipara*. Herpetologica, 1987; 43: 405-415.

—**van Marken Lichtenbelt, WD:**
Digestion in an ectothermic herbivore, the green iguana (*Iguana iguana*): effect of food composition and body temperature. Physiological Zoology, 1992; 65: 649-673.

—**Vaughn, LK; Bernheim, HA; Kluger, MJ:**
Fever in the lizard *Dipsosaurus dorsalis*. Nature, 1974; 252: 473-474.

—**Viets, BE; Ewert, MA; Talent, LG; Nelson, CE:**
Sex-determining mechanisms in squamate reptiles. Journal of Experimental Zoology, 1994; 270: 45-65.

—**Viets, BE; Tousignant, A; Ewert, MA; Nelson, CE; Crews, D:**
Temperature-dependent sex determination in the leopard gecko, *Eublepharis macularius*. Journal of Experimental Zoology, 1993; 265: 679-683.

—**Vinegar, A; Hutchison, VH; Dowling, HG:**
Metabolism, energetics, and thermoregulation during brooding of snakes of the genus *Python*. Zoologica, 1970; 55: 19-48.

—**Vogt, RC; Bull, JJ:**
Temperature controlled sex-determination in turtles: ecological and behavioral aspects. Herpetologica, 1982; 38: 156-164.

—**Wagner, EL; Gleeson, TT:**
Low temperature and exercise recovery in the desert iguana. Physiological Zoology, 1996; 69: 168-190.

—**Waldschmidt, SR; Jones, SM; Porter, WP:**
The effect of body temperature and feeding regime on activity, passage time, and digestive coefficient in the lizard *Uta stansburiana*. Physiological Zoology, 1986; 59: 376-383.

—**Webb, GJG; Cooper-Preston, H:**
Effects of incubation temperature on crocodiles and the evolution of reptilian oviparity. American Zoologist, 1989; 29: 953-971.

—**Werner, YL:**
Temperature effects on the inner-ear sensitivity in six species of iguanid lizards. Journal of Herpetology, 1972; 6: 147-177.

—**Werner, YL:**
Optimal temperatures for inner-ear performance in gekkonid lizards. Journal of Experimental Zoology, 1976; 195: 319-352.

—**Wilson, KJ; Lee, AK:**
Energy expenditure of a large herbivorous lizard. Copeia, 1974; 1974: 338-348.

—**Wilson, MA; Echternacht, AC:**
Geographic variation in the critical thermal minimum of the green anole, *Anolis carolinensis* (Sauria: Iguanidae), along a latitudinal gradient. Comparative Biochemistry and Physiology, 1987, 87A: 757-760.

—**White, FN:**
Circulation. In, Biology of the Reptilia, C Gans; WR Dawson (Eds). Academic Press, London, 1976, 5: 275-334.

—**Zari, TA:**
The influence of body mass and temperature on the standard metabolic rate of the herbivorous desert lizard, *Uromastyx microlepis*. Journal of Thermal Biology, 1991; 16: 129-133.

—**Zimmerman, LC; Tracy, CR:**
Interactions between the environment and ectothermy and herbivory in reptiles. Physiological Zoology, 1989; 62: 374-409.

—**Zug, GR:**
Herpetology. Academic Press, San Diego, 1993, 527 pp.

—**Zurovsky, Y; Mitchell, D; Laburn, H:**
Pyrogens fail to produce fever in the leopard tortoise *Geochelone pardalis*. Comparative Biochemistry and Physiology, 1987; 87A: 467-469.

HEARING, TASTE, TACTILE RECEPTION, AND OLFACTION

Bruce A. Young
Department of Biology
Lafayette College
Easton, PA 18042

Bruce A. Young received his Ph.D. in Biology from the University of Calgary in 1989. His research work centers on the evolution of morphological complexity, and the functional morphology and behavioral ecology of snakes.

INTRODUCTION

The four sensory modalities (audition, gustation, tactile, and olfaction) yield clear examples of reptilian specialization. The loss of the external ear, the pronounced development of the vomeronasal organ, and other reptilian specializations can tell us a great deal about the evolutionary history and ecology of reptiles. Unfortunately, even with the increasing attention accorded reptilian olfaction during the last two decades, our understanding of the role of these sensory modalities in the life of reptiles is still quite limited.

AUDITION (HEARING)

ANATOMY OF THE EAR

The ear of extant reptiles includes a great deal of morphological variation. This chapter will first present a generalized description of the reptilian ear to establish a framework within which this variation can be understood. Following this, the major variations that have been observed will be described. Major reviews of the reptilian ear, from which this generalized description has been taken, include Bellairs (1970), Wever (1978), and Baird (1970).

The tympanic membrane, a thin, circular, often pigmented structure visible near the back of the animal's head, is the most external component of the ear. The tympanic membrane forms the outer boundary of the middle-ear cavity; the middle-ear cavity is linked to the pharynx by the eustachian tube (Fig. 1). The deep or medial boundary of the middle-ear cavity is pierced by

two openings: the round window, which is covered by a thin membrane; and the more dorsal, oval window, which is open. Into the oval window is fitted the expanded footplate of a long rod of bone: the stapes (Fig. 1). The stapes spans the middle-ear cavity and forms a link between the oval window and the inner surface of the tympanic membrane. The distal or lateral portion of the stapes supports a cap of cartilage, termed the extrastapes. The extrastapes forms the actual con-

Figure 1.
Diagrammatic representation of a transverse section through the ear of a "typical" lizard with a tympanic membrane. C - cochlear duct; E - extrastapes; ET - eustachian tube; I - inner-ear cavity; M - middle-ear cavity; O - oval window; Q - quadrate; R - round window; S - stapes; T - tympanic membrane.

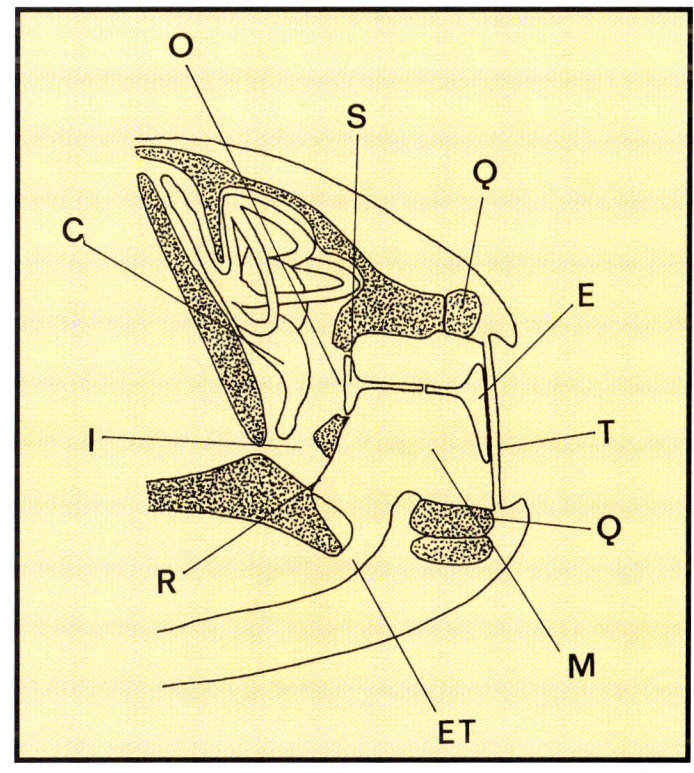

tact with the tympanic membrane, and is also frequently attached to the adjacent primary support of the lower jaw, the quadrate bone (Fig. 1).

Deep or medial to the oval window and round window is the inner-ear cavity. This is where the organs for balance (the semicircular canals, the utricle, and the saccule) and hearing (the cochlear duct) are located. The cochlear duct is normally an ovoid body connected to the larger saccule, both of which are suspended in a bath of perilymphatic fluid which fills the inner-ear cavity (Fig. 1). The cochlear duct is filled with perilymphatic fluid, and its inner surface supports two specialized regions, the large papilla basilaris and the smaller macula lagenae. The macula lagenae is located at the tip of the cochlear duct. Both the papilla basilaris and the macula lagenae are clusters of sensory cells. The apical (free) surfaces of these clusters support sensory cilia. The cilia are embedded within a thin membrane (the tectorial membrane) that is located within the perilymphatic-filled cavity of the cochlear duct. It is from these numerous sensory cells that the fibers of the acoustic branch of the VIIIth cranial nerve (the auditory nerve) arise.

In order to put the morphological variation observed in the ear of reptiles into a biological context, it is necessary to briefly sketch how this system functions. Vibrations, whether airborne against the tympanic membrane or groundborne against the quadrate, are transmitted to the stapes. The vibrations cause the stapes to move. The movement of the stapes causes the footplate of the stapes to move against the oval window. This latter movement produces pressure waves within the perilymphatic fluid. Since the cochlear duct is suspended within, and filled with, this perilymphatic fluid, these pressure waves are transmitted to the interior of the cochlear duct. The wave motion of perilymphatic fluid within the cochlear duct causes a displacement of the tectorial membrane.

The frequency of movement of the tectorial membrane is determined by the frequency of the waves in the perilymphatic fluid. The frequency of the waves in the perilymphatic fluid is ultimately determined (via the stapes) by the frequency of vibration from the external source. The sensory cells that contact the tectorial membrane are stimulated by the vibration of the tectorial membrane. This stimulation gives rise to nerve impulses. Thus, this system can encode different vibration patterns into different patterns of neural impulses. The pressure waves in the perilymphatic fluid are dissipated at the round window where they are "shed" into the middle-ear cavity.

The tympanic membrane is lost in a number of fossorial or semi-fossorial lizards (e.g., the earless monitor *Lanthanotus*, the slow-worm *Anguis*, and the legless lizards, *Anniella*), snakes, amphisbaenids, and the tuatara: it is also absent from some nonfossorial lizards, such as the chameleons. The tympanic membrane that is present in turtles and lizards exhibits considerable morphological variation (Fig. 2) in terms of its relative depth from the surface of the head, its size, and

Nile Crocodile, *Crocodylus niloticus*. Photo by Mark Smith.

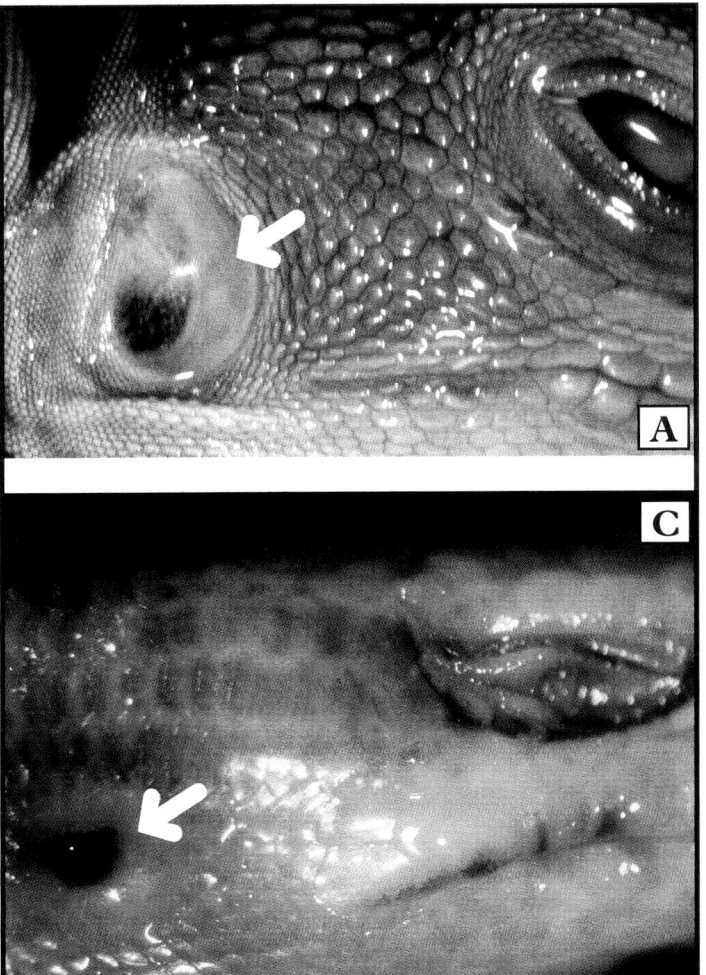

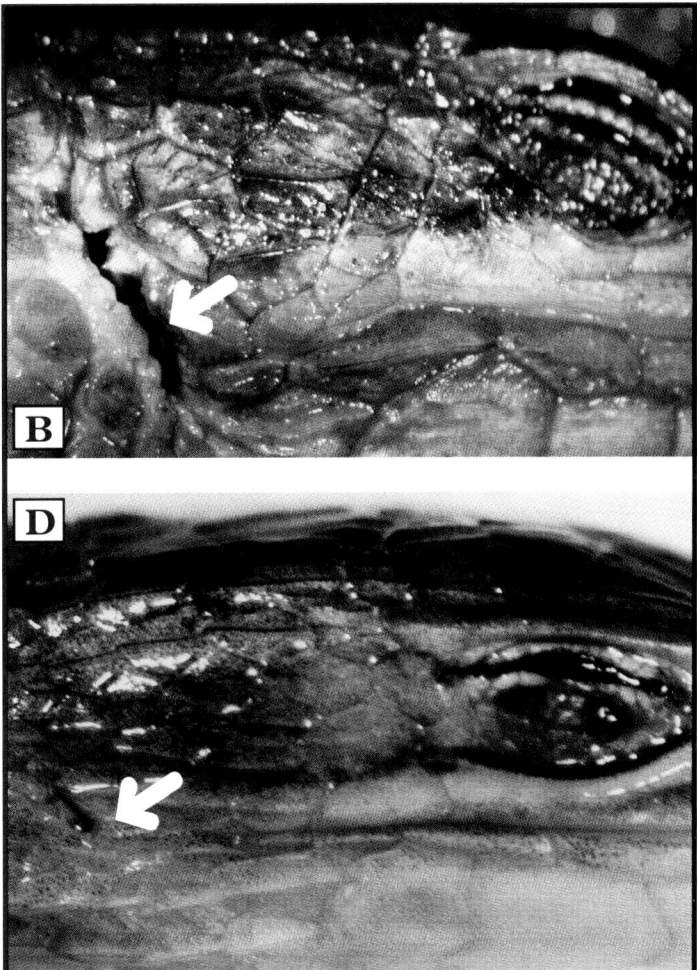

Figure 2.
Variations in the tympanic membrane (arrow) of lizards. A - *Ctenosaura pectinata*; B - *Cordylus cordylus*; C - *Diploglossus warreni*; D - *Chamaesaura anguina*.

the apparent thickness or texture of the membrane (Versluys, 1898). Crocodilians are the only reptiles with an external ear. The tympanic membrane of crocodilians is covered dorsally by a distinct ear flap (Fig. 3), which is under muscular control. The lowering of this ear flap reduces the exposure of the tympanic membrane to a horizontal slit (Shute and Bellairs, 1955).

The stapes-extrastapes complex also exhibits considerable morphological variation (Fig. 4) in reptiles (Olson, 1966). In those reptiles lacking a tympanic membrane, the extrastapes (or its analog) connects with the medial surface of the quadrate (Norris and Lowe, 1951; Earle, 1961; Toerien, 1963). In crocodilians and geckos, a small muscle inserts adjacent to, or upon, the stapes. Presumably, this small muscle is the functional equivalent of the mammalian stapedius muscle, and it protects the ear by dampening strong vibrations (Wever, 1965, 1978). In the tuatara (*Sphenodon punctatus*), the stapes is continued distally by a cartilaginous rod (not considered the homolog of the

extrastapes). This rod is in contact with not only the quadrate, but also the squamosal and hyoid bones (Wyeth, 1924; Gans and Wever, 1976). In some amphisbaenids (e.g., *Bipes*), the stapes has been reduced to little more than the footplate, while the extrastapes extends to the quadrate (Wever and Gans, 1972). In other amphisbaenids, the extrastapes extends beyond the quadrate along the lateral surface of the lower jaw. There, it ter-

Figure 3.
The external ear of *Crocodylus moreleti*. The dorsal ear flap has been raised to expose the tympanic membrane. E - eye; F - dorsal ear flap; T - tympanic membrane.

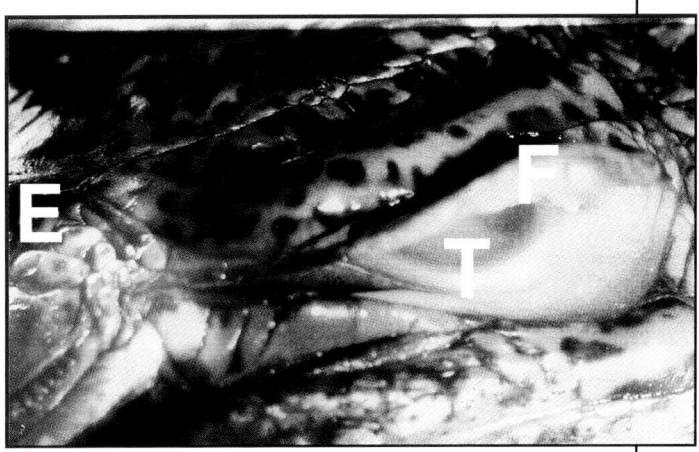

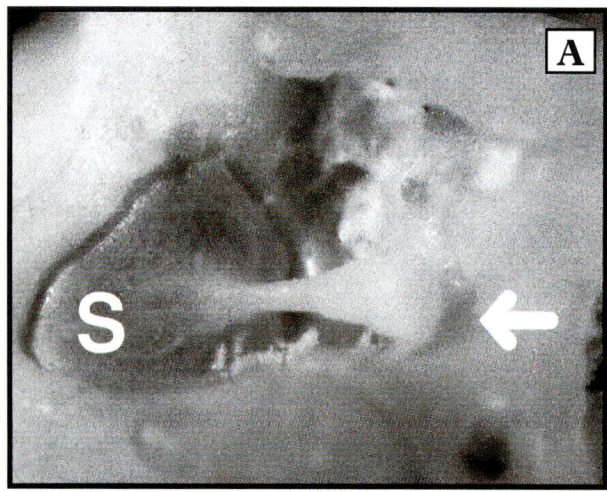

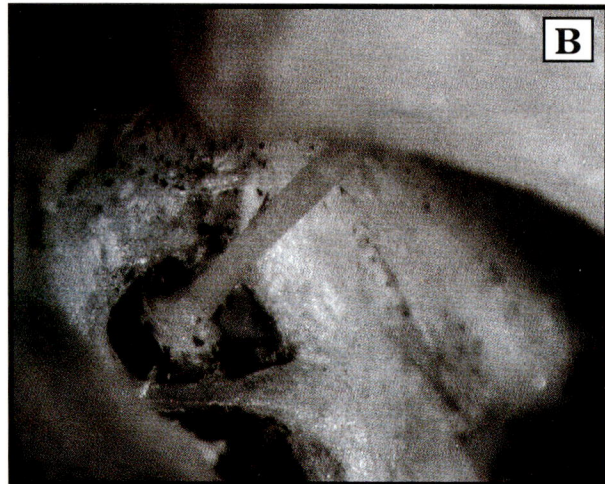

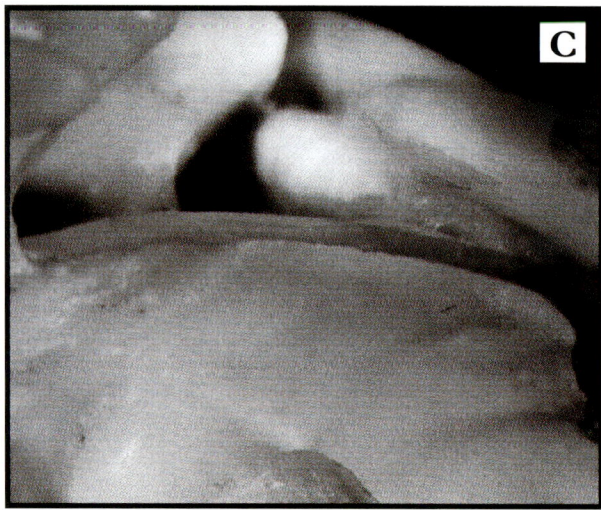

Figure 4.
Variations in the stapes of reptiles. A - the stapes of the amphisbaenid *Rhineura floridana*; note the expanded footplate of the stapes (S) and the groove in the quadrate (arrow) for the extensive extrastapes. B - the stapes of *Varanus acanthurus*; note that the footplate of the stapes is visible within the oval window. C - the stapes of *Ophiophagus hannah*; note that the footplate of the stapes is obscured by the bony partitions which form the small middle ear cavity of snakes.

minates in a band of connective tissue which extends further anteriorly along the jaw (Gans and Wever, 1972).

Three main variations are observed in the middle-ear cavity of reptiles. The tuatara has a poorly defined middle cavity which, rather than being empty, is filled with loose tissue, especially adipose tissue (Gans and Wever, 1976). Crocodilians show almost the opposite extreme in that their middle cavity is a strong, bony labyrinth of air-filled passages and dual, branching eustachian tubes (Colbert, 1946). The branches of the eustachian tubes have many interconnections. These connections link the contralateral middle-ear cavities independent of the pharynx (van Beneden, 1882). Perhaps the most common specializations of the middle-ear cavity (found, presumably independently, in lizards lacking a tympanic membrane, snakes, and turtles) is a bony partitioning of that cavity into an outer chamber and an inner cham-

Figure 5.
Diagrammatic representation of a transverse section through the ear of a "typical" reptile without a tympanic membrane. C - concha; E - extrastapes; I - Inner ear cavity; M - middle ear cavity; Q - quadrate; S - stapes.

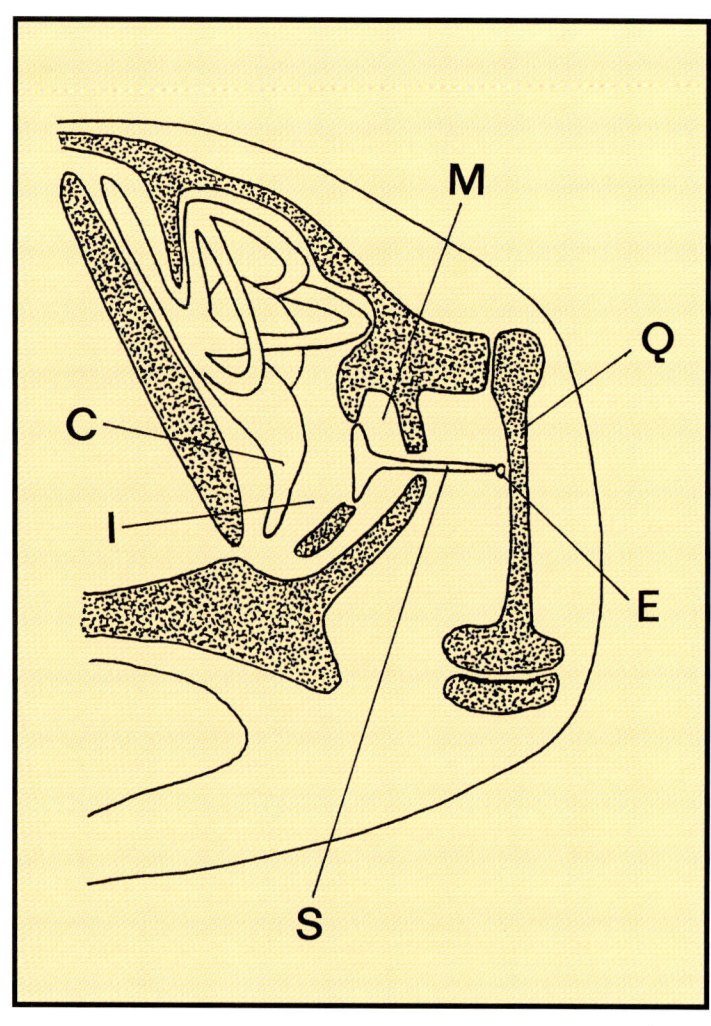

Lesser Earless Lizard, *Holbrookia maculata*. Photo by R. D. Bartlett.

ber. The extrastapes passes through the outer chamber, and the eustachian tube opens into this outer chamber. The inner chamber is called the the pericapsular sinus in lizards; the juxtastapedial sinus in turtles; and the pericapsular recess in snakes. In lizards and turtles, this inner chamber is filled with perilymphatic fluid; in snakes, the inner chamber is filled with air (Baird, 1960a,b; McDowell, 1961; Wever, 1978). In many of these lizards and in all snakes, the outer larger portion of the middle-ear cavity has been lost, so that only the small inner cavity or sinus remains (Fig. 5).

A recurring morphological variation in the inner ear of reptiles is the loss of the round window. This is seen in turtles, snakes, amphisbaenids, and the tuatara. Without the round window, other mechanisms must develop for dissipating the vibrations of the perilymphatic fluid. These other mechanisms normally involve complex "recycling" patterns of fluid movement (Gans, 1978; Wever, 1969; Wever, 1978). The cochlear duct of crocodiles is elongate and divided into two limbs (Baird, 1970; von Düring, 1974), presumably reflecting phylogenetic relationships and the well developed vocalization in this group. The structure of the cochlear duct in other groups has received considerable attention (see Miller, 1966, 1968, 1980, 1992). Among other things, these studies have shown that the cochlear duct of turtles differs from that of all other reptiles in that the papilla basilaris is not isolated from the macula lagenae.

Many of the comparative studies of reptilian auditory anatomy have focused on the papilla basilaris. These studies have looked at its size and hair cell population (Miller, 1966; Wever, 1978), the nature and attachments of the tectorial membrane (Wever, 1967a,b,1978), the directionality of the hair cells (Miller, 1992), and the relationship between the hair cells and the afferent and efferent nerve fibers (Sneary, 1988; Mulroy, 1986; Miller and Beck, 1988). Many of the patterns that emerge from these studies of the inner ear have

taxonomic and phylogenetic significance (see Miller, 1992). There are also some basic functional patters; in lizards with vocal communication (e.g., geckos) the papilla basilaris is much larger than in fossorial forms. Interestingly, snakes differ from this pattern in that the fossorial snakes exhibit the largest papilla basilaris.

AUDITORY PHYSIOLOGY

You can determine the physiological response of the ear by recording the electrical activity of the sensory cells indirectly or directly. Indirect recordings measure the charge on the perilymphatic fluid and are recorded at the round window or directly from the fluid. Direct recordings measure the charge from the sensory cells or acoustic branch of the auditory nerve. The use of both methods allows you to quantify both the frequency range over which the ear responds, and the amplitude of sound necessary to invoke that response.

Alligator lizard, *Gerrhonotus* sp. Photo by R. D. Bartlett.

The auditory physiology of reptiles has been treated in detail by several workers (e.g., Manley, 1970, 1981; Belekhova, 1979; Köppl and Manley, 1992, Turner, 1980; Patterson, 1966). The values given in the following summary of auditory physiology, which is restricted to airborne stimuli, have for the sake of consistency all been taken (following conversion of units into SPL) from the major work of Wever (1978).

There is substantial variation in the acoustic sensitivity of lizards (Fig. 6). The majority of lizards for which data are available show a pattern similar to that of *Iguana iguana* (Fig. 6), with auditory responses spanning from 500-4,000Hz, and a peak sensitivity at 700Hz equal to 24db. In fossorial forms such as *Holbrookia maculata*, or others such as *Chamaelo chamaeleon* in which the tympanic membrane is lost, the auditory response is limited to lower frequencies and requires stronger stimulation (Fig. 6). Some lizards (such as *Gerrhonotus*

Fan-footed Gecko, *Ptyodactylus hasselquisti*. Photo by Paul Freed.

Figure 6.
Auditory sensitivity of selected lizards (data taken from Wever, 1978 and converted into SPL). Solid square - *Iguana iguana*; open square - *Holbrookia maculata*; open triangle - *Chamaelo chamaeleon*; solid triangle - *Lepidophyma sylvaticum*; open circle - *Ptyodactylus hasselquistii*; solid circle - *Gerrhonotus multicarinatus*.

multicarinatus) show high auditory sensitivity over a wide frequency range. In other species (such as *Lepidophyma sylvaticum*) with similarly high auditory sensitivity, the frequency range is restricted to only the lower frequency sounds. Lastly, as a clear specialization, the vocal gekkonid species (such as *Ptyodactylus hasselquistii*) have high auditory sensitivity and a frequency-response range that extends up to 10,000Hz (Fig. 6).

The auditory physiology of the remaining reptilian groups has not been studied in as much detail, nor do these other groups appear to include as much variation in auditory physiology as do the lizards. In snakes, the auditory frequency range normally spans from below 100Hz to slightly over 1,000Hz. Auditory sensitivity in snakes varies considerably. Most forms are similar to *Elaphe gutatta*, with an auditory sensitivity of 25db at 200Hz. However, fossorial forms (such as *Rhinophis drummondhayi*) have greatly reduced auditory sensitivities (Fig. 7). Crocodilians have a fairly broad range of frequency response—from 50-3,000Hz in *Alligator mississippiensis*, extending up to 6,000Hz in other species—coupled with an auditory sensitivity of 4db at 200Hz (Fig. 7).

The frequency-response ranges of the chelonians which have been studied have been similar to crocodilians. In chelonians, the frequency-response ranges indicates a response to low-fre-

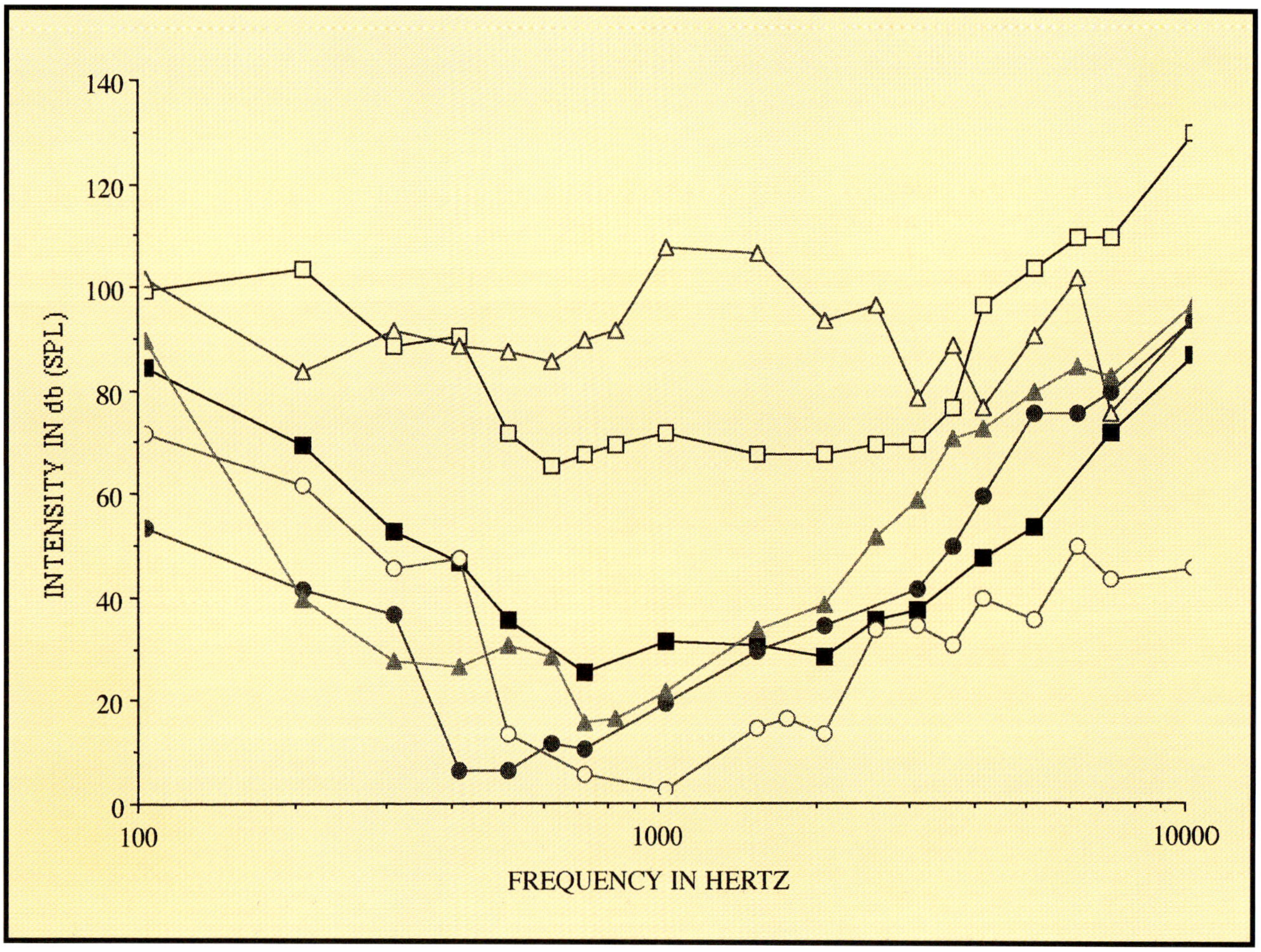

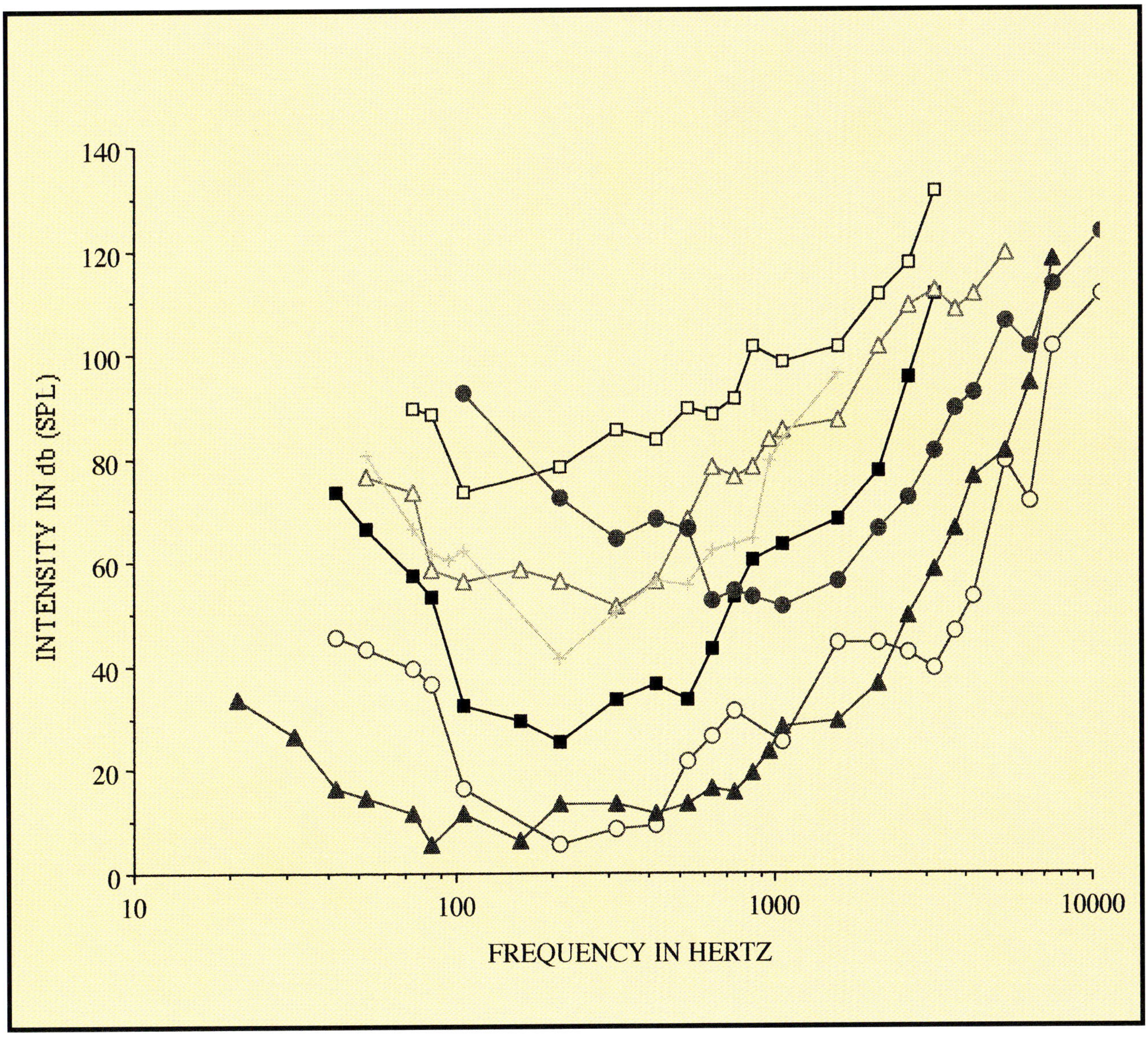

Figure 7.

Auditory sensitivity of selected reptiles (data taken from Wever, 1978 and converted into SPL). Solid square - *Elaphe obsoleta*; open square - *Rhinophis drummondhayi*; solid circle - *Amphisbaena manni*; open circle - *Alligator mississippiensis*; X - *Sphenodon punctatus*.

Corn Snake, *Elaphe guttata*. Photo by R. D. Bartlett.

quency sounds from 50-1,500Hz. Chelonians do show variation in their auditory sensitivity. While most turtles have an auditory sensitivity similar to that of *Clemmys guttata*, with peak sensitivity of 4db at 80Hz, some species (such as *Geochelone carbonaria*) have a much lower sensitivity, with a peak of 50db at 300Hz (Fig. 7). The auditory response of amphisbaenids is typically restricted to frequencies below 2,000Hz, with a low sensitivity of 50db at 1,000Hz for *Amphisbaena manni* (Fig. 7). The tuatara (*Sphenodon*) has a frequency response from 100 to 800Hz, with a peak auditory sensitivity of 40db at 200Hz (Fig. 7).

Groundborne Vibrations

The preceding discussion of auditory physiol-

Spotted Turtle, *Clemmys guttata*. Photo by R. T. Zappalorti.

ogy focussed exclusively on airborne stimuli. However, for many reptiles—especially fossorial forms—response to groundborne vibrations may be of equal or greater importance. The exact pathways for transmission of groundborne stimuli vary, and may or may not include the stapes.

Applying local mechanical vibration to the body of a snake results in neural excitation at the tectum similar to that recorded during airborne stimuli (Hartline and Campbell, 1969; Hartline, 1971a,b). Responses to groundborne vibrations extend to lower frequencies (50-1,000Hz) and have lower sensitivity than do those for airborne stimuli. It appears that special receptors in the snake's skin (Proske, 1969a) respond to these groundborne vibrations, and that output from these mechanoreceptors are transported to the tectum via the spinal nerves (Hartline, 1971b). Hartline has argued that these two classes of receptors (the auditory and the somatic) can not distinguish between groundborne or airborne stimuli, but that processing at higher levels could enable the snake to determine the relative stimulatory contribution of these two sources.

Gans and Wever (1972) have shown that amphisbaenids, particularly those forms in which the extrastapes extends along the lower jaw, are sensitive to groundborne vibration. In some species, the frequency range and sensitivity to groundborne vibrations was very similar to that for airborne vibrations. These mechanical stimuli appeared to be transmitted as much through the tissues of the lower jaw as through the extrastapes itself. Severing the extrastapes caused a drop in sensitivity to airborne stimuli of approximately 30db, but had no impact on sensitivity to groundborne stimuli. Response to groundborne stimuli is greatest near the distal tip of the lower jaw, and drops some 10db proximally where the extrastapes lies deep to muscle tissue.

Unfortunately the sensitivity of other reptiles to groundborne stimuli has been little-studied. The studies of Gans and Wever (1972) and Hartline (1971b) clearly demonstrate that reception of vibratory stimuli can occur through the body—a point demonstrated for the turtle shell by Lenhardt et al (1986). It is possible that other vibratory receptor systems are present in reptiles.

Red-footed Tortoise, *Geochelone carbonaria*. Photo by Aaron Norman.

ROLE OF HEARING IN THE BIOLOGY OF REPTILES

As noted above, and in Figures 6 and 7, at least some members of three reptilian groups—gekkonid lizards, crocodilians, and turtles—can perceive sounds over a wider frequency than other reptiles. These same three groups exhibit distinctive intraspecific acoustic communication (Frankenberg and Werner, 1992; Marcellini, 1978). The next four paragraphs summarize communication methods in crocodilians, chelonians, geckos, and snakes.

Crocodilians. Crocodilians produce a variety of vocalizations, most of which function in intraspecific socialization (Garrick et al, 1978; Campbell, 1973). The bellows, bellow/growls, and coughs of crocodilians are part of the courtship and mating behaviors (Joanen and McNease, 1976; Neil, 1971; Garrick and Lang, 1977; Garrick et al, 1978). Additionally, crocodilians use deep grunting sounds to maintain social contact between adult and young (Garrick et al, 1978). They also appear to use sound as a signal to free the hatched young from the nest (Alderton, 1991).

Chelonians. Chelonian acoustic communication is still relatively understudied, but appears to be a common component of their behavioral repertoire. The variety of turtle sounds described include those that appear to have a role in courtship or mating, group contact, and distress calls (Campbell and Evans, 1967,1972; Frazier and Peters, 1981; Harless, 1979; Frankenberg and Werner, 1992).

Geckos. Marcellini (1977, 1978) divided the vocalization of *Hemidactylus* and other geckos into three types of calls. Other workers have described more variation and a richer vocal repertoire (e.g., Frankenberg, 1982; Frankenberg and Werner, 1984, 1992). Most of the calls reported from geckos appear to function as alarm signals, although the multiple-chirp call plays a broader role in territoriality and social grouping (Marcellini, 1978).

Snakes. The potential for acoustic communication in snakes has normally been dismissed, although at least in the King cobra (*Ophiophagus hannah*) the defensive sounds overlap the auditory sensitivity, and a biological context of nest defense make acoustic communication plausible (Young, 1991).

Though not discussed as often as intraspecific acoustic communication, interspecific acoustic communication is used by many reptiles for foraging and avoidance. Reptilian ears can respond to seismic stimuli (Hartline, 1971b; Narins and Lewis, 1985). For example, the sandfish lizard, *Scincus scincus* exploits this ability while foraging (Hetherington, 1989, 1992). Similarly, Gans (1960) has argued that the fossorial amphisbaenids use sound to locate their prey. Tests conducted with experimentally deafened geckos, *Hemidactylus frenatus* and *Cosymbotus playturus*, revealed a significant decrease in prey capture when compared to controls (Chou et al, 1988). Aquatic turtles show a clear avoidance response to low-frequency sound (Vogt, 1980; O'Hara, 1990).

TASTE (GUSTATION)

Taste in reptiles has been neglected in favor of studies on the olfactory system. The extent to which oral-based taste and vomeronasal-based smell are integrated in the higher brain centers is not clear. Accordingly, and in part for organizational clarity, this description of the sense of taste

Sand fish, *Scincus scincus*. Photo by R. D. Bartlett.

King Cobra, *Ophiophagus hannah*. Photo by Zoltan Takacs.

in reptiles will exclude the vomeronasal organ and focus on the taste buds located on the tongue and oral epithelium.

MORPHOLOGY AND LOCATION OF THE TASTE BUDS

If the common designator of "taste bud" is applied to receptors on the oral epithelium and the tongue, then taste buds have been reported from all major groups of reptiles:
—turtles (Korte, 1980)
—crocodiles (Bath, 1906; Weldon and Ferguson, 1993)
—amphisbaenids (De La Serna De Esteban, 1959)
—tuatara (Osawa, 1897; Schwenk, 1986)
—snakes (Kroll, 1973; Burns, 1969)
—lizards (Nonoyama, 1936; Schwenk, 1985; Mohammed, 1992)

However, of these studies, only that of Schwenk (1985) approaches a broad survey; the remainder of the studies represent isolated reports. As a result, the form, abundance, and taxonomic distribution of taste buds in most reptilian groups is still poorly known.

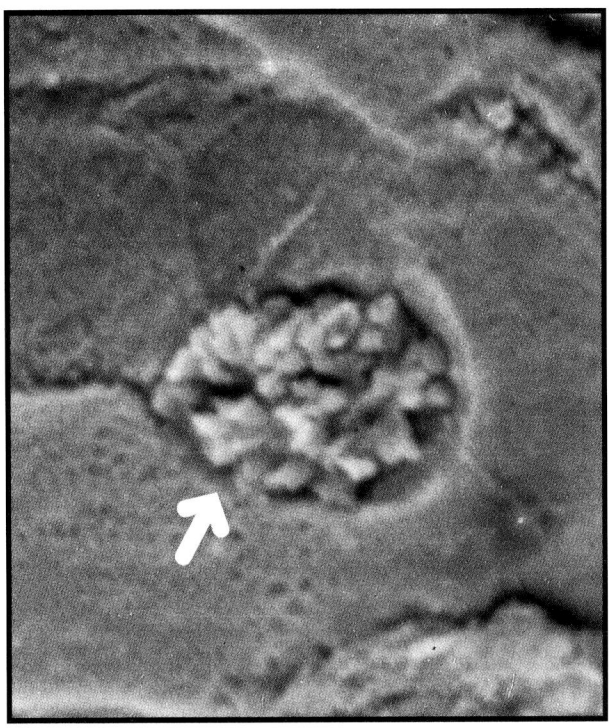

Figure 8.
Taste buds (arrow) from the fore-tongue of
Amphibolurus nuchalis.

Reptilian taste buds show the same structural features found in the taste buds of other vertebrates. The taste buds are shaped like compressed ovoids of 30-40um in diameter (Nonoyama, 1936; Korte, 1980), with the base of the taste buds located on the basal membrane of the epithelium. The sensory cells of the taste bud are oriented perpendicular to the basal membrane. These sensory cells taper towards their apical surface. The cell nucleus is located in the basal portion of the cell. The apical surface of the sensory cells supports numerous microvilli. The epithelium is discontinuous over the sensory cells, forming the taste pore. Thus, the microvilli are in direct contact with chemical environment of the oral cavity (Fig. 8). An additional smaller class of cells is located around the base of the taste bud. Korte (1980) was able to distinguish three different cell types within those cells reaching the taste pore, and two cell types within the population of basally located cells.

Taste buds have been reported from the oral epithelium, normally the roof of the mouth and adjacent to the tooth rows. The morphology of taste budes in the oral epithelium may differ from the morphology of taste buds located on the tongue (Ferguson, 1981). Crocodiles and most lizards have taste buds on both the oral epithelium and the tongue (Bath, 1906; Schwenk, 1985; Willard, 1915). In snakes, and within some Gekkonidae (e.g., *Gonatodes antillensis*) taste buds are found in the oral epithelium, but have not been recorded

from the epithelium of the tongue (Schwenk, 1985; Kroll, 1973; Burns, 1969). The converse pattern has also been documented, Jackson's chamaeleon (*Chamaeleo jacksoni*) has lingual taste buds, but no taste buds on the oral epithelium (Schwenk, 1985). Among lizards which have been examined, the Varanidae appear to be unique in lacking taste buds on both the oral and lingual surfaces (Schwenk, 1985).

Substantial variation has been reported for those taste buds located on the tongue of reptiles. While it appears that these taste buds always occur singly, the total number of taste buds supported by the tongue varies. Nonoyama (1936) estimated 100 taste buds on the tongue of *Takydromus tachydromoides*; Schwenk (1985) estimated up to 600 taste buds in some species. Nonoyama (1936) also claimed that young specimens show fewer taste buds than do the adults. Taste buds appear to be concentrated at the tongue tip, which has stratified squamous epithelium, low levels of keratinization, and absence of glandular epithelium. Schwenk (1985) argued that these three factors are correlated with increased density of taste buds. Unfortunately, while the interfamilial variation in taste buds (e.g., the abundance of taste buds in the Iguanidae and their absence in the Varanidae; Schwenk, 1985) is intriguing, the phylogeny and biological role of these receptors are too poorly known to justify any conclusions.

BIOLOGICAL ROLE OF TASTE IN REPTILES

Burghardt (1970), while reviewing chemical perception in reptiles, lamented the dearth of experimental studies on the role of gustation in reptiles. Two factors seem to account for the almost total neglect of this system. Firstly, the vomeronasal system has been, and continues to be, viewed as the dominant chemosensory organ in reptiles—so much so that the tongue has often been seen as nothing more than a cog in the mechanism for delivering external stimuli to the vomeronasal organ. (For a discussion of this preoccupation in snakes see Young, 1993.) Secondly, many of the early studies in chemosensory behavior had methodological problems. These problems often prevented isolation of a single sensory system or mandated the anthropomorphizing of the results (reviewed by Burghardt, 1970). Rensch and Eisenkraut (1927) did show differential reaction of three lizards to drinking water containing different compounds, but the methodology employed in this study clouded the results. Schwenk (1985) has argued that gustation may be the dominant sensory mode operating during periods of substrate licking in lizards. As such, gustation presumably plays an important part in social behaviors involv-

194

ing cloacal licking (e.g., Tollestrup, 1981). Conditioning experiments with garter snakes (*Thamnophis*) led to the conclusion that gustation may play a role in prey recognition (Burghardt et al, 1973).

TOUCH (TACTILE SENSE)

MORPHOLOGY AND DISTRIBUTION OF THE TACTILE RECEPTORS

Since Leydig (1868) first described the tactile sense organs in reptiles, there has been a slow but steady increase in our understanding of the morphology, distribution, and physiology of these receptors. The following list shows references for descriptions of touch receptors by reptilian group:
—Crocodiles: Hulanicka, 1913; Jaburek, 1926; von Düring, 1973, 1974
—Turtles: Jaburek, 1926; Hin-Ching and Maneely, 1962; Rosenberg, 1986
—Tuatara: Osawa, 1897
—Lizards: Hiller, 1976; Schmidt, 1912, 1920; Jaburek, 1926; Miller and Kasahara, 1967; Landmann, 1975; Grandison, 1968; Maclean, 1980; Pác, 1984; Perret, 1986; Bauer and Russell, 1988; Ananjeva et al, 1991
—Snakes: Landmann, 1975; Aota, 1940; Proske, 1969b, von Düring, 1973; Jackson, 1975, 1977; Jackson and Sharawy, 1980

Tactile receptors are not evenly distributed over the body. As a general rule, they are most frequently encountered along the outer margins of the oral cavity. Aota (1940) examined the distribution of tactile receptors over the head of the Bramina blind snake (*Ramphotyphlops braminus*) and reported 636 receptors from the rostral portion of the head, 194 from the dorsal and dorsolateral surfaces, and 276 from the ventral and ventrolateral surfaces. Breyer (1929) reported the distribution of tactile receptors on the surface of three species of Lacerta. In each case, the density of receptors was greatest over the back, and least over the head, with substantial interspecific variation evident in the distribution pattern. The number of receptors for *L. muralis* was recorded as: head = 266, back = 3,702, and side = 1,842. Touch receptors appear to be lacking in amphisbaenids (Gans, 1978).

Tactile receptors are comprised of both dermal and epidermal components. There are three basic patterns of epidermal specialization associated with touch receptors. The upper and lower jaws of crocodilians bear distinctive, elevated, touch pa-

Bramina Blind Snake, *Ramphotyphlops braminus*. **Photo by R. D. Bartlett.**

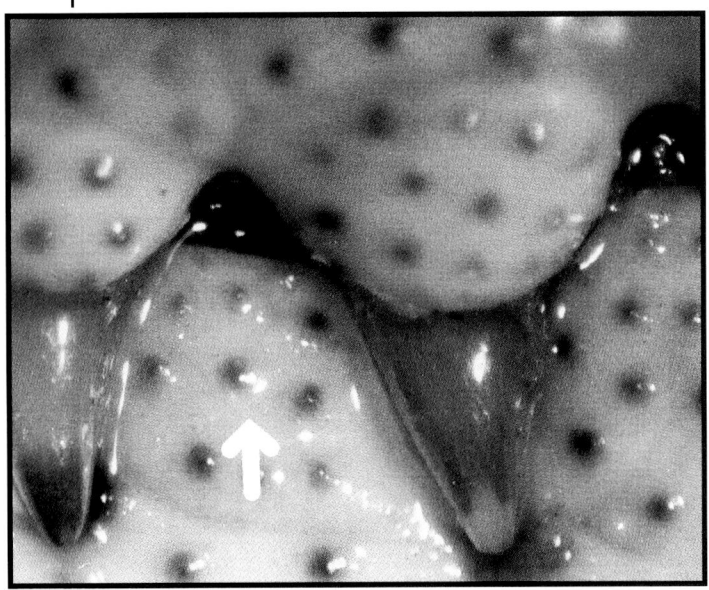

Figure 9.
Touch papillae (arrow) on the jaws of *Crocodylus moreleti.*

pilla (Fig. 9). In these papilla, the stratum corneum is thinned to an extent that the underlying tissues are visible (von Düring, 1973). Superficially similar sensory tubercles have been described from the head of some snakes (Fig. 10) (Jackson, 1977; Jackson and Sharawy, 1980). In most snakes and lizards, the b-keratin layer is reduced over the touch receptor (Fig. 11). In many lizards (but not in snakes) this region of the b-keratin takes on a more organized lenslike appearance (Miller and

Figure 11.
Transverse section through the lower jaw of *Nerodia rhombifera* **showing two tactile receptors. Note the Merkel-like arrangement of the cells within the receptor and the deformation of the b-keratin layer over the receptor (arrow).**

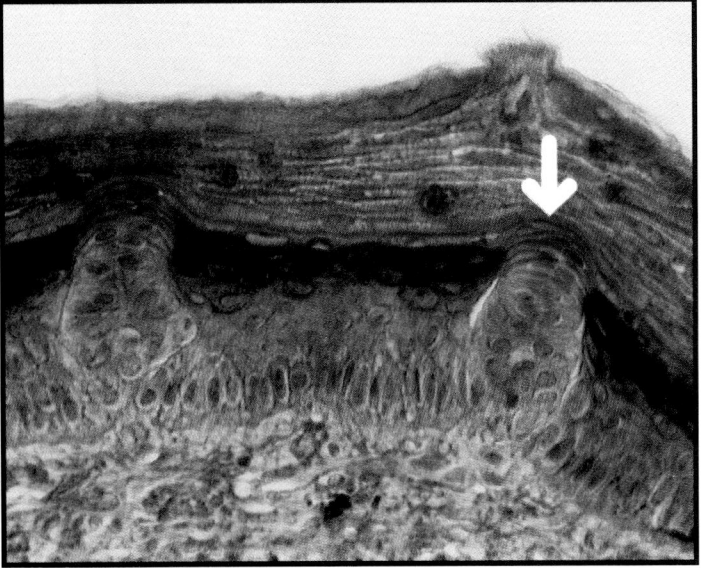

Kasahara, 1967; Landmann, 1975). In three lizard families (Agamidae, Gekkonidae, and Pygopodidae) the b-keratin layer over the touch receptor gives rise to a specialized expanded bristle (Landmann, 1975; Hiller, 1976).

The dermal papilla associated with the tactile receptor varies considerable in size and shape. Landmann (1975) recognized six different types of touch receptor, based in part on the size of the papilla. Most of the characteristic axons of the touch recepter are located within this dermal papilla. These axons can be divided into three different categories:

—individual free nerve endings, which terminate in discoidal receptors

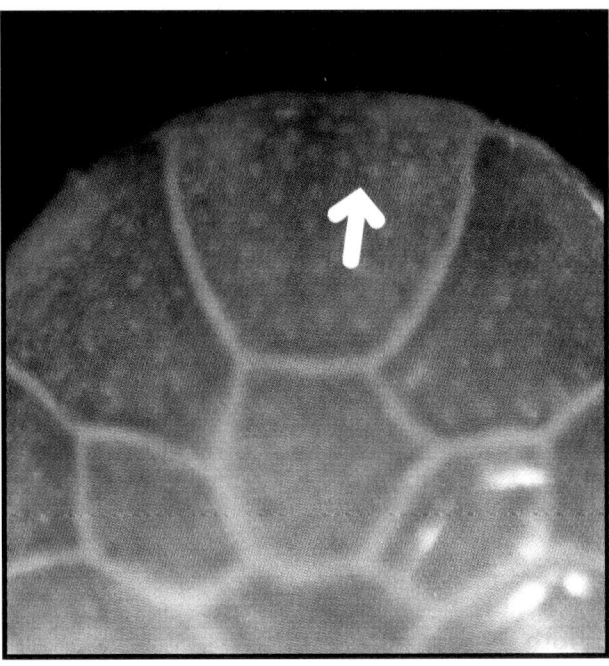

Figure 10.
Touch papillae (arrow) on the head of *Leptotyphlops dulcis.*

—clusters of terminal receptors, which are normally associated with fibrocytes and Schwann cells
—lamellated axons

Free Nerve Endings. The discoidal receptors of the individual free nerve endings extend from the dermis into the epidermis. The density of these free nerve endings is especially high in the touch receptors, but they also appear throughout the skin of reptiles (Miller and Kasahara, 1967; Proske, 1969b). The number of discoid terminals within a touch receptor varies interspecifically (numbering 6-8 in *Boa constrictor* and 60-100 in *Caiman crocodilus*) and intraspecifically by size (von Düring and Miller, 1979). The abundance of these free nerve endings, and their associated discoidal receptors, appears to be a common characteristic of reptilian skin (Miller and Kasahara, 1967; von

Düring and Miller, 1979). However, Landmann (1975) claimed they were absent from several lizard families (Anguidae, Lacertidae, Teiidae, and Xantusiidae), and absent from two families of snakes (Boidae and Elapidae). It remains to be seen to what extent these exceptions are the result of preservation and fixation techniques. Hiller (1976) has documented the pattern of regeneration of these receptors associated with the shedding of the skin.

Terminal Receptors. The second type of axon are the clusters of terminal receptors that are associated with the fibrocytes located within the dermal papilla (Fig. 11). The close association between these terminal receptors and the fibrocytes results in a superficial resemblance to Merkel cells. *Caiman crocodilus* appears to be an exception, in that the dermal papilla of the touch organ in this species supports true Merkel cells (von Düring,

Spectacled Caiman, *Caiman crocodilus.*
Photo by Aaron Norman.

1973). Independent of the touch receptors, Merkel cells have been identified in the epidermis and dermis of reptiles (e.g., Proske, 1969b; von Düring and Miller, 1979).

Schwann Cells. The third receptors described are characterized by their lamellation produced by processes of Schwann cells. There are several classes of these lamellated receptors, based on the presence of a capsule and a perineural sheath (von Düring, 1973,1974; von Düring and Miller, 1979). These lamellated receptors, which normally are located outside of the dermal papilla, have been described in turtles, lizards, snakes, and crocodilians. Lamellated receptors are most evident in *Caiman crocodilus*, where they extend distally to the tip of the touch papilla (von Düring, 1973).

PHYSIOLOGICAL PERFORMANCE OF REPTILIAN TACTILE RECEPTORS

Physiological studies have revealed two different classes of mechanoreceptors within the skin of reptiles. The two classes of mechanoreceptors appear to be analogous to the mammalian pressure and touch receptors (Kenton et al, 1971; Bailey, 1969; Siminoff and Kruger, 1968). Compared to the pressure receptors, the tactile receptors have larger fibers, lower thresholds, smaller receptive fields (about 2mm^2 in *Lacerta viridis*), and a shorter discharge period (Bailey, 1969).

Kenton et al (1971) divided the mechanoreceptors of crocodilians into two classes. These classes did show different discharge patterns, recovery rates, and sensitivity to lateral stretching, Kenton et al (1971). However, in contrast, Bailey (1969), did not find any difference in the size of the receptive field between the two types of receptors. What remains to be explored, is the precise linkage between these physiological properties and the different types of receptors associated with the tactile organ.

SPECIALIZED TACTILE ORGANS

In addition to these specific tactile organs there are a number of additional, larger, structural features of reptiles which have been regarded as specializations for gathering tactile stimuli (Fig. 12). These proposed mechanoreceptor organs include:
—the elongate rostral tentacles of the tentacle snake, *Erpeton tentaculatum*, (Winokur, 1977)
—the epithelial sheaths surrounding the tongue of sea snakes (Hibbard,1975)
—the spinous scales of *Lapemis hardwickii* (Gopalakrishnakone, 1985)

Tentacled Snake, *Erpeton tentaculatum.*
Photo by J. K. Langhammer.

—the tubercles and barbels found on the neck and lower jaw (respectively) of some aquatic turtles (Winokur, 1982)
—the supracloacal tubercles of some Natricine snakes (Noble, 1937)
—the broadened tail tip of the knob-tailed geckos (Russell and Bauer, 1987)

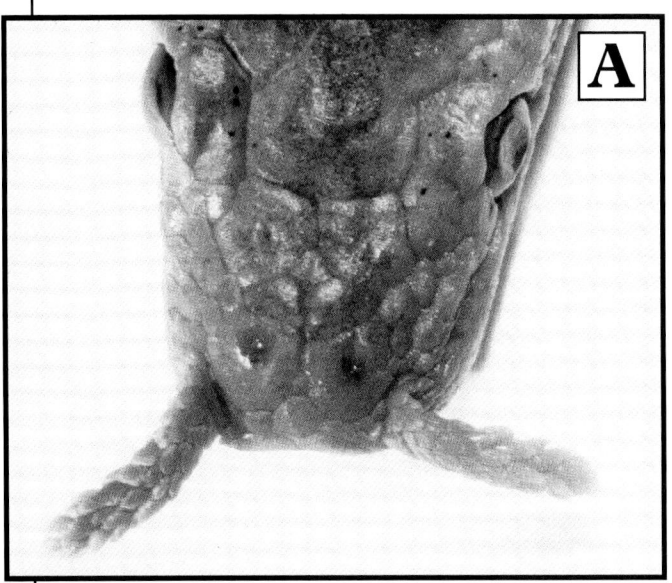

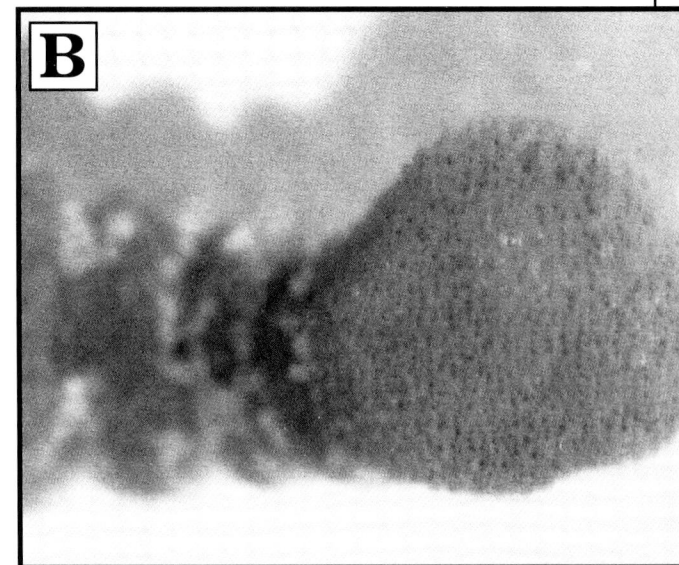

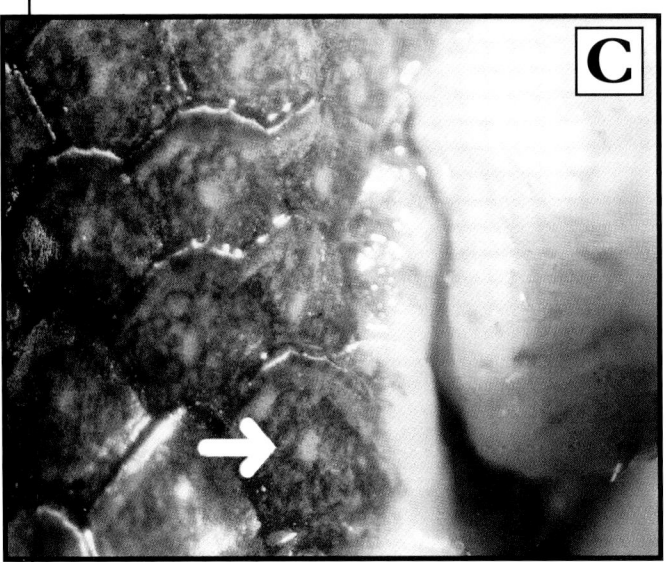

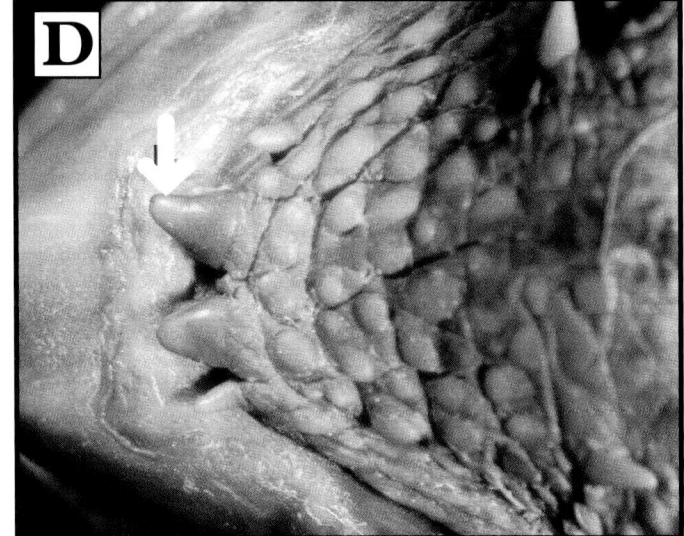

Figure 12.
Specializations for tactile reception in reptiles. A - the "tentacles" *of Erpeton tentaculatum*; **B - the "knob-tail" of** *Nephrurus levis*; **C - Supracloacal polyps (arrow) of** *Diadophis punctatus* **(H - hemipenis); D - barbels (arrow) of** *Sternotherus odoratus.*

ROLE OF TACTILE STIMULI IN THE BIOLOGY OF REPTILES

Courtship in squamates often involves activities that are presumably rich in tactile stimuli. For example, courtship in lizards often involves bouts of grappling; courtship in snakes involves repeated rubbing of one snake's head along its potential mate's body (see the review by Carpenter and Ferguson, 1977). Noble (1937) discussed the role of tactile information in the courtship rituals of snakes, but few other studies have focussed on the biological context of tactile stimuli in reptiles. Rosenberg (1986) argued that tactile receptors in turtles could function during courtship and mat-

ing, and could also function to localize innocuous stimuli. Whitaker and Whitaker (1984) proposed that tactile stimuli were important in underwater feeding in *Crocodylus palustris*. Conversely, Ferguson (1981) has proposed that when the young are carried in the mother's mouth, they generate tactile stimuli which inhibits the mouth from closing. Chiszar et al (1987) has argued that tactile stimuli are used by cobras to assay den quality. Sprackland (1990) claims that varanids rely on tactile information to assay food quality.

SMELL (OLFACTION)

MORPHOLOGY OF THE NASAL PASSAGE

The terminology used to describe this region in the older literature is often confusing, if not contradictory. For consistency, this chapter uses the terminology of Parsons (1970).

The typical reptilian nasal passageway can be divided into three components (Figure 13A):
—the cavum nasi proprium, an expanded chamber that supports the sensory epithelium

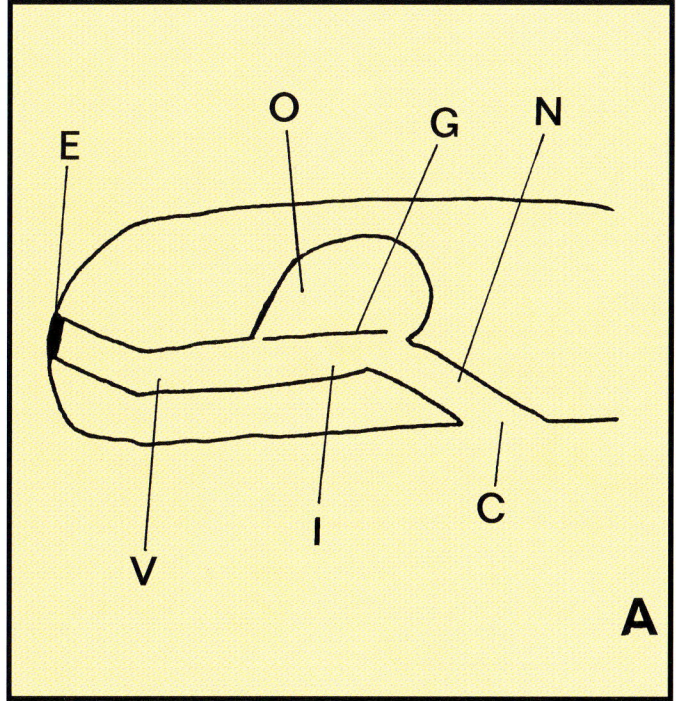

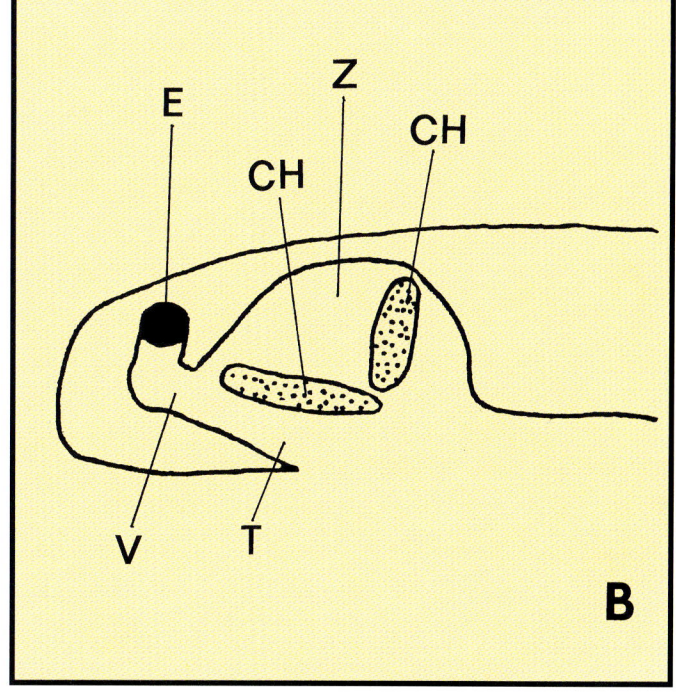

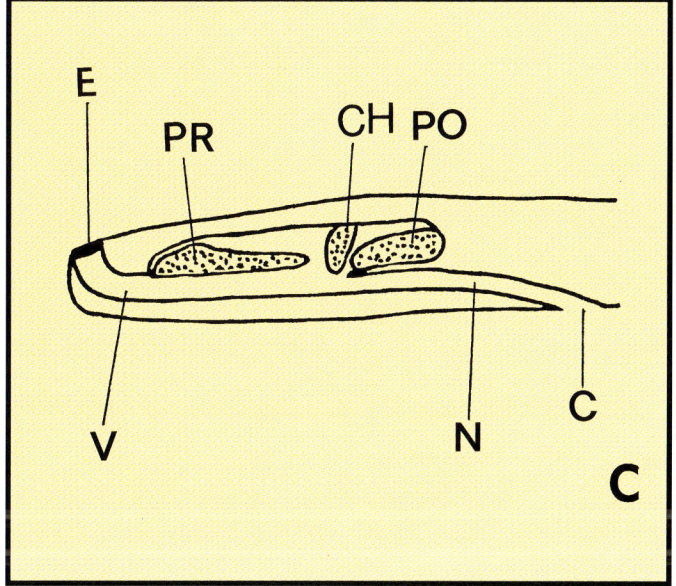

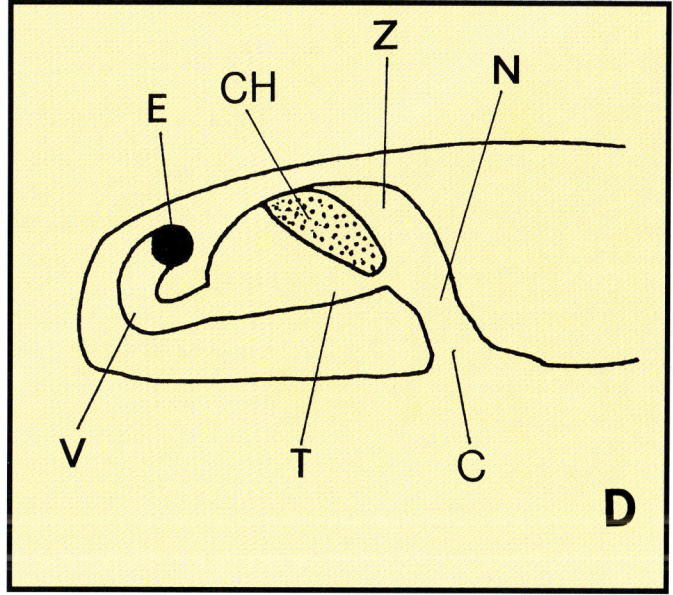

Figure 13.
Diagrammatic representations of the nasal passageways in certain reptile groups. A - turtles; B - the tuatara; C - crocodilians; and D - lizards and snakes. C - choana; CH - concha; E - external nares; G - Grenzfalte; I - intermediate region; N - nasopharyngeal duct; O - olfactory region; PO - postconcha; PR - preconcha; T - choanal tube; V - nasal vestibule; Z - choanal zone.

—the vestibulum nasi, a tubular passageway that connects the cavum nasi proprium with the external nares
—the nasopharyngeal duct, a tubular passageway that connects the internal nares (or choana) with the cavum nasi proprium

TAXON-SPECIFIC MORPHOLOGY

Chelonians. In turtles, the vestibulum nasi is a fairly short tube that extends posteriorly from the external nares (Fig. 13A). It is slightly longer in forms like the trionychids, which have an elongate snout (Parsons, 1970). The cavum nasi propium of turtles is subdivided by two horizontal ridges: the medial and lateral Grenzfalten. The portion of the cavum nasi propium dorsal to the Grenzfalten is termed the olfactory region and supports the sensory epithelium. Ventral to the

199

Grenzfalten is the intermediate region. This region is lined by both sensory epithelium and respiratory epithelium, and this region directly connects the vestibulum nasi with the nasopharyngeal duct. In marine turtles, the olfactory region is reduced in size, and the intermediate region supports paired diverticula (Parsons, 1970). The nasopharyngeal duct of chelonians extends for a variable distance posteriorly before opening into the elongate choana. In turtles, the lateral margins of the choana support a variety of tissue flaps or papillae (Parsons, 1968).

Tuatara. In the tuatara, *Sphenodon punctatus*, the vestibulum nasi is a short, medially directed tube; the medial portion of this tube is expanded. The cavum nasi propium of the tuatara supports two projections of the nasal capsule: the anterior and posterior concha (Fig. 13B) (Hoppe, 1934; Parsons, 1970). The anterior concha is oriented roughly horizontally, slightly ventral to the midpoint of the cavum nasi propium. The posterior concha extends posterodorsally from the caudal end of the anterior concha. The anterior concha divides the cavum nasi propium into a choanal tube and the choanal zone. The choanal tube is located ventral to the anterior concha and continuous with the vestibulum nasi. The choanal zone is located above the anterior concha. Much of the choanal zone is lined with sensory epithelium; whereas the choanal tube supports respiratory epithelium. The nasopharyngeal duct is absent in the tuatara. In tuatara, the choanal tube extends to the choana, which are elongate wide slits. The true dimensions of these slits are obscured by the prominent lateral choanal folds and midline vomerine cushion (Parsons, 1970).

Crocodilians. In crocodiles, the vestibulum nasi is a short, ventrally directed tube. The cavdal portion of this tube curves posteriorly to join the cavum nasi proprium (von Wettstein, 1954; Parsons, 1970). The lateral wall of the cavum nasi proprium supports three projections (from anterior to posterior): the preconcha, the concha, and the postconcha (Fig. 13D) (Parsons, 1970). These three projections effectively partition the dorsal portion of the cavum nasi propium into seven chambers or recesses (Wegner, 1958). Two of these chambers—the preconchal and extraconchal recesses—support sensory epithelium, as do the walls of the cavum nasi propium dorsal to the conchae. Ventral to the conchae, the cavum nasi propium forms a fairly simply tube lined with respiratory epithelium (Parsons, 1970). The nasopharyngeal duct is an elongate, but simple, tubular duct that extends from the posterior portion of the cavum to the choana on the caudal margin of the secondary palate.

Amphisbaenids. In amphisbaenids, the vestibulum nasi extends for a short distance medi-ally—or dorsally in those forms with ventral external nares—then curves rather abruptly posteriorly. The cavum nasi proprium is large, and supports a single distinct concha (Fischer, 1900; Bellairs and Boyd, 1950; Parsons, 1970; Gans, 1978). Amphisbaenids lack a nasopharyngeal duct; instead, the posteroventral portion of the cavum extends to the choana. The size of the choanal fold and vomerine cushion varies in the amphisbaenids. Corresponding to these variations are differences in the anterior extension of the choana, which forms the choanal groove, toward the duct of the vomeronasal organ (Bellairs and Boyd, 1950).

Lizards. In lizards, the vestibulum nasi normally extends for a short distance medially from the laterally positioned external nares, then turns abruptly posteriorly to join the cavum nasi proprium (Parsons, 1970). The exact pattern of the vestibulum varies, both in terms of diameter and course. The vestibulum is most pronounced in the Varanidae, Chamaeleonidae, Iguanidae, and Agamidae (Bellairs, 1949; Haas, 1937; Stebbins, 1943, 1948; Pratt, 1948; Parsons, 1970). Stebbins (1943) argued that the distinct curvature in the vestibulum near the nares represented an anatomical means of restricting sand and other foreign matter to the distal portion of the nasal passageway. The cavum nasi proprium of most lizards supports a single concha (of variable size and attachment) which divides the cavum into the ventral choanal tube and the dorsal conchal zone where the sensory epithelium is located (Fig. 13A) (Parsons, 1970). In chameleonids, the concha is missing (as it is in *Anolis* and other iguanids), the cavum is greatly reduced and supports little sensory epithelium. Agamids also have a reduced cavum, although they retain the concha. In the Varanidae, and in *Iguana* and other Iguanidae, the cavum is large, the concha distinct, and a pronounced subconchal recesses is present ventral to the concha.

In most lizards, the choanal tube extends ventrally or posteroventrally to connect with the choana. Along its course, the choanal tube is bordered by two tissue masses, the vomerine cushion (medially) and the choanal fold (laterally). The contact and fusion between the choanal fold and the vomerine cushion will determine the extent of the choana. In groups with little fusion—Iguanidae, Agamidae, Chamaeleonidae, Gekkonidae, and Pygopodidae—a distinct choanal groove extends from the choana anteriorly as far as the duct to the vomeronasal organ. Fusion between the vomerine cushion and the choanal fold is most pronounced in the Varanidae, in which the choanae are fairly small and well isolated from the duct to the vomeronasal organ. The extent of the choanal groove can be quite variable in some families. Parsons (1970) separated the earlier descriptions of this region in scincids (Busch,

1898; Göppert, 1903; Malan, 1946) into seven types ranging from choanal grooves to fusion forming nasopharyngeal ducts.

Snakes. In snakes, the vestibulum is a short, simple tube coursing medially, or coursing ventrally in the case of aquatic snakes. The cavum is similar to that of a typical lizard. Snakes have a single concha (variable in size and position) which divides the cavum into the dorsal conchal zone (with its sensory epithelium) and the ventral choanal tube. In aquatic snakes, the cavum is more simplified. For example, in *Acrochordus*, *Pelamis*, and *Laticauda* the concha is lacking, the cavum is reduced in size, and the amount of sensory epithelium is reduced (Kathariner, 1900). Snakes possess nasopharyngeal ducts connecting the cavum with the distinct choana. The associated fusion of the vomerine cushion and the choanal fold has eliminated the choanal groove (Parsons, 1970).

GENERAL MORPHOLOGY

Reptiles have a number of mechanisms for controlling the diameter of the external nares. In most squamates, the vestibulum is surrounded by erectile vascular tissue which is apparently capable of constricting the external nares. In many lizards and aquatic snakes, this constriction is enhanced by the presence of fleshy valves on the posterior wall of the external nares (Kathariner, 1900; Bruner, 1907; Stebbins, 1948). Similar erectile tissue has been reported from the external nares of some aquatic turtles (Walker, 1959; Nick, 1912; Fuchs, 1915). Smooth muscle has been described surrounding the vestibulum of snakes and lizards (Lapage, 1928; Malan, 1946). This smooth muscle appears to function as a constrictor muscle on the deeper erectile tissue. Crocodilians have distinctive dilator and constrictor muscles surrounding the external nares; these smooth muscles form the elevated narial projections on the snout (Bellairs and Shute, 1953; Parsons, 1970).

The sensory epithelium of reptiles is similar to the typical vertebrate pattern of three cell types (Gabe and Saint Girons, 1964, 1976; Ferri et al, 1982; Iwahori et al, 1987; Saint Girons, 1991):
—the sensory (receptor) cells
—the sustentacular cells
—and the basal cells

The apical surface of the sensory cells support from 8-12 cilia, which are referred to as olfactory hairs (Parsons, 1970), although these show considerable variation (Wang and Halpern, 1980). The sensory cells give rise to the olfactory nerve, which extends caudally to the olfactory bulb (Crosby and Humphrey, 1939; Rubin, 1974). The fibers project back from the olfactory bulb into the telencephalon—especially the anterior olfactory nucleus, olfactory tubercle, lateral pallium, pyriform cortex, and the amygloid nuclei (Northcutt, 1978; Halpern, 1980 - for a review see Halpern, 1992).

MORPHOLOGY OF THE VOMERONASAL ORGAN

The vomeronasal organ (Jacobson's organ) develops as a ventromedial outpocketing of the nasal pit. In turtles, this outpocketing is greatly reduced or absent, with the result that the apparent homolog of the vomeronasal organ is located along a portion of the wall of the cavum nasi proprium (see Parsons, 1959, 1970; Bertmar, 1981). Adult crocodilians do not have a vomeronasal organ. There is some disagreement amongst researchers as to whether a vomeronasal organ is formed during development in crocodilians. In the tuatara, the vomeronasal organ is tubular in shape. Also in tuatara, the organ retains a connection to the nasal passageway, as well as to the oral cavity (Parsons, 1959; Bellairs and Boyd, 1950). In amphisbaenids, lizards, and snakes, the vomeronasal organ is fully separate from the nasal passageway. In these squamates, the vomeronasal organ connects to the oral cavity by way of the small Jacobson's duct, which is derived from the choana. The duct leading to the vomeronasal organ is located near the midline of the palate. This duct follows an often convoluted dorsolateral course to open into the medial portion the organ. The size of the lumen of the vomeronasal organ is greatly reduced in most squamates by the presence of the large "mushroom body" which invaginates into the lumen from the ventral surface (Fig. 14).

The size of the vomeronasal organ varies in squamates. It is well-developed in all snakes, in-

Cameroon Sailfin Chameleon, *Chamaeleo montium*. **Photo by K. H. Switak.**

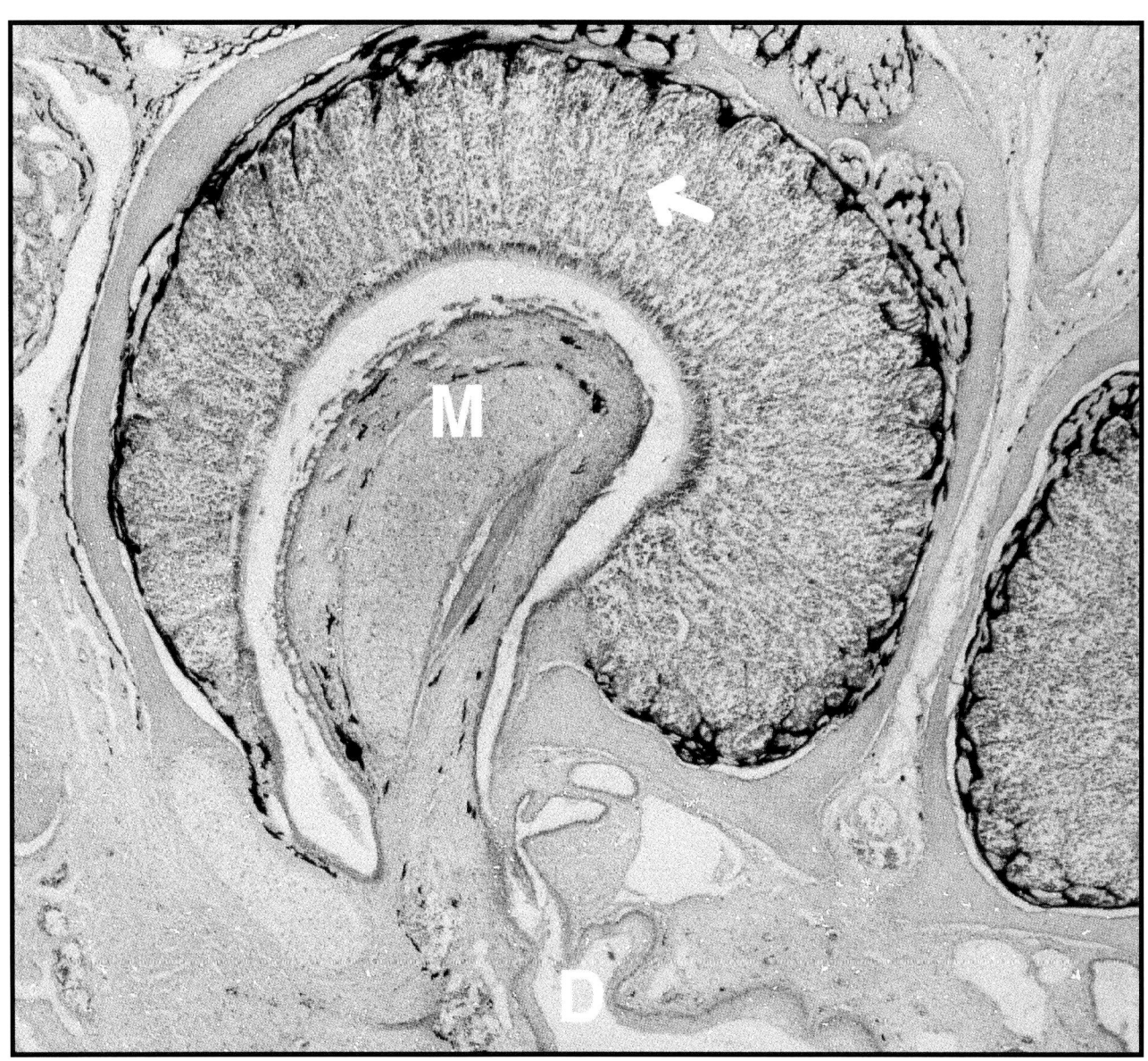

Figure 14.
Transverse section through the vomeronasal organ of *Aipysurus eydouxii*; note the distincitve columnar arrangement of the sensory epithelium (arrow). D - duct to the vomeronasal organ; M - mushroom body.

cluding the aquatic forms (Platel, 1986). While some variations have been noted, this organ is also well-developed in the amphisbaenids (Gans, 1978). In lizards, the vomeronasal organ is well-developed in varanids, but greatly reduced in at least some members of Iguanidae, Agamidae, and Chamaelonidae (Gabe and Saint Girons, 1976). This reduction in size of the vomeronasal organ can involve a simple decrease in the luminal volume, an absence of the mushroom body, and, for all practical purpose, the complete absence of the organ (Pratt, 1948; Stimie, 1966; Eckart, 1922; Haas, 1947). In *Anolis* and *Chamaeleon*, as well as some related genera, the vomeronasal organ is generally considered to be nonfunctional (Stimie, 1966; Haas, 1947).

The periphery of the squamate's vomeronasal organ, but not the surface of the mushroom body, supports the sensory epithelium. This sensory epithelium contains the same three cell types found in the sensory epithelium of the cavum nasi proprium (Parsons, 1970; Halpern, 1992). In many squamates, but especially in most snakes, this sensory epithelium is partitioned by indentations of the basal lamina. The indentations give the sensory epithelium the appearance of distinct columns (Fig. 14). In *Sphenodon*, the sensory epithelium is only found in the dorsal portion of the vomeronasal organ. The sensory epithelium gives rise to the vomeronasal nerve, which passes posteriorly to form the accessory olfactory bulb. The size of this accessory olfactory bulb varies with the development of the vomeronasal organ (Rubin, 1974; Halpern, 1992).

ROLE OF OLFACTION IN THE BIOLOGY OF REPTILES

The importance of olfactory information to reptilian behavior has been the focus of considerable research during the last decade (see Halpern and Holtzman, 1993; and for reviews Simon, 1983; Halpern, 1992). Through laboratory and field analyses, squamates have emerged as model systems for chemosensory studies. Unfortunately, far less attention has been paid to turtles and crocodilians; also, amphisbaenids have been virtually ignored.

Olfaction plays an important role during the courtship and mating rituals of most reptiles. This has been most thoroughly studied in *Thamnophis*, where the courtship and mating rituals appear to be governed by a variety of pheromones. Mature females secrete (from their skin) pheromones which attract the males (Mason, 1992; Crews, 1980; Garstka and Crews, 1986). The males preferentially respond to phermones from conspecifics (Ford, 1982; Ford and O'Bleness, 1986). However, males will also court other males and inanimate objects which have been coated with the pheromone (Gillingham and Dickinson, 1980; Mason et al, 1989). After mating, the male deposits a cloacal plug in the female. This plug appears to include a courtship-inhibiting pheronone (Devine, 1977; Ross and Crews, 1977).

In *Eumeces*, the females have a urodaeal gland, which is secretory during the reproductive season (Cooper et al, 1986; Trauth et al, 1987). Courting males lick the cloacal region of females and can distinguish and follow cloacal trails of conspecific females (Cooper and Vitt, 1984, 1986a,b,d). Additional examples of the importance of olfaction to mating in lizards come from *Sceloporus* (Duvall, 1982), *Gerrhosaurus* (Cooper and Trauth, 1992), and *Phrynosoma* (Tollestrup, 1981). Male turtles show a variety of behaviors during courtship and mating. These behaviors have been interpreted as responses to the secretions of the chin and cloacal glands of the female. Severing the vomeronasal or olfactory nerve in male *Emys orbicularis* produces a drastic reduction in mating behavior. Severing both nerves in male *E. orbicularis* eliminates mating behavior (Boiko, 1984).

Olfactory stimuli are also important in conspecific interactions outside of courtship and mating. Chemosensory information is important for the

Desert Horned Lizard, *Phrynosoma platyrhinos*. **Photo by R. D. Bartlett.**

formation of aggregations of conspecific snakes (Noble and Clausen, 1936; Halpern, 1992). While the behavioral mechanisms responsible for the formation of these aggregates is uncertain, evidence suggests that it could be chemical trailing (Costanzo, 1986, 1989; Gehlbach et al, 1971). The chemical trail being followed appears to be skin lipids from conspecific snakes (Graves and Halpern, 1988; Graves et al, 1986,1991). *Dipsosaurus* shows similar responses to femoral gland secretions (Alberts, 1989), and conspecific preference mediated by chemical signals from feces has been shown in *Sceloporous* (Duvall, 1979) and *Iguana* (Werner et al, 1987). Exposing *Alligator mississippiensis* to conspecific glandular secretions produces a distinct increase in the rate of gular pumping (Johnsen and Wellington, 1982). Chemical signals, especially from feces, have also been implicated in social groupings of turtles (Harless, 1979; Vogt, 1979).

Olfactory information is also important during predation. Turtle foraging is impaired by severing the vomeronasal and olfactory nerve (Boiko, 1983). *Alligator mississippiensis* responds to chemical stimuli in the water and on land (Weldon et al, 1990; Scott and Weldon, 1990). However, the best information on the role of the chemosensory system in predation comes from squamates, especially snakes (Burghardt, 1970). In some lizards, the response to prey odors is innate, as evident by the behavior of naive hatchlings (Burghardt, 1973). While interspecific differences exist, chemical stimuli have been shown to be an important trigger to the feeding behavior in some lizards (e.g., Cooper, 1990; Cooper and Vitt, 1989). Newborn, ingestively naive specimens from several species of snakes have shown behavioral preferences for the chemical extracts of their normal diet (Burghardt, 1970, Halpern, 1992).

There is also evidence that snakes respond to the chemical trail of prey items, whether the trail is on the ground, in the air, or in the water. Ground trails have been described by Kubie and Halpern (1975, 1978); Watkins et al (1969); and Webb and Shine (1992). Air trails have been described by Burghardt (1977, 1980); and Halpern and Kubie (1983). Water trails have been described by Rudiger (1986). One of the most heavily studied systems is the strike-induced chemosensory searching (SICS) whereby rattlesnakes (or other venomous snakes) use chemosensory stimuli to locate the specific prey item they have previously envenomated and released (see Halpern, 1992; Chiszar and Scudder, 1980; Chiszar et al, 1983; Lavin-Murcio et al, 1993).

The chemosensory system, in addition to its importance during mating, conspecific interactions, and predation, appears to have additional behavioral influences. Turtles show olfactory imprinting (Owens et al, 1982, 1986) which may play a role in migration (Grassman et al, 1984; Koch et al, 1969). *Lacerta vivipara* exhibits avoidance behaviors when exposed to chemical stimuli from its natural predators (Thoen et al, 1986). *Eumeces laticeps* (Cooper, 1990) and *Varanus albigularis* (Phillips and Alberts (1992) also react to chemical stimuli from predators. Graves and Duvall (1988) have argued for the presence of an alarm pheromone in *Crotalus v. viridis*.

Many, if not most, of the studies on the relationship between chemosensory stimuli and behavior in reptiles have not differentiated between vomeronasal and olfactory stimuli. Claims for the dominance of either of these two receptor areas have been based on the relative size of the organs to each other, as in Schwenk's (1993) claim that geckos are olfactory specialists. Recent work has highlighted the functional segregation between the vomeronasal and olfactory system, with the olfactory system responding primarily to volatile compounds, and the vomeronasal organ responding to nonvolatile substances (Inouchi et al, 1993).

White-
throated
Monitor,
*Varanus
albigularis*.
Photo by
R. D.
Bartlett.

REFERENCES AND RECOMMENDED READING

—**Alberts, A:**
Ultraviolet visual sensitivity in desert iguanas: implications for pheromone detection. *Anim Behav*, 1989; 38: 129-137.

—**Alderton, D:**
Crocodiles and alligators of the world. Blandford Publishing, New York, 1991.

—**Ananjeva, N;**
Dilmuchamedov, M; Matveyeva, T: The skin sense organs of some Iguanian lizards. *J Herpet*, 1991; 25(2): 186-199.

—**Aota, S:**
An histological study on the integument of a blind snake, *Typhlops braminus* (Daudin), with special reference to the sense organs and nerve ends. J Sci Hiroshima Univ Ser. B, 1940; 7: 1-16.

—**Bailey, S:**
The responses of sensory receptors in the skin of the green lizard, *Lacerta viridis*, to mechanical and thermal stimulation. Comp Biochem Physiol, 1969; 29: 161-172.

—**Baird, I:**
Observations on the auditory apparatus in typhlopid snakes. Anat Rec, 1960a; 138: 332.

—**Baird, I:**
A survey of the periotic labyrinth in some representative recent reptiles. Kansas Univ Sci Bull, 1960b; 41: 891-981.

—**Baird, I:**
The anatomy of the Reptilian ear. In, Biology of the Reptilia, Gans, C; Parsons, T (Eds.) Academic Press, New York, 1970, pp. 193-275.

—**Bath, W:**
Die Geschmacksorgane der Vögel und Krokodile. Arch für Biont, 1906; 1: 1-47.

—**Bauer, A; Russell, A:**
Morphology of gekkonid cutaneous sensilla, with comments on function and phylogeny in the Carphodactylini (Reptilia: Gekkonidae). Can J Zool, 1988; 66: 1583-1588.

—**Belekhova, M:**
Neurophysiology of the forebrain. In, Biology of the Reptilia, Gans, C; Northcutt, G; Ulinski, P (Eds.), vol. 10, 1979, Academic Press, New York, pp. 287-359.

—**Bellairs, A:**
Observations on the snout of *Varanus*, and a comparison with that of other lizards and snakes. J Anat, 1949; 83: 116-146.

—**Bellairs, A:**
The life of reptiles. 2 vol. Universe Books, New York, 1970.

—**Bellairs, A; Boyd, J:**
The lachrymal apparatus in lizards and snakes. - II. The anterior part of the lachrymal duct and its relationship with the palate and with the nasal and vomeronasal organs. Proc Zool Soc Lond, 1950; 120: 269-310.

—**Bellairs, A; Shute, C:**
Observations on the narial musculature of Crocodilia and its innervation from the sympathetic system. J Anat, 1953; 87: 367-378.

—**Beneden, E van:**
Recherches sur l'oreille moyenne des Crocodiliens et ses communications multiples avec le pharynx. Arch de Biol, 1882; 3: 497-560.

—**Bertmar, G:**
Evolution of the vomeronasal organs in vertebrates. Evolution, 1981; 35: 359-366.

—**Boiko, V:**
The jaw testing movements and role of sensory systems in food searching behavior of *Emys orbicularis* (Testudines, Emydidae). Zool Zh, 1983; 62: 1528-1532.

—**Boiko, V:**
The participation of chemoreception in the organization of reproductive behavior in *Emys orbicularis* (Testudines, Emydidae). Zool Zh, 1984; 63: 584-589.

—**Breyer, H:**
Über Hautsinnesorgane und Häutung bei Lacertilien. Zool Jahrb Anat, 1929; 51: 549-580.

—**Bruner, H:**
On the cephalic veins and sinuses of reptiles, with a description of a mechanism for raising the venous blood-pressure in the head. Am J Anat, 1907; 7: 1-117.

—**Burghardt, G:**
Chemical perception in reptiles. In, Communication by chemical signals, J Johnston, Jr.; D Moulton; A Turk (Eds.). Appleton-Century-Crofts, New York, 1970, pp. 241-308.

—**Burghardt, G:**
Chemical release of prey attack: Extension to naive newly hatched lizards, *Eumeces fasciatus.* Copeia, 1973; 1973: 178-181.

—**Burghardt, G:**
Learning processes in reptiles. In, Biology of the Reptilia, Gans, C; Tinkle, D (Eds.). Academic Press, New York, 1977, vol. 7, pp. 555-681.

—**Burghardt, G:**
Behavioral and stimulus correlates of vomeronasal functioning in reptiles: feeding, grouping, sex, and tongue use. In, Chemical signals of vertebrates and aquatic inverte-

brates, Müller-Schwarze, D; Silverstein, R (Eds.). Plenum Press, New York, 1980, pp. 275-301.

—**Burghardt, G; Wilcoxon, H; Czaplicki, J:** Conditioning in garter snakes: Aversion to palatable prey induced by delayed illness. Anim Learn Behav, 1973; 1: 317-320.

—**Burns, B:** Oral sensory papillae in sea snakes. Copeia, 1969; 1969: 617, 619.

—**Busch, C:** Beitrag zur Kenntniss der Gaumenbildung bei den Reptilien. Zool Jahrb Abst Anat, 1898; 11: 441-500.

—**Campbell, H:** Observations on the acoustic behavior of crocodilians. Zoologica, 1973; 58: 1-11.

—**Campbell, H; Evans, W:** Observations on the vocal behavior of chelonians. Herpetologica, 1972; 28: 277-280.

—**Campbell, H; Evans, W:** Sound production in two species of tortoises. Herpetologica, 1967; 23: 204-209.

—**Carpenter, C; Ferguson, G:** Variation and evolution of stereotyped behavior in reptiles. In, Biology of the Reptilia, Gans, C; Tinkle, D (Eds.). vol. 7, 1977, Academic Press, New York, pp. 355-554.

—**Chiszar, D; Scudder, K:** Chemosensory searching by rattlesnakes during predatory episodes. In, Chemical signals. Vertebrates and aquatic invertebrates, Müller-Schwarze, D; Silverstein, R (Eds.), Plenum Press, New York, 1980, pp. 125-139.

—**Chiszar, D; Radcliffe, C; Boyer, T; Behler, J:** Cover-seeking behavior in red spitting cobras (*Naja mossambica pallida*): Effects of tactile cues and darkness. Zoo Biol, 1987; 6:161-167.

—**Chiszar, D; Radcliffe, C; Scudder, K; Duvall, D:** Strike-induced chemosensory searching by rattlesnakes: the role of envenomation- related chemical cues in the post-strike environment. In, Chemical signals in vertebrates. 3, Müller-Schwarze, D; Silverstein, R (Eds.). Plenum Press, New York, 1983, pp. 1-24.

—**Chou, L; Leong, C; Choo, B:** The role of optic, auditory and olfactory senses in prey hunting by two species of geckos. J Herpet, 1988; 22(3): 349-351.

—**Colbert, E:** The eustachian tubes in the Crocodilia. Copeia, 1946; 1946: 12-14.

—**Cooper, W:** Chemical detection of predators by a lizard, the broad-headed skink *(Eumeces laticeps)*. J Exp Zool, 1990; 256:162-167.

—**Cooper, W; Trauth, S:** Discrimination of conspecific male and female cloacal chemical stimuli by males and possession of a probable pheromone gland by females in a cordylid lizard, *Gerrhosaurus nigrolineatus*. Herpetologica, 1992; 48(2): 229-236.

—**Cooper, W; Vitt, L:** Conspecific odor detection by the male broad-headed skink, *Eumeces laticeps*: effects of sex and site of odor source and of male reproductive condition. J Exp Zool, 1984; 230: 199-209.

—**Cooper, W; Vitt, L:** Interspecific odour discriminations among syntopic cogeners in scincid lizards (genus *Eumeces*). Behaviour, 1986a; 97: 1-9.

—**Cooper, W; Vitt, L:** Interspecific odour discrimination by a lizard (*Eumeces laticeps*). Anim Beh, 1986b; 34: 367-376.

—**Cooper, W; Vitt, L:** Tracking of female conspecific odor trails by broad-headed skinks (*Eumeces laticeps*). Ethology, 1986c; 71: 242-248.

—**Cooper, W; Vitt, L:** Prey odor discrimination by the broad-headed skink *(Eumeces laticeps)*. J Exp Zool, 1989; 249: 11-16.

—**Cooper, W; Garstka, W; Vitt, L:** Female sex pheromone in the lizard *Eumeces laticeps*. Herpetologica, 1986; 42: 361-366.

—**Costanzo, J:** Influences of hibernaculum microenvironment on the winter life history of the garter snake (*Thamnophis sirtalis*). Ohio J Sci, 1986; 86: 199-204.

—**Costanzo, J:** Conspecific scent trailing by garter snakes (*Thamnophis sirtalis*) during autumn. Further evidence for use of pheromones in den location. J Chem Ecol, 1989; 15: 2531-2538.

—**Crews, D:** Studies in squamate sexuality. Bioscience, 1980; 30: 835-838.

—**Crosby, E; Humphrey, T.** Studies on the vertebrate telencephalon. I. The nuclear configuration of the olfactory and accessory olfactory formations and of the nucleus olfactorius anterior of certain reptiles, birds and mammals. J Comp Neurol, 1939; 71: 121-213.

—**De La Serna De Esteban, C:** Anatomía microscópica de la lengua de Amphisbaena vermicularis darwini (D. y B.).

Actas Trab Primer Congr Sulamer Zool, 1959; 5: 143-150.

—**Devine, M:**
Copulatory plugs, restricted mating opportunities and reproductive competition among male garter snakes. Nature, 1977; 267: 345-346.

—**Düring, M von:**
The ultrastructure of lamellated mechanoreceptors in the skin of reptiles. Z Anat EntwGesch, 1973; 143: 81-94.

—**Düring, M von:**
The radiant receptor and other tissue receptors in the scales of the upper jaw of *Boa constrictor*. Z Anat EntwGesch, 1974; 145: 299-319.

—**Düring, M von; Miller, M:**
Sensory nerve endings of the skin and deeper structures. In, Biology of the Reptilia, Vol. 9, Gans, C; Northcutt, G; Ulinski, P (Eds.). Academic Press, New York, 1979, pp. 407-441.

—**Duvall, D:**
Western fence lizard (*Sceloporus occidentalis*) chemical signals. I. Conspecific discriminations and release of a species-typical visual display. J Exp Zool, 1979; 210: 321-326.

—**Duvall, D:**
Western fence lizard (*Sceloporus occidentalis*) chemical signals. III. An experimental ethogram of conspecific body licking. J Exp Zool, 1982; 221: 23-26.

—**Earle, A:**
The middle ear of *Holbrookia maculata*, the northern earless lizard. Copeia, 1961; 1961: 68-74.

—**Eckart, H:**
Das Geruchsorgan einiger ceylonischer Eidechsen (Agamidae). (Fauna et Anatomia ceylonica, Bdf. II, Nr. I). Jena Zeits Naturw, 1922; 58: 271-318.

—**Ferguson, M:**
The structure and development of the palate in *Alligator mississippiensis*. Arch Oral Biol, 1981; 26: 427-443.

—**Ferri, D; Liquori, G; Labate, M:**
La mucosa del cavum nasi proprium della lucertola campestre (*Podarcis sicula campestris* de betta). Atti Soc Pelorit Sc Fis Mat Natur, 1982; 28: 75-81.

—**Fischer, E:**
Beiträge zur Kenntniss der Nasenhöhle und des Thränennasenganges der Amphisbaeniden. Arch Mikrosk Anat EntwMech, 1900; 55: 441-478.

—**Ford, N:**
Species specificity of sex phermone trails of sympatric and allopatric garter snakes (*Thamnophis*). Copeia, 1982; 1982: 10-13.

—**Ford, N; O'Bleness, M:**
Species and sexual specificty of pheromone trails of garter snake, *Thamnophis marcianus*. J Herpet, 1986; 20: 259-262.

—**Frankenberg, E:**
Vocal behavior of the Mediterranean house gecko, *Hemidactylus turcicus*. Copeia, 1982; 1982: 770-775.

—**Frankenberg, E: Werner, Y:**
The defensive vocal "distress" repertoire of gekkonid lizards: Intra- and inter-specific variation. Amph-Rept, 1984; 5: 109-124.

—**Frankenberg, E; Werner, Y:**
Vocal communication in the reptilia - facts and questions. Acta Zool Lilloana, 1992; 41: 45-62.

—**Frazier, J; Peters, G:**
The call of the Aldabra tortoise (*Geochelone gigantea*) (Reptilia, Testudinidae). Amph-Rept, 1981; 2: 165-179.

—**Fuchs, H:**
Über den Bau und die Entwicklung des Schädels der Chelone imbricata. Ein Beitrag zur Entwicklungsgeschichte und vergleichenden Anatomie des Wirbeltierscädels. Erster Teil: Das Primordialskelett des Neurocraniums und des Kieferbogens. In, Reise in Ostrafrika in den Jehren 1903-1905, Wissenschaftliche Ergebnisse, Voeltzkow, A (Ed.). vol. 5. Schweizerbart, Stuttgart. pp. 1-325.

—**Gabe, M; Saint Girons, H:**
Contribution à l'Histologie de *Sphenodon punctatus* Gray. Centre National de la Recherche Scientifique, Paris. 1964.

—**Gabe, M; Saint Girons, H:**
Contribution a la morphologie comparée des fosses nasales et de leur annexes chez les lépidosoriens. Mem Mus Nat d'Hist Nat Paris, 1976; 98(A): 1-87.

—**Gans, C:**
Studies on amphisbaenids (Amphisbaenia, Reptilia). Bull Amer Mus Nat Hist, 1960; 119: 131-204.

—**Gans, C:**
The characteristics and affinities of the Amphisbaenia. Trans Zool Soc Lond, 1978; 34: 347-416.

—**Gans, C; Wever, E:**
The ear and hearing in Amphisbaenia (reptilia). J Exper Zool, 1972; 179: 17-34.

—**Gans, C; Wever, E:**
The ear and hearing in *Sphenodon punctatus*. Proc Natl Acad Sci USA, 1976; 73: 4244-4246.

—**Garrick, L; Lang, J:**
Social signals and behaviors of adult alligators and crocodilians. Amer Zool, 1977; 17: 225-239.

—**Garrick, L; Lang, J; Herzog, H:**
Social signals of adult american alligators. Bull Amer Mus Nat Hist, 1978; 160(3): 153-192.

—**Garstka, W; Crews, D:**
Phermones and reproduction in garter snakes. In, Chemical signals in Vertebrates. 4. Ecology, evolution and comparative biology, Duvall, D; Müller-Schwarze, D; Silverstein, R (Eds.). Plenum Press, New York, 1986, pp. 243-260.

—**Gehlbach, F; Watkins, J; Kroll, J:**
Pheromone trailing studies of typhlopid, leptotyphlopid, and colubrid snakes. Behaviour, 1971; 40: 282-294.

—**Gillingham, J; Dickinson, J:**
Postural orientation during courtship in the eastern garter snake, *Thamnophis s. sirtalis*. Behav Neur Biol, 1980; 28: 211-217.

—**Gopalakrishnakone, P:**
Study of the spinous scales of *Lapemis hardwickii*. 1. Light, transmission electron and scanning electron microscopic study. Snake, 1985; 17(2): 148-155.

—**Göppert, E:**
Die Bedeutung der Zunge für den sekundären Gaumen und den Ductus naso-pharyngcus. Beobachtungen an Reptilien und Vögeln. Morph Jahrb, 1903; 31: 311-359.

—**Grandison, A:**
Nigerian lizards of the genus *Agama* (Sauria: Agamidae). Bull Brit Mus Nat Hist, 1968; 17(3): 65-90.

—**Grassman, M; Owens, D; McVey, J; Marquez, M:**
Olfactory-based orientation in artificially imprinted sea turtles. Science, 1984; 224: 83-84.

—**Graves, B; Duvall, D:**
Evidence of an alarm pheromone from the cloacal sacs of prarie rattlesnakes. Southwest Nat, 1988; 33: 339-345.

—**Graves, B; Halpern, M:**
Neonate plains garter snakes (*Thamnophis radix*) are attracted to conspecific skin extracts. J Comp Psychol, 1988; 102: 251-253.

—**Graves, B; Duvall, D; King, M; Lindstedt, S; Gern, W:**
Initial den location by neonatal prarie rattlesnakes: functions, causes, and natural history in chemical ecology. In, Chemical signals in vertebrates. 4. Ecology, evolution and comparative biology, Duvall, D; Müller-Schwarze, D; Silverstein, R (Eds.). Plenum Press, New York, 1986, pp. 285-304.

—**Graves, B; Halpern, M; Friesen, J:**
Snake aggregation pheromones: source and chemosensory mediation in western ribbon snakes (*Thamnophis proximus*). J Comp Psychol, 1991; 105(2): 140-144.

—**Haas, G:**
The structure of the nasal cavity in *Chamaeleo chameleon* (Linnaeus). J Morph, 1937; 61: 433-451.

—**Haas, G:**
Jacobson's organ in the chameleon. J Morph, 1947; 81: 195-207.

—**Halpern, M:**
The telencephalon of snakes. In, Comparative neurology of the telencephalon, Ebbeson, S (Ed.). Plenum Press, New York, 1980, pp. 257-295.

—**Halpern, M:**
Nasal chemical senses in reptiles: Structure and function. In, Biology of the Reptilia, Gans, C; Crews, D (Eds.). University of Chicago Press, Chicago, 1992, pp. 423-523.

—**Halpern, M; Holtzman, D (Eds.):**
Chemosensing and chemosignaling in reptiles. Brain Beh Evol, 1993; 41.

—**Halpern, M; Kubie, J:**
Snake tongue flicking behavior: clues to vomcronasal system functions. In, Chemical signals in vertebrates. III, Silverstein, R; Müller-Schwarze (Eds.) Plenum Press, New York, 1983, pp. 45-72.

—**Harless, M:**
Social behavior. In, Turtles: perspectives and research, Harless, M; Morlock, H (Eds.), Wiley and Sons, New York, 1979, pp. 475-492.

—**Hartline, P; Campbell, H:**
Auditory and vibratory responses in the midbrains of snakes. Science, 1969; 163: 1221-1223.

—**Hartline, P:**
Physiological basis for detection of sound and vibration in snakes. J Exp Biol, 1971a; 59: 349-371.

—**Hartline, P:**
Midbrain responses of the auditory and somatic vibration in snakes. J Exp Biol, 1971b; 54: 373-390.

—**Hetherington, T:**
Use of vibratory cues for detection of insect prey by the sandswimming lizard *Scincus scincus*. Anim Behav, 1989; 37: 290-297.

—**Hetherington, T:**
Behavioral use of seismic cues by the

sandswimming lizard *Scincus scincus*. Ethol Ecol Evol, 1992; 4: 5-14.

—**Hibbard, E:**
Eyes and other sense organs of sea snakes. In, The biology of sea snakes, W Dunson (Ed). University Park Press, Baltimore, 1975, pp. 355-382.

—**Hiller, U:**
Ultrastruktur und Regeneration mechanorezeptiver Hautsinnesorgane bei Gekkoniden. Naturwissenschaften, 1976; 63: 200-201.

—**Hin-Ching, L; Maneely, R:**
Some cutaneous nerve endings in the soft-shelled turtle of South China. J Comp Neurol, 1962; 10: 159-208.

—**Hoppe, G:**
Das Geruchsorgan von *Hatteria punctata*. Z Anat EntwGesch, 1934; 102: 434-461.

—**Hulanicka, R:**
Recherches sur les Terminaisons nerveuses dans la langue, le palais et la peau du crocodile. Arch Zool expér gén, 1913; 53: 1-14.

—**Inouchi, J; Wang, D; Jiang, X; Kubie, J; Halpern, M:**
Electrophysiological analysis of the nasal chemical senses in garter snakes. Brain Behav Evol, 1993; 41: 171-182.

—**Iwahori, N; Kiyota, E; Nakamura, K:**
Olfactory and respiratory epithelia in the snake, *Elaphe quadrivirgata*. Neurosci Res, 1987; 6: 411-425.

—**Jaburek, L:**
Über Nervenendigungen in der Epidermis der Reptilien. Zeitsch f Mikr-Anat Forsch, 1926; 10: 1-49.

—**Jackson, M:**
Cutaneous corpuscles within the cephalic integument of the rat snake. Anat Rec, 1975; 181: 382-383.

—**Jackson, M:**
Histology and distribution of cutaneous touch corpuscles in some leptotyphlopid and colubrid snakes. J Herpet, 1977; 11: 7-15.

—**Jackson, M; Sharawy, M:**
Scanning electron microscopy and distribution of specialized mechanoreceptors in the Texas rat snake, *Elaphe obsoleta lindheimeri* (Baird and Girard). J Morph, 1980; 163: 59-67.

—**Joanen, T; McNease, L:**
Notes on the reproductive biology and captive propagation of the American alligator. Proc SEast Assoc Game and Fish Comm, 29th Ann Conf, 1976, pp. 407-415.

—**Johnsen, P; Wellington, J:**
Detection of glandular secretions by yearling alligators. Copeia, 1982; 1982: 705-708.

—**Kathariner, L:**
Die Nase der im Wasser lebenden Schlangen als Luftweg und Geruchsorgan. Zool Jahrb Abst Syst, 1900; 13: 415-442.

—**Kenton, B; Kruger, L; Woo, M:**
Two classes of slowly adapting mechanoreceptor fibers in reptile cutaneous nerve. J Physiol Lond, 1971; 212: 21-44.

—**Koch, A; Carr, A; Ehrenfeld, D:**
The problem of open-sea navigation: The migration of the green turtle to Ascension Island. J Theor Biol, 1969; 22: 163-179.

—**Köppl, C; Manley, G:**
Functional consequences of morphological trends in the evolution of lizard hearing organs. In, The evolutionary biology of hearing, Webster, D; Fay, R; Popper, A (Eds.), Springer-Verlag, New York, pp. 489-509.

—**Korte, G:**
Ultrastructure of the tastebuds of the red-eared turtle, *Chrysemys scripta elegans*. J Morph, 1980; 163: 231-252.

—**Kroll, J:**
Taste buds in the oral epithelium of the blind snake, *Leptotyphlops dulcis* (Reptilia: Leptotyphlopidae). SouthWest Nat, 1973; 17: 365-370.

—**Kubie, J; Halpern, M:**
Laboratory observations of trailing behavior in garter snakes. J Comp Physiol Psychol, 1975; 89: 667-674.

—**Kubie, J; Halpern, M:**
Garter snake trailing behavior: effects of varying prey-extract concentration and mode of prey-extract presentation. J Comp Physiol Psychol, 1978; 92: 362-373.

—**Landmann, L:**
The sense organs in the skin of the head of squamata (Reptilia). Israel J Zool, 1975; 24: 99-135.

—**Lapage, E:**
The septomaxillary of the Amphibia Anura and the Reptilia. II. J Morph, 1928; 46: 399-430.

—**Lavin-Murcio, P; Robinson, B; Kardong, K:**
Cues involved in relocation of struck prey by rattlesnakes, *Crotalus viridis oreganus*. Herpetologica, 1993; 49(4): 463-469.

—**Lenhardt, M; Klinger, R; Musick, J:**
Marine turtle middle-ear anatomy. J Aud Res, 1986; 25(1): 66-72.

—**Leydig, F:**
Über Organe eines sechsten Sinnes (zugleich ein Beitrag zur Kenntnis des feineren Baues der Haut bei Amphibien und Reptilien). Dresden, 1868.

—**Maclean, S:**
Ultrastructure of epidermal sensory receptors in *Amphibolurus barbatus* (Lacertilis: Agamidae). Cell Tissue Res, 1980; 210: 435-445.

—**Malan, M:**
Contributions to the comparative anatomy of the nasal capsule and the organ of Jacobson of the Lacertilia. Annale Univ Stellenbosch, 1946; (A)24: 69-137.

—**Manley, G:**
Comparative studies of auditory physiology in reptiles. Z Vergl Physiol, 1970; 67: 363-381.

—**Manley, G:**
A review of the auditory physiology of the reptiles. *Prog Sens Physiol*, 1981; 2: 49-134.

—**Marcellini, D:**
The function of the vocal display of the lizard *Hemidactylus frenatus* (Sauria: Gekkonidae). Anim Beh, 1977; 25(2): 414-417.

—**Marcellini, D:**
The acoustic behavior of lizards. In, Behavior and neurology of lizards, Greenberg, N; MacLean, P (Eds.), National Institute of Mental Health, Rockville, Maryland, 1978, pp. 287-300.

—**Mason, R:**
Reptilian phermones. In, Biology of the Reptilia, Gans, C; Crews, D (Eds.). University of Chicago Press, Chicago, 1992; vol. 18, pp. 114-228.

—**Mason, R; Fales, H; Jones, T; Pannell, L; Chinn, J; Crews, D:**
Sex pheromones in snakes. Science, 1989; 245: 2909-293.

—**McDowell, S:**
On the major arterial canals in the ear region of testudinoid turtles, and the classification of the Testudinoidea. Bull Mus Comp Zool Harvard. 1961; 125: 23-39.

—**Miller, M:**
The cochlear duct of lizards. Proc Calif Acad Sci, 1966; 33: 255-359.

—**Miller, M:**
The cochlear duct of snakes. Proc Calif Acad Sci, 1968; 35: 425-476.

—**Miller, M:**
The reptilian cochlear duct. In, Comparative studies of hearing in vertebrates, Popper, A; Fay, R (Eds.). Springer-Verlag, New York, 1980.

—**Miller, M:**
The evolution implications of the structural variations in the auditory papilla of lizards. In, The evolutionary biology of hearing, Webster, D; Fay, R; Popper, A (Eds.), Springer-Verlag, New York, 1992, pp. 463-487.

—**Miller, M; Beck, J:**
Auditory hair cell innervational patterns in lizards. J Comp Neurol, 1988; 271: 604-628.

—**Miller, M; Kasahara, M:**
Studies on the cutaneous innervation of lizards. Proc Cal Acad Sci, 1967; 34: 549-568.

—**Mohammed, W:**
Structure and function of the tongue and hyoid apparatus in *Acanthodactylus boskianus* (Lacertidae, Reptilia). J Egypt Ger Soc Zool, 1992; 7B: 335-354.

—**Mulroy, M:**
Pattern of afferent synaptic contacts in the alligator lizard's cochlea. J Comp Neurol, 1988; 248: 263-271.

—**Narins, P; Lewis, E:**
The vertebrate ear as an exquisite seismic sensor. J Acoust Soc Amer, 1985; 76: 1384-1387.

—**Neil, W:**
The last of the ruling reptiles: alligators, crocodiles and their kin. Columbia University Press, New York, 1971.

—**Nick, L:**
Das Kopfskelet von *Dermochelys coriacea* L. Zool Jahrb Abst Anat, 1912; 33: 1-238.

—**Noble, G:**
The sense organs involved in the courtship of *Storeria, Thamnophis* and other snakes. Bull Amer Mus Nat Hist, 1937; 73: 673-725.

—**Noble, G; Clausen, H:**
The aggregation behavior of *Storeria dekayi* and other snakes, with especial reference to the sense organs involved. Ecol Monog, 1936; 6: 269-316.

—**Nonoyama, J:**
The distribution of the taste-buds on the tongue of some Reptilia. J Sci Hiroshoma Univ Ser B, 1936; 5:57-66.

—**Noris, K; Lowe, C:**
A study of the osteology and musculature of *Phryosoma m'calli* pertinent to its systematic position. Bull Chicago Acad Sci, 1951; 9: 117-125.

—**Northcutt, G:**
Forebrain and midbrain organization in lizards and its phylogenetic significance. In, Behavior and neurology of lizards, Greenberg, N; MacLean, P (Eds.). National Institutes of Mental Health, Bethesda, Maryland, 1978, pp. 11-64.

—**O'Hara, J:**
Avoidance responses of loggerhead turtles, *Caretta caretta*, to low frequency sound. Copeia, 1990; 1990: 564-567.

—Olson, E:
The middle ear: morphological types in amphibians and reptiles. Am Zool, 1966; 6: 399-419.

—Osawa, G:
Beitrage zure Lehre ven den Eingeweiden der *Hatteria punctata*. Arch für Mikro Anat, 1897; 49: 113-126.

—Owens, D; Comuzzie, D; Grassman, M:
Chemoreception in the homing and orientation behavior of amphibians and reptiles, with special reference to sea turtles. In, Chemical signals in vertebrates. 4. Ecology, evolution and comparative biology, Duvall, D; M_ller-Schwarze, D, Silverstein, R (Eds.) Plenum Press, New York, 1986, pp. 341-355.

—Owens, D; Grassman, M; Hendrickson, J:
The imprinting hypothesis and sea turtle reproduction. Herpetologica, 1982; 38: 124-135.

—Pác, L:
Nerve endings in the lizard skin (lacerta viridis). Zeits Mikr-Anat Forsch, 1984; 98: 939-950.

—Parsons, T:
Studies on the comparative embryology of the reptilian nose. Bull Mus Comp Zool Harvard, 1959; 120: 101-277.

—Parsons, T:
Variation in the choanal structure of recent turtles. Can J Zool, 1968; 46: 1235-1263.

—Parsons, T:
The nose and Jacobson's organ. In, Biology of the Reptilia, Gans, C; Parsons, T (Eds.) vol.2. Academic Press, New York, 1970, pp. 99-191.

—Patterson, W:
Hearing in the turtle. J Aud Res, 1966; 6: 453-464.

—Perret, J:
Revision des especes africaines du genre *Cnemaspis* Strauch, sous-genre *Ancylodactylus* Muller (Lacertilia, Gekkonidae), avec la description de quarte especs nouvelles. Rev Suisse Zool, 1986; 208(3): 443-455.

—Phillips, J; Alberts, A:
Naive ophiophagus lizards recognize and avoid venomous snakes using chemical cues. J Chem Ecol, 1992; 18(10): 1775-1783.

—Platel, R:
Donnes recentes sur l'organe vomero-nasal des serpents. J Psychol Norm Pathol, 1986; 81(3-4): 199-219.

—Pratt, C:
The morphology of the ethmoidal region of *Sphenodon* and lizards. Proc Zool Soc Lond, 1948; 118: 171-201.

—Proske, U:
Vibration-sensitive mechanoreceptors in snake skin. Exp Neurol, 1969a; 23: 187-194.

—Proske, U:
Nerve endings in skin of the Australian black snake. Anat Rec, 1969b; 164: 259-266.

—Rensch, B; Eisentraut, M:
Experimentelle Untersuchungen über den Geschmackssimn der Reptilien. Z Vergl Physiol, 1927; 5: 607-612.

—Rosenberg, M:
Carapace and plastron sensitivity to touch and vibration in the tortoise *(Testudo hermanni* and *T. graeca)*. J Zool Lond, 1986; 208: 443-455.

—Ross, P, Jr; Crews, D:
Influence of the seminal plug on mating behavior in the garter snake. Nature, 1977; 267: 344-345.

—Rubin, W:
Untersuchungen am olfaktorischen System der Reptilien. III. Differenzierungsformen einiger olfaktorischen Zentren bei Reptilien. Acta Anat, 1974; 89: 481-515.

—Rudiger, A:
Schlangen mit Heckantrieb. Kosmos, 1986; 82(7): 38-43.

—Russell, A; Bauer, A:
Caudal morphology of the knob-tailed geckos, genus *Nephrurus* (Reptilia: Gekkonidae), with special reference to the tail tip. Aust J Zool, 1987; 35: 541-551.

—Saint Girons, H:
Histologie comparee des fosses nasales de guelgues tortues marine (Dermochelys coriacea et Chelonia mydas) et d'eaux douces (Emys obicularis et Pseudemys scripta) (Reptilia, Dermochelyidae, Chelonidae, Emydidae). Bijdr Dierkd, 1991; 61(1): 51-61.

—Schmidt, W:
Studien am Integument der Reptilien. I. Die Haut der Geckoniden. Z Wiss Zool, 1912; 101: 139-258.

—Schmidt, W:
Einiges über die Hautsinnesorgane der Agamiden, insbesondere von Calotes, nebst bemerkungen über diese Organe bei Geckoniden und Iguaniden. Anat Anz, 1920; 53: 113-139.

—Schwenk, K:
Occurrence, distribution and functional significance of taste buds in lizards. Copeia, 1985; 1985(1): 91-101.

—Schwenk, K:
Morphology of the tongue of the tuatara, *Sphenodon punctatus* (Reptilia, Lepidosauria), with

comments on function and phylogeny. J Morphol, 1986; 188: 129-156.

—**Schwenk, K:**
Are geckos olfactory specialists? J Zool London, 1993; 229: 289-302.

—**Scott, T; Weldon, P:**
Chemoreception in the feeding behavior of adult American alligators, *Alligator mississippiensis.* Anim Behav, 1990; 39: 398-405.

—**Shute, C; Bellairs, A:**
The external ear in crocodilia. Proc Zool Soc London, 1955; 124: 741-749.

—**Siminoff, R; Kruger, L:**
Properties of reptilian cutaneous mechanoreceptors. Exp Neur, 1968; 20: 403-414.

—**Simon, C:**
A review of lizard chemoreception. In, Lizard ecology: Studies of a model organism, Huey, R; Pianka, E; Schoener, T (Eds.). Harvard University Press, Cambridge, 1983, pp. 119-133.

—**Sneary, M:**
Auditory receptor of the red-eared turtle: II. Afferent and efferent synapses and innervation patterns. J Comp Neurol, 1988; 276: 588-606.

—**Sprackland, R:**
A preliminary study of food discrimination in monitor lizards. Bull Chic Herpet Soc, 1990; 25(10): 181-183.

—**Stebbins, R:**
Adaptations in the nasal passages for sand burrowing in the saurian genus Uma. Am Nat, 1943; 77: 38-52.

—**Stebbins, R:**
Nasal structure in lizards with reference to olfaction and conditioning of the inspired air. Am J Anat, 1948; 83: 183-221.

—**Stimie, M:**
The cranial anatomy of the iguanid *Anolis carolinensis* (Cuvier). Annale Univ Stellenbosch, 1966; 41(A): 239-268.

—**Thoen, C; Bauwens, D; Verheyen, R:**
Chemoreceptive and behavioral responses of the common lizard *Lacerta vivipara* to snake chemical deposits. *Anim Behav,* 1986; 34: 1805-1813.

—**Toerien, M:**
The sound-conducting systems of lizards without tympanic membranes. Evolution, 1963; 17: 540-547.

—**Tollestrup, K:**
The social behavior and displays of two species of horned lizards, *Phrynosoma platyrhinos* and *Phrynosoma coronatum.* Herpetologica, 1981; 37: 130-141.

—**Trauth, S; Cooper, W; Vitt, L; Perrill, S:**
Cloacal anatomy of the broad-headed skink, *Eumeces laticeps,* with a description of a female pheromonal gland. Herpetologica, 1987; 43: 458-466.

—**Turner, R:**
Physiology and bioacoustics in reptiles. In, Comparative studies of hearing in vertebrates, Popper, A; Fay, R (Eds.), Springer-Verlag, New York. pp. 205-237.

—**Versluys, J:**
Die mittlere und äussere Ohrsphäre der Lacertilia und Rhynchocephalia. Zool Jahrb Abt Anat, 1898; 12: 161-406.

—**Vogt, R:**
Spring aggregating behavior of painted turtles, *Chrysemys picta* (Reptilia, Testudines, Testudinidae). J Herpetol, 1979; 13: 363-365.

—**Vogt, R:**
New methods for trapping aquatic turtles. Copeia, 1980; 1980: 368-371.

—**Walker, W:**
Closure of the nostrils in the Atlantic loggerhead and other sea turtles. Copeia, 1959; 1959: 257-259.

—**Wang, R; Halpern, M:**
Scanning electron microscopic studies of the surface morphology of the vomeronasal epithelium and olfactory epithelium of garter snakes. *Am J Anat,* 1980; 157: 399-428.

—**Watkins, J; Gehlbach, F; Kroll, J:**
Attractant-repellent secretions in the intra-ans interspecific relations of blind snakes (*Leptotyphlops dulcis*) and army ants (*Neivamyrmex nigrescens*). Ecology, 1969; 50: 1098-1104.

—**Webb, J; Shine, R:**
To find an ant: trail-following in Australian blindsnakes (Typhlopidae). Anim Behav, 1992; 43: 941-948.

—**Wegner, R:**
Die Nebenhöhlen der Nase bei den Krokodilen (Studien über Nebenhöhlen des Schädels, 2 Teil). Wiss Z Ernst Moritz Arndt-Univ Greifswald, 1958; 7: 1-39.

—**Weldon, P; Ferguson, M:**
Chemoreception in crocodilians: Anatomy, natural history, and empirical results. Brain Beh Evol, 1993; 41: 239-245.

—**Weldon, P; Swenson, D; Olson, J; Brinkmeier, W:**
The American alligator detects food chemicals in aquatic and terrestrial environments. Ethology, 1990, 85: 191-198.

—**Werner, D; Baker, E; Gonzalez, E; Sosa, I:**
Kinship recognition and grouping in

hatchling green iguanas. Behav Ecol Sociobiol, 1987; 21: 83-89.

—**Wettstein, O von:**
Sauropsida: Allgemeines-Reptilia. In, Handbuch der Zoologie. Eine Naturgeschichte der Stämme des Tierreiches, Kükenthal, W; Krumbach, T; Helmcke, J; Lengerken, H von (Eds.). vol. 7(2). de Gruyter, Berlin, 1954, pp. 321-424.

—**Wever, E:**
Structure and function of the lizard ear. J Aud Res, 1965; 5: 331-371.

—**Wever, E:**
The tectorial membrane of the lizard ear: Types of structures. J Morphol, 1967a; 122: 307-320.

—**Wever, E:**
The tectorial membrane of the lizard ear: Species variations. J Morphol, 1967b; 123: 355-372.

—**Wever, E:**
The ear of the chameleon: the round window problem. *J Exp Zool*, 1969; 171: 1-6.

—**Wever, E:**
The reptile ear: Its structure and function. Princeton University Press, Princeton, 1978.

—**Wever, E; Gans, C:**
The ear and hearing in *Bipes biporous*. Proc Natl Acad Sci USA, 1972; 69: 2714-2716.

—**Whitaker, R; Whitaker, Z:**
Reproductive biology of the Mugger (*Crocodylus palustris*). J Bombay Nat Hist Soc, 1985; 81: 297-317.

—**Willard, W:**
The cranial nerves of *Anolis carolinensis*. Bull Mus Comp Zool, 1915; 59: 15-116.

—**Winokur, R:**
The integumentary tentacles of the snake *Erpeton tentaculatum*: Structure, function and evolution. Herpetologica, 1977; 33: 247-253.

—**Winokur, R:**
Integumentary appendages of chelonians. J Morph, 1982; 172: 59-74.

—**Wyeth, F:**
The development of the auditory apparatus in *Sphenodon punctatus*. Phil Trans Royal Soc London, 1924; 212(B): 259-368.

—**Young, B:**
Morphological basis of "growling" in the king cobra, *Ophiophagus hannah*. J Exp Zool, 1991; 260: 275-283.

—**Young, B:**
Evaluating hypotheses for the transfer of stimulus particles to Jacobson's organ in snakes. Brain Beh Evol, 1993; 41: 203-209.

ACKNOWLEGEMENTS

The author is indebted to Bill Yost and the faculty and staff of the Parmly Hearing Institute for their assistance and support. Special thanks to Alan Resetar and Harold Voris of the Field Museum of Natural History for their continued cooperation and generosity.

VENOMS AND ENVENOMATION

P Gopalakrishnakone
Chairman, Venom and Toxin Research Group
Faculty of Medicine
National University of Singapore
Singapore 119260

THE CLASSIFICATION AND DISTRIBUTION OF VENOMOUS SNAKES

Snakes are classified under the suborder Serpentes that belongs to the order Squamata, of the class Reptilia (Kochva, 1987). It is now generally agreed that the snakes arxe a monophyletic group (Rieppel, 1979) that has originated from lizard or prelizard ancestors, during the late Cretaceous period, some 65—135 million years ago (Russell, 1980). Much snake taxonomy to this day rests upon the morphological characters of the snake. The morphological characters which are useful in the classification of snakes include maxillary dentition, skull and bone structure, scalation (squamation), shape and form of hemipenis, as well as features of the retina. Based on these, snakes are classified as shown below. The Caenophidia are the more advanced snakes (Webb et al., 1978), and all venomous snakes belong to this infraorder.

There are about 3,200 species of snakes. Approximately 1,300 species are venomous (Hider et al., 1991). Venomous snakes are usually defined as those which possess venom glands and specialized venom-conducting fangs, which enable them to inflict serious bites upon their victims (Klemmer, 1968). Generally, there are five recognized families of venomous snakes: the Colubridae,

Ringed Turtlehead Sea Snake, *Emydocephalus annulatus*. Photo by Dr. Sherman A. Minton.

which possess small rear fangs; the front-fanged Elapidae and Hydrophidae; and the viper group, which consists of the Viperidae and Crotalidae.

Venomous snakes are widespread throughout the world. They have successfully colonized the varied habitats found in most parts of the world with the exception of lakes and the sea depths (Phelps, 1981). However, it is interesting to note that land snakes do not occur in several islands, including New Zealand, Ireland, Iceland, the Azores and Canaries (Phelps, 1981).

CLASS : Reptilia		
ORDER : Squamata		
SUBORDER : Serpentes		
INFRAORDER	INFRAORDER	INFRAORDER
Scolecophidia	Henophidia	Caenophida
FAMILY	**FAMILY**	**FAMILY**
Typhlopidae	Aniliidae	Elapidae
Leptotyphlopidae	Uropeltidae	Hydrophiidae
	Boidea	Viperidae
	Xenopeltidae	Crotalidae
	Acrochordidae	Colubridae

VENOMOUS SNAKE FAMILIES

ELAPIDAE

This is a large family that includes the kraits, cobras, mamba, and coral snakes. It is a widespread family represented in the Americas, Africa, Asia, and Australasia. Members of this family typically have a small head with short, fixed fangs mounted at the front of the jaw (proteroglyphous). All mem-

Black Mamba, *Dendroaspis polylepis*. Photo by C. Banks.

bers of this family are venomous and potentially dangerous to humans.

HYDROPHIIDAE

This family comprises the sea snakes. Sea snakes are similar in general form to the elapids, except that sea snakes have evolved a number of special features which allow them an almost exclusively marine existence:

Annulated Sea Snake, *Hydrophis cyanocinctus*. Photo by Dr. Sherman A. Minton.

Texas Coral Snake, *Micrurus fulvius tener*. Photo by R. T. Zappalorti.

—The nostrils are mounted dorsally on the head, and they are equipped with a closing mechanism
—The tail is laterally flattened.
—The tongue is reduced.
—Salt glands have evolved.

Most sea snakes are found in the coastal waters of Asia and Australasia but some are found far out into Oceania. However, no sea snakes are found in the Atlantic Ocean.

VIPERIDAE

The Viperidae (true vipers) is the most widespread family of venomous snakes. It is represented throughout Europe, Africa, Asia, and the Americas; but it is absent from Australasia. The vipers tend to be of heavier and bulkier build than the elapids and many are remarkably sluggish. They possess a large, flattened triangular head and a characteristic dentition. The venom fangs are large and often grooved, rather than truly hollow. The venom fangs are mounted on the maxillary bone, which is mobile and can rotate 90 degrees on the prefrontal bone. The snake accomodates its fangs within its mouth by folding the fangs flat against the upper jaw. When the fangs are to be used, the snake opens its jaw and the fangs are erected.

CROTALIDAE

The snakes comprising the Crotalidae are similar in all but one respect to those of family Viperidae. Crotalidae possess heat-sensitive pits situated on each side of the head between the nostril and the eye. This facility is used for hunting warm-blooded prey at night. The Crotalidae are well represented in the Americas and parts of Southeast Asia but absent from Australasia and Europe.

COLUBRIDAE

This family is the largest of all venomous snake families. It is the dominant family of snakes in all

Queretaran Dusky Rattlesnake, *Crotalus aquilus*. Photo by R. D. Bartlett.

parts of the world (except for Australasia). Most snakes in this family are harmless but some are venomous. The venomous colubrids have venom fangs that are typically grooved and are mounted at the rear of the upper jaws (opisthoglyphous), rather than at the front, as in all other venomous snakes. Some of the venomous colubrids are extremely dangerous, such as the boomslang of South Africa.

VENOM

VENOM GLAND

Venom glands are modified or specialised salivary glands which are situated on either side of the head. These glands include a posterior portion known as the main gland, which tapers ante-

riorly into the fang. At the region where the duct enters the fang, there is a collection of glandular tissue known as the accessory gland.

The fang is a specialised tooth which is usually larger than the other teeth. The fang possesses a deep groove, a closed groove, or a tubelike canal. The groove or tube runs through the fang from its base almost to the tip, and the venom is injected into the victim's system through this fang. The fang may be situated in the anterior or in the posterior region of the upper jaw. In some snakes, these fangs could be moved by the action of muscles.

The structure of venom glands of the land snakes have been extensively studied and published (see reviews by Bdolah, 1979; Kochva 1987). Recently, sea-snake venom glands also have been studied in detail (Gopalakrishnakone, Wollberg and Kochva 1994).

Northern Vine Snake, *Thelotornis kirtlandi*. Photo by R. D. Bartlett.

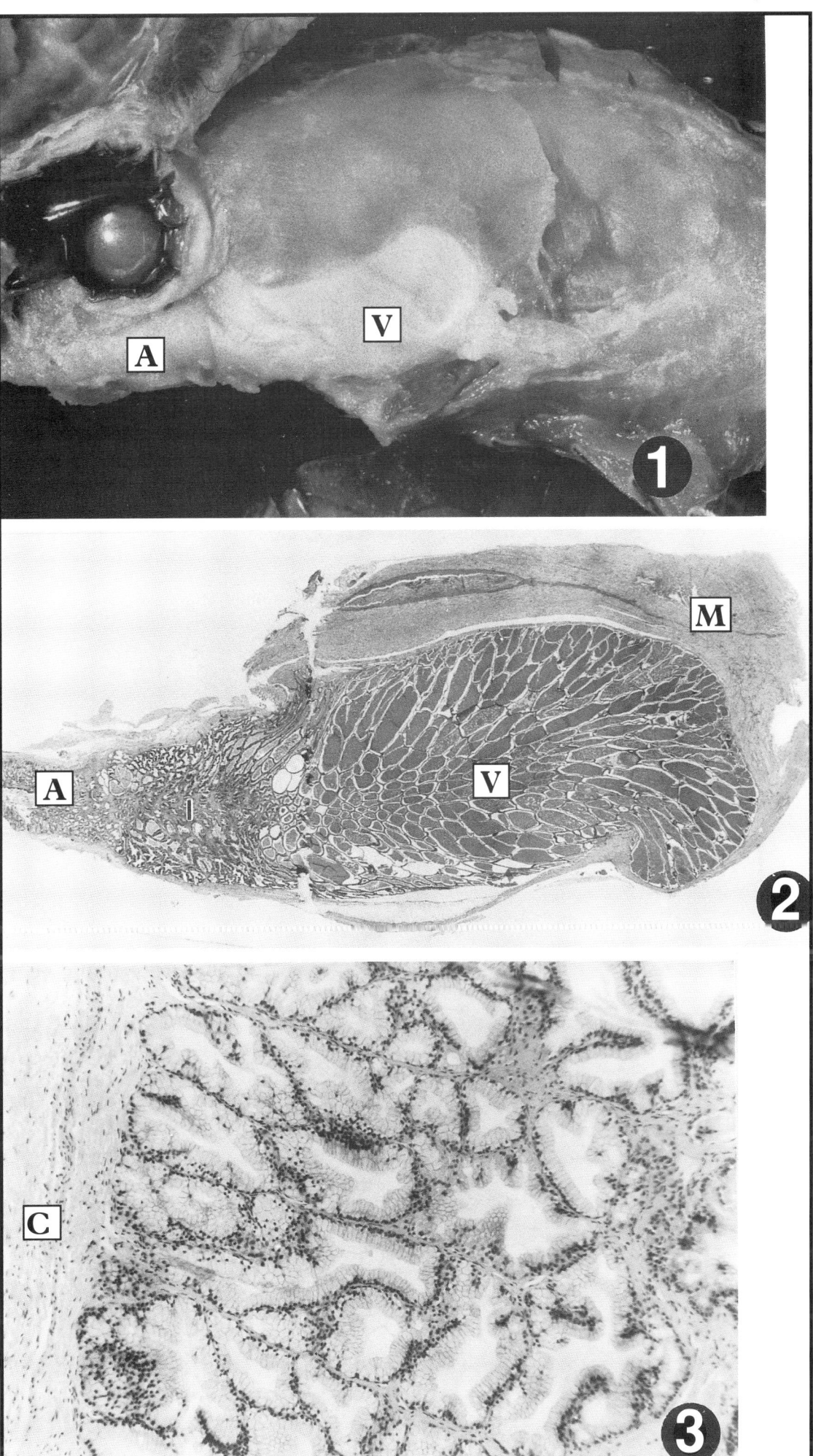

Figure 1 :
Lateral view of venom gland of the spitting cobra, *Naja naja sputartrix*, and the muscles associated with the venom gland. In this figure, you can see the venom gland proper or main gland (V) and the accessory gland (A).

Figure 2 :
Lower-power light micrograph of the sagittal section of the whole venom gland showing the main gland (V), the accessory gland (A) and the intermediate or transition region (I). You can also see the skeletal muscle (S) associated with the main gland (M). (X10).

Figure 3 :
Light micrograph of a portion of the accessory gland, showing the capsule (C); and the mucous acini, showing the lightly stained mucous cells, with well-stained basally situated nuclei. (X110).

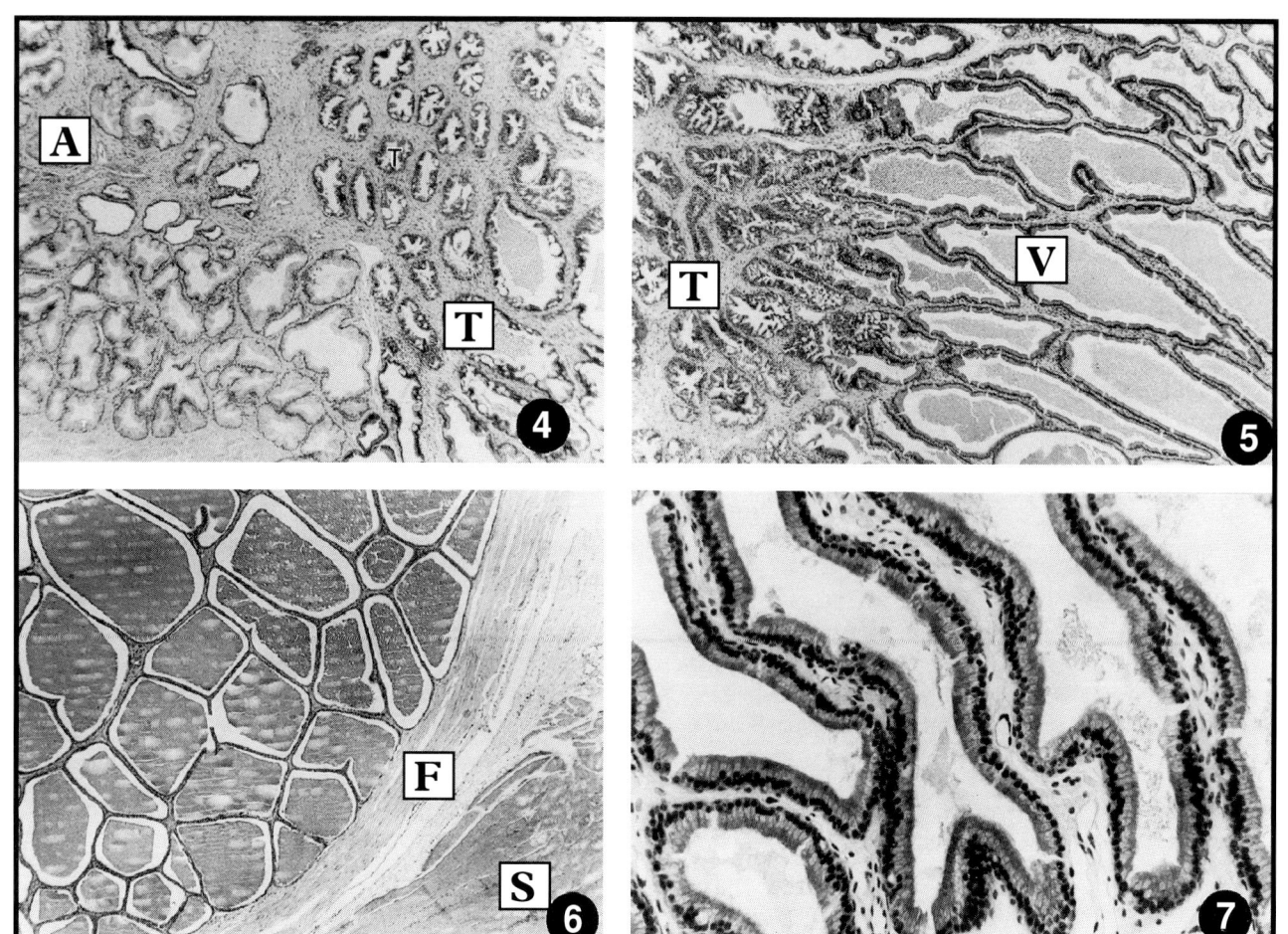

Figure 4 :
Light micrograph showing the portion of the accessory gland (A) and the transition zone (T) between the accessory gland and the main gland (X88).

Figure 5 :
Light micrograph showing the main venom gland (V) and the transition zone (T) between the main gland and the accessory gland. (X88).

Figure 6 :
Light micrograph of the posterior portion of the main venom gland showing the acini, lined with single layer of epithelium, and showing the lumen filled with venom secretion. Note the close association of the fibrous capsule (F) and the skeletal muscle (S). (X88).

Figure 7 :
Light micrograph of a magnified area of the main venom gland showing the secretory tubules cut in longitudinal section and the connective tissue in between. The epithelium is simple columnar epithelium with prominent nuclei. (X352).

Generally, the venom gland includes a posterior main gland and an anterior accessory gland. The anterior gland leads to the venom duct and finally opens into the fang. The posterior main gland is surrounded by a skeletal muscle. The entire venom gland is covered by a tough capsule with septae dividing the gland into many lobes and lobules. The capsule consists of connective tissue containing blood vessels, lymphatics, and nerves.

The anterior accessory gland contains mainly mucous-secreting cells. In hematoxylin-eosin staining, the mucous-secreting cells stain very lightly, and the nuclei are not prominent; however, the acini pattern can be observed in transverse section.

The main gland consists of many branching tubules, which open into a wide lumen. The lumen continue anteriorly as the primary duct. The appearance of the glandular epithelium varies with the stage of activity at which the gland was fixed for specimen preservation. Glands which have been milked before fixing show short, almost flattened epithelium. Glands which were not milked and were not actively secreting at the time they were fixed show tall, columnar epithelium, sometimes with the lumen of the acini filled with secretion.

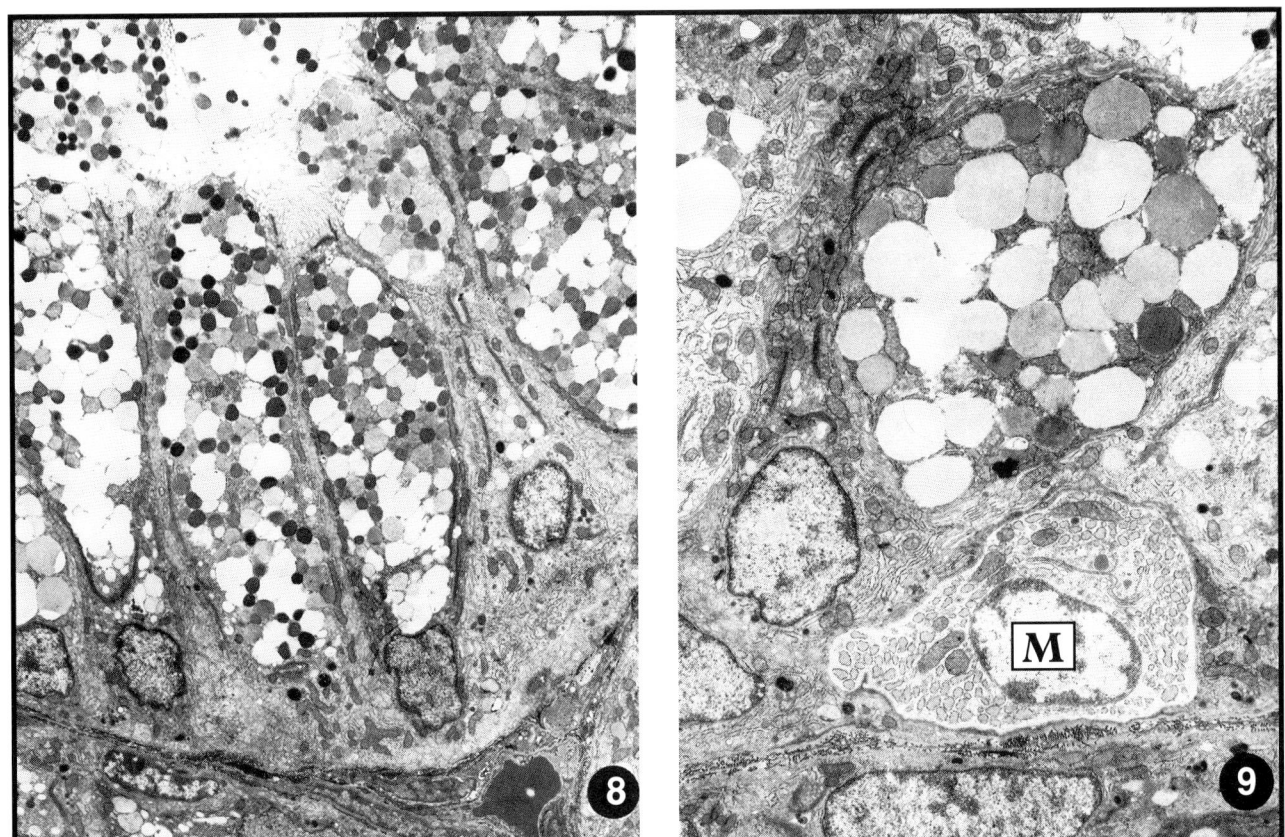

Figure 8 :
Electron micrograph a portion of the mucous acini from the accessory gland. The cells contain a large amount of secretory granules of varying electron density, which occupy the entire cytoplasm. This figure shows that the nuclei are closer to the base. (X4725).

Figure 9 :
Electron micrograph showing a mucous-secreting cell and another cell, possibly a migratory cell (M) in between the mucus cell and the basement membrane in the mucous acinus. (X6035).

Electron-microscopic observations of the venom gland show the anterior mucous gland with the mucus-secreting cell. The nuclei of the cells are towards the base and are located at the periphery. The mucus-containing vesicles are membrane-bound, and there are aggregations of these vesicles. Some of these vesicles appear to be coalescing with each other. Few mucus-secreting cells show microvilli. There is very little cytoplasm and few cytoplasmic organelles.

In the main gland, many types of cells are seen, but out of those many types, only two types are constantly observed: tall, columnar cells, and horizontal cells. The principal cell which forms the bulk of the cellular element appears as a tall, columnar cell with prominent nuclei. It shows well-developed, rough endoplasmic reticulum (RER), golgi apparatus, and microvilli. The nucleus shows evenly distributed chromatin. Two types of vesicles are seen in the cytoplasm: one membrane-bound,

empty vesicles; and the other, membrane-bound electron-dense vesicles.

The second type of cell is the horizontal cell. It is seen in between the base of the principal cells and the basement membrane. These horizontal cells are semilunar or spindle-shaped. They show a large, prominent nucleus with a thin rim of cytoplasm that has no visible cytoplasmic organelles.

The skeletal muscle fibers associated with the posterior part of the main gland are of the "twitch" variety. The elements of the sarcotubular "triad" (sarcoplasmic reticulum and the T system) are clearly seen. Mitochondrial profiles are seen closely associated with sarcoplasmic reticulum. Two types of nuclei lie within the cytoplasm of the muscle fiber, while the satellite cell lies outside the sarcolemmal membrane, but inside the basement membrane. The satellite cells are semilunar in shape, with a large nucleus that has a thin rim of cytoplasm containing very few mitochondria.

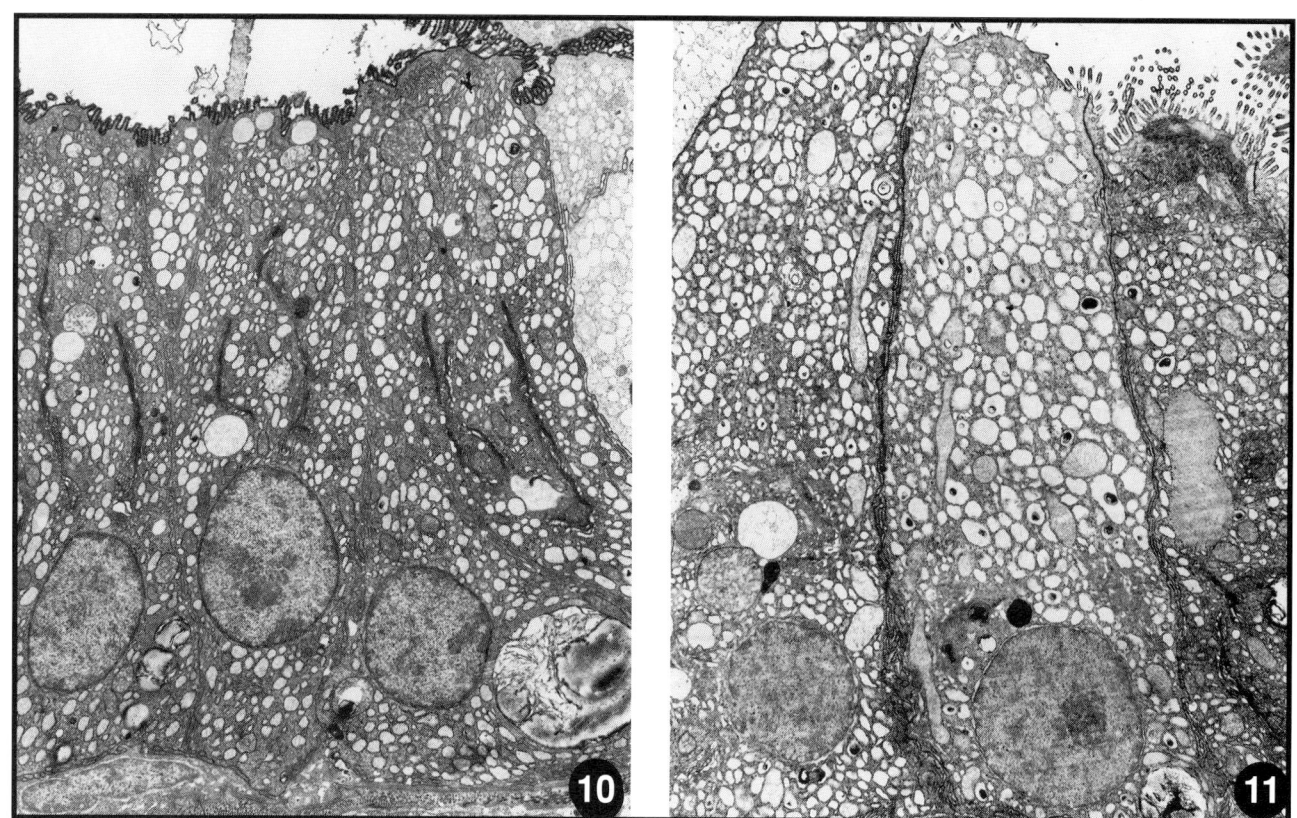

Figure 10 :
Electron micrograph showing columnar cells, a secretory epithelium from the main venom gland. The tall columnar cells have the free secretory border with some microvilli. The cytoplasm contains large number of membrane-bound vacuoles and vesicles and Golgi apparatus. (X4725).

Figure 11 :
Another region from the main venom gland showing the large number of membrane-bound vacuoles and vesicles, and also showing some vacuoles which contain electron-dense granules. (X4725).

SNAKE VENOM

Snake venom is a toxic substance produced in a highly developed secretory organ or group of cells, and one which the animal delivers during a biting act (Russell, 1980). Venom in snakes evolved as an adaptation for subduing prey. This remains the primary role of venom in nearly all snake species; venom serves only secondarily as a defensive adaptation (Minton, 1974). Another likely function of snake venom is in the digestion of the prey (Zeller, 1977; Thomas et al., 1979).

Snake venom is a complicated mixture of various substances. This mixture has attracted special attention because of the complexity of the chemical and biochemical composition of those substances, and because of the broad spectrum of their pharmacological actions. No other natural product constitutes such an effective mixture of different factors that directly influence vital body functions or that initiate autopharmacological mechanisms which can lead to the death or severe impairment of its victim.

Snake venom is colorless to a dark amber shade. It is a viscous fluid with a viscosity of 1.5 to 2.5 (Devi, 1968) and a specific gravity of 1.03 to 1.12 (Minton, 1974). You can dry snake venom in vacuum without loss of its toxicity, and you can refrigerate the dried venom for years without appreciable destruction of toxicity (Devi, 1968). Currently, freeze-drying is the method of choice for presentation and storage of venom.

RESEARCH IN SNAKE VENOMS AND TOXINS

In the past two decades, there has been an explosion of knowledge of the chemistry, biochemistry, and pharmacology of snake venoms and toxins. Snake venoms are complex mixtures, chiefly of proteins, many of which have enzymatic properties. The venoms of many snakes contain about 26 enzymes, and 10 enzymes can be found in almost all snake venoms (Russell, 1984). The mode of action of many of these venoms and toxins has been largely elucidated by the concerted efforts of

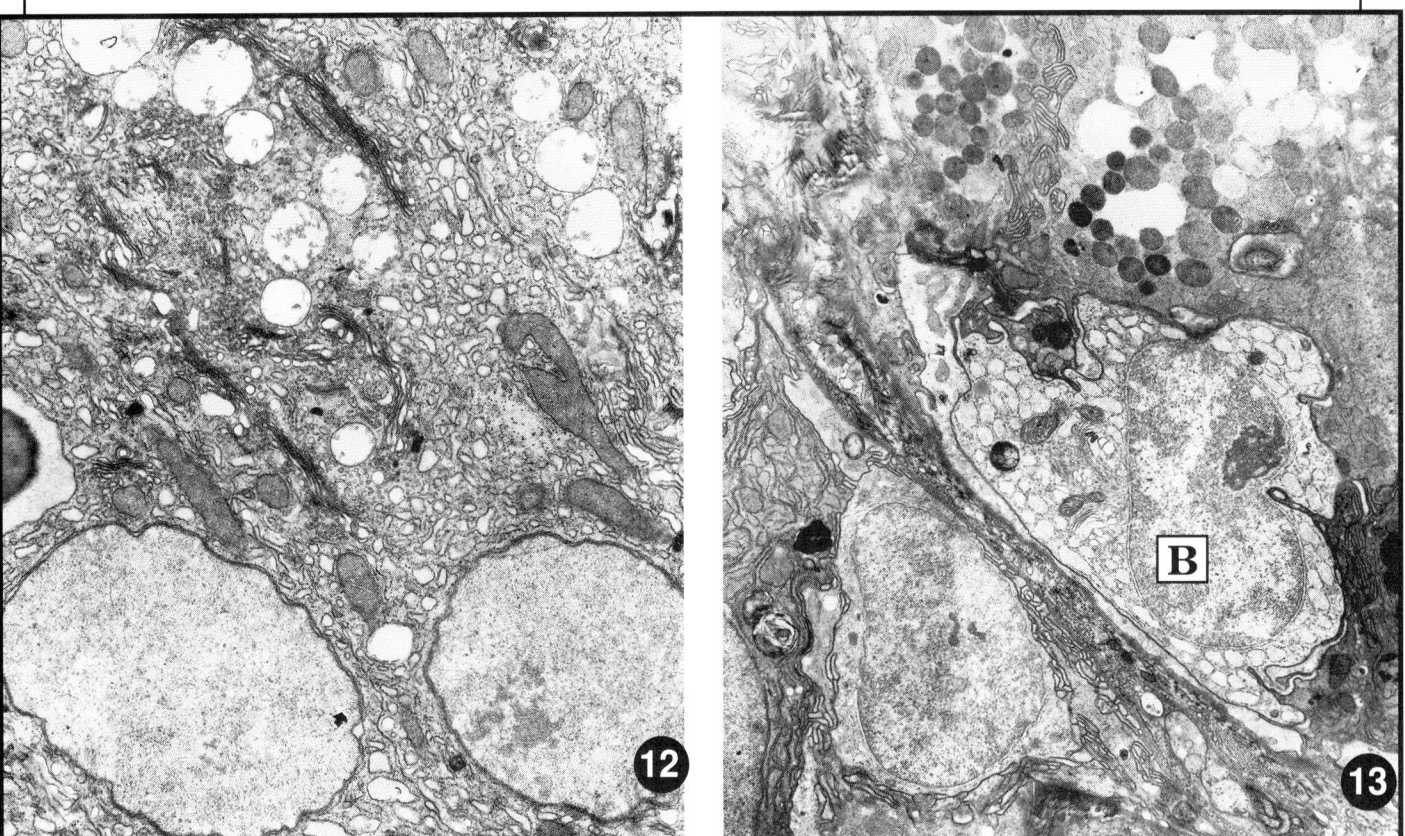

Figure 12 :
Higher-magnification electron micrograph of the basal region of the secretory cell. This figure shows the nuclei, Golgi apparatus, rough endoplasmic reticulum, membrane-bound vacuoles and vesicles, and some mitochondria. (X8500).

Figure 13 :
Appearance of the basal cell (B) in the main venom gland. The cell is triangular in shape with a well-developed nucleus and few cytoplasmic organelles (X8500).

pharmacologists, electrophysiologists, electron microscopists and biochemists.

Being one of the most concentrated enzyme sources in nature, snake venoms are valuable tools in biochemical research. Today, many bioscientists throughout the world have been using chemicals derived from snake venoms for various purposes in biological research. These chemicals include phosphodiesterase, phospholipase A2, proteinase, L-amino acid oxidase, and other enzymes. Some components from certain snake venoms (such as presynaptic neurotoxins and cardiotoxins) are of current interest as potential tools for studies of transmitter release, ion channel, and biomembrane structure. Furthermore, snake venoms can be made to serve as therapeutic agents, such as vaccines, anticoagulants and anti-cancer drugs, to fight modern diseases.

There have been many books published in the past few years, emphasizing the explosion of knowledge in this field. The following books (for com-

plete citations, see the list of references) will provide a starting point for research into details on a specific toxin or enzyme:

—Snake Venoms, Lee CY, Editor, 1979
—Snake Venom Poisoning, Russell FE, 1980
—Handbook of Toxinology, Shier TW and Mebs D, Editors, 1990
—Snake Toxins; International Encyclopaedia of Pharmacology and Therapeutics, Harvey AL, Editor, Vol. 134, 1990
—Handbook of Natural Toxins, Tu AT, Editor, Vol. 5, 1991

The following account is an overview of the chemistry of snake venom.

COMPOSITION AND PROPERTIES OF SNAKE VENOM

Snake venom has protein, as well as nonprotein, components. The protein components constitute about 90 to 95% of the dry weight of the venom. These protein components include en-

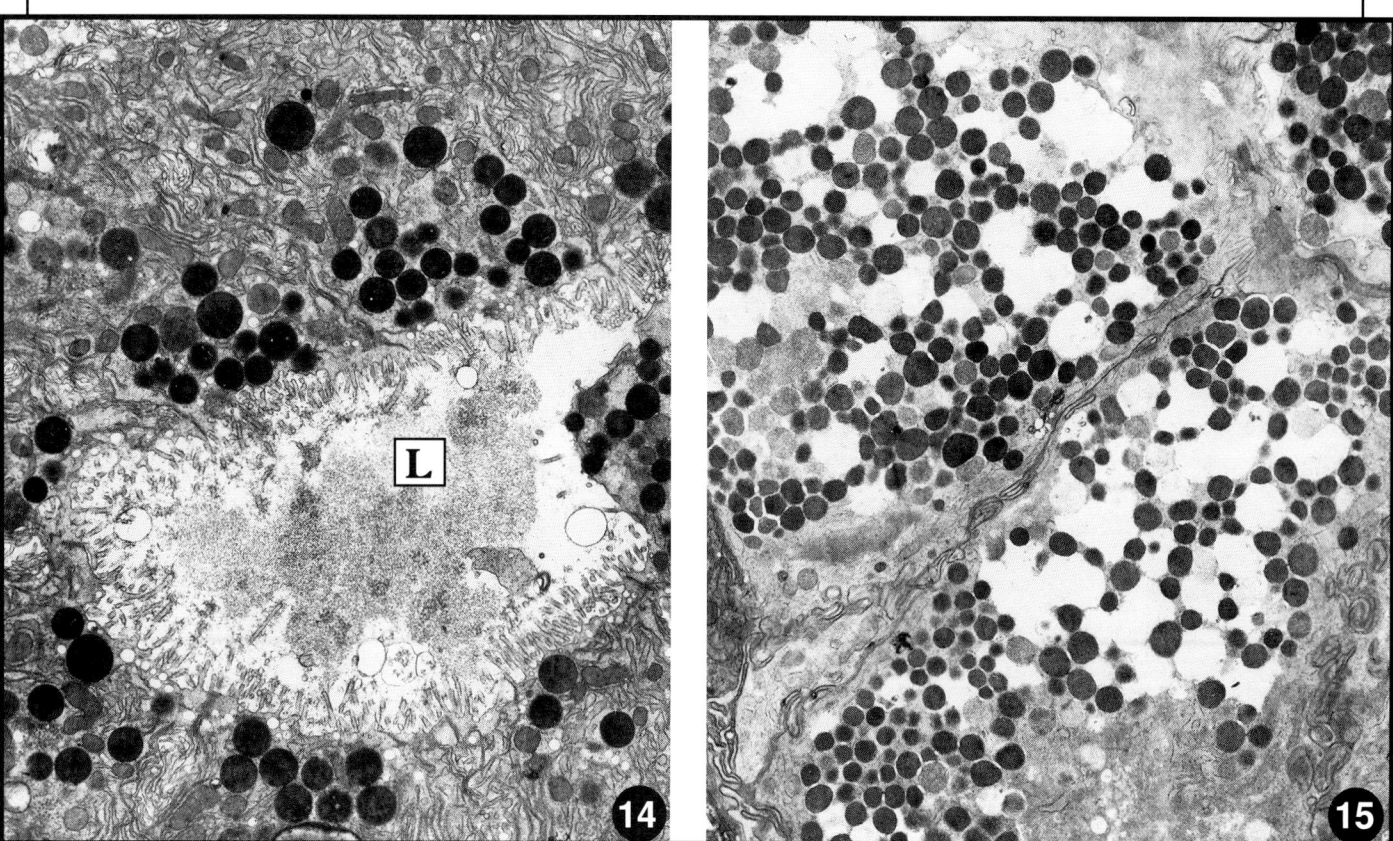

Figure 14 :
Electron micrograph of a portion of the transverse section of the duct, showing the lumen (L) of the duct. Note the venom secretion in the lumen and also the microvilli projecting into the lumen. The cells showed well-developed, rough, endoplasmic reticulum, mitochondria, and electron-dense secretory granules, closer to the apical region of the cell. The secretory granules were electron-dense, round, and membrane bound. (X1250).

Figure 15 :
Electron micrograph of a basal portion of the cells lining the duct region. You can see a large amount of granules, which are electron-dense and membrane-bound. Inbetween the granules, you can see the membrane-bound vacuoles. (X11250).

zymes and polypeptide toxins. In general, the enzymes appear to play a more important role than polypeptide toxins in the lethal action of the viperid and crotalid venoms. In constrast, the polypeptide toxins dominate the lethal actions of elapid venoms.

The minor, nonprotein components of snake venom include inorganic and organic constituents. These components have a low-molecular weight of less than 1,500 daltons. The organic constituents include free amino acids, peptides, nucleosides, carbohydrates (largely glycoproteins), lipids (phospholipids), and biogenic amines (Devi, 1968; Bieber, 1979). The inorganic constituents include sodium, calcium, potassium, magnesium, zinc, and small amounts of cobalt and nickel (Rodriguez et al., Russell, 1980). A large proportion of each of the metal ions is associated with

the protein fraction, presumably acting as enzyme cofactors.

POLYPEPTIDE TOXINS IN SNAKE VENOM

Venoms of the Elapidae usually contain large amounts of low-molecular-weight polypeptide toxins having a molecular weight of 5,000 to 10,000 daltons. They include post-synaptic (or curare-like) alpha-neurotoxins, presynaptic neurotoxins, and cardiotoxins. Snake venom neurotoxins can be classified into two groups, alpha-neurotoxins and presynaptic neurotoxins, according to their mode of action.

Alpha-neurotoxins have been isolated from venoms of many Elapidae and Hydrophiidae. Alpha-neurotoxins (or a-neurotoxins) produce a nondepolarizing neuromuscular block. These toxins produce this block by binding specifically to

222

Western Coral Snake, *Micruroides euryxanthus*. Photo by Paul Freed.

Monocled Cobra, *Naja kaouthia*. Photo by David Dube.

the post-synaptic membrane of the motor end plate. The toxin does not inhibit acetylcholine release from the motor nerve terminal into the synapse. Rather, the binding of the acetylcholine to the receptor is blocked. These toxins are thus curare-like in action.

In general, the a-neurotoxins in snake venom are basic polypeptides with isoelectric points in the vicinity of pH 9 -10 and composed of 60 - 70 amino acids. They have a molecular weight of 7000 daltons. Based on their size, they can be further divided into two distinct groups by length: the short and long a-neurotoxins. Short a-neurotoxins contain 60 - 62 amino acids, with four disulfide bonds. Long a-neurotoxins usually have 71 - 74 amino acids, with five disulfide bonds. Both long and short a-neurotoxins have been found in cobra (*Naja*) and mamba (*Dendroaspis*) venom. Only long alpha-neurotoxins have been isolated from krait (*Bungarus*) and king cobra (*Ophiophagus hannah*) venom (Lee, 1972; Yang, 1974).

The second group of neurotoxins is the presynaptic neurotoxins. These toxins produce neuromuscular blockade by acting primarily on the motor nerve endings. They decrease the frequency of the motor end-plate potentials by interfering with the release of acetylcholine from the motor nerve terminals. Their molecular weight usually

Banded Krait, *Bungarus fasciatus*. Photo by W. Wuster.

exceeds 10,000, and all of them exhibit phospholipase A2 activity. Some of the presynaptic neurotoxins also display myotoxicity. Myonecrotic toxins damage muscle fibers and can give rise to myoglobinuria.

In addition to a-neurotoxins and presynaptic toxins, venoms of the Elapidae also contain various pharmacologically active, basic polypeptides. In cobra venom, the most abundant basic polypeptide is cardiotoxin, with a molecular weight of 6,000 - 7,000. Cardiotoxins affect both excitable and nonexcitable cells. They cause irreversible depolarization of the cell membrane. By impairing the structure and function of various cells, the cardiotoxins contribute to muscle paralysis, which leads to circulatory and respiratory failure and systolic arrest (Lee, 1972).

ENZYMES IN SNAKE VENOM

Snake venoms are rich sources of water-soluble enzymes (Zeller, 1977). Many of these enzymes are hydrolases, and they possess a digestive role; Examples include: proteinases, exo- and endopeptidases, phosphodiesterases, and phospholipases. The one hydrolase that does not possess a digestive role is L-amino acid oxidase. The L-amino acid oxidase causes oxidative deamination of amino acids.

It is also generally agreed that, besides functioning in the digestion of the prey, enzymes are also involved in the toxic action of the snake venom. The enzymes may act in the following ways:

—cause local capillary damage and tissue necrosis by the actions of proteinases, phospholipases, arginine ester hydrolases, and hyaluronidases (Slotta, 1995; Suzuki and Iwanaga, 1970).

—cause diverse coagulant and anticoagulant actions by various proteinases, arginine ester hydrolases, and phospholipases A2 (Iwanaga and Suzuki, 1979).

—induce acute hypertension and pain due to release of vasoactive peptides by the kinin-releasing enzyme, kininogenase (Suzuki and Iwanaga, 1970).

In general, elapid venoms contain fewer enzymes than viperid and crotalid venoms.

Twenty-six different types of enzymes have been reported to be present in snake venoms. However, no single venom contains all 16 enzymes. Twelve enzymes are found in all venoms (Table 1), although the levels at which they are present differ markedly. The enzyme levels of viperid and crotalid venoms fall in the range 80% to 95% of the total dry matter. The enzyme levels in elapid venoms is 25 to 70% of the total dry matter (Mebs, 1968). The rest of the enzymes occur mainly in certain families, subfamilies, and genera, or they are characteristic of only a few species.

Many elapid venoms are characterized by high activity of acetylcholinesterase, an enzyme which is seldom found in viperid and crotalid venoms (Zeller, 1948). On the other hand, endopeptidase, arginine ester hydrolase, thrombinlike enzyme, and kininogenase are found in many viperid and crotalid venoms, but usually are not present in the elapid venoms (Deutsch and Diniz, 1955). Compared to the role of polypeptide toxins, the role of most enzymes in the pathophysiological action of snake venom is still not well understood.

Proteolytic enzymes

Proteolytic enzymes of molecular weight ranging from 20,000 - 95,000 daltons (Russell, 1980) are commonly found in snake venoms. The occurrence of proteolytic activity in snake venom shows some correlation to the family of snakes. The strength of the proteolytic activity has been reported to decrease in the following order: Crotalidae, Viperidae, and Elapidae (Tu, 1977). Reports have shown that the procoagulant, anticoagulant, and haemorrhagic effects of snake venom may be due to the presence of these proteolytic enzymes (Furukawa et al., 1976; Daoud et al., 1986; Civello et al., 1983; Nikai et al., 1986).

Phosphodiesterase

Phosphodiesterase, with a molecular weight of about 115,000 daltons, has been found in the venoms of most snakes. It is an orthophosphate diester phosphohydrolase that acts on deoxyribonucleic acids, ribonucleic acids, and their derivatives (Russell, 1980). It catalyses the release of 5' mononucleotide units from the polynucleotide chain in stepwise fashion from the 3'-hydroxyl end. The pharmacological role of phosphodiesterase is, however, not well understood.

Phosphomononesterase

Both specific and nonspecific phosphomonoesterases (phosphatases) are widely distributed in all families of venomous snakes. In general, these phosphomonoesterases have a molecular weight of approximately 100,000 daltons. Depending on the optimum pH of its action, the enzyme is also called an acid phosphatase or alkaline phosphatase (Tu, 1977). Thus far, there has been no reports associating any biological effect of this enzyme with the toxic action of snake venom (Russell, 1980).

Figure 16 :
Scanning electron micrograph of the fangs of various species of spitting cobras. (X50).
(a) *Naja naja sputatrix.*
(b) *Naja nigricollis.*
(c) *Hemachatus haemachatus.*
(d) *Naja melanoleuca.*

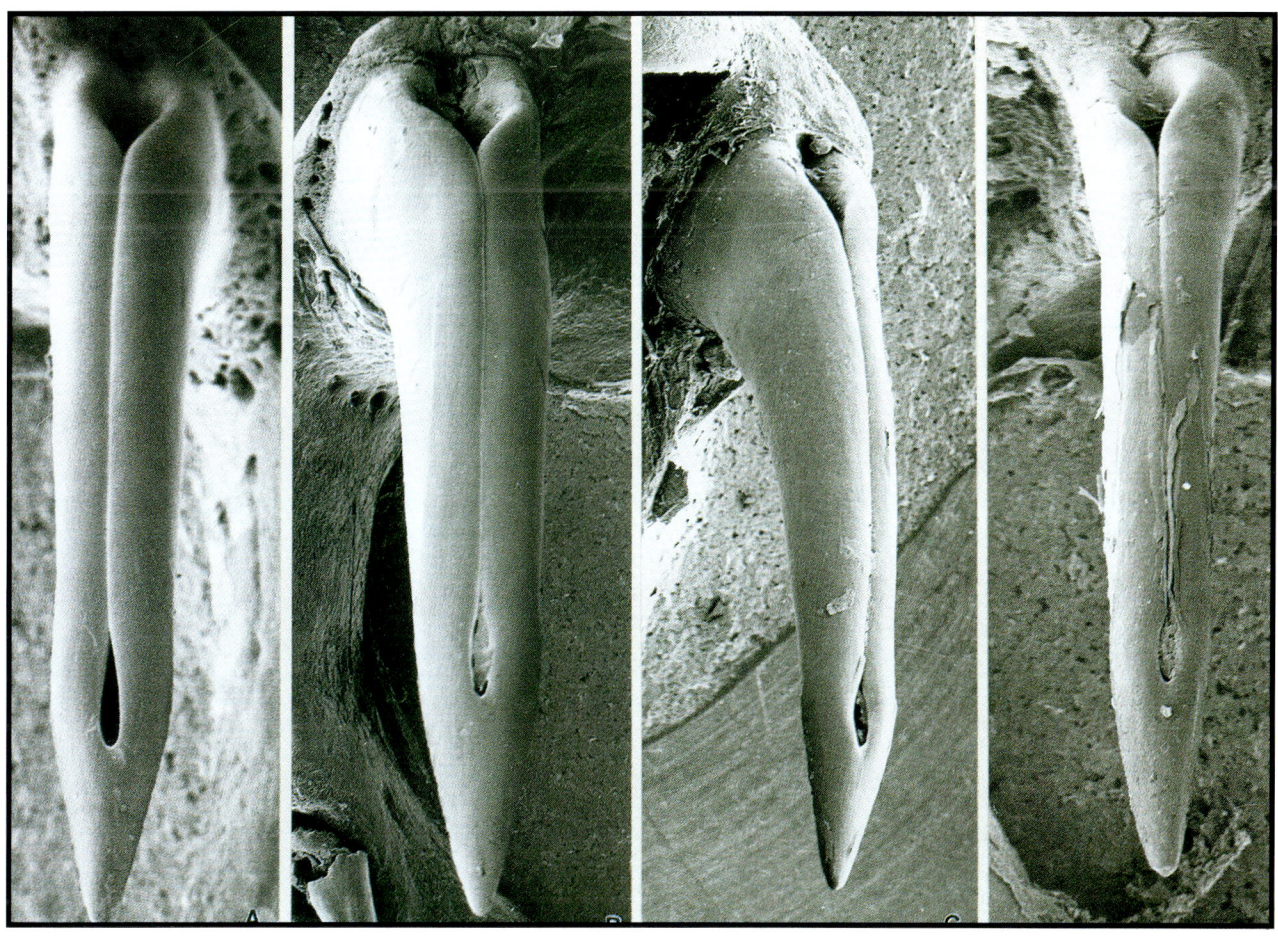

Meadow Viper, *Vipera ursini*. Photo by Zoltan Takacs.

5'-Nucleotidase

A 5'-nucleotidase is a phosphomonoesterase that specifically hydrolyses phosphate monoester. Phosphate monoester links with a 5'-position of deoxyribonucleic acid and ribonuclei acid. Most 5'-nucleotidases have a molecular weight around 100,000 daltons. Mebs (1970) reported that the 5'-nucleotidase activity is comparatively higher in viperid and crotalid venoms than in elapid venoms. Little is known of the pharmacological role of this enzyme.

Arginine ester hydrolase

All known snake-venom thrombinlike enzymes exhibit arginine ester hydrolase activity. These enzymes may also be related to the hypotensive, bradykinin-releasing and capillary permeability-increasing activities of snake venoms. Snake-venom arginine ester hydrolases usually have molecular weight of 27,000 - 30,000 daltons. They are widely distributed in the venoms of Crotalidae and Viperidae, but not in the venoms of Elapidae. It is known that arginine ester hydrolase catalyses the hydrolysis of ester or peptide linkages to which an arginine residue contributes the carboxyl group. However, the biological activities of most arginine esterases are still unknown.

Acetylcholinesterase

Acetylcholinesterase, with an approximate molecular weight of 126,000 daltons, is found only in elapid venoms, and not in viperid venoms (Zeller, 1948; Chang and Lee, 1955). Although the pharmacological role of the enzyme is not clear, it does not seem to contribute significantly to venom toxicity (Yang et al., 1960).

Phospholipase A2

Phospholipase A2 has an approximate molecular weight of 11,000-15,000 daltons (Tu et al., 1970: Iwanaga and Suzuki, 1979). This enzyme is widely distributed throughout the families Elapidae and Viperidae, and even Colubridae. Phospholipase A2 hydrolyses selectively the 2-acyl group from sn-3-phosphoglycerides. This gives rise to 1-acyl-3-sn-lysophospholipids and fatty acids.

In addition to aiding the digestion of prey (Tu, 1977), snake venom phospholipase A2 also exhibits the following effects:
—neurotoxic (Kini and Iwanaga, 1986)
—myotoxic (Fohlman and Eaker, 1977)
—cardiotoxic (Fletcher et al., 1981)
—haemolytic (Condrea et al., 1980)
—anticoagulant (Condrea et al., 1981)
—convulsant (Condrea et al., 1980)
—hypotensive (Huang and Lee, 1984)
—haemorrhagic (Condrea et al., 1980b)

It may also induce liver necrosis (Viswanath et al., 1985).

Hyaluronidase

Hyaluronidase is present in all venoms so far examined. However, it is found in higher concentrations in viperid and crotalid venoms than in elapid venoms (Zeller, 1948; Favilli, 1956). Hyaluronidase catalyses the cleavage of internal glycosidic bonds of certain acid mucopolysaccharides of animal connective tissues that serve to promote intercellular adhesion. Because the hydrolysis of hyaluronic acid facilitates toxin diffusion into the tissues of the victim (Duran-Reynals, 1939), this enzyme is also referred to as the "spreading factor." In addition, hyaluronidase may also be related to the extent of edema produced by snake venoms (Russell, 1980).

L-Amino acid oxidase

Most snake-venom L-amino acid oxidases have a molecular weight of approximately 100,000 - 130,000 daltons (Iwanaga and Suzuki, 1979). The enzyme is a flavoprotein, with a high content of amino acids (Kurht and Aurich, 1973; Ueda et al., 1988). It is responsible for the yellow colour of snake venoms. It is a nonhydrolytic enzyme which catalyses the oxidative deamination of L-

Common Viper, *Vipera berus*. Photo by W. Wuster.

amino acids to produce the corresponding oxo acids and ammonia. L-Amino acid oxidase has not been shown to have any effect on neuromuscular transmission (Russell et al., 1963).

Hemorrhagins

Hemorrhagin refers to a venomous agent which causes bleeding by a direct action on the blood vessel wall. Hemorrhagins are usually found in viperid and crotalid venoms (Tu, 1977). The only elapid venom known to have a relatively strong haemorrhagic effect is the Ophiophagus hannah (king cobra) venom (Ohsaka et al., 1966, Ohsaka, 1979).

Many snake venom hemorrhagins have been isolated in homogeneous forms. They are generally metallo-proteases with molecular weight ranging from 20,000 - 100,000 daltons (Bjarnason and Fox, 1978; Nikai et al., 1986).

Coagulant and Anticoagulant Activities

Many venoms exert profound effects on a victim's blood coagulation system. Snake venoms can generally be divided into two types: coagulant and anticoagulant venoms, depending on whether they accelerate or retard the coagulation process (Tu, 1977). Both coagulant and anticoagulant factors can also occur simultaneously in the same venom. Sometimes a venom becomes coagulant or anticoagulant, depending on the concentration used (Tu, 1977).

Various mechanisms can induce procoagulant or anticoagulant effect. A venom may act as a coagulant for the following reasons;
—It has thromboplastin activity
—It contains a factor X activator
—It can activate factor V
—It can activate prothrombin
—It has thrombinlike activity

Similarly, a venom may serve as an anticoagulant for these reasons:
—It contains fibrinolytic activity
—It has fibrinogenolytic activity
—It has inhibitory or destructive action towards any of the blood coagulation factors preceding thrombin
—It has antithrombic action (Tu, 1977)

When fibrinolytic activity is stronger than coagulant activity, clots are not observed, since the fibrin is hydrolyzed as soon as it is formed. However, when coagulant action is stronger than fibrinolytic action, a fibrin clot is first formed, and then it slowly disappears.

Thrombin-like enzyme

Thrombinlike enzyme is found in many viperid but not elapid venoms. Thrombinlike enzyme in snake venom has a molecular weight of 28,000 - 33,000 daltons (Iwanaga and Suzuki, 1979). This enzyme hydrolyses fibrinogen, but the mechanism of fibrinogen clot formation is different from that produced by thrombin. Many venom thrombinlike enzymes preferentially release only fibrinopeptide A or B (Markland and Pirkle, 1977), while thrombin releases fibrinopeptides A and B.

MAIN CLINICAL FEATURES OF SNAKE BITE (REID AND THEAKSTON, 1983)

Snake	Percentage capable of poisoning	Local Effects	Systemic Effects	Approximate natural mortality (%)	Average time to death (h)
Elapids	50 necrosis with Asian	Slow swelling, then ptosis, cobras, African spitting cobras. Usually no local effects with other elapids.	Neurotoxic effects glosso-pharyngeal palsy. Respiratory paresis. Cardiac effects.	10	5.20
Sea snakes	80	None	Myotoxic effects: myalgia on moving, paresis, myoglobinuria, hyperkalemia	10	15
Vipers	30	Rapid swelling. Necrosis in 5-10% (some vipers only).	Abnormal bleeding, non-clotting blood (some vipers only), shock.	1.15	48

TREATMENT OF VENOMOUS SNAKE BITES

GENERAL FIRST AID MEASURES

1. Do not panic. Keep calm.
2. Reassure the individual who has been bitten.
3. Lie the patient down to ensure minimal activity by the patient.
4. Keep the bitten limb at rest.
5. Wash the bite with care, because washing might disfigure or deface the original bite marks. Use an antiseptic such as povidone-iodine, if available. In some areas, authorities recommend no washing of the site since they may need to obtain traces of venom residue at or near the skin surface for testing by ELISA to determine the specific species of offending snake.
6. Apply a broad firm bandage, covering the bite area, as well as above and below the site. Tourniquets are dangerous and should not be used as a means of containing the spread of venom.
7. If the bite occurred on either an upper or lower limb, the extremity should be immobilized with splints.
8. The victim should be transported to the nearest hospital as soon as possible.
9. If the snake has been killed or captured, bring it to the hospital for identification. Do not waste time or take any unnecessary risks doing this as a good description of the snake and where the bite occurred can suffice, if necessary.

> ### Warnings
> Do not pack ice on the wound. When the ice pack is removed, reflex vasodilation can result in rapid absorption of venom. This undesired sequelae may also follow the application of arterial tourniquet.
>
> In general, do not apply a tourniquet to a snake-bite victim. Tourniquets are useful only when a patient can reach a medical authority within a few minutes after the application of the tourniquet.

TREATMENT IN THE EMERGENCY/ CASUALTY DEPARTMENT

1. Establish one or more intravenous sites in the non-bitten limb.
2. If possible, take a detailed history from the patient or companion.
3. Determine the location where the snake-bite occurred (land or sea) and obtain details of the habitat to aid in identification of the snake, if it has not been killed or captured. Ask for the color, size, and peculiar characteristics of the snake. Immediately contact the nearest Poison Control Center or a recognized expert on venomous snakebite for information of specific treatments and availability of anivenom.
4. Estimate the time interval between the incident and arrival at the hospital.
5. Remove dressings, if necessary and examine the site of the snake bite and note characteristics and pattern of the bite mark.
6. Ask the patient directly for symptoms of snake bite envenomation.
7. Perform a complete, clinical examination of the patient, noting: vital signs (temperature, pulse, respirations, blood pressure). Note carefully any signs or symptoms of either neurotoxic or hemotoxic poisoning. Shock should be treated according to protocols. Anti-venom should be adminstered immediately and according to protocols. If deemed necessary, give the patient an antitetanus toxoid.
8. Do not give any sedatives or analgesics which may depress or otherwise affect respirations and blood pressure. If necessary, tranquilize the patient with an injection of diazepam (Valiumâ).
9. Do not give the patient anything to eat or drink as this increases the risk of vomiting and consequent aspiration pneumonia. Ice chips or small sips of water may be allowed.
10. Packing the snakebite in ice is not advised because there may be subsequent rapid spread of the venom when the ice is removed and the constricted vessels vasodilate.
11. The patient should be maintained and monitored in an intensive care setting. Frequent laboratory testing is necessary, including blood cell counts (red blood cell count, platelet count, hemoglobin, hematocrit), coagulation studies (prothrombin time, activated partial thromboplastin time), urinalysis (including urine myoblobin), arterial blood gases, and blood chemistries, including electrolytes, urea (BUN), fibrinogen, fibrin degradation products, pH and glucose. All patients should have thorough cardiac and blood pressure assessment and be continously monitored, if possible. Respiratory or cardiac irregularities or arrest should be treated according to protocol.

GRADING SEVERITY OF VENOMOUS SNAKEBITES

In mild cases, there are minimal local signs, little or no swelling except at the bite site and no significant or discernible systemic or laboratory abnormalities. However, all patients with snake bites should be kept under hospital evaluation for a minimum of 24 hours.

In severe cases, pain may be great, swelling is extreme and progressive from the site, shock or impending shock may be discernible and there is laboroatroy evidence of blood cell destruction (hemolysis), prolonged coagulation time, disseminated intravascular coagulopathy (DIC) or defibrination. Neurologic signs and symptoms must be evaluated frequently. Early signs of impending neuromuscular failure incude ptosis (drooping) of the eyelid and difficulty swallowing. Elective endotracheal intubation and respiratory support must be considered when these symptoms appear.

SNAKE ANTIVENOMS

The availability of snake antivenoms depends on the location at which the patient is being treated for snake bite. To obtain an antivenom, contact your hospital's pharmaceutical department, or contact the poison-information center for the country in which the patient is being treated

In general, antivenoms should be stored in accordance with the manufacturer's recommendations. Most should be stored, protected from light, at 2°C to 8°C. They must be frozen. When an antivenom is brought to the hospital ward, you must use the serum quickly; otherwise, it will deteriorate and lose its effectiveness at room temperature.

You must also closely follow the instructions for reconstituting the lyophilized product for use. These instructions are provided in the accompanying leaflet of each antivenom ampule. The instructions may vary from country to country. Local Poison Control Centers can assist in guiding the appropriate administration and dosing of these products. Since all snakebites vary in severity as well as to species and victim, one of the best rules to follow is to administer as much as necessary, slowly and "to effect".

Before administration of horse sera-based antivenom, it is necessary to inquire from the patient whether or not he/she has had any vaccinations against tetanus or diptheria as these may have sensitized the patient to horse serum-based products and greatly increase the likelihood of anaphylaxis once the antivenom is administered. These risks are also increased in patients with a personal or family history of allergies. Patients with asthma, eczema or a history of allergic drug reactions also stand a greater chance of an allergic reaction to antivenom.

To test a patient's sensitivity to serum, follow these steps:
1. Create a 1:10 serum dilution.
2. Subcutaneously inject 0.1 ml of the dilute serum.
3. Observe the patient for 30 minutes for local and general reactions. Look for local reactions, such as wheal and flare; and watch for general anaphylactic reactions, such as pallor, sweating, nausea and vomiting, urticaria, and fall of blood pressure.
4. Local and general reactions should be countered immediately by an intramuscular injection of 1 ml of 1:1000 epinephrine (adrenaline), and with corticosteroids, which should always be kept handy.

In allergic or sensitive patients, it is better to inject the antivenom serum together with antihistamine and/or rapid-acting corticosteroids. Some authorities feel that if antivenom needs to be given anyway, it is best to dispense with sensitivity testing and administer antihistamines and corticosteroids empirically with the antivenom. It is best to administer the anti-inflammatory therapies prior to giving the antivenom.

Administration of Antivenom.

Bolus Dose. Intravenous administration of the standard dose of antivenom can be used in very serious cases of envenomation where a large, concentrated amount of antivenom is required in the shortest possible time. As a first dose, administer up to 20 ml of the reconstituted serum intravenously over 15-20 minutes. If symptoms persist, repeat the second dose 2 hours later. Following this, if symptoms still indicate persistence of venom action, repeat further doses every 6 hours, until symptoms are relieved. In the case of a viper bite, antivenoms are given in such short periods of time that patient reactions to serum (serum sickness) are likely. Because of this, antihistamines/corticosteroids may be required concurrently with the administration of serum.

Slow-Infusion Drip. When given intravenously via an infusion drip, you can adequately regulate antivenoms over a prolonged period of time. In cases where allergy is likely, you can inject antihistamines/steroids into the infusion set prophylactically. Intravenous administration should be a regulated drip over half an hour to one hour with the required dose given in 200 ml of 5% dextrose in water. Children usually respond well to doses of antivenom similar to those required by adults.

Intramuscular or Subcutaneous Injections. Intramuscular or subcutaneous injections of antivenom are never as effective as intravenous administration. However, in cases where expert medical aid is unavailable, the serum can be administered by the intramuscular or subcutaneous routes.

Anticholinesterase. In patients bitten by snakes which have venoms with a preponderence of neurotoxic action such as most Elapids, a test dose of edrophonium (Tensilonä) 10 mg may be given intravenously with 0.6 mg of atopine. If response is convincing, neostigmine should be infused.

Airway Management. Maintain a clear airway in the patient. If there is danger of bulbar or respiratory paralysis, intubate and start mechanical ventilation or ventilate via tracheostomy.

Intravenous fluids. You may administer crystalloids—and sometimes colloids—for hypotensive states. In general, crystalloids are used initially and then, after 40% of the fluid volume has been replaced, whole blood or colloids are used instead. You should monitor the ventral venous pressure to help prevent volume overload.

Surgical. Surgical debridement, split-skin grating, and broad-spectrum antibiotic cover are indicated where signs of local tissue necrosis are present. Occasionally, fasciotomy may be needed in cases of fascial compartment syndromes.

Antibiotic Therapy. Broad-specturm coverage with antibiotics is indicated to control infectious sequelae, especially if significant tissue necrosis is present.

Renal Dialysis. Some patients will have persistent renal dysfunction after rehydration, or will have generalized rhabdomyolysis, hyperkalemia, and myoglobinuria. For these patients, alkalinization of urine (e.g., mannitol) will be useful. Peritoneal dialysis/hemodialysis may be necessary if this fails to correct renal failure.

Eye Irrigation. Where snake-venom ophthalmia occurs from venom being squirted into the victim's eyes (a habit of several species of cobra), eye-irrigation with water, milk, normal saline or other bland substance is necessary. A follow-up ophthalologic evaluation is then warranted. Rarely, systemic absorption of venom occurs as a result of snake venom ophthalmia. this should be dealt with as if it were a regular snake bite envenomation where signs and symptoms indicate.

FOLLOW-UP TREATMENT SUBSEQUENT TO DISCHARGE FROM HOSPITAL

Follow-up treatment (outpatient investigations) are required for those who have received a poisonous snake bite. Follow-ups ensure that the patient's blood chemistries and hematological parameters have returned to normal. Investigations must evaluate the effect of paralysis, the recovery of the muscles, and the recovery of organs (such as kidneys). You must also look for late allergic symptoms and subsequent delayed-type hypersensitivity. The patient must be warned of the possibility of hypersensitivity if he is to receive horse-serum globulin or vaccines in the future. The wound, if sacerized for gangrene, may occasionally require surgical reconstruction.

IDENTIFICATION OF THE SNAKE

Venomous snakes constitute only a small minority of the large number of land snakes; however, all sea snakes are considered venomous. The venomous snakes can be classified according to the toxic effects of their venom :

Neurotoxic: cobras, kraits and coral snakes
Haemolytic: vipers
Neurotoxic and haemolytic: sea snakes

If the snake is available for identification, follow these steps:
1. Confirm with the patient whether the snake is truly dead.
2. Use a set of colored charts for gross identification of the snake.

If the snake is not available for identification, follow these steps to try to identify the snake:
1. Get a detailed description of the snake from the patient and any eye witnesses..
2. Identify the location at which the snake-bite occurred to separate land snakes from sea snakes. The habitat will also suggest the type of snake.
3. Examine the bite marks, which may indicate whether it is a venomous or nonvenomous snake.
4. Determine the type of poisoning the patient is experiencing: neurotoxic, hemolytic or both. This may help in the identification of the snake.

PRECAUTIONS TO AVOID SNAKE BITES

Ninety-five percent of snake bites occur on the lower limbs. To avoid snake bites, you should be careful to protect your feet and legs when venturing into snake-infested terrains. Follow these precautions:

—Always wear thick, heavy shoes and long, loose trousers when walking through undergrowth and bushes.

—Use a flashlight to focus onto the ground ahead of you so that you can see where you are stepping.

—Beat the ground with a long stick as you walk. The vibrations will tell nearby snakes that you are coming, and they will usually then slither away without confrontation.

—Never pick up or handle any snake, dead or alive. "Dead" reptiles have a way of coming to life when handled.

—Never step over a pile of rocks or logs, etc. as there can be snakes on the blind side.

—Never put your hands into thick grass or hollow logs.

—Spread sulfur powder around the perimeter of your tent when you are camping. This may help to repel snakes during the night.

—When camping, always shake your clothes and shoes before putting them on.

—When confronted by a snake, stay calm and immobile. Snakes seldom attack without provocation.

—Do not try to disturb, attack, or kill an unoffending snake. Keep your distance and slowly move away from it. Snakes usually strike in self-defence; they prefer escape to engagement if given a good margin of distance.

—Do not swim in shallow water and river mouths known to be inhabited by snakes.

—Do not attempt to grab or poke at a nearby snake, as this could easily provoke an attack. Sea snakes are well known for their vindictive nature.

—If you encounter large numbers of sea snakes, try to avoid them by going around the group or possibly by going under them if they are on the surface.

—When bitten by a snake, keep calm and walk for help if you are alone. Never run for help. Running serves to speed up the action of the venom.

PREVENTING SNAKES FROM ENTERING HOUSES

Snakes are usually encountered after heavy rains, when they leave their hiding places (commonly vacated rat burrows, crevices and trees) in search of drier and more sheltered areas. Also, during breeding periods, young snakes can move great distances, and they are usually attracted to areas with an abundance of food (such as rats, chickens, etc.). Take the following precautions to help discourage snakes from taking up residence in or near a house:

Indian Cobra, *Naja naja*. Photo by R. T. Zappalorti.

—Make sure that grass is well-kept and regularly trimmed.

—Remove all unwanted timber and rubbish to deny snakes nearby hiding places.

—Use good hygiene and cleanliness procedures to minimize the rodent population, as they tend to attract snakes.

—Note that rearing chickens, pigeons, and other small animals may attract snakes since they are a source of food for snakes.

—Regularly drain and clean nearby ponds and keep the perimeter free of tall grass. Improperly kept ponds harbor frogs, toads and fish, which in turn attract snakes.

—Make sure that all doors are close-fitting. The slit along the bottom of each door should have as narrow a slit as possible.

—Cut off all overhanging branches of trees which are in contact with roofs, balconies, windows, and walls.

REFERENCES AND RECOMMENDED READING

—**Aloof-Hirsch S, De-Vries A and Berger A, (1968).**
The direct lytic factor of cobra venom: purification and chemical characterization. Biochim. Biophys. Acta 154, 53-60.

—**Aye Maung Maung**
"Snakes of Burma with Venomology and Envenomation." M.Sc thesis, Rangoon University, Burma, 1976.

—**Bdolah A (1979).**
The venom gland of snakes and venom secretion. In "Snake Venoms", Ed. C Y Lee. Pubs Springer-Verlag, Berlin, Heidelberg, New York, pp. 41-57.

—**Bergmeyer HV, (1983).**
L-Amino acid oxidase. In : Methods in enzymatic analysis. Vol.2, pp. 149-150.

—**Weinheim: Verlag Chimie, GmbH. Bieber AL, (1979).**
Metal and non-protein constituents in snake venoms. In : Snake venoms. Handbook of experimental pharmacology. Vol. 52, pp. 295-306. Lee C.Y. (ed.) Springer-Verlag, Berlin.

—**Bjarnason JB and Fox JW (1987).**
Characterization of two hemorrhagic zinc proteinase, toxin-c and toxin-d from western diamondback rattlesnake (*Crotalus atrax*) venom. Biochim. Biophys. Acta. 911, 356-363.

—**Borkow G and Ovadia M (1992).**
Inhibition of Sendai virus by various snake venom. Life Sciences. 51:1261-1267.

—**Chang CC and Lee CY (1955).**
Cholinesterase and anticholinesterase activities in snake venom. J. Formosan. Med. Assoc. 54, 103-112.

—**Condrea E, Yang CC and Rosenberg P (1980a).**
Comparison of a relatively toxic phospholipase A_2 from *Naja nigricollis* snake venom with that of a relatively non-toxic phospholipase A_2 from *Hemachatus haemachatus* snake venom. I. Enzymactic activities on free and membrane bound substrates. Biochem. Pharmac. 29, 1555-1563.

—**Condrea E, Yang CC and Rosenberg P (1980b).**
Comparison of a relatively toxic phospholipase A_2 *Naja nigricollis* snake venom with that of a relatively non-toxic phospholipase A_2 from Hemachatus haemachatus snake venom. II. Pharmacological properties in relationship to enzymatic activity. Biochem. Pharmac. 29, 1564-1574.

—**Condrea E, Yang CC and Rosenberg P (1981).**
Lack of correlation between anticoagulant activity and phospholipid hydrolysis by snake venom phospholipase A_2. Thromb. Haemast. 45, 82-85.

—**Curti B, Massey V and Zmudka M (1968).**
Inactivation of snake venom L- amino acid oxidase by freezing. J. Biol. Chem. 243, 2306-2314.

—**Daoud E, Tu AT and El-Asmar MF, (1986).**
Isolation and characterization of an anticoagulant proteinase, cerastase F-4 from *Cerastes cerastes* (Egyptian sand viper) venom. Thromb. Res. 42, 55-62.

—**Deutsch HF and Diniz CR (1955).**
Some proteolytic activities of snake venoms. J. Biol. Chem. 216, 17-26.

—**Devi A (1968).**
The protein and non-protein constituents of snake venoms. In : Venomous animals and their venom. Vol. 1, pp.119-165. Bucherl W, Buckley EE and Deulofeu V. (eds). Academic Press, London and New York.

—**Dimitrov GD and Kankonkar RC (1968).**
Fractionation of *Vipera russelli* venom by gel filtration-II. Comparative study of yellow and white venom of *Vipera russelli* with special reference to the local necrotizing and lethal actions. Toxicon. 5, 283-288.

—**Duran-Reynals F (1939).**
A spreading factor in certain snake venoms and its relation to their mode of action. J. Exp. Med. 69, 81.

—**Favilli G (1956).**
Occurrence of spreading factors and some properties of hyaluronidases in animal parasites and venoms. In : Venom. Buckley EE and Porges N (Eds.). pp.28-289. American Association for the Advancement of Science, Washington, D.C.

—**Fletcher JE, Rapuano BE, Condrea E, Yang CC and Rosenberg P (1981).**
Relationship between catalysis and toxicological properties of three phospholipase A_2 from elapid snake venoms. Toxic. Appl. Pharmac. 59, 375-388.

—**Fohlman J and Eaker O (1977).**
Isolation and characterization of a lethal myotoxic phospholipase A_2 from the venom of the common sea snake Enhydrina schistosa causing myoglobinuria in mice. Toxicon. 15, 385-393.

Furukawa Y, Matsunaga Y and Hagashi K (1976).
Purification and characterization of a coagu-

lant protein from the venom of Russell's Viper. Biochim. Biophys. Acta. 453, 48-61.

—**Gopalakrishnakone P, Chou LM, Aye MM, Lim FLK,Cheng CT, Lim SK and Anantharaman S (1990).**
Snake bites and their treatment. Pubs. Singapore University Press, Kent Ridge, Singapore, pp 53.

—**Gopalakrishnakone P, Wollberg M and Kochva E (1994).**
In: Sea snake toxinology (Ed : P. Gopalakrishnakone). Pubs. Singapore University Press, NUS, pp. 37-65.

—**Harvey AL (1990).**
Cytolytic toxins. In : Handbook of toxinology. pp.1-66. ShierWT and Mebs D (eds). Marcel Dekker, Inc., New York and Basel.

—**Harvey AL (ed) (1990).**
Snake toxins. International encyclopaedia of pharmacology and therapeutics, Vol. 134, Pergamon Press, NewYork, pp. 460.

—**Hider RC, Karlsson E and Namiranian S (1991).**
Snake toxins. In : International encyclopedia of pharmacology and therapeutics. Section 134, pp.1-34. Harvey AL (ed). Pergamon Press, NewYork.

—**Iwanaga S and Suzuki T (1979).**
Enzymes in snake venom. In : Handbook of experimental pharmacology. Vol. 52, pp. 61-158. Lee CY (ed). Springer-Verlag, NewYork.

—**Kini RM and Iwanaga S (1986).**
Structure-function relationship of phospholipase : prediction of presynaptic neurotoxicity. Toxicon. 24, 527-542.

—**Klemmer K (1968).**
Classification and distribution of European, North African and North and West Asiatic venomous snakes. In :Venomous animals and their venoms. Vol. 1 : pp.309-325. Bucherl W, Buckley EE and Deulofeu V (Eds.). Academic Press, London and New York.

—**Kochva E (1987).**
The origin of snakes and evolution of the venom apparatus. Toxicon 25(1), 65-106.

—**Kochva E (1978).**
The origin of snakes and evolution of the venom apparatus. Toxicon. 9, 43-51.

—**Kornalik F and Master RWP (1964).**
A comparative examination of yellow and white venom of *Vipera ammodytes*. Toxicon. 2, 109-115.

—**Kurth J and Aurich H (1973).**
Purification and some properties of L- amino acid oxidase from the venom of sand viper (*Vipera ammodytes*). Acta. Bio. Med. Ger. 31, 641-653.

—**Lee CY (1972).**
Chemistry and pharmacology of polypeptide toxins in snake venoms. Ann. Rev. Pharmacol. 12, 265-281.

—**Lee CY (Ed) (1979).**
Snake venoms. Springer-Verlag, Berlin, Heidelberg, NewYork, pp 1130.

—**Lim BL (1990).**
Venomous land snakes of Malaysia. In : Snakes of medical importance (Asia-Pacific region). pp.387-417. Gopalakrishnakone P and Chou LM (eds). Venom and Toxin Research Group and International Society on Toxinology, Singapore.

—**Markland FS and Pirkle H (1977).**
Thrombin-like enzyme from the venom of *Crotalus adamanteus* (eastern diamondback rattlesnake).Thrombosis Res. 10, 487-494.

—**Mebs D (1969).**
Preliminary studies on small molecular toxic compounds of elapid venoms. Toxicon. 6, 247-253.

—**Mebs D (1970).**
A comparative study of enzyme activities in snake venoms. Int. J. Biochem. 1, 355-342.

—**Minton SA Jr (1974).**
Snake and snake venoms. In : Venom diseases. pp. 107-144. I. Newton Kuyelmass (ed). Charles C Thomas (pub.), Illinois, USA.

—**Mirtschin PJ, Crowe GR and Davis R (1990).**
Dangerous snakes of Australia. In : Snakes of medical importance (Asia-Pacific region). pp. 1-173. Gopalakrishnakone P and Chou LM (eds.).Venom andToxin Research Group and International Society on Toxinology, Singapore.

—**Nikai T, Oguri E, Kishida M, Sugihara H, Mori N andTu AT, 1986.**
Reevaluation of hemorrhagic toxin, HR-1, from *Agkistrodon halys blomhoffi* venom : proof of a proteolytic enzyme. Int. J. Biochem. 18, 103-108.

—**Ohsaka A, Omari-Satoh T, Kondo S and Murata R (1966).**
Biochemical and pathological aspects of hemorrhagic principles in snake venoms with special reference to Habu (*Trimeresurus flavoviridis*) venom. Mem. Inst. Butantan. Simp. Internac. 33, 193-205.

—**Ohsaka A (1979).**
Hemorrhagic, necrotizing and edema-forming effects of snake venoms. In : Snake venoms. Handbook of experimental pharmacology. Vol. 52 : pp. 480-546. Lee C.Y. (ed), Springer-Verlag, Berlin.

233

—Oshima G, Omori-Satoh T, Iwanaga S and Suzuki T (1972).
Studies on snake venom hemorrhagic factor I (HR-I) in the venom of Agkistrodon halys blomhoffii. Its purification and properties. J. Biochem. 72, 1483-1444.

—Phelps T (1981).
Poisonous snakes. Blandford Press, Dorset. Reid HA and Theakston RDG. "The Management of Snake Bite." Bulletin of the World Health Organization 1983 61(6) : 885-895.

—Rieppel O (1979).
A cladistic classification of primitive snakes based on skull structure. Z. Zool. Syst. Evol Forsch. 17, 140-150.

—Rodriguez OG, Scannone HR and Parra ND (1974).
Enzymatic activities and other characteristics of *Crotalus durissus cumanensis* venom. Toxicon 12, 297-302.

—Russell FE, Buess FW, Woo MY and Eventon R (1963).
Zootoxicological properties of venom L-amino acid oxidase. Toxicon 1, 229-234.

—Russell FE (1980).
Chemistry and pharmacology of snake venom. In : Snake venom poisoning pp. 139-234. Scholium International Inc., New York.

—Russell FE (1980).
Snake venom poisoning. Scholium International, Inc. New York, USA, pp. 562.

—Shier TW and Mebs D (ed), (1990).
Handbook of toxinology. Marcel Dekker Inc., New York and Basel, pp. 814.

—Skarnes RC (1970).
L-Amino acid oxidase, a bactericidal system. Nature 225, 1072-1073.

—Slotta K (1955).
Chemistry and biochemistry of snake venoms. Prog. Chem. Org. Nat. Prod. 12, 406-465.

—Stiles BG, Sexton FW and Weinstein SA (1991).
Antibacterial effects of different snake venoms : purification and characterization of antibacterial proteins from *Pseudechis australis* (Australian king brown or mulga snake) venom. Toxicon 29, 1129-1141.

—Suzuki T and Iwanaga S (1970).
Snake venoms. Bradykinin, Kallidin and Kallikrein. In : Handbook of experimental pharmacology. Vol. 25, pp. 193-213. Erdos, EG (ed). Springer, Berlin-Heidelberg, New York, Springer.

—Thomas RG and Pough FH (1979).
The effect of rattlesnake venom on digestion of prey. Toxicon 17, 221-228.

—Tu AT, Passey RB and Too PM (1970).
Isolation and characterization of phospholipase A$_2$ from sea snake, *Laticauda semifasciata*, venom. Arch. Biochem. Biophys. 140, 96-106.

—Tu AT (1977).
In : Venoms : Chemistry and molecular biology. pp 1- 153. John Wiley and Sons, Inc., New York.

—Tu AT (ed) (1991).
Handbook of natural toxins, Vol. 5. Reptile venoms and toxins, Marcel Dekker Inc., New York, Basel, Hong Kong, pp. 826.

—Tweedie MWF.
The Snakes of Malaya 3rd ed. Singapore National Printers (Pte) Ltd. 1983.

—Ueda M, Chang CC and Ohno M (1988).
Purification and characterization of L-amino acid oxidase from the venom of *Trimeresurus mucrosquamatus* (Taiwan habu snake). Toxicon 26, 695-706.

—Viswanath BS, Kini RM and Godwa TV (1985).
Purification of an edema inducing phospholipase A$_2$ from *Vipera russelli* venom and its interaction with aristolochic acid. Toxicon 23, 617-625.

—Warrell DA.
"Snakes" in Hunters Tropical Medicine Textbook 6th ed. W. B. Saunders and Company, 1984.

—Warrell DA (1990).
Treatment of snake bite in the Asia-Pacific region - A personal view. In : "Snakes of Medical Importance - Asia-Pacific Region". Ed. P. Gopalakrishnakone and LM Chou. Pubs. VTRGp, National University of Singapore, pp. 641-670.

—Webb JE, Wallwork JA and Elgood JH, 1978.
In : Guide to living reptiles. pp. 118-151. The Macmillan Press Ltd., London and Basingstoke.

—Yang CC, Chiu WC and Kao KC (1960).
Biochemical studies on snake venoms. VII. Isolation of venom cholinesterase by zone electrophoresis. J. Biochem. 48, 706-713.

—Yang CC, 1974.
Chemistry and evolution of toxins in snake venom. Toxicon. 12, 1-43.

—Zeller EA, 1948.
Enzymes of snake venoms and their biological significance. Adv. Enzymol. 8, 459-495.

—Zeller EA, 1972.
Snake venom actions : are enzymes involved in it? Experientia 30, 143-284.

WORLDWIDE CONSERVATION BREEDING OF THREATENED REPTILIAN SPECIES

Craig Hassapakis
Founder, Editor, and Publisher
AMPHIBIAN AND REPTILE CONSERVATION
The International Journal Devoted to the Worldwide Preservation
and Management of Amphibian and Reptilian Diversity
2255 North University Parkway Suite 15
Provo Utah 84604-7506 USA
Tel: (801) 375-1620
Email: ARC@byu.edu

Craig Hassapakis obtained his Bachelor of Science degree in zoology from Brigham Young University in 1988. He continued his interest in herpetology (as an independent researcher at Brigham Young University) focusing on captive population management and conservation of amphibians and reptiles. This work led to this resource chapter and a new journal, Amphibian and Reptile Conservation—The International Journal Devoted to the Worldwide Preservation and Management of Amphibian and Reptilian Diversity, *for which he is the founder, editor, and publisher. His research interests include herpetological diversity, distribution, and conservation of reptiles and amphibians worldwide, the wildlife trade, chemical communication, animal behavior, captive population management and the role of captive breeding programs for* ex-situ *preservation of threatened species, particularly reptiles and amphibians.*

INTRODUCTION

The field of reptilian conservation encompasses scientific, economic, and policy and a substantial body of literature and disciplines. This review provides selected bibliographical references in the areas of biological conservation, reptilian conservation (for each taxonomic family), populations in the wild and captivity, the wildlife trade, re-introduction of captive animals to the wild, legislation, small population management, software for small population management and field work, and species management plans. A brief action plan for private sector contributions to conservation breeding is proposed. Nine appendices and 5 tables summarize the status of reptilian species and list the US Fish and Wildlife Service (USFWS) recovery plans for reptiles

BIOLOGICAL CONSERVATION

Conservation of biodiversity is concerned with the preservation of genetic uniqueness of all life. To reach this goal it is imperative that entire ecological processes be preserved. Without healthy, functioning ecosystems, all life to some degree is threatened. While trying to *save* a single species from extinction is commendable, it is much more important to save ecosystem processes which support all life. When keeping species in captivity for any purpose (conservation breeding or propagation), one must never forget the animal's connection to its natural habitat.

Habitat is the physical environment in space and time where wild animals and plants live out their lives. Destruction of any part of the animal's habitat often results in population declines. Some animals thrive in disturbed habitats but most need specific requirements to maintain healthy and viable populations. Any disruption of their habitat, social structure, or food supply will most likely lead to a decline in population numbers. If the population numbers of the species become low enough, then it can be defined as threatened with extinction and will need outside help to exist. The World Conservation Union (IUCN) [IUCN 1987a] has determined that any species falling below 1,000 in number are good candidates for intervention with captive breeding. If population numbers of the species in the wild are known (often they are not), low enough, and the species is one deemed important to save, then outside help comes to the rescue in the form of captive breeding. It is wiser to maintain the proper functioning of habitat and wild populations in nature than to intervene with captive breeding and its practical difficulties and financial implications

(Conway 1986). Knowing where the animals are and in what numbers is the best place to start any species conservation effort.

Captive breeding is only one aspect of species conservation. No captive breeding project should be conducted in isolation if conservation is the intended goal. Captive breeding specialists need to complement their efforts with other breeders and projects by cooperative coordination to maximize effectiveness. The ultimate goal should be to recreate self-sustaining wild populations. This only, can then be labeled *conservation breeding* (Ebenhard 1995; Hutchins and Wiese 1991; Wiese and Hutchins 1994).

Fig. 2
Flat-tailed Gecko, *Uroplatus* sp? A newly found and yet to be described *Uroplatus* lizard species found in Madagascar. Many species new to science are being found there each year. Photo by W.B. Love/Blue Chameleon Ventures

Fig. 1
New Caledonia Bumpy Gecko, *Rhacodactylus auriculatus*. A common New Caledonian gecko now being bred in captivity. It grows to about 6-7 inches in total length. Photo by W.B. Love/Blue Chameleon Ventures

Conservation International (CI) has constructed a Global Biodiversity Hotspots Map, which shows that more than 50 percent of the earth's terrestrial biodiversity is found within these hotspots, which cover only 1.32 percent of the planet's land surface. Almost 40 percent of all terrestrial plants and 25 percent of terrestrial vertebrate species are endemic to these areas (i.e. found nowhere else). The top 17 priority global biodiversity hotspots, with their respective number of reptile and amphibian species, are: (1) The tropical Andes (Venezuela, Colombia, Ecuador, Peru, and Bolivia) [558] (2) Meso-American forests [400] (3) The island of Madagascar [450] (4) Cape and Western Cape floristic region (South Africa) [66] (5) Antilles [148] (6) Western Sundaic region (Indonesia, Malaysia, and Brunei) [108] (7) Philippines [175] (8) Atlantic Coastal Forest region (Brazil, Paraguay, and Argentina) [260] (9) Brazil's Cerrado [under final study] (10) The Darién (Panama), the Chocó (Colombia-Ecuador), and

Western Ecuador [304] (11) Polynesia and Micronesian Island complex, including Hawaii and Fiji [11] (12) Eastern Sundaic region (Indonesia) [58] (13) Southwestern Australia [47] (14) Mediterranean region [11] (15) Western Ghats (India) & the island of Sri Lanka [253] (15) New Caledonia [48] and (16) Guinean forests of Western Africa (under final study) [97]. Approximately 3,000 species of reptiles and amphibians could be protected in only 1.32 percent of the earth's land surface. Management of these areas could protect between 25 to 30 percent, or more, of the world's herpetofauna in less than two percent of the land surface. In just the top ten Hotspots, 2,714 species could be protected in only 0.72 percent of the earth's land surface. More research should be committed to determining *reptilian Hotspots*, so conservation of these areas can maximize preservation efforts.

The countries with 10 or more threatened reptilian species are Australia (37), USA (28), Myanmar (20), Indonesia and South Africa (19), Mexico (18), Madagascar (17), India and Thailand (16), China, Brazil , and Columbia (15), Venezuela (14), Malaysia (14), Bangladesh (13), Turkey, Ecuador, and Viet Nam (12), New Zealand (11), and Papua New Guinea and Dominican Republic (10) [IUCN 1996].

The nature of habitat loss and destruction is of a global scale. Those interested in contributing to conservation efforts should try to focus on species preservation from a worldwide perspective. This could start by the understanding of a species' country geography, factors involved in habitat destruction, local and country economies, environmental conditions, as well as location, distribution and number of species and how these factors relate to ecosystem preservation. A significant contribution to this holistic understanding of ecosystems and species preservation comes through further education, for which this chapter introduces.

Bibliographic Summaries. Some of the references do not deal specifically with reptiles, but do provide an excellent general background that can be applied to reptile populations and conservation. This selected bibliography should be a considered starting point or introduction to the literature. Overlaps in subject matter do occur because some publications cover more than one topic.

Selected Bibliography—Biological Conservation. General (Soulé 1986; Majumdar et al. 1994; WCMC and Groombridge 1994; Western and Pearl

Fig. 3
Rhinoceros Iguana (juvenile), *Cyclura cornuta.* **This species is a member of the most endangered group of lizard species in the world. It is only found on Hispaniola in the Caribbean Sea. Photo by W.B. Love/Blue Chameleon Ventures**

1989; Wilson and Peter 1988). Global Biodiversity Strategies (Groombridge 1992b; IUCN et al. 1993; WRI et al. 1992). Global Biodiversity Assessment (Haywood 1995). Protected Areas (IUCN 1992; IUCN et al. 1992). Hotspots (Myers 1990). Rainforests (Newman 1990; Robinson and Redford 1991). Science for Conservation (Tudge 1991; Tudge 1992; Moore et al. 1992; Hutchins 1988).

REPTILIAN CONSERVATION

It is estimated that of the 6000 plus species of known living reptiles, only 20 percent have received adequate conservation evaluation for threat determination and status in the wild (Groombridge 1993). Of the 4,014 named amphibian species listed in Frost (1985), about 700 are reportedly known only from the type locality. Many species have yet to be col-

lected, described by science or have become extinct unnoticed. Changes in taxonomy, especially at the species level, have a significant effect on the data presented. Estimates of threatened reptilian taxa are highly underestimated. Not all reptile species have been assessed, but of those that have been evaluated, rough estimates of the percent that are threatened are 20% (IUCN 1996). Table 1 is provided to give a general picture of the possible deficiencies in estimating the threat to reptilian species from different sources.

The categories used in the IUCN Red Lists are defined in IUCN/SSC (1994), and detailed in Mace and Lande (1991), Mace (1994), and explained in Stattersfield (1996). The 1996 IUCN Red List of Threatened Animals include 428 reptilian species (20 extinct, 1 extinct in the wild, 41 critically endangered, 59 endangered, 153 vulnerable, 1 least concern: conservation dependent, 79 least concern: near threatened, and 74 data deficient) [IUCN 1996] (a). The IUCN 1994 Red List record 316 reptilian species in five threat categories (47 endangered, 88 vulnerable, 79 rare, 43 indeterminate and 59 insufficiently known) [Groombridge 1993] (b). The Convention on International Trade in Endangered Species of Wild Fauna and Flora (CITES), the treaty that regulates the international trade of endangered species, include 478 species [WCMC 1995] (d). The United States include 102 species of reptiles on the US Endangered Species List [USFWS 1994b] (h).

THREATENED SPECIES KEPT AND/OR BRED IN CAPTIVITY

In Captivity. The private sector and/or zoological parks and institutions keep 1,010 different

Fig. 4
Reticulate Gila Monster, *Heloderma suspectum suspectum.* **This popular species is held in captivity by numerous zoos and individuals. Found in the southwestern United States and one of only two venomous species of lizards in the world. Photo by W.B. Love/ Blue Chameleon Ventures**

TABLE 1

THREATENED REPTILES

Source	Status	Reptiles	Lizards	Snakes	Chelons	Crocs	Tuatars
	EX	20	11	3	6	0	0
	EW	1	1	0	0	0	0
	Subtotal	21	12	3	6	0	0
	CR	41	15	12	10	4	0
a	EN	59	15	13	28	3	0
	VU	153	66	25	58	3	1
	Subtotal	253	96	50	96	10	1
	LR:cd	1	0	0	1	0	0
	LR:nt	79	23	9	47	0	0
	DD	74	35	13	23	3	0
	Totals	428	166	75	173	13	1
	E	47	18	10	11	7	1
	V	88	47	15	21	5	0
b	R	79	45	24	9	0	1
	I	43	18	11	14	0	0
	K	59	21	11	27	0	0
	Totals	316	149	71	82	12	2
c	Totals	547	272	139	111	15	2
d	Totals	478	258	117	78	23	2
	Totals	878	335	338	182	22	1
e	Totals	1010	431	378	179	21	1
	Bred	337	131	115	84	6	1
	I	69	16	12	24	15	2
f	II	368	220	90	52	6	0
	III	20	0	13	7	0	0
	Totals	457	236	115	83	21	2
	E	74	18	11	28	16	1
g	T	23	9	6	6	2	0
	Totals	97	27	17	34	18	1
	E	76	20	9	28	18	1
h	T	29	13	6	8	2	0
	Totals	102	30	15	36	20	1
	E	9	1	0	3	5	0
	V	9	3	1	3	2	0
	R	7	2	3	1	0	1
i	I	5	1	2	2	0	0
	K	5	0	5	0	0	0
	T	1	0	1	0	0	0
	r	1	2	1	0	2	0
	Totals	40	8	13	9	9	1
	E	10	1	0	5	4	0
	V	21	8	2	8	3	0
	R	7	1	1	4	0	1
j	I	7	3	3	1	0	0
	K	11	0	4	7	0	0
	T	0	0	0	0	0	0
	Totals	55	13	10	24	7	1

TABLE 1 - SOURCE KEY
(a) - 1996 IUCN RED LIST (IUCN 1996), **(b)** - 1994 IUCN RED LIST (Groombridge 1993), **(c)** - WORLD CHECK-LIST (WCMC 1993), **(d)** - CITES CHECKLIST (WCMC 1995), **(e)** - ISIS (ISIS 1995), **(f)** - SLAVEN'S REPORT (Slavens and Slavens 1994). **(g)** - USFWS COMBINED SPECIES REPORT (USFWS/DLE 1995), **(h)** - CITES SPE-CIES LIST [50 CFR 17.11 & 17.12] (USFWS 1994b), **(i)** - RARE REPTILES IN CAPTIVITY (Olney et al. 1994b), **(j)** - RARE REPTILES BRED IN CAPTIVITY (Olney et al. 1994b).

Table Key: The latest IUCN Red List of Threatened Animals (IUCN 1996). Categories: EX = Extinct, EW = Extinct in the Wild, CR = Critically Endangered, EN = Endangered, VU = Vulnerable, LR = Lower Risk (cd = Conservation Dependent, nt = Near Threatened, and lc = Least Concern), DD = data Deficient, and NE = Not Evaluated. Other definitions (IUCN/SSC. 1994) Categories: (E) = Endangered, (V) = Vulnerable, (R) = Rare, (I) = Indeterminate, (K) = Insufficiently Known, (T) = Threatened; (r) = rare, as defined by the International Zoo Yearbook (IZY), which, although not necessarily rare and endangered in the wild, are rare in zoos. Only species were counted. For example, *Cyclura nubila caymanensis* and *Cyclura nubila nubila* were only counted as one species in the tabled results. CITES: (I) = Appendix 1, (II) = Appendix II, and (III) = Appendix 3. Source = Source of data in table (see next paragraph, Sources). Status = threat category as defined by source. Reptiles = total number of reptile species in each category. Lizards = total number of lizard species in each category. Snakes = total number of snake species in each category. Chelons = total number of turtle and tortoise species in each category. Crocs = total number of crocodilian species in each category. Tuatars = total number of tuatara species in each category.

Sources: (a) 1996 IUCN Red List (IUCN 1996). Published every two years. (b) 1994 IUCN Red List (Groombridge 1993). (c) World Checklist of Threatened Amphibians and Reptiles (WCMC 1993). Checklist of reptiles and amphibians appearing in Appendices I, II, and III of CITES together with those included in the 1990 edition of the IUCN Red List of Threatened Animals. (d) Checklist of Amphibians and Reptiles Listed in the CITES Appendices. (WCMC 1995). (e) ISIS (ISIS 1995). Reports published every six months. (f) Slaven's Report (Slavens and Slavens 1994). Published annually. (g) USFWS Combined Species Report (USFWS/DLE. 1995). This species report is the latest version (August 11, 1995) of a computer generated report taken from the US Fish and Wildlife Service Division of Law Enforcement's Protected Species Computer File of Protected and Commonly Traded Non-protected Species. CITES and US Endangered Species List totals were easily counted from this list (also compare h). (h) US Endangered Species List [50 CFR 17.11 & 17.12, August 20, 1994] (USFWS 1994b). Published irregularly. (i) Rare Reptiles in Captivity (Olney et al. 1994b). Census of Rare Animals in Captivity. Published annually. (j) Reptiles Bred in Captivity (Olney et al. 1994b). Species of wild animals bred in captivity during 1992 and multiple generation captive births. Published annually.

Notes: The CITES List (CITES 1995) were not included for comparison due to the difficulty of determining the exact number of species on the list. For example, the following groups were listed as: Varanus spp. (all species except those in App. 1) and Boidae spp. (all species except those in App. 1 or with earlier date in App. 11). This type of listing of whole animal groups together made it difficult to determine species numbers directly from the report. The USFWS Combined Species Report (g) data was sorted by Class, genus, species, and subspecies. Therefore, species numbers in CITES and US Endangered Species List categories were easily counted from this source. The World Checklist [WCMC 1993] (c) also lists individual species into CITES categories but no attempt was made here to compare their results with those in the USFWS Combined Species Report (g). The most reliable numbers for CITES species counts can be obtained from [WCMC 1995] (d). Results from (h) were determined as follows: When subspecies are listed as both threatened (T) and endangered (E) they are counted once in the results as an endangered species. When a species was listed as endangered in the United States but threatened elsewhere it was counted once in the results as endangered. When the table was compiled, an effort was made to use the most current sources available at the time. Prior to publication of this report the IUCN 1996 Red List (IUCN 1996) was added to these relative comparisons in table 1 but due to time constraints the other sources were not updated. The most current sources should be consulted to supplement or replace this table.

species according to Slavens and Slavens [1994] (f). The International Species Information System (ISIS) include 878 species being kept in captivity in zoological institutions [ISIS 1995] (e). ISIS also report, as of December 31, 1995, a total of 33,796 (9,674 males, 13,871 females and 13,871 of unknown sex) reptile specimens. Groombridge (1992b—table 34.15) include a worldwide total of 74,416 reptile specimens and a total of 6,187 specimens (36 species—table 34.16) with threat-

Mugger Crocodile, *Crocodylus palustris*. Photo by Aaron Norman.

ened status according to the IUCN and reported by ISIS, being held in captivity by zoos. Olney (1994b) include 40 rare species being kept in captivity by zoological parks (j).

Bred in Captivity. Olney (1994b) include 55 rare species being bred in captivity (i). Groombridge (1992b—table 34.16) include a total of 4,279 specimens (of which 2,913 are *Crocodylus palustris*) being bred in captivity by zoos from 31 species. Slavens and Slavens (1994) include 337 species bred in 1993 (f).

Using the source with the highest number of threatened species listed, 547 [WCMC 1993] (c), this number is roughly one-half of the number of species kept in captivity—reference [ISIS 1995] (e) and Slavens and Slavens [1994] (f). Of these a smaller fraction are being bred in captivity (forty threatened or rare species bred in zoos [Olney 1994*b*] (i) and 337 species reported from Slavens and Slavens [1994] (f) being bred by zoos and the private sector). Only a small fraction of reptilian species are being bred in captivity—0.5 percent [Olney 1994*b*] (j) of rare reptilian species and 5.6 percent reported by Slavens and Slavens [1994] (f).

Total number of reptile specimens in zoos reported to ISIS [ISIS 1995] (e) are 33,796 from 470 institutions. Depending on species-specific parameters such as life span a captive population of 250-500 animals is required to maintain approximately 90 percent of the population's gene diversity for 100 years.

Assuming that one-half the space in zoological parks could be set aside for threatened species propagation, it is estimated that approximately 75-150 species respectively could be held by institutions that report to ISIS (approximately 500 of 1000 total). This number could greatly increase by involving additional institutions and the private sector in conservation breeding (see also the Private Sector Action Plan in this chapter). The number of animals needed to be kept in captivity could be somewhat reduced by such techniques as introducing new blood lines from animals in the wild into captive populations (Willis and Wiese 1993). Space and long term commitment to breeding threatened species are the main limiting factors to how many species can be potentially helped through conservation breeding.

Selected Bibliography—Reptilia Conservation. General (Pritchard 1995; Mittermeier and Carr 1994; Mittermeier et al. 1992; Murphy and Collins 1980; Lawler 1992; Groombridge 1992a). Species Lists and Checklists (CITES 1995; USFWS 1994b; WCMC 1993; WCMC 1995; Groombridge 1982; Groombridge 1993; Honegger 1975/1979; King and Burke 1989). IUCN Threat Categories (IUCN/SSC 1994; Stattersfield 1996; Mace and Lande 1991; Mace 1994). Species in Captivity (ISIS 1995; Olney et al. 1994b; Lawler 1994; Slavens and Slavens 1994). Extinct Species (Groombridge 1993; Honegger 1980-81; Richman et al. 1988; Case et al. 1992). Mexico (Anonymous 1994; Flores-Villela 1993a; Flores-Villela 1993b; Flores-Villela and Gerez 1994). Australia (Cogger et al. 1993). European (Corbett 1989). New Zealand (Daugherty 1994). Madagascar (Raxworthy 1988). Common Names for Reptiles (Frank and Ramus 1995).

Blue-gray Sea Snake, *Hydrophis inornatus*. Photo by Dr. Sherman A. Minton.

TABLE 2

USFWS LIZARD RECOVERY PLANS

Plan Name	Common Name	Scientific Name	Plan Date	Plan Status	List Date	Listed As
Blunt-nosed Lepoard Lizard	Blunt-nosed Lepoard Lizard	*Gambelia (=Crotaphytus) silus*	04/18/80	Final	03/11/67	Endangered
California Channel Islands (7ssp.) ++	Island Night Lizard	*Xantusia (=Klauberina) riversiana*	01/26/84	Final	08/11/77	Threatened
Coachella Valley Fringe-toed Lizard	Coachella Valley Fringe-toed Lizard	*Uma inornata*	09/11/85	Final	09/25/80	Threatened Critical Habitat
Culebra Island Giant Anole	Culebra Island Giant Anole	*Anolis roosevelti*	01/28/83	Final	07/21/77	Endangered Critical Habitat
Mona Ground Iguana	Mona Ground Iguana	*Cyclura stejnegeri*	04/19/84	Final	02/03/78	Threatened Critical Habitat
Monito Gecko	Monito Gecko	*Sphaerodactylus micropithecus*	03/27/86	Final	10/15/82	Endangered Critical Habitat
Saint Croix Ground Lizard	Saint Croix Ground Lizard	*Ameiva polops*	03/29/84	Final	06/03/77	Endangered Critical Habitat
Sand/Blue-tailed Mole Skinks (2 spp.)	Bluetail (=blue-tailed) Mole Skink	*Eumeces egregius lividus*	12/23/93	Final	11/06/87	Threatened
Sand/Blue-tailed Mole Skinks (2 spp.) ++	Sand Skink	*Neoseps reynoldsi*	12/23/93	Final	11/06/87	Threatened

Source: USFWS Division of Endangered Species, October 11, 1995.

Notes: List Date = Date that the recovery plan was published in the Federal Register. Plan Date = Date recovery plan was approved. Threatened and Endangered = As defined by the USFWS. Critical Habitat = Habitat specifically designated as part of the species recovery plan. Spp = subspecies.

SAURIANS

The 1996 IUCN Red List of Threatened Animals include 166 lizard species (11 extinct, 1 extinct in the wild, 15 critically endangered, 15 endangered, 66 vulnerable, 0 least concern: conservation dependent, 23 least concern: near threatened, and 35 data deficient) [IUCN 1996] (a). The 1994 IUCN Red List record 149 saurian species in five threat categories (18 endangered, 47 vulnerable, 45 rare, 18 indeterminate and 21 insufficiently known) [Groombridge 1993] (b). CITES Appendices include 258 species [WCMC 1995] (d). The United States include 27 species on the US Endangered Species List [USFWS 1994*b*] (h).

THREATENED SPECIES KEPT AND/OR BRED IN CAPTIVITY

In Captivity. The private sector and/or zoological parks and institutions keep 431 different species according to Slavens and Slavens [1994] (f). ISIS include 335 species being kept in captivity in zoological institutions [ISIS 1995] (e). Groombridge (1992b—table 34.16) include a worldwide total of 419 specimens with threatened status according to the IUCN and reported by ISIS being held in captivity by zoos. Olney (1994*b*) in-

Cayman Islands Ground Iguana, *Cyclura nubila*. Photo by R. D. Bartlett.

clude 8 rare species being kept in captivity by zoological parks (j).

Bred in Captivity. Olney (1994*b*) include 13 rare species being bred in captivity (i). Slavens and Slavens (1994) include 131 species bred in 1993 (f).

Selected Bibliography—Sauria Conservation. General (see also above Reptilia Conservation: General; Bauer and Sadlier 1993). North American Regional Collection Plan (AZA/LAG 1995). Management (Alberts 1994). Iguanas and Varanids (Seal 1992b; Seal 1993a; Hudson et al. 1994; Burghardt and Rand 1982). Conservation Assessment and Management Plan [CAMP] (Seal 1992b). Popula-

Chinese Crocodile Lizard, *Shinisaurus crocodilurus*. Photo by R. W. Van Devender.

tion Habitat Viability Analysis (PHVA) (Seal 1993a). Studbook (Perry-Richardson and Ivanyi 1995). New Caledonia (Bauer and Sadlier 1993).

AZA/Wildlife Conservation and Management Committee (WCMC) Studbooks Approved for Lizards

Source: AZA
(R) = Regional, (I) = International
Total Number of Studbooks = 8

SAURIANS

Asian Forest Monitors *(Varanus sp.)* (R), Winston Card, Dallas Zoo.

Chinese Crocodile Lizard *(Shinisaurus crocodilurus)* (R), Andrew Snider, Detroit Zoological Park.

Fiji Banded Iguana (*Brachylopus fasiatus*) (R),

American Sand Skink, *Neoseps reynoldsi*. Photo by R. D. Bartlett.

John Kinkaid, San Diego Zoo.

Komodo Dragon (*Varanus komodoensis*) (R), Johnny Arnett, Cincinnati Zoo & Botanical Garden.

Malagasy Leaf Geckos (*Uroplatus sp.*) (R), Sean Foley, Riverbanks Zoological Park and Botanical Garden.

Komodo Dragon, *Varanus komodoensis*. Photo by John Coborn.

Cayman Islands Ground Iguana, *Cyclura nubila*.
Photo by K. H. Switak.

Cayman Islands Ground Iguana, *Cyclura nubila.* **Photo by K. H. Switak.**

Mexican Beaded Lizard (*Heloderma horridum*) (R), Janice Perry-Richardson, Arizona-Sonora Desert Museum.

Prehensile-Tailed Skink (*Corucia zebrata*) (R), Frank Slavens, Woodland Park Zoological Gardens.

Rock Iguanas (*Cyclura sp.*) (R), Bill Christie, Indianapolis Zoo.

AZA Lizard Species Survival Plans© (SSP©): 0

International Lizard Studbooks
Source: Olney et al. (1994)
Beaded Lizard (*Heloderma horridum*). Studbook Keeper: Vacant.
Gila Monster (*Heloderma suspectum*). Studbook Keeper: Vacant.

SERPENTS

The 1996 IUCN Red List of Threatened Animals include 75 snake species (3 extinct, 0 extinct in the wild, 12 critically endangered, 13 endangered, 25 vulnerable, 0 least concern: conservation dependent, 9 least concern: near threatened, and 13 data deficient) [IUCN 1996] (a). The 1994 IUCN Red List report 71 serpent species in five threat categories (10 endangered, 15 vulnerable, 24 rare, 11 indeterminate and 11 insufficiently known) [Groombridge 1993] (b). CITES Appendices include 117 species [WCMC 1995] (d). The United States include 17 species on the US Endangered Species List [USFWS 1994*b*] (h).

THREATENED SPECIES KEPT AND/OR BRED IN CAPTIVITY

In Captivity. The private sector and/or zoological parks and institutions keep 378 different

Mexican Beaded Lizard, *Heloderma horridum.* **Photo by M. P. and C. Piednoir.**

species according to Slavens and Slavens [1994] (f). ISIS include 338 species being kept in captivity in zoological institutions [ISIS 1995] (e). Groombridge (1992*b*—table 34.16) include a worldwide total of 921 specimens with threatened status according to the IUCN and reported by ISIS being held in captivity by zoos. Olney (1994*b*) include 13 rare species being kept in captivity by zoological parks (j).

Bred in Captivity. Olney (1994*b*) include 10 rare species being bred in captivity (i). Slavens and Slavens (1994) include 115 species bred in 1993 (f).

Selected Bibliography—Serpent Conservation: General (see also above Reptilia Conservation: General; Dodd 1987; Dodd 1993; Brown 1993). Regional Collection Plan (AZA/Snake Tag 1995). Conservation Assessment and Management Plan

Eastern Indigo Snake, *Drymarchon corais couperi*. **Photo by R.D. Bartlett.**

TABLE 3

USFWS SNAKE RECOVERY PLANS

Plan Name	Common Name	Scientific Name	Plan Date	Plan Status	List Date	Listed As
Atlantic Salt Marsh Snake	Atlantic Salt Marsh Snake	*Neoodica clarkii taeniata*	12/15/93	Final	11/12/77	Threatened
Concho Water Snake	Concho Water Snake	*Nerodica paucimaculata*	09/27/93	Final	09/03/86	Threatened
Eastern Indigo Snake	Eastern Indigo Snake	*Drymarchon corais couperi*	04/22/82	Final	01/31/78	Threatened
Giant Garter Snake	Giant Garter Snake	*Thamnophis gigas*	//	Under Development	10/20/93	Endangered
Mona Boa	Mona Boa	*Epicrates monensis monensis*	04/19/84	Final	02/03/78	Threatened Critical Habitat
New Mexico Ridge-nosed Rattlesnake	New Mexico Ridge-nosed Rattlesnake	*Crotalus willardi obscurus*	3/22/85	Final	08/04/78	Endangered Critical Habitat
Puerto Rican Boa	Puerto Rican Boa	*Epicrates inornatus*	03/27/86	Final	10/13/70	Endangered
San Francisco Garter Snake	San Francisco Garter Snake	*Thamnophis sirtalis tetrataenia*	09/11/85	Final	03/11/67	Endangered
Virgin Islands Tree Boa	Virgin Islands Tree Boa	*Epicrates monensis (=inornatus) granti*	03/27/86	Final	10/13/70	Endangered

Source: USFWS Division of Endangered Species, October 11, 1995.

Notes: List Date = Date that the recovery plan was published in the Federal Register. Plan Date = Date recovery plan was approved. Threatened and Endangered = As defined by the USFWS. Critical Habitat = Habitat specifically designated as part of the species recovery plan.

San Francisco Garter Snake, *Thamnophis sirtalis tetrataenia*. Photo by W. B. Allen, Jr.

(CAMP) (Seal 1992b). Population Habitat Viability Assessment (PHVA) (Seal 1992a). Boas and Pythons (Seal 1992b). Species Survival Plan (Odum 1992). International Studbook (Peterson 1992).

AZA/WCMC Studbooks Approved for Snakes
Source: AZA
(R) = Regional, **(I)** = International
Total Number of Studbooks = 12

SERPENTS

Annulated Boa (*Corallus annulatus*) (R), David Blody, Fort Worth Zoological Park.

Aruba Island Rattlesnake (*Crotalus durissus unicolor*) (I), Karl Peterson, Houston Zoological Gardens.

Blood Python (*Python curtus*) (R), Jeff Ettling, Sedgewick County Zoo & Botanical Garden.

Central American Dwarf Boa (*Ungaliophis sp.*) (R), David Blody, Fort Worth Zoological Park.

Common Anaconda (*Eunectes murinus*) (R), William Holmstom, Wildlife Conservation Park/Bronx Zoo.

Dumeril's Ground Boa (*Acrantophis dumerili*) (R), Terrence Fisher, San Antonio Zoo & Aquarium.

Virgin Islands Tree Boa, *Epicrates monensis granti*. Photo by Roberta Kayne.

Jamaican Boa (*Epicrates subflavus*) (R), Vacant.

King Cobra (*Ophiophagus hannah*) (R), Scott Pfaff, Riverbanks Zoological Gardens.

Palm Viper (*Bothriechis sp.*) (R), Michael Chadwell, Houston Zoological Gardens.

Pine Snakes (*Pituophis melanoleucus lodingi; P.m. ruthveni*) (R), Steve Reichling, Memphis Zoological Garden & Aquarium.

Reticulated Python (*Python reticulatus*) (R), Steve Conners, Birmingham Zoo.

Virgin Islands Boa (*Epicrates monensis*) (R), Peter Tolson, Toledo Zoological Gardens.

AZA Snake SSPs

Aruba Island Rattlesnake (*Crotalus durissus unicolor*)

Durmeril's Ground Boa (*Acrantophis dumerili*)

Mona/Virgin Islands Boa (*Epicrates monensis*)
International Snake Studbook
Source: Olney et al. (1994)

Aruba Island Rattlesnake (*Crotalus durissus unicolor*). Studbook Keeper: Karl H. Peterson, Houston Zoological Gardens.

CHELONIANS

The 1996 IUCN Red List of Threatened Animals include 173 turtle and tortoise species (6 extinct, 0 extinct in the wild, 10 critically endangered, 28 endangered, 58 vulnerable, 1 least concern: conservation dependent, 47 least concern: near threatened, and 23 data deficient) [IUCN 1996] (a). The 1994 IUCN Red List report 82 chelonian species in five threat categories (11 endangered, 21 vulnerable, 9 rare, 14 indeterminate and 27 insufficiently known) [Groombridge 1993] (b). CITES Appendices include 78 species [WCMC 1995] (d). The United States include 34 species on the US Endangered Species List [USFWS 1994*b*] (h).

Dumeril's Ground Boa, *Acrantophis dumerili*. Photo by K. H. Switak.

Louisiana Pine Snake, *Pituophis ruthveni*. Photo by Paul Freed.

Aruba Island Rattlesnake, *Crotalus durissus unicolor*. Photo by R. D. Bartlett.

Black Pine Snake, *Pituophis melanoleucus lodingi*. Photo by Louis Porras.

THREATENED SPECIES KEPT AND/OR BRED IN CAPTIVITY

In Captivity. The private sector and/or zoological parks and institutions keep 179 different species according to Slavens and Slavens (1994) (f). ISIS include 182 species being kept in captivity in zoological institutions [ISIS 1995] (e). Groombridge (1992b—table 34.16) include a worldwide total of 951 specimens with threatened status according to the IUCN and reported by ISIS being held in captivity by zoos. Olney (1994b) include 9 rare species being kept in captivity by zoological parks (j).

Desert Tortoise, *Gopherus agassizi.* **Photo by Jim Merli.**

Bred in Captivity. Olney (1994b) include 24 rare species being bred in captivity (i). Slavens and Slavens (1994) 84 species bred in 1993 (f).

Selected Bibliography—Chelonia Conservation. General (see also above Reptilia Conservation: General; Bjorndal 1995; Bjorndal 1987; NRC 1990; Beaman 1991; Swingland 1994; Swingland and Klemens 1989; Pritchard and Anders In Press). Proceedings (Richardson and

Eastern Painted Turtle, *Chrysemys picta picta.* **Photo by M. Smith.**

Loggerhead Sea Turtle, *Caretta caretta.* **Photo by J. Visser.**

Kemp's Ridley Turtle, *Lepidochelys kempi.* **Photo by Dr. Peter Pritchard.**

Gopher Tortoise, *Gopherus polyphemus.* **Photo by R. T. Zappalorti.**

248

Richardson 1995). Checklists (Iverson 1992; Iverson 1985; Marquez M. 1990). Action Plan (IUCN/SSC/TFTSG 1991; Stearns 1989). Conservation Assessment and Management Plan (CAMP) (Ellis and Donnelly 1995). Recovery Plan (Balazs 1991). North America (Bury 1982). Galápagos (Pritchard 1996).

AZA/WCMC Studbooks Approved for Turtles and Tortoises

Source: AZA
(R) = Regional, **(I)** = International
Total Number of Studbooks = 7

CHELONIANS

African Spurred Tortoise (*Geochelone sulcata*) (R), Brett Stearns, Institute for Herpetological Research.

TABLE 4

USFWS TURTLE AND TORTOISE RECOVERY PLANS

Plan Name	Common Name	Scientific Name	Plan Date	Plan Status	List Date	Listed As
Desert Tortoise (Mojave Population)	Desert Tortoise	*Gopherus (=Scaptochelys, =Xerobates) agassizlii*	06/28/94	Final	08/20/80	Threatened Critical Habitat
Gopher Tortoise	Gopher Tortoise	*Gopherus polyphemus*	12/26/90	Final	04/02/90	Threatened
Alabama Red-bellied Turtle	Alabama Red-bellied Turtle	*Pseudemys alabamensis*	01/08/90	Final	06/16/87	Endangered
Flattened Musk Turtle	Flattened Musk Turtle	*Sternotherus depressus*	02/26/90	Final	06/11/87	Threatened
Plymouth Redbelly Turtle	Plymouth Redbelly Turtle (=red-bellied)	*Pseudemys (=Chrysemys) rubriventris bangsi*	07/29/93	Revised Draft No. 1★	04/02/80	Endangered Critical Habitat
Ringed Sawback Turtle	Ringed Sawback Turtle	*Graptemys oculifera*	04/08/88	Final	12/23/86	Threatened
Yellow-Blotched Map Turtle	Yellow-Blotched Map Turtle (= sawback)	*Graptemys flavimaculata*	03/15/93	Final	01/14/91	Threatened
Kemp's Ridley Sea Turtle	Kemp's (=Atlantic) Ridley Sea Turtle	*Lepidochelys kempii*	08/29/92	Final	12/02/70	Endangered
Leatherback Sea Turtle	Leatherback Sea Turtle	*Dermochelys coriacea*	04/06/93	Final	06/02/70	Endangered Critical Habitat
Loggerhead Sea Turtle	Loggerhead Sea Turtle	*Caretta caretta*	12/26/91	Final	07/28/78	Threatened
Olive Ridley Sea Turtle	Olive (Pacific) Sea Turtle	*Lepidochelys olivacea*	09/26/85	Revised Draft No. 1★	07/28/78	Endangered Threatened
Green Sea Turtle	Green Sea Turtle	*Chelonia mydas*	10/29/91	Final	10/13/70	Endangered Threatened
Hawksbill Sea Turtle	Hawksbill Sea Turtle (=carey)	*Eretmochelys imbricata*	08/05/92	Draft	06/02/70	Endangered Critical Habitat

Source: USFWS Division of Endangered Species, October 11, 1995.

Notes: List Date = Date that the recovery plan was published in the Federal Register. Plan Date = Date recovery plan was approved. Threatened and Endangered = As defined by the USFWS. Critical Habitat = Habitat specifically designated as part of the species recovery plan.

★ Revision of a previously approved program.

Pancake Tortoise, *Malacochersus tornieri.* **Photo by K. H. Switak.**

Asian Brown Tortoise (*Manouria sp.*) (R), Becky Heller, Minnesota Zoological Garden.

Black-Breasted Leaf Turtle (*Geomyda spengleri*) (R), Rick Haeffner, Denver Zoological Gardens.

Galapagos Tortoise (*Geochelone elephantopus ssp.*) (R), Colette Hairston, Gladys Porter Zoo.

Pancake Tortoise (*Malacochersus tornieri*) (R), Rusty Grimpe, Tulsa Zoological Park.

Radiated Tortoise (*Geochelone radiata*) (R), William Holmstrom, Wildlife Conservation Park/Bronx Zoo.

Side-Necked Turtle (*Podocnemis sp.*) (R), Richard Sajdak, Milwaukee County Zoological Gardens.

AZA Tortoise SSP

Radiated Tortoise (*Geochelone radiata*)
International Turtle and Tortoise Studbooks**: 0**

Radiated Tortoise, *Geochelone radiata.* **Photo by R. D. Bartlett.**

African Spurred Tortoise, *Geochelone sulcata.* **Photo by R. D. Bartlett.**

CROCODILIANS

The 1996 IUCN Red List of Threatened Animals include 13 Crocodilian species (0 extinct, 0 extinct in the wild, 4 critically endangered, 3 endangered, 3 vulnerable, 0 least concern: conservation dependent, 0 least concern: near threatened, and 3 data deficient) [IUCN 1996] (a). The 1994 IUCN Red List report 12 crocodilian species in five threat categories (7 endangered, 5 vulnerable, 0 rare, 0 indeterminate and 0 insufficiently known) [Groombridge 1993] (b). CITES Appendices include 23 species [WCMC 1995] (d). The United States include 18 species on the US Endangered Species List [USFWS 1994*b*] (h).

THREATENED SPECIES KEPT AND/OR BRED IN CAPTIVITY

In Captivity. The private sector and/or zoological parks and institutions keep 21 different species according to Slavens and Slavens [1994] (f). ISIS include 22 species being kept in captivity in zoological institutions [ISIS 1995] (e). Groombridge (1992*b*—table 34.16) include a worldwide total of 3,833 specimens with threatened status according to the IUCN and reported by ISIS being held in captivity by zoos. Olney (1994*b*) include 9 rare species being kept in captivity by zoological parks (j).

Bred in Captivity. Olney (1994*b*) include 7 rare species being bred in captivity (i). Slavens and Slavens (1994) include 6 species bred in 1993 (f).

Selected Bibliography—Crocodylia Conservation. General (see also above Reptilia Conservation: General; Webb et al. 1987; Ross and Garnett 1989). Action Plan (Thorbjarnarson 1992). Proceedings (CSG 1990). Farming (Luxmoore et al. 1985; Revol 1995). Population Habitat Viability Assessment (PHVA) (Rao 1995; Ellis 1996).

TABLE 5

USFWS CROCODILE RECOVERY PLAN

Plan Name	Common Name	Scientific Name	Plan Date	Plan Status	List Date	Listed As
American Crocodile	American Crocodile	*Crocodylus acutus*	02/02/84	Revised Draft No. 1★	09/25/75	Endangered Critical Habitat

Source: USFWS Division of Endangered Species, October 11, 1995.

Notes: List Date = Date that the recovery plan was published in the Federal Register. Plan Date = Date recovery plan was approved. Threatened and Endangered = As defined by the USFWS. Critical Habitat = Habitat specifically designated as part of the species recovery plan.

★ Revision of a previously approved program.

Chinese Alligator, *Alligator sinensis*. Photo by R. D. Bartlett.

American Crocodile, *Crocodylus acutus*. Photo by K. H. Switak.

Cuban Crocodile, *Crocodylus rhombifer*. Photo by R. D. Bartlett.

AZA/WCMC STUDBOOKS APPROVED FOR ALLIGATORS AND CROCODILES
    Source: AZA
    (R) = Regional, **(I)** = International
    Total Number of Studbooks = 7

CROCODILIANS

    Chinese Alligator (*Alligator sinensis*) (I), John Behler, Wildlife Conservation Park/Bronx Zoo.
    Cuban Crocodile (*Crocodylus rhombifer*) (R), Michael Davenport, National Zoological Park.
    Dwarf Caiman (*Paleosuchus palpebrosus*) (R), Dale Belcher, Rio Grande Zoological Park.

    Gharial (*Gavialis gangeticus*) (R), Vacant.
    Morelet's Crocodile (*Crocodylus moreletii*) (R), E. Howard Hunt, Zoo Atlanta.
    Siamese Crocodile (*Crocodylus siamensis*) (R), Vacant.
    Tomistoma (*Tomistoma schlegelii*) (R), William Zeigler, Miami Metrozoo.
    AZA Alligator and Crocodile SSPs
    Chinese Alligator (*Alligator sinensis*)
    Cuban Crocodile (*Crocodylus rhombifer*)
    International Alligator Studbook
    Source: Olney et al. (1994)
    Chinese Alligator (*Alligator sinensis*). Studbook Keeper: John L. Behler, Wildlife Conservation Society.

Fig. 17
False Gharial, *Tomistoma schlegeli*. Even the larger species of reptiles (such as alligators and crocodiles) could be bred by serious amateur breeding specialists. There is now the opportunity to breed threatened and endangered species and raise needed revenue to help augment conservation program efforts. Photo by W.B. Love/Blue Chameleon Ventures

RHYNCHOCEPHALIANS

The 1996 IUCN Red List of Threatened Animals include 1 Tuatara species (0 extinct, 0 extinct in the wild, 0 critically endangered, 0 endangered, 1 vulnerable, 0 least concern: conservation dependent, 0 least concern: near threatened, and 0 data deficient) [IUCN 1996] (a). The 1994 IUCN Red List record both existing tuatara species in two threat categories (1 endangered and 1 rare) [Groombridge 1993] (b). CITES Appendices include both species [WCMC 1995] (d). The United States include 1 species on the US Endangered Species List [USFWS 1994b] (h).

THREATENED SPECIES KEPT AND/OR BRED IN CAPTIVITY

In Captivity. The private sector and/or zoological parks and institutions keep 1 species according to Slavens and Slavens (1994) (f). ISIS include 1 species being kept in captivity in zoological institutions [ISIS 1995] (e). Groombridge (1992b—table 34.16) include a worldwide total of 63 specimens reported by ISIS being held in captivity by zoos. Olney (1994b) include 1 species being kept in captivity by zoological parks (j).

Bred in Captivity. Olney (1994b) include 1 rare species being bred in captivity (i). Slavens and Slavens (1994) include 1 species bred in 1993 (f).

Selected Bibliography—Rhynchocephalia Conservation. General (**see also above Reptilia Conservation:** General; Newman 1987). Captive Breeding and Management (Cree and Daugherty 1990; Cree et al. 1994). Recovery Plan (Cree and Butler 1993).

Fig. 6
Guyana Caiman Lizard, *Dracaena guianensis*. Caiman lizard from the Amazon basin in Peru. It grows to nearly 5 feet in length and loves to feed on snails. Photo by W.B. Love/Blue Chameleon Ventures

Fig. 7
Four-eyed Day Gecko, *Phelsuma quadriocellata lepida*. This group of lizards (day Geckos) is very popular in the commercial pet industry. These species would benefit from private sector breeding programs for conservation. Photo by W.B. Love/Blue Chameleon Ventures

WILD POPULATIONS— SIZE ESTIMATES

For most animal populations in the wild, the actual numbers are unknown or, at best, can only be estimated. A starting point for obtaining estimates of species numbers in the wild are from the Conservation Breeding Specialist Group's (CBSG) Conservation Assessment and Management Plans

Fig. 5
Ornate Mastigure, *Uromastyx ornatus*. This unique group of lizard species from the Old World has benefitted by private sector contributions in developing captive breeding and husbandry protocols. Photo by W.B. Love/Blue Chameleon Ventures

Fig. 8
Green Tree Monitor, *Varanus prasinus.*
Monitors are difficult to breed in captivity with many species having never bred. Monitor lizards could benefit tremendously by cooperative efforts by the private and professional conservation community. Photo by W.B. Love/Blue Chameleon Ventures

(CAMPs), Population Habitat Viability Analysis (PHVAs) and Action Plans published by the various IUCN/Species Survival Commission (SSC) Specialist Groups. For example, Crocodiles: An Action Plan for their Conservation is published by the IUCN/SSC Crocodile Specialist Group (CSG). This action plan lists species country accounts, survey data, status of wild populations, and various management and conservation programs for crocodilian species worldwide. Great care should be taken when using data on species population numbers from

Fig. 9
Antsingy Leaf Chameleon, *Brookesia perarmata.* **Is the largest of Madagascar's odd leaf chameleons. Much remains to be learned about this rare and unique chameleon species. Photo by W.B. Love/Blue Chameleon Ventures**

some of these sources. Often they are mere guesses and until verified by further research they should be considered best ball park estimates.

Extremely valuable sources of information are state and federal governmental agencies such as State Departments of Natural and Wildlife Resources and the USFWS. These important sources of information are often not widely publicized and these organizations should be contacted directly in locating unpublished or hard to find reports.

The most important source of valuable data on wild populations are published scientific papers and reports. These are often the most accurate source of numbers on species populations. Any good science librarian can help you location these sources by using techniques as computer aided literature searches.

The Nature Conservancy (TNC), Natural Heritage Programs exist throughout much of the Western Hemisphere. Collectively, they represent the largest ongoing effort to gather standardized data on endangered plants, animals, and ecosystems. For more information about this program see Appendix 5—Worldwide Web Pages, The Natural Heritage Network Central Server.

Make efforts to locate taxon specialists to aid your research. Many of these people are associated with such groups as the American Zoo and Aquarium Association (AZA) Taxon Advisory Groups (TAGs) and professional herpetological organizations like the Society for the Study of Amphibians and Reptiles (SSAR), the world's largest reptile and amphibian association.

Selected Bibliography—Populations. General (Bezzel 1994; Ceballos and Brown 1995; Dunham 1988; Osborne 1995). Measuring and Monitoring (Heyer et al. 1994; Dunham 1988). Definitions of Threat (IUCN/SSC 1994; Stattersfield 1996; Mace and Lande 1991; Mace 1994).

WILDLIFE TRADE

The wildlife trade in reptiles is enormous. This activity includes the trading of millions of animals and animal parts in the commerce of skin and live animals. Trade often has a significant effect on wild populations, even causing wild populations to decline to the point of possible extinction. For example, all marine turtles are listed as CITES Appendix 1 species due to human exploitation and incidental catch of sea turtles which causes huge mortality. Accurate population numbers must be determined well before the species are threatened with possible extinction, to avoid the need for recovery programs.

Wild animals in trade can be of greater conservation benefit if they are placed in programs where they can yield data on how to maintain and breed them in captivity and/or become part of regulated captive breeding programs. More effort should be committed to these goals. The private sector can do the most good in these areas by reporting valuable captive husbandry data and working with recognized breeding programs associated with the professional conservation community.

Fig. 11
Blunthead Tree Snake, *Imantodes cenchoa.* **This uncommon Belize snake could benefit by private sector efforts in the collection of breeding and husbandry data from captive populations. In the event that this species becomes threatened in the future this type of knowledge might be very essential to conservation efforts. Photo by W.B. Love/Blue Chameleon Ventures**

Fig. 10
Petter's Chameleon, *Chamaeleo petteri* **(male). A little known chameleon species from Madagascar which could benefit from conservation breeding. Males have two nasal "horns," while females lack them completely. Photo by W.B. Love/Blue Chameleon Ventures**

3) Country Reports. The annual report format provides a complete printout of all CITES trade for a particular year and reported by a specific CITES party. Where parties are unable to produce their own annual report, WTMU can produce one based on that country's returned permits.

Selected Bibliography—Wildlife Trade. General (Fitzgerald 1989; Bolze 1992; HSUS and HSI 1994; Luxmoore et al. 1988; USFWS 1993). CITES (USFWS 1983; Trexler and

Fig. 12
Borneo Short-tailed Python (juvenile), *Python curtis breitensteini.* **A very popular species in the pet trade. It is built short and stocky, unlike most python species. Photo by W.B. Love/Blue Chameleon Ventures**

The World Conservation Monitoring Centre (WCMC), Wildlife Trade Monitoring Unit (WTMU) has maintained the international trade statistics on behalf of the CITES Secretariat since 1980. Statistics are submitted from CITES member states, compiling the largest database of wildlife trade information in the world. With permission from the CITES Secretariat, WTMU can provide data in various formats to the public, generally in one of three formats below:

1) Gross/Net Trade Tabulations. Provides gross or net import/export data for a specific year(s), country, species and/or product, allowing yearly trends to be monitored.

2) Comparative Tabulations. Provides data from corresponding importing and exporting countries for a specific year, species, product, etc. Data allows comparison of reporting, between the two parties and a chance to identify any potentially illegal trade.

Fig. 13
Bothrops (nigroviridis) aurifer (Guatemala).
A rare inhabitant of isolated cloud forests in Guatemala. Logging of such habitats threatens its continued survival. Photo by W.B. Love/Blue Chameleon Ventures

Kosloff 1987; Luxmoore et al. 1988; Hemsley 1994; Gray-Schofield 1983; Faure 1989; Wijnskekers 1992). Regulations (AZA 1994). Reptilia (Luxmoore et al. 1988; see Madagascar below). Chelonia (Groombridge and Luxmoore 1989; HSUS and HSI 1994). Sauria (Luxmoore and Groombridge 1990). Serpent (Groombridge and Luxmoore 1991). Madagascar (IUCN/SSC Trade and Madagascar Reptile and Amphibian Specialist Group 1993). Reptile Skin Trade (Jenkins and Board 1994).

REINTRODUCTIONS

Reintroductions of animals is controversial

Fig. 14
Indian Tent Turtle, *Kachuga tecta tecta*. Rare and threatened reptile species, such as this turtle from rivers of India, can all potentially benefit from private sector contributions. Photo by W.B. Love/Blue Chameleon Ventures

and success has been limited. Though reintroductions are not a panacea to the problems of endangered species, if captive populations are to have any positive effect, they should be managed to support the survival of species in the wild (Hutchins and Wiese 1991; Wiese and Hutchins 1994). Individuals should envision how their work directly relates to the survival of the animal in the wild. The ultimate goal is to blend the activities and goals of captive breeding to those of reintroducing animals back into the wild if reintroduction is deemed necessary.

The science of reintroduction of animals back into the wild is only in the early stages of research and development. More effort and research is needed to advance this link between captive breeding and placing animals in the wild. Working with others such as the IUCN/SSC Reintroduction Specialist Group is imperative when considering the re-introduction of captive animals back into the wild.

Selected Bibliography—Reintroductions. General (Olney et al. 1994a; Wiese and Hutchins 1993; Gipps 1991; IUCN 1987b; IUCN/SSC/RSG 1995; Ralls and Ballou 1992). Disease (Cunningham 1996). Reptilia (Case and Bogler 1991; Goodyear and Lazell 1994; Reinert 1991; Dodd 1991).

LEGISLATION

The keeping of animals in captivity has been under attack by various animal rights groups for some time. They are campaigning to encourage lawmakers to pass legislation to stop this activity. Groups are now forming to protect the captive animal keeper and breeder (see the National Herpetological Alliance and the California Herpetological Advisory Council). Any serious animal keeper or breeder should lend their support to such groups as mentioned above.

Selected Bibliography—Legislation. General (Klemms 1993a; Levell 1995). CITES (Klemm 1993b). Australia (Ehmann and Cogger 1985; Jenkins 1985).

SMALL POPULATION MANAGEMENT

Small population management is the science of managing small populations in captivity. The genetic goal for many captive populations is to maintain 90 percent of the genetic variation (measured as the gene diversity) present in the wild population for 100-200 years. Goals and objectives of a particular breeding program require periodic adjustments. The minimum number of animals that will accomplish the genetic and demographic goals for the program is termed the *Minimum Viable Population* (MVP). MVP depends on parameters such as the generation time of the species, number of effective founders and other biological characteristics of the population. Computer software is available to determine the number of founders, target population size, etc. needed for managing the species in captivity (see below—Computer Software). As a rule of thumb, 20 to 30 unrelated founders are sufficient to represent the genetic variation from the wild population and meet the requirements for most captive breeding programs.

Systematic and directed breeding must be performed with captive populations so the intended target size of the population can be reached and that individual genetic contributions from generation to generation are evenly distributed in the population. Software programs can determine the target population size needed to keep a species in captivity. There is no simple formula to determine the ultimate target population size due to the numerous population variables and constant changes in a dynamic population. Factors as the number of unrelated founders with which the captive population began will have a profound effect on the target population size. The best paper to consult before under taking any captive breeding program is Ballou (1987). Otherwise, it is most useful to learn and use the software programs listed in the Software section below.

Other demographic factors, unique genetic and population factors such as varying sex ratios, number of animals that reproduce, etc. all have a profound effect on all captive population management decisions. These decisions are most easily aided by computer analysis. Many private individuals starting new captive breeding programs will not have the expertise in small population management that is required to manage animals in captivity. An early working relationship with such groups as the AZA Small Population Management Scientific Advisory Group and the CBSG should be initiated. Further study of the important references listed here would be extremely beneficial.

Selected Bibliography—Small Population Management. General (see also Software; Species Management Strategies; Ballou et al. 1995; Ballou 1987; Olney et al. 1994*a*; Foose and Ballou 1988; McCullough and Barrett 1992; Soule 1987; Willis and Wiese 1993; Wiese et al.1994). Technology (Moore et al. 1992). Captivity (Ralls and Ballou 1992; Ballou 1987; Huntley and Langton 1994).

SOFTWARE

Computer programs allow for complicated mathematical computations to be performed quick and easily. Software programs come with instruc-

Fig. 15
Madagascar Radiated Tortoise, *Geochelone radiata*. CITES appendix 1 species. This beautiful creature is now scarce in its range impacted by habitat destruction and over-collection for food. Photo by W.B. Love/Blue Chameleon Ventures

tions or manuals. Any person serious about conservation breeding must learn the basic programs—CAPACITY, SPARKS, DEMOG, and GENES. The other programs listed below could apply to your specific program and needs.

Selected Bibliography—Software. Small Population Biology (Ballou; Bingaman; Ballou). Population Viability Analysis (PVA) (Lacy 1993; Lacy*b*). Genes (Lacy*a*; Mace). Animal Management Systems (ISIS*a*, ISIS*b*, ISIS*c* and Slavens and Slavens). Conservation (Gilpin). Field Notes (GECKO and Slavens and Slavens).

Fig. 16
Kleinmann's Tortoise, *Testudo kleinmanni*. An example of a rare species being kept by the private sector. This species from Egypt rarely exceeds 4-5 inches in length. Photo by W.B. Love/Blue Chameleon Ventures

SPECIES MANAGEMENT PLANS

Species management plans organize and manage threatened species in captivity through the world's global zoo programs (Appendix 2) and key conservation organizations. Examples of zoos that keep diverse groups of reptile species are listed in Appendix 1. Emphasis was given to zoos that specialize in reptiles and/or associated with auxiliary conservation programs.

A key conservation breeding organization is the IUCN/SSC/CBSG. This group works with many individuals and organizations concerned with the survival of threatened species and are in need of captive breeding. Critical to the support of CBSG's programs are the expertise of the IUCN/SSC/TAGs such as the Crocodile Specialist Group.

Fig. 18
***Uroplatus phantasticus* (male and female). The pet industry should foster the selling of paired animal species to facilitate conservation breeding by the private sector. These lizards live in moist forests of Madagascar. Photo by W.B. Love/Blue Chameleon Ventures**

These groups lend valuable expertise when determining species priorities for conservation breeding and develop *Action Plans* for the taxonomic group. Presently, only two plans have been developed by the Specialist Groups (IUCN/SSC/TFTSG 1991; Thorbjarnarson 1992) and one by the Australian Nature Conservation Agency (Cogger et al. 1993).

CBSG's programs consist of 4 types of planning tools:

1) Population and Habitat Viability Assessments (PHVAs). PHVAs are a single species approach to saving species and its corresponding habitat. Workshops are developed around the concept of assessing the extinction risk and developing better management strategies.

2) Conservation Assessment Management Plans (CAMPs). Detailed lists of threatened species are not available for most regions of the world. The CAMP process is designed to assess and compile the status and degree of threat of a group of taxa or a particular region so management actions can be developed. Species' status in the wild and captivity, degree of endangerment, and the need for research or PHVAs are reported. These reports are used in setting global conservation priorities as well as management recommendations. Three CAMPs are available for reptiles (Ellis and Donnelly 1995; Hudson et al. 1994; Seal 1992*b*).

3) Global Captive Action Recommendations (GCARs). GCARs summarize the captive status and captive breeding priorities for recommended animals on a worldwide scale.

4) Global Animal Survival Plans (GASPs). GASPs are a collaborative process for managing species at an international level emphasizing the linkage of captive populations to the conservation of wild populations.

Other services available through CBSG are essential training, meetings, workshops and communication. CBSG membership is open to all for a fee.

The primary AZA program for endangered species is the Species Survival Plan©. SSP©s are developed to ensure the survival of selected wildlife species through demographic and genetic management of small populations. SSP programs have been listed under each reptile family respectively.

The *SSP Master Plans* outline the goals for the SSP population. They are designed to retain maximum gene diversity. One aspect of the program includes the coordinated breeding of the species at each member institution. SSPs also encompass programs for species in the wild such as habitat protection, reintroduction programs, public education and basic and applied research.

Studbooks are animal registries containing the vital records of an entire captive population of a species. Information collected includes births, deaths, transfers and family lineage. The AZA/WCMC approved studbooks have been listed under each reptile family respectively.

Other AZA groups established to assist conservation efforts within the AZA are the Taxon Advisory Groups (TAGs), Fauna Interest Groups (FIGs), and Scientific Advisory Groups (SAGs)—(Appendix 9). TAGs examine the conservation needs of a entire taxon including species selection for conservation programs, developing husbandry protocols and developing *Regional Collection Plans* (RCPs). FIGs are designed to help coordinate the conservation and science activities of AZA institutions working in specific geographical regions of the world. FIGs encourage the host country's conservation efforts through training, technology transfer and other forms of support. SAGs were began to collaborate with the greater academic community and increase the use of science in the management of captive populations.

Other global zoological associations are starting to establish conservation programs similar to those in the AZA (Appendices 3 and 4). As more of these programs develop and greater cooperation ensues conservation efforts can save increasing numbers of endangered species and habitats worldwide.

Species management in the wild is often the responsibility of local and federal governmental agencies. The USFWS has published 32 Recovery Plans, including 9 saurian, 9 serpent, 13 chelonian, and 1 crocodilian plans. Tables of these Recovery Plans are listed under each reptile family respectively.

Space is the key limiting factor for breeding threatened species in captivity. The inability of wild species to acclimate to and breed in captivity is also a challenge. Species priorities are set by governing organizations to maximize the use of the limited space in zoological parks and aquariums. The need to increase this capacity could be increased many fold if the private sector would increase and focus its efforts on conservation breeding. Developing husbandry protocols for rarely-kept species and working closely with the professional conservation community would facilitate these efforts in *ex-situ* conservation of threatened species.

Selected Bibliography—Species Management Plans. General (Bowles and Whelan 1994; Gibbons et. al. 1995; Jones 1992; IUDZG/CBSG (IUCN/SSC) 1993; Wiese and Hutchins 1994)*. Directories (CBSG 1996; Bowdoin et al. 1994). Conservation Breeding (see also CAMPs and GCAR; Boer 1992; Gibbons 1995; Butler 1992; Lawler 1992; Lawler 1994; Foose et al. 1986; Hutchins et al. In Press; Hutchins and Wiese 1991; Hutchins and Wemmer 1991; Marcellini 1994; Derrickson and Snyder 1992; Wiese et al. 1993; Wiese and Hutchins 1994; Wiese et al. 1996; Wiese and Hutchins 1993; Stevens et al. 1996b; Bowdoin et al. 1994; Murphy et al. 1994; Alberts 1994; Butler 1992). Zoological Parks [IUDZG/CBSG (IUCN/SSC) 1993; Hutchins and Conway 1995;

Hutchins et al. 1995; Koebner 1994; CBSG 1996, and Tudge 1992]. GCAR and CAMPs (Byers 1994; Seal 1992b; Hudson et al. 1994; Ellis and Donnelly 1995; Ellis and Seal 1995). CAMPs and GCAPs (Seal et al. 1994). Species Survival Plans (Wiese and Hutchins 1994; Stevens, et al. 1996a; Stearns 1989; Odum 1992; Odum and Goode 1994). Action Plans (Foose and Seal 1991; Cogger et al. 1993; IUCN/SSC/TFTSG 1991; Thorbjarnarson 1992). Recovery Plans (Cree and Butler 1993; Balazas et al. 1991; USFWS 1994a; Speake et al. 1981). Studbooks (Perry-Richardson and Ivanyi 1995; Peterson 1992; Rockwell and Teere 1986). PHVAs (Rao 1995; Ellis 1996; Seal 1992a; Seal 1993a; Seal 1993b; Shaffer 1990). Workshop (OPWT 1991).

★ **Note.** Volume 14 (1), 1995 of the journal

Fig. 19
Redtail Boa Constrictor, *Boa constrictor.* **Boa Constrictors are traded by the hundreds of thousands each year but even with these numbers few serious conservation breeding efforts have resulted. The country of Columbia now mass-produces their local race of Boa Constrictor for export as pets. Photo by W.B. Love/Blue Chameleon Ventures**

Zoo Biology has been devoted entirely to the single topic of Collection Planning: Theory and practice. Copies are available from the publisher (John Wiley & Sons) at special discount prices. To obtain additional information email: nadams@jwiley.com.

PRIVATE SECTOR ACTION PLAN

Private sector involvement in organized captive breeding programs is meant to increase the ability of the professional conservation community in efforts to enhance the status of endangered species. Though many obstacles remain to be overcome the private sector does have the resources to make significant contributions to worldwide conservation efforts.

Conservation breeding is only one of the many possible conservation strategies in endangered species programs and is limited by a variety of significant difficulties. Of special concern are problems in: (1) obtaining consistent reproduction in some species; (2) controlling disease confinement and transmission; (3) avoiding detrimental genetic and behavioral changes; (4) meeting long-term financial and logistical requirements; (5) securing administrative continuity and commitment (Derrickson and Snyder 1992); (6) sequestering and dealing with potential problems unique to private sector efforts i.e. (7) resolving conflicts over ownership and control of animals; (8) mutual distrust and fear between conservationists and private breeders; (9) overcoming traditional attitudes of independence and secrecy (Clubb 1992), lack of private sector commitment to organized and cooperative breeding plans, and (10) various financial considerations. Other problems which exist are inadequate habitat to reintroduce captive bred animals, political obstacles, and renewed poaching. If these problems such as those noted above can be solved, to the satisfaction of all parties, then truc cooperative efforts by the private sector and the professional conservation community can achieve progress toward the conservation of endangered and threatened species.

The private sector has the ability to increase the carrying capacity of threatened species now being bred in zoological parks and aquariums. Often private breeders have valuable space, time and resources that are in scarce supply in the professional zoo community. The professional zoo community harbors much of the technical knowledge in areas such as small population management. Effective transfer of this knowledge to the private sector could result in a tremendous boon in worldwide breeding capacity of captive animals. The following is a brief suggested outline on how the private sector and professional zoo community can unite together in the common goal of the conservation breeding of threatened and endangered species.

The prerequisite for any positive action to occur between the private sector and the professional zoo community must be a renewed commitment toward conservation breeding of species from the private sector arena. The professional zoo community should facilitate this new movement through technology transfer and moral support. An organization dedicated to these specific goals is paramount to the success of such a venture. One such organization which is making progress toward the cooperation of professional and nonprofessional efforts in breeding programs is the Chameleon Conservation Society (CCS), [see Appendix 5—Worldwide Web Pages]. Professional support would greatly facilitate these efforts in all phases of planning and implementation of such cooperative ventures. Without the structure and direction that a nonprofessional/professional organization would provide, chances of success are greatly reduced for private sector contributions to conservation breeding.

Another integral part of the successful harnessing of the private sector's talent and resources is the use of the Internet. It is now possible to communicate with others worldwide with ease. Mailing lists could be established by the one participating organization for the exchange of information among species breeding groups, advisory committees, taxon experts, individuals located in foreign countries with expert knowledge, or anyone else needed to implement the programs. Worldwide Web (WWW) home pages can be repositories for valuable member information. These pages can be interactive information exchange services.

For such an organization to develop there must be support from the professional zoo community and a new conservation ethic fostered in the private sector, namely private breeders and keepers. Both groups must decide on mutual goals and evaluate progress toward them often.

Selected Bibliography—Private Sector Action Plan. General (Clubb 1992; Backner 1994). Captive Breeding (Derrickson and Snyder 1992). Organizational Cooperation (Trebbau et al. 1994; Mallinson 1991).

CONCLUSION

Conservation breeding remains controversial and problems exist that must be resolved. Regardless of these potential and real problems, private sector efforts should be harnessed for conservation purposes. This could be facilitated by redirecting emphasis from commercial breeding to conservation breeding, organizing activities under a new, nonprofit foundation, recruiting new members, coordinating projects with those of the professional conservation community, and effective problem resolution.. The result would be a tremendous expansion of current carrying capacity for threatened reptilian species. At the least, private breeders should focus their attention on supplying the pet trade with significant numbers of common species at competitive prices and developing husbandry protocols for species not currently kept in zoos but are likely to become threatened in the near future. Priority should be placed on species whose habitats are being destroyed rapidly.

Fig. 20
An Australian Bearded (*Pogona*) Lizard at sunset. McDonell's Ridge, Australia. The future of many rare and threatened reptilian species would benefit by increased development of conservation breeding and husbandry protocols by the private sector. How many species will benefit remains to be determined by the enthusiasm and concerted efforts of private individuals toward conservation breeding of reptilian species. Photo by Jamie K. Reaser/Stanford University

ACKNOWLEDGEMENTS

Special thanks is due to and credit is acknowledged for the following individuals and organizations: Robert Wiese, Fort Worth Zoo, Frank Slavens, Woodland Park Zoological Gardens, William Kramer, USFWS/DES, and the excellent staffs at ISIS, the IUCN/SSC/CBSG, and the World Conservation Monitoring Centre (WCMC).

SELECTED BIBLIOGRAPHY

—**Alberts, A.C. 1994.**
Dominance hierarchies in male lizards: Implications for zoo management programs. *Zoo Biology* 13: 479-490.

—**Anonymous. 1994.**
NORMA Oficial Mexicana NOM-059-ECOL-1994, que determina las especies y subespecies de flora y fauna silvestres terrestres y acuaticas en peligro de extincion, amenazadas, raras y las sujetas a proteccion especial, y que establece especificaciones para su proteccion. Diario Oficial De La Federacion, Organo Del Gobierno Constitucional De Los Estados Unidos Mexicanos, Tomo Cdlxxxviii No. 10, Mexicao, D.F., Lunes 16 De Mayo De 1994: 2-60.

—**AZA. 1994.**
AZA Manual of Federal Wildlife Regulations. American Zoo and Aquarium Association (AZA), Bethesda, Maryland.

—**AZA/LAG. 1995.**
American Association of Zoos and Aquariums Lizard Advisory Group Regional Collection Plan. American Association of Zoos and Aquariums (AZA), Lizard Advisory Group (LAG).

—**AZA/Snake TAG. 1995.**
American Association of Zoos and Aquariums Snake Advisory Group Regional Collection Plan. American Association of Zoos and Aquariums (AZA), Snake Taxon Advisory Group (TAG). 26 pp.

—**Backner, B.P. 1994.**
The future role of the private sector in breeding endangered species, pp. 387-390 IN Murphy, B. et al. (editors). Captive Management and Conservation of Amphibians and Reptiles. Society for the Study of Amphibians and Reptiles, Ithaca, New York. Contributions to Herpetology, Volume 11. 488 pp.

—**Balazs, G.H. et al. 1991.**
Draft recovery plan for Hawaiian sea turtles, pp. 16-52 IN Uchida, I. (editor). International Symposium on Sea Turtles. Himeji City Aquarium and the Hiwasa Chelonian Museum.

—**Ballou, J.D.**
Capacity 3.0. National Zoological Park, Washington, DC 20008-2958. Software to establish target population sizes for managed species.

—**Ballou, J.D. 1987.**
Small populations, genetic diversity and captive carrying capacities. *Annual Proceedings of the American Association of Zoological Parks and Aquariums* 1987: 33-47.

—**Ballou, J.D. et al. (editors). 1995.**
Population Management for Survival and Recovery: Analytical methods and strategies in small population conservation. Columbia University Press, New York. 375 pp.

—**Bartholomew, B. 1996.**
1995 Herpetological Index. American Federation of Herpetoculturists, Escondido, California.

—**Bauer, A.M. and Sadlier, R.A. 1993.**
Systematics, biogeography and conservation of lizards of New Caledonia. *Biodiversity Letters* 1: 107-122.

—**Beaman, K.R. et al. 1991.**
International Symposium on Turtles & Tortoises: Conservation and captive husbandry. California Turtle & Tortoise Club, Executive Board, PO Box 7300, Van Nuys, California. 171 pp.

—**Bezzel, E. 1994.**
Small world populations in birds: An attempt of a brief general survey, pp. 23-32 IN Hermann, R. (editor). Minimum Animal Populations. Springer-Verlag, Berlin. 156 pp.

—**Bingaman, L. and Ballou, J.D.**
Demog. National Zoological Park, Washington, DC. Lotus 123 spreadsheet demographic model.

—**Bingaman, L. 1987.**
Herpetological collection composition: Recent and future. *Annual Proceedings of the American Association of Zoological Parks and Aquariums*: 844-861.

—**Bjorndal, K. (editor). 1995.**
Biology and Conservation of Sea Turtles. Smithsonian Press, Washington, DC.

—**Bjorndal, K.A. 1987.**
Manual of Sea Turtle Research and Conservation Techniques. Center for Environmental Education, Washington, DC.

—**Boer, L.E.M. de. 1992.**
Ex situ propagation programmes as a contribution to the conservation of biodiversity IN

Sandlund, O.T. et al. Conservation of Biodiversity for Sustainable Development. Scandinavian University Press, Oslo.

—**Bolze, D. 1992.**
The Wildlife Bird Trade: When a bird in the hands means none in the bush. Wildlife Conservation Society, New York. 24 pp.

—**Bowdoin, J. et al. 1994.**
AZA Annual Report on Conservation and Science 94. American Association of Zoological Parks and Aquariums (AAZPA), Bethesda, Maryland.

—**Bowles, M.L. and Whelan, C.J. (editors). 1994.**
Restoration of Endangered Species: Conceptual issues, planning, and implementation. Cambridge University Press, Cambridge, England. 394 pp.

—**Brown, W.S. 1993.**
Biology, Status, and Management of the Timber Rattlesnake (*Crotalus horridus*): A guide for conservation. Society for the Study of Amphibians and Reptiles, Herpetological Circulars No. 22. 84 pp.

—**Burghardt, G.M. and Rand, A.S. 1982.**
Iguanas of the World: Their behaviour, ecology, and conservation. Noyes Publications, Park Ridge, New Jersey. 472 pp.

—**Bury, R.B. (editor). 1982.**
North American Tortoises: Conservation and ecology. United States Department of the Interior, Fish and Wildlife Service, Wildlife Research Report 12, Washington, DC. 126 pp.

—**Butler, D.J. 1992.**
The role of zoos in the captive breeding of New Zealand's threatened fauna. *International Zoo Yearbook* 31: 4-9.

—**Byers, O. 1994.**
Global Captive Action Recommendations (GCAR): Reference material packet. IUCN/SSC Conservation Breeding Specialist Group, Apple Valley, Minnesota. 15 pp.

—**Carr, A.F. 1967.**
So Excellent a Fish: A natural history of sea turtles. Scribner, New York.

—**Case, T.J. and Bogler, D.T. 1991.**
The role of introduced species in shaping the distribution and abundance of island reptiles. *Evolutionary Ecology* 5: 272-290.

—**Case, T.J. et al. 1992.**
Reptilian Extinctions: The last ten thousand years, pp. 91-125 IN Fiedler, P.L. and Jain, S.K. (editors). Conservation Biology: The theory and practice of nature conservation, Preservation, and Management. Chapman and Hall, New York. 507 pp.

—**CBSG. 1996.**
Global Zoo Directory. IUCN/SSC/ Conservation Breeding Specialist Group (CBSG), Apple Valley, Minnesota.

—**Ceballos, G. and Brown, J.H. 1995.**
Global patterns of mammalian diversity, endemism, and endangerment. *Conservation Biology* 9(3): 559-568.

—**CITES. 1995.**
Appendices I, II, and III to the Convention on International Trade in Endangered Species of Wild Fauna and Flora, February, 16, 1995. Geneva, Switzerland. 23 pp.

—**Clubb, S.L. 1992.**
The role of private aviculture in the conservation of Neotropical Psittacines, pp. 117-131 IN Beissinger, S.R. and Synder, N.F.R. New World Parrots in Crisis: Solutions from conservation biology. Smithsonian Institution Press, Washington, DC. 288 pp.

—**Cogger, H. et al. 1993.**
The Action Plan for Australian Reptiles. Australian Nature Conservation Agency, Canberra, ACT. 254 pp.

—**Conway, W.G. 1986.**
The practical difficulties and financial implications of endangered species breeding programmes. *International Zoo Yearbook* 24/25: 210-219.

—**Corbett, K. (editor). 1989.**
The Conservation of European Reptiles and Amphibians. Christopher Helm, London, England. 274 pp.

—**Cree, A. and Butler, D. 1993.**
Tuatara Recovery Plan (*Sphenodon* spp.). Threatened Species Recovery Plan No. 9. New Zealand Department of Conservation, Wellington. 71 pp.

—**Cree, A. and Daugherty, C.H. 1990.**
Captive breeding of the New Zealand Tuatara: Past results and future directions, pp. 477-491 IN Dresser, B.L. et al. (editors). Proceedings of the Fifth World Conference on Breeding Endangered Species in Captivity. Cincinnati Zoo and Botanical Garden, Cincinnati, Ohio.

—**Cree, A. et al. 1994.**
The contribution of captive management to the conservation of Tuatara (*Sphenodon*) in New Zealand, pp. 377-385 IN Murphy, B. et al. (editors). Captive Management and Conservation of Amphibians and Reptiles. Society for the Study of Amphibians and Reptiles, Ithaca, New York. Contributions to Herpetology, Volume 11. 488 pp.

—**CSG. 1990.**
Crocodiles: Proceedings of the 10th Work-

ing Meeting of the Crocodile Specialist Group, International Union for Conservation of Nature and Natural Resources. Crocodile Specialist Group (CSG), World Conservation Union, Gland, Switzerland, 2 Volumes.

—**Cunningham, A. 1996.**
Disease risks of wildlife translocations. *Conservation Biology* 10(2): 349-353.

—**Da Silva, Jr., N.J. and Sites, Jr., J.W. 1995.**
Patterns of diversity of Neotropical squamate reptile species with emphasis on the Brazilian amazon and the conservation potential of indigenous reserves. *Conservation Biology* 9(4): 873-901.

—**Daugherty, C.H. et al. 1994.**
Taxonomic and conservation review of New Zealand herpetofauna. *New Zealand Journal of Zoology* 21(4): 317-323.

—**Derrickson S.R. and Snyder, N.F.R. 1992.**
Potentials and limits of captive breeding in Parrot conservation, pp. 133-163 IN Beissinger, S.R. and Synder, N.F.R. New World Parrots in Crisis: Solutions from conservation biology. Smithsonian Institution Press, Washington, DC. 288 pp.

—**Dodd, C.K., Jr. 1993.**
Strategies for snake conservation, pp. 363-393 IN Seigel, R.A. and Collins, J.T. (editors). Snakes: Ecology and behavior. McGraw-Hill Book Co., New York.

—**Dodd, C.K., Jr. 1987.**
Status, conservation, and management, pp. 478-513 IN Seigel, R.A. et al. (editors). Snakes: Ecology and evolutionary biology. MacMillan Publishing Co., New York.

—**Dodd, C.K., Jr. and Seigel, R.A. 1991.**
Relocation, repatriation, and translocation of amphibians and reptiles: Are they conservation strategies that work? *Hereptologica* 47: 336-350.

—**Dunham, A.E. et al. 1988.**
Methods for the study of reptile populations, pp. 331-386 IN Gans, C. and Huey, R.B. (editors). Biology of the Reptilia, Volume 16. Alan R. Liss, New York, New York.

—**Ebenhard, T. 1995.**
Conservation breeding as a tool for saving animal species from extinction. *Trends in Ecology & Evolution* 10 (11): 438-443.

—**Ehmann, H.F.W. and Cogger, H.G. 1985.**
Australia's endangered herpetofauna: A review of criteria and policies, pp. 435-447 IN Grigg, G.C. et al. (editors). The Biology of Australian Frogs and Reptiles. Surrey Beatty and Sons with Royal Zoological Society, New South Wales, Sydney. 527 pp.

—**Ellis, S. (editor). 1996.**
Population and Habitat Viability Assessment for the Orinoco Crocodile. IUCN/SSC Conservation Breeding Specialist Group, Apple Valley, Minnesota.

—**Ellis, S. and Donnelly, M. (editors). 1995.**
Conservation Assessment and Management Plan (CAMP) and Population and Habitat Viability Assessment for Marine Turtles in Indonesia. IUCN/SSC Conservation Breeding Specialist Group, Apple Valley, Minnesota.

—**Ellis, S. and Seal, U.S. 1995.**
Conservation Assessment and Management Plan (CAMP): Reference material packet. IUCN/SSC Conservation Breeding Specialist Group, Apple Valley, Minnesota.

—**Faure, D.S. 1989.**
International Trade in Endangered Species: A guide to CITES. Martinus Nijhoff, Dordrecht.

—**Fitzgerald, S. 1989.**
International Wildlife Trade: Whose business is it? World Wildlife Fund, Washington, DC. 459 pp.

—**Flores-Villela, O. 1993***a***.**
Herpetofauna Mexicana. Carnegie Museum of Natural History, Pittsburgh, Pennsylvania.

—**Flores-Villela, O. 1993***b***.**
Herpetofauna of Mexico: Distribution and endemism, pp. 253-280 IN Ramamoorthy, T.P. et al. Biological Diversity of Mexico: Origins and distribution. Oxford University Press, New York. 812 pp.

—**Flores-Villela, O. and Gerez, P. 1994.**
Biodiveridad Y Conservacion En Mexico: Vertebrados, Vegetacion Y Uso Del Suelo. Comision Nacional para el Conocimiento y Uso de la Biodiversidad and Universidad Nacional Antonoma de Mexico D.F. 439 pp.

—**Foose, T.J. 1986.**
Riders of the last ark: The role of captive breeding in conservation strategies, pp. 14-65 IN Kaufman, L. and Mallory, D. The Last Extinction. MIT Press, Cambridge, Maryland.

—**Foose, T.J. and Ballou, J.D. 1988.**
Management of small populations. *International Zoo Yearbook* 27: 26-41.

—**Foose, T.J. and Seal, U.S. 1991.**
Action Plans. Captive Breeding Specialist Group IUCN/SSC/ Conservation Breeding Specialist Group, Apple Valley, Minnesota.

—**Foose, T.J. et al. 1986.**
Propagation plans. *Zoo Biology* 5: 139-146.

—**Frank, N. and Ramus, E. 1995.**
A Complete Guide to Scientific and Common Names of Reptiles and Amphibians of

the World. N G Publishing Incorporated, Pottsville, Pennsylvania.

—**Frost, D.R. 1985.**
Amphibian Species of the World: A taxonomic and geographic reference. Allen Press, Incorporated and the Association of Systematic Collections, Lawrence, Kansas. 732 pp.

—**GECKO.**
Sandpiper Software, 153 Michele Circle, Novato, California 94947. Personalize your field notes and collections.

—**Gibbons, E.J., Jr. et al. 1995.**
Conservation of Endangered Species in Captivity: An interdisciplinary approach. State University of New York Press, Ithaca, New York. 675 pp.

—**Gilpin, M.**
Nemesis: Conservation Biology Software. 419 West Harrison, Bozeman, Montana 59715.

—**Gipps, J.H.W. (editor). 1991.**
Beyond Captive Breeding: Reintroducing endangered species to the wild. Clarendon Press, Oxford, England. 284 pp.

—**Goetz, B. 1994.**
A Study on the Captive Maintenance of Tuatara (*Sphenodon punctatus*). Landcare Research New Zealand, Native Plants and Animals Division, Auckland, New Zealand.

—**Goodyear, N.C. and Lazell, J. 1994.**
Status of a relocated population of endangered *Iguana pinguis* on Guana Island, British Virgin Islands. *Restoration Ecology* 2: 43-50.

—**Gray-Schofield, G. 1983.**
CITES Appendix I Species in Captivity 1977-1981: A survey of the maintenance and breeding of captive mammals, birds, reptiles, and amphibians from three data sources. Traffic USA, World Wildlife Fund—US, Washington, DC. 29 pp.

—**Groombridge, B. (editor). 1993.**
1994 IUCN Red List of Threatened Animals. The World Conservation Union (IUCN), Gland, Switzerland. 286 pp.

—**Groombridge, B. 1992***a.*
Endangered Species, pp. 42-49 IN Cogger, H. G. and Zweifel, R.G. (editors). Reptiles & Amphibians. Smithmark, New York, New York. 240 pp.

—**Groombridge, B. (editor). 1992***b.*
Global Biodiversity: Status of the earth's living resources. Chapman and Hall, London, England. 614 pp.

—**Groombridge, B. 1982.**
The IUCN Amphibia-Reptilia Red Data Book. Part 1, Testudines, Crocodylia, Rhynchocephalia, IUCN, Gland.

—**Groombridge, B. and Luxmoore, R. 1989.**
The Green Turtle and Hawksbill (Reptilia: Chelonidae): World status, exploitation and trade. CITES Secretariat, Lausanne, Switzerland.

—**Groombridge, B. and Luxmoore, R. 1991.**
Pythons in South-East Asia: A review of distribution, status and trade in three selected species. CITES Secretariat, Lausanne, Switzerland.

—**Haywood, V.H. (editor). 1995.**
Global Biodiversity Assessment. Cambridge University Press, Cambridge, United Kingdom.

—**Hemley, G. 1994.**
International Wildlife Trade: A CITES sourcebook. Island Press, Washington, DC. 180 pp.

—**Heyer, W.R. et al. (editors). 1994.**
Measuring and Monitoring Biological Diversity: Standard methods for amphibians. Smithsonian Institution Press. Washington, DC. 364 pp.

—**Honegger, R..E. 1980-81.**
List of amphibians and reptiles either known or thought to have been extinct since 1600. *Biological Conservation* 19: 141-158.

—**Honegger, R. 1975/1979.**
Red Data Book, Volume 3—Amphibia and Reptilia. Second Edition. IUCN, Gland.

—**HSUS and HSI 1994.**
Preliminary Report: Live freshwater turtle and tortoise trade in the United States. The Humane Society of the United States (HSUS) and Humane Society International (HSI), November 1994. 38 pp.

—**Hudson, R. et al. 1994.**
Conservation Assessment and Management Plan for Iguanidae and Varanidae. IUCN/ SSC Conservation Breeding Specialist Group, Apple Valley, Minnesota.

—**Huntley, R.V. and Langton, R.W. 1994.**
Captive Breeding Guidelines. Aquatic Conservation Network. Ottawa, Ontario, Canada. 62 pp.

—**Hutchins. M. et al. *In Press.***
Why we need captive breeding. *1996 AZA Regional Conference Proceedings.*

—**Hutchins, M. and Conway, W.G. 1995.**
Beyond Noah's ark: The evolving role of modern zoological parks and aquariums in field conservation. *International Zoo Yearbook* 34: 85-97.

—**Hutchins, M. et al. 1995.**
Zoos, ecotourism and conservation: A panel discussion, pp. 229-255 IN AZA Annual Conference Proceedings. American Associa-

tion of Zoological Parks and Aquariums, Wheeling, West Virginia.

—**Hutchins, M. and Wemmer, C. 1991.**
In defense of captive breeding. *Endangered Species Update* 8(9-10):5-6.

—**Hutchins, M. and Wiese, R.J. 1991.**
Beyond genetic and demographic management: The future of the Species Survival Plan and related AAZPA conservation efforts. *Zoo Biology* 10:285-292.

—**Hutchins, M. 1988.**
On the design of zoo research programs. *International Zoo Yearbook* 27: 9-19.

—**ISIS***a.*
Animal Records Keeping System (ARKS). International Species Information System (ISIS), Apple Valley, Minnesota.

—**ISIS***b.*
Medical Animal Records Keeping System (MEDARKS). International Species Information System (ISIS), Apple Valley, Minnesota.

—**ISIS***c.*
Single Population Analysis and Record Keeping System (SPARKS). International Species Information System (ISIS), Apple Valley, Minnesota.

—**ISIS. 1995.**
ISIS Reptile Abstract: As of 30 June 1995. International Species Information System (ISIS), Apple Valley, Minnesota. 185 pp.

—**IUCN. 1996.**
1996 IUCN Red List of Threatened Animals. IUCN, Gland, Switzerland. 368 pp.

—**IUCN. 1992.**
Protected Areas of The World: A review of national systems. Volume 1—Indomalaya, Oceania, Australia, and Antarctic. 352 pp.; Volume 2—Palaearctic. 556 pp.; Volume 3—Afrotropical. 360 pp.; Volume 4—Nearctic and Neotropical. 460 pp. The World Conservation Union (IUCN), Gland, Switzerland.

—**IUCN. 1987***a.*
The IUCN Policy Statement on Captive Breeding. The World Conservation Union (IUCN), Gland, Switzerland.

—**IUCN. 1987***b.*
The IUCN Position Statement on Translocation of Living Organisms: Introductions, re-introductions and restocking. The World Conservation Union (IUCN), Gland, Switzerland.

—**IUCN/SSC. 1994.**
IUCN Red List Categories. The World Conservation Union (IUCN), Gland, Switzerland. 21 pp.

—**IUCN/SSC/RSG. 1995.**
IUCN/SSC/RSG Guidelines for Re-Introductions. The World Conservation Union (IUCN), Species Survival Commission (SSC), Re-Introduction Specialist Group (RSG), Nairobi, Kenya. 4 pp.

—**IUCN/SSC/TFTSG. 1991.**
Tortoises and Freshwater Turtles: An action plan for their conservation. Tortoises and Freshwater Turtle Specialist Group of the Species Survival Commission, The World Conservation Union (IUCN), Gland, Switzerland. 48 pp.

—**IUCN/SSC Trade and Madagascar Reptile and Amphibian Specialist Groups. 1993.**
A preliminary review of the status and distribution of reptile and amphibian species exported from Madagascar. IUCN/BIODEV Joint Nature Conservation Committee.

—**IUDZG/CBSG (IUCN/SSC). 1993.**
The World Zoo Conservation Strategy: The role of the zoos and aquaria of the world in global conservation. Chicago Zoological Society, Brookfield, Illinois. 76 pp.

—**IUCN et al. 1993.**
Caring for the Earth: A strategy for sustainable living. The World Conservation Union (IUCN), Gland, Switzerland. 228 pp.

—**IUCN et al. 1992.**
Masterworks of Man and Nature: Preserving our world heritage. Harper-MacRae, Patonga, Australia. 447 pp.

—**Iverson, J.B. 1985.**
Checklist of the Turtles of the World with English Common Names. Society for the Study of Amphibians and Reptiles, Oxford, Ohio. 14 pp.

—**Iverson, J.B. 1992.**
A Revised Checklist with Distribution Maps of the Turtles of the World. J. Iverson, Richmond, Indiana. 363 pp.

—**Jenkins, R.W.G. 1985.**
Government legislation and conservation of endangered reptiles and amphibians, pp. 431-433 IN Grigg, G.C. et al. (editors.). The Biology of Australian Frogs and Reptiles. Surrey Beatty and Sons with Royal Zoological Society, New South Wales, Sydney. 527 pp.

—**Jenkins, M. and Board, S. (editors). 1994.**
International Trade in Reptile Skins: A review and analysis of the main consumer markets, 1983-1991. Traffic International, Cambridge, United Kingdom.

—**Jones, S.R. 1990.**
Overview of the goals and activities of the IUCN Captive Breeding Specialist Group and International Species Information System. *Endangered Species Update* 8(1): 8-9.

—**King, F.W. and Burke, R.L. (editors). 1989.**
Crocodilian, Tuatara, and Turtle Species of the World: A taxonomic and geographic reference. Association of Systematic Collections, Washington, DC. 216 pp.

—**Klemm, C. 1993*a*.**
Biological Diversity Conservation and the Law: Legal mechanisms for the conserving species and ecosystems. The World Conservation Union, Gland, Switzerland and Cambridge, United Kingdom.

—**Klemm, C. 1993*b*.**
Guidelines for Legislation to Implement CITES. The World Conservation Union, Cambridge, England. 107 pp.

—**Koebner, L. 1994.**
Zoo Book: The Evolution of Wildlife Conservation Centers. Forge, New York, New York. 192 pp.

—**Lacy, R.C.*a*.**
Genes. Chicago Zoological Society, Chicago, Illinois 60513.

—**Lacy, R.C.*b*.**
Vortex. Population modeling software & manual. IUCN/SSC Conservation Breeding Specialist Group, Apple Valley, Minnesota.

—**Lacy, R.C. 1993.**
Vortex: A computer simulation model for population viability analysis. *Wildlife Research* 20: 45-65.

—**Langerwerf, B. 1991.**
A large scale lizard breeding facility in Alabama. *British Herpetological Society Bulletin* 36: 43-46.

—**Langerwerf, B. 1984.**
Techniques for large-scale breeding of lizards from temperate climates in greenhouse enclosure (breeding many species of lizards in captivity, aiming the maintenance of populations of each species outside their natural habitat). *Acta Zoologica Et Pathologica Antverpiensia* No. 78: 163-176.

—**Langerwerf, B. 1980.**
The successful breeding of lizards from temperate regions, pp. 37-46 IN Townson, S. et al. The Care and Breeding of Captive Reptiles. British Herpetological Society, London, United Kingdom. 98 pp.

—**Lawler, H.E. 1994.**
Applications of field herpetology in captive management programs for endangered herpetofauna, pp. 273-286 IN Brown, P.R. and Wright, J.W. (editors). Herpetology of The North American Deserts. Southwestern Herpetological Society, Special Publication No. 5, Santa Barbara, California. 300 pp.

—**Lawler, H.E. 1992.**
Advanced protocols for the management and propagation of endangered and threatened reptiles, pp. 57-66 IN Uricheck, M.J. (editor). Proceedings of the 15th International Herpetological Symposium on Captive Propagation and Husbandry. International. Herpetological Symposium, Danbury, Connecticut.

—**Levell, J.P. 1995.**
A Field Guide to Reptiles and the Law. Serpent's Tale Natural History Book Distributors, Excelsior, Minnesota. 240 pp.

—**Luxmoore, R.A. 1992.**
A Directory of Crocodilian Farming Operations. World Conservation Union, Gland, Switzerland. 352 pp.

—**Luxmoore, R. and Groombridge, B. 1990.**
Asian Monitor Lizards: A review of distribution, status, exploitation and trade in four selected species. CITES Secretariat, Lausanne, Switzerland.

—**Luxmoore, R. et al. (editors). 1988.**
Significant Trade in Wildlife: A review of selected species in CITES appendix II. Reptiles and Invertebrates, Volume. 2. World Conservation Monitoring Centre, Cambridge, England. 306 pp.

—**Mace, G.**
Genedrop. Computer software for gene drop analysis. Zoological Society of London, United Kingdom.

—**Mace, G.M. 1994.**
Definitions and categories for describing the conservation status of species, IN Edwards, P.J. et al. (editors). Large Scale Ecology and Conservation Biology. Blackwell Scientific Publications, Cambridge, Massachusetts.

—**Mace, G.M. and Lande, R. 1991.**
Assessing extinction threats: Toward a reevaluation of IUCN threatened species categories. *Conservation Biology* 5: 148-157.

—**Majumdar, S.K. et al. (editors). 1994.**
Biological Diversity: Problems and challenges. Pennsylvania Academy of Sciences, Easton, Pennsylvania.

—**Mallinson, J.J.C. 1991.**
Partners for conservation between zoos, local governments and non-governmental organizations, pp. 57-74 IN Gipps, J.H.W. (editor). 1991. Beyond Captive Breeding: Reintroducing endangered species to the wild. Clarendon Press, Oxford, England. 284 pp.

—**Mallinson, J.J.C. 1988.**
Collaboration for conservation between the Jersey Wildlife Preservation Trust and countries where species are endangered. *International Zoo Yearbook* 27: 176-191.

—**Marcellini, D.L. 1994.**
Collection-management, captive-breeding, and conservation programs in zoo herpetological collections, pp. 397-400 IN Murphy, B. et al. (editors). Captive Management and Conservation of Amphibians and Reptiles. Society for the Study of Amphibians and Reptiles, Ithaca, New York. Contributions to Herpetology, Volume 11. 488 pp.

—**Marquez M., R. 1990.**
FAO Species Catalogue. Volume 11: Sea Turtles of the World. An annotated and illustrated catalogue of sea turtle species known to date. FAO Fisheries Synopsis, No. 125, Volume 11, FAO, Rome. 81 pp.

—**McCullough, D.R. and Barrett, R.H. (editors). 1992.**
Wildlife 2001: Populations. Elsevier Applied Science, London, England.

—**Mittermeier, R.A. and Carr, J.L. 1994.**
Conservation of Reptiles and Amphibians: A global perspective, pp. 27-36 IN Murphy, B. et al. (editors). Captive Management and Conservation of Amphibians and Reptiles. Society for the Study of Amphibians and Reptiles, Ithaca, New York. Contributions to Herpetology, Volume 11. 488 pp.

—**Mittermeier, R.A. et al. 1994.**
Lemurs of Madagascar. Conservation International, Washington, DC. 356 pp.

—**Mittermeier, R.A. et al. 1992.**
Conservation of amphibians and reptiles, pp. 59-80 IN Adler, K. (editor). Herpetology: Current research on the biology amphibians and reptiles. Proceedings of the First World Congress of Herpetology. Society for the Study of Amphibians and Reptiles, Oxford, Ohio.

—**Moore, H.D.M., et. al. 1992.**
Biotechnology and the Conservation of Genetic Diversity. Clarendon Press, New York. 256 pp.

—**Murphy, J.B. and Collins, J.T. (editors). 1980.**
Reproduction Biology and Diseases of Captive Reptiles. Society for the Study of Amphibians and Reptiles, Contributions to Herpetology 1, Oxford, Ohio. 287 pp.

—**Murphy, J.B. et al. 1994.**
Captive Management and Conservation of Amphibians and Reptiles. Society for the Study of Amphibians and Reptiles, Ithaca, New York. Contributions to Herpetology, Volume 11. 408 pp.

—**Myers, N. 1990.**
The Biodiversity Challenge: Expanded Hot-Spots analysis. *The Environmentalist* 10(4): 243-256.

—**Newman, A. 1990.**
Tropical Rainforest: A world survey of our most valuable and endangered habitat with a blueprint for its survival. Eddison-Sadd, New York, New York. 256 pp.

—**Newman, D. 1987.**
Tuatara. John McIndoe and Department of Conservation, Dunedin, New Zealand.

—**NRC. 1990.**
Decline of the Sea Turtles: Causes and prevention. National Research Council (NRC). National Academy Press, Washington, DC. 259 pp.

—**Odum, R.A. 1992.**
Crotalus durissus unicolor Species Survival Plan, Master Plan, Status and Recommendations, 1992-93. Toledo Zoo, Toledo, Ohio.

—**Odum, R.A. and Goode, M.J. 1994.**
The Species Survival Plan for *Crotalus durissus unicolor*: A multifaceted approach to conservation of an insular rattlesnake, pp. 363-368 IN Murphy, B. et al. (editors). Captive Management and Conservation of Amphibians and Reptiles. Society for the Study of Amphibians and Reptiles, Ithaca, New York. Contributions to Herpetology, Volume 11.

—**Olney, P.J.S. et al. (editors). 1994*a*.**
Creative Conservation: Interactive management of wild and captive animals. Chapman & Hall. London, England. 517 pp.

—**Olney, P.J.S. et al. (editors). 1994*b*.**
1993 International Zoo Yearbook—Volume 33. Zoological Society of London, London, England. 492 pp.

—**OPWT. 1991.**
Proceedings of New Zealand Giant Skink Workshop, March 1991. Orana Park Wildlife Trust (OPWT), Christchurch, New Zealand.

—**Osborne, R. 1995.**
The world Cycad census and a proposed revision of the threatened species status for Cycad taxa. *Biological Conservation* 71(1): 1-12.

—**Perry-Richardson, J. and Ivanyi, C. 1995.**
Beaded Lizard (*Heloderma horridum*) North American Regional Studbook. Arizona-Sonora Desert Museum, Tucson, Arizona. 83 pp.

—**Peterson, K.H. 1992.**
International Studbook for the Aruba Island Rattlesnake, 1992 Edition. Houston Zoological Gardens, Houston, Texas. 55 pp.

—**Pindee, N.T. and Barkham, J.P. 1978.**
An assessment of the contribution of captive breeding to the conservation of rare mammals. *Biological Conservation* 13: 187-245.

—Pritchard, P.C.H. and Anders, G.J.R. (editors). *In Press.*
The Conservation Biology of Freshwater Turtles: Volume 1—Old World Turtles (Palearctic, Afrotropical, Indomalayan, and Australasian Realms). Chelonian Research Monographs.

—Pritchard, P.C.H. 1996.
The Galápagos Tortoises: Nomenclature and survival status. *Chelonian Research Monographs Number 1.* Chelonian Research Foundation. 85 pp.

—Pritchard, P.C.H. 1995.
Conservation of reptiles and amphibians, pp. 147-167 IN Gibbons, E.J., Jr. et al. 1995. Conservation of Endangered Species in Captivity: An interdisciplinary approach. State University of New York Press, Ithaca, New York. 675 pp.

—Quinn, H. and Quinn, H. 1993.
Estimated number of snake species that can be managed by species survival plans in North America. *Zoo Biology* 12: 243-255.

—Ralls, K. and Ballou, J.D. 1992.
Managing genetic diversity in captive breeding and reintroduction programs. *Transactions of the North American Wildlife and Natural Resources Conference* 57: 263-282.

—Rao, R.J. 1995.
Population and Habitat Viability Assessment for Gharial: Briefing book. IUCN/SSC Conservation Breeding Specialist Group, Apple Valley, Minnesota.

—Raxworthy, C.J. 1988.
Reptiles, rainforest and conservation in Madagascar. *Biological Conservation* 43: 181-211.

—Reinert, H.K. 1991.
Translocation as a conservation strategy for amphibians and reptiles: Some comments, concerns and observations. *Herpetologica* 47: 357-363.

—Revol, B. 1995.
Crocodile farming and conservation, the example of Zimbabwe. *Biodiversity and Conservation* 4(3): 299-305.

—Richardson, J.I. and Richardson, T.H. 1995.
Proceedings of the Twelfth Annual Workshop on Sea Turtle Biology and Conservation. NOAA Technical Memorandum NMFS-SEFSC-361. 274 pp.

—Richman, A.D. et al. 1988.
Natural and unnatural extinction rates of reptiles on islands. *American Naturalist* 131: 611-630.

—Robinson, J.G. and Redford, K.H. (editors). 1991.
Neotropical Wildlife Use and Conservation. University Chicago Press, Chicago. 520 pp.

—Rockwell, R. and Teere, A. 1986.
Studbook Management System. Henry Doorly Zoo. Omaha, Nebraska.

—Ross, C.A. and Garnett, S. 1989.
Crocodiles and Alligators. Facts on File, New York, New York. 240 pp.

—Seal et al. 1994.
Conservation Assessment and Management Plans (CAMPs) and Global Captive Action Plans (GCAPs), pp. 312-325 IN Olney, P.J.S. et al. (editors). 1994. Creative Conservation: Interactive management of wild and captive animals. Chapman & Hall. London, England. 517 pp.

—Seal, U.S. 1993*a.*
Jamaican Iguana Population and Habitat Viability Assessment Workshop, Briefing Book. IUCN/SSC Captive Breeding Specialist Group. Apple Valley, Minnesota.

—Seal, U.S. 1993*b.*
Population and Habitat Viability Assessment (PHVA): Reference material packet. IUCN/SSC Conservation Breeding Specialist Group (CBSG), Apple Valley, Minnesota.

—Seal, U.S. 1992*a.*
Aruba Island Rattlesnake Population and Habitat Viability Assessment. IUCN/SSC Captive Breeding Specialist Group, Apple Valley, Minnesota.

—Seal, U.S. 1992*b.*
Conservation Assessment and Management Plan (CAMP) for Varnidae, Iguanidae, Pythonidae, Boidae, Tropidipheridae, and Bolyeriidae: Briefing book. IUCN/SSC Conservation Breeding Specialist Group, Apple Valley, Minnesota.

—Shaffer, M.L. 1990.
Population viability analysis. *Conservation Biology* 4: 39-40.

—Sheppard, C. 1995.
Propagation of endangered birds in US institutions: How much space is there? *Zoo Biology* 14: 197-210.

—Slavens, F.L. 1989.
The Inventory of Live Reptiles and Amphibians in Captivity: A brief history. *International Zoo Yearbook* 28: 7-9.

—Slavens, F. and Slavens, K.
Animal Tracks. Slaveware, Seattle, Washington. Complete animal management software package for managing your personal animal collection and field notes.

—Slavens, F.L. and Slavens, K. 1994.
Reptiles and Amphibians in Captivity: Breeding—Longevity and Inventory Current January 1, 1994. Slaveware, Seattle, Washington. 532 pp.

—Soulé, M.E. (editor). 1987.
Viable Populations for Conservation. Cambridge University Press, Cambridge, England. 189 pp.

—Soulé, M.E. (editor). 1986.
Conservation Biology: The science of scarcity and diversity. Sinauer. Sunderland, Massachusetts. 584 pp.

—Soulé, M. et al. 1986.
The millennium ark: How long a voyage, how many staterooms, how many passengers? *Zoo Biology* 5: 101-113.

—Speake, D.W. et al. 1981.
Eastern Indigo Snake Recovery Plan. United States Fish and Wildlife Service, Atlanta, Georgia.

—Stattersfield, A.J. 1996.
Applying the new IUCN threatened species categories, pp. 67-70 IN IUCN. 1996 IUCN Red List of Threatened Animals. IUCN, Gland, Switzerland. 368 pp.

—Stevens, E.F., Hutchins, M., and Maple, T. 1996*a*.
The AZA's conservation programs: How are they organized? *Endangered Species Update* 13: 10-12.

—Stevens, E.F., Hutchins, M., and Maple, T. 1996*b*.
Zoos, aquariums and endangered species. *Endangered Species Update* 13: 7-9.

—Stearns, B.C. 1989.
Chelonian Species Survival Plans: Present status and future directions. *Annual Proceedings of the American Association of Zoological Parks and Aquariums.* 1989: 24-35.

—Swingland, I. 1994.
International conservation and captive management of Tortoises, pp. 99-108 IN Murphy, B. et al. (editors). Captive Management and Conservation of Amphibians and Reptiles. Society for the Study of Amphibians and Reptiles, Ithaca, New York. Contributions to Herpetology, Volume 11. 488 pp.

—Swingland, I.R., and Klemens, M.W. (editors). 1989.
The Conservation Biology of Tortoises. Occasional Papers of the International Union Conservation Nature Natural Resources, Species Survival Commission, World Conservation Union, Gland, Switzerland No. 5. 204 pp.

—Thorbjarnarson, J.B. 1992.
Crocodiles: An action plan for their conservation. International Union for the Conservation of Nature, Species Survival Commission, Crocodile Specialist —Group, Gland, Switzerland. 136 pp.

—Trebbau et al. 1994.
The potential for captive breeding programmes in Venezuela—efforts between zoos, government and non-governmental organizations, pp. 487-494 IN Olney, —P.J.S. et al. (editors). 1994. Creative Conservation: Interactive management of wild and captive animals. Chapman & Hall. London, England. 517 pp.

—Trexler, M. and Kosloff, L. 1987.
The Wildlife Trade and CITES: An annotated bibliography for the Convention on International Trade in Endangered Species of Wild Fauna and Flora. Traffic USA, World Wildlife Fund, Washington, DC.

—Tudge, C. 1992.
Last Animals at the Zoo: How mass extinction can be stopped. Island Press, Washington, DC. 266 pp.

—Tudge, C. and Flint, A.P.F. 1991.
Science for Conservation: Research of the Zoological Society of London. Zoological Society of London, London, England.

—USFWS/DLE. 1995.
Combined Species Report (Dated August 11, 1995). This computer generated report taken from the US Fish and Wildlife Service Division of Law Enforcement's Protected Species Computer File of Protected and Commonly Traded Non-protected Species. Unpublished report, United States Fish and Wildlife Service (USFWS), Office of Management Authority, Arlington, Virginia. 26 pp.

—USFWS. 1994*a*.
Desert Tortoise (Mojave Population) Recovery Plan. United States Fish and Wildlife Service (USFWS), Portland, Oregon. 73 pp.

—USFWS. 1994*b*.
Endangered and Threatened Wildlife and Plants: 50 CFR 17.11 & 17.12, August 20, 1994. Copies are available from the Publications Unit, United States Fish and Wildlife Service (USFWS), 130-WEBB, Washington, DC 20240.

—USFWS. 1993.
Cargo for Conservation: An information kit about wildlife. United States Fish and Wildlife Service (USFWS), Arlington, Virginia.

—USFWS. 1983.
US CITES Annual Report for 1981. Wildlife Permit Office, United States Fish and Wildlife Service (USFWS), Department of the Interior, Washington, DC 20240. Note: This data is now sent out on electronic computer tape and no longer printed in published form.

—WCMC. 1995.
Checklist of Amphibians and Reptiles Listed

in the CITES Appendices. Joint Nature Conservation Committee, Peterborough, United Kingdom. Report No. 237.

—WCMC. 1993.
World Checklist of Threatened Amphibians and Reptiles. 5th Edition. World Conservation Monitoring Centre (WCMC). Joint Nature Conservation Committee, Peterborough, United Kingdom. 99 pp.

—WCMC (compiled by) and Groombridge, B. (editor). 1994.
Biodiversity Data Sourcebook. World Conservation Press, Cambridge, United Kingdom. 155 pp.

—Webb, G.J.W. et al. (editors). 1987.
Wildlife Management: Crocodiles and alligators. Surrey Beatty and Sons, New South Wales, Sydney and Conservation Commission of the Northern Territory. 552 pp.

—Western, D. and Pearl, M.C. (editors). 1989.
Conservation for the Twenty-first Century. Oxford University Press, New York, New York. 365 pp.

—Wiese, R.J. and Hutchins, M. 1994.
Species Survival Plans: Strategies for wildlife conservation. American Zoo and Aquarium Association, Wheeling, West Virginia.

—Wiese, R.J. and Hutchins, M. 1994.
The role of zoos and aquariums in amphibian and reptilian conservation, pp. 37-46 IN Murphy, B. et al. (editors). Captive Management and Conservation of Amphibians and Reptiles. Society for the Study of Amphibians and Reptiles, Ithaca, New York. Contributions to Herpetology, Volume 11. 488 pp.

—Wiese, R.J. and Hutchins, M. 1993.
The role of captive breeding and reintroduction in wildlife conservation, pp. 16-23 IN

AAZPA 1993 Regional Conference Proceedings. American Association of Zoological Parks and Aquariums, Wheeling West Virginia.

—Wiese, R.J., Willis, K., and Hutchins, M. 1996.
Conservation breeding in 1995: An update. trends in Evolution and Ecology 11(5): 218-219.

—Wiese, R.J. et al. 1994.
Is genetic and demographic management conservation? Zoo Biology 13:297-299.

—Wiese, R.J. et al. 1993.
The AAZPA Conservation Program: There is a method to our madness, pp. 1-13 IN American Association of Zoological Parks and Aquariums Conservation Program Resource Guide. American Association of Zoological Parks and Aquariums (AAZPA), Executive Office/Conservation Center, Bethesda, Maryland.

—Wijnskekers, W. 1992.
The Evolution of CITES: A reference to the Convention on International Trade in Endangered Species of Wild Fauna and Flora. Third revised edition. CITES Secretariat, Lausanne, Switzerland.

—Willis, K. and Wiese, R.J. 1993.
Effect of new founders on retention of gene diversity in captive populations: A formalization of the nucleus population concept. Zoo Biology 12: 535-548.

—Wilson, E.O. and Peter, F.M. (editors). 1988.
Biodiversity. National Academy Press. Washington, DC. 521 pp.

—WRI et al. 1992.
Global Biodiversity Strategy: Guidelines for action to save, study and use earth's biotic wealth sustainably and equitably. World Resources Institute, Washington, DC. 244 pp.

West Midland Safari Park
Spring Grove
BEWDLEY
Worcestershire
DY12 1LF

THE USE OF REPTILES IN PUBLIC EDUCATION

Melissa Kaplan
RepEnvirEd
6366 Commerce Blvd #216
Rohnert Park CA 94928

Kaplan's work and practical experience includes six years in wildlife rehabilitation, with emphasis on reptiles; behavior observation in zoo and field settings; and oil-spill bird recovery. Currently completing a masters thesis on the selection, care, and use of animals in the classroom, Ms. Kaplan works as a freelance educator, presenting programs on reptiles and their environment, and developing integrated curricula based on animal and plant life. She is also a freelance author, writing articles on reptile rehabilitation, reptile pet care, and related issues. Ms. Kaplan has extensive consulting experience, both on- and offline, on reptile care and behavior, with an emphasis on the green iguana.

REPTILES AND EDUCATION

The use of animals in education is not new, nor is the controversy surrounding such use. The effectiveness of educational programs using animals has recently been studied to determine if students are learning what the program developers intended and, in the case of wildlife education programs, whether the desired attitudinal shifts are being made.

The issues concerning the use of reptiles in education programs are the same issues concerning the use of other animals by educators. Reptiles are neither more nor less dangerous than other animals and, as with other animals, some reptiles are more appropriate than others for use in certain educational settings. However, given the largely negative view of reptiles held by the general public (i.e. they are often afraid of them; that reptiles are inherently dangerous to humans), the use of reptiles may provide more opportunities for growth in awareness and changes in attitude.

Adams (1986) described wildlife education as "those teaching and learning processes that introduce information about specific wildlife resources, habitats, ecological relationships, conservation, and management strategies into public school and community educational programs." To be worthwhile, the educational process must result in lasting changes in the learner's knowledge, attitude and awareness (Kellert, 1989; Sherwood, 1989).

Recently, filmmakers found they were producing material that much of their potential audience failed to understand or did not watch because some footage offended the sensibilities of the audience. Biologists and humane educators have become aware that what they assumed children and adults knew, thought, or felt about animals was incorrect. They had assumed that the general public thought and felt as they themselves thought and felt about animals and the environment. Biology teachers presumed and assumed that students knew and under-

Sinaloan Milk Snake, *Lampropeltis triangulum sinaloae*. Photo by Susan Miller.

Ball Python, *Python regius*.
Photo by Isabelle Francais.

stood what they in fact did not. Thus, biology teachers were trying to teach concepts for which their students were not intellectually prepared. Research suggests that the priority of learning about animals decreases as people age (Kellert, 1989; Paterson, 1989).

In the past, animal welfare organizations have produced educational materials that were poorly researched. Most of these materials grossly underestimated the public's background knowledge of animals. Educational programs were not assessed to determine if the material presented was being absorbed and retained beyond the giving of correct answers on tests which may have been administered at the time the material was presented (Paterson, 1989; Kellert, 1989).

In the 1980's, research in the United States and Britain found that all of the most popular animals were mammals with large eyes and cuddly, rounded bodies—in a word, humanoid. The least popular animals lacked easily anthropomorphic features and were described in pejorative terms such as slimy, dirty, or dangerous (Paterson, 1989).

Middle-childhood-aged children (ages 10-12) rated high in naturalistic views of anthropomorphically charged animals. Younger children (aged 6-8) were highly negativistic—some even dominionistic—in their attitudes towards wildlife. Overall, children up to age 10 years old were found to be more exploitative, harsh, and unfeeling in their attitude towards animals, generally lacking empathy and emotional identification with nonanthropomorphically charged animals. Negativism, however, encompasses two attitudes: neutralistic, characterized by avoidance due to indifference; and negativism based on an active dislike or fear (Kellert, 1989). Younger children are less informed about animals and the natural environment than are older children, but their negativism, based on fear or lack of exposure can be mediated through controlled, positive exposure to live animals more effectively than by rote or didactic learning of facts (Morgan, 1989; Skeen, 1987).

Kellert (1981) also found that not only was basic identification and understanding of animals lacking, especially in urban children and adults, but so, too, was their understanding of the ecology of animals. Predation and nutrient cycles were viewed in predominantly negative terms, with animals such as dung beetles considered "disgusting" and predation as being inherently wrong. Nature was viewed as good or bad rather than merely neutral. Both Patterson (1989) and Kellert (1981) found that children from rural areas and those children who engaged in wildlife contact or observation activities were better disposed towards wildlife and knew more about wildlife and animal activities. These children also understood that most wild animals were not dangerous to people.

GOALS OF EDUCATION

While large mammalian predators are admired, the role of reptilian predators is often lost in the revulsion and fear many people feel when thinking about those least anthropomorphic animals that test low on popularity (Kellert, 1981; Patterson, 1989). People who would think nothing of reaching out and touching a mammal or bird if given the opportunity may shriek and shy away, or look on with morbid fascination, when faced with a creature with scales instead of feathers or fur. Controlled contact with reptiles, however, can help dispel the fears and misunderstandings (Caras, 1980; Golden, 1989; Morgan, 1992).

When live reptiles are used in an educational setting, learning occurs in both the cognitive and affective realms. This provides the opportunity for almost immediate personal growth and development. Not only does the learner begin to understand facts about reptiles and their classification, behavior and ecology; he also begins to see how the animal functions as a member of an ecosystem. As information is integrated into the learner's cognitive system, he is able to take in more and increasingly complex information.

Personal and interpersonal growth occurs as the learner makes use of the opportunity to overcome fear and resistance to touching the animal. This builds self-confidence and self-esteem that is strengthened through others' recognition of the accomplishment and positive reinforcement of appropriate handling. Cooperation and sharing when interacting with the reptiles are important skills learned by school-aged children. Late childhood and adolescent learners may develop leadership skills through working with others, supervising younger children and interacting with peers and adults in the learning and teaching about reptiles (Hodges, 1991; Patterson-Morris, 1993; Skeen, et al., 1987).

The goal of a positive learning encounter is to change the learner's perception of reptiles from one of fearsome predator or mindless nonsentience to the recognition and acceptance of life. The learner should come to understand that, cold-blooded or warm, living things are deserving of respect, both individually, wherever they are encountered, and as an important member species in the maintenance of a health ecosystem.

DIRECT CONTACT WITH LIVE ANIMALS VS. MERE EXPOSURE

With television and computer videography making inroads into homes and schools, student and

Iguanas are inappropriate pets for young children, who are generally not suited to holding them without close adult supervision. Photo by Isabelle Francais.

adult learners are exposed as never before to a wealth of information and visuals. In one evening, the viewer may see tuataras in Tasman Bay and gavials in the Ganges, with stops in between in Indonesia and Africa. Ultimately it may be too much. The overstimulation can result in the reader tuning out the information or message of the show. Wildlife at risk can become just another installment of Wile Coyote getting squashed by yet another Acme anvil—yet another plea to give, stop, or do something for someone somewhere. Having seen it all, there is little left to challenge, create dissonance, or stimulate learning in those with little prior interest or commitment to animals and their environment. What does create dissonance and stimulate growth and learning is exposure to the real thing: contact with live animals (Gibson, 1994b; Morris, 1990; Paterson, 1989).

Kreger, et al. (1995) found that zoo visitors desire more contact with the animals. Typically zoo contacts have included petting zoos, the public feeding of animals, and animal rides. These contact opportunities have been reduced or stopped in many zoos. Contact has decreased not only because of concern with the animal's welfare, but also because of the lack of research on the effect of such interactions. Information on the behavioral and physiological responses in animals is emerging, however, through controlled physiological studies and practical applications in the training of animals and environmental enhancements in zoos and wildlife parks (Laule, 1993; Kreger, 1993b; Reichard, et al., 1992; Warwick, 1990a, b).

Most zoos' energies and monies are concentrated on those few (usually mammalian) species that best draw in the paying public. Most zoos also now offer only superficial educational opportunities to their visitors. Typically, visitors spend 30-120 seconds at any one zoo exhibit, and during that time, the public is exposed to information rather than allowed to interact with the animals. This reduces the acquisition of information to an intellectual activity (Kreger, et al., 1995).

Studies have found that learners' knowlege and negativistic scores depend greatly on the type of animal-related activities use to teach them biology and ecology. Students whose animal-related activities involved zoo visits and classroom learning had relatively low knowledge scores and the highest negativistic scores. Also, ethnic and urban/rural differences showed the need to focus on the children's perceptions of animals. Both surveys found boys more knowledgeable about predators (47%:42%). Both studies also found that non-whites (32%:47%) and white, urban youth (38%:51%) scored lower overall in knowledge than white, rural youth. Paterson found that more than half of the rural students were comfortable in proximity to wildlife; only 37% of rural youth thought most wild animals were dangerous to humans, compared to 53% of urban youth believing so. Kellert found that 75% of his respondents had participated in some animal-related activity during the previous two-year period, including visiting zoos (93%), learning about animals in school (83%), reading books and magazines about animals (76%), and watching "Wild Kingdom" on television (74%). Most of these students had pets at home (87%); and many went fishing (87%). A far smaller number of students were involved in family livestock raising, hunting (18%), or trapping (13%). A small number (8%) belonged to an animal-related club.

In the United States and Great Britain, the regular school curricula for animal information is divorced from direct experience with animals. In those countries, studies strongly indicate that the regular school curricula has failed to present material in such a way as to promote affective and cognitive learning about animals and the environment (Kellert, 1989; Paterson, 1989).

Gentle handling of "tame" snakes such as kingsnakes, *Lampropeltis*, often helps convince an audience that not all snakes are dangerous. Photo by W.P. Mara

Ball Python, *Python regius*.
Photo by Isabelle Francais.

Children who participated in animal-care activities, spent time birdwatching, belonged to animal-related clubs, or hunted were more appreciative, knowledgeable and concerned about animals. The difference between the passive (zoos, schools) and active (self-directed and group participation) animal-learning activities is that active learning provides opportunities for experiential contact and involvement. This in turn facilitates and enhances the affective and cognitive development of learners of all ages (Kellert, 1989).

One often-used alternative to the hands-on approach is modeling by an authority figure. Modeling is based on the informational approach to teaching and learning. Subjects are presented with information and are shown an object or animal being held by the speaker. Subjects are expected to modify their behavior or attitudes due to the persuasiveness of the information presented and the credibility or respectability of the presenter. In studies with snake-phobic adults in controlled settings, with modeling done by a non-phobic presenter, the adults were able to make some improvement in their attitude towards snakes. When a presenter exhibited fear during the presentation, the modeling failed to produce attitudinal change. Modeling by peers or respected adults, however, did not effect any attitude change in children (Morgan, et al., 1989). The children did not make changes in their perception or in their fear-response, despite being presented with information or despite watching someone handle the snake without fear or harm.

Some educators advocate the use of preserved specimens and artifacts including bones, skins, shells, and products (such as clothing and accessories) made from animals. The use of preserved specimens is an active learning method and can greatly enhance knowlege and attitudes. However, one research study found through pre- and posttesting that cognitive and attitudinal changes in students who handled preserved specimens were somewhat less than the learning and attitudinal changes in students who handled live specimens (Sherwood, 1989). After-contact testing showed that the learners who handled the live specimens retained more information (from 56% on posttest to 55% on the later retention test) and sustained attitudinal changes (scoring 85% on posttest and 87% on the retention test). Learners who handled only preserved specimens regressed in their knowledge (from 51% on posttest to 49% on the retention test) and made only a minor gain in attitude (from 82% on the posttest to 83% on the retention test).

TYPES OF EDUCATION EVENTS

Wildlife and conservation education now takes place in a wide variety of settings. From schools to parks, libraries to birthday parties, the opportunities for teaching and learning often take place under the guise of having fun. The number of animals and depth of information will vary depending upon the target audience.

From preschool (age 3 years) up through high school (age 18 years), learners can be taught a wealth of information. Information and concepts must be kept to that which the children are developmentally able to understand. Given the often wide range of ages, cognitive development, and attention spans often found in any one group, the educator must feel his or her way, keeping things moving along for the younger children while keeping the older children challenged.

In the United States, the people and organizations who are presenting educational programs includes free-lance educators specializing in wildlife in general, or reptiles in particular; herpetological societies; humane societies; teachers who keep reptiles in their classrooms or have them as frequent visitors; nature centers; zoos; and museums. Parents of school-aged children may often find themselves playing the role of educator when they are invited by their child's teacher to make a presentation to the class. Groups of age-related or mixed ages will be found in schools, summer school programs, and library lectures. The focus for these audiences should be on reptiles as a class, with the audience learning about reptile characteristics, defenses, reproduction, feeding, and environment. In these situations, the audiences should also learn about the characteristics of specific types of reptiles which do or do not make good pets.

Birthday-party programs should be little lighter in tone than the more formal programs presented at schools and libraries. Often times, the educator will have an opportunity to talk with the parents of the children attending the party before presenting the program. This allows the educator to find out if any of the parents or children are interested in a specific reptile as a possible pet. This also allows the educator to address particular concerns relating to reptiles and children. Depending upon the age and interest level of the party guests, more emphasis may be put on the contact and handling part of the presentation. The information provided during the presentation should be communicated on two levels: one to the children, and one to the parents (who may be looking for guidance on what kind of animals would and would not make suitable pets).

Lectures focusing more on the selection and care of reptiles may be arranged for by pet stores or humane societies as part of the services they provide to their customers or their community. Class characteristics will be covered more briefly; the way in which the reptile lives within its native environment, its

Minor bites from small non-venomous snakes can be a teaching tool allowing a lecturer to open a discussion. Photo by W.P. Mara.

captive requirements, and temperament tend to be the focus in these settings. Since the audience represents such a varied background of interests and existing knowledge, the questions may range from the very basic to quite technical.

Programs for veterinary office staff, pet-store employees and animal-shelter staff will have a slightly different focus from all other programs. Such animal-care workers need to know not only about natural history and captive care of the reptiles, but also handling and restraint techniques. The need to teach appropriate handling and restraint techniques may justify the inclusion in the program of animals who, because of their more active nature, are not normally used in education programs, such as hissing, thrashing monitors, iguanas, and snakes. While the author does not necessarily advocate encouraging an animal to bite during a presentation, when one does bite, it can be particularly useful in terms of the presenter modeling appropriate bite and post-bite behavior to the audience. Such behavior also allows the presenter to launch a discussion on how to handle biters and discuss treating the bites themselves.

Exhibitions may range from very small thematic exhibits where the small number of attendees are focused on a certain topic (rainforest; temperate forests; mimicry; indigenous to state or locale, etc.), to large exhibitions with hundreds or thousands of people attending. These may be fund-raisers for animal-welfare and wildlife groups or special programs for museums, science and nature centers, and parks. Exhibitions and fund-raisers can help raise awareness for environmental causes. The education at these events will run the gamut

Bite from nonvenomous snake (Northern Pine Snake, *Pituophis melanoleucus melanoleucus*). Photo by W. P. Mara.

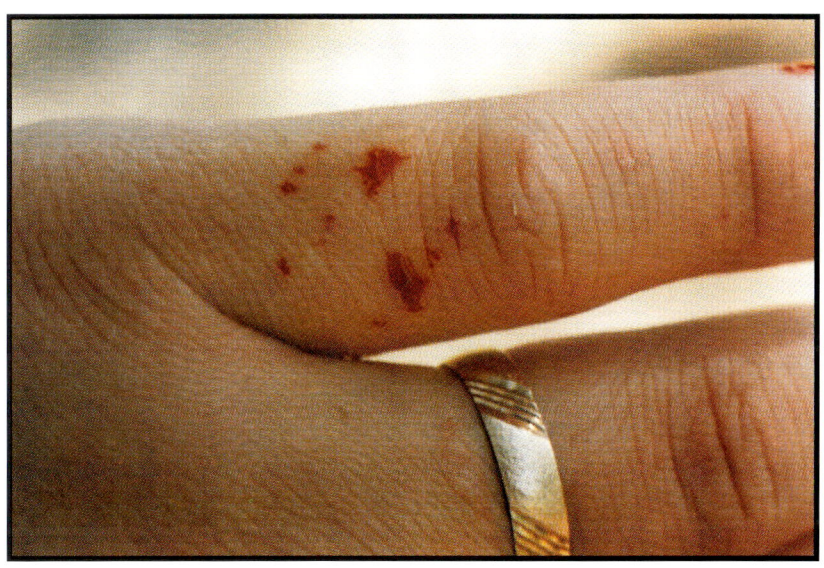

from simple animal identification (what is it; where it is from) to extensive conversations on the animal's required care, natural history, temperament, species status, etc.

Whatever the setting or focus, the opportunity to touch and hold reptiles has the greatest impact in promoting cognitive and affective development. To aid in the success of the program or exhibition, it is essential to use a selection of reptiles who are comfortable being handled, who are used to being manipulated during modeling presentations, and which can be handled by several people during the course of an hour or day.

SELECTION AND USE OF EDUCATION ANIMALS

Wildlife educators are generally the primary caretakers of the animals they use in their education programs. The animals may have been selected specifically for educational purposes or may have been acquired from other educators, reptile owners or wildlife rehabilitators.

One of the goals of wildlife education is to teach the audience respect for animals, not just for the individuals used in the program, but also generally—for the species or family of reptiles. Information is presented both verbally (through the dissemination of facts and clarifying misconceptions) and physically (in the appearance of the animals). This requires that the animals be healthy. That in turn requires that the educator knows what each animal needs. Educators must be able to provide the proper housing, environment, diet, and stimulation to keep the education animals healthy. Educators must also know what constitutes normal behavior for the species—both in the wild, and in captivity—and be able to identify abnormal behavior and its causes. Through such intimate knowledge of the species and individual animals, educators can assess the suitability of an animal for use in education, can determine the level at which that animal will be used, and can make day-to-day determinations as to the fitness of any of the animals to be used (Gibson, 1994b).

The criteria by which education animals are selected are geared to the animal's welfare, the comfort of both the handler and the animal, and the message to be conveyed to the public.

The education animal should be representative of a normal form of the species (Gibson, 1994a; San Francisco Zoological Society, 1983). One of the goals of reptile education is to teach not only about the reptile itself, but how that species lives in its environment, including how it is camouflaged from predator and prey. In the case of indigenous species, normal forms will help the audience identify the species when they see it in their yards, parks, or in wild areas. Captive-bred color and pattern morphs are best saved for use in teaching the basics of genetics and heredity. Educators can also use captive-bred color and pattern morphs in lectures which address reptiles as pets rather than where the focus is on creating an awareness of wildlife and conservation. An exception to these two types of lectures would be the use of a small albino snake, such as a corn or rat snake (*Elaphe guttata*), in working with severely phobic individuals in an educational setting, as they seem to invoke less fear, possibly due to their albino rabbit-like skin and red eyes.

The education animal must be well adapted to captivity. It must also be comfortable with being on view and, in the case of animals to be touched and held, comfortable with physical contact with strangers. Not all members of a species may be equally well adapted for educational purposes, and not all education animals may be suited for all educational settings. If the choice is between a representative who is not well adapted or doing without that species for the time being, then the program should do without that species until a well-adapted representative can be obtained or one socialized and habituated to contact or setting type.

The animal must be healthy and in good physical shape; injuries which may have precipitated the reptile's being brought into captivity and which prevents its release should be well-healed and no longer painful. While pity may be useful for raising concern for an individual, it may not engender concern for a species or for the environment in which the species lives (Gibson, 1994a, b). Special-focus programs, such as those for pet-store employees or animal-shelter adoption and animal-care staff, may benefit from the includsion of animals who have been permanently disfigured by the effects of inappropriate captive care. Such disfigurement includes: scoliosis from metabolic bone disease; gross scarring from rat bites, snout-rubbing trauma, thermal burns, etc.

The animal should stimulate learning about some aspect of wildlife or habitat. The animal's story, how it or its parents came to be in captivity, is often useful in illustrating issues and concerns (Gibson, 1994b). When possible, use captive-bred or captive-born exotics. This enables communication, on verbal and nonverbal levels, that such animals are being bred, are available (in the case of reptiles suitable as pets), and for many reasons may be preferable to wild-caught members of the same species. When native species are used, they should, when possible, be nonreleasable animals. It is difficult to teach

nonconsumptive wildlife uses when the educator's animals are wild-collected native species who were collected for the sake of collection. The educator may work into the presentation the reasons the native species are not releasable, and the reasons why nonnative species cannot be released. Including such information will reinforce environmental and species issues (such as the introduction of disease pathogens) and responsible ownership (such as long-term commitment, the effect of nonnative species on indigenous populations, inappropriate habitat for the species, etc.).

The handler should work with, not dominate, the animal; the audience should learn respect, not fear. The audience will learn how to hold the reptile in part by watching how the educator holds and interacts with the animal as it moves about. When both the reptile and the handler are comfortable with their interaction, it helps relax those members of the audience who will, often for the first time, touch or hold the reptile (Gibson, 1994b; Morgan, et al., 1989).

TYPES OF USE

More than one animal is brought to an education event to reduce the amount of time the animal is out or being handled. This also provides the flexibility to change an animal from being used to being placed off exhibit without unduly affecting the diversity or quality of the program. For a classroom or lecture, 12-15 reptiles are typically included in the program. Exhibitions may include the use of 15-20 or more reptiles, with duplicates rotated on and off exhibit to reduce stress or fatigue as necessary.

The animals themselves may be classed into one of four categories:
1. No contact: animal off exhibit.
2. Minimum contact: animal is looked at, not touched.
3. Moderate contact: animal is looked at and touched.
4. Maximum contact: animal is held by the learners.

The reptiles are routinely classified into one of the four categories. As the animals in the minimum contact category become acclimated to human contact, they may be changed to moderate contact, and perhaps ultimately to being held by learners. Reptiles in the third and fourth contact categories may be temporarily moved down one or more categories depending upon their individual status on any given day. During long events, some reptiles may be taken off exhibit for rest periods as needed.

Some animals may tolerate intermittent contact or exposure, and so are kept off exhibit, brought out at intervals for viewing and, if suitable, touching and then returned to their off-exhibit holding area. For example, an alligator might be brought out for fifteen minutes every hour for lecture and touching, then returned to his off-exhibit holding enclosure, and kept in a quiet area away from the exhibition, until the next appearance.

ANIMAL WELFARE

One of the most common questions asked about education animals, especially reptiles who are not generally known for their sociable natures, is "how do you know they are not stressed all the time?" Working with reptiles is no different from working with mammals or birds. Working with a species over time, and with individual representatives of the species, one learns to recognize normal behaviors and signs of well-being and discomfort. Reptiles appear inscrutable to those who have little or no experience with them. Most, however, are just as expressive as any mammal or bird, communicating through their behavior, posture, appetite, color and other key and subtle indicators (Kreger, 1993a; Duncan, 1993; Laule, 1993). Key indicators (Chiszar et al., 1993; Kreger, 1993a) of well-being include:

- —normal activity
- —thermoregulation
- —feeding
- —elimination
- —shedding
- —reproduction for the species

Reptiles may appear to be unsuitable as education animals to those whose jobs include laboratory research and clinical treatment of these animals. However, research indicates that reptiles, like other animals, can and do become habituated to regular human contact (Reichard, et al., 1992; Bowers, et al., 1992; Laule, 1993a). Kreger, et al. (1993c) studied ball pythons *(Python regius)* and blue-tongued skinks *(Tiliqua scincoides)*. Their studies found that there was no change in the python or skink plasma corticosterone levels and heterophil/lymphocyte ratios when the animals were handled as pets or

as during gross veterinary examinations. It was further found that such handling did little to change the animals' post-treatment feeding and activity levels.

Kreger (1995) makes the salient point that context and habituation are important factors in handling and stress reduction. The effects of regular handling of a lizard or snake kept as a pet or education animal are sure to be greatly different than when the same type of animal is hurriedly selected from a study group or noosed in the wild, a cloacal thermometer thrust in, the animal then quickly slung from a scale and measured several different ways before being released. Such treatment would likely cause stress in a tame, habituated animal of any species, let alone in a wild animal or laboratory research subject handled only when put through its paces or during invasive or noninvasive measurement and data recording sessions.

ANTHROPOMORPHISM

Humans are perhaps coming full circle in their view and understanding of animals. At one time, the study of animals and their habits was essential to human survival. Then superstition, utilitarianism and negativism took hold, condemning animals as unthinking, unfeeling beasts which should be subjected to total domination. The tide of negativism is slowing changing, however. Scientists are beginning to realize that animals think, communicate, and play, and that individuals may display distinct personalities (Arluke, 1990; Bowers, et al., 1992; Griffin, 1992). The relatively new (and often disparaged) fields of ethology (the study of behavior and motivation) and sociobiology have greatly improved our understanding of species and have shown us how little we still know (Griffin, 1992); Wilson, 1994)

Despite ethological findings, educators and pet owners are castigated for the sin of anthropomorphising whenever they make reference to what they believe an animal is thinking or feeling. Living closely with an animal, caring for it, and observing it for many years, does give one insight (Dawkins, 1990). While the terms a pet owner may use, or an educator may use when dealing with the lay public, may not be the same as those used by an ethologist or biologist, they often convey the same meaning and intent. This then is not a case of anthropomorphism but of semantics. Educators must remember to address the target audience in such as way as to ensure understanding.

In another example, in the above section on animal welfare, the text states that reptiles are "expressive...communicating through their behavior" etc. Does this mean that the author thinks the reptile is intentionally acting in some way to tell the handler "I don't want to work today?" The reader may argue with the choice of words, but the meaning was clearly and quickly communicated. For example, when a snake or lizard who normally exhibits alert attention to surroundings and active tongue-flicking when picked up is, instead subdued and inattentive, with little or no tongue-flicking, it is signaling that something is wrong. In this example, it could be too cold (something that the handler may immediately feel) or it may be getting ready to shed (prior to color changes associated with ecdysis becoming immediately apparent). A green iguana, with no change in ambient air temperature, who changes from her normal bright, vivid green to a dull green may be signaling fatigue. A highly socialized box turtle or tortoise who normally presents with head fully extended and exhibits exploratory behavior, but who keeps its head in, may not wish any contact that day. A normally docile and easily handled lizard who suddenly becomes extremely unsettled and tries to escape from one's hold, may see an animals which it perceives to be a potential predator; or it may merely have a pressing need to defecate, and is trying not to do it on the handler. These deviations in behavior and color are easily and quickly noticed by the experienced handler; they provide clues as to what the animal is "feeling."

An educator must be able to assess his or her animals before, during, and after every education event. An educator must be able to quickly and effectively stop an attempted interaction or initiate a change in status. A simple "He's a little tired and cranky; don't you get tired and want to be left alone sometimes?" may work better when telling a six-year old why a snake cannot be handled than a discussion as to all the reasons why this usually well-adapted and placid animal is acting uncomfortable with being handled that particular day. Such an explanation, along with a caution for the need of parental supervision and oversight, is best reserved for the parents considering such an animal a pet for their child.

People who visit reptile education events do not always have the same concerns for the environment and conservation in mind as they might when

Sinaloan Milk Snake, *Lampropeltis triangulum sinaloae*. **Photo by Susan Miller.**

approaching a wildlife exhibit featuring well- and comfortably-known mammals and birds. Describing and explaining reptile behavior in "human" terms understandable by those who are not ethologically or behaviorally oriented may help tip the balance between their seeing a "dangerous" snake and an interesting and nonthreatening animal who plays an important role in helping to maintain a healthy ecosystem. On many occasions, homeowners who call to demand traps, poisons, or relocation services to rid their property of snakes, can be educated to change their attitude, as well as their landscaping and garbage storage routines. By giving them the information they need to understand the natural habits and preferences of the snakes in question, they are able to make changes without serious threat to the well-being of the animals, seen and unseen, who share their property.

learning to take place. Names need not be exotic. For example, to people who do not know the genus name of the bearded dragon, *Pogona* sounds exotic. Names which highlight fearsome aspects of the animal, such as Killer or Fang, prey on fears rather than help to instill a sense of connection or respect. A chocolate-brown and yellow California kingsnake named Banana is innocuous and familiar, yet not intrusive. A vividly striped and colored garter snake named Magic can be used to highlight how well garter snakes are camouflaged in their natural environment.

Overuse of the animal's name, however, may detract from the species as a whole by focusing all attention on the individual, especially in groups of very young children (Gibson, 1994b). In most instances, the educational goal may be accomplished with no or minimal use of the animal's name. Introducing an animal by saying, "This is Pogona,

Eastern Garter Snake, *Thamnophis sirtalis sirtalis*. Photo by Susan Miller.

NAMES

Names may be very important for some children and adults. While not always possible, naming a reptile by its native name or a name that, in an indigenous language, represents a characteristic of the species, is often a good launching point for instruction and discussion. Names also enable a personal identification with an animal. When identification forms with an animal typically reviled or grossly misunderstood, that animal becomes less threatening and the stage is set for real

an Australian bearded dragon. Bearded dragons are..." gives the individual animal's name and immediately moves from the individual to the species. This may be the only time the individual's name is used in the presentation. Some audiences—especially those composed of very young children—may demonstrate, through their questions or reactions, a greater need to hear the name used as a way to reduce the level of fear or apprehension as they become comfortable with seeing and initially touching the animal.

A WORD FOR EDUCATORS

Educational efforts directed toward children aged 6-10 should focus on affective development, emphasizing emotional concern and sympathy for animals. Children aged 10-13, with their increased cognitive abilities, are ready to develop a more factual understanding of animals and their environment. High school students are more ecologistic, naturalistic, and moralistic in their attitudes, able to take in and assimilate more complex issues. Kellert (1985) found that this group was far more interested in direct contact with wildlife and outdoor recreation. Their increasing ability to deal with abstracts, such as biodiversity and ecosystems, coupled with their greater knowledge about animals and their environment, supports providing increased interactive learning opportunities for this group to deepen and strengthen their knowledge and understanding.

Wildlife education, regardless of the animals used, must be an ongoing, regularly repeated process, increasing in complexity and scope based on stages of child cognitive and affective development. Learning is further enhanced when the animals and their environment are used as a pivotal point on which the curriculum can be based. There is a growing body of work that focuses on bringing animals into the classroom and the curriculum to create an integrated learning experience. By use of creative curriculum, media, classroom animals, animal visitors, and varied animal encounters, wildlife education will build on the learner's prior experiential and encourage further growth through continued experience and exposure.

HEALTH RISKS

Mammals, birds and reptiles all have the potential for zoonotic transmission of pathogens. Healthy animals, including humans, are generally successful in keeping pathogen loads under control through normal immune system functioning. When animals are stressed, either psychologically or environmentally, immunosuppression results as does the risk of illness and cross-infection.

Risks are mitigated by using healthy animals who have been under observation for some time. Fecal and other examinations should be done initially to determine basal levels of organisms in the blood and feces. Regular retesting, along with close observation of the animal, should be done to ensure the animal continues in good health. (Despite being kept in clean environ-

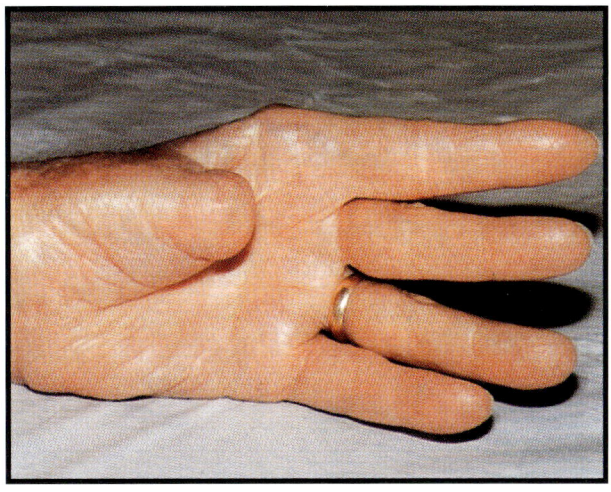

Amputated thumb, the result of improper treatment and an ensuing infection after a rattlesnake bite. Photo by W. P. Mara.

ments, reptiles may contract pathogens or parasites through ingestion of infected prey or water.) Education animals should be clean before being packed up for transport to the educational site. Cleaning and disinfecting supplies, both for the animals, their carriers and the handlers, should be part of the regular gear.

If there is a possibility that the audience has handled substances that may be harmful to the education animals (hand and skin lotions, topical pesticides or medications, disinfectants, cosmetics, or perfumes), they should be instructed to thoroughly wash their hands before handling the reptiles. They should also be instructed to wash their hands before handling or putting their hands near the reptiles if they have been handling animals that may be considered prey by the reptiles. In general, learners should wash their hands before and after handling reptiles or any other animal.

To keep zoonotic risk in perspective, it may be necessary to point out to concerned parents and teachers that of some 240 infectious zoonotic diseases, 65 are transmitted by dogs and 39 by cats (Gittleman, 1995). There are 110 million pet dogs and cats in the United States. The chances, then, of contracting feline and canine hookworm, roundworm, and feline toxoplasmosis are higher than contracting host-specific parasites and Salmonella from the far-less common pet and education reptiles. Those individuals at high risk for contracting reptile salmonellosis are also at high risk for contracting *Salmonella* from eating poorly cooked poultry and for contracting other zoonotic diseases from other animals. If there are members of a lecture audience who are in the high risk category (pregnant women, newborns, toddlers, immunosuppressed and frail elderly) the educator may make a blanket cautionary statement advising the risks and what can be done to mitigate the risks. In other settings, where the contact is more one-on-one, such cautions may be discussed on an as-needed basis as well as being conspicuously posted.

A first aid kit should also be part of the regular gear, including alcohol that may be used to detach a reptile that has become clamped to some part of the handler or educator.

This is a young adult Australian Water Python, *Liasis fuscus*. Photo by K. H. Switak.

DEALING WITH FEAR

Reptiles are often feared by people. Their reasons may be based on an early negative experience, acquired from their parents who themselves are fearful, or due to the belief that all reptiles—especially snakes—are inherently dangerous, unpredictable and, more often than not, venomous.

Fear can and should be addressed when working with any age group. This can be done matter-of-factly by stating that no one has to touch any of the animals. If someone is particularly phobic in their response, they can be gently told that they are free to move as far away as they need to feel comfortable. In some groups, especially in classroom settings, the individuals who admit to their fears are often teased. This behavior should be stopped and can be done so by saying that it is "okay" to be afraid. At this point, it is helpful for the educator or handler to admit to a personal fear themselves and unobtrusively get the attention of the teacher or group leader to get a non-

verbal cue from them, or to urge them, verbally or non-verbally, to participate in the discussion. It is often helpful for the educator to find out if the teacher or leader is themself afraid of any of the reptiles before the program begins, and to ascertain whether the teacher or leader may be drawn in and would be willing to hold or touch the animal if deemed beneficial.

Quite often, once a person accepts their fear and knows that their fear is acceptable to others, their initial aversion will abate. After watching everyone else touch or handle the reptiles without incident, they are often able to encourage themselves to reach out and, however briefly, touch one of the animals. Such overcoming of fear should be acknowledged and praised, not enough so that they are embarrassed by their earlier fear or embarrassed in front of their peers, but enough so that the encounter becomes a positive learning and growth experience.

When meeting fearful parents who nonetheless let their children explore by touching and holding reptiles, it is often beneficial to quietly praise the parents for overcoming their fear enough to not impart it to their children. These adults often overcome their own anxieties when they see their children's guided interaction with the animals. Often, these adults will also soon touch the animals themselves.

Another way to mitigate fear is to not abruptly spring new animals on the audience. When giving an organized lecture or program, the author starts off with lizards, moving to chelonians before finishing with snakes, with this order of progression announced at the start of the program. When providing exhibits, the snakes are placed at one end of the area, with the chelonians in between the snakes and the lizards; when possible, the snakes are arranged according to size to ease the transition for those nervous around large boids. When a separate chelonian area is set aside, the area between the snakes and lizards is filled with artifacts, books, and educational materials. This enables those individuals who are fearful of certain animals to still enjoy and learn from the rest of the program or exhibit.

CONCLUSION

When early humans hunted with spear and club, animals—especially the large and potentially dangerous ones—were respected and feared. The earliest images that exist today are of such animals carved or painted on cave walls. Subtle changes in human-animal relationships began to appear as animals were domesticated and weaponry improved a hunter's kill ability. No longer mysterious or brutal, humans began to lose their fear or reverence of animals. Lore and respect became lost as cultures became increasingly isolated from nature and became self-sufficient through breeding food animals and growing—rather than gathering—plants. Successive generations became desensitized to animals, dismissing any reference to an animal's thoughts or feelings or any concern for their basic welfare (Morris, 1990). With reptiles, this distance and disdain is reinforced through such acts as the exclusion of reptiles from protection under animal welfare laws and approved public displays of cruelty such as rattlesnake roundups (Kreger, 1992).

Wildlife educators who use reptiles, either solely or as part of a larger group of animal representatives, have a great opportunity to help individuals overcome fears and learn facts about reptiles to replace myths. By using reptiles who are secondary and tertiary consumers, the educator is also uniquely placed to reach both up and down the food chain, to pluck all the threads within the energy web. Sparking a learner's imagination and teaching respect for wildlife is one of the best subjective experiences an educator can have.

GLOSSARY TERMS:

Dominionistic: Primary interest in the mastery and control of animals typically in sporting situations.

Naturalistic: Primary interest in, and affection for, wildlife and the outdoors.

Negativistic: Primary orientation an active avoidance due to indifference, dislike or fear.

REFERENCES AND RECOMMENDED READING

—**Arluke, A:**
The significance of seeking the animal's perspective. *Behavioral and Brain Sciences*, 1990, 13(1):13-14.

—**Bowers, BB; Burgardt, GM:**
The scientist and the snake. In, The Inevitable Bond: Examining Scientist-Animal Interactions. H Davis, D Balfour (Eds.), Cambridge University Press, New York, NY, 1992, pp. 250-263.

—**Cantor, D.**
Animals don't belong in school. *The American School Board Journal*, October 1992, pp. 39-40.

—**Caras, R.**
A guide to managing your classroom pets. *Instructor*, September 1980, pp. 48-51, 54-55.

—**Chiszar, D; Murphy, JB; Smith, HM:**
In search of zoo-academic collaborations: A research agenda for the 1990's. *Herpetologica*, 1993, 49(4):488-500.

—**Dawkins, MS:**
From an animal's point of view: Motivation, fitness and animal welfare. *Behavior and Brain Science*, 13(1):1-5.

—**Duncan, IJH:**
The science of animal well-being. *AWIC*, 1993, 4(1):1, 4-7.

—**Gibson, M:**
Let's Get Real: Using live animals in wildlife education. *Journal of International Wildlife Education*, 1994a, 17(2):11-13,18.

—**Gibson, M:**
You and your wildlife education program. *Journal of International Wildlife Education*, 1994b, 17(2):6-10.

—**Gittleman, AL:**
Parasites: Alive and well in the U.S.A. *Health Counselor*, 1995, 7(2):15-18.

—**Golden, J.A.**
Child-focused programming on human/animal interactions. [Abstract] Massachusetts Society for the Prevention of Cruetly to Animals, 1989.

—**Griffin, D.**
Animal Minds. University of Chicago Press, Chicago, IL, 1992.

—**Hodges, JL:**
Spiders and boas and rats, oh my! *Science and Children*, 1991, pp. 22-25.

—**Kellert, S.R:**
Attitudes toward animals: age-related development among children. *Journal of Environmental Education*, 1985, 16, pp. 29-39.

—**Kreger, MD:**
Regarding Reptiles. *Science of Animal Care*, 1992, pp. 1-4.

—**Kreger, MD:**
The psychological well-being of reptiles. *Humane Innovations and Alternatives*, 1993a, pp. 519-523.

—**Kreger, MD:**
Zoo-Academic Collaborations: Physiological and psychological needs of reptiles and amphibians. *Herpetologica*, 1993b, 49, pp. 509-512.

—**Kreger, MD; Mench, JA:**
Physiological and behavioral effects of handling and restraint in the ball python (*Python regius*) and the blue-tongued skink (*Tiliqua scincoides*). *Applied Animal Behaviour Science*, 1993c, 38, pp. 323-336.

—**Kreger, MD; Mench, JA:**
Visitor-animal interaction at the zoo: Animal welfare. Unpublished paper presented before the AZA, 1995, 5 pp.

—**Laule, G:**
Using training to enhance animal care and welfare. NAL Animal Welfare Information Center, 1993a, 4(1):2, 8-9.

—**Laule, G:**
The use of behavioral management techniques to reduce or eliminate abnormal behavior. NAL Animal Welfare Information Center, 1993b, 4(4):1-2, 8-11.

—**Morgan, JM; Gramann, JH:**
Predicting effectiveness of wildlife education programs: a study of students' attitudes and knowledge toward snakes. *Wildlife Society Bulletin*, 1989, 17, pp. 501-509.

—**Morris, D:**
The Animal Contract. Warner Books, New York, NY, 1990, 169 pp.

—**Nebbe, LL:**
The human-animal bond and the elementary school counselor. *The School Counselor*, 1991, 38, 362-371.

—**Paterson, D:**
Assessing children's attitudes towards animals. In, The Status of Animals: Ethics, Education and Welfare, CAB International, Wallingford, Oxon, UK, 1989, pp. 58-63.

—**Patterson-Morris, L:**
Fostering autonomy in the four and five year old with animals in the classroom. Pacific Oaks College, Pasadena, CA, 1993. Thesis

—**Reichard, T; Shellabarger, W; Laule, G:**
Training for husbandry and medical purposes. AAZPA Annual Conference Proceedings, Toronto, Canada. Wheeling, WV, 1992, pp. 396-402.

—**San Francisco Zoological Society.**
Use of animals in public relations. Unpublished policy. 1983, pp. 4.23-4.24.

—**Sherwood, KP; Rallis, SF; Stone, J:**
Effects of live animals vs preserved specimens on student learning. *Zoo Biology*, 1989, 8, pp. 99-104.

—**Skeen, P; Wallinga, C; Hodson, D:**
Enhancing children's physical, intellectual, social, and emotional development through the inclusion of animals in the curriculum. Delta Society Annual Conference, Vancouver, B.C., 1987. Abstract.

—**Warwick, C:**
Reptilian ethology in captivity: Observations of some problems and an evaluation of their aetiology. *Applied Animal Behaviour Science*, 1990a, 26, pp. 1-13.

—**Warwick, C:**
Important ethological and other considerations of the study and maintenance of reptiles in captivity. *Applied Animal Behaviour Science*, 1990b, 27, pp. 363-366.

—**Wilson, E.O.**
Naturalist. Island Press, Washington, DC, 1994.

WELFARE ISSUES

Michael D. Kreger, M.S*.
Technical Information Specialist,
Animal Welfare Information Center,
National Agricultural Library,
10301 Baltimore Blvd.,
Beltsville, Maryland 20705

Michael Kreger is a technical information specialist at the Animal Welfare Information Center at the National Agricultural Library, U.S. Department of Agriculture. He served as a Peace Corps Volunteer in Honduras (1984-86) where he worked on wildlife management and zoo-related projects. He serves on the Board of Directors of the Center for the Study of Tropical Birds, Inc. and Vice President of the World Nature Association. As a Masters student at the University of Maryland's Department of Poultry Science, he investigated the physiological and behavioral effects of handling and restraint in reptiles. He can be reached at the Animal Welfare Information Center in Beltsville Maryland.

INTRODUCTION

At the breeder expo, baby milksnakes are kept in plastic pint-size coleslaw containers ready for sale. Except for its writhing contents, the container is empty. At the zoo Reptile House, a small monitor lizard strides along the front of the exhibit only to get its rostrum wedged into a glass corner. It nods its head repeatedly, bloodying the surface of its skin. These are animal welfare issues. They concern the physical and mental health of the individual animal. They can be scientifically evaluated with results used to improve management and husbandry or provide the facts needed in making legislative decisions. Without scientific evaluation, welfare issues may lead to regulatory guidelines and legislation based on human emotion and philosophy.

This chapter will outline some of the concepts associated with animal welfare and its importance in making husbandry decisions. The relevance of welfare considerations in crafting guidelines, legislation, and research policy will also be discussed. Several other chapters in this publication address particular animal welfare issues in great detail (i.e. humane transport, euthanasia) so they will not be emphasized here.

Pale Milk Snake, *Lampropeltis triangulum multistrata*. Photo by Paul Freed.

The views expressed here are those of the author and do not represent those of the US Department of Agriculture or the Animal Welfare Information Center.

WHAT IS ANIMAL WELFARE?

The science of animal welfare incorporates the disciplines of ethology (animal behavior), neuroscience, endocrinology, and immunology, and aims to identify how an animal perceives and responds to stimuli (Mench, 1993). Its application to herpetology can be viewed as serving four main functions:

1. It can lead to improved husbandry by eliminating stressors that may impair feeding, growth, reproduction, and normal behaviors (and thus improve the quality of the individual's life).

2. It can help eliminate maladaptive behaviors which affect the quality of data collected (Dawkins, 1980) for basic herpetological research.

3. It can form a framework for rational, scientifically-based guidelines on animal care and use by professional societies or for potential legislation.

4. Animal welfare research can also be used to assure the public and animal protection groups that animal programs provide optimal husbandry based on the animal's identified needs (Kreger, 1992).

Animal welfare encompasses values. It is more than provision of food, water, living space and veterinary care. However, because it is laden with human values, it is difficult to define (Fraser, 1995). To many veterinarians, for example, housing a snake in a sterile tank with a waterbowl and newspaper substrate would be acceptable because the animal is protected from disease and predation. The tank can be thoroughly cleaned and the animal easily manipulated for veterinary procedures (Cooper and Williams, 1995). The applied ethologist (one who studies the behavior of animals in human-imposed environments such as zoos, farms, and laboratories), however, would argue that meeting the most basic health and safety needs is not enough. Such an environment impedes the snake's natural behavior and some risk of disease would be acceptable in order for the animal to accomplish a greater repetoire of behaviors (i.e., supply a more natural substrate for burrowing, add perches for climbing) (Warwick, 1995).

Although many definitions of animal welfare have been put forward by philosophers, veterinarians, and applied ethologists, most share the concept that captive animals should be as free as possible from pain and suffering. That pain and suffering occur in the wild in instances such as being devoured alive by predators or being infested by internal parasites is no justification for its existance in the vivarium. Unlike life in the wild, the survival of captive animals is entirely dependant on human caretakers.

Animals can suffer from "stress". The stress response is a coping mechanism that allows animals to adapt to a variety of unpredictable environmental or social changes. It is normal and beneficial for any species to experience some stress daily. Brief changes in biological function can be caused by positive stress such as exploration of a novel, but non-threatening environment or copulation. Stress in the negative sense (often called "distress"), however, refers to the magnitude of the stressor being so great as to cause a biological "cost" to the animal (Moberg, 1993). Costs may be short-term or long-term and include psychological impairment, greater susceptibility to disease and bacterial infections, slower growth, and failure to reproduce. The toad that refuses to feed due to its being housed with an aggressive mate, would be an example of when an animal is suffering from stress. Although poor health and productivity are indicators of poor welfare, when animal suffer from stress, thus reducing general welfare, they may still be healthy and productive (Mench, 1993). Pain caused by acute stress may be transient and not affect long-term health and reproduction. More chronic stress can be masked by management practices such as using antibiotics to fight infections and improving growth by force-feeding an animal that refuses to eat. In this chapter, "stress" will refer to the failure of an animal to adapt to stimulus without compromising its biological functions.

Suffering also implies sentience or consciousness. Thus, some animal welfare researchers believe that welfare is based on feelings (Dawkins, 1990; Duncan, 1993). This assumes that animals, including reptiles and amphibians, do not simply react to a stimulus, but actually think about the stimulus and react according to their perceptions (Rogers, 1994). They often learn survival skills from experience such as what prey to avoid; and they can demonstrate preferences. In birds and mammals emotional states such as fear, frustration, and boredom from the lack of environmental stimuli or overstimulation may result in stereotypies such as pacing, redirected behaviors such as feather plucking and self-mutilation, and vacuum behaviors such as going through the motions of burrowing behavior in the absences of burrowing substrate (e.g. a concrete floor) (Fraser, 1984; Markowitz, 1982; Novak and Suomi, 1988).

There are few systematic efforts to examine the welfare of reptiles and amphibians. However, the increasing use of these taxa as alternative models to birds and mammals in biomedical research, as companion animals, as exhibit animals, and conservation tools have provided information (often through trial and error) about some of their behavioral and physiological needs. Knowledge of their species-specific anatomy, physiology, and behavior have allowed researchers to study anti-tumor and analgesic properties of venom, cloning (some species are parthenogenic), Parkinson's disease, stress-related disorders, developmental biology, genetics, neurology, endocrinology, ecology, and ethology (Frye, 1981; Greenberg et al., 1989). Such studies, as well as those specifically designed to measure different aspects of welfare such as stress, are providing evidence that reptiles and amphibians can suffer, experience pain, and learn (Berry et al., 1995; Lance, 1990; Lance, 1992; Suboski, 1992).

STRESS AND WELFARE

How an animal responds to a stressor (any real or perceived threat to homeostasis) depends on many factors: genetics, previous experience, social situation, perception, and characteristics unique to the individual (Dantzer and Mormede, 1985; Greenberg and Crews, 1990; Moberg, 1985). Defensive behaviors of eastern garter snakes (*Thamnophis sirtalis*) in response to a perceived stressor (i.e., handling, harassing, or no treatment) can be manipulated by experience (Herzog, 1990). In Mexican aquatic garter snakes (*Thamnophis melanogaster*), defensive temperament varies across litters and individuals in response to the presence of the human hand for up to a year (Herzog and Burghardt, 1988).

As previously mentioned, birds and mammals may respond behaviorally to chronic stressors by self-mutilation, stereotypies, abnormal body movements, and hyperactivity or depression (Duncan, 1992; Moberg, 1993). Similar reactions have been observed in reptiles and amphibians; most notably hypo- and hyperactivity, escape attempts, refusal to feed, and aggression (Frye, 1981; Greenberg, 1992; Guillette et al., 1995; Lance, 1990, 1992; Warwick, 1990; Wright, 1994). Physiologically, stressed reptiles and amphibians may briefly or chronically show immunosuppression, nutritional wasting, and suppression of thermoregulatory and reproductive functions (Frye, 1981; Guillette et al., 1995). American alligators (*Alligator mississippiensis*) maintained at high stocking densities, for example, show chronic corticosterone secretion, growth and reproductive inhibition, and immunosuppression as a result of stress from overcrowding (Elsey et al., 1990).

There is no single parameter that, by itself, is a measure of stress. Although measurement of adrenal hormones such as corticosterone and epinephrine are commonly used indicators of stress in reptiles, non-endocrine indicators such as changes in behavioral patterns or immune response have also been used (Guillette et al., 1995; Lance, 1990). Behavioral patterns have the advantages of being non-invasive and easy to measure. Warwick (1995) lists a series of behavioral indicators that might be used as "signs of psychological quiescence and comfort" (ie normal feeding, normal alertness) and "signs of psychological arousal and discomfort" (ie hissing, hyper-alertness). The examination of non-endocrine parameters, such as behavior, are necessary to give a more complete picture because corticosterone levels are known to vary as a result of individual and environmental factors (e.g. sex, season, day, nutritional status, reproductive status) in reptiles that may not be related to stressful events (Chan and Callard, 1972; Cooper and Jackson, 1981; Grassman and Crews, 1990; Greenberg and Wingfield, 1987).

Few published herpetology papers attempt to identify chronic stress resulting from husbandry. To identify such stressors, it is useful to know what the animal does in the wild so that provisions can be made to fill behavioral needs before the stress response reaches a pre-pathological state from which it will be difficult to recover (Moberg, 1985). The absence or presence of normal behavior is often seen as a window into the psychological welfare of the animal. Knowledge of what constitutes "normal" behavior can sometimes be difficult due to lack of species-specific field behavioral and ecological data as well as differences among individuals of the same species (Burghardt and Layne, 1995; Kreger, 1993b).

Green Anoles, *Anolis carolinensis*. Photo by Michael Gilroy.

Figure 1.
Handling herpetofauna may help educate and create positive attitudes towards these animals, but how does it physiologically and behaviorally affect the animal? (Photo by M. Kreger)

In some cases, this difficulty may be overcome by preference testing. By providing the animal with choices such as which environment or social situation it prefers and noting the time spent in each option and its behavior in each, stressful husbandry situations can often be avoided. If the results of preference testing are applied to husbandry situations, good observational monitoring is essential. Preference testing has its limitations. The selected option may only be a short-term or seasonal preference or there may be also be risks to growth and reproduction over the long-term (Fraser et al., 1993). For example, imagine that a snake is given equal access to chambers except that one contains a single mouse and the other contains four mice. Although its selection of chambers may be dependant on its appetite at the time or inability to voluntarily restrain itself,

assume the snake selects the chamber with the four mice. In the wild, food is not always plentiful, so the snake may eat many prey animals when they are available to improve chances of survival in leaner times (ie dry season, torpor, etc.). While this is evolutionarily advantageous in the wild, in captivity such overeating can lead to a variety of health risks including those associated with obesity. Overeating tends to be a problem in large boids, particularly in restrictive captive environments where physical activity is limited (Frye, 1981).

Whether or not handling is perceived as a stressor is still in question (Figure 1). Chiszar et al. (1993) suggests that one cause of reproductive suppression in reptiles may be due to the perception of the handler as the dominant animal. There is evidence that plasma testosterone levels decreases when plasma corticosterone increases due to handling in male tree lizards (*Urosaurus ornatus*), Moore et al., 1991). Capture and repeated blood sampling decreased plasma testosterone levels in male painted turtles (*Chrysemys picta*) (Licht et al., 1985) and male tuataras (*Sphenodon punctatus*) (Cree et al., 1990). The depression of testosterone in these studies, however, cannot be directly attributed to handling since other factors were involved: capture, repeated blood sampling, possibly of variation in sampling technique, season or time of day for sampling, or lack of acclimation to the laboratory environment.

It may be that the context of the handling is what is important, i.e., what additional procedures accompany the handling, the frequency and predictability of handling, type of handling used, and what rewards or punishments reinforce the behavioral response. The fear response of the green anole (*Anolis carolinensis*) to a handler, for example, when measured by the duration of tonic immobility (the amount of time an animal will lie motionless on its back after being manipulated), is reduced by gentle regular handling (McKnight et al., 1978). Bowers and Burghardt (1992) observe that snakes tend to become less defensive after prolonged handling by student caretakers. At the University of Maryland, Joy Mench and I found that the ball python (*Python regius*) and the blue-tongued skink (*Tiliqua scincoides*) show no changes in basal plasma corticosterone level, gross activity levels, or heterophil/lymphocyte ratio in response to regular gentle handling, manual restraint, or container restraint. This was possibly due to habituation to handling, since animals were handled during routine enclosure maintenance for several months preceeding the experiment (Kreger and Mench, 1993). Indeed, the only evidence of stress was when a snake was manually forced out of a PVC tube container. In that instance, there was a brief corticosterone increase, but appetite and pre- and post-treatment behaviors remained un-

Ball Python, *Python regius*. Photo by David Dube.

affected. Whether or not habituation to handling can actually increase breeding success in some species is worthy of investigation.

WELFARE AND HUSBANDRY

The key to successful husbandry as well as meeting the welfare needs of reptiles and amphibians is more than reducing stress. It involves stimulating as much of the normal behavior as possible without causing physical or psychological damage to the animal itself or cagemates. The failure of an animal to adapt to a new environment has been called "Acclimation-Maladaptation Syndrome" or "AMS" by herpetological veterinarians (Cowan, 1980). Often the herpetoculturist encourages "enforced idleness" in which the animal is provided only with accommodations for eating, drinking, and shedding (Frye, 1995) (Figure 2). This can lead to repetitive locomotor behaviors such as frustrated escape attempts and rostrum rubbing or "pica" (a condition where reptiles ingest non-food material possibly due to lack of stimulation)(Frye, 1995; Warwick, 1990). Particularly important is provision of the animal's microhabitat including the appropriate thermal gradient, humidity level, and lighting (Pough, 1991; 1992). The moist world of the salamander that thrives under leaf litter, for example, is sig-

nificantly different from the microhabitat of an arboreal tree frog. Because thermoregulation, lighting, and humidity are dealt with in detail elsewhere in this book they will not be discussed here, but their relevance to animal welfare should not be overlooked.

Herpetoculturists and herpetologists refer to the need for these species to feel psychologically secure in the captive environment (Demeter,

Figure 2.
This circus enclosure for a large python contains lighting, temperature, and humidity control. There is also little utilizable space and no retreat or shelter. The "enforced idleness" is an animal welfare concern. (Photo by M. Kreger)

293

Eastern Blue-tongued Skink, *Tiliqua scincoides*. Photo by K. H. Switak.

1989; Warwick, 1990, Wright, 1994). The animals must be able to hide from perceived predators such as conspecifics or the human attendant. Hideboxes or shelters and other retreats using a variety of cage furniture have met this need. Because each animal must have the opportunity to escape heat or cold so proper thermoregulation can occur, the thermal gradient becomes a major factor in housing and husbandry (see section on thermoregulation in this book). Therefore, retreats reflecting the animal's lifestyle should run the length of the thermal gradient so the individual will not have to choose between thermoregulation and psychological

Red Spitting Cobra, *Naja mossambica pallida*. Photo by S. Kochetov.

security (Demeter, 1989; Mattison, 1987; Pough, 1991). Red spitting cobras (*Naja mossambica pallida*) have shown a preference for opaque plastic boxes with a small opening in front to transparent ones (Chiszar et al., 1987). Demeter (1989) suggests using tight-fitting retreats that allow the animal to be completely contained as well as tactually aware of all sides of the interior thus providing security through familiarity of the immediate environment.

Western Rattlesnake, *Crotalus viridis*. Photo by Ron Everhart.

Another method used to increase psychological security is reducing the number of transparent sides on an enclosure (Wright, 1991; 1994). This is especially useful when new animals are introduced to an enclosure. Newly introduced anurans are highly susceptible and often jump into glass walls of the tank as if the barriers were invisible. Such escape attempts often result in rostral lesions. By covering transparent walls with material such as opaque plastic and providing appropriate retreats, the risk of AMS is reduced (Wright, 1994). Wall coverings also remove visual cues from animals in adjacent en-

Baja California Rattlesnake, *Crotalus enyo*. Photo by K. H. Switak.

closures that may elicit frustrated escape or aggressive behaviors.

Olfactory cues should also be considered in husbandry regimens. Western rattlesnakes (*Crotalus viridis*) spend more time attempting escape when their feces are removed during routine cleaning (Chizsar et al., 1980). Therefore, even at the risk of potential pathogens, it may be better from the welfare viewpoint to leave a small amount of feces in the enclosure when cleaning rather than to disinfect the entire tank and its props. There is also more investigatory behavior (number of tongue-flicks) when individual western rattlesnakes and timber rattlesnakes (*Crotalus horridus*) are introduced to a cage containing the scent of feces from a conspecific rather than its own. The olfactory cues from the feces may possibly indicate an individual animal's recognition of self or others (Chiszar et al, 1991) and serve to identify terri-

tory thus providing security to the individual..

More arboreal species require perches for escape, security, basking sites, and territory. Perch diameters, angles, and placement for basking and retreat depends on the individual animal's size and particular preferences (Demeter, 1989; Mattison, 1987). They should have diameters that will support the weight of the animal (Frye, 1981). Perches are especially important to species that rarely spend time on the ground. In the wild, Solomon Islands Prehensile-tailed skinks *(Crucia zebrata)* seek shelter in tree cavities and forage mainly on leaves and some fruits (see review by Balsai, 1995). Therefore, in captivity, perches should ideally contain retreats (De Vosjoli, 1993) positioned vertically, diagonally and horizontally to mimic the forest habitat. Although anoles species can perch on glass walls, they prefer more natural sites which include branches, cinderblock, and rocks (Greenberg,

1992). Crevices within and around perches provide shelters for small lizard species. A functional but less naturalistic cage for single-housed arboreal reptiles has been designed by Mason et al. (1992) for use in research facilities.

The availability of perches is a consideration when group-housing species. In the male green anole, occupation of higher perches contributes to determining the the social status of the individual. Lizards that occupy the higher sites tend to be dominant, while those on lower sites have depressed courtship rates and become social subordinates (Greenberg and Crews, 1990).

The social environment, as illustrated in the perch example, also affects the welfare of the animal. Herpetofauna interact either continually or infrequently, but most are territorial (Bowers and Burghardt, 1992; Mattison, 1987). Social interactions ranging from behaviors learned from parental care (e.g., American alligators) to group housing with appropriate sex and age ratios affect how an individual feeds, reproduces, and defends itself or its young (see review and citations in Burghardt and Layne, 1995). Some social groupings may be important to the development and survival of neonates or adults while others may have no effect. When litters of captive-raised neonate lower California rattlesnakes (*Crotalus enyo*) are reared individually in small plastic boxes or in a group in a large cage, exploration of a novel environment does not differ between groups or between the two groups and wild-caught counterparts (Marmie et al., 1990). Although this may indicate that there is no advantage to group housing this species, other species are more social in the wild and there may be benefits to group-housing them in captivity. Social feeding occurs in some lizards. One animal will try to steal food from another which may provide information about a new or novel food source to the thief (Greenberg, 1976).

The social environment is an extremely relevant consideration that should be viewed in the context of the reason for confinement. Certainly, neonates bred for release into the wild or rehabilitation animals, for example, should not be imprinted on humans and should be given the benefit of living in a social structure similar to that found in the wild (ie with parental care for the appropriate time period, etc.). Conversely, some individuals kept in the hobbyist's vivarium may suffer from being maintained in a social group, particularly if there is overcrowding.

Territory and dominance are important in an enclosed system like captivity where resources such as basking sites and retreats are limited. There is strong physiological and behavioral evidence that subordinate animals become chronically stressed

Brown Anole, *Anolis sagrei.*
Photo by R. D. Bartlett.

Six-lined Racerunner, *Cnemidophorus sexlineatus*. Photo by R. T. Zappalorti.

which results in suppression of reproductive, appetitive, and immune functions (Brackin, 1978; Greenberg and Crews, 1990; Greenberg and Wingfield, 1987). Dominance status and aggression among green anoles affect androgen levels and may suppress reproduction (Greenberg and Crews, 1990). Low social status is associated with large adrenals in whiptail lizards (*Cnemidophorus sexlineatus*) (Bracken, 1978). Male brown anoles *Anolis sagrei* implanted with corticosterone show a decrease in aggression and assume a more subordinate position in territorial competition (Tokarz, 1987). In the wild, a male Jackson's chameleon (*Chamaeleo jacksonii*) tosses intruders from of his tree (territory). Their success in captive husbandry requires that conspecifics be able to find visual isolation from each other. Simple posturing of a dominant animal can suppress feeding of a subordinate in a separate tank where there is visual access (Ferguson and Blades, 1991). Even olfactory cues where snakes are housed in the same room without visual access to each other can cause intimidation of a subordinate animal or trauma from individuals striking against a transparent wall of the enclosure towards an unseen foe (Wright, 1991). Seasonal aggression also has its psychological considerations. A green anole female observing two males in combat shows suppressed ova-

rian development and sexual behavior, whereas the opposite is true for the female observing male to female courtship behavior (Crews, 1975).

Although overcrowding, in general, tends to lead to increased fighting, injury, and death (Elsey et al., 1990; Mattison, 1987), there are benefits to social housing if all individuals, including subordinates, are provided for in terms of thermoregulation, access to feed, and psychological security. Placing animals together only when they would normally socialize, court, and mate in the wild has facilitated captive breeding of species that were considered difficult to breed (Mattison, 1987).Non-social species, including those that aggregate seasonally in nature for hibernation or courtship and breeding, should not be forced into social environments.

Another husbandry condition related to animal welfare is the size and complexity of the captive environment. The size of the enclosure depends on the size and activity of the individual animal. Cage size must allow for a thermal gradient, room for exercise, cage furnishings, and establishment of territory if more than one animal is present (Demeter, 1989). A small tank with a complex or enriched vertical dimension for arboreal species that includes perches, foliage, etc. has more utilizable space than a larger tank which contains only horizontal space with little complexity or novelty. Other design factors such as "haul-out" sites for turtles, rough objects for rubbing during ecdysis, and increasing the number and variety of basking or perching sites and retreats, allow the animals some control over their environments in captivity according to their preferences.

Other effects of routine husbandry techniques have shed light on animal perception moreso than on stress effects. Chiszar and colleagues have routinely monitored the number of tongue-flicks snakes emit in response to husbandry manipulations (Chiszar et al, 1995). Because tongue-flicks are related to vomeronasal chemoreception in snakes and lizards, it has been used as an indicator of investigatory behavior. For example, red spitting cobras (*Naja pallida*), western rattlesnakes (*Crotalus viridis*), and bull snakes (*Pituopis melanoleucus*) show no significant difference in the number of tongue-flicks when the cage is moved to a new location or replaced in a former location. However, a significantly higher number of tongue-flicks are observed after cage contents are rearranged versus leaving the contents in their original places following routine cage cleaning. When the cage rearrangement experiment is replicated by using blindfolded versus non-blindfolded bullsnakes, the blindfolded animals show no effect from cage rearrangement. The results suggest that these animals are sensitive not only to chemical cues in the environment, but also to the visual arrangement of objects within the environment (Chiszar et al, 1995). Whether the increase in exploratory behavior via tongue-flicks is indicative of stress remains to be tested.

Many of the basic husbandry needs of reptiles and amphibians can be met with what, to human eyes, may seem like a stark and sterile enclosure. Hygenic cages or tanks in research facilities or off-exhibit areas at zoos have had major breeding and longevity successes. Newspaper is a highly recommended substrate due to its sterility, availability, and ease of change (Demeter, 1989). Furnishings can be simple washable plastic. Thermal gradients and full spectrum lighting are easily established. For research purposes (depending on the context of the study), such a simple, low maintenance enclosure provides easy capture of the animal, repeated handling, ease of sampling if the animal is cannulated, and a low pathogen environment (Cooper and Williams, 1995). Conversely, it could be argued that such an enclosure might meet the animals minimal needs, but not its optimal needs. Human hospital patients are provided with food, water, a place to rest, limited physical activity, and some social contact, but most healthy people would not want to live there. The environmental complexity denied to patients in hospitals is also denied to animals in stark, sterile enclosures. Although ideally animals should be able to express their normal range of behaviors to the greatest extent possible, this should, however, be weighed against the merits and type of research being done (Cooper and Williams, 1995). For example, an animal in quarantine or one held briefly for an invasive study could have a hygienic environment (including thermal gradient, retreat, and appropriate lighting and water conditions). However, in the case of behavioral research, exhibition, and herpetoculture, it should not be the presence of health risks that decide whether the naturalistic or clinical enclosure should be used, but the extent of those risks (Kreger, 1993a, Warwick, 1995).

ANIMAL WELFARE REGULATIONS AND GUIDELINES

What are the minimum housing, husbandry, and welfare standards for captive herpetofauna? Currently, there is no national legislation that specifically recognizes the welfare of reptiles and amphibians with the exception of international animal transport. The International Air Transportation Association (IATA) provides minimal shipping conditions that include substrate, ventilation, temperature, water, and restraint for closely related reptiles. These regulations have been adopted and are required by the Convention on the International Trade in Endangered Species (CITES) member nations—including the United States.

The Animal Welfare Act which is enforced by the U.S. Department of Agriculture only extends to warm-blooded species (*Title 7, U.S. Code, Sections 2131-2157*). However, amphibians and reptiles are covered under the *PHS Policy on Humane Care and Use of Laboratory Animals* (1986) if a research project is receiving funds from the U.S. Public Health Service (PHS) which is enforced by the Office for Protection from Research Risks (OPRR). Therefore, National Institutes of Health-supported projects involving these species must comply. The policy sets general standards for PHS contractors and grantees. Its specific rules are explained in *Guide for the Care and Use of Laboratory Animals* (National Research Council, 1996, currently under revision). The guide does not give specific recommendations for reptile and amphibian care so compliance officers rely on the expertise of the

Jackson's Chameleon, *Chamaeleo jacksoni*. Photo by Aaron Norman.

investigator. The 1984 guidelines in the Canadian Council on Animal Care's (CCAC) *Guide to the Care and Use of Experimental Animals* contains chapters on reptiles and amphibians and the 1987 *Guidelines for Use of Live Amphibians and Reptiles in Field Research* is published and endorsed by The American Society of Ichthyologists and Herpetologists (ASIH), The Herpetologists' League (HL), and The Society for the Study of Amphibians and Reptiles (SSAR) (McCarthy, 1992). The CCAC guide gives recommendations specific to taxonomic groups and relates to care of the animals in the laboratory, while the ASIH/HL/SSAR guide pertains only to field research and does not taxonomically group animals due to the lack of known cross-species needs.

The diversity of reptile and amphibian species makes development of stringent regulations on animal care and use very difficult. There are no hard and fast engineering-based rules governing enclosure size, substrate type, appropriate temperature, etc. for animals in captivity. Performance standards that list a set of behavioral or physiological conditions that could be used to identify whether or not an animal is welfare-compromised are also difficult due to the variety of species adaptations and microenvironments (Pough, 1992) (although Warwick (1995) provides a general checklist that could be used as a starting point). Nevertheless, many Institutional Animal Care and Use Committees (IACUC) at university, zoo, and private sector research facilities evaluate the care and use of herpetofauna in proposed research projects as they would any species that falls within the realm of the Animal Welfare Act. The purpose of the IACUC is not to be a barrier to useful research, but to ensure that the research is as humane as possible. Therefore, when it comes to animal welfare, why give mammals and birds preferential treatment? Unfortunately, however, there are far fewer resources available to IACUC members about humane euthanasia, appropriate anaesthesia, and basic animal care for reptiles and amphibians in the laboratory than there are for more typical laboratory species like rodents, rabbits, and non-human primates.

The whole concept of using reptiles and amphibians in research raises ethical questions. In our handling study, for example (Kreger and Mench, 1993), the IACUC prohibited feeding live rodents to the study animals. Although the ball python feeds only on live animals in the wild, the committee felt uncomfortable having "higher" vertebrates fed to "lower" ones. There was also the ethical question of not knowing how much pain and suffering the prey species would have to endure; particularly since there was no way it could escape. The committee was trying to balance the stress to the prey versus the stress to the predator.

There are several arguments for feeding live prey. Some snakes must hunt and attack in order to stimulate feeding behavior (Chiszar, et al., 1983; Chiszar, et al., 1994). It gives the predatory animal a novel stimulus similar to what it experiences in the wild and helps decrease the "enforced idleness" seen in captivity (Frye, 1995). Our study animals had to be trained to eat thawed mice even if it meant occasional force feeding.

Answers to the ethical dilemmas faced by the IACUC are not easy to find. This is where professional guidelines could be most useful. Guidelines would have to be based on scientific research and peer-reviewed. Although there have been many studies that use reptiles and amphibians in genetic, behavioral, and biomedical research, few have examined the impact of the laboratory, zoo, or herpetoculture environment on the individual animals involved. How should prey species be presented to captive predators? Is there a core body temperature below which hypothermia would be considered an acceptable anaesthetic? What are the best methods of marking or blood sampling an animal which minimize pain and stress and what are their long-term effects? How do the animals feel about the naturalistic or clinical enclosures in which they are housed? Experiments that examine their preferences and motivations are few. Those who regulate or judge the care of these less familiar study species at research facilities must have easily accessible answers to these questions.

CONCLUSIONS

Despite their reverence as deities and protectors of ancient and recent cultures, their value as biological pest control, and their exploitation as a biomedical, food, and fashion resource, reptiles and amphibians do not carry the same weight as cats, dogs, and nonhuman primates in animal welfare discussions. The fear of snakes tops the 1992 list of the nation's top ten phobias (which also includes public speaking, getting fat, and your own death) according to the Roper Organization's *Roper Report Survey* which polled 2,000 adults nationwide. Reptiles and amphibians lack the facial features, social nature, and body covering of mammals. The young are often miniature versions of adults, or go through a series of drastic morphological changes that make them appear like they might be from some other planet. They lack the large eyes and head that endear us to offspring of more closely related species. Venomous adults produce fully venomous young. With the exception of marine turtles, animal protectionists are unlikely to campaign for improved captive conditions for herpetofauna.

Even within the herpetological community, there are mixed feelings about imposing welfare guidelines. Animal welfarists have been accused of thrusting emotion-based rules upon the academic herpetologist (via the IACUC) that make research cost-prohibitive to the point where conservation decisions so urgently needed are delayed (Gans, 1994). Meeting the animal's physical and psychological needs, however, can only serve to improve research through less confounded data and, perhaps, improved competence and breeding success in conservation-oriented studies (Chiszar et al, 1993b). Another criticism of animal welfare is the question of why researchers should follow guidelines to collect and experiment on a few salamanders when a construction team outside the laboratory can destroy many more salamanders with the sweep of a bulldozer (Gans, 1994). Here, the scientist should take the moral high ground. The scientist may have no control over the lives of animals in the field, but, in the laboratory (or zoo or private collection), the welfare of the animal is entirely dependant on the human custodian.

The American Federation of Herpetoculturists has consistently supported groups that oppose blatantly cruel events such as rattlesnake round-ups or animal abuses in the entertainment industry. It also supports and documents successful husbandry efforts and innovations. Zoos, universities, and private herpetoculturists should support welfare-related research that may lead to breeding success of endangered species or healthy animals that behave normally and provide good educational exhibits. In 1991 and 1996, the Scientists Center for Animal Welfare held conferences on the care and use of amphibians, reptiles, and fish in research where authorities in each field were able to present and exchange current information.

The welfare of captive herpetofauna depends on meeting the physiological and behavioral needs of the individual. These needs can be largely identified by knowledge of the animal's evolutionary adaptations to its habitat. Failure to provide animals with the ability to choose appropriate temperatures, retreats, basking sites, and social situation result in egg retention (Mader, 1990), reproductive, appetite, and immune suppression, and other stress-related disorders including mortality (Frye, 1981; Greenberg and Wingfield, 1987; Lance, 1990; and Wright, 1991). Benefits of welfare considerations to reptiles

Western Rattlesnake, *Crotalus viridis*. **Photo by Paul Freed.**

and amphibians include improved health, less pain and suffering, and perhaps even pleasure. Benefits to their human custodians include better research, scientifically-based guidelines, successful husbandry and conservation efforts, and winning the support of a public fearful of these creatures and in favor of humane treatment of animals. Captive animal welfare is more than animal care and meeting minimal needs. It is housing and caring for the animal from the animal's perception of what is important—not based on the constraints we impose. We must adapt our research and husbandry to fit their optimal needs; not the other way around.

ACKNOWLEDGEMENTS

The author thanks Joy A. Mench, D.Phil., Department of Animal Science, University of California, Davis for her review and suggestions for this manuscript.

REFERENCES

—**Balsai, MJ:**
Husbandry and breeding of the Solomon Is-
lands Prehensile-tailed skink *Corucia zebrata*. *The Vivarium*, 1995, 7 (1) : 4-11.

—**Berry, DJ, MD Kreger, and JL Lyons-Carter:**
Information Resources for Reptiles, Amphibians, Fish, and Cephalopods Used in Biomedical Research. National Agricultural Library, US Department of Agriculture, Beltsville, MD, 1995, 92pp.

—**Bowers, BB and GM Burghardt:**
The scientist and the snake: relationships with reptiles. In, The Inevitable Bond: Examining Scientist-Animal Interactions, H Davis and D Balfour (Eds). Cambridge University Press, Cambridge/New York/Victoria, 1992, pp. 250-263.

—**Brackin, MF:**
The reaction of rank to physiological state in *Cnemidophorus sexlineatus* dominance hierarchies. *Herpetologica*, 1978, 34 (2) : 185-219.

—**Bowers, BB and GM Burghardt 1992.**
The scientist and the snake: relationships with reptiles. In: The Inevitable Bond: Examining Scientist-Animal Interactions, H Davis and

D Balfour (Eds). Cambridge University Press, Cambridge/New York/Victoria, 1992, pp. 250-263.

—**Burghardt, GM and DG Layne:**
Effects of ontogenetic processes and rearing conditions. In, Health and Welfare of Captive Reptiles, C Warwick, FL Frye, and JB Murphy (Eds). Chapman & Hall, London, UK, 1995, pp. 165-185.

—**Chan, SWC and IP Callard:**
Circadian rhythm in the secretion of corticosterone by the Desert Iguana, *Dipsosaurus dorsalis. General and Comparative Endocrinology*, 1972, 18 (3): 565-568.

—**Chiszar, D, D Belcher, SP Mackessy, A Petkus, and HM Smith:**
Stimulation of ingestion in solenoglyphous snakes. *Herpetological Review*, 1994, 25 (4) : 158-159.

—**Chiszar, D, JB Murphy, and HM Smith:**
In search of zoo-academic collaborations: a research agenda for the 1990s. *Herpetologica*, 1993, 49 (4) : 488-500.

—**Chiszar, D, CW Radcliffe, and KM Scudder:**
Strike-induced chemosensory searching by rattlesnakes: the role of envenomation-related chemical cues in the post-strike environment. In, Chemical Signals of Vertebrates III, RM Silverstein and D Müller-Schwarze (Eds). Plenum Press, New York, 1983, pp. 1-24.

—**Chiszar, D, CW Radcliffe, T Boyer, and JL Behler:**
Cover-seeking behavior in red spitting cobras (*Naja mossambica pallida*): effects of tactile cues and darkness. *Zoo Biology*, 1987, 6 (2) : 161-167.

—**Chiszar, D, HM Smith, CM Bogert, and J Vidaurri:**
A chemical sense of self in timber and prairie rattlesnakes. *Bulletin of the Psychonomic Society*, 1991, 29: 153-154.

—**Chiszar, D, HM Smith, and CW Radcliffe:**
Zoo and laboratory experiments on the behavior of snakes: assessments of competence in captive-reared animals. *American Zoologist*, 1993b, 33 (2) : 109-116.

—**Chiszar, D, WT Tomlinson, HM Smith, JB Murphy, and CW Radcliffe:**
Behavioural consequences of husbandry manipulations: indicators of arousal, quiescence and environmental awareness. In, Health and Welfare of Captive Reptiles, C Warwick, FL Frye, and JB Murphy (Eds). Chapman & Hall, London, UK, 1995, pp. 186-204.

—**Chiszar, D, S Wellborn, MA Wand, KM Scudder, and HM Smith:**
Investigatory behavior in snakes. II. Cage cleaning and the induction of defecation in snakes. *Animal Learning and Behavior*, 1980, 8 (3) : 505-510.

—**Cooper, JE and OF Jackson:**
Miscellaneous diseases. In, Diseases of the Reptilia. Vol. 2, JE Cooper and OF Jackson (Eds). Academic Press, NY, 1981, pp. 488-491.

—**Cooper, JE and DL Williams:**
Veterinary perspectives and techniques in husbandry and research. In, Health and Welfare of Captive Reptiles, C Warwick, FL Frye, and JB Murphy (Eds). Chapman & Hall, London, UK, 1995, pp. 98-112.

—**Cowan, DF:**
Adaptation, maladaptation and disease. In, Reproductive Biology and Diseases in Captive Reptiles, SSAR Contributions to Herpetology, Number 1, JB Murphy and JT Collins (Eds). Society for the Study of Amphibians and Reptiles, Meseraull Printing, Lawrence, KS, 1980, pp. 191-196.

—**Cree, A, L.J. Guillette, Jr, JF Cockrem, and J Joss:**
Effects of plasma and temperature stresses on plasma steroid concentrations in male tuatara (*Sphenodon punctatus*). *Journal of Experimental Zoology*, 1990, 253 (1) : 38-46.

—**Dantzer, R and P Mormede:**
Stress in domestic animals: a psychoneuroendocrine approach. In, Stress in Animals, G Moberg (Ed). American Physiological Society, Bethesda, MD, 1985, pp. 81-95.

—**Dauphin-Villemant, C and F Xavier:**
Nychthermal variations of plasma corticosteroids in captive female *Lacerta vivipara* Jacquin: influence of stress and reproductive state. *General and Comparative Endocrinology*, 1987, 67 (3) : 292-230.

—**Dawkins, MS:**
Animal Suffering. Chapman & Hall, London, UK, 1980, 149 pp.

—**Dawkins, MS:**
From an animal's point of view: motivation, fitness, and animal welfare. *Behavioral and Brain Science*, 1990, 13: 1-9, 54-61.

—**Demeter, B:**
Herpetological Husbandry for the Naturalist. Department of Herpetology, National Zoological Park, Washington, DC, 1989, 99 pp.

—**Duncan, IJH:**
Behavioral assessment of welfare. In, The Well-being of Agricultural Animals in Biomedical and Agricultural Research, JA Mench, SJ Mayer and L Krulisch (Eds.). Scientists Center for Animal Welfare, Greenbelt, MD, 1992, pp. 62-68.

—**Duncan, IJH:**
Welfare is all to do with what animals feel. *Journal of Agricultural and Environmental Ethics*, 1993, 6 (Supplement 2): 8-14.

—**Elsey, RM, T Joanen, L McNease, and V Lance:**
Growth rate and plasma corticosterone levels in juvenile alligators maintained at different stocking densities. *Journal of Experimental Zoology*, 1990, 255 (1) : 30-36.

—**Fraser, AF:**
The behaviour of suffering in animals. *Applied Animal Behaviour Science*, 1984, 13 (1984/85) : 1-6.

—**Fraser, D:**
Science, values and animal welfare: Exploring the 'inextricable connection'. *Animal Welfare*, 1995, 4 (2): 103-117.

—**Fraser, D, PA Phillips, and BK Thompson:**
Environmental preference testing to access the well-being of animals - An evolving paradigm. *Journal of Agricultural and Environmental Ethics*, 1993, 6 (Supplement 2): 104-114.

—**Frye, FL:**
Biomedical and Surgical Aspects of Captive Reptile Husbandry. Veterinary Medicine Publishing Co., Edwardsville, KS, 1981, pp. 61-94.

—**Frye, FL:**
Nutritional considerations. In, Health and Welfare of Captive Reptiles, C Warwick, FL Frye, and JB Murphy (Eds). Chapman & Hall, London, UK, 1995, pp. 82-97.

—**Grassman, M and D Crews:**
Ovarian and adrenal functions in the parthenogenic whiptail lizard *Cnemidophorus uniparens* in the field and laboratory. *General and Comparative Endocrinology*, 1990, 76 (3) : 444-450.

—**Greenberg, N:**
Observations of social feeding in lizards. *Herpetologica*, 1976, 32 (3): 349-352.

—**Greenberg, N:**
The saurian psyche revisited: Lizards in research. In, The Care and Use of Amphibians, Reptiles and Fish in Research, DO Schaeffer, KM Klienow and L Krulisch (Eds). Scientists Center for Animal Welfare, Greenbelt, MD, 1992, pp. 75-91.

—**Greenberg, N, GM Burghardt, D Crews, E Font, RE Jones, and G. Vaughan:**
Reptile models for biomedical research. In, Nonmammalian Animal Models for Biomedical Research, AD Woodhead and K Vivirito (Eds). CRC Press, Inc., Boca Raton, FL, 1989, pp. 289-308.

—**Greenberg, N and D Crews:**
Endocrine and behavioral responses to aggression and social dominance in the green anole lizard, *Anolis carolinensis*. *General and Comparative Endocrinology*, 1990, 77 (2) : 246-255.

—**Greenberg, N and JC Wingfield:**
Stress and reproduction: reciprocal relationships. In, Hormones and Reproduction in Fishes, Amphibians, and Reptiles, DO Norris and RE Jones (Eds). Plenum Press, NY, 1987, pp. 461-503.

—**Guillette Jr, LJ, A Cree, and AA Rooney:**
Biology of stress: interactions with reproduction, immunology and intermediary metabolism. In, Health and Welfare of Captive Reptiles, C Warwick, FL Frye, and JB Murphy (Eds). Chapman & Hall, London, UK, 1995, pp. 32-81.

—**Herzog, HA, Jr:**
Experiential modification of defensive behaviors in garter snakes (*Thamnophis sirtalis*). *Journal of Comparative Psychology*, 1990, 104 (4) : 334-339.

—**Herzog, HA, Jr and GM Burghardt:**
Development of antipredator responses in snakes III: stability of individual and litter differences over the first year of life. *Ethology*, 1988, 77 (3) : 250-258.

—**Kreger, MD:**
Regarding reptiles. *Science and Animal Care*, 1992, 3 (3) : 1,4.

—**Kreger, MD:**
The psychological well-being of reptiles. *Humane Innovations and Alternatives*, 1993a, 7: 519-523.

—**Kreger, MD:**
Zoo-academic collaborations: physiological and psychological needs of reptiles and amphibians. *Herpetologica*, 1993b, 49 (4) : 509-512.

—**Kreger, MD and JA Mench:**
Behavioral and physiological effects of handling and restraint in the ball python (*Python regius*) and the blue-tongued skink (*Tiliqua scincoides*). *Applied Animal Behaviour Science*, 1993, 38 (3-4) : 323-336.

—**Lance, VA:**
Stress in reptiles. In, Progress in Comparative Endocrinology, A Epple, CG Scanes, and MH Stetson (Eds). Wiley-Liss, Inc, NY, 1990, pp. 461-466.

—**Lance, VA:**
Evaluating pain and stress in reptiles. In, The Care and Use of Amphibians, Reptiles and Fish in Research, DO Schaeffer, KM Klienow, and L Krulisch (Eds). Scientists Center for Animal Welfare, Greenbelt, MD, 1992, pp. 101-106.

—**Licht, P:**
Reptiles. In, Marshall's Physiology of Repro-

duction, Reproductive Cycles of Vertebrates, GE Lamming (Ed). Vol. 1, Churchill Livingston, Edinburgh, 1985, pp. 206-272.

—**Markowitz, H:**
Behavioral Enrichment in the Zoo. Van Nostrand Reinhold, Co., NY, 1982, 210pp.

—**Marmie, W, S Kuhn, and D Chiszar:**
Behavior of captive-raised rattlesnakes (*Crotalus enyo*) as a function of rearing conditions. *Zoo Biology*, 1990, 241-246.

—**Mason, RT, RF Hoyt, Jr, LK Pannell, EF Wellner, and B Demeter:**
Cage design and configuration for arboreal reptiles. In, The Care and Use of Amphibians, Reptiles and Fish in Research, DO Schaeffer, KM Klienow, and L Krulisch (Eds). Scientists Center for Animal Welfare, Bethesda, Maryland, 1992, pp. 72-74.

—**Mattison, C:**
The Care of Reptiles and Amphibians in Captivity. Blandford Press, London, U.K., 1987, 317pp.

—**McCarthy, CR:**
Regulations and guidelines: the National Institutes of Health. In, The Care and Use of Amphibians, Reptiles and Fish in Research, DO Schaeffer, KM Klienow, and L Krulisch (Eds). Scientists Center for Animal Welfare, Greenbelt, MD, 1992, pp. 5-6.

—**McKnight, RR, GF Copperberg, and EJ Ginter:**
Duration of tonic immobility in lizards (*Anolis carolinensis*) as a function of repeated immobilization, frequent handling, and laboratory maintenance. *Psychological Record*, 1978, 28: 549-556.

—**Mench, JA:**
Assessing animal welfare: An overview. Journal of Agricultural and Environmental Ethics, 6 (Supplement 2) : 69-73.

—**Moberg, GP:**
Biological response to stress: Key to assessment of animal well-being? In, Stress in Animals, G Moberg (Ed), American Physiological Society, Bethesda, MD, 1985, pp. 27-51.

—**Moberg, GP:**
Scientific perspectives: Defining welfare. *Journal of Agricultural and Environmental Ethics*, 6 (Supplement 2) : 1-7.

—**Moore, MC, CW Thompson, and CA Marler:**
Reciprocal changes in corticosterone and testosterone levels following acute and chronic handling stress in the Tree Lizard *Urosaurus ornatus*. *General and Comparative Endocrinology*, 1991, 81 (2) : 217-226.

—**National Research Council:**
Guide for the Care and Use of Laboratory Animals. National Academy Press, Washington, DC, 1996, 128 pp.

—**Novak, M and S Suomi:**
Psychological well-being of primates in captivity. *American Psychologist*, 1988, 43 (10) : 765-773.

—**Public Health Service:**
Public Health Service Policy on Humane Care and Use of Laboratory Animals. Washington, DC, US Department of Health and Human Services, 1986.

—**Pough, HF:**
Recommendations for the care of amphibians and reptiles in academic institutions. *ILAR News*, 1991, 33 (4) : S3-S21.

—**Pough, HF:**
Setting guidelines for the care of reptiles, amphibians and fishes. In, The Care and Use of Amphibians, Reptiles and Fish in Research, DO Schaeffer, KM Klienow, and L Krulisch (Eds). Scientists Center for Animal Welfare, Greenbelt, MD, 1992, pp. 7-14.

—**Rogers, LJ:**
What do animals think and feel? *ANZCCART News*, 1994, 7 (4) : 1-3.

—**Suboski, MD:**
Releaser-induced recognition learning by amphibians and reptiles. *Animal Learning and Behavior*, 1992, 20 (1) : 63-82.

—**Tokarz, RR:**
Effects of corticosterone treatment on male aggressive behavior in a lizard (*Anolis sagrei*). *Hormones and Behavior*, 1987, 21 (3) : 358-370.

—**Warwick, C:**
Reptilian ethology in captivity: observations of some problems and an evaluation of their aetiology. *Applied Animal Behaviour Science*, 1990, 26 (1-2) : 1-13.

—**Warwick, C:**
Psychological and behavioral principles and problems. In, Health and Welfare of Captive Reptiles, C Warwick, FL Frye, and JB Murphy (Eds). Chapman & Hall, London, UK, 1995, pp. 205-238.

—**Warwick, C. and C. Steedman:**
Naturalistic versus clinical environments in husbandry and research. In, Health and Welfare of Captive Reptiles, C Warwick, FL Frye, and JB Murphy (Eds). Chapman & Hall, London, UK, 1995, pp. 113-130.

—**Wright, K:**
Husbandry an essential component of diagnosing disease in reptiles and amphibians. *The Vivarium*, 1991, 3 (3) : 23-27.

—**Wright, K:**
Acclimation-Maladaptation Syndrome in captive amphibians. *The Vivarium*, 1994, 6 (3) 12-13.

304

SAFE AND HUMANE TRANSPORT

Lowell Ackerman DVM PhD
P.O. Box 12093
Scottsdale AZ 85267-2093

Dr. Lowell Ackerman is a practicing veterinarian, consultant, author, lecturer and radio personality. To date he has written 34 books and over 150 book chapters and articles dealing with animal health care issues.

INTRODUCTION

Every year thousands of reptiles perish needlessly by being shipped inappropriately between locations. This is not only disgraceful from an animal welfare standpoint, but, in most cases, is completely preventable. The following information has been extracted from the International Air Transport Association (IATA) Live Animals Regulations. The current 22nd Edition became available in October, 1995 and permission has been kindly granted by IATA to reproduce an overview of the information here. This summary does not reflect all the species-specific requirements included in the regulatory guidelines. For anyone that might be shipping animals, order your copy directly from IATA, 2000 Peel Street, Montreal, Quebec, CANADA, H3A 2R4

CONTAINER DESIGN AND CONSTRUCTION

When constructing containers for shipment of reptiles, make sure they are closed and sturdy, yet well-ventilated. Keep in mind that your container is not the only one being transported and that it might be damaged by other freight if not sturdily constructed. The door or lid must be access-proof so that it can't accidentally open due to actions of personnel or the animals themselves. The container must be suitable to keep the species inside at all times and to protect them from unauthorized access. Similarly, it must be impossible for animals to escape through cracks and crevices or gaps at the seams or joints. Fashion handles or spacer bars on the container that will not only make

Mangrove Salt Marsh Snakes, *Nerodia clarki compressicauda*. **Photo by W. P. Mara.**

transportation easier but also help ensure that the ventilation holes don't become blocked by other freight being loaded adjacent. If there is the likelihood of extreme temperature variance during shipment, the container must be insulated by an outer ventilated polystyrene box. If the temperature is likely to rise, it may be necessary to put some ice in a sealed polyethylene/ waterproof bag or bags around the inner container. There must never be direct contact between the ice and the animal. The International

Boa constrictor. Photo courtesy of Dr. Lowell Ackerman.

SUMMERY OF IATA REGULATIONS

Species	Container Requirement	Other notes
Agama	41	
Alligator species	42	IATA recommends that large animals have their mouths tied with sealing tape and be blindfolded with a soft material.
Anaconda (small)	41	
Anaconda (large)	42	
Anole	41	
Boa species	41	
Boa constrictor	41	
Caiman	42	IATA recommends that large animals have their mouths tied with sealing tape and be blindfolded with a soft material.
Caiman lizard	42	
Chameleon species	41	May be placed individually in linen or cotton bags in which case the container does not need to be lined with nylon mesh or gauze. Chameleons require a system of brushwood perches. These animals must be sprayed with warm fresh water at the time of packing.
Crocodile lizard	41	
Crocodile species	42	IATA recommends that large animals have their mouths tied with sealing tape and be blindfolded with a soft material.
Egg-eating Snake	41	
Gavial	42	
Gecko	41	May be placed individually in linen or cotton bags in which case the container does not need to be lined with nylon mesh or gauze. Travel well in plenty of crumpled paper.
Gila monster	41	
Heloderma	41	
Iguana species	42	
Komodo Dragon	42	
Lizards (most)	41	May be placed individually in linen or cotton bags in which case the container does not need to be lined with nylon mesh or gauze. Small lizards need dry leaves or moss to provide a foothold.
Monitor Lizard	42	
Mussurana	41	
Olive Ridley	43	
Python	41	
Reptile (most)	41	
Skink	41	
Snake (most)	41	See Exceptions TW-01 and UA-02 in IATA Regs.
Tegu	42	
Teiid	41	
Terrapin species	43	Must be packed in damp (not wet) wood wool or moss.
Tortoise species	43	
Tuatara	41	
Turtle species	43	Must be packed in damp (not wet) wood wool or moss.
Watersnake (small)	41;51	May be packed in bags which have been thoroughly dampened, but this is not a requirement if total transportation time is less than 72 hours.
Watersnake (large)	42;51	May be packed in bags which have been thoroughly dampened, but this is not a requirement if total transportation time is less than 72 hours.
Watersnake (South East Asian)	51	Must be packed in plastic bags containing 1/3 water in which the snake is immersed. The space above the water must be filled with normal air, not oxygen

Savannah Monitor. Photo courtesy of Dr. Lowell Ackerman

Burmese Mountain Tortoise. Photo courtesy of Dr. Lowell Ackerman

Yellow Anaconda, *Eunectes notaeus*. **Photo by Paul Freed.**

Air Transport Association (IATA) provides specific Container Requirements in its Live Animals Regulations. The 22nd edition of these Regulations was in effect on 1st October, 1995

The container must allow the animal to lie in a natural manner with enough space that stacking is avoidable. The height of the container must permit an air flow over the animals but prevent excess stacking. A clearance of 3 cm (1.2 inches) above the highest point of the animal is recommended. The container must be adequately ventilated on at least three sides, with the majority of the ventilation being provided on the upper part of the container. The ventilation openings must be small enough to prevent the animal's escape and never more than 2.5 cm (one inch) in diameter. Very fine nylon gauze should cover the ventilation holes on the inside container. Meshed openings must be added to the outer container to prevent possible occlusion of inner ventilation holes by the outer container.

It may seem unnecessary to mention here, but the enclosure must be safe for the animals you are transporting. Make sure that there are no nails, screws or other sharp surfaces extending into the container. Also ensure that the enclosure is made of non-toxic materials. Chemically-impregnated wood may be poisonous to reptiles and must never be used. Since reptiles are cold-blooded, metal must not be used in the construction of the inner container. Strong plywood or expanded polystyrene/styrofoam boxes are the best materials to use in construction. Containers manufactured of or lined with styrofoam reduce the effects of sudden temperature changes. There are several commercial products available that meet transport requirements; a container need not be constructed.

Hygiene is extremely important when it comes to containers. They must be clean and leak-proof and must be made of waterproof material for species that urinate. If you are re-using a container it must be thoroughly disinfected or sterilized. Check with your veterinarian and only use products that are non-toxic for reptiles. Preferably, clean or sterilize the containers several days before shipping to minimize exposure risks. The containers should be insulated or lined to help prevent temperature fluctuations and bedding should be provided that is suitable for the given species. Where necessary, moss or suitable brushwood may be placed in the box. Straw is not acceptable and many countries prohibit its importation.

Finally, safety for transport personnel must be considered. Venomous reptiles must be individually packed in styrofoam containers placed within a wooden container; both containers must be appropriately labeled. Each bag must carry a label "poisonous" or "Nonpoisonous" as appropriate. If your reptile harms someone because of your failure to ship safely, you might not only lose your animal(s) but risk potential liability and litigation.

SPECIAL ATTENTION

Be aware of the special needs of any animal before you consider shipping it. Also be aware that the animals will not have access to food or water during the entire time in transit. Therefore, don't plan on taking the container to the airport more than four hours before the scheduled departure time. Arrangements must be made for animals to be delivered to the consignee or his agent as soon as possible upon arrival at destination. Whenever possible, avoid connecting flights in favor of direct non-stop routes.

Many reptiles are CITES-listed species and must be shipped in accordance with strict standards and according to IATA Live Animals Regulations. In most cases, import/export licenses or permits are required for international shipment. Make sure you are in compliance. If you are sending your reptiles by air, you will need to complete a "Shipper's Certification for Live Animals" which is available from IATA and its member airlines. You will need to provide information on the number of containers, the specific Container Requirement Number (see table on page 317), species description, name and address of shipper, CITES requirements, airport of departure and airport of destination. It also asks for assurances that arrangements and packaging has been made in accordance with IATA Live Animals Regulations and all applicable carrier and governmental regulations.

The container must be correctly labeled and marked with the consignee's name, address and telephone number. Make sure that these labels do not block the ventilation holes, especially on small containers.

Argus Monitor, *Varanus panoptes*. **Photo by K. H. Switak.**

Boa Constrictor, *Boa constrictor*. **Photo by R. D. Bartlett.**

High-casqued Chameleon, *Chamaeleo hoehneli*. **Photo by Aaron Norman.**

Tokay Gecko, *Gekko gecko*. **Photo by Zoltan Takacs.**

PAIN SENSATION AND ANALGESIA

Craig W. Stevens PhD*
Stan Willenbring PhD
Department of Pharmacology and Physiology
Oklahoma State University,
College of Osteopathic Medicine,
Tulsa, OK 74107

Craig W. Stevens received his Ph.D. in Pharmacology from the Mayo Graduate School of Medicine at Rochester, Minnesota in 1988. He completed postdoctoral training at the University of Minnesota in Minneapolis and joined the faculty at the OSU, College of Osteopathic Medicine in 1990. His research interests include opioid analgesia and tolerance and alternative models for biomedical research. He is currently an Associate Professor of Pharmacology.

Stan Willenbring received his doctorate in physiology from Dartmouth Medical School in 1994. His research explores the peripheral and central mechanisms of neuropathic pain, particularly the neural changes that underlie the development of behavioral and pharmacological abnormalities following peripheral nerve injury. He is currently an Assistant Professor of Physiology at the College of West Virginia, where he is conducting research to develop an amphibian model for the study of neuropathic pain.

INTRODUCTION

This chapter presents a summary of the existing scientific literature on pain sensation and analgesia in amphibians and reptiles. It should be noted that there is relatively little data available on pain transmission in nonmammalian vertebrates, and even less data on the action of analgesic agents. However, the basic plan of the amphibian and reptile vertebrate nervous system is consistent with that of mammals. It appears that neural pathways subserving pain transmission arise early in phylogeny; pain transmission at lower levels in the nervous system may share common features with homologous structures in mammals. In contrast, pain processing at higher, supraspinal centers (which arise later in vertebrate phylogeny) may not

* Address all correspondence to Dr. Craig W. Stevens, Department of Pharmacology and Physiology, Oklahoma State University, College of Osteopathic Medicine, Tulsa OK 74107

Eastern Box Turtle, *Terrapene carolina*. Photo by M. P. and C. Piednoir.

Green Tree Python, *Chondropython viridis*. Photo by K. H. Switak.

Green Iguana, *Iguana iguana*. Photo by U. E. Friese.

be present in amphibians and reptiles which do not share homologous supraspinal structures.

This chapter first introduces pain terminology and modalities. (In this chapter, the term animals refers to nonhuman animals unless otherwise stated.) This chapter then presents evidence for pain sensation processing through the following pathways:

—peripheral nerves
—spinal cord
—ascending spinal pain pathways
—supraspinal processing
—descending neurotransmitter systems that may modulate pain in the spinal cord

The chapter closes with a review of herpetological animal studies to assess the analgesic action of opioids and other pharmacological agents.

PAIN SENSATION IN ANIMALS

The first issue to be considered when reviewing pain sensation and analgesia is one of semantics. The word pain is not correctly applied to animals. Pain refers to a complex perceptual and emotional experience in humans that is largely subjective (Kitchell and Erickson, 1983; IASP, 1986). In the truest sense, what we commonly call pain in animals is nociception—a term that refers only to the physiological processes of sensing and reacting to noxious stimuli prior to the supraspinal events associated with the experience of pain. However, for ease of use and to make research findings accessible to a general audience, the term pain is generally used instead of nociception, and analgesia instead of antinociception. Researchers accept this less-than-precise usage of the word pain in deference to the benefit of the general readership; however, this does not imply that these researchers believe that animals experience pain as we do. Thus, for general discussions and in this chapter, the

American Alligator, *Alligator mississippiensis.* **Photo by R. T. Zappalorti.**

Gila Monster, *Heloderma suspectum.* **Photo by R. S. Simmons.**

terms pain and analgesia are used to refer to any level of nociceptive processing and abatement of this processing.

MODALITIES OF PAIN SENSATION

Animals use a variety of physical and neural adaptations to discriminate between modalities of peripheral stimuli. All vertebrates seem to be able to distinguish thermal, tactile and chemical stimulation at the skin surface. The noxious level of any modality is defined as the intensity of stimulus (threshold) that causes the animal to withdraw, or defined as the duration of time (latency) until the animal withdraws from a suprathreshold stimulus.

Thermal sensations range from noxious cold, through the nonnoxious cool and warm sensations, to the burning sensations of noxious heat. We measure noxious heat and noxious cold as withdrawal latencies to a suprathreshold stimuli. However, you can calibrate the temperature ramp of a thermal stimulus apparatus to allow conversion from latency to relative temperature.

As poikilotherms, the image of reptiles and amphibians is that of being slow to respond to gradual changes in environmental temperature. However, both classes of animals demonstrate organized behaviors indicating well-defined abilities to discriminate among thermal stimuli. Infrared detectors in the facial pits of snakes are known to be exquisitely sensitive. Crocodiles placed on a hot plate attempt to guard their foot pads by lifting them alternately as well as attempting to escape the heated surface (Kanui et al., 1990).

Figure 1 shows that amphibians respond to a noxious radiant heat stimulus in a manner virtually identical to rodents. The only difference is a shift in the mean response threshold between the two groups, with amphibians responding at a lower mean temperature than rodents.

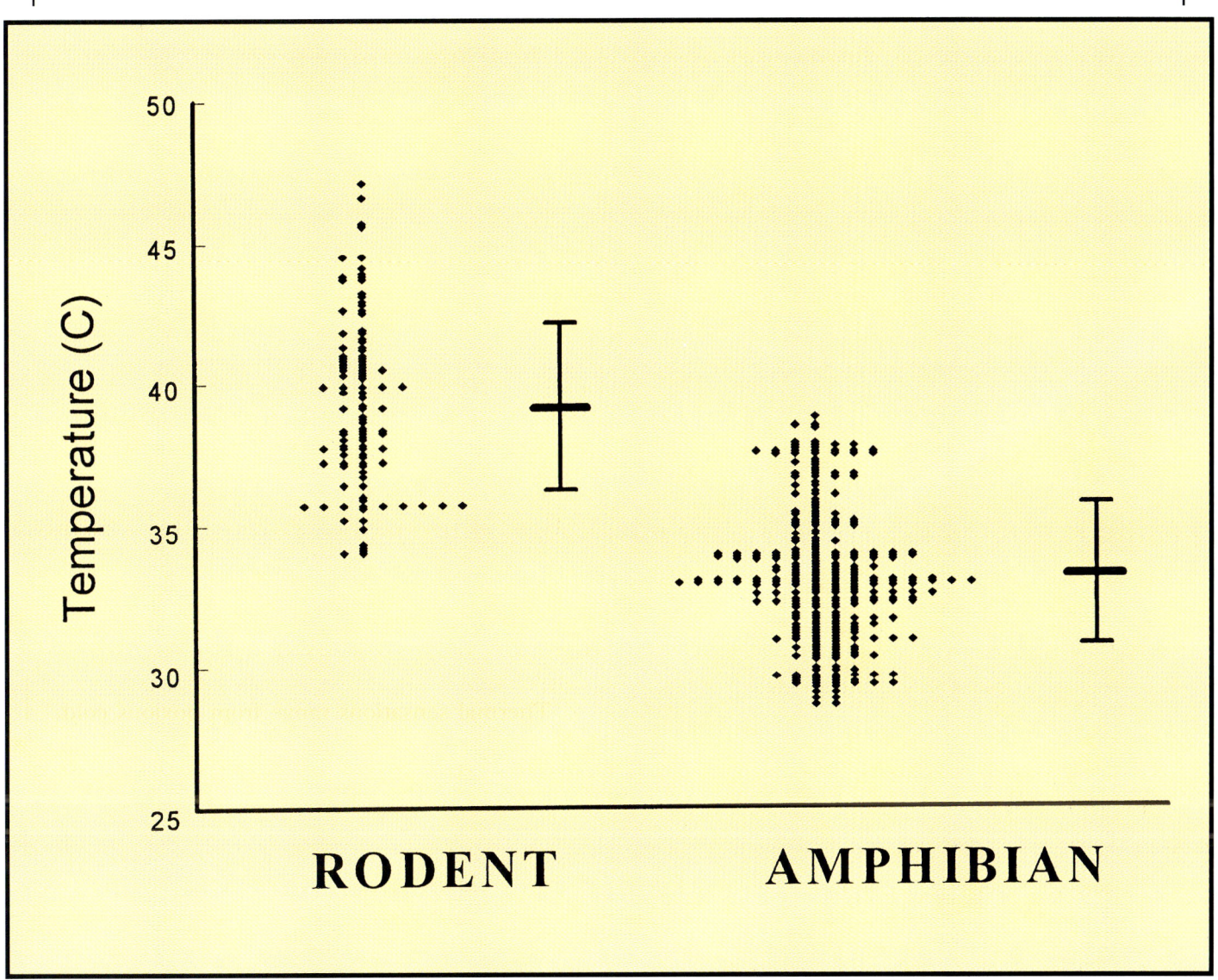

Fig.1:
Comparison of thermal response thresholds in normal rodents and amphibians using a modification of the Hargreave's thermal stimulator apparatus: Holtzman Sprague Dawley rats (*Rattus norvegicus*; n=108, mean 39.3 C, s.d. 3.0 C) and Northern grass frogs (*Rana pipiens*; n=323, mean 33.1 C, s.d. 2.3 C).

Discernible tactile stimuli include categories of light touch, vibration and deep pressure. The first two groupings of tactile stimuli are invariably nonnoxious (under normal physiological conditions). Deep pressure on the peripheral tissues in the forms of crush or pinch is invariably noxious. To our knowledge, no work has been done with noxious mechanical stimulation in either amphibians or reptiles. However, preliminary data indicates the development of abnormal nociceptive responses to previously nonnoxious mechanical stimuli following peripheral nerve injury in frogs (Willenbring and Stevens, 1995b).

Chemical stimuli are always noxious at the levels at which they become perceptible. In the acetic acid test (AAT), dilute acetic acid is ap-

Northern Leopard Frog, *Rana pipiens*. **Photo by David Green.**

plied to the skin of an animal. In amphibians, the wiping response of frogs to the AAT is a well-established nociceptive test (Pezalla, 1983; Stevens, 1992). The AAT has been used to produce a significant body of work regarding pain sensation and analgesia in amphibians (see below).

The data regarding peripheral chemosensitivity in reptiles are not as abundant. A dilute capsaicin solution instilled in the eye of the crocodile produces behavioral responses, including blinking, rubbing and head shaking (Kanui et al., 1990). Injection of formalin in the crocodile forepaw results in the development of paw guarding behaviors (Kanui et al., 1990). However, pain-related responses to formalin injection may be mediated more through the induction of inflammation than by direct chemical stimulation.

At noxious levels in humans, the discrimina-

Nile Crocodile, *Crocodylus niloticus*. **Photo by Mark Smith.**

tion between modalities of sensation becomes less distinct. Thus noxious cold or chemical stimuli may be perceived as burning. This might be due to common secondary pathways, aberrations in intrinsic modulatory systems, or both. Based on the observed conservation of neural systems between lower vertebrates and mammals, it is conceivable that the same phenomenon exists in the nociceptive processing of amphibians and reptiles.

PAIN PATHWAYS
TRANSDUCTION OF PAIN FROM THE PERIPHERY

Underlying the perception of these various modalities of sensation are neural structures and fiber types. Neural structures and fiber types permit an animal to detect and transmit noxious and nonnoxious stimuli. Mammals have a variety of specialized end-organs on their afferent fibers. In contrast, only three groups of afferent nerve endings have been identified in amphibians. The nerve endings that transduce noxious stimuli are called nociceptors.

In amphibians, the three groups of afferent nerve endings include:
—one type of expanded tip ending, primarily located in the superficial level of the dermis
—two groups of free nerve endings:
    one group located in the epidermis
    one group located in the deeper layers of the dermis

(Roberts and Hayes, 1977; Fox and Whitear, 1978; Spray, 1976).

Natterjack Toad, *Bufo calamita*. Photo by Mark Smith.

Reptiles also appear to possess only simple nonencapsulated corpuscular endings and free nerve endings. Both endings are distributed throughout the dermis and epidermis (Landmann and Halata, 1980; Pac, 1984).

The expanded tip endings seen on both reptile and amphibian sensory afferents are varieties of Merkel cell complexes. In amphibians, detection of mechanical stimuli is associated with the Merkel cell structures and the superficial free nerve endings. In particular, detection of mechanical stimuli is associated with nonnoxious constant pressure, phasic touch, and vibration (Yamashita and Ogawa, 1991).

Pain perception is most readily associated with the free nerve endings of the deeper dermis, which primarily transduce temperature. Under normal physiological conditions, it is likely that these nerve endings also transduce noxious mechanical stimuli, such as pinching and pin pricks.

In reptiles, the separation of receptor structures into categories of noxious and nonnoxious sensory function is less discrete. Reptiles also have Merkel cell complexes. In reptiles, these complexes are associated with myelinated fibers known to transmit signals elicited by nonnoxious mechanical stimuli. The presence of these complexes suggests an association in the reptile (Kenton et al., 1971; Landmann and Halata, 1980) similar to that in the amphibian. However, thus far, no stimulus-specific receptor structures have been identified (Kenton et al., 1971).

It is as yet unclear if chemical sensitivity is mediated exclusively by these nerve endings associated with thermal stimuli. Early electrophysiological work indicated that the detection of all noxious sensory stimuli (including chemical) was attributed exclusively to the same free nerve endings associated with thermal sensitivity in amphibians (Adrian et al., 1931). However, recent findings demonstrate the continued presence of chemical sensitivity responses in the absence of thermal sensitivity following peripheral nerve injury in some frogs (Willenbring and Stevens, 1995c). This indicates that chemical stimuli may be transduced by more than one receptor structure, and transmitted by more than one fiber type in the amphibian. Receptor structures associated specifically with chemical sensitivity in reptiles have not been identified.

PERIPHERAL PAIN FIBERS

Table 1 delineates the various peripheral sensory fibers and receptor structures in amphibians and reptiles. Amphibians possess both myelinated and unmyelinated afferent fibers running concurrently in mixed-fiber peripheral sensory nerves (Spray, 1976). Investigators delineate these fibers into three general classes based on morphology,

Water-holding frog, *Cyclorana* sp. Photo by Paul Freed.

conduction velocities, latency of response, and action potential characteristics:
—large heavily myelinated A fibers
—thinly myelinated B fibers
—small unmyelinated C fibers

Fiber characteristics correlate well with those observed in corresponding classes of somatic sensory afferents in mammals: Aβ,Aδ, and C fibers respectively.

In general, the cutaneous nociceptors in frog skin (those responding to noxious thermal, mechanical and chemical stimuli) arise from peripheral terminations of the thinly myelinated C fibers. Maruhashi (Maruhashi et al., 1952; Adrian et al., 1931) separated fibers both by conduction velocity and fiber diameter in amphibians. Those studies found that small, slowly-conducting fibers transmitted the majority of all impulses induced by noxious heat, pinching, pin pricks and the application of dilute acid to the skin (Maruhashi et al., 1952; Adrian et al., 1931).

Table 1. Characteristics of afferent fiber types and associated structures in amphibians and reptiles.

Fiber Type		Fiber Size (μm)	Conduction Velocity (m/sec)	Associated Nociceptors	Strata	Stimuli Transduced	Terminal Laminae	References
AMPHIBIAN								
A (large myelinated)		6 - 12	15 - 35	Merkel complexes and free nerve endings	Epidermis	pressure, pricking, vibration	IV - VIII	Adrian et al., 1931; Catton, 1966, 1976; Maruhashi et al., 1952; Spray and Chronister, 1974;
B (small myelinated)		2 - 6	3 - 14	Merkel complexes and free nerve endings	Epidermis	light pressure, vibration, cold	IV - VIII	Spray, 1976; Szekely, 1976; Szekely et al., 1982
C (small unmyelinated)		0.1 - 2	0.1 - 4	Free nerve endings	Dermis	noxious heat, pinching, deep pressure, chemical	I - III	
REPTILE	unimodal grouping; mostly myelinated	0.9 - 6.3	5 - 25	Merkel complexes and free nerve endings; slowly adapting mechanoreceptors	Dermis and Epidermis	deep pressure, cold	I - III	Kenton et al., 1971; Kusuma and ten Donkelaar, 1980; Landmann and Halata, 1980; Pac, 1984; Ruigrok et al., 1985
		10 - 35		Merkel complexes and free nerve endings; rapidly adapting mechanoreceptors	Dermis and Epidermis	fine touch, vibration	IV - VII	

314

Criolla Frog, *Leptodactylus ocellatus*. Photo by Paul Freed.

There is a controversy over the central terminations of primary afferent fibers within the amphibian spinal gray (Nikundiwe et al., 1982). Most studies indicate that sensory afferents from the skin terminate in areas of the dorsal spinal cord that correspond to laminae I-IV. Some studies describe small-diameter primary afferent fibers (which carry information of a noxious nature) terminating primarily within the dorsal field, and to a lesser extent, in the central field surrounding the central canal (Nikundiwe et al., 1982). Other studies suggest that the end-branches of small-caliber fibers associated with nociception terminate exclusively in the superficial dorsal laminae (the substantia gelatinosa); while only larger fibers associated with transmission of nonnoxious information penetrate to the deeper laminae (Szekely, 1976; Szekely et al., 1982). Electrophysiological evidence supports the existence of primary afferent synapses on motoneuron dendrites within the amphibian dorsal horn.

Likewise, there is remarkably little data available concerning peripheral fiber types in reptiles. For reptiles, researchers report only a unimodal distribution of sensory fiber sizes, which extends over the sizes of the B and C classes of amphibian fibers. In contrast to amphibian fibers, these reptilian fibers do not fall into distinct classes based on associated conduction velocities or stimulus-specific responses. Conduction velocities range from <1 to 35 m/sec, with the majority of fibers conducting in the amphibian, B-fiber range. However, no correlation is noted between fiber size and conduction velocity. Furthermore, all stimulus modalities elicit responses throughout both ranges of conduction velocity and fiber size. Additionally, the dorsal roots containing peripheral sensory afferents entering the spinal cord do not clearly segregate according to large and small fibers as they do in higher vertebrates (Kusuma and Ten Donkelaar, 1980).

Thus it is difficult to classify any specific subgroup of reptilian sensory afferents as primarily nociceptive. However, in chelonians at least, it has been suggested that peripheral fiber types are separated according to their sites of termination in the spinal cord. In this format, smaller, type-A fibers associated with cutaneous sensation and nociception arborize primarily in the superficial laminae (I - III). This is in comparison to muscle-spindle and joint proprioceptive fibers, which penetrate to the deeper laminae (IV - VII) where they form monosynaptic reflex pathways with the dendritic endings of motor neurons (Ruigrok et al., 1985).

PROCESSING OF PAIN IN THE SPINAL CORD

The pain signal is carried from the peripheral nociceptor to the spinal cord by the primary afferent nerve fiber in all vertebrates. This fiber terminates in the dorsal horn. There, it releases pain-signaling neurotransmitters such as substance P, calcitonin gene-related peptide (CGRP) and glutamate. Using immunohistochemical techniques, all of these substances are readily identified in abundance in the spinal dorsal horn of both amphibians and reptiles (Inagaki et al., 1981; Lorez and Kemali, 1981; Wolters et al., 1986; Luthman et al., 1991). Substance P and glutamate excite second-order neurons which have their cell bodies in the dorsal horn and which send long fibers upward to form the ascending pain pathway. Research has not identified in either amphibians or reptiles such second-order neurons within the dorsal horn which receive direct dorsal root input (Simpson, 1976).

Also present in the spinal cord are endorphinergic neurons which release met-enkephalin, an endogenous opioid peptide. Met-enkephalin inhibits the release of substance P and decreases the firing of the second-order pain neuron. Met-enkephalin and opioid receptors have been detected by immunohistochemical means in the spinal cord of amphibians and reptiles (Stevens, 1988; Luthman et al., 1991; Naik et al., 1981). Additionally, using in-situ hybridization to stain neurons expressing mRNA for met-enkephalin, endorphinergic neurons have been identified throughout the brain and spinal cord of *Rana pipiens* (Rothe-Skinner and Stevens, 1995). In amphibians, immobilization stress produces analgesia by release of an opioid peptide, demonstrating that endorphinergic neurons are functional (Stevens et al., 1995; Pezalla and Dicig, 1984). Thus, while the most detailed studies have only been performed in mammals, the existence of these key pain neurotransmitters and endogenous opioid analgesics suggests that basic mechanisms of pain transmission within the spinal cord are common throughout the vertebrate classes.

ASCENDING PAIN PATHWAYS

Pain is transmitted from the spinal cord to the brain by ascending pain pathways. In mammals, fibers from the second-order neurons cross to the opposite side (decussate) and ascend in the ventrolateral quadrant, which conveys pain information. Similar decussating fibers are scarce in amphibians.

In general, spinal morphology of the amphibian and reptilian do not show the highly-defined laminar patterns observed in mammals. However, the primary afferent fibers associated with noxious stimuli terminate similarly in reptiles and amphibians as in mammals. Termination is primarily in the superficial dorsal horn areas of spinal cords. This similarity between amphibian and mammalian nociceptive anatomy again indicates that the nociceptive structures are a highly conserved physiological organization throughout the vertebrata.

To provide a workable morphological scheme, the amphibian spinal gray was subdivided into the following fields: dorsal, lateral, central, ventrolateral, and ventromedial fields (Ebbesson, 1976). Fibers from these second-order neurons ascend to midbrain somatosensory areas via two distinct tracts: the dorsal column nucleus and the spinal tracts. These ascending tracts are predominantly ipsilateral. The ascending tracts travel within the dorsal and lateral funiculi, although some dorsal column fibers decussate prior to innervating their supraspinal targets in the midbrain. Intersegmental tracts, comparable to Lissauer's tract in mammals, are also seen in frogs. However, the amphibian tracts are composed of both large and small diameter fibers.

The above results are observed after hemisection of the spinal cord. The only somatosensory ascending tracts identified in the reptile are those of the dorsal column nucleus that project to the midbrain and subsequently to the thalamus (Pritz and Stritzel, 1989; Pritz and Strizel, 1990). However, these tracts are not identified as exclusively nociceptive. Exact location of the second-order neurons giving rise to these tracts is yet unknown.

SUPRASPINAL PROCESSING OF PAIN STIMULI

Pain transmission in vertebrates is parallel-processed throughout the nervous system, with separate pathways for the sensory-discriminative and motivational-affective aspects of pain. At present, we only have adequate neurological data of pain transmission in mammals. However, insofar as pain pathways are contained within sensory tracts in lower vertebrates, an examination of ascending sensory tracts and their brain connections can provide a basis for comparison.

Ascending the phylogeny of vertebrates, the sensory-discriminative pathway originating from spinal neurons makes direct connections with neuron groups farther towards the front of the brain (Sarnat and Netsky, 1981). Fish and amphibians have direct spinal connections to the brainstem. Reptiles and birds have direct spinal connections to the brainstem and the dorsal thalamus in the midbrain. Mammals have connections to brainstem, thalamus, and primary cortex. Pathways that appear to contribute to the motivational-affective dimension of pain follow a similar evolutionary pattern. The exception to this is that more medial target sites are contacted in the brain: the medial thalamic nuclei in reptiles and the limbic cortex in mammals. Throughout phylogeny, all the target sites of spinal tracts in the brain increase in complexity, specialization, and number of neurons. This suggests that even pain messages to the thalamus in a reptile and mammal may not be comparable.

Brown House Snake, *Lamprophis fulginosus.* **Photo by Marius Burger.**

In amphibians and reptiles, the majority of ascending spinal pathways terminate in the medullary reticular formation. Other terminations are: spinocerebellar, spinomesencephalic, spinovestibular, and spinothalamic. There is a lack of functional studies of evoked responses in supraspinal sites after specific noxious stimulation of peripheral fibers. However, electrical stimulation of the sciatic produces evoked potentials in posterior thalamic nuclei and primordial hippocampal structures in frogs (Vesselkin et al., 1971).

Comparing amphibian and reptile brains with those of mammals, there are significant differences in both the discriminative and affective pathways. While sensory-discriminative information from the spinal cord does indirectly reach the dorsal thalamus in frogs by way of the brainstem-thalamus tract, amphibian thalamic nuclei are diffuse and are not entirely organized as seen in mammals. In amphibians, there are only scant fibers coursing from the thalamus to an unspecialized area of the forebrain olfactory lobe. However, thalamic projections to cortex in mammals is prominent. There is no strong thalamus-to-cortex connection in amphibians. This is because a cortex, which evolves from the olfactory area, does not appear in phylogeny until the class Reptilia. The primordial cortex in reptiles is considered primitive and lacking the complex laminar structure seen in mammals. Amphibians simply have a brain without cortical tissue.

The phylogenetic development of the medial pathway correlated with motivational-affective aspects of pain in mammals is similar to the discriminative pathway in amphibians. In amphibians, the most rostral projection of the discriminative pathway reaches to a diffuse olfactory area with little

Boomslang, *Dispholidus typus*. **Photo by Marius Burger.**

organization of neurons (Sarnat and Netsky, 1981). In mammals, the most rostral target of this pathway is the highly-organized limbic cortex. Again, the beginning of even a primitive laminar organization of the limbic area does not appear until reptiles. The amphibian brain does not contain a limbic cortex.

Cortical tissue, whether in limbic or cerebral regions, is a highly complex and laminated structure, which is a relatively recent development in the evolution of the nervous system. From human experience, we know that decreasing the activity of cortical neurons by anesthesia or surgical lesion results in a loss of the full appreciation of nociception. Patients report an awareness of pain "but it no longer bothers them" (White and Sweet, 1969). Recent studies using positron imaging techniques also show specific areas of the cortex activated by noxious stimuli in awake humans (Talbot et al., 1991). For these reasons, there is widespread agreement among various investigators and scientific organizations that an intact limbic and primary sensory cortex is essential for the full appreciation of pain.

DESCENDING MODULATION OF PAIN TRANSMISSION

In mammals, descending pathways from brain structures above the spinal cord act to inhibit pain transmission in the spinal cord. The most studied pathways have cell bodies in the brainstem of mammals. These pathways contain the neurotransmitters serotonin (5-hydroxytryptamine, 5-HT) or the catecholamine norepinephrine. Numerous studies have shown that application of 5-HT or norepinephrine directly to the spinal cord produce analgesia in mammals. There is little functional data in amphibians and reptiles, but descending pathways (and the neurotransmitters released from their spinal terminals) probably also play a role in pain inhibition.

The anatomy of descending pathways from brainstem reticular nuclei in lower vertebrates has been reviewed (Newman et al., 1983). In anuran amphibians and reptiles, reticular nuclei maintain strong ipsilateral and bilateral projections to the spinal cord via the ventral and lateral funiculi. As in mammals, there is much evidence that these pathways contain 5-hydroxytryptamine (5-HT) and catecholamines, either norepinephrine or epinephrine. Thus both 5-HT and norepinephrine are found within separate, discrete reticular nuclei, with perikarya containing 5-HT especially rich in the raphe region of the medulla in amphibians (Parent, 1973; Tan and Miletic, 1990b; Ueda et al., 1984).

Mensah (Mensah et al., 1974; Soller, 1977) administered intracranial injections of 5,6-dihydroxytryptamine (a neurotoxin which selectively destroys serotonergic fibers) into lesions of the raphe nuclei and used reduced silver staining techniques. After the injections, two divisions of descending 5-HT pathways are seen. Electrical stimulation of these descending pathways in *Rana pipiens* demonstrated that enhancement of 5-HT pathways increases motoneuronal activity; whereas catecholaminergic pathways suppress motoneuronal activity (Soller and Erulkar, 1979). These authors conclude that, descending systems increase motoneuronal activity and may also reduce peripheral input.

With regard to descending catecholaminergic pathways, there is immunohistochemical evidence of the existence of epinephrine-containing pathways in amphibians (Parent, 1973). However there is recent functional data showing that spinal administration of norepinephrine and epinephrine produce analgesia (Stevens et al., 1996). Such studies of spinally administered 5-HT in amphibians has not been performed. However, electrophysiological studies showed that dorsal horn neurons in *Rana pipiens* decrease firing when 5-HT or norepinephrine are applied to their vicinity by a micropipette (Tan and Miletic, 1990a; Caulford and Coceani, 1977).

ANALGESIA

The final section of this chapter presents findings from animal research studies that used amphibians and reptiles to assess the analgesic action of various pharmacological agents. Analgesia is a selective loss of pain transmission, without loss of other sensory sensations. Thus, an analgesic animal should appear normal, without sedation, and respond to nonnoxious stimuli and perform routine behaviors in an unaltered fashion. This is in contrast to anesthesia, which is loss of all sensations, and is discussed in other chapters in this volume.

Given that investigators cannot gain access into the sensorium of an animal, a behavioral assessment of analgesia must be made using a pain test. As the gold standard of analgesic agents remains morphine and other opioids, this class of agents is presented first.

ANALGESIC ACTION OF OPIOIDS

In order to demonstrate an analgesic action in an animal model, an appropriate test has to be developed to assess the behavioral response (i.e. the pain threshold, PT) to a painful stimulus. For amphibians, much work has been done using the acetic acid test (AAT) on the Northern grass frog, *Rana pipiens*. The AAT to assess the PT in frogs was recently elaborated (Stevens, 1992). Briefly, 10 solutions of acetic acid were serially-diluted from glacial acetic acid and given a code number from 0 to 10. The lowest code number was equal to the lowest concentration of acetic acid.

Testing was done by placing, with a Pasteur pipette, a single drop of acid on the dorsal surface of the frog's thigh. Testing began with the lowest concentration of acid and proceeded with increasing concentrations until the PT was reached. The PT was defined as the code number of the lowest concentration of acid which caused the frog to vigorously wipe the treated leg with either hindlimb,

Green Anole, *Anolis carolinensis*. Photo by Michael Gilroy.

Northern Leopard Frog, *Rana pipiens*. Photo by Aaron Norman.

known as the wiping response. To prevent tissue damage, the acetic acid was immediately washed off with a gentle stream of distilled water once the animal responded, or was washed off after 5 sec if the animal failed to respond. In the latter case, testing continued on the opposite hindlimb with the next higher concentration of acid. By obtaining the PT before injection of analgesic agents, and at various times after injection, the analgesic effects can be measured and quantified.

Using *Rana pipiens*, a number of opioid agents commonly used in the clinic were administered by the subcutaneous route and assayed on the AAT (see Table 2 for references). These results showed that the rank order of potency of clinical opioids like morphine, meperidine, methadone, and codeine, was similar in amphibians and rodents, and indeed the same as in humans. Full dose-response curves, as well as antagonism studies using the opioid antagonist, naltrexone, were obtained for each of these opioids. This suggests that opioid analgesia is common to all classes of vertebrates, although this remains to be demonstrated by suitable analgesic assays appropriate for each species. This commonality might not be unexpected, given the demonstration of endogenous opioid peptides and opioid receptors in brain and spinal cord tissue from each species examined throughout phylogeny.

With regard to behavioral effects of opioids in reptiles, a tail-flick apparatus was used for studies of immobility in the lizard, *Anolis carolinensis* (Mauk et al., 1981). Intraperitoneal injection of morphine (5 mg/kg) produced a significant increase in the latency of the lizard to remove its tail from a noxious heat stimulus. However, the authors did not complete dose-response analysis, nor assess the opioid nature of the analgesic effect by pretreatment with an opioid antagonist, such as naloxone or naltrexone. In the crocodile (*Crocodylus niloticus africana*), morphine or meperidine (pethidine) produced an elevation of the latency for the animal to lift its leg in a hot-plate test (Kanui and Hole, 1992).

TABLE 2.
Existing pharmacological studies of analgesia in amphibians and reptiles.

Analgesic	Route[a]	Species	Assay	References
Opioids				
Morphine	s.c.	*Rana pipiens*	Acetic acid test	Pezalla, 1983; Pezalla and Stevens, 1984; Stevens et al., 1994
Levorphanol, fentanyl, methadone, meperidine, codeine, buprenorphine, nalorphine, bremazocine	s.c.	*Rana pipiens*	Acetic acid test	Pezalla and Stevens, 1984; Stevens et al., 1994
Morphine, Ethylketocyclazocine	s.c.	*Bufo marinus*	Electrified floor	Carr et al., 1984
Oxymorphazone	s.c.	*Rana esculenta*	Acetic acid test	Benyhe et al., 1989
Morphine	i.p.	*Anolis carolinensis*	Tail-flick test	Mauk et al., 1981
Morphine	i.p.	*Crocodylus niloticus*	Hot plate test	Kanui and Hole, 1992
Morphine	i.s.	*Rana pipiens*	Acetic acid test	Stevens and Pezalla, 1983
Morphine, and comparison of *mu*, *delta*, and *kappa* opioids	i.s.	*Rana pipiens*	Acetic acid test	Stevens, 1996
Levorphanol	i.s.	*Rana pipiens*	Acetic acid test	Stevens and Pezalla, 1984
Adrenergics				
Noreprinephrine, epinephrine, dexmedetomidine, clonidine	s.c.	*Rana pipiens*	Acetic acid test	Brenner et al., 1994
Noreprinephrine, epinephrine, dexmedetomidine, clonidine	i.s.	*Rana pipiens*	Acetic acid test	Stevens and Brenner, 1996
Cholinergics				
Oxytremorine	s.c.	*Rana pipiens, Salamandra salaman.*	Electrified floor	Leslie et al., 1969

[a] s.c. = subcutaneons; i.p. = intraperitoneal; i.s. = intraspinal

ANALGESIC ACTION OF ADRENERGIC AGENTS

Nociceptive systems in the amphibian respond to adrenergic and sympathetic modulations in a manner comparable to similar modulatory mechanisms in mammals. Systemic administrations of adrenergic agonist drugs produce significant dose-related elevations of response thresholds in the AAT (Brenner et al., 1994). The rank order of potency for agents studied was as follows, with dexmedetromidine being the most potent.

1. dexmedetomidine
2. epinephrine
3. norepinephrine
4. clonidine

These analgesic effects are diminished by pretreatment with atipamezole and yohimbine (alpha$_2$ antagonists). To a lesser extent, the analgesic effects are also diminished by idazoxan, though not at all by prazosin (alpha1 antagonists).

Longtail Whip Lizard, *Tetradactylus tetradactylus.* **Photo by Marius Burger.**

These findings support the interpretation that adrenergic analgesia in the amphibian is a receptor-mediated phenomenon. Also, the results support the theory that the predominant mechanisms in the amphibian are mediated through alpha$_2$ receptor systems as in mammals.

A separate study demonstrates that dexmedetomidine raises chemical and thermal— but not mechanical—response thresholds in the amphibian (Willenbring and Stevens, 1995a). While morphine diminishes all three sensory modalities equivalently, dexmedetomidine had its greatest effect in elevating acetic acid test response thresholds. Dexmedetomidine had a lesser, but still significant, effect on thermal response latencies.

In contrast, the adrenergic agonist had no effect on responses to nonnoxious mechanical stimulation. Pretreatment with atipamezole erradicated the dexmedetomidine effects on thermal and mechanical resonses but also did not effect mechani-

Yellow-spotted Night Lizard, *Lepidophyma flavimaculatum.* **Photo by R. W. Van Devender.**

cal sensitivity. In keeping with these findings, stimulation of sympathetic efferents increases the reponse characteristics of mechanoreceptors activated with mild mechanical stimulation. Stimulation of sympathetic efferents decreases responses of mechanoreptors activated with deeper (ostensibly noxious) mechanical stimuli (Calof et al., 1981).

Thus in amphibians, as in mammals, pharmacological manipulation of adrenergic mechanisms appears to simulate an endogenous modulation of nociception. Modulation of nociception is stimulated by the sympathetic nervous system, which does not inhibit the perception of nonnoxious stimuli. To our knowledge, nonopioid analgesia has not been investigated in reptiles.

NEUROPATHIC PAIN IN AMPHIBIANS AND REPTILES

Neuropathic pain is a pathological condition in which there are pronounced increases in sensitivity to one or more modalities of somatic sensation. In humans, it occurs as chronic, debilitating pain associated with:

Crag Lizard, *Pseudocordylus microlepidotus.* **Photo by Marius Burger.**

Leopard Tortoise, *Geochelone pardalis*. Photo by Marius Burger,

—peripheral or central nerve injury
—diabetic or other ischemic neuropathies
—degenerative nerve disease
—cancer

The classic evidence of neuropathic pain is observably lowered response thresholds or decreased response latencies to mechanical, thermal, chemical and electrical stimulation concurrent with a refractory response to standard analgesics. These behavioral changes result from increased spontaneous activity, increased synaptic efficacy, and disinhibition of endogenous modulatory systems in the nociceptive pathway. Chronic somatic hypersensitivity (interpreted as evidence of neuropathic pain state) has been successfully modeled in mammals from rodents to primates.

Several lines of evidence suggest that, following certain neurological manipulations, similar conditions occur in amphibians and reptiles. In amphibians, decreases in response thresholds to mechanical, thermal, and chemical stimulation have been observed following freeze or constriction injuries of the sciatic nerve (Willenbring and Stevens,

Armadillo Spinytail Lizard, *Cordylus cataphractus.* **Photo by Marius Burger.**

1996). Electrical stimulation of mechanically sensitive receptive areas of the turtle shell produce prolonged (multisecond) increases in excitability of second-order target neurons in the spinal dorsal horn (Currie and Stein, 1990). For an in-vitro turtle spinal cord preparation, electrical stimulation of the associated intact presynaptic dorsal root fibers results in a similar increase in responsiveness of dorsal horn neurons (Russo and Hounsgaard, 1994). Certainly, much work remains to be done in investigating neuropathic phenomena in amphibians and reptiles. Nonetheless, the remarkable homology with mammalian nociceptive systems combined with an overall neurological simplicity in these species offers many potential advantages in their employment as models in this difficult area of research.

CLINICAL IMPLICATIONS AND CONCLUDING REMARKS

This chapter has reviewed the processing of pain information and mechanisms of analgesia in amphibians and reptiles from a basic research perspective. With regard to clinical treatment strategies for veterinarians, herpetologists and other animal-care personnel, this chapter provides a tentative guideline for therapeutic treatment of possible pain states in amphibians and reptiles. Whether or not the capacity for pain in these animals is even remotely similar to that experienced by humans and possibly other mammals, treatment of injury or surgical incision with suitable analgesic agents may provide for a better prognosis.

The information presented above suggests that a number of agents used in mammals and in the clinic might also be effective analgesics in amphibians and reptiles. However, these studies are performed in experimental situations. More studies need to be done with clinically-relevant states which have different types of noxious stimulation. Rigorous scientific experimentation is needed to assess anecdotal accounts using various analgesics for the clinical treatment of amphibians and reptiles. The simple finding that opioid analgesics used in humans and other mammals show the same relative potency in amphibians suggests that analgesic agents used in mammals may also be employed in amphibian and reptile care. Given the basic mechanisms of pain and analgesia that appear consistent throughout phylogeny, nonmammalian models may provide a simpler system for further investigations. This supports the use of nonmammalian models for pain research on ethical and economic grounds, especially for pilot studies testing numerous potential compounds (Stevens, 1995).

REFERENCES AND RECOMMENDED READING

—**Adrian ED; Cattell M; Hoagland H:**
Sensory discharges in single cutaneous nerve fibres. *J Physiol* 1931; 72: 377-391.

—**Benyhe S; Hoffmann G; Varga E et al.:**
Effects of oxymorphazone in frogs: long-lasting antinociception in vivo, and apparently irreversible binding in vitro. Life Sci 1989; 44: 1847-1857.

—**Brenner GM; Klopp AJ; Deason LL et al.:**
Analgesic potency of alpha adrenergic agents after systemic administration in amphibians. J Pharmacol Exp Ther 1994; 270: 540-545.

—**Calof AL; Jones RB; Roberts WJ:**
Sympathetic modulation of mechanoreceptor sensitivity in frog skin. J Physiol 1981; 310: 481-499.

—**Carr KD; Aleman DO; Holland MJ et al.:**
Analgesic effects of ethylketocyclazocine and morphine in rat and toad. Life Sci 1984; 35: 997-1003.

—**Caulford PG; Coceani F:**
Microiontophoresis of 5-hydroxytryptamine, epinephrine, and prostaglandin E1 on spinal neurons in the frog. Can J Physiol Pharmacol 1977; 55: 293-300.

—**Currie SN; Stein PS:**
Cutaneous stimulation evokes long-lasting excitation of spinal interneurons in the turtle. J Neurophysiol 1990; 64: 1134-1148.

—**Ebbesson, SOE:**
Morphology of the Spinal Cord. In, Frog Neurobiology: A Handbook, R Llinas, W Precht, (Eds).Springer-Verlag, Berlin, 1976, pp. 679-706.

—**Fox H; Whitear M:**
Observations of Merkel cells in amphibians. Biol Cell 1978; 32: 223-232.IASP subcommittee on Taxonomy: Classification of Chronic Pain: description of chronic pain syndromes and definitions of pain terms. Pain Suppl 1986; 3: 5217

—**Inagaki S; Senba E; Shiosaka S et al.:**
Regional distribution of substance P-like immunoreactivity in the frog brain and spinal cord: immunohistochemical analysis. J Comp Neurol 1981; 201: 243-254.

—**Kanui TI; Hole K; Miaron JO:**
Nociception in crocodiles: capsaicin instillation, formalin and hot plate tests. Zoological Science 1990; 7: 537-540.

—**Kanui TI; Hole K:**
Morphine and pethidine antinociception in the crocodile. J Vet Pharmacol Ther 1992; 15: 101-103.

—**Kenton B; Kruger L; Woo M:**
Two classes of slowly adapting mechanoreceptor fibres in reptile cutaneous nerve. J Physiol 1971; 212: 21-44.

—**Kitchell RL; Erickson HH:**
What is Pain? In, Animal Pain: Perception and Alleviation, RL Kitchell, HM Erickson, (Eds).Waverly Press, Baltimore,M.D. 1983, pp. vii-viii.

—**Kusuma A; Ten Donkelaar HJ:**
Dorsal root projections in various types of reptiles. Brain Behav Evol 1980; 17: 291-309.

—**Landmann L; Halata Z:**
Merkel cells and nerve endings in the labial epidermis of a lizard. Cell Tissue Res 1980; 210: 353-357.

—**Leslie GB; Ireson JD; Tattersall ML:**
Some central actions of a potent muscarinic agent in lower vertebrates. Comp Biochem Physiol 1969; 31: 571-574.

—**Lorez HP; Kemali M:**
Substance P, met-enkephalin and somatostatin-like immunoreactivity distribution in the frog spinal cord. Neurosci Lett 1981; 26: 119-124.

—**Luthman J; Fernandez A; Radmilovich M et al.:**
Immunohistochemical studies on the spinal dorsal horn of the turtle Chrysemys d'orbigny. Tissue Cell 1991; 23: 515-523.

—**Maruhashi J; Mizuguchi K; Tasaki I:**
Action currents in single afferent nerve fibres elicited by stimulation of the skin of the toad and the cat. J Physiol 1952; 117: 129-151.

—**Mauk MD; Olson RD; LaHoste GJ et al.:**
Tonic immobility produces hyperanalgesia and antagonizes morphine analgesia. Science 1981; 213: 353-354.

—**Mensah PL; Glanzman DL; Levy WB et al.:**
The effects of 5,6-dihydroxytryptamine in the amphibian spinal cord using silver staining techniques. Brain Res 1974; 78: 255-261.

—**Naik DR; Sar M; Stumpf WE:**
Immunohistochemical localization of enkephalin in the central nervous system and pituitary of the lizard, *Anolis carolinensis*. J Comp Neurol 1981; 198: 583-601.

—**Newman DB; Cruce WLR; Bruce LL:**
The sources of supraspinal afferents to the spinal cord in a variety of limbed reptiles. I. Reticulospinal systems. J Comp Neurol 1983; 215: 17-32.

—**Nikundiwe AM; De Boer-van Huizen R; Ten Donkelaar HJ:**
Dorsal root projections in the clawed toad *(Xenopus laevis)* as demonstrated by

anterograde labeling with horseradish peroxidase. Neuroscience 1982; 7: 2089-2103.

—**Pac L:**
Nerve endings in the lizard skin *(Lacerta viridis)*. Z Mikrosk Anat Forsch 1984; 98: 939-950.

—**Parent A:**
Distribution of monoamine-containing neurons in the brain stem of the frog, *Rana temporaria.* J Morph 1973; 139: 67-78.

—**Pezalla PD:**
Morphine-induced analgesia and explosive motor behavior in an amphibian. Brain Res 1983; 273: 297-305.

—**Pezalla PD; Dicig M:**
Stress-induced analgesia in frogs: evidence for the involvement of an opioid system. Brain Res 1984; 296: 356-360.

—**Pezalla PD; Stevens CW:**
Behavioral effects of morphine, levorphanol, dextrorphan and naloxone in the frog *Rana pipiens.* Pharmacol Biochem Behav 1984; 21: 213-217.

—**Pritz MB; Stritzel ME:**
Reptilian somatosensory midbrain: identification based on input from the spinal cord and dorsal column nucleus. Brain Behav Evol 1989; 33: 1-14.

—**Pritz MB; Strizel ME:**
Thalamic projections from a midbrain somatosensory area in a reptile, *Caiman crocodilus.* Brain Behav Evol 1990; 36: 1-13.

—**Roberts A; Hayes BP:**
The anatomy and function of free nerve endings in an amphibian skin sensory system. Proc R Soc Lond 1977; 196: 415-420.

—**Rothe-Skinner KS; Stevens CW:**
Distribution of opioid-expressing neurons in the frog: an in situ hybridization study. Analgesia 1995;

—**Ruigrok TJ; Crowe A; Ten Donkelaar HJ:**
Morphology of primary afferents to the spinal cord of the turtle *Pseudemys scripta elegans.* Anat Embryol Berl 1985; 171: 75-81.

—**Russo RE; Hounsgaard J:**
Short-term plasticity in turtle dorsal horn neurons mediated by L-type Ca2+ channels. Neuroscience 1994; 61: 191-197.

—**Sarnat HB; Netsky MG:**
Evolution of the Nervous System. Oxford University Press, New York, 1981, 3pp.

—**Simpson JI:**
Functional Synaptology of the Spinal Cord. In, Frog Neurobiology: A Handbook, R Llinas, W Precht, (Eds).Springer-Verlag, Berlin, 1976, pp. 728-749.

—**Soller RW:**
Monoaminergic inputs to frog motoneurons: an anatomical study using fluorescence histochemical and silver degeneration techniques. Brain Res 1977; 122: 445-458.

—**Soller RW; Erulkar SD:**
The bulbo-spinal indoleaminergic pathway in the frog. Brain Res 1979; 172: 277-293.

—**Spray DC:**
Cutaneous Receptors: pain and temperature receptors of anurans. In, Frog Neurobiology: a handbook, R Llinas, W Precht, (Eds).Springer-Verlag, Berlin, 1976, pp. 607-628.

—**Stevens CW:**
Opioid antinociception in amphibians. Brain Res Bull 1988; 21: 959-962.

—**Stevens CW:**
Alternatives to the use of mammals for pain research. Life Sci 1992; 50: 901-912.

—**Stevens CW:**
Alternatives in action: amphibian model for pain research. Lab Animal 1995;

—**Stevens Cal:**
Relative analgesic potency of mu, delta, and kappa aproids after spinal administration in zmphibinus. J. Pharm. Exp Ther 1996; 276:440-449.

—**Stevens CW; Sangha S; Ogg BG:**
Analgesia produced by immobilization stress and an enkephalinase-inhibitor in amphibians. Pharmacol Biochem Behav 1995; 51: 675-680.

—**Stevens CW; Brenner GM: A**
Spinal administration of adrenergic agents produces analgesis in amphibians. Eur. Journal Pharm, in press 1996.

—**Stevens CW; Pezalla PD:**
A spinal site mediates opiate analgesia in frogs. Life Sci 1983; 33: 2097-2103.

—**Stevens CW; Pezalla PD:**
Naloxone blocks the analgesic action of levorphanol but not of dextrorphan in the leopard frog. Brain Res 1984; 301: 171-174.

—**Szekely G:**
The morphology of motoneurons and dorsal root fibers in the frog's spinal cord. Brain Res 1976; 103: 275-290.

—**Szekely G; Matesz K; Baker RE et al.:**
The termination of cutaneous nerves in the dorsal horn of the spinal cord in normal and in skin-rotated frogs. Exp Brain Res 1982; 45: 19-28.

—**Talbot JD; Marrett S; Evans AC et al.:**
Multiple representations of pain in human cerebral cortex. Science 1991; 251: 1355-1358.

—**Tan H; Miletic V:**

Electrophysiological properties of frog spinal dorsal horn neurons and their responses to serotonin: an intracellular study in the isolated hemisected spinal cord. Brain Res 1990a; 528: 344-348.

—**Tan H; Miletic V:**
Bulbospinal serotoninergic pathways in the frog *Rana pipiens.* J Comp Neurol 1990b; 292: 291-302.

—**Ueda S; Nojyo Y; Sano Y:**
Immunohistochemical demonstration of the serotonin neuron system in the central nervous system of the bullfrog, *Rana catesbeiana.* Anat Embryl 1984; 169: 219-229.

—**Vesselkin NP; Agayan AL; Nomokonova LM:**
A study of thalamo-telencephalic afferent systems in frogs. Brain Behav Evol 1971; 4: 295-306.

—**White JC; Sweet WH;**
Pain and the Neurosurgeon. Thomas, Springfield, 1969,

—**Willenbring S; Stevens CW:**
Thermal, mechanical and chemical periph-eral sensation in amphibians: opioid and adrenergic effects. Life Sci 1995a;

—**Willenbring S; Stevens CW:**
Effects of morphine or nerve injury on mechanical, thermal and chemical response thresholds in frogs. Society for Neuroscience 1995b; 21: 1168

—**Willenbring S; Stevens CW:**
Somatic hypersensitivity following peripheral nerve injury in frogs: a novel model for studying neuropathic pain. American Pain Society 1995c;

—**Wolters JG; Ten Donkelaar HJ; Verhofstad AAJ:**
Distribution of some peptides (substance P,[Leu]enkephalin,[Met]enkephalin) in the brain stem and spinal cord of a lizard, *Varanus exanthematicus.* Neuroscience 1986; 18: 917-946.

—**Yamashita Y; Ogawa H:**
Slowly adapting cutaneous mechanoreceptor afferent units associated with merkel cells in frogs and effects of direct currents. Somatosens Mot Res 1991; 8: 87-95.

THE VISUAL SYSTEM AND NON-VISUAL PHOTORECEPTION

Michael S. Grace, Ph.D.
Dept. of Biology
University of Virginia
Charlottesville, Virginia 22903

Dr. Michael Grace investigates the functional anatomy and molecular mechanisms underlying sensory systems and biological timing. Dr. Grace earned a B.S. in Applied Biology from the Georgia Institute of Technology, and M.S. and Ph.D. degrees in Neuroscience from the Emory University School of Medicine. At Emory and the University of Kansas Medical Center he studied retinal cell biology in the clawed frog, Xenopus laevis, *and melatonin biochemistry in the retina, pineal, and brain of* Xenopus, *iguanid lizards, and other vertebrates. Dr. Grace is currently Research Assistant Professor at the University of Virginia, where he studies photoreception and circadian rhythmicity in the green iguana and hamster. He also leads an effort to define the molecular mechanisms of infrared "vision" in boid and crotalid snakes. Dr. Grace and his wife, Tanya, operate a facility for captive reproduction of boid and colubrid snakes for research and education.*

INTRODUCTION

Reptiles are a diverse group of vertebrate animals that have evolved to take advantage of numerous types of very different environments. The different niches each impose their own constraints on the visual system. An understanding of reptilian vision is interesting from the perspectives of both evolution and natural history of reptiles, and important for the successful maintenance of reptiles in captivity.

The goals of this chapter are to: (1) describe the reptilian retina and it variation among taxonomic groups, (2) show how retinal morphology and function determines a given reptile's visual niche, and (3) describe two corollary senses in reptiles: non-visual photoreception and infrared detection.

ANATOMY OF REPTILIAN VISION

THE EYE

The eye is composed of an anterior segment including an optical apparatus that restricts and focuses incoming light, and a posterior segment that includes the retina, which is the first neural stage of visual image formation. The most anterior portion of the eye is the cornea, a transparent dome covering the iris and pupil, and the first stage of light refraction in the eye. In diurnal reptiles, the cornea is usually highly convex and is maintained in this shape partly by scleral ossicles, small overlapping bony plates that form a ring at the scleral-corneal border. Scleral ossicles are found

Figure 1: Microscopic section of the eye of the green Iguana (*Iguana iguana*), stained with Giemsa stain. The front of the eye is toward the bottom of this photomicrograph. Visible structures (beginning at the bottom of the micrograph) include the retina (R), retinal pigmented epithelium(RPE), choroid (C), sclera (S), and ocular muscle (M).

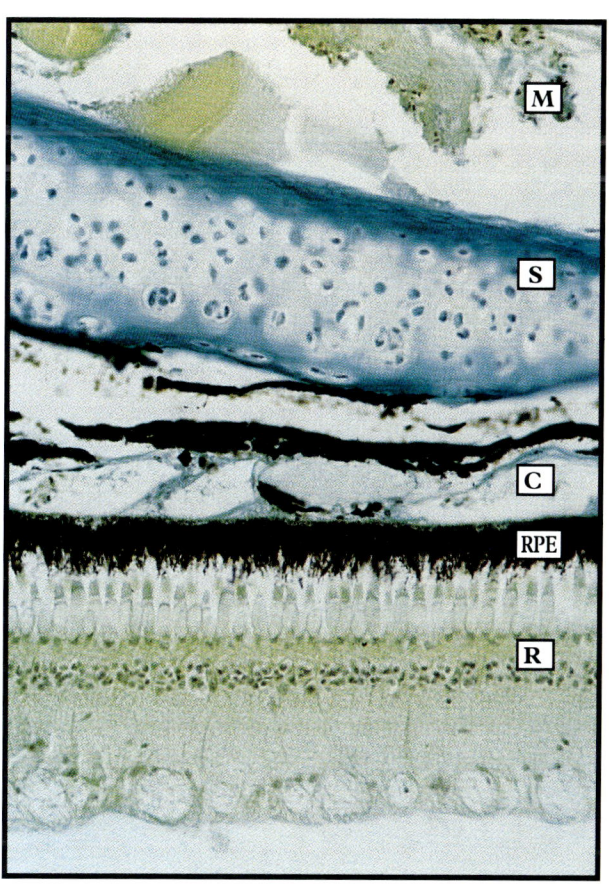

in all living groups of reptiles except snakes and crocodilians, which underwent subterranean and nocturnal "bottlenecks", respectively (that is, all living snakes and crocodilians apparently are derived from ancestors which were either fossorial or nocturnal; see below for more details on the ocular effects of these histories).

The anterior segment of the eye also includes the iris and its pupil. Muscles of the iris respond autonomically to the intensity of incident light by contracting or relaxing, thereby changing the diameter of the pupil. In addition to controlling the amount of light entering the eye, pupil diameter helps determine the depth of field (range of focus) of the eye. Pupil shapes exhibit remarkable diversity among reptiles, ranging from slit-like pupils to circular ones. Generally, slit-shaped pupils are associated with nocturnality (see below).

Visual accommodation refers to the mechanism whereby an animal focuses an image upon its retina. In many reptiles, as in mammals and birds, this is accomplished primarily by changing the

Figure 2: Light micrograph of the retina of the green Iguana (*Iguana iguana*), stained with Mallory's trichrome. Light would enter the eye from the direction of the bottom of the micrograph. RPE, retinal pigmented epithelium; OS, photoreceptor outer segments; IS, photoreceptor inner segments; PR, photoreceptor nuclei; INL, inner nuclear layer; IPL, inner plexiform layer; GC, ganglion cell layer.

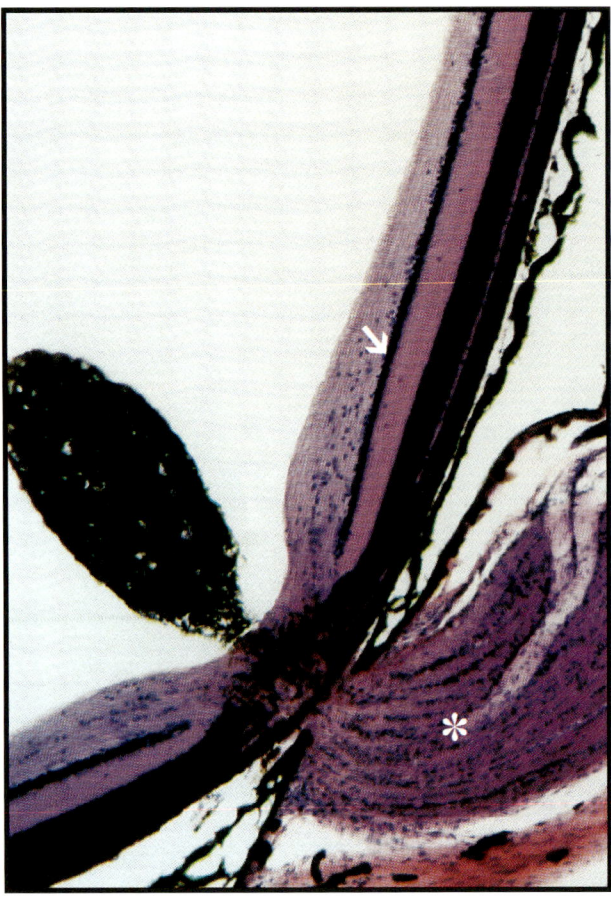

Figure 3: Low-power light micrograph of the rear of the eye of Carolina anole (*Anolis carolinensis*), stained with hematoxylin and eosin. The layers of the retina (arrow) are clearly visible. The large stained structure (asterisk) in the lower left of the micrograph is the optic nerve exiting the rear of the eye.

shape and thereby the refractive angles of the lens. All reptile eyes contain a lenses, suspended by ciliary muscles just below the iris and pupil within the posterior chamber of the eye. Even so, snakes have completely lost key anatomical requirements of visual accommodation. The cornea also plays an important role in accommodation, but aquatic reptiles are presented with a special problem in that refraction at the interface of the cornea and environment is greatly reduced in water. To cope with these problems, both snakes and aquatic reptiles have developed other, albeit less effective, methods of accommodation (discussed further below).

THE RETINA

The retina of the eye is an extension of the brain (literally and embryologically), and has much of the same complexity as is found in the central nervous system. The same classes and arrangement of cells found in the retinas of other vertebrate are found in reptilian retinas. The retina is divided into neural and non-neural components. The non-neural retina consists of a single layer of epithelial cells, the retinal

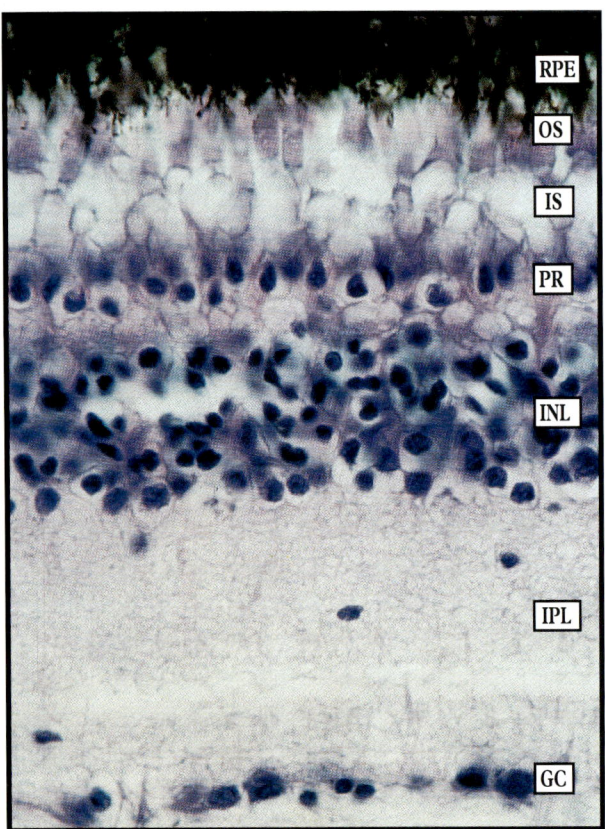

pigmented epithelium (RPE), so-called because of its high content of melanin pigment granules, lining the rear of the ocular cavity and underlying the neural retina. The RPE provides both structural and nutritive support to the neural retina. Cells of the neural retina fall under six general types: (1) photoreceptors, (2) bipolar cells, (3) horizontal cells, (4) amacrine cells, (5) interplexiform cells, and (6) ganglion cells. Each cell type is defined by structure and function, and has a unique location within the highly ordered laminar arrangement of the retina. In addition, each of these cell types can be further subdivided based upon their structure, and/or function. Because the retina is arranged with the photoreceptors farthest from the anterior of the eye, light must travel through all of the retinal layers before striking the photoreceptors. Photic information then travels in the reverse direction through the retina, an is ultimately relayed to the brain through the ganglion cell axons which together form the optic nerves.

PHOTORECEPTION AND PHOTORECEPTORS

PHOTORECEPTOR MECHANISMS

The initial step in retinal image formation occurs within the photoreceptors. The cells determine, at least at the first approximation, spatial acuity, and allow discrimination of color. Photoreceptors are highly specialized cells which convert photons of light into electrochemical neural signals. These cells are distinctly polarized with a synapse at one end of the cell, and the photoreceptive outer segment at the other. The membrane of the outer segment forms an array of flattened disks that are oriented perpendicular to the plane of incoming light. Within this disk membrane is the visual pigment opsin and its constituent chromophore 11-*cis*-retinaldehyde, together called rhodopsin (in rod photoreceptors). A photon of light changes the conformation of a chemical bond within the 11-*cis*-retinaldehyde, resulting in the formation of all-*trans*-retinaldehyde. This photoconversion causes a change in the conformation of the opsin protein, which in turn changes the interaction of opsin with other proteins within the outer segment. A photon of light striking rhodopsin thus activates a series of sequential protein-protein interactions, ultimately leading to reduction of the concentration of the chemical cyclic guanosine monophosphate (cGMP) in the photoreceptor. It is this change in cyclic GMP levels that causes a change in the activation state of the photoreceptor.

While the general features of this chemical signaling system is essentially the same among all photoreceptors, different classes of photoreceptors are defined by the levels of light to which they respond, and by the wavelengths of light to which they respond. Two general classes of photoreceptors can be distinguished on the basis of structure and their differing sensitivities to the amount of light entering the eye. Rods are very sensitive cells, functioning at relatively low light levels (scotopic vision). They have cylindrical outer segments containing membranous disks free of the plasma membrane. Cones, on the other hand, are much less sensitive to light, and therefore are functional only at relatively high (daytime) light levels (photopic vision). The classical arrangement of cone outer segments consists of a stack of membranous disks, all of which are confluent with, and therefore form, the plasma membrane.

PHOTORECEPTOR TYPE AND NOCTURNALITY

The relative abundance of rods and cones has a profound impact on the light environment in which a given reptile can function effectively. Conversely, the light environment in which a reptile has evolved constrains the relative abundance of rods and cones. In general, nocturnal reptiles have a high percentage of rods relative to cones, while diurnal reptiles have a higher relative abundance of cones. However, this observation is based upon photoreceptor morphology which has a high degree of variability among reptiles.

Most lizards studied have photoreceptors with cone-like morphologies, and the photoreceptors of some nocturnal lizards have features characteristic of both rods and cones (see below). All diurnal lizards, and some nocturnal forms, like *Heloderma*, contain classical cones (see (Underwood, 1970)). On the other hand, some nocturnal lizards including many geckos have photoreceptors with distinctly rod-like outer segments. Electron microscopic analysis reveals, however, that the outer segments are not completely rod-like: they contain multiple regions of continuity between the disk membranes and the plasma membrane (Pedler and Tiley, 1964; Yoshida, 1978). Similarly, retinal photoreceptors in the tuatara have cone-like features (see below), but the outer segments of many of its photoreceptors have rod-like morphology (Underwood, 1970).

All turtles studied with the exception of *Emys orbicularis*, have both rod-like and cone-like photoreceptors in their retinas. The rod-like cells are characterized on the gross morphology of their outer segments, but have cone-like features as well. The rod-like cells are especially abundant (about 40% of photoreceptors) in the benthic snapping turtle, *Chelydra serpentina* (Underwood, 1970). The

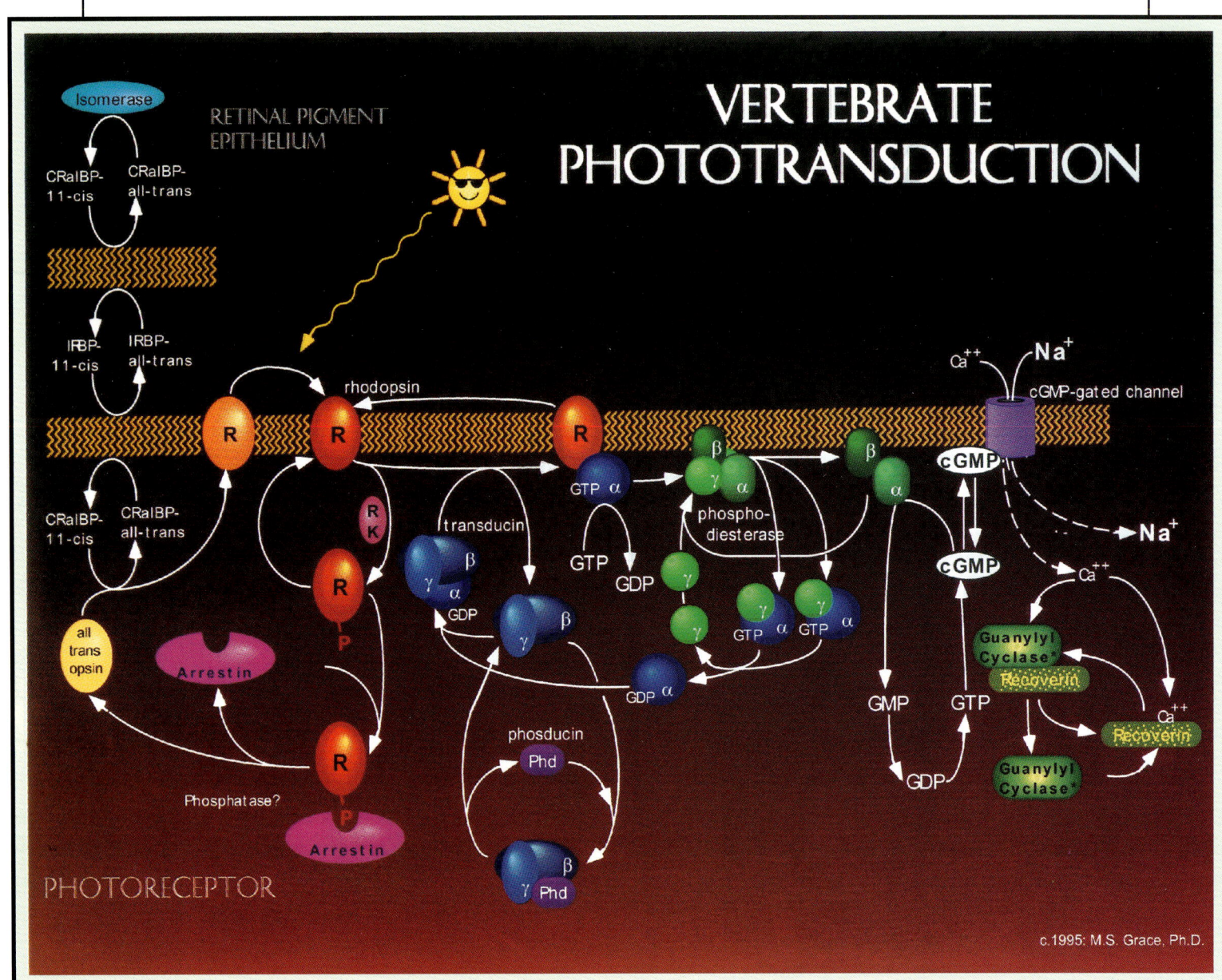

Figure 4: Mechanism of phototransduction in vertebrate retinal photoreceptors. Light activates the photopigment rhodopsin, which initiates a cascade of molecular events that ultimately leads to closure of a cyclic GMP-gated channel in the photoreceptor outer segment membrane. Closure of the channel leads to hyperpolarization of the cell and decreased transmitter release. The retinal pigmented epithelium re-isomerizes the photo-isomerized chromophore, retinaldehyde, thus returning it to its photoactive form.

retinas of crocodilians are also duplex, with rod-like cells predominating over cones (Underwood, 1970). Interestingly, cones are more highly concentrated in the ventral half of the retina, the area that would be illuminated by the sky, and therefore presumably more important for daytime vision. Different groups of snakes exhibit very different complements of photoreceptors, consistent with the idea that snake ancestors were nocturnal and/or fossorial (see below). Many snakes have duplex retinas (i.e., they contain both rods and cones), but some appear to be either all-cone or all-rod. The fossorial *Typhlops* and *Leptotyphlops* have only a single type of rod-like photoreceptor (Underwood, 1970). In many diurnal snakes, including the colubrids *Nerodia* and *Thamnophis*, and some elapids, rods appear to be completely lost, such that these snakes have an all-cone retina.

VISUAL PIGMENTS AND OIL DROPLETS: COLOR VISION

Color vision requires at least two types of photoreceptor, each of which responds maximally to different regions of the electromagnetic spectrum. Cones (and perhaps in some cases rods) can be subdivided into different classes on the basis of wavelength sensitivity (the different wavelength sensitivities are a product of subtle differences in the structure of the opsin proteins; thus each cone class has a unique opsin sequence). Each type of cone responds maximally to a certain wavelength, and responsiveness declines at wavelengths above and below this maximum.

Turtle photopigments have been relatively well-studied. Microspectrophotometry (a method for measuring the spectral absorbance of photopigments in single cells either *in situ* or isolated; for reviews, see (Liebman, 1972; Bowmaker, 1984)) was used to identify three different visual pigments in cones of the turtle *Pseudemys* (Liebman and Granda, 1971). The lizard *Anolis* also has three different photopigments with response maxima in the visible spectrum. Recently, a fourth *Anolis* photopigment, sensitive to ultraviolet light, has been identified (Fleishman et al., 1993). The UV photoreceptor is thought to play an important role in communication using the UV-reflective dewlap (Fleishman et al., 1993).

Oil droplets within photoreceptors may also contribute to color vision. Because they are situated between the incoming light and the photoreceptor outer segment, oil droplets serve as wavelength cutoff filters. Thus, the presence of multiple different oil droplets in a single class of photoreceptor (having a single type of opsin) could confer wavelength sensitivity since the spectral quality of light available to each different photoreceptor will be different. Both turtle and lizard retinas contain multiple types of oil droplets within the photoreceptors. The UV-sensitive cone of

Figure 5: Head of an amelanistic California kingsnake (*Lampropeltis getula califomiae*). Note that melanin is absent from both the skin and the eye. Oculocutaneous amelanism is the most common form of albinism.

Figure 6: Lateral view of the head of an amelanistic Burmese python (*Python molurus bivittatus*).

Anolis contains only clear oil droplets which transmit UV light down to 320nm (Fleishman et al., 1993). The morphologically rod-like, but physiologically cone-like gecko photoreceptors contain oil droplets. Many tuatara photoreceptors (including rod-shaped ones) also contain oil droplets. Turtles retinas contain an abundance of oil droplets, the spectral properties of which appear to be matched to habitat. The freshwater turtle *Pseudemys* has many red and orange oil droplets, which would serve well since freshwater transmits predominantly longer wavelengths, while the marine green turtle has few or no red/orange oil droplets, and lives in an environment rich in shorter wavelength light (which would be highly filtered by red or orange oil droplets) (Liebman and Granda, 1971). Neither snake nor crocodilian photoreceptors contain oil droplets.

PHOTORECEPTORS, RETINAL PIGMENTED EPITHELIUM, AND ALBINISM

Closely associated with the outer segments of photoreceptors is the retinal pigmented epithelium (RPE), so named because of the high concentration of melanin pigment granules within its cells. Photoreceptor outer segments interdigitate with apical microvilli of the RPE. The RPE serves several functions associated with the retina. The vasculature on the photoreceptor side of the retina lies within the choroid. Nutrients arriving from and metabolic waste products carried away by this blood supply must cross the cytoplasm of the RPE, since adjacent RPE cells are connected by tight junctions. Thus, the RPE regulates communication between the choroid and neural retina. Photoreceptors constantly renew their outer segment membrane, and the RPE phagocytoses and degrades shed outer segment membrane. Finally, the melanin pigment granules within the RPE absorb light and therefore serve to protect the retina from light-induced damage, and also increase visual acuity by reducing the amount of light scatter.

Albinism refers to any change in pigmentation, but is most often used when referring to amelanism (loss of melanin production) in both the skin and eye (oculocutaneous albinism). Ocular albinism (amelanism) may also occur, causing a loss of melanin in the eye without affecting the skin. Either condition may affect vision. Loss of melanin from the retinal pigmented epithelium may reduce spatial resolution of the retina (see above). Melanin probably protects against damage caused by high light intensity; thus ocular amelanism may predispose the retina to light-induced damage. Amelanistic rats raised in constant light at normal room intensities causes severe retinal degeneration within only a few days. Oculocutaneous albinism is common occurrence among reptiles, and has been propagated frequently in recent years by selective breeding. In reptiles, like mammals, it is likely that albinism affecting the eye results in both increased rates of retinal degeneration and loss of visual acuity, although this has yet to be documented.

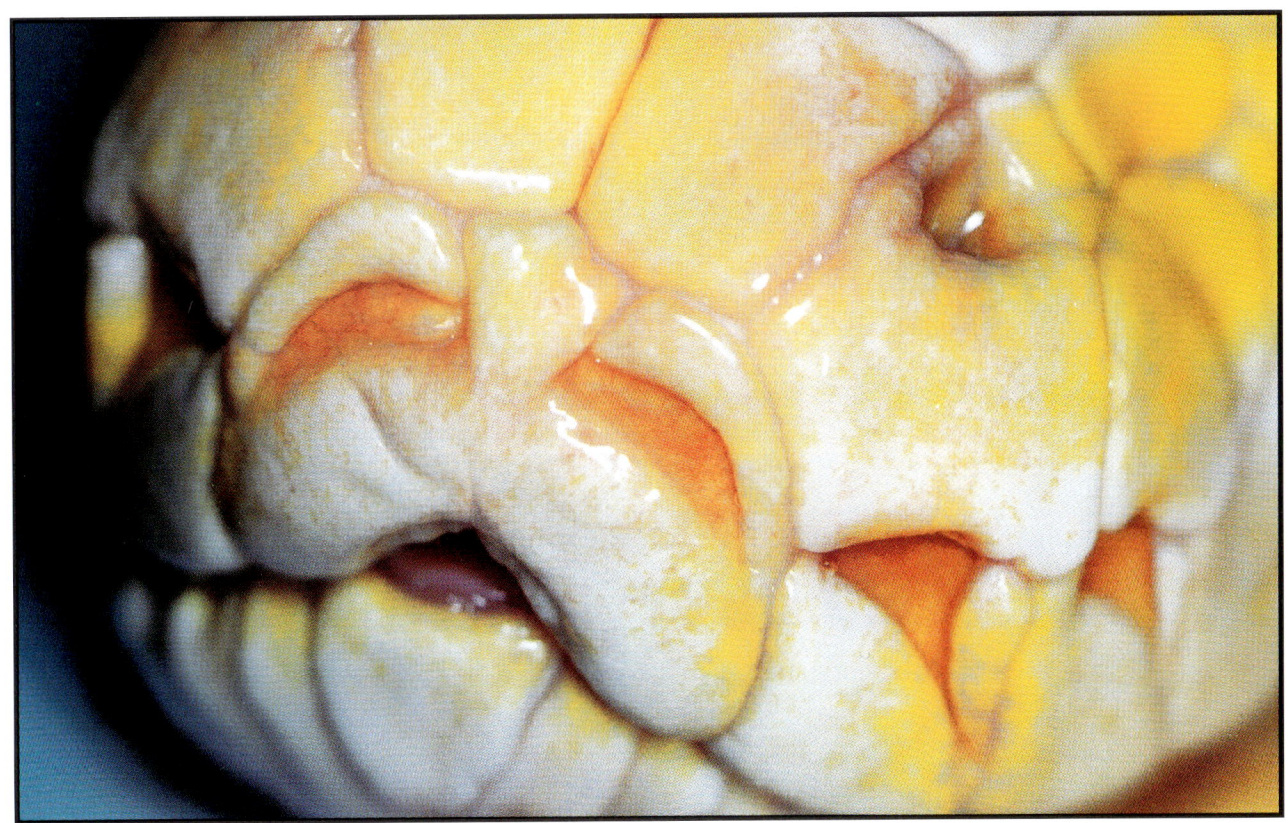

Figure 7: Infrared-sensitive pits in the labial scales of an amelanistic Burmese python (*Python molurus bivittatus*).

VISUAL ACCOMMODATION

Accommodation refers to the mechanical process resulting in greater visual acuity and a focused representation of visible objects on the retina. This is accomplished in lizards, *Sphenodon*, terrestrial turtles, and crocodilians (although accommodation in crocodilians is probably limited), as in mammals and other vertebrates, by deformation of the lens. Muscles of the ciliary body (which underlies the iris) contract, causing the lens to change shape, thereby altering its focal length.

Interestingly, in snakes the mechanics of this system have been lost, but are replaced by several completely different (albeit less effective) mechanisms. Snake lenses are nearly spherical and comparatively hard, making deformation much more difficult. The ciliary body of snakes is highly reduced, or even absent in some burrowing forms (for example *Typhlops*), and even where it exists, the ciliary muscles responsible for lens deformation are absent. Snakes exercise a form of accommodation by contracting muscles of the iris, which causes increased intraocular pressure. The increased pressure forces the lens farther from the retina, thereby changing the plane of focus. Aquatic animals have an even greater problem with accommodation, since the refractive function of the cornea is lost underwater (the refractive index of the cornea approximates that of water). The semi-aquatic *Thamnophis melanogaster* uses some unknown mechanism to gain an extended range of accommodation, while *Thamnophis couchii* increases depth of focus underwater by greatly constricting its pupil (Schaeffel and de Queiroz, 1990). Sea snakes apparently have completely lost the ability to focus in air (Walls, 1942).

Aquatic turtles use a similar mechanism to increase accommodation underwater. Marine turtles are so completely adapted to life underwater that the cornea has become greatly flattened, and therefore has little function in air. None of these adaptations can give the range of focus or the acuity produced by ciliary muscle-induced deformation of the lens, and as such, snakes and aquatic turtles must have significantly lower visual acuity than other reptiles.

NOCTURNAL ADAPTATIONS OF THE EYE

Nocturnal reptiles generally exhibit reduction in overall size of the eye, and increases in (1) pupillary aperture, (2) lens aperture, and (3) corneal area relative to size of the eye. All of these serve to increase the ability of the eye to gather light under scotopic conditions, but result in reduced visual acuity (and therefore also reduced importance of accommodation). The slit-shaped pupils of nocturnal reptiles allow for much greater aperture under low levels of illumination, thereby increasing visual sensitivity. The nocturnal geckos have slit-like pupils, some of which, as in *Tarentola*, close to multiple pinhole apertures. Other geckos have reverted to diurnality, and have re-acquired circular pupils. Two Madagascan species, *Phelsuma guentheri* and *P. newtonii*, have pupils in a simple vertical arrangement, while all others in this genus have circular pupils (see Underwood, 1970).

Since the corneal area is increased relative to the overall size of the eye in nocturnal reptiles, the scleral sulcus is reduced in angle (i.e. the circumference of the cornea begins to approach that of the sclera). For this reason, the importance of scleral ossicles in maintaining the acute angle of the scleral sulcus in diurnal forms is reduced in nocturnal forms. Scleral ossicles are absent in extant crocodilians, but have been found in fossil crocodilians. Scleral ossicles are completely absent in snakes as well.

The nocturnal *Heloderma* retains scleral ossicles, but the eye has been greatly reduced in size relative to diurnal lizards. In addition, the ciliary muscle and fovea are absent, so visual accommodation and acuity are probably very much reduced. The reduced size of the eye of the mata mata, *Chelus fimbriatus*, may also indicate visual adaptation to the very dim light of its riverbottom niche.

ADAPTATIONS OF THE VISUAL SYSTEM IN FOSSORIAL REPTILES

A fossorial existence poses some of the same problems as a nocturnal existence, along with other problems not encountered by nocturnal animals. It is generally thought that snakes have had a complicated evolutionary history. Most authors agree that snakes, lizards, and amphisbaenids arose from a common diurnal ancestor (although some argue origins from lacertilians and others from burrowing lizards), but that snakes first became nocturnal, and then fossorial. They then re-emerged from their subterranean existence as primarily surface-dwelling forms. As a consequence, the visual system of snakes has undergone tremendous change, resulting in an eye unlike that in any other reptilian group. The lenses of snakes are relatively large and essentially spherical, and the ciliary muscles responsible for accommodation are absent (but see above for alternate mechanisms of accommodation in snakes). The overall reduction in the size of the eye, and the relatively large cornea produce an eye with essentially no change in curvature between the sclera and cornea. As a result, scleral ossicles would be functionless, and have disappeared.

Figure 8: Lateral eye of the green iguana (*Iguana iguana*). The small opening of the lateral eye is deceptive: the lateral eyes are so large in this diurnal species that they nearly touch in the center of the head.

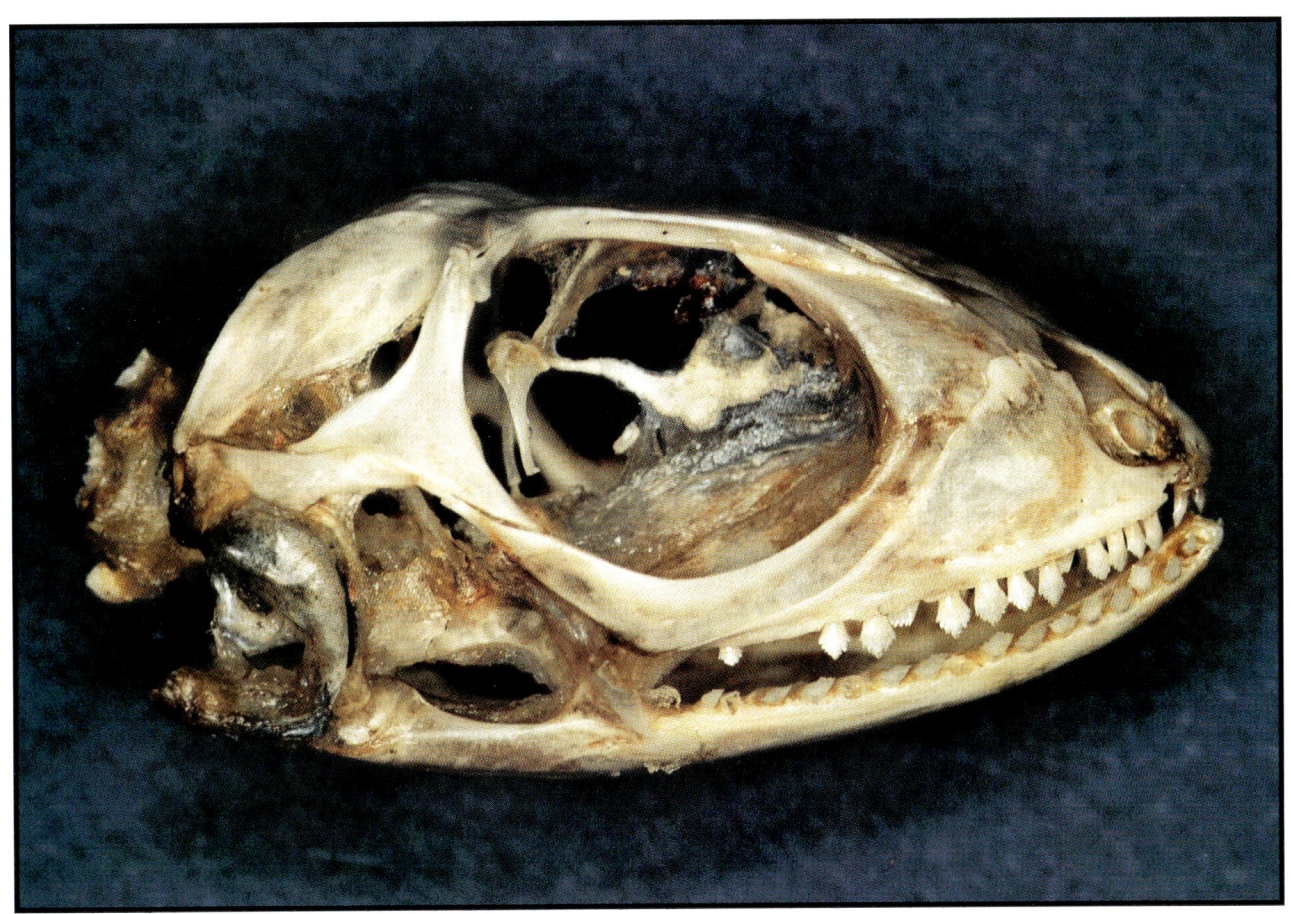

Figure 9: Skull of the green iguana (*Iguana iguana*) showing the extremely large ocular orbits. The bone in the center of the skull between the two orbits is less than 0.5mm thick.

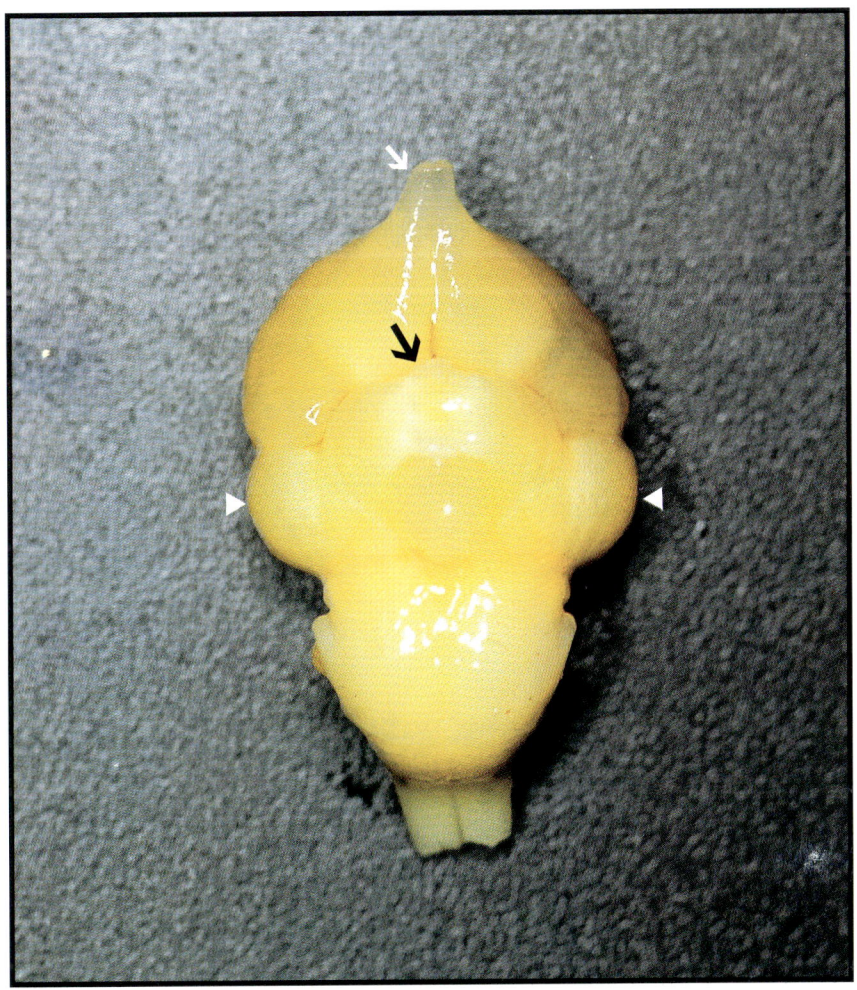

Figure 10: Ventral view of a paraformaldehyde/picric acid-fixed brain from the green iguana (*Iguana iguana*). The large white area in the center of the ventral surface (large arrow) is the optic chiasm. Compare the size of the optic chiasm to that of the olfactory nerves (small arrow). Also visible are the very large optic lobes (arrowheads) of this strictly diurnal lizard.

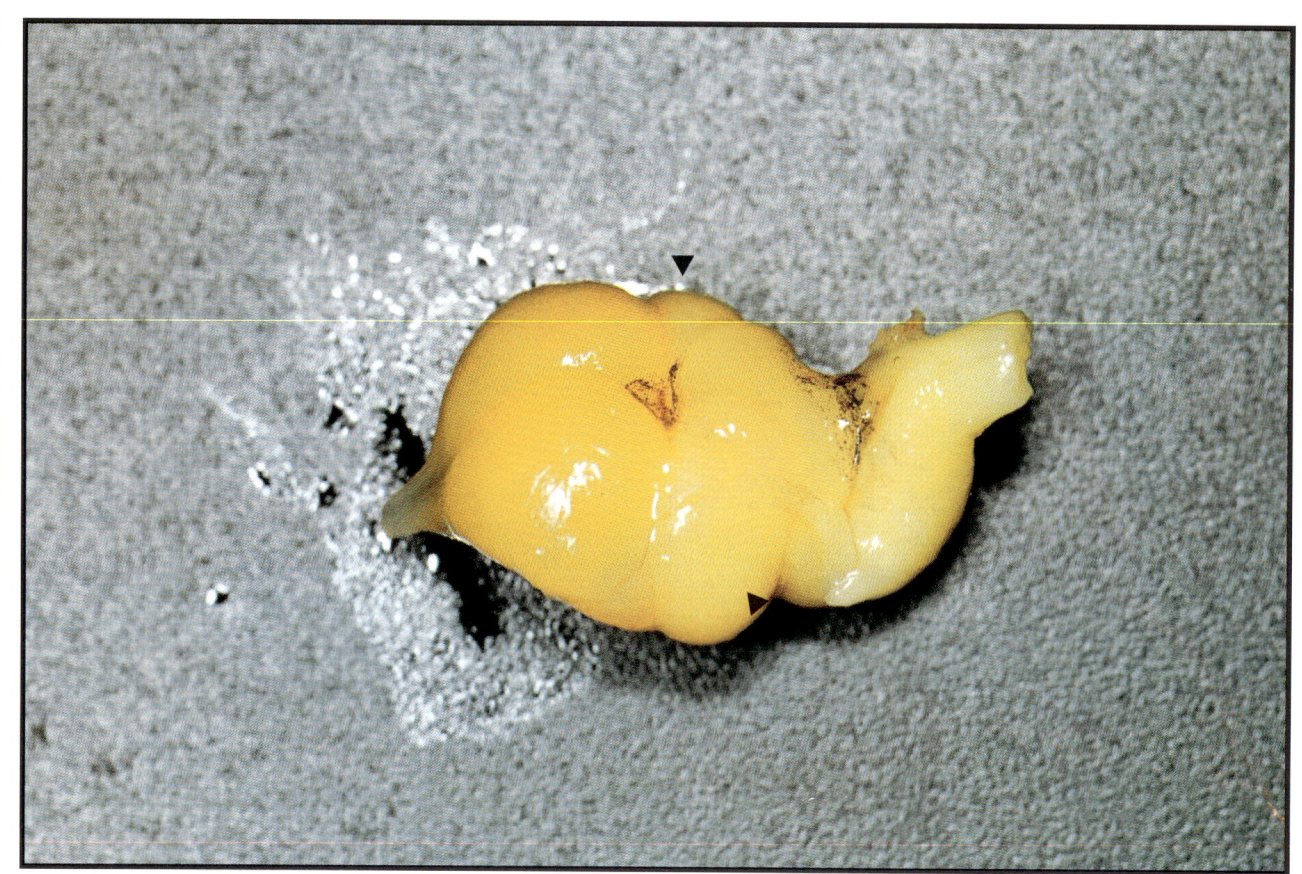

Figure 11: Dorsal view of a paraformaldehyde/picric acid-fixed green iguana (*Iguana iguana*) brain. Note that the optic lobes (arrowheads) of this animal occupy a significant volume of the brain.

Figure 12: Lateral eye of the South American red-footed tortoise, *Geochelone carbonaria*.

334

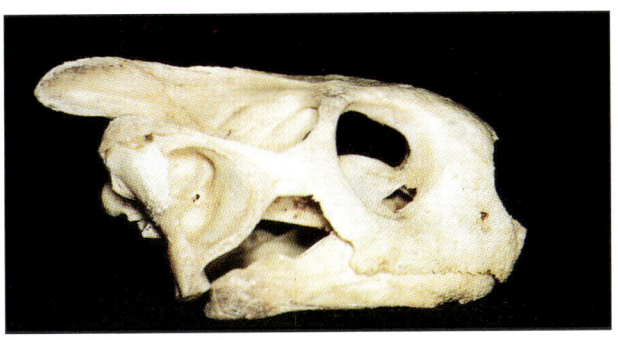

Figure 13: Lateral view of the skull of an adult African leopard tortoise, *Geochelone pardalis*. Note the size of the orbits (compare with photo of the Iguana skull.

The low or nonexistent levels of light underground must tremendously reduce the importance of the eye for visual function, and the eye is continually subjected to mechanical stress. Perhaps the most important physical change outside the eyeball is the development of a clear spectacle replacing the eyelids. This adaptation prevents the accumulation of debris within the eye. Both mechanical stress and reduced importance of vision probably led to the drastic reduction in the overall size of the eye in fossorial species. In addition, reduced importance of the eyes has probably led to a reduction in spatial resolution, and a reduction in the importance of accommodation.

EXTRA-RETINAL PHOTORECEPTION

Photoreception can be divided into two categories: radiance detection and irradiance detection. Radiance detection refers to the spatial mapping of light information from the environment onto the brain. Irradiance detection, on the other hand, refers to the detection of overall light levels. The retina of the lateral eyes is the first anatomical step in the formation of visual images, but probably also contains irradiance detectors as well (this is known

Figure 14: Orbit of the lateral eye of the musk turtle, *Stenotherus odoratus*. Note that the orbit in this benthic turtle is significantly smaller than in diurnal lizards such as *Iguana*.

for mammals and some birds and is probably also true for reptiles and other vertebrates). Irradiance detection in all non-mammalian vertebrate classes also occurs via extra-ocular photoreceptors, and some taxa have multiple anatomically-distinct populations of extra-ocular irradiance detectors. Iguanid lizards, for example, have irradiance-detecting photoreceptors located within the pineal organ, parietal eye, and basal brain, and probably in the eye as they do in mammals.

The parietal eye, also known as the "third eye", is an archaic structure, that was once much more widely distributed among reptiles than it is today (see (Quay, 1979) for a more detailed discussion of the pineal-parietal complex of reptiles). The parietal eye is located at the junction of the frontal and parietal bones of the skull, and can be seen as a small clear window in the central head scale of smaller lizards such as some iguanids, and as a relatively large window in larger lizards such as the monitors (genus

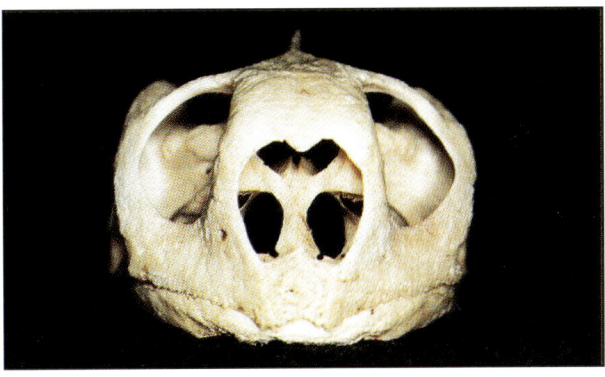

Figure 15: Frontal view of the skull of an adult African leopard tortoise, *Geochelone pardalis*. Note the large size of the nasal opening.

Varanus) and in the tuatara. The structure of the parietal eye is in many ways similar to the lateral eye, but it also has several distinctive features. Most importantly, the arrangement of the cellular layers with respect to incoming light is the reverse of that in the lateral eyes. Here, the photoreceptors are closest to the incoming light, and signals from them are processed through successively deeper layers of the retina before leaving via the axons of ganglion cells which are located farthest from the incoming light (in the lateral eye, this arrangement is reversed).

While the exact function of the parietal eye is unclear, other extra-retinal photoreceptors are known to be involved in the control of circadian (daily) rhythms. Circadian rhythms are endogenously-generated rhythms that persist in the absence of external time cues. Circadian clocks have periods of nearly, but not exactly, 24-hours. In order to be useful, they must be re-set each day so that they are entrained or synchronized to environmental (astronomical) time. The pineal organ or pineal gland contains both irradiance-detecting circadian photoreceptors and a circadian clock. Menaker and Wisner (Menaker and Wisner, 1983) showed that the isolated pineal of the lizard *Anolis carolinensis* produces the hormone melatonin rhythmically and that this rhythm is entrained (synchronized to a daily light-dark cycle. Experiments on cultured dissociated pineal cells (non-reptilian species) have shown that individual pinealocytes are both photoreceptive and clock-containing. Photoreceptors within the pineal are arranged radially around a central lumen, and sometimes project a rudimentary outer segment into the lumen. The role of the pineal gland in circadian timing was discussed in the previous chapter.

Photoreceptors are also located deep within the brains of non-mammalian vertebrates. Their existence has been postulated for nearly a century, since von Frisch (von Frische, 1911) discovered that light-induced color changes in the European minnow (*Phoxinus phoxinus*) persisted in the absence of both the lateral eyes and pineal. He found that lesions in the diencephalic region of the brain abolished this response. One of the most elegant demonstrations of extra-retinal, -pineal, and -parietal photoreception in a reptile was performed using the lizard *Sceloporus olivaceous*. Underwood and Menaker (Underwood and Menaker, 1970) showed that lizard locomotor activity remained entrained to a light-dark cycle (lizards were active in the day) even after removal of the lateral eyes, pineal, and parietal eye.

Recently, candidate "deep brain photoreceptors" of iguanid lizards have been found (Foster et al., 1993; Foster et al., 1994) and characterized (Foster et al., 1993; Grace et al., 1993; Foster et al., 1994; Grace et al., 1996). Opsin-like immunoreactivity was found in a small subset of neurons located adjacent to the lateral ventricles of the lizards *Anolis carolinensis* and *Iguana iguana*. These cells send a ciliated process (rudimentary outer segment?) into the lumen of the ventricle (hence the term "cerebrospinal fluid-contacting neurons"). It is possible that the ventricle acts as a light guide from the upper part of the brain to the "outer segments" of these cells. Birds have two sets of putative deep brain photoreceptors, but there is only one class of these cells in iguanid lizards studied thus far (Grace et al., 1996).

INFRARED DETECTION

Certain snakes "see" not only "visible" light, but also form spatial images of the world using infrared energy. The infrared portion of the electromagnetic spectrum lies in wavelengths longer than about 700nm (the visible spectrum lies between 400 and 700nm), and infrared radiation is emitted by warm objects including endothermic prey of infrared detecting snakes. Boids (boas and pythons) and pit vi-

Figure 16: Lateral eye of the Dumeril's ground boa (*Acrantophis dumerili*). Note the small size of the eye relative to that in *Iguana*, for example.

pers (rattlesnakes, for example) can accurately detect and strike prey even at night when no visible cues are available. In order to locate warm objects (including prey and perhaps basking sites) in their environments, these snakes utilize a system of receptor neurons that are sensitive in the infrared region of the electromagnetic spectrum.

Both the infrared and visual systems (along with chemical and tactile cues) are involved in prey detection by boids and pit vipers, but prey detection and localization do not require the eyes. A congenitally blind rattlesnake was shown to accurately strike prey with an efficiency and precision comparable to sighted animals of the same species (Kardong and Makessey, 1991). When this snake's pits were covered, the snake struck prey with much less frequency and accuracy, indicating that the infrared detectors play an important role in prey detection and localization.

In pit vipers, a single infrared-sensitive pit is located below and between the eye and nostril on each side of the face. Most pythons and some boas (for example, the arboreal *Corallus*) have elaborate arrays of infrared-sensitive labial pits along the edges of both the upper and lower jaws. Other boas and a few pythons (for example, the woma and

Figure 17: Dorsal view of the head of a Burmese python (*Python molurus bivittatus*) congenitally lacking the left eye. The animal's left eye was completely absent from birth.

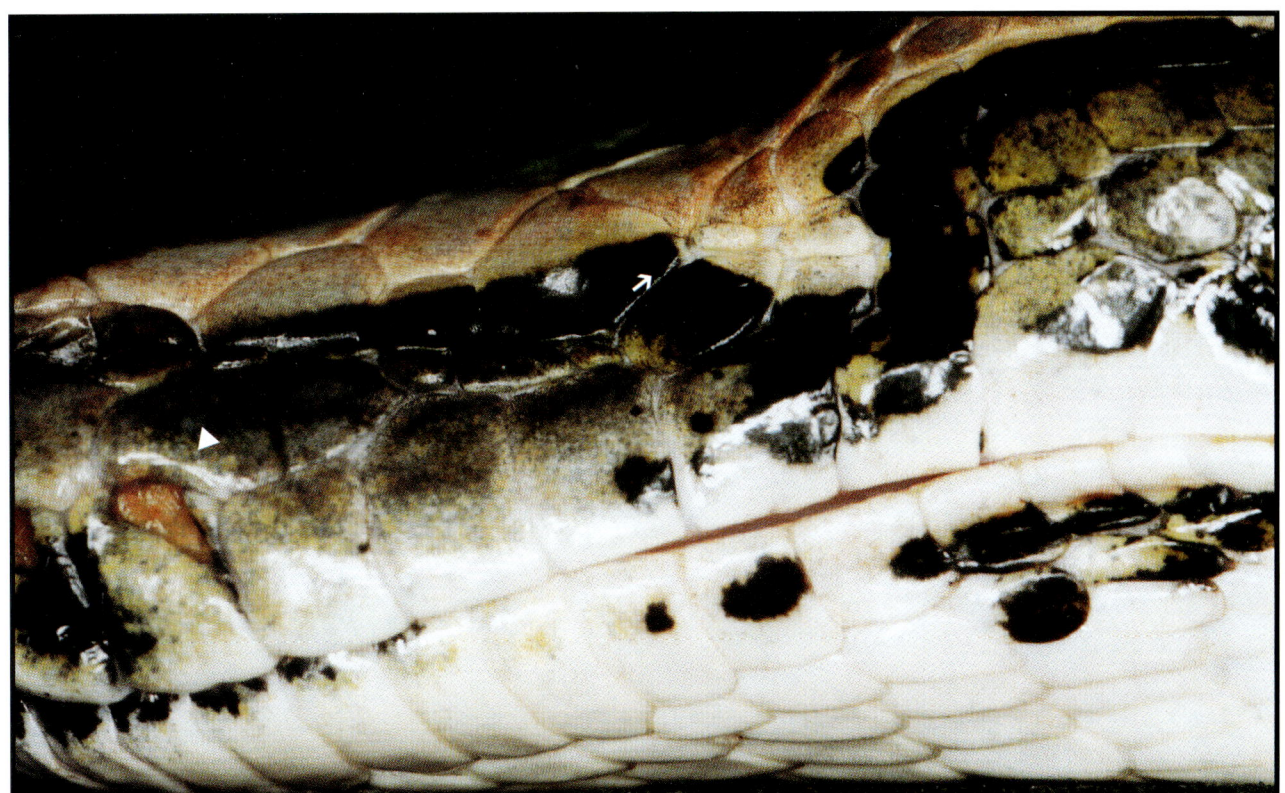

Figure 18: Lateral view of the snake (*Python molurus bivittatus*) shown in Figure 17. Note complete absence of the eye (arrow indicates the normal position of the eye), but apparently normal infrared-sensitive pits (arrowhead).

black-headed pythons, genus *Aspidites*) lack the pit structure, but possess infrared-sensitive patches of labial skin in an arrangement analogous to that of boids with pits. The infrared-sensitive membrane of pit vipers is suspended within the pit. This membrane consists of a central layer containing the receptor afferents and terminals, and outer and inner layers of epithelium. The pits of boas and pythons also contain the terminals of infrared-sensitive fibers, but these terminals lie in an epithelium that is not suspended within the pit. Otherwise, the structure of infrared-sensitive membrane is very similar in pythons, boas, and pit vipers. The infrared-sensitive areas of both boids and pit vipers contain a rich capillary bed. Myelinated infrared receptor fibers of about 2-6 μm diameter lose their myelin and taper to about 1mm diameter before forming the terminal nerve mass (Hirosawa, 1980). This terminal mass consists of fibers that branch several times to form a large palmate structure of numerous fine free nerve endings (Bullock and Fox, 1957).

The pits of both boids and pit vipers are innervated by branches of the trigeminal nerve (for review, see (Molenaar, 1992)). These are the same nerve branches that subserve the sensory roles of pressure, pain, and thermoreception in the facial region of reptiles, mammals, and other vertebrates, suggesting that infrared sensitivity may have evolved from other sensory modalities. Sensory fibers arising from the trigeminal nerve in infrared-sensitive snakes follow two distinct pathways after entering the brain: the common sensory trigeminal system, and the lateral descending trigeminal system. The common sensory trigeminal system subserves such sensory functions as mechanoreception, thermoreception, and nociception, and in infrared-sensing snakes appears essentially identical to that in other vertebrate animals. The lateral descending trigeminal system, on the other hand, appears specific to infrared-sensing snakes, and consists of a large descending tract that terminates in a very large nucleus, the lateral descending nucleus of the trigeminal nerve (Stanford et al., 1981). This nucleus is present in all infrared-sensitive snakes studied thus far, and is absent from animals not infrared-sensitive. Ultimately, infrared information reaches the optic tectum, forming a spatial map of the infrared environment on the tectum. In fact, this map overlays the spatial map of the visual world; individual fibers in the optic tectum may be stimulated by both visual and infrared energy arising from the same point in space (Hartline et al., 1978). Finally, two well-developed pathways convey information from the tectum to the telencephalon. One, via the dorsal geniculate nucleus, conveys visual information, while the other, via the nuclei rotundus/pararotundus, conveys infrared information (Berson and Hartline, 1988).

Figure 19: Infrared-sensitive pit (arrow) in an amelanistic Eastern diamondback rattlesnake (*Crotalus adamanteus*). Note that only a single deep pit is present on each side of the head.

It is unclear how important the infrared sense is to reptiles that possess it. These snakes rely on visual and chemosensory information in addition to infrared information for prey detection. Infrared-sensing snakes can accurately detect and strike prey as well as warm non-prey objects (heated metal, for example) in the absence of visible light, so the infrared system is obviously valuable to these animals. Boids and pitvipers may also use their infrared sense in thermoregulation, although this has not been demonstrated experimentally.

SUMMARY AND CONCLUSIONS

Vision and the detection of electromagnetic radiation outside the visible spectrum are profoundly important sensory systems in reptiles. Vision mediates prey and predator detection in many reptiles, and is involved (at least in some taxa) in inter- and intraspecific communication. Different reptilian groups have evolved strikingly different adaptations of their visual systems based upon their evolutionary histories. Specialized radiant energy receptors (circadian photoreceptors and infrared receptors) are relatively little understood, but probably also have great functional importance to reptiles. For example, non-visual photoreception probably plays a critical role in both daily and reproductive rhythms. Therefore, both the quality of light and its temporal pattern should be considered as important components of optimal reptile husbandry.

REFERENCES AND RECOMMENDED READING

—Berson, D. M. and P. H. Hartline:
A tecto-rotundo-telencephalic pathway in the rattlesnake: evidence for a forebrain representation of the infrared sense. J. Neurosci., 1988, 8:1074-1088.

—Bowmaker, J. K.:
Microspectrophotometry of vertebrate photoreceptors. Vision Res., 1984, 24: 1641-1650.

—Bullock, T. H. and W. Fox:
The anatomy of the infrared sense organ in the facial pit of pit vipers. Quarterly Journal of the Microscopical Society, 1957, 98:219-234.

—Fleishman, L. J., E. R. Loew and M. Leal:
Ultraviolet vision in lizards. Nature, 1993, 365:397.

—Foster, R. G., J. M. Garcia-Fernandez, I. Provencio and W. J. DeGrip:
Opsin localization and chromophore retinoids identified within the basal brain of the lizard *Anolis carolinensis*. Journal of Comparative Physiology A, 1993, 172:33-45.

—Foster, R. G., M. S. Grace, I. Provencio, W. J. DeGrip and J. M. Garcia-Fernandez:
Identification of vertebrate deep brain photoreceptors. Neuroscience and Biobehavioral Reviews, 1994, 18:541-546.

—Grace, M. S., V. Alones and M. Menaker:
Correlated light and electron microscopy of opsin-immunoreactive neurons in lizard basal brain. Soc. Neurosci. Abstr., 1993, 19:1201.

—Grace, M. S., V. Alones and M. Menaker:
A single population of photoreceptor-like cerebrospinal fluid-contacting neurons in the lizard *Iguana iguana*, 1997 (in preparation).

—Grace, M. S., V. Alones, M. Menaker and R. G. Foster:
Light perception in the vertebrate brain: an ultrastructural analysis of opsin-immunoreactive neurons in iguanid lizards. J. Comp. Neurol., 1996, 367:575-594.

—Hartline, P. H., L. Kass and M. S. Loop:
Merging modalities in the optic tectum: infrared and visual integration in rattlesnakes. Science, 1978, 199:1225-1229.

—Hirosawa, K.:
Electron microscopic obsevations on the pit organ of a crotaline snake (*Trimeresurus flavoviridis*). Arch. Histol. Japan, 1980, 43:65-78.

—Kardong, K. V. and S. P. Makessey:
The strike behavior of a congenitally blind rattlesnake. J. Herpetology, 1991, 25:208-211.

—Liebman, P. A.:
Microspectrophotometry of photoreceptors. In, Handbook of Sensory Physiology. M. G. Fuorter, (Ed.). Springer-Verlag, Berlin, New York, 1972, VII: 481-528.

—Liebman, P. A. and A. M. Granda:
Microspectrophotometric measurements of visual pigments in two species of turtle, *Pseudemys scripta* and *Chelonia mydas*. Vision Res., 1971, 11:105-114.

—Menaker, M. and S. Wisner:
Temperature-compensated circadian clock in the pineal of *Anolis*. Proc. Natl. Acad. Sci. U.S.A., 1983, 80:6119-6121.

—Molenaar, G. J.:
Anatomy and physiology of infrared sensitivity of snakes. In, Biology of the Reptilia. C. Gans and P. S. Ulinski (Eds.), University of Chicago Press, Chicago, 1992, 17: 367-453.

—Pedler, C. and R. Tiley:

Figure 20: Infrared-sensitive pits in the labial scales of a normally-colored Burmese python (*Python molurus bivittatus*).

Figure 21: Infrared-sensitive pits in the labial scales of the carpet python (*Morelia spilotes*). Snakes of this genus have a more elaborate array of pits on the lower jaw than do some other snakes (the *Python molurus*, for example).

Figure 22: Lateral view of the head of the Brazilian rainbow boa (*Epicrates cenchria cenchria*). Labial pits are present, but are only shallow depressions in the labial scales (arrows). Note that many individual scales have a pair of infrared-sensitive pits: one directed forward, and the other directed rearward.

The nature of the gecko visual cell: a light and electron microscopic study. Vision Res., 1964, 4:499-510.

—**Quay, W. B.:**
The parietal eye-pineal complex. In, Biology of the Reptilia. C. Gans, R. G. Northcutt and P. Ulinski, (Ed.). Academic Press, London, New York, 1979, 9:245-406.

—**Schaeffel, F. and A. de Queiroz:**
Alternative mechanisms of enhanced underwater vision in the garter snakes *Thamnophis melanogaster* and *T. couchii*. Copeia, 1990, 1990:50-58.

—**Stanford, L. R., D. M. Schroeder and P. H. Hartline:**
The ascending projection of the nucleus of the lateral descending trigeminal tract: a nucleus in the infrared system of the rattlesnake (*Crotalus viridis*). J. Comp. Neurol., 1981, 201:161-174.

—**Underwood, G.:**
The eye. In, Biology of the Reptilia. C. Gans and T. S. Parsons (Eds.), Academic Press, New York, 1970, 2:1-98.

—**Underwood, H. and M. Menaker:**
Extraretinal light perception: entrainment of the biological clock controlling lizard locomotor activity. Science, 1970, 170:190-193.

—**von Frische, K.:**
Beitrage zur Physiologie der Pigmentzellen in der Fischhaut. Pfluger's Archiv, 1911, 138:319-387.

—**Walls, G. L.:**
The vertebrate eye and its adaptive radiation. Hafner Publishing Co., New York, 1942.

—**Yoshida, M.:**
Some observations on the patency in the outer segments of the photoreceptors of the nocturnal gecko. Vision Res., 1978, 18:137-143.

BIOLOGICAL RHYTHMS IN REPTILES

Michael S. Grace, Ph.D.
Dept. of Biology
University of Virginia
Charlottesville, Virginia 22903

All photographs and illustrations courtesy of Michael S. Grace, Ph.D.

Dr. Michael Grace investigates the functional anatomy and molecular mechanisms underlying sensory systems and biological timing. Dr. Grace earned a B.S. in Applied Biology from the Georgia Institute of Technology, and M.S. and Ph.D. degrees in Neuroscience from the Emory University School of Medicine. At Emory and the University of Kansas Medical Center he studied retinal cell biology in the clawed frog, Xenopus laevis, *and melatonin biochemistry in the retina, pineal, and brain of* Xenopus, *iguanid lizards, and other vertebrates. Dr. Grace is currently Research Assistant Professor at the University of Virginia, where he studies photoreception and circadian rhythmicity in the green iguana and hamster. He also leads an effort to define the molecular mechanisms of infrared "vision" in boid and crotalid snakes. Dr. Grace and his wife, Tanya, operate a facility for captive reproduction of boid and colubrid snakes for research and education.*

INTRODUCTION

Biological clocks probably exist in all organisms, from fungi to plants to vertebrate animals, and the clocks of laboratory mammals and birds have been rather well-studied because of their relatively close relationship to man. Even so, reptiles and amphibians have served as important model systems for the study of biological timing. In particular, the reproductive rhythms of iguanid lizards have been intensively studied. Certain iguanids, including *Anolis carolinensis* and *Iguana iguana*, are becoming an important model systems for the study of circadian rhythms. The African clawed frog *Xenopus laevis* is also intensively studied in attempts to understand the circadian clock contained within the eye. There are two major values of these organisms as model systems for circadian biology. First, as opposed to the situation in mammals, reptiles and amphibians have multiple distinct oscillators (actually mammals may also, but they are much more difficult to study separately). Second, clock-containing tissues in reptiles and amphib-

ians are relatively easy to keep alive and functioning in culture, separated from confounding influences of other organs and processes in the intact organism. Also, because of the evolutionary positions of reptiles and amphibians, it is important to understand rhythms in these animals from a comparative standpoint. Finally, since reproduction in these animals is often seasonal, an understanding of their endogenous clocks is important for successful captive propagation.

The purpose of this chapter is to provide an overview of what is known about biological rhythms in reptiles, and to point out their importance to normal function, both under natural conditions and in the vivarium. A major emphasis is placed upon circadian rhythms since circadian clocks are ubiquitous among species, have profound influence on many behaviors and physiological processes, and underlie seasonal rhythmicity. This discussion of reptilian rhythms will include an analysis of the rhythm-generating systems of reptiles, beginning with the observable rhythms themselves, and then the clocks that generate them. Finally, the mechanisms of synchronizing biological rhythms with cyclic changes in the environment will be discussed, since entrainment is required for biological clocks to be useful (and indeed not harmful) to organisms. As part of the discussion of entrainment, the very important role of temperature will be considered. Temperature has little effect on clocks themselves (this is a hallmark of biological clocks), but may have profound effects on the expression biochemical, physiological, and behavioral rhythms.

OVERVIEW OF BIOLOGICAL TIMING

The physical environment undergoes periodic changes that drastically alter the ability of organisms to function and even survive. As the earth rotates, any given point on its surface is subjected to a light-dark cycle, the period of which is 24 hours. Along with this change in light level comes

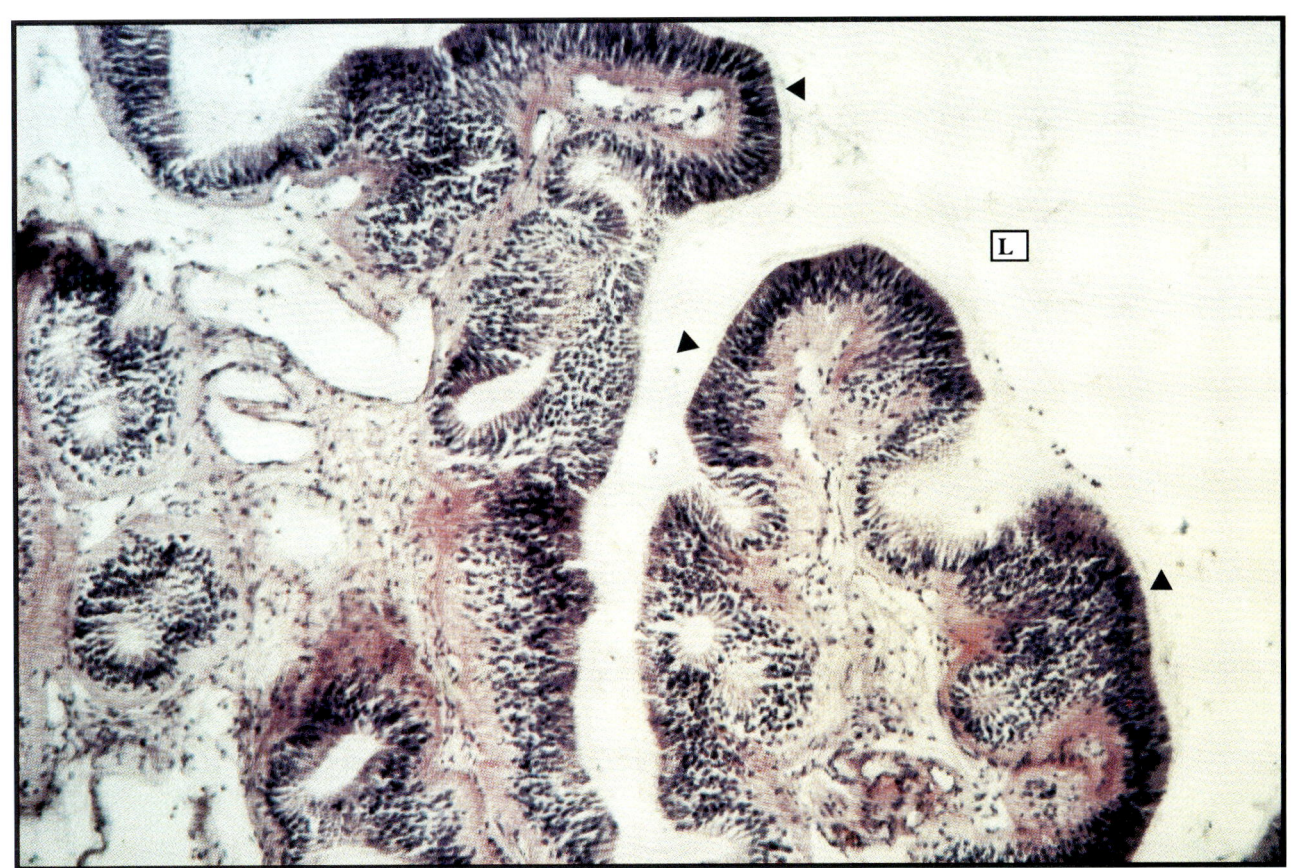

Fig. 1. Low-power light micrograph of the pineal organ of the green iguana (*Iguana iguana*), stained with hematoxylin and eosin. Note the convoluted structure of the pineal with pinealocytes (arrowheads) surrounding a central lumen (L).

several other important physical parameters. In particular, humidity and temperature vary according to time of day (although these cyclic changes are less reliable as indicators of time than is the level of light). Daily cycles are not the only periodic events in the environment, however. As the earth rotates around the sun, it's tilted axis causes seasonal changes in temperature, humidity, rainfall, and daylength.

Animals have responded to the daily light-dark cycle by evolving to become diurnal, nocturnal, and sometimes crepuscular (active at dawn and/or dusk). Similarly, organisms respond to seasonal cycles most obviously by reproducing at the time of the year that is optimal for survival of offspring. Seasonal and daily changes in physiology and behavior are not simply driven by environmental changes, however. All organisms thus far studied (from the simplest taxa such as fungi and protists, to vertebrates including reptiles, amphibians, and even man) have biological clocks that generate rhythmic biological changes.

Biological rhythms are regularly-occurring changes in an organism's physiology or behavior that are generated by clocks contained within the organism ("endogenous oscillators"). The hallmark of biological rhythms is that they persist in the absence of external time cues. In the laboratory, organisms (or their clock-containing tissues) held in constant conditions (i.e. no light cycle, temperature cycle, or other

indicator of environmental time) continue to express rhythmic changes similar to those seen in the natural environment.

Biological rhythms are defined by their cycle lengths (periods). Rhythms are described as ultradian (less than a day in period length), circadian (period of about a day), or infradian (period greater than a day). Heartbeat is an example of an ultradian rhythm. In the reproductive system, there are ultradian rhythms of hormone release, and of course reproduction is very often seasonal, an example of an infradian rhythm. Circadian rhythms, however, are perhaps the most widely studied by those scientists interested in biological clocks. Examples of circadian rhythms include the daily sleep-wake cycle, and rhythms of feeding and locomotor activity. Many physiological processes undergo rhythmic daily changes also. For example, visual sensitivity changes over the course of the day, even in the absence of a light-dark cycle. The effectiveness of certain drugs has been shown to vary according to time of day. In my own laboratory, I find that the sensitivity to anesthetics varies with time of day. A dose that safely induces anesthesia at one time of day may be lethal at others. These facts point out the ubiquity and functional relevance, as well as the importance of understanding biological rhythms and their consequences.

SURVEY OF RHYTHMS IN REPTILES

CIRCADIAN RHYTHMS IN MELATONIN

Circadian rhythms of biochemical changes, changes in cell morphology, structure, or function, and locomotor activity are the most commonly studied. The best-studied biochemical rhythm is that of melatonin synthesis and release. Not only is melatonin production a relatively easily-measured output of a circadian oscillator, but it also provides an important link between circadian clocks and rhythmic changes in other biochemical processes, as well as physiological changes and behaviors. Melatonin is synthesized in the pineal gland, within photoreceptive pinealocytes. In fact, melatonin synthesis may commonly occur in photoreceptors including those of the lateral eyes and parietal eye (although not all reptiles species may produce melatonin in all photoreceptive organelles).

Rhythmic pineal melatonin production has been documented in all turtle and tortoise species studied. Melatonin in the blood and cerebrospinal fluid was shown to exhibit daily fluctuations in the sea turtle *Chelonia mydas* (Owens et al., 1980). Other circadian biochemical changes have been docu-mented in the softshell turtle *Lissemys punctata*: the neurotransmitters serotonin, norepinephrine, and epinephrine exhibit circadian fluctuations in its pineal (Mahapatra et al., 1986). The only crocodilian studied thus far is the American alligator, a species with no morphologically apparent pineal. Only very low levels of melatonin were found in the circulation, and no rhythm was apparent (Roth et al., 1980).

Daily fluctuations in the level of melatonin have been observed in a number of lizard species. Most of these studies were done under conditions of cyclic light, but in a few species, truly rhythmic melatonin has been demonstrated. Pineal melatonin in *Anolis carolinensis* exhibits a circadian rhythm under constant conditions (Underwood and Calaban, 1987), as does plasma melatonin in *Trachydosaurus rugosus* (Firth et al., 1979). The mechanisms of entraining melatonin rhythms have been examined in lizards with some very interesting results. Both daily light-dark cycles and cycles of temperature entrain the rhythm, and the relative strength of the two signals varies with the amplitude of the stimulus. That is, while the light-dark cycle is considered to be the most important entraining stimulus in many organisms, cycles of temperature with sufficient amplitude are more effective in reptiles than is the light-dark cycle (see

Fig. 2. High-power light micrograph of the pineal of the green iguana *(Iguana* iguana), stained with hematoxylin and eosin. Pinealocytes (P) each send a rudimentary outer segment into the lumen (L) of the pinneal.

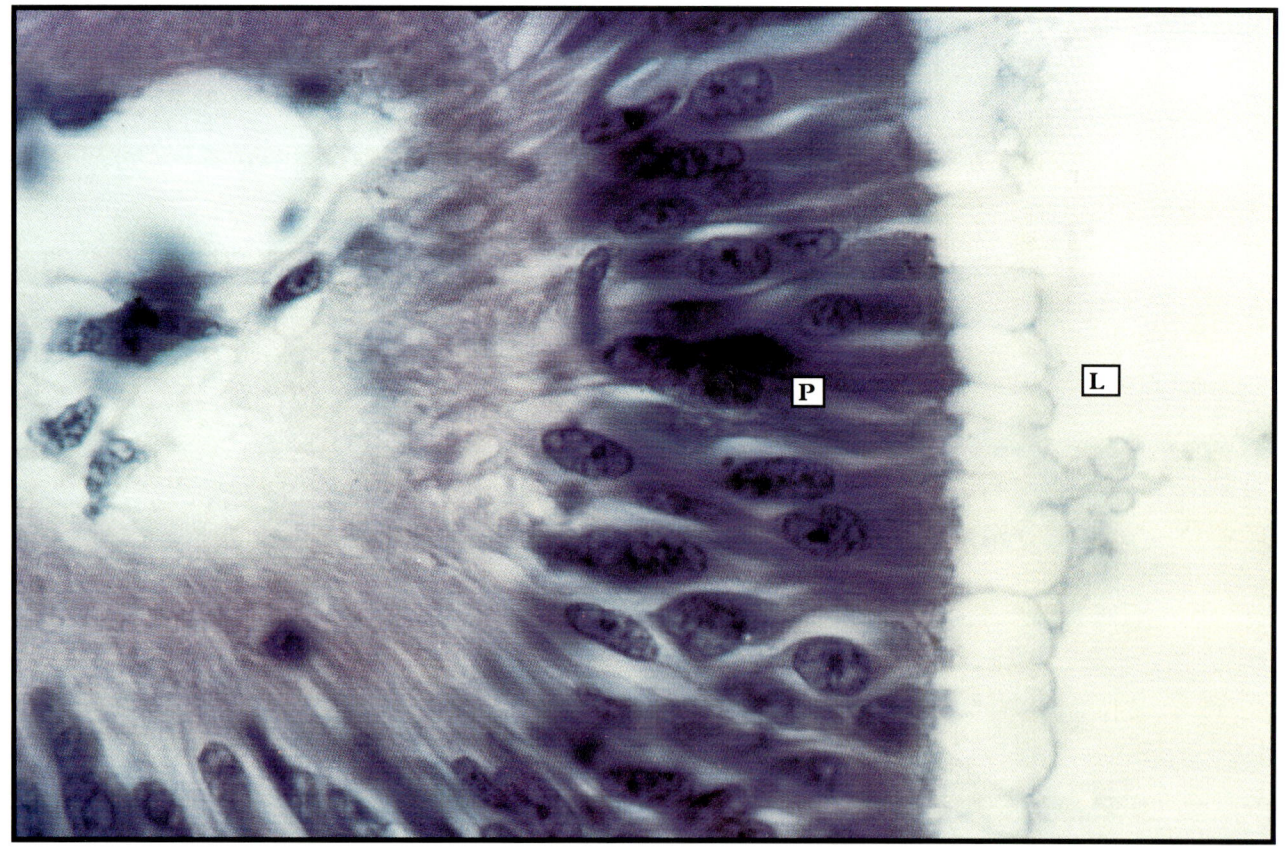

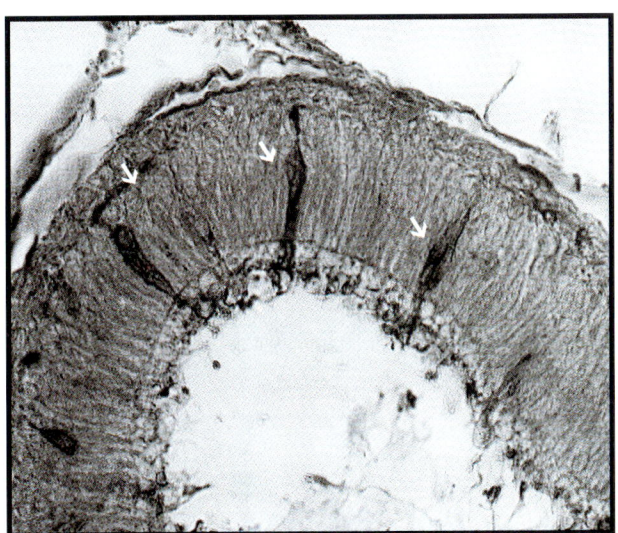

Fig. 3. Light micrograph of the pineal of the green iguana (*Iguana iguana*), immunostained (arrows) with an antiserum against the retinal cone photoreceptor photopigment opsin. Iguana pinealocytes (like those of many non-mammalian species) are photoreceptive.

below). In both the field and in the captive environment, temperature is a very important input pathway to reptilian biological clocks.

CIRCADIAN RHYTHMS IN THE EYE

The eyes are important components of circadian systems in vertebrate animals. In all vertebrate classes, they may be a part of the light input pathway to the clock(s) (in mammals, they are probably the only input pathway). In addition, eyes themselves contain clocks (see below for evidence in reptiles), and exhibit rhythmic changes in sensitivity and structure.

The normal function of photoreceptors in the retina includes the renewal of photoreceptor outer segment membrane. The outer segment, the part of the photoreceptor that transduces light into an electrochemical neural signal (see chapter on reptilian vision), undergoes addition of new membrane at its base, and periodically sheds packets of disk membrane which are degraded by the adjacent retinal pigmented epithelium. This process is essential for normal photoreceptor function, and is regulated by light and a biological clock. In the lizard *Sceloporus olivaceous*, the rate of disk shedding peaks just after light offset in a light-dark cycle (Young, 1977; Bernstein et al., 1984), and persists with a period of about 24 hours in constant conditions (Bernstein et al., 1984). It is interesting to note that *Sceloporus* has an all-cone retina (see chapter on reptilian vision), and in mammals with duplex retinas, cones shed outer segment material in the early night, at the light-to-dark transition, while rods shed in the morning, at the dark-to-light transition. Rhythmic disk shedding has been little studied in reptiles, but in those with duplex retinas, there are likely to be two peaks

of disk shedding, each associated with a different class of photoreceptor. It would be particularly interesting to investigate rhythmic disk shedding in nocturnal geckos, the photoreceptors of which have characteristics of both rods and cones (see chapter on reptilian vision).

The morphology of photoreceptor synapses also changes over the course of the day. It was shown that rod synapses in the turtle *Pseudemys* exhibit daily changes in the structure of their synaptic ribbons (Abe and Yamamoto, 1984), sites of neurotransmitter release from the photoreceptor. Whether this change is actually rhythmic (fluctuates in the absence of external time cues) is unknown. It may be either a response to changing light levels and photoreceptor activity. Alternatively, if daily changes in rod synaptic morphology are truly rhythmic, they may underlie rhythmic changes in retinal sensitivity.

A rhythm of retinal sensitivity, as measured by electrical activity, has been reported in *Anolis carolinensis* and *Gekko gecko* (Fowlkes et al., 1984; Fowlkes et al., 1987). The amplitude of the electroretinogram (ERG, an electrical response of the retina to a flash of light) changes with time of day, and this rhythm persists in the absence of external time cues. Shaw et al. (Shaw et al., 1993) provided evidence that there is also a seasonal rhythm in ERG amplitude in *Anolis*.

Figure 4: Rhythmic photoreceptor outer segment disk shedding in the eye of the lizard Sceloporus occidentalis. Bar at top indicates lighting conditions. Lizards were held in cyclic light (12hr light:12hr dark). At time 12 (normal time of dark onset), lizards were placed in constant darkness. Note that the rhythm persists with an approximately 24-hour period in the absence of time cues. Data from Bernstein et al., 1984.

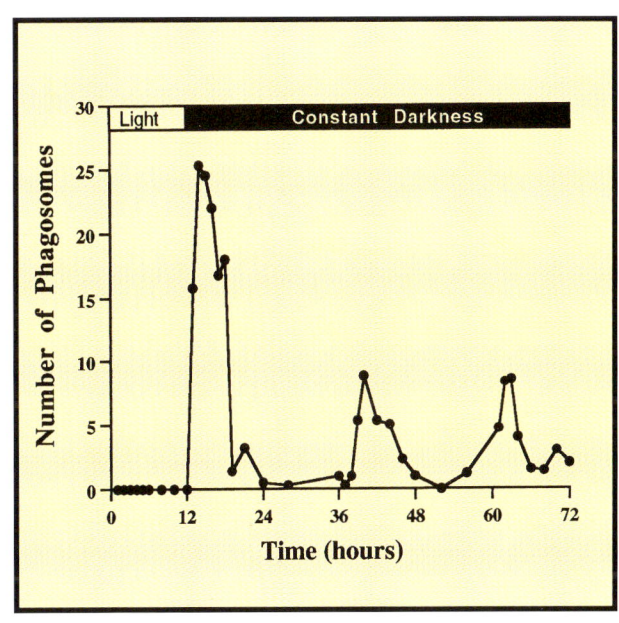

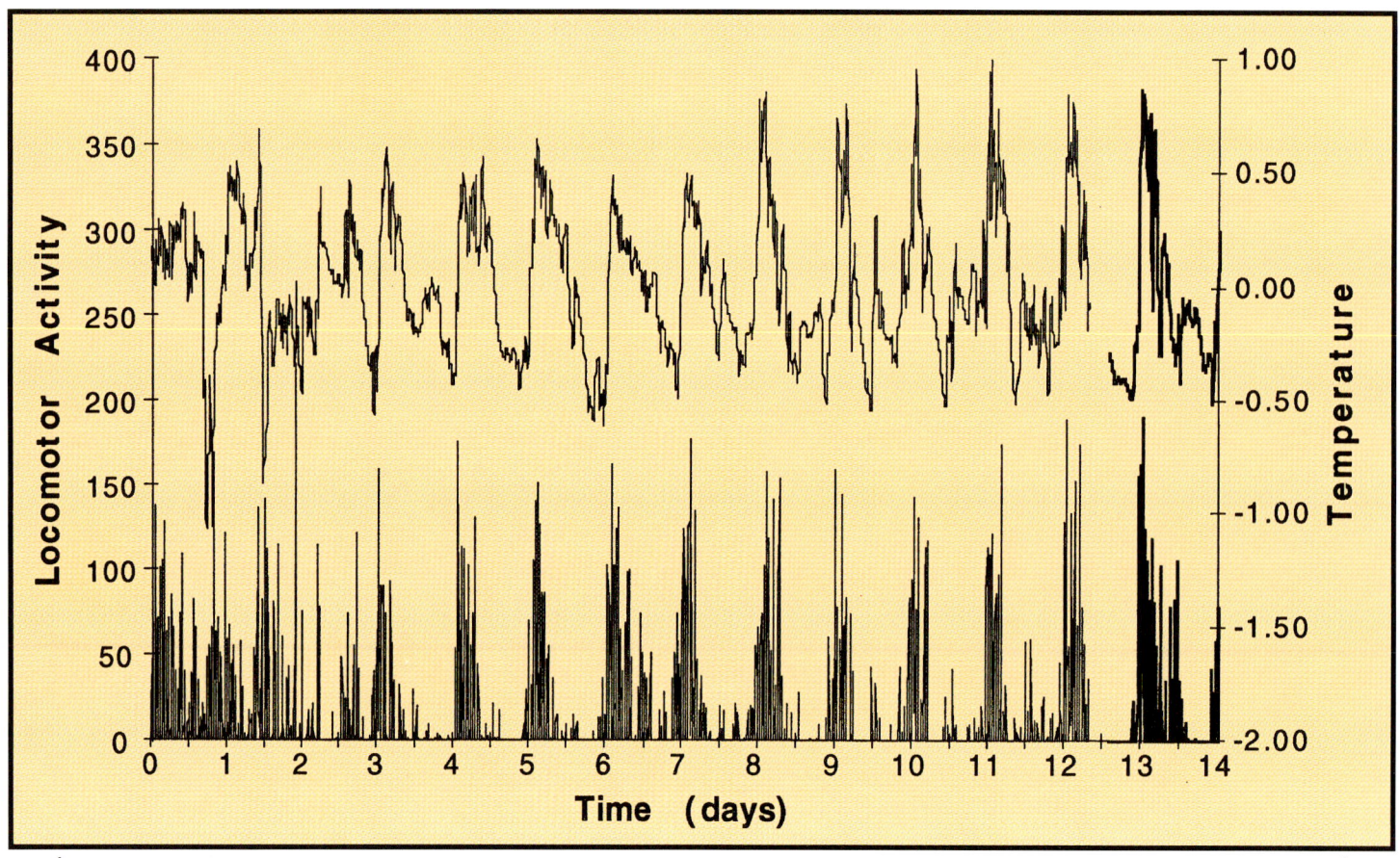

Figure 5: Rhythmic locomotor activity (lower trace) and body temperature (upper trace) in a green iguana (*Iguana iguana*) held in constant darkness and constant temperature for 14 days (L.F.S. Moreira and M.S. Grace, unpublished data). Data were collected using an intraperitoneal radio-frequency transmitter. The rhythm of body temperature is not simply a product of rhythmic locomotor activity.

CIRCADIAN ACTIVITY RHYTHMS

One of the most easily studied outputs of circadian clocks is the circadian rhythm of locomotor activity. Circadian clocks drive rhythms of locomotor activity, and like other rhythms, that of activity is entrained to environmental time in reptiles by the daily light-dark cycle, and by daily changes in temperature. It must be remembered however, that both light and temperature can have acute effects on locomotor activity, independent of their effects on clocks, especially in ectotherms such as reptiles. For example, both low and high temperatures (significantly outside a given reptile's thermal preference range) can cause reptiles to become lethargic, "masking" the circadian rhythm of locomotor activity.

The role of circadian clocks as regulators of locomotor activity is apparent both in the laboratory and in the field. Under natural conditions, reptiles will emerge from burrows or dens even when the ambient temperature is far below preferred body temperature and locomotor activity is otherwise minimal. After a period of basking, body temperature rises to the preferred range for activity, and normal locomotor activity begins.

In the field, the patterns of locomotor activity may change dramatically with changes in temperature. Tortoises, for example, can exhibit a unimodal peak of locomotor activity when temperatures are low, but at higher temperatures activity becomes bimodal: animals are active in the morning and late in the day, but inactive during the heat of midday. This phenomenon is not simply a response to the changing temperature over the course of the day, however, since even at high but constant daily temperatures (i.e. the temperature does not change over the course of the day), tortoises still exhibit a bimodal pattern of activity (M.S. Grace, personal observations).

Snakes have been far less studied than lizards, but they are very interesting in that the phase relationship of activity to the light-dark cycle is very labile. Like the rhythm of melatonin production in the lizard pineal, temperature has profound effects on the patterns of snake locomotor activity. Many casual observers in the field have noted apparent shifts from diurnality to nocturnality in many snake species, and this phenomenon has been documented in water snakes (*Nerodia cyclopion, N. fasciata, N. rhombifera*: (Mushinski et al., 1980)), the copperhead (*Agkistrodon contortrix*: (Sanders and Jacob, 1981), and rattlesnakes (*Crotalus mitchelli, C. cerastes*: (Moore, 1978)); *C. atrox*: (Landreth, 1973)). Finally, the garter snake

Thamnophis radix held in captivity remains diurnal at 15°C, but become nocturnal when held at 31°C (Heckrotte, 1975).

THERMOREGULATORY RHYTHMS

Ectotherms including reptiles depend largely on environmental heat since their metabolism has little effect on body temperature. Even so, reptiles are able to thermoregulate by behaviorally changing their physical relationship with the thermal environment. This behavioral thermoregulation exhibits circadian regulation. Daily variations in self-selected body temperature have been reported in turtles and lizards, and at least in some reports, true circadian rhythms in constant conditions have been reported (see for example (Cowgell and Underwood, 1979; Jarling et al., 1989)). Snakes have been little studied with regard to rhythms in thermal preference. This is surprising in light of the fact that snakes can completely change the active phase of their activity rhythms between diurnality and nocturnality according to the environmental temperature. Even so, both daily and circadian rhythms in behaviorally-selected body temperatures have been reported in the snake *Vipera aspis* (Naulleau, 1976; Naulleau, 1979).

PHOTOPERIODISM AND SEASONAL/ CIRCANNUAL RHYTHMS

Just as circadian rhythms prepare an organism for anticipated daily changes in its environment, seasonal or circannual rhythms prepare an organism for seasonal changes in its environment. Obviously such changes are critical for survival and reproduction, particularly in ectotherms which are more critically subject to such seasonal changes as temperature. Two rhythmic processes effect seasonal changes: circannual rhythms, and photo- or thermoperiodism.

Photo- and thermoperiodism refer to processes mediated by the circadian system that ultimately produce seasonal changes in such things as reproductive function and fat accumulation. That is, animals sense the seasonal change in the relative amounts of light and dark in the day/night cycle, or high and low temperatures over the course of the day as signals to time seasonal events. One model of this process holds that there is an endogenous circadian rhythm of responsiveness to the periodic stimulus (light or temperature). For example, when light falls in the sensitive phase of the circadian rhythm of photosensitivity (during the long days of summer) it has physiological effects that are absent during the short days of winter when light is absent from the sensitive phase. Alternatively, animals may measure the absolute length of the light or high temperature portion on the day.

Reproduction has been relatively well-studied in reptiles. Generally, temperate zone reptiles exhibit seasonal reproduction with the timing of gonadal growth and egg/sperm production varying with latitude such that mating occurs in spring. Tropical reptiles vary from being distinctly seasonal breeders to continuous or acyclic breeders. A detailed analysis of reproductive cyclicity is beyond the scope of this paper, but a few examples will be used to illustrate the nature of reptilian reproductive cycles. For a more detailed treatment of reptilian reproductive cyclicity, see reviews by Duvall et al. (Duvall et al., 1982) and Whittier and Crews (Whittier and Crews, 1987); for a discussion of reproduction-associated behavior in reptiles, see reviews by Whittier and Tokarz (Whittier and Tokarz, 1992) and Moore and Lidzey (Moore and Lindzey, 1992).

Temperate-zone lizards exhibit an annual cycle of reproductive function; the best studied lizard in this respect is *Anolis carolinensis* (see for example (Underwood, 1978). In late summer its testes regress, while in winter and early spring they recrudesce in anticipation of the breeding season. *Anolis* exhibits a critical photoperiod (the minimum daylength required) for testicular recrudescence or maintenance of about 13.5 hours. The reproductive system and fat stores of *Anolis* are also sensitive to temperature. Noeske and Meier (Noeske and Meier, 1977; Noeske and Meier, 1982) showed that photoperiod and temperature interact in the control of these seasonal variables, and suggested that *Anolis* also exhibits a circadian rhythm of thermosensitivity. Seasonal cycles of reproductive activity also occur in the tropical lizard *Anolis aeneus*, but *Anolis trinitatus*, which lives in the same region, breeds throughout the year. Snakes, turtles, crocodilians, and the tuatara are generally seasonal breeders, but continuous reproductive activity occurs in some including the tropical water snake *Homalopsis buccata*. Interestingly, certain sea turtles (*Chelonia mydas, C. depressa*) have been seen to nest throughout the year in tropical parts of their ranges, but seasonally in temperate regions.

True circannual rhythms, characterized by continuing cyclicity in the absence of seasonal time cues, have been demonstrated in lizards. Stebbins (Stebbins, 1963) reported a circannual rhythm of activity in the lizard *Sceloporus virgatus*. A circannual rhythm of reproductive function (ovulation) has been demonstrated in *Cnemidophorus uniparens* (Cuellar and Cuellar, 1977; Cuellar, 1981). In experiments on both of these species, animals were held under daily cycles of light and temperature, but these cycles were invariant over the course of the year. Interestingly, the reproductive rhythm seen in *C. uniparens* held under constant conditions has a period of significantly lees than one year (2 or 3 cycles of ovulation were seen in 20 months: (Cuellar and Cuellar, 1977)), but this is not unexpected, as similar phenomena occur in mammals.

Figure 6: The roof of the skull of the green iguana (*Iguana iguana*). The pineal organ is the oval-shaped yellow structure (arrow) in the center of the tissue. The two oval depressions in the bone overlie the frontal cortex of the brain. The parietal window in the skin is visible at the anterior margin of this piece of skull (arrowhead). The parietal eye itself has been removed. Snout-vent length of this animal was approximately 23cm; pineal dimensions were approximately 1mm x 2mm.

Figure 7: Dorsal view of a paraformaldehyde/picric acid-fixed green iguana (*Iguana iguana*) brain. The pineal would lie at the junction (arrow) of the frontal cortical hemispheres (CH), the optic lobes (OL), and the cerebellum (Ce). The black pigment is melanin from the (mostly removed) pigmented meninges.

COMPONENTS OF THE CIRCADIAN SYSTEM

The circadian system can be modeled simply as a clock (often termed a "black box" because the basic mechanisms underlying the clock mechanism are essentially unknown) with one or more inputs and one or more outputs. Inputs to the clock are the stimuli and the pathways they take in changing clock function. An example of an input pathway includes the light-dark cycle, photoreceptors, and pathway(s) from the photoreceptors to the clock. Clock outputs are the observable effects of the clock on behavior, physiology, and biochemistry, as well as the neural and chemical pathways that link the clock to the overt rhythm. Circadian clock outputs include the phenomena described above (locomotor activity, melatonin rhythmicity, etc.).

A great deal of research is currently aimed at understanding the functional mechanisms within clocks themselves, and the most promising results are coming from attempts to identify clock genes; however, none of this research currently involves reptiles (but see companion volume for interesting new information coming from amphibian systems). On the other hand, certain reptiles have been and are becoming more important for the study of the anatomy of the circadian system, and for the study of circadian photoreception.

THE PINEAL ORGAN

The pineal is the best studied circadian structure in non-mammalian vertebrates. In lizards, there is conflicting information on the clock function of the pineal, though. In lizards the necessity of the pineal for circadian rhythmicity varies across taxa. Removal of the pineal from lizards of the genus *Sceloporus* has a slight effect on the circadian rhythm of locomotor activity (the period of the rhythm in constant conditions changes, but this could be due to the surgical procedure itself rather than to pinealectomy), but does not abolish it (Underwood, 1977; Underwood, 1981). On the other hand, pinealectomy abolishes the circadian rhythm of locomotor activity in *Anolis* (Underwood, 1983).

In culture, the *Anolis carolinensis* pineal continues to produce melatonin rhythmically, under conditions of cyclic light or in constant conditions (Menaker and Wisner, 1983). In fact, individual *Anolis* pinealocytes must contain clocks, since when isolated, they still produce melatonin rhythmically under constant conditions. The cultured pineal of the gecko *Christinus marmoratus* apparently does not contain a clock coupled to melatonin synthesis, but maintains its photoreceptive capacity, since melatonin levels cycle under 12-hour light/12-hour dark conditions, but not in constant darkness (Moyer et al., 1995). Thus, while both *Anolis* and *Christinus*

Figure 8: The parietal eye of the green iguana (*Iguana iguana*). The parietal eye is located just under a translucent scale in the center of the head (arrow), between and just behind the lateral eyes.

Figure 9: The parietal eye (arrow) of the Cuban ground iguana (*Cyclura nubila nubila*).

pineals are photoreceptive, only *Anolis* exhibits clock function with respect to melatonin synthesis. It is possible that the gecko pineal contains a clock, but melatonin production is not under direct clock control. On the other hand, there may be significant differences among reptilian taxa in the relative importance of the pineal as a clock-containing structure. Still, pineal melatonin under natural conditions of cyclic light is likely an important effector of cyclic phenomena including reproductive cyclicity, even in reptiles whose pineal melatonin is not under clock control.

THE PARIETAL EYE

The parietal eye, also known as the "third eye", is an archaic structure that was once much more widely distributed, but today is found only in some lizards and the tuatara (see (Quay, 1979) for a more detailed discussion of the pineal-parietal complex of reptiles). The parietal eye is located at the junction of the frontal and parietal bones of the skull, and can be seen as a small clear window in the central head scale of smaller lizards such as some iguanids, and as a relatively large window in larger lizards such as the monitors (genus *Varanus*), as wel as the tuatara (*Sphenodon*). The structure of the parietal eye is in many ways similar to the lateral eye: it has a lens and a retina composed of photoreceptors and second order neurons. The structure of the retina is radically different from that in the lateral eye, however. The arrangement is much simpler; photoreceptors synapse directly onto ganglion cells which send their axons out as the parietal nerve (see chapter on reptilian vision). In addition, the arrangement of the cellular layers with respect to incoming light is the reverse of that in the lateral eyes. Parietal eye photoreceptors are closest to the incoming light, while in the lateral eye, photoreceptors are located at the back of the retina.

The parietal eye is thought to function in the control of thermoregulation and seasonal reproduction. Consistent with a role in circadian and seasonal processes, the parietal has very unusual electrical response properties to light which have led some authors to suggest that it functions as a "dawn and dusk detector" (Solessio and Engbretson, 1993). These authors showed that there are two distinct electrical responses to light, each activated at different wavelengths. They propose that, because of the changing quality of light over the course of the day, parietal photoreceptors only discharge at dawn and dusk. This mechanism would function to encode not only dawn and dusk which could entrain circadian rhythms, but the length of the day as a cue for seasonal reproduction.

THE LATERAL EYES

As discussed above, lateral eyes in many if not all vertebrate animals contain circadian clocks that affect processes occurring within the eye. However, the eyes are not known to be critically important for circadian function in the whole animal. While the eyes often do synthesize melatonin, little or none is released into the circulation. In fact, the eyes have a very efficient system that degrades melatonin (Grace et al., 1991), suggesting that melatonin synthesized there has only local functions (melatonin is also degraded within the lizard pineal, but the levels of degradation apparently do not prevent release of melatonin into the circulation (Grace and Besharse, 1994). Removal of the lateral eyes has negligible effect on the circadian rhythm of locomotor activity, in some cases changing the period of the rhythm, but not abolishing it (Underwood, 1981; Janik and Menaker, 1990).

While veretbrate eyes are known to contain competent circadian oscillators, they may in some species be under control of the pineal. For example, the retinal electroretinogram of the lizard *Anolis carolinensis* exhibits a circadian rhythm in amplitude (see above). However, this rhythm is in some way affected by the pineal: removal of the parietal eye has no effect, but removal of the pineal nearly abolishes the ERG rhythm (Shaw et al., 1993).

THE SUPRACHIASMATIC NUCLEI

The suprachiasmatic nuclei (SCN) are known as the location of the "master clock" in mammals. These two small clusters of cell bodies lie at the base of the mammalian brain adjacent to the third ventricle, and just above the junction of the two optic nerves as they enter the brain, the optic chiasm (hence the name "suprachiasmatic": above the optic chiasm). The SCN may not be the only site of a circadian clock in mammals, but if other clocks do exist (the probably do), the SCN control or synchronize the outputs of them. Many mammals exhibit robust rhythms of locomotor activity. Nocturnal rodents are most commonly studied because they have a high amplitude rhythm of activity on a running wheel. The active portion of the cycle is confined to the night on a light-dark cycle, but rodents continue to run rhythmically with a period of about 24 hours in the complete absence of external time cues. If the SCN is completely destroyed, the rhythm is abolished; animals still run on their wheels, but the timing of activity is random. SCN-containing brain tissue can be transplanted from donor animals to those whose SCN was destroyed, and the activity rhythm returns.

Despite the fact that so much consideration is given to the mammalian SCN, it has largely been neglected in reptiles and other non-mammalian vertebrates. An SCN-like structure may exist, however, but its role in the reptilian circadian system has never been tested. Janik et al. found an SCN-like structure in the lizard *Dipsosaurus dorsalis*. The

brain region they implicated has biochemical similarities to the mammalian SCN, and receives direct input from the retina, just as the mammalian SCN does. However, other common biochemical markers of the mammalian SCN were not found. Subsequently, Grace et al. (Grace and Menaker, 1996) found an SCN-like region in the brain of *Iguana iguana*. This region appears immunologically similar to that in *Dipsosaurus*, and also receives direct retinal input. Interestingly, though, certain common chemical markers of the mammalian SCN were absent. The *Iguana* brain also contains an area immunologically and anatomically similar to the mammalian lateral geniculate nucleus (Grace et al., 1996), a structure involved in light input to the SCN. These studies of the iguanid circadian system may be very important to the overall understanding of circadian timing in vertebrates, since they may help determine which neurochemical markers are functionally important components of the SCN.

The importance of the SCN in reptilian rhythms has been little investigated. One report is instrumental, however. In the iguanid lizard *Dipsosaurus dorsalis*, removal of both the lateral eyes and pineal fails to abolish rhythmic locomotor activity (Janik and Menaker, 1990), but electrolytic destruction of the SCN region can produce arrhythmic locomotor activity (Janik and Menaker, 1990). This procedure could have simply interrupted a clock output rather than destroying the clock itself, but the fact that the mammalian SCN is required for circadian rhythms of locomotor activity suggests that the lizard SCN may also control rhythmic activity. Even so, other clocks located in other organs may be more important in the control of other rhythmic outputs.

The preceding discussion points out the fact that reptiles contain multiple distinct clocks. A given individual may have as many as six separate clock-containing structures (one in the pineal, one in the parietal eye, one in each of the lateral eyes, and one in each of the SCN; there may be other undiscovered clocks as well). The relative importance of the different clock-containing structures apparently varies greatly among reptiles: eyes are not required for expression of activity rhythms, while the pineal is in certain species but not others. In the intact animal, all of the clocks obviously function in synchrony. It is possible that the endogenous periods of the oscillator are independent of each other, but under conditions of cyclic light, temperature, or other stimuli, all of the clocks should entrain or be driven by one or more dominant (master) oscillators. All of the clocks are not required for expression of rhythmic outputs, how-

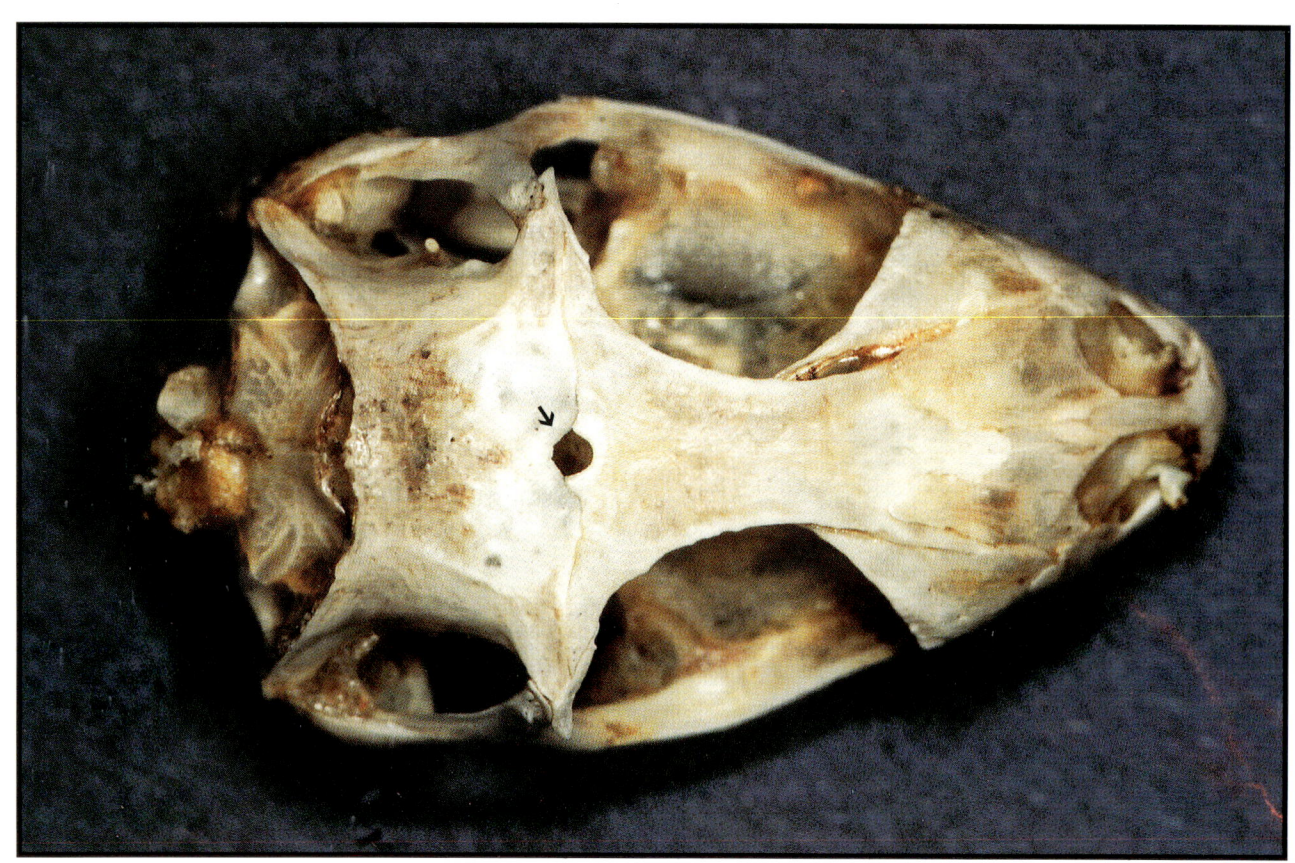

Figure 10: The parietal foramen (arrow) in the skull of the green iguana (*Iguana iguana*). The parietal lies within this foramen, and is covered by a lens and a clear scale in the skin. The parietal nerve exits the parietal eye and travels caudally toward the pineal organ.

Figure 11: Dorsal view of the head of the African spurred tortoise, *Geochelone sulcata*. Note the absence of a parietal window.

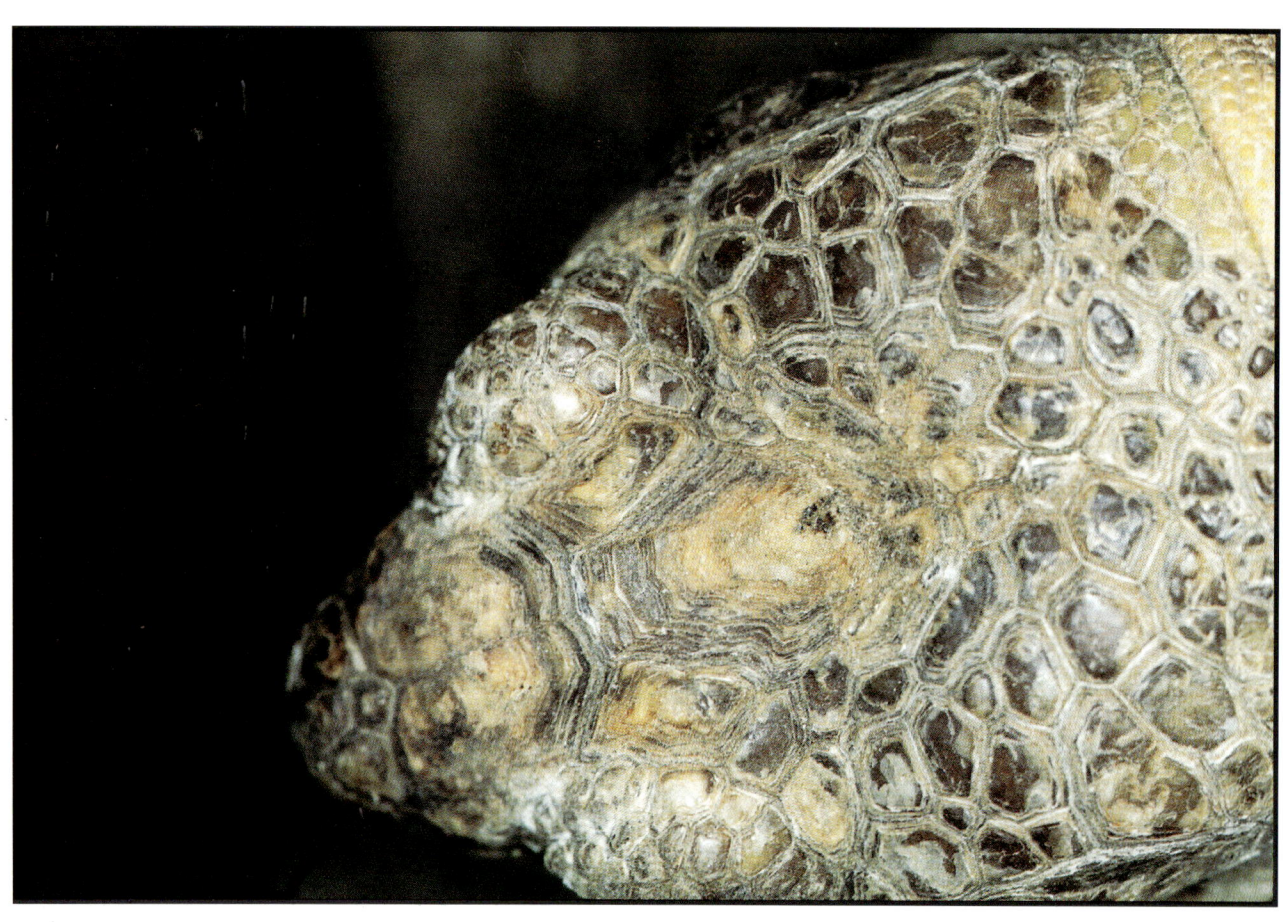

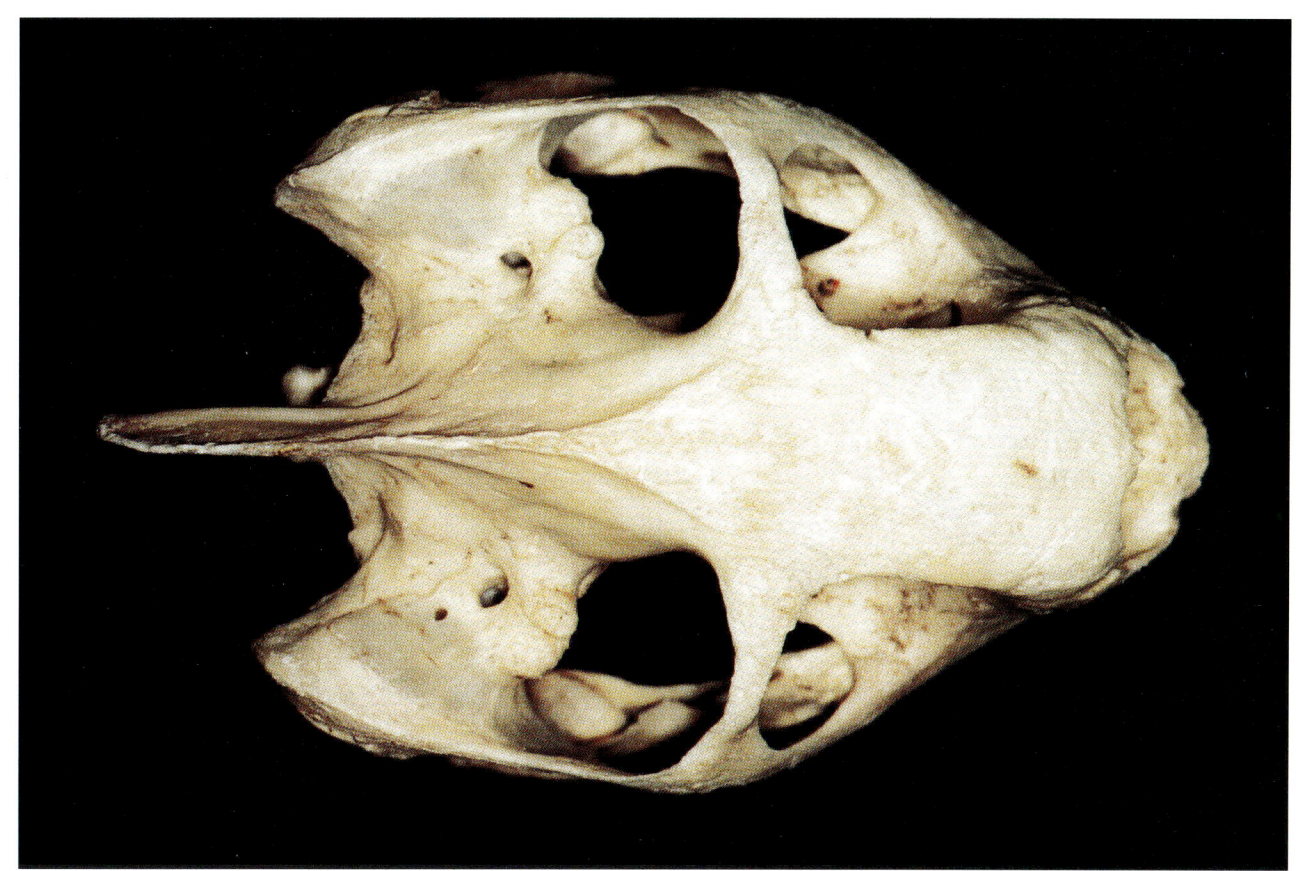

Figure 12: Dorsal view of the skull of the African leopard tortoise, *Geochelone pardalis*. Note the absence of a parietal foramen. Parietals were once more common among reptiles than they are today, as evidenced by parietal foramena in the skulls of many extinct reptiles.

Figure 13: Light micrograph of the retina of the green iguana (*Iguana iguana*), stained with Mallory's trichrome. Photoreceptors develop a large and highly-ordered photoreceptive outer segment (arrows) which is partially embedded in the apical microvilli of the retina pigmented epithelium (asterisk).

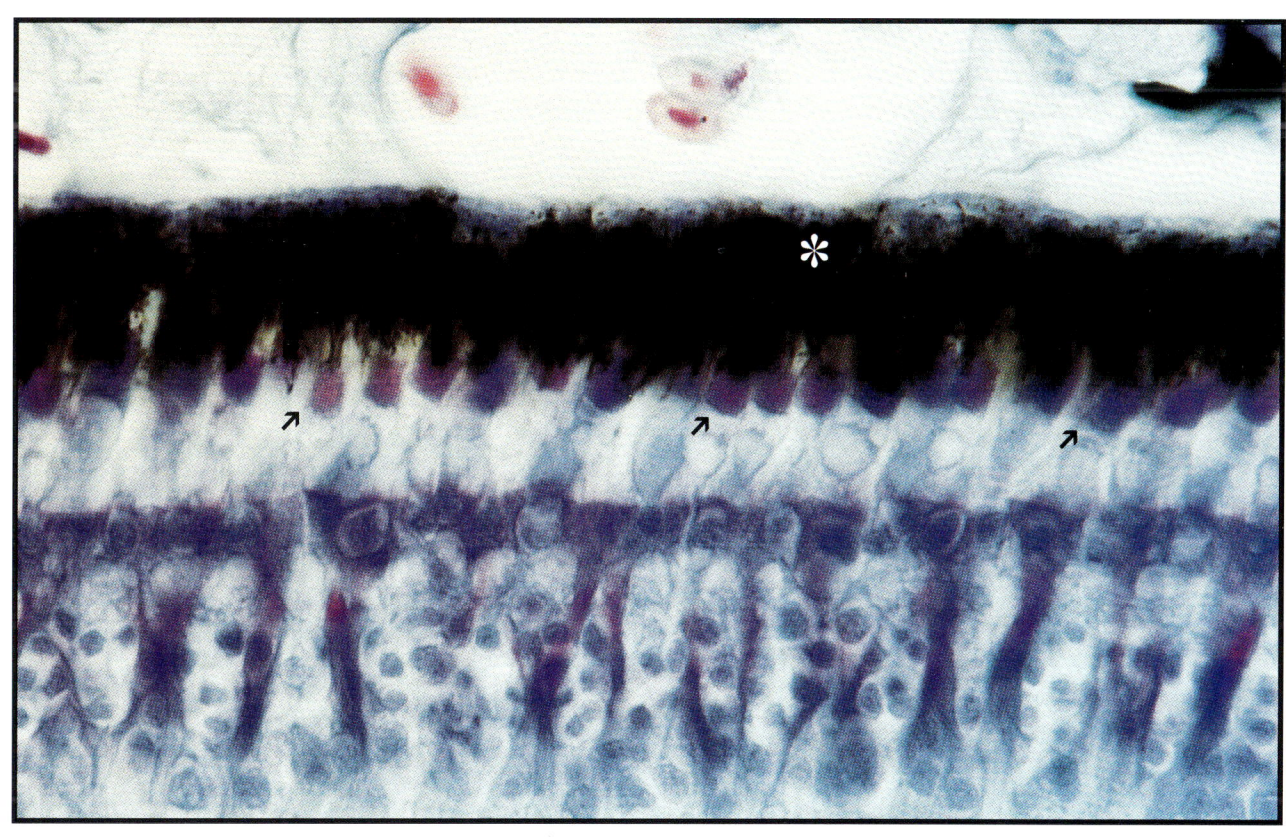

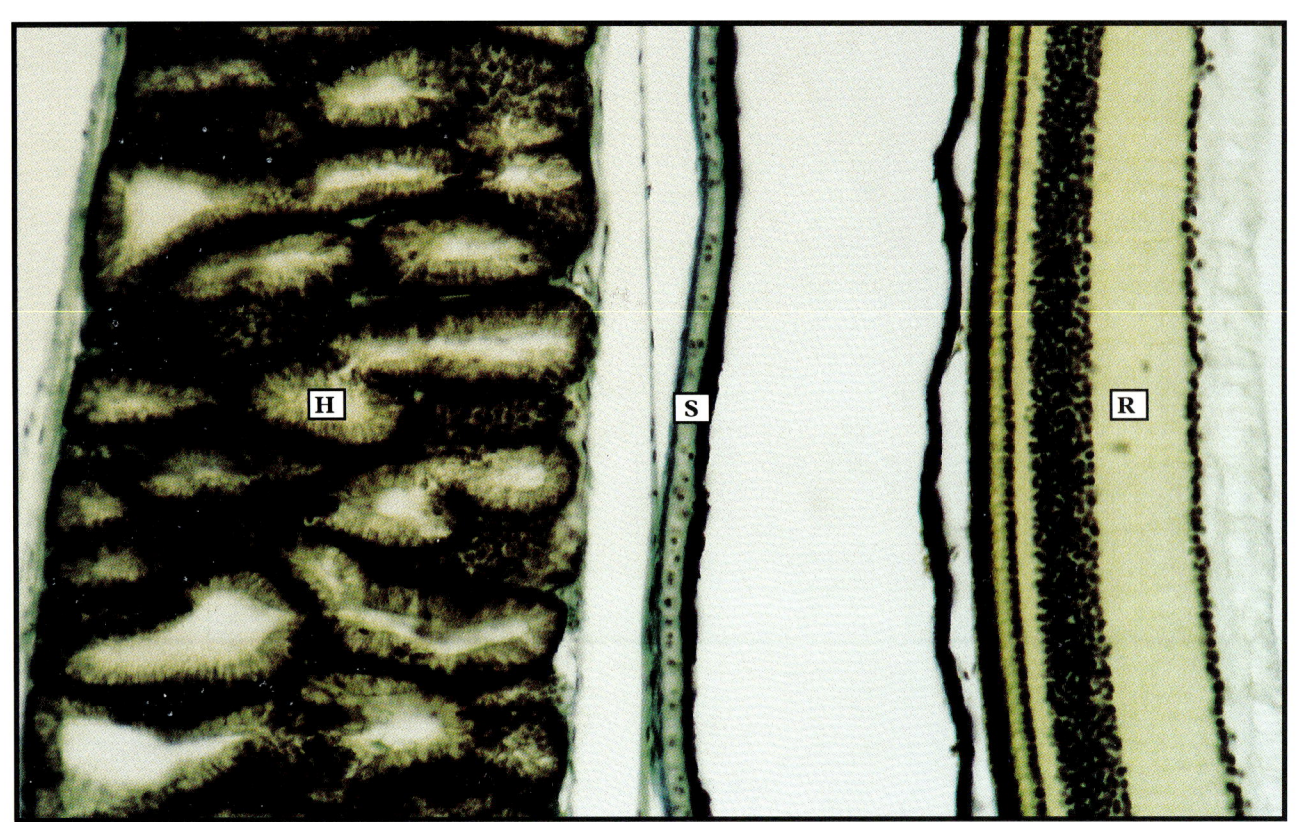

Figure 14: Low-power light micrograph of the eye of the Carolina anole (*Anolis carolinensis*). The large convoluted structure is the Harderian gland (H). It is located just outside the orbit of the eye. The Harderian gland may be a component of the circadian system, as several reports indicate that it produces melatonin. Note the multi-layered retina (R) and the sclera (S).

Figure 15: The suprachiasmatic nuclei (arrows) of the green iguana *(Iguana iguana)* stained with an antiserum against neuropeptide Y (M.S. Grace, unpublished results). Frozen 20mm frontal section of the brain. 3V: third ventricle; OC: optic chiasm.

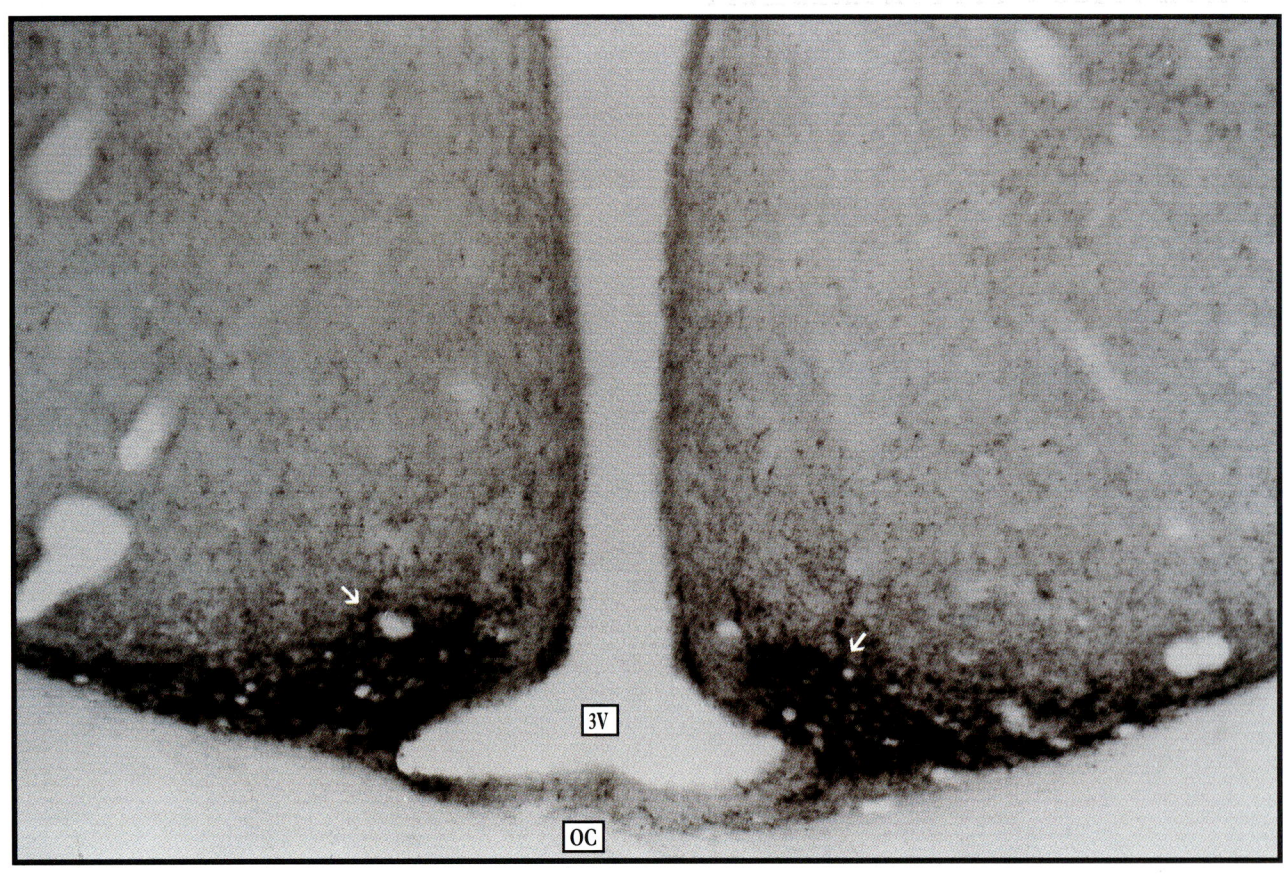

354

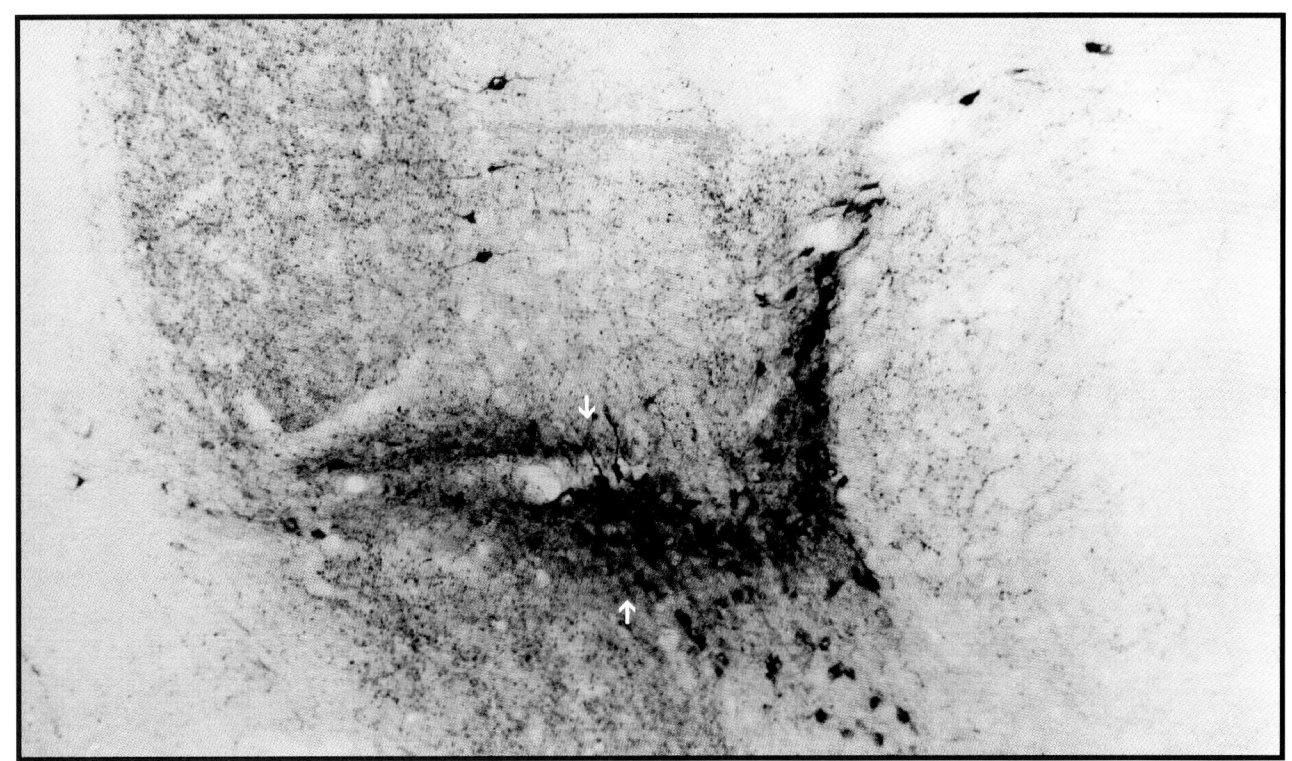

Figure 16: The intergeniculate leaflet (arrows) of the green iguana (*Iguana iguana*) stained with an antiserum against neuropeptide Y (M.S. Grace, unpublished results). Frozen 20 μm frontal section of the brain.

ever. For example, rhythmic and entrainable locomotor activity in lizards continues even in the absence of the lateral eyes, pineal, and/or parietal (Underwood and Menaker, 1970; Janik and Menaker, 1990).

RHYTHM ENTRAINMENT MECHANISMS

Clocks function to prepare an organism for upcoming changes in the environment. For example, an animal adapted to nocturnal activity would be subject to predation by diurnal predators if it had to periodically emerge from its burrow to determine whether night had begun. However, biological clocks are not precisely matched to environmental time. Circadian clocks have periods near, but not exactly 24 hours. Similarly, in the few cases where endogenous circannual clocks have been investigated, their periods are not exactly 1 year. Therefore, to be useful to the organism, endogenous clocks must be synchronized or entrained to environmental time. Many environmental parameters oscillate, but very few are precisely regular. Humidity is generally higher at night, for example, but the pattern of humidity changes depends to a great degree on variable air currents and other weather conditions. Rainfall often varies with season, but it too is an imprecise measure of time. The most reliable rhythmic environmental stimulus is the daily light-dark cycle. The length

of the day remains 24 hours throughout the year, and the light-dark cycle remains regular and observable even on overcast days (the only real exceptions to the regularity of the light-dark cycle are eclipses, but these are so infrequent and short-lived that they are inconsequential.

Because of its ease of manipulation, and because of its ubiquitous importance from the simplest to the most complex organisms, light has been by far the most thoroughly studied rhythm-entraining agent. For ectotherms, such as reptiles and amphibians, the influence of the physical environment is more complex than the daily light-dark cycle. Because their body temperature depends largely on environmental temperature, thermal cues have become important inputs to their circadian systems.

RHYTHM-ENTRAINING PHOTORECEPTORS

Photoreceptors mediating light's influence on the circadian system are located exclusively in the eyes of mammals (although there is some evidence for photosensitivity in the neonatal mammalian pineal). In all non-mammalian vertebrates, however, rhythm-entraining photoreceptors exist outside the eyes, and almost certainly within them as well.

It seems likely that all photoreceptive organs contain clocks, and that the clocks may in fact be located within photoreceptors (see companion volume for a discussion of clock and photoreceptor functions in the eyes of the African clawed frog

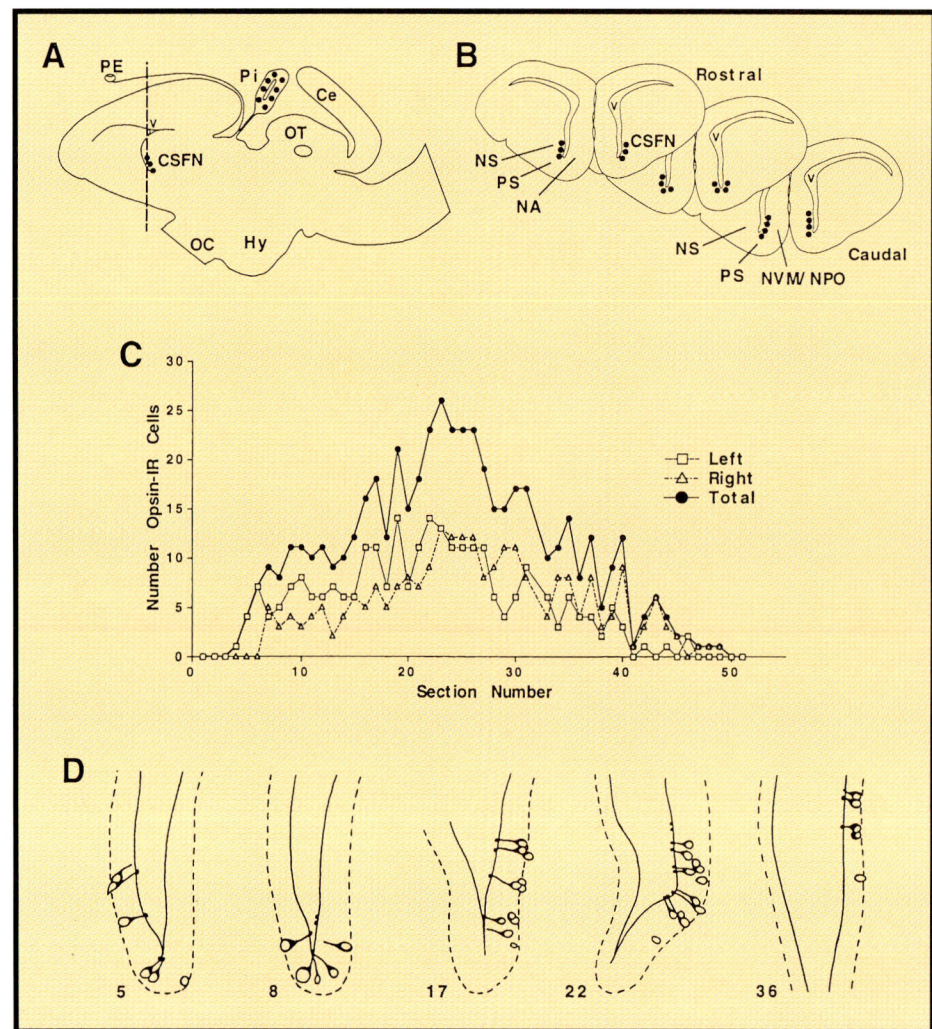

Figure 17: The locations of opsin-immunoreactive cells in the brains of iguanid lizards. These results are based upon studies in *Iguana iguana* and *Anolis carolinensis*. A: parasagital view of the brain showing opsin-immunoreactive cells (filled circles) in the basal forebrain and pineal. B: frontal sections showing the locations of immunoreactive cells at different levels of the *Iguana* brain. C: Counts of opsin-immunostained cells in each hemisphere of the brain. D: Camera lucida drawings of frontal sections of Iguana brain showing the locations and shapes of stained cells at different levels of the brain. Left is rostral; right is caudal. From M.S. Grace et al., J. Comparative Neurology, 1996.

Xenopus laevis). The lizard pineal is photoreceptive and contains a clock. Menaker and Wisner (Menaker and Wisner, 1983) showed that the isolated pineal of the lizard *Anolis carolinensis* produces the hormone melatonin rhythmically and that this rhythm is entrained (synchronized) to a daily light-dark cycle. Experiments on cultured dissociated pineal cells (non-reptilian species) have shown that individual pinealocytes are both photoreceptive and clock-containing. While this has not been done with reptilian pineals, it seems likely that individual pinealocytes contain all three components of the circadian system: a clock controlling an output of rhythmic melatonin production, and a photoreceptive entraining input pathway.

Even though we know that the parietal eye is photoreceptive, its involvement in clock function has not been directly demonstrated. One report suggests a functional role in circadian timing and seasonal rhythmicity based upon the unusual response properties of *Anolis* parietal photoreceptors (Solessio and Engbretson, 1993). These unusual response properties may allow *Anolis* parietal photoreceptors to serve as dawn and dusk detectors (see above).

While the eyes are not required for at least one behavioral rhythm (locomotor activity), there are circadian fluctuations within the eye (see above). Presumably, these phenomena, including rhythmic disk shedding and melatonin synthesis, are controlled by clocks located within the eye, and possibly within the photoreceptors themselves. It is possible that ocular rhythms in the intact animal are also under the control of extra-ocular oscillators, but this question has never been investigated in reptiles.

"DEEP BRAIN" PHOTORECEPTORS

Photoreceptors are also located within the basal brain of non-mammalian vertebrates. Their existence has been postulated for nearly a century, since (von Frische, 1911) discovered that light-induced color changes in the European minnow (*Phoxinus phoxinus*) persisted in the absence of both the lateral eyes and pineal. He found that lesions in the diencephalic region of the brain abolished this response. One of the most elegant demonstrations of extra-retinal, -pineal, and -parietal photoreception in a reptile was performed using the lizard *Sceloporus olivaceous*. Underwood and Menaker (Underwood and Menaker, 1970)

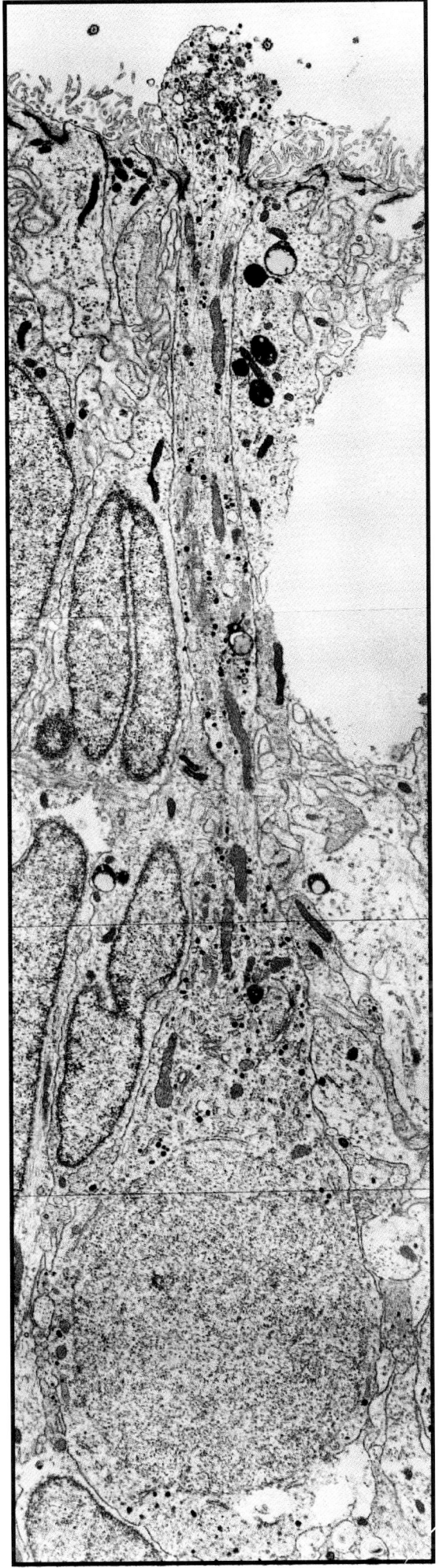

showed that lizard locomotor activity remained entrained to a light-dark cycle (lizards were active in the day) even after removal of the lateral eyes, pineal, and parietal eye. Since then, Underwood has extended these observations to many lizard species in four different families.

Recently, candidate "deep brain photoreceptors" of iguanid lizards have been found (Foster et al., 1993; Foster et al., 1994) and characterized (Grace et al., 1993; Grace et al., 1996). Opsin-like immunoreactivity was found in a small subset of neurons located adjacent to the lateral ventricles of the lizards *Anolis carolinensis* and *Iguana iguana*. These cells send a ciliated process (rudimentary outer segment?) into the lumen of the ventricle where they contact cerebrospinal fluid (hence the term "cerebrospinal fluid-contacting neurons"). It is possible that the ventricle acts as a light guide from the upper part of the brain to the "outer segments" of these cells. Birds have two sets of putative deep brain photoreceptors, one in an analogous location, and the other in the hypothalamus, but there is only one class of these cells in the iguanid lizards studied thus far (Grace et al., 1996).

The putative encephalic photoreceptors found in lizards and other non-mammalian vertebrates may be the most primitive photoreceptors known in vertebrates. Certain features of their morphology are reminiscent of visual photoreceptors (they have a cilium and are longitudinally polarized), but they are most similar to extra-retinal photoreceptors found in the brains of crayfish and associated with the eye of certain marine snails. Even though these cerebrospinal fluid-contacting neurons in the lizard brain have biochemical and structural features in common with other photoreceptive cells, it must be noted that the physiological role of these cells remains to be determined.

TEMPERATURE AS AN ENTRAINING SIGNAL

Temperature can also serve as an effective entraining agent in reptiles, and under certain conditions can override the role of the light-dark cycle.

Figure 18: Electron micrograph of an opsin-immunostained cerebrospinal fluid-contacting neuron of the basal forebrain of *Iguana iguana*. These cells more closely resemble pinealocytes than retinal photoreceptors. They also share an important structural feature, the numerous large electron-dense vesicles, with extra-retinal photoreceptors of invertebrates. These vesicles are thought to be the photoreceptive organelles in extra-retinal photoreceptors of crayfish and gastropod mollusks.

Under laboratory conditions of constant light and cyclic temperature, normally diurnal lizards (including *Anolis carolinensis* (Underwood, 1985), and *Acanthodactylus schmidti* (Constantineau and Cloudsley-Thompson, 1985)) are active during the high temperature portion of the cycle, while normally nocturnal lizards (including *Tarentola annularis* (Cloudsley-Thompson, 1965) and *Ptyodactylus hasselquisti* (Frankenberg, 1979)) are active during the low temperature portion of the cycle. Biochemical rhythms in reptiles are also entrained by temperature cycles. The pineal melatonin rhythm in *Anolis* shows peak melatonin levels during the night under normal conditions of low temperature correlated with darkness in a cyclic light and temperature environment. However, if the two cycles are reversed with respect to each other (low temperature during the day, high at night), lizards are active during the high temperature, but dark, phase of the cycle (Underwood and Calaban, 1987).

Temperature obviously has a very important role in reproductive cyclicity in ectotherms. The role of thermoperiodism in seasonal reproduction has been investigated recently in the lizard *Lacerta vivipara*. Females of this species require a period of hibernation for spring vitellogenesis. The ovarian cycle is completely abolished by keeping lizards in a constantly warm environment. Gavaud reported that a period of cold temperatures stimulates vitellogenesis during a subsequent warm (spring-like) period, even when the cold occurs only during part of the day every 24 hours (Gavaud, 1991). Under the conditions of the experiments, longer and cooler cold portions of the daily cycle were more effective than shorter or warmer cool portions. Gavaud also provided evidence that the reproductive cycle in *L. vivipara* is a true circannual rhythm, and that this rhythm is entrained by the seasonally changing thermoperiod.

SUMMARY AND CONCLUSIONS

Reptiles, and particularly iguanid lizards, have been and continue to be important model systems for the study of biological timing. Iguanids are particularly interesting because of the high number of known clock- and photoreceptor-containing organs. These animals present perhaps the best opportunity to understand how multiple clocks and photoreceptive systems function together. On the other hand, circadian biology has been relatively neglected in other reptilian taxa. Snakes in particular, have been very little studied. Reptilian rhythms are also interesting because temperature cycles can be important entraining signals. A better knowledge of the relative importance of light and temperature cycles would be valuable to reptile husbandry, especially with regard to captive reproduction.

REFERENCES AND RECOMMENDED READING

—**Abe, H. and T. Y. Yamamoto:**
Diurnal changes in synaptic ribbons of rod cells of the turtle. J. Ultrastruct. Res., 1984, 86:246-251.

—**Bernstein, S. A., D. J. Breding and S. K. Fisher:**
The influence of light on cone disk shedding in the lizard, *Sceloporus olivaceous*. J. Cell Biol., 1984, 99:379-389.

—**Cloudsley-Thompson, J. L.:**
Rhythmic activity, temperature tolerance, water relations, and mechanism of heat death in a tropical skink and gecko. J. Zool. (London), 1965, 146:55-69.

—**Constantineau, C. and J. L. Cloudsley-Thompson:**
The circadian rhythm of locomotor activity in the desert lizard *Acanthodactylus schmidti*. J. Interdisciplin. Cycle Res., 1985, 16:107-111.

—**Cowgell, J. and H. Underwood:**
Behavioral thermoregulation in lizards: a circadian rhythm. J. Exp. Zool., 1979, 210:189-194.

—**Cuellar, H. S. and O. Cuellar:**
Evidence for endogenous rhythmicity in the reproductive cycle of the parthenogenetic lizard *Cnemidophorus uniparens*. Copeia, 1977, 1977:554-557.

—**Cuellar, O.:**
Long-term analysis of reproductive periodicity in the lizard *Cnemidophorus uniparens*. Am. Mid. Naturalist, 1981, 105:93-101.

—**Duvall, D., L. J. Guillette and R. E. Jones:**
Environmental control of reptilian reproductive cycles. In, Biology of the Reptilia. C. Gans, (Ed.). Academic Press, London, New York, 1982, 13: 201-232.

—**Firth, B. T., D. J. Kennaway and M. A. M. Rozenbilds:**
Plasma melatonin in the scincid lizard, *Trachydosaurus rugosus*: diel rhythm, seasonality, and the effects of constant light and constant darkness. Gen. Comp. Endocrinol., 1979, 37:493-500.

—**Foster, R. G., J. M. Garcia-Fernandez, I. Provencio and W. J. DeGrip:**
Opsin localization and chromophore retinoids

identified within the basal brain of the lizard *Anolis carolinensis*. Journal of Comparative Physiology A, 1993, 172:33-45.

—**Foster, R. G., M. S. Grace, I. Provencio, W. J. DeGrip and J. M. Garcia-Fernandez:**
Identification of vertebrate deep brain photoreceptors. Neuroscience and Biobehavioral Reviews, 1994, 18:541-546.

—**Fowlkes, D. H., C. L. Karwoski and L. M. Proenza:**
Endogenous circadian rhythm in electroretinogram of free-moving lizards. Visual Sci., 1984, 25:121-124.

—**Fowlkes, D. H., C. L. Karwoski and L. M. Proenza:**
Circadian modulation of the electroretinogram (a- and b-waves) in the diurnal lizard *Anolis carolinensis*. J. Interdiscipl. Cycle Res., 1987, 18:147-168.

—**Frankenberg, E.:**
Influence of light and temperature on daily activity patterns of three Israeli forms of *Ptyodactylus* (Reptilia: Gekkonidae). J. Zool. (London), 1979, 189:21-30.

—**Gavaud, J.:**
Cold entrainment of the annual cycle of ovarian activity in the lizard *Lacerta vivpera*: thermoperiodic rhythm vs. hibernation. J. Biol. Rhythms, 1991, 6:201-215.

—**Grace, M. S., V. Alones and M. Menaker:**
Correlated light and electron microscopy of opsin-immunoreactive neurons in lizard basal brain. Soc. Neurosci. Abstr., 1993, 19:1201.

—**Grace, M. S., V. Alones and M. Menaker:**
The intergeniculate leaflet: a component of the circadian system of *Iguana iguana*? (in preparation), 1997.

—**Grace, M. S., V. Alones and M. Menaker:**
A single population of photoreceptor-like cerebrospinal fluid-contacting neurons in the lizard *Iguana iguana*. (in preparation), 1997.

—**Grace, M. S., V. Alones, M. Menaker and R. G. Foster:**
Light perception in the vertebrate brain: an ultrastructural analysis of opsin-immunoreactive neurons in iguanid lizards. J. Comp. Neurol., 1996,367:575-594.

—**Grace, M. S. and J. C. Besharse:**
Melatonin deacetylase activity in the pineal glands and brains of the lizards *Sceloporus jarrovi* and *Anolis carolinensis*. Neuroscience, 1994, 62:615-623.

—**Grace, M. S., G. M. Cahill and J. C. Besharse:**
Melatonin deacetylation: retinal vertebrate class distribution and *Xenopus laevis* tissue distribution. Brain Res., 1991, 559:56-63.

—**Grace, M. S. and M. Menaker:**
The suprachiasmatic nucleus of the lizard *Iguana iguana* as defined by retinal tract tracing and NPY, VIP, and AVP immunocytochemistry. (in preparation), 1997.

—**Heckrotte, C.:**
Temperature and light effects on the circadian rhythm and locomotor activity of the plains garter snake (*Thamnophis radix haydeni*). J. Interdiscipl. Cycle Res., 1975, 6:279-290.

—**Janik, D. S. and M. Menaker:**
Circadian locomotor rhythms in the desert iguana. I. The role of the eyes and pineal. J. Comp. Physiol. A, 1990, 166:803-810.

—**Janik, D. S. and M. Menaker:**
Circadian locomotor rhythms in the desert iguana. II. Effects of electrolytic lesions to the hypothalamus. J. Cmp. Physiol. A, 1990, 166:811-816.

—**Jarling, C., M. Scarperi and A. Bleichert:**
Circadian rhythm in the temperature preference of the turtle, *Chrysemys* (=*Pseudemys*) *scripta elegans*, in a thermal gradient. J. Thermal Biol., 1989, 14:173-178.

—**Landreth, H. F.:**
Orientation and behavior of the rattlesnake, *Crotalus atrox*. Copeia, 1973, 1973:26-31.

—**Mahapatra, M. S., S. K. Mahata and B. R. Maiti:**
Circadian rhythms in serotonin, norepinephrine, and epinephrine content of the pineal-paraphyseal complex of the softshell turtle (*Lissemys punctata punctata*). Gen. Comp. Endocrinol., 1986, 64:246-249.

—**Menaker, M. and S. Wisner:**
Temperature-compensated circadian clock in the pineal of *Anolis*. Proc. Natl. Acad. Sci. U.S.A., 1983, 80:6119-6121.

—**Moore, M. C. and J. Lindzey:**
The physiological basis of sexual behavior in male reptiles. In, Hormones, Brain, and Behavior. C. Gans and D. Crews, (Ed.). University of Chicago Press, Chicago, 1992, 18:70-113.

—**Moore, R. G.:**
Seasonal and diel activity patterns and thermoregulation in the southwestern speckled rattlesnake (*Crotalus mitchelli pyrrhus*) and the Colorado desert sidewinder (*Crotalus cerastes laterorepens*). Copeia, 1978, 1978:439-442.

—**Moyer, R. W., B. T. Firth and D. J. Kennaway:**
Effects of constant temperatures, darkness and light on the secretion of melatonin by pineal explants and retinas in the gecko *Christinus marmoratus*. Brain Res., 1995, 675:345-348.

359

—**Mushinski, H. R., J. J. Hebrard and M. G. Walley:**
The role of temperature on the behavioral and ecological associations of sympatric water snakes. Copeia, 1980, 1980:744-754.

—**Naulleau, G.:**
La thermoregulation chez vipere aspic (*Vipera aspis*) etudiee par biotelemetrie dans differente conditions artificielles experimentales. Bull. Soc. Zool. France, 1976, 101:726-728.

—**Naulleau, G.:**
Etude biotelemetrique de la thermoregulation chez *Vipera aspis* (L.) elevee on conditions artificielles. J. Herpetol., 1979, 13:203-208.

—**Noeske, T. A. and A. H. Meier:**
Photoperiodic and thermoperiodic interaction affecting fat stores and reproductive indices in the male green anole, *Anolis carolinensis*. J. Exp. Zool., 1977, 202:97-102.

—**Noeske, T. A. and A. H. Meier:**
Thermoperiodic and photoperiodic influences on daily and seasonal changes in the physiology of the male green anole, *Anolis carolinensis*. J. Exp. Zool., 1982, 226:177-184.

—**Owens, D. W., W. A. Gern and C. L. Ralph:**
Melatonin in the blood and cerebrospinal fluid of the green sea turtle (*Chelonia mydas*). Gen. Comp. Endocrinol., 1980, 40:180-187.

—**Quay, W. B.:**
The parietal eye-pineal complex. In, Biology of the Reptilia. C. Gans, R. G. Northcutt and P. Ulinski, (Ed.). Academic Press, London, New York, 1979, 9:245-406.

—**Roth, J. J., W. A. Gern, E. C. Roth, C. L. Ralph and E. Jacobson:**
Nonpineal melatonin in the alligator (*Alligator mississippiensis*). Science, 1980, 210:548-550.

—**Sanders, J. S. and J. S. Jacob:**
Thermal ecology of the copperhead (*Agkistrodon contortrix*). Herpetologica, 1981, 37:264-270.

—**Shaw, A. P., C. R. Collazo, K. Easterling, C. D. Young and C. J. Karwoski:**
Circadian rhythm in the visual system of the lizard *Anolis carolinensis*. J. Biol. Rhythms, 1993, 8:107-124.

—**Solessio, E. and G. A. Engbretson:**
Antagonistic chromatic mechanisms in photoreceptors of the parietal eye of lizards. Nature, 1993, 364:442-445.

—**Stebbins, R. C.:**
Activity changes in the striped plateau lizard with evidence on influence of the parietal eye. Copeia, 1963, 1963:681-691.

—**Underwood, H.:**
Circadian organization in lizards: the role of the pineal. Science, 1977, 195:587-589.

—**Underwood, H.:**
Photoperiodic time measurement in the male lizard *Anolis carolinensis*. J. Comp. Physiol., 1978, 125:143-150.

—**Underwood, H.:**
Circadian organization in the lizard *Sceloporus occidentalis*: the effects of blinding, pinealectomy and melatonin. J. Comp. Physiol., 1981, 141:537-547.

—**Underwood, H.:**
Circadian organization in the lizard *Anolis carolinensis*: a multioscillator system. J. Com. Physiol., 1983, 152:265-274.

—**Underwood, H.:**
Pineal melatonin rhythms in the lizard *Anolis carolinensis*: effects of light and temperature cycles. J. Comp. Physiol. A, 1985, 157:57-65.

—**Underwood, H. and M. Calaban:**
Pineal melatonin rhythms in the lizard *Anolis carolinensis* I. Response to light and temperature cycles. J. Biol. Rhythms, 1987, 2:179-193.

—**Underwood, H. and M. Menaker:**
Extraretinal light perception: entrainment of the biological clock controlling lizard locomotor activity. Science, 1970, 170:190-193.

—**von Frische, K.:**
Beitrage zur Physiologie der Pigmentzellen in der Fischhaut. Pfluger's Archiv, 1911, 138:319-387.

—**Whittier, J. M. and D. Crews:**
Seasonal reproduction: patterns and control. In, Hormones and Reproduction in Fishes, Amphibians, and Reptiles. D. O. Norris and R. E. Jones, (Ed.). Plenum, New York, 1987, pp.385-410.

—**Whittier, J. M. and R. R. Tokarz:**
Physiological regulation of sexual behavior in female reptiles. In, Hormones, Brain, and Behavior. C. Gans and D. Crews, (Eds.). University of Chicago Press, Chicago, 1992, 18:24-69.

—**Young, R. W.:**
The daily rhythm of shedding and degradation of cone outer segment membranes in the lizard retina. J. Ultrastruct. Res., 1977, 61:172-185.

INDEX

Please Note: This Index includes page references for all three volumes of
The Biology, Husbandry and Health Care of Reptiles.